DEVELOPING A CURRICULUM FOR MODERN LIVING

THE HORACE MANN-LINCOLN INSTITUTE
OF SCHOOL EXPERIMENTATION
TEACHERS COLLEGE, COLUMBIA UNIVERSITY

DEVELOPING A CURRICULUM FOR MODERN LIVING

Second Edition, Revised and Enlarged

FLORENCE B. STRATEMEYER
Teachers College, Columbia University

HAMDEN L. FORKNER
Teachers College, Columbia University

MARGARET G. McKIM
University of Cincinnati

A. HARRY PASSOW
Teachers College, Columbia University

BUREAU OF PUBLICATIONS
TEACHERS COLLEGE, COLUMBIA UNIVERSITY
NEW YORK

LIBRARY OF CONGRESS CATALOG CARD NUMBER: 57–11371
MANUFACTURED IN THE UNITED STATES OF AMERICA
BY H. WOLFF, NEW YORK

SECOND PRINTING, 1963

FOREWORD

This book is a thorough revision of an unusually successful text written by three of the four authors and published ten years ago. The present volume deals with the curriculum as an entity. The main argument is related to a set of beliefs which have at their core a broad conception of democracy and of the importance of cooperative planning in bringing about instructional change. Much attention is paid to principles of curriculum construction that make it possible to relate the needs of the individual to those of society. The "persistent life situation" concept is further developed in relation to the major issues in curriculum building —scope, sequence, continuity, balance, and depth.

Part Four of DEVELOPING A CURRICULUM FOR MODERN LIVING presents illustrative curriculum designs that are in harmony with the authors' basic point of view. These are worked out in detail for the first-, fifth-, and tenth-grade levels. They lend concrete specificity to conceptions about the curriculum which are carefully derived from a broad and deep sociological, psychological, and philosophical orientation.

The Horace Mann–Lincoln Institute of School Experimentation is proud to present this revision of DEVELOPING A CURRICULUM FOR MODERN LIVING. We are certain that its influence will be beneficent and pervasive.

STEPHEN M. COREY
Director, Horace Mann–Lincoln Institute of School Experimentation

ACKNOWLEDGMENT

We wish to express our appreciation and indebtedness to the large number of classroom teachers, curriculum coordinators, and college teachers who have over the years offered pointed and constructive suggestions based on their use of the earlier edition. In addition we wish to acknowledge the help given by the selected group of educators whose general comments as well as reactions to specific points of inquiry also guided us in identifying aspects of the original volume which were most helpful, others which needed further clarification, and new areas which should be considered.

We wish to acknowledge the helpful criticism of the many who read parts or all of the manuscript, including Professors William L. Carter, Gordon Hendrickson, and Ralph L. Pounds, of the University of Cincinnati; Mr. Norman J. Niesen, Assistant Supervisor of Special Education of the Cincinnati Public Schools; Dean Stephen M. Corey, Professors Arno A. Bellack, Max R. Brunstetter, and Dorothy M. McGeoch, and Dr. Hamden L. Forkner, Jr., of Teachers College, Columbia University.

Special recognition is also due to Mrs. Shirley O'Donnol and Miss Beth Drake for their careful and generous assistance in the preparation of the manuscript. Appreciation is extended to the publishers of copyrighted materials who have given permission to quote from their publications.

THE AUTHORS

CONTENTS

FOREWORD by Stephen M. Corey v

Part I : FOUNDATIONS OF CURRICULUM DEVELOPMENT

1. Basic Curriculum Issues 3

The Challenge to Education 4
Consistent Responses to Basic Curriculum Problems an Impelling Need 6
Toward a Curriculum for Modern Living 21

2. Society a Guide to Curriculum Development 26

Democratic Values—The Foundation of American Society 26
America—A Machine-Powered and Industrial Civilization 34
Interdependence—A Characteristic of Today's Civilization 43

3. Children and Youth a Guide to Curriculum Development 51

The Maturing Learner—A Guide to Curriculum Development 53
The Learning Process—A Guide to Curriculum Development 66

Part II : A CURRICULUM FOR LEARNERS IN OUR TIMES

4. An Analysis of Major Approaches to Designing the Curriculum 85

Varied Proposals of Scope, Sequence, and Organization 86
Common Goals and Points of Difference 106
The Proposal of the Writers of This Volume 110

5. A Proposal for Designing a Curriculum for Living in Our Times 113

A Proposal for a Curriculum for Learners in Our Times 114
The Persistent Life Situations Concept and the Essentials of Curriculum Development 121
A Summary Look 140

6. The Scope of Persistent Life Situations and Ways in Which Learners Face Them 146

The Scope of Persistent Life Situations 146
The Analysis of Persistent Life Situations 151
Typical Situations of Everyday Living in Which Persistent Life Situations Appear 167
Using the Charts of Persistent Life Situations as Learners Face Them 322

Part III : DEVELOPING THE CURRICULUM WITH LEARNERS

7. Selecting Curriculum Experiences 335

Identifying the Concerns of Learners 336
Determining the Place of an Experience in the Curriculum 344
Providing Effective Experiences for Children in the Elementary School 352
Providing Effective Experiences for High School Youth 355
Making a Start Toward the Proposed Design from More Traditional Types of Organization 362

8. Guiding the Experiences of Learners 369

Developing Experiences with Learners 370
Planning for and with Learners 379
Scheduling the Day's Activities 397
Using Organized Bodies of Subject Matter 403
Developing Fundamental Skills 409
Materials and Equipment for Maximum Growth 418
Beginning the School Year 426

9. Providing for Individual Differences 432

Functional Grouping of Learners 433
Meeting Individual Needs Within the Classroom Setting 438
Making Adjustments for Exceptional Pupils 446

10. Using the Resources of the Whole School and the Community 459

Making Effective Use of Specialization 459
Programing to Meet Learners' Needs 465

Providing Continuity of Growth Through Articulation 468
Using the Whole School and the Community as Sources of Learning Experiences 471

11. Making Evaluation an Integral Part of the Curriculum 476

The Nature of Evaluation in Curriculum Development 476
Determining the Values Sought 479
Gathering Data on Which to Base Evaluation 484
Keeping Functional Records 491
Reporting Pupil Progress 499
Evaluating the Educational Program 510

Part IV : TEACHERS AND LEARNERS AT WORK

12. Guiding a Year's Work in a Fifth Grade 521

The Children and Their School 522
Beginning the Year's Work 525
The Next Milestone—Getting Ready for Christmas 548
Continuing Problems Take on Added Meaning in the New Year 554
Spring Brings New Problems 565
A Summary Look 570

13. Caring for Youth's Special Needs—A Tenth-Grade Program 578

The Setting for This Tenth-Grade Program 579
The Activities of the Core Program 589
Providing for Needs Through Service Courses and Laboratory Activities 610
A Summary Look 613

14. A First Grade Deals with Persistent Life Situations 616

The Children and Their School 617
The Way They Work 618
Experiences Through Which Persistent Life Situations Were Faced 621
A Summary Look 654

Part V : WORKING COOPERATIVELY FOR CURRICULUM IMPROVEMENT

15. Stimulating and Guiding Curriculum Change 661

The Process of Improving the Curriculum 662
Organizing for Curriculum Improvement 670
Planning Effective Procedures for Improving the Curriculum 681
Providing Leadership for Curriculum Improvement 692
Securing Necessary Personnel Resources 696
Developing a Curriculum in Terms of Persistent Life Situations 699

16. Improving the Curriculum Through Research 705

Developing Skill in and Understanding of the Research Process 708
Using Research in Developing a Curriculum Based on Persistent Life Situations 716
Providing Conditions Conducive to Research and Experimentation 722
Building a Research Base for a Curriculum for Modern Living 727

INDEX 731

Part I

FOUNDATIONS OF CURRICULUM DEVELOPMENT

1

BASIC CURRICULUM ISSUES

In a world of change and invention, of movement and tensions, of hope and promise, schools play an increasingly important role. Schools can and have been used for both good and evil—freeing the minds of some and giving them a vision of a world of peace and justice while, almost at the same time, firing the minds of others and giving them a thirst for power and a hunger for domination. Schools have helped build good will, healthy interpersonal relations, respect for individual rights and personal dignity, and understanding of other cultures. But they have also fostered thought control, mistrust of others, antagonisms toward other cultures, and subservience of individuals to the state. Through schools, health, prosperity, and peace have been and are being brought to some peoples long used to plagues, misery, and unrest. But schools have also been used to fan the flames of hatred which lead eventually to carnage and destruction.

Schools are organized and maintained by societies to enhance values and knowledge important to them. To a degree, schools both reflect and alter the culture of which they are a part—they can build as well as perpetuate civilizations. Developed constructively, schools can create civilizations of responsible peoples who are at home in a world of change and who want to and can solve life's problems for the well-being of all.

The Challenge to Education

Contemporary civilization relies upon organized education to help enlarge the range of competencies needed for living in today's world. In the social, political, and economic upheavals which are characteristic of the twentieth century, schools can be a major force. At no time has the challenge to education been greater.

SCHOOLS ARE AN INTEGRAL PART OF THE AMERICAN WAY OF LIFE

The American school system, so called, actually consists of thousands of separate systems throughout the nation, each locally controlled. The public schools, comprising the bulk of these many systems, are free—open to all regardless of race, religion, ethnic origin, wealth, or social status. They are supported by public funds and each is independent of the others. While every state exercises some supervisory functions, the people control their own schools through a board of education whose members are either elected by popular vote or appointed by officials who are themselves elected. This public control of education makes the United States unique among the nations of the world. It evolved, not without struggle, during the years since colonial times and is an important factor in determining the nature of our schools.

Many forces helped shape this design of free public education. Just as all schools reflect the purposes of the societies which found and support them, the American school system is rooted in the philosophy that sustained the establishment of the nation. In the early days of the republic, Thomas Jefferson wrote: "If a nation expects to be ignorant and free, in a state of civilization, it expects what never was and what never will be." Other founding fathers voiced similar faith in an enlightened citizenry as assurance of democracy's survival.

The history of public education in the United States records the development of a school system whose ideal accomplishment would be a way of life based on freedom, equality, and self-government. This ideal has guided a steady expansion of public schools to include all children and youth and to provide them with equal educational opportunities. The underlying concept of providing free and equal opportunities for each individual to develop his potential in so far as possible is a prevailing reason for the unique design of American education.

Though schools expose their disparities, inequalities, and inadequacies in attaining the ideal, basically the American dream dominates and guides the public school system. Schools have moved beyond the founding fathers' concern with a means for developing an informed and literate citizenry and have played an integral role in establishing a society marked by mobility and a fluid social structure.

School programs are influenced rather directly by the ideals, attitudes, and pressures of the individuals and groups in the community. The gradual upward extension of the common school through the secondary level, the prolongation of compulsory attendance, the lengthening of the school year, all necessitated re-examination of the kinds of experience being provided for children and youth. When business and industry began to demand more years of schooling and when the monetary value of a high school diploma became apparent, school attendance and program development were affected. Promulgation of child labor laws, sometimes for humanitarian reasons and often to remove children from the competitive labor market, changed the nature of the student population. America's cultural pluralism—the respect for and acceptance of contributions from the many heterogeneous groups comprising the American people—is another important aspect of society affecting education. The way in which the many cultures blend into a synthesis which preserves elements of the old and, at the same time, adds to a new whole, is a facet of American democracy which influences school program development.

The unique relationship between the American people and their schools affects the nature of the educational program. Schools literally belong to the people who, because they are close to the boards wherein legal control rests, can make known the purposes which they want the school to consider as it develops a program. The goal of equal educational opportunities has already been translated into the same amount of education for all youth. Now it is being converted into appropriate kinds of education for all. To provide experiences of a quality which will make education a positive social force is today's challenge to both layman and educator.

EDUCATION MUST BE A POSITIVE SOCIAL FORCE

Modern living is more complicated with each new day. Our democratic and social institutions are dependent, as never before, upon a greater diffusion of knowledge and understanding. Active, intelligent citizens require honest and accurate information, if they are to participate in government and community affairs. Shrinking distances mean new and complicated cultural contacts. Peoples from all over the world need to, and at some points do, come together to build common policies. International affairs have become vitally important to each individual, for happenings thousands of miles away in other lands have a direct bearing on his life. Science has shaken individual and group composure with the development of the means for total world destruction. Unless institutions and individuals come to understand and accept the sacrifices necessary for continuing peace, civilization as it is known today can disappear from the globe.

The problems of everyday living have never seemed more relentless. At a time when our nation is advancing boldly in physical medicine and overtaking disease, mental health is more vulnerable daily. Social problems related to urbanization have multiplied as metropolitan centers grow. Increased command of material power has brought a multitude of new problems, including those of increased leisure. At no period have these and other problems called for a wider range of information and for greater ability to see relationships and to make choices in terms of sound social and human values. Never has the urgency for understanding oneself and others been sharper. At no other time has there been a greater need for realistic education of all individuals—children, youth, and adults. The dynamics of the times call for persons able to deal with the complexity of everyday living.

Throughout the world there is reflected a growing faith in the power of education—faith in education as the source of environment and guidance to give children and youth a share in today's world and leadership in tomorrow's. It is up to schools to respond to the challenge of that faith. It is essential that education become a positive social force, and this can only happen as teachers and others charged with guiding the educative process critically examine and appraise the proposals they make for dealing with basic curriculum problems.

Consistent Responses to Basic Curriculum Problems an Impelling Need

Consciously or unconsciously teachers make choices which affect the kinds of experiences they provide for children and youth. These choices range from the selection of the very goals the school seeks to attain and the relations maintained with other community agencies, to organization of the educational program, the methods employed, the materials used, and the provision made for differences among pupils. The quality of the learning experiences is derived from the choices made. All theories and their practices cannot produce the same quality of education nor can they equally nurture individual and social growth.

To meet the challenge of the twentieth century, and to provide an education that will function effectively in the lives of all children and youth, there is need to re-examine the basic curriculum problems and issues which lie back of the choices made by teachers and administrators in elementary and secondary schools. The discussion which follows seeks, by looking at schools in action, to point to some of the issues and related problems that must be faced. Although each issue is treated separately, in practice all operate together. A position taken on any one issue influences the decisions made in relation to all the others.

WHAT SHALL BE THE ROLE OF THE SCHOOL IN ACHIEVING EDUCATIONAL GOALS?

The changes brought about in all aspects of daily living by the scientific and technological revolution and the pressures for preserving and nurturing democratic values in a world of tensions have resulted in demands being made on the school to accept new and different responsibilities for the development of children and youth. The early and distinctive role of the school—to teach reading, writing, arithmetic, citizenship—soon began to be altered. As the common school came to be extended upwards for children and youth, it accepted varying degrees of responsibility for the intellectual, social, physical, aesthetic, and moral development of boys and girls.

Schools today reflect these new responsibilities in many ways. Some endeavor to provide for all aspects of living, others focus chiefly on development of intellectual power. In one situation courses in driver training, typewriting, and home management are considered essential in the education of modern youth. In another, these courses are available as electives when requirements in the traditional subjects have been met. One school provides an extended recreational program, even though community agencies sponsor similar activities. In another school a representative of the student council regularly meets with representatives of other groups to coordinate the activities in a recreational center. Some schools operate for five or six hours a day—the duration of classes—while other schools serve their communities from early morning to late in the evening on a year-round basis, providing organized educational activities for youth, children, and adults.

Schools cannot possibly do all the things various persons would assign to them. Accepting some responsibilities means sacrificing other functions, or accomplishing them less adequately. In judging the patchwork of roles and responsibilities currently assumed by the school, at least three basic questions must be carefully thought through by teachers and other curriculum workers.

What shall be the nature of educational goals? Perhaps the most fundamental question relates to the nature of the educational goals themselves. All educators agree on the need for learning experiences that will attune the young individual to an active and productive role in society. But what does this mean in action? Answers range from the transmission of the cultural heritage to the reconstruction of society. Is it the role of education to attempt to shape character, personality, and attitudes toward democracy as a way of life? What place should controversial issues be accorded? What room should be made for the recognized and accepted problems of today's world—using leisure time effectively, driving a car safely, purchasing goods and services wisely?

In the total process of achieving educational goals, does the school have a distinctive part to play? This is a second basic question. Some educators believe that the all-round growth of the learner is the proper concern of the school and that there should be provision for all aspects of living, regardless of what is being done in the home and in the community. Others hold that the peculiar jurisdiction of the school is limited to such functions as the transmission of the cultural heritage, the cultivation of the intellect, and the development of critical thinking. These educators maintain that, while other institutions may perform some of these functions in varying degrees, the school provides the setting for doing these things in a systematic fashion which insures their being done well. Still other educators believe the school should share responsibility with agencies such as the home and the church, and vary its role to supplement the functions effectively provided by other sources. They point out that the school should not accept sole responsibility for total development, but should see that total development of children and youth is provided for.

Who shall determine the role of the school? This third question is closely related. By tradition and by law, schools are the agents to which society has delegated responsibility for the education of children and youth. What does this delegation entail? Should such specially designated groups as boards of education set basic policy, leaving to the professional staff the final decisions on what to teach and how it should be taught? What should be the function of the professional staff in determining the role of the school? Should pupils of all ages have a share? If the responsibility for clarifying the role of the school is a cooperative one, what parts should teachers, parents, children, others in the community play in the process?

Because communities differ, the kind and number of educational influences that affect children and youth also vary. In some places agencies and institutions richly support the schools' activities; in others they may directly or indirectly compete and contradict. Some functions of the school may be common to all communities; others may vary because of the differences in the agencies to which specific educational assignments can be made. Whatever the needs of a particular community, the school will play its role most effectively if thoughtful and analytical consideration determines that role.

WHAT TO TEACH—TOWARD WHAT KNOWLEDGE, UNDERSTANDINGS, AND SKILLS SHALL EXPERIENCES BE GUIDED?

The curriculum is currently defined in three ways: the courses and class activities in which children and youth engage; the total range of in-class and out-of-class experiences sponsored by the school; and the total life experiences of the learner. Whatever definition is accepted, educators must decide toward which knowledge, understandings, and skills the learner's experiences shall be directed. These decisions determine the **scope** of the school curriculum.

Differing conceptions regarding the school's role in a democratic society lead to differing decisions about the scope of the curriculum. Educators who see the unique role of the school as transmitting the cultural heritage tend to stress the understandings and skills that acquaint learners with important aspects of that heritage—history, literature, government, science, art, music, languages, mathematics. This position on "what to teach" differs from that of educators who would emphasize experiences designed to help children and youth cope with the problems of everyday living. And there are points of difference within this latter group. Some feel it is enough to help learners adjust to well-established present-day trends; others believe that in a world of change it is fundamental to understand how a democracy deals with controversial issues. Whatever the emphasis, educators concerned with situations of everyday living would have learners draw on the heritage whenever it casts light on their problems, but they would not attempt to systematize cultural achievements. The past is considered of merit in so far as it clarifies contemporary trends and movements.

Defining the unique role of the school is only the take-off point for determining the scope of a school curriculum. There must be specific delineation of these basic goals. Even when values are held in common, this delineation has resulted in a rainbow of practices. Some schools place major emphasis on the skills of reading, spelling, writing, and speaking. Other schools are equally concerned with listening skills, active and intelligent observation, techniques of effective group discussion, social competencies, and individual creativity. There are differences in the degree to which there is emphasis on specific knowledge and skills and on the methods of work through which these specifics are acquired; in stress on learning how to think as against what to think; in decisions regarding the proper balance between facts and the generalizations drawn from the study of these facts. The effective translation of goals into specific learnings requires thoughtful answers to two fundamental questions.

Are there certain understandings and skills needed by all children and youth growing up in our society? Some teachers feel that democratic values—freedom to act on thinking and respect for each unique personality—mean that specific goals can be attained only by helping learners develop experiences in terms of their own purposes and problems. These teachers consider the situations surrounding learners as the best guides to the understandings and skills to be taught. Others see the learner's immaturity as giving little guidance in the selection of what to teach; they feel that at least minimum understandings and skills should be specified. Courses of study show great diversity as to both the range of specific knowledge and skills needed by all learners and the ways used for developing them. Some list facts and skills grade by grade in considerable detail; some provide general statements of concepts and ways of behaving but leave particulars for the teacher to decide and adapt to the needs and abilities of his group. In some schools adopted texts or the contents of standardized tests dictate the approved understandings and skills.

What shall be the sources of experiences which determine the knowledge, understandings, and skills toward which the educational program is directed? This question is equally important in determining the actual scope of the curriculum for any given grade. In one school adolescents acquire health concepts through working on their own problems of physical appearance. In another, they study a list of problems related to diet, exercise, and rest provided by the teacher. Fifth-graders in one school learn about their community by exploring the possible impact of the expressway under construction in their neighborhood, while the pupils in another fifth grade read about community structure as outlined in their textbook. Within the same classroom there may be different bases for determining experiences. In creative drama what is learned may be bounded only by the children's interests and their decisions in pursuing these. The same children may be following step by step the lists in a spelling text, with only secondary emphasis upon the words they need in daily writing. Their science activities may start with interesting objects they bring to school but be guided by the teacher toward concepts, understandings, and skills decided by curriculum committees to be important objectives of the science program. Even though over-all purposes may be essentially the same, the actual curricula differ for youngsters in classrooms where there are such varied means of reaching these goals.

Learning activities may be guided in many directions. Curriculum planners should give careful thought to the understandings and abilities one needs to function effectively as an individual and as a citizen. Because all experiences are not equally effective in reaching goals, the choice of experiences merits as much consideration as the ends themselves.

HOW SHALL THE CURRICULUM BE ORGANIZED?

Teachers and other curriculum planners must do more than outline the broad goals and the specific knowledge, understandings, and skills which make up the scope of the curriculum. Decisions must be made regarding the ways in which those understandings and skills are to be related and grouped for teaching. This is a question of the **organization** of the curriculum. Decisions must also be made regarding the order in which proposed learnings are to be developed—which are most appropriate for younger children, which for adolescents; in what order the activities of a given group of children or youth are to unfold. Answers to this second set of questions determine the **sequence** of the curriculum.

What shall be the basis for organizing school experiences? Practices differ widely. The program of one high school is so organized that history, mathematics, Latin, French, English, science, art, music, and other fields are studied as separate courses. Students planning on college elect courses to achieve a balance among natural sciences, social sciences, languages, English, and mathematics. For those who are not college bound, typewriting, home economics, and vocational education are offered. In another community's high school a generous block of time is set aside for a series of related experiences called the core program. Here the focus is on the solution of problems selected as common to the needs of all group members. No subject-matter area is barred to exploration if it seems to contribute to the problem at hand. In a third high school there is also a core program, but here the core consists of an integration of concepts from the fields of mathematics and science. Here, too, problems of concern in the lives of the learners are the starting point, but these problems lie within the designated fields. Other subject-matter areas may be touched on as needed, but these contacts are limited.

The elementary schools of one community have self-contained classrooms in which teacher and children work on a variety of problems of concern to individuals or groups, drawing upon one, several, or all fields of human knowledge as needed. In another elementary school, history and geography are combined in the social studies; oral and written composition make up the language arts; reading, science, art, arithmetic, and other subject areas remain distinct. In a third, centers of study are listed in terms of such areas as transportation, housing, and communication.

What shall determine the sequence and continuity of experiences? School practices show equally great variety in attempting to provide practical answers to this question. **Continuity** involves sustaining and reenforcing learnings as they emerge in the program. When experiences are organized around separate subjects, the sequence of experience is based largely on the increasing difficulty of materials and concepts while the continuity stresses reiteration of important insights and skills as the learner moves through the grades. Where curriculum choices are made in terms of problems of everyday living, the order of experiences—the steps in the study of a problem and the sequence of problems studied—is determined by the nature of the problem and the learner's grasp of it. This is rarely the continuity of material as it would be set up by specialists in a particular discipline or organized in textbooks. The continuity lies within the learner as he is helped to extend his understandings, to see relationships among experiences, and to apply the generalizations from one experience to another.

How shall in-class and out-of-class experiences be brought into relationship? If the curriculum is thought of as the class activities of children and youth, in-class and out-of-class experiences will be dealt with as separate and distinct units. In some cases, the school may make little or no provision for guiding out-of-class activities. If the curriculum is conceived as all the experiences for which the school assumes responsibility, the organization must relate in-class and out-of-class experiences as interlocking parts of the same whole. If the learner's total life experiences are to comprise his curriculum, there are additional problems of relating life in and outside school so that effective continuity and integration are provided.

Through all the variations of theory and practice runs the common desire to plan and implement an organization which will furnish the sequence, continuity, and integration necessary for a rich and well-rounded education. All plans recognize the need to help the learner build on and extend insights and skills as he moves through the educational program. However, all plans cannot achieve with equal facility the same goals.

Which organization and sequence will lead most effectively to desired goals? Answers to this question will vary as goals differ. Nevertheless, all educators need to appraise the value of keeping school experiences within separate subjects. If it is important to help the learner see relationships among areas of knowledge, how can these relationships best be understood? While the maturity of learners always requires adjustments in sequence, how should the experiences, capacities, and needs of particular learners be reflected in the proposed sequence of experiences? Should there be grade-by-grade designation of sequence? If so, how much freedom should a teacher have to move beyond the activities designated for his grade? If not, how can duplication and repetition from year to year be avoided?

The traditional curriculum organization is by separate subjects. Some of these—mathematics, music, grammar, rhetoric, physical education—have been part of the school curriculum since ancient times. While subjects have multiplied, serious challenges to their role as the organizing elements of the curriculum are recent. A curriculum organization is not necessarily desirable merely because it is either traditional or new. Thoughtful appraisal is needed to determine the effectiveness with which various proposals for curriculum organization and sequence actually achieve desired goals.

HOW TO TEACH—HOW SHALL CURRICULUM EXPERIENCES BE GUIDED?

Teachers guide curriculum experiences according to their concepts of the nature of the learner and of the learning process. Although sound concepts about learning enter every curriculum issue, they are central to the questions of how to teach—how to guide curriculum experiences. While this is an area to which psychological, biological, and sociological research have contributed many insights, there are questions of how best to implement these findings and of how to help teachers translate what they know about the learning process into classroom behavior. Four major problem areas about which there is controversy as to how to interpret research findings can be identified: the role that learners' purposes are to play in the choice and development of experiences; the place of firsthand in contrast to vicarious experience; the relative effectiveness of "verbalizing" as against "doing"; and the degree to which the social climate in the classroom needs to be taken into account. Answers to these questions influence the quality of the learning. They also help to determine the choice of school experiences.

What is the significance of the learner's purposes in the guidance of curriculum experiences? One point of view is that if the learner is interested, effective learning is guaranteed—and the learner can become interested in any experience if it is "attractively" presented. A modification of this position is found in the belief that the individual learns just as effectively if he understands the teacher's purpose and follows it. In contrast are those who hold that the meaning a learner sees in a situation will determine what he gets out of it. Among teachers who select and develop learning experiences in terms of the purposes of children and youth, there are those who believe that all learning must stay close to the original purposes recognized by the learner. Others hold that the learner's immediate concerns are the starting point but that the teacher must help him widen his purposes and sense new problems. Thus one finds in one classroom an attractive bulletin board prepared by the teacher to arouse interest in the next topic to be studied. In a second, youngsters are working, each at his own rate of speed, on teacher-prepared contracts or worksheets which outline questions to be answered and sources to be consulted. In a third, committees are left almost entirely to themselves to prepare lists of problems they would like answered in relation to the topic that is the current center of interest. In a fourth, teacher and children together are planning the details of a project, each contributing from his insights and background.

What is the place of direct and of vicarious experience in learning? Certainly, the question of balance between direct and vicarious experience depends in part upon the learner's maturity, for one characteristic of intellectual growth is increased ability to deal with abstract ideas. However, for every maturity level educators differ on the necessity for learners to have some firsthand experiences in contrast to using the symbolism of language, art, and other media to change their behavior. In some classes pupils go through elaborate activity to set up mock conditions or engage in firsthand experiences which some teachers feel provide relatively little insight or understanding beyond what might have been acquired by reading a description of the real situation. There are teachers who believe that learning requires overt action, and they exclude certain experiences because the learners can do nothing directly about solving the problems involved. On the continuum between this position and abstract verbalization is one that views active learning as coming through the use of intellectual processes, including reflection which both deepens basic understanding and clarifies the process of purposeful thinking. How far to go in time and space from learners' lives here and now;

what types of visual or other aids to use; how to adjust to differences in maturity and background are related parts of this question.

What is desirable balance between verbalizing and doing? One group may be engaged in a panel discussion of what they have read about proposals for preventing erosion in their community. In another classroom, several students may be demonstrating the effects of water on eroded soil with models they have prepared by following the instructions in their science textbook. Elsewhere, a group may be working at the edge of the school property planting shrubs and grass and providing drainage for the playing field. In many classrooms all these approaches will be used in connection with a single project. These varied procedures raise the question of how to develop attitudes and understandings that lead to intelligent action. Direct action does not, in and of itself, guarantee understanding and insights, nor do certain kinds of verbalization necessarily preclude growth.

What constitutes an effective learning environment—human and material? Effective teachers have, over the years, provided stimulating physical environments in classrooms. Conscious attention to creating an equally effective social and emotional environment is a more recent concern. Some research indicates that classroom interaction is a major influence on children's learning, with social and emotional needs affecting progress and achievement. Teachers who feel this is important try to evaluate the interpersonal relationships, emotional climate, and other aspects of the program which affect learning. Those who are not impressed with these studies concern themselves with their teaching procedures, giving less attention to the dynamics of the group situation. There are also questions regarding the relative importance of various kinds of motives and the effects upon learning of rewards and punishment. Teachers are also concerned with problems of how best to deal with subsurface motives—desire for acceptance by teachers and peers, security needs, pressures of home and community.

Whether or not ultimate goals are achieved depends, in the end, on the quality of teaching. There is need for a careful appraisal of the effectiveness with which schools are applying what is known about children and youth, the way they grow and the way they learn.

WHO SHOULD BE TAUGHT WHAT UNDER A CURRICULUM THAT PROVIDES FOR ALL PUPILS?

An important aspect of guiding learning is providing for the kaleidoscope of personalities, abilities, and aptitudes in our schools. There are great variations in any group of children. Within a single class there may be a range of several years in intellectual, physical, emotional, and social maturity. The evident upward expansion of the educational program to include all children and youth has increased this range. A high school diploma is a prerequisite for employment in many kinds of business and industry. On the horizon are junior colleges, fast becoming the right of every youth. Never have schools been faced with a more stupendous task in meeting individual needs. How to provide for differences in interests, needs, drives, and abilities within experiences of common concern; how to provide for special interests and abilities; how to relate the demands of general and special education are some of the questions to which teachers give varying answers.

How shall the curriculum be differentiated to provide for all learners? Administrative efforts to provide for the range of individual differences are varied. In some schools there are so-called homogeneous classes in which pupils have been classified on the basis of one or more sets of test scores. In some, the determining factor in setting up two or more classes at a single grade level is age—younger children going to one teacher, older to another. At the primary levels particularly, age and grade lines are disappearing in some schools. In other schools children go from teacher to teacher in order to work with persons who are specialists in their fields. Some classes have specialists come to them. There are remedial clinics and helping teachers. There are special classes of various kinds—"honors" classes for college-bound youth of unusual ability and "opportunity" courses for those whose achievement is limited. If the needs of children and youth are truly to be met, the effectiveness of these and many other procedures must be carefully appraised.

Attempts to solve the problem of providing for differences in interests, needs, and abilities within the classroom setting have resulted in equally varied practices. One class divides into small interest groups, each working on one aspect of the area of study in keeping with the members' judgments of the contributions they can best make to the total class project. In another class, differentiation is provided through free and unassigned periods when individuals can pursue special needs and interests, and through widely varied assignments. One teacher plans home assignments so that, although no two children are doing exactly the same assignment, each is working within the same general area. Another uses workbooks and job sheets to allow individuals to progress at their own rates. In one room learners work as a total class until certain basic information is secured and then divide for special projects. In another, work is almost entirely in groups, and all-class activities come at the point where information is to be shared. Almost every aspect of the teaching–learning process has been modified to provide for individual differences —differentiated activities, assignments, methods, materials, tests, groupings, drill, and promotion. Each of these procedures is not likely to be equally effective. Further, what is effective in one situation may not be as successful in another.

How are the needs of learners with exceptional talent and ability and of those with special needs to be met? This is another major question. Some educators have strong convictions that the child who is gifted intellectually should not be placed much ahead of his social-age group while others would accelerate such children to match their intellectual capacities. Most would consider each child on his own merits. Similar diversity characterizes points of view regarding youngsters classified as mentally retarded, although special classes for this group now have more widespread approval. Whether to offer the same kinds of experiences for all learners, merely adjusting standards, or whether to develop new and distinct programs for these youngsters represents a major problem area for the curriculum worker. A similar range of problems emerges in relation to the role of the school in providing for the learner with special talent. Critical shortages in some areas of specialized talents have focused public and professional attention on the means for developing outstanding potentials.

What part of the educational program shall be allotted to general and what to specialized education, and when should the latter begin? Some educators feel that a good educational framework incorporates specialization. Others argue that education should be general to a particular rung on the educational ladder, such as the secondary school, with specialization following after this point. Still others believe that specialized and general education should move along together, with decreasing time for common study and a corresponding increasing emphasis upon specialized education as the learner proceeds up the educational ladder. The school's role in specific occupational preparation is also being reconsidered. Some educators feel that a program in general education should include various types of work experiences. Others consider vocational education, with instruction in specific work skills, to be a legitimate part of the school program. For some youth, work experience is a reason for staying in school. Re-examination of such problems becomes urgent in a society that requires its citizens to have both a wide range of general competence and a high degree of specialization.

The problem of tailoring a program to the needs of children and youth is a complex one. It is not going to be solved by focusing attention on administrative adaptation alone. Basically, it calls for a rethinking and restructuring of instruction to provide adequate and appropriate experiences for children and youth with all levels of potential.

In a nation which values the unique worth of each individual and recognizes both his right and his obligation to make his maximum contribution to common problems, the basic question of how best to meet the needs of individuals assumes major importance.

HOW SHALL PUPIL GROWTH AND PROGRESS BE EVALUATED?

Progress toward educational goals must be evaluated. In some schools, the primary means of evaluation are tests designed to check the pupil's acquisition of knowledge and skills; in others, evaluation includes the use of anecdotal and other types of records, day-to-day observation of the way learners deal with varied problems they face, and oral and written examinations calling for reasoned judgments of specific situations. Some schools view regular tests and report cards to parents as comprising an adequate evaluation of student growth and even of the curriculum itself. In other schools parent–pupil–teacher conferences are held as needed to evaluate pupil progress and to plan ways in which school and home can supplement each other's efforts in guiding the learner toward agreed-upon goals. Both the evidence collected and the way in which it is appraised must reflect educational goals. Nevertheless, such divergent practices suggest several questions.

What evidence of individual growth shall be gathered and appraised? Some educators would base evaluation on pupil responses to paper-and-pencil tests focused primarily upon factual knowledge; others would use similar instruments but stress questions that require the use of knowledge in meeting a prescribed situation. Still others believe that such means of evaluation should be supplemented by behavioral responses as observed and recorded in cumulative records. This group tends to favor the use of a number of additional evaluative instruments including sociograms, projective techniques, and evaluative conferences. From school to school the variety of combinations in which these and other techniques are used is infinite.

Measurement alone is not evaluation. When the evidence of progress is in, there is still much soul-searching and sometimes heartache when the time comes to translate this evidence into an evaluative statement for an individual student. Some teachers hold that pupil progress should be judged in terms of certain standards determined by educators. Other teachers believe that evaluation should be focused upon progress in terms of individual capacities and without reference to predetermined inclusive standards. Still others argue that evaluation should consider both the learner's progress in terms of his possible growth and how that progress relates to general expectancies for individuals of his age range and general ability. Decisions regarding promotion are closely related to the foregoing. Some educators would promote a pupil only when pre-set standards are met, some favor automatic promotion, others would base a decision on action that promises most for individual growth in the future.

How are learners and other persons to be involved in the evaluation process? In one classroom the teacher grades all papers to insure accurate marking. The teacher's record book contains the evidence of growth, entered in letter grades. In another, teacher and learners together appraise written work. Pupils' notebooks contain a variety of evaluation devices—individual spelling lists, check lists of oral-reading needs, reminders of special English errors. In one classroom, pupils help to phrase letters to their parents reporting their progress; in another, pupils wait anxiously at report time to see what grades they will be given. Parents visit some schools frequently and are called to others only when problems arise. Community members may or may not share their knowledge of learners with teachers.

Such varied procedures indicate that some teachers see evaluation as an integral part of the learning process with teacher and learners reflecting on work done and planning next steps. Others see evaluation as periodic stocktaking by the teacher who then informs the pupil and his parents. Some teachers make evaluation an important part of daily learning experiences while others divorce the evaluative process from other activities. These differing positions not only lead to varied judgments regarding the effectiveness with which the curriculum is meeting the needs of children and youth, but they result in significantly different day-to-day experiences for learners.

Which viewpoints regarding the nature of evaluation adequately judge the competencies required of today's citizens?

HOW SHALL CURRICULUM IMPROVEMENT BE ASSURED?

No matter how carefully decisions are made regarding the curriculum issues discussed in the preceding sections, there is always need to appraise curriculum development critically. Evaluation of the educational program is as basic to the work of the teacher as is self-evaluation to the learner. Teachers, too, are learners as they test the soundness of their decisions on curriculum issues and seek to find ways more fully to implement those decisions. Problems of whom to involve in curriculum improvement; how to assure that proposed changes are actually steps forward; what to foresee as the end product of a curriculum improvement program are crucial in increasing the effectiveness of the curriculum in meeting the needs of children and youth.

Who shall be involved in curriculum improvement? Traditionally, this responsibility was assigned to research bureaus, to curriculum directors, and to committees of teachers whose main function was to install and to test the proposed changes. Over the years, as a consequence of new insights into the process of bringing about change, there has been increasing concern with the involvement of teachers. But many questions have been raised. Is involvement to be on a voluntary or required basis? Should all professional personnel participate or only selected key individuals? What is the most effective unit for curriculum development—the building or the school system? How should committees be selected and organized? Should parents and other lay persons be represented? If so, when and on what bases? Do children and youth have a part? How is consultant help to be used? How should time and funds be provided for curriculum improvement activities? The practices in our schools today are as varied as the answers to these questions.

What procedures make for the most effective changes? The early involvement of teachers, and still the most commonly used method, is at the discussion level. Other procedures, focused directly on behavioral change—new teaching skills, responses reflecting change in attitudes—have been used but not nearly as extensively. Some teachers and other educators believe that direct involvement of the teacher is central in improving educational practice; that the process of curriculum change is, in essence, the application of principles of learning to instructional problems. These educators see experimentation and action research as an integral part of teaching. Those taking a different position ask how the evidence on which change should be based can be secured in the complex classroom setting. To what extent can teachers carry on effective research? Both groups foresee the need for using research techniques in curriculum change. Some would assign to research the role of appraising present practices. Others stress the need for answers to basic curriculum issues based on research. Still others point to the importance of individual and group exploration and testing of ideas in classroom situations. If curriculum revision is to result in improvement, not merely in change, it is important to consider the means through which it is accomplished.

Few studies have tested the effectiveness of the various techniques used to bring about curriculum change.

What shall be the end result of a curriculum improvement program? Some school systems aim for the publication of courses of study and their periodic revision. Others see curriculum improvement as a continuous process and set up the machinery for the constant evaluation of present practices and the testing of new proposals. Some see the process largely as a means of in-service education and care less about the end product than about the experiences of those involved.

Bringing about curriculum change is central to any forward-moving educational program. What is done and how it is done make a fundamental difference in the way in which the whole range of curriculum issues are conceived and dealt with.

Toward a Curriculum for Modern Living

If sound proposals for curriculum design and effective educational practices are to result, teachers and administrators must consider the basic issues involved. Every aspect of education—defining the role of the school, deciding what to teach, determining bases for organizing the curriculum, selecting ways of guiding experiences, evaluating pupil growth—requires a choice among alternatives. Over the years, educators, together with specialists in related fields, have developed a body of research and experience. These are helpful in understanding the issues, in indicating what the alternative choices are and where each may lead, and in making decisions for action. But the soundest research seldom provides final answers to curriculum problems. Research must still be interpreted and eventually translated into practice. Curriculum development and even day-to-day teaching, therefore, involve a great many value judgments.

An analytical look at classroom practice often fails to reveal sharply etched solutions to curriculum problems. What actually is being done in the classroom frequently represents a compromise or merging of judgments—often without identification of the basic issues, sometimes without clear understanding that such issues even exist or without consideration of the assumptions underlying the several possible alternative resolutions of these issues. The wide range of curriculum practices which has been identified in this chapter, and the obvious differences from one school to another, between classrooms in the same school, and even within a single classroom, point to the central role of value judgments in decision-making in education.

THREE FOUNDATIONAL AREAS CONTRIBUTE TO DECISION-MAKING IN EDUCATION

Educators can turn to three foundational areas as they examine alternative proposals on any of the curriculum issues and problems identified in this chapter and make the many choices required in developing an adequate program for children and youth. The first relates to the nature of society and the values it holds and seeks to attain (the **social foundations**); the second, to the learner as a developing organism and to the nature of the learning process (the **psychological foundations**); and the third, to the values and beliefs which make up one's philosophies of life and of education (the **philosophical foundations**). Chapters 2 and 3 examine in detail the social and psychological areas. The third area, philosophy, in a sense overarches the others.

Philosophical thinking involves clarifying one's concepts and beliefs, analyzing and criticizing the assumptions underlying alternative proposals, and using these as a basis for choice-making. Schools of philosophy represent attempts by philosophers to systematize and organize this process into sets of beliefs that will yield consistent answers to basic issues. From such a process may come new alternative proposals as well as insights into the assumptions underlying existing alternatives. The individual's philosophy of education is usually related to, or part of, a larger philosophy of life. It emerges for some individuals on an intuitive basis, the product of an accumulation of experiences since childhood which have resulted in beliefs with various degrees of personal commitment. For others, philosophies of life and of education have evolved from rather conscious attempts to order beliefs into some unified scheme which might guide their decision-making.

It is quite likely that many individuals select from various possible alternatives without too much conscious attention to the bases underlying their choices. And yet they are undoubtedly influenced by values assimilated and internalized to a point where many day-to-day decisions are made without apparent recourse to a very elaborate deductive process which begins with reference to basic beliefs about education. The fact that some individuals operate effectively without rational examination of their value systems while others are vocal about a philosophical scheme without its affecting their behavior does not minimize the importance of clarifying one's concepts and critically analyzing the underlying assumptions in order to sift alternatives and develop sound educational programs. A carefully thought through set of beliefs provides a basis for consistent action in dealing with curriculum issues.

Comprehensive statements of educational philosophy represent the systematic efforts of philosophers to examine values, to derive meanings from facts, to organize experiences so they are useful, to justify one belief as better than another, and sometimes to develop new proposals for translation into practice. Several careful delineations of the various schools of philosophical thought are available.[1] These analyses are an important resource for educators as they test the assumptions which underlie their practical decisions about what and how to teach.

The various schools of philosophy are not detailed in this volume in the same way as Chapter 2 examines the nature of our society and Chapter 3 discusses the learner and the learning process. Rather than ascribing certain positions on curriculum issues to various schools of philosophy or individual philosophers, the basic values underlying the decisions which lead to the authors' proposal for a curriculum design are identified as specific problems and issues are considered, the alternative solutions are critically analyzed, and justifications for the choices are made. Thus, in effect, the authors apply the philosophical method to the issues of curriculum development throughout the volume.

THIS VOLUME IS AN APPLICATION OF A SET OF BELIEFS

This volume is an attempt to look at the curriculum as a whole and in terms of a particular set of beliefs. It is focused upon a particular curriculum design and the ways in which this design may be put into practice. The purpose is to spell out, first, general principles of curriculum development that recognize the importance of relating individual needs to those of society, and, second, suggestions as to the implications of this relationship for each of the basic curriculum issues discussed in this chapter.

[1] For discussions of viewpoints of several major philosophical schools see: J. Donald Butler, *Four Philosophies and Their Practice in Education and Religion* (New York: Harper & Brothers, 1951); John S. Brubacher, *Modern Philosophies of Education,* Second Edition (New York: McGraw-Hill Book Company, Inc., 1950); Sidney M. Hook, *Education for Modern Man* (New York: The Dial Press, Inc., 1946); National Society for the Study of Education, *Modern Philosophies and Education,* Fifty-fourth Yearbook, Part I (Chicago: The University of Chicago Press, 1955), and *Philosophies of Education,* Forty-first Yearbook, Part I (Chicago: The University of Chicago Press, 1942).

For discussion of particular schools see: CLASSICAL REALISM: Harry S. Broudy, *Building a Philosophy of Education* (New York: Prentice-Hall, Inc., 1954); EXPERIMENTALISM: John L. Childs, *American Pragmatism and Education* (New York: Henry Holt and Company, Inc., 1956); RECONSTRUCTIONISM: Theodore Brameld, *Toward a Reconstructed Philosophy of Education* (New York: The Dryden Press, Inc., 1956); PERENNIALISM: Robert M. Hutchins, *The University of Utopia* (Chicago: The University of Chicago Press, 1954); and THOMISM: Jacques Maritain, *Education at the Crossroads* (New York: Newson & Company, 1943).

Part I deals with the foundations of the curriculum just noted as basic to developing a set of educational beliefs—the nature of our society and its values and the nature of the learner and the learning process.

Part II analyzes current proposals for designing the curriculum, provides the details of the authors' concept of the curriculum for learners in our times, and relates this concept to the essential elements of a desirable curriculum design. In this part, we indicate how our proposed curriculum answers the questions of scope, sequence, continuity, balance, and depth with which all designs must deal.

In Part III the relationship between what and how to teach is developed through discussion of the selection and guidance of learning experiences and provisions for individual differences. Because we believe evaluation is an integral part of the curriculum, specific suggestions are included for evaluating both individual growth and the effectiveness of the school program.

Part IV contains detailed descriptions of what the proposed curriculum design might look like in a first, fifth, and tenth grade.

The final section, Part V, offers suggestions for working cooperatively in curriculum improvement. The role of the teacher and of leadership in implementing the proposed design is discussed as well as the methods for initiating programs for curriculum improvement. Finally, because of the authors' conviction of the importance of an experimental approach, attention is given to the role of research in curriculum development.

The problem of developing a curriculum for modern living is not new. All teachers and other curriculum workers have faced it in varied ways. Changes of many types have been made in educational programs during the years of school expansion. While the significance of these changes is not to be minimized, the development has been so rapid and the problems and pressures so great that the many parts have not always been synthesized into a whole related to the central purposes of education and the principles for achieving them.

America is a giant in the world of today and is likely to continue to be so tomorrow. If it plays the giant heroically, it will be because educators have learned to help each individual develop his personal resources as effectively as scientists and industrialists have learned to develop material resources. The school can be important in shaping the thinking and behavior of the young. The school, at its best, can prepare learners to take their places in new world relationships, as producers and consumers of the culture and society. To do the job, the school must be equipped to study every learner carefully, to guide him according to his own capabilities and talents, and to provide experiences that call forth each person's maximum effectiveness.

Curriculum improvement is a major obligation of every educator and of many lay persons as well, if schools are to achieve the kind of education that will fit young people to join adult society with satisfaction and self-fulfillment, with loyalty and a spirit of active contribution. The individual teacher must become a curriculum worker constantly examining, testing, and evaluating his own practices and procedures as these affect the total educational program, if society's faith in the school as a positive social force is to be justified. Whatever other issues may exist among educators, all are agreed that the key to a good educational program is an effective teacher.

Related Readings

BRAMELD, THEODORE. *Philosophy of Education in Cultural Perspective.* New York: The Dryden Press, Inc., 1955.

CASWELL, HOLLIS L., AND ARTHUR W. FOSHAY. *Education in the Elementary School.* Third edition. New York: American Book Company, 1957.

DEWEY, JOHN. *Experience and Education.* New York: The Macmillan Company, 1938.

GWYNN, J. MINOR. *Curriculum Principles and Social Trends.* Revised edition. New York: The Macmillan Company, 1950.

HERRICK, V. E., AND R. W. TYLER. *Toward Improved Curriculum Theory.* Supplementary Edition, Monograph No. 71. Conference on Curriculum Theory, 1947. Chicago: University of Chicago Press, 1950.

KEARNEY, NOLAN C. *Elementary School Objectives.* New York: Russell Sage Foundation, 1953.

LEONARD, J. P. *Developing the Secondary School Curriculum.* Revised edition. New York: Rinehart & Company, Inc., 1953.

NATIONAL SOCIETY FOR THE STUDY OF EDUCATION. *Modern Philosophies of Education.* Fifty-fourth Yearbook, Part 1. Chicago: University of Chicago Press, 1955.

SAYLOR, J. GALEN, AND WILLIAM M. ALEXANDER. *Curriculum Planning for Better Teaching and Learning.* New York: Rinehart & Company, Inc., 1954.

SMITH, B. OTHANEL, WILLIAM O. STANLEY, AND J. HARLAN SHORES. *Fundamentals of Curriculum Development.* Revised edition. Yonkers-on-Hudson, N.Y.: World Book Company, 1957.

2

SOCIETY

A GUIDE TO CURRICULUM DEVELOPMENT

Society and contemporary life outside of the school can and do act as guides to curriculum development. Society provides the framework within which children and youth live and learn, and inevitably affects what they bring to school and the ways in which they put their school experiences to work. The kind of society from which learners come points to the values they must live by as they share with others the task of building their country and their world. A study of society can indicate the understandings and competencies children and youth are likely to need just as it can bring into focus the problems with which they are dealing and with which they will have to cope. An examination of society also suggests the environments out of which come the citizens who mold the world of today and tomorrow. Cultural values, societal needs, and learners' backgrounds serve as guides to curriculum development.

Democratic Values—The Foundation of American Society

Free peoples have set democracy as their goal. Any society grows in the direction of democracy to the extent that each individual and group in that society can put basic democratic values into action in every aspect of daily living. Living and participating in a democracy require skills and understandings far more complex and difficult than those required in a society dominated and controlled by a select few. The individual in a democracy is charged with the responsibility of making that democracy function for the good of all. The school's obligation is to build curricula and establish the conditions under which individuals can acquire values and needed competencies and be able to translate them into action. To provide the guide lines for the education of all citizens, the basic characteristics of a democratic society must be examined and understood. The characteristics set forth in the following pages are not all-inclusive but are illustrative of democratic values which serve as guides to the development of skills and understandings needed by all.

FREEDOM TO CHOOSE THOSE WHO WILL GOVERN

Citizens in a democratic society are individually responsible for selecting those who will develop and administer governmental policies. Before the individual can meet intelligently his obligations toward his government, he must know what it is like. He must understand its weaknesses and its strengths. He must know its organization, responsibilities, ways of operation, and goals. Likewise, he must know how his participation can effectively promote better government through the selection of able persons to establish policies and administer them. He must be aware of and willing to accept his own responsibility to take appropriate leadership roles. He must recognize that democratic governments express the will of the people. He must understand, also, that society is dynamic and that what was good for one period in our history may not be desirable as times and conditions change. The individual must recognize the qualities that make for leadership so that when he makes his choices through the ballot, or offers himself as a candidate, he does so on the basis of sound principles rather than of emotion or traditional patterns of acting.

To accomplish these ends, the curriculum worker needs to answer such questions as . . .

What should children and youth understand about democratic governments as compared with totalitarian governments?

What should children and youth know about the ways and means that have brought about democracy in government?

How can children and youth be helped to develop the skills and understandings that are basic to strengthening democratic governments?

How can the school and the community provide children and youth with firsthand experiences of democracy in government?

What experiences can be provided children and youth in selecting leaders and in evaluating their choices?

FREEDOM TO INITIATE NEEDED CHANGE

Local, national, and world conditions change rapidly. As these changes occur, new problems arise, new situations emerge, and old patterns of action may no longer be the best patterns. In a totalitarian state, the decisions to effect change rest with a small group of self-appointed and self-perpetuating individuals. In a democracy, the power and the obligation to initiate change rest with the people. Change for the sake of change is unrealistic. But a society that clings to yesterday's patterns when change would improve the lot of all ceases to be a dynamic society. Among the blocks in the way of change when it is needed are tradition, fear, ignorance, apathy, and administrative controls. These blocks to change need to be examined and children and youth should be helped to understand how these obstacles originate and how they prevent society from meeting the needs of the modern world.

Clearly, a changing world makes fixed and patterned ways of behaving of little worth. Each individual must be able to sense the new elements in situations, must be flexible in responding to them, and must be willing to approach life with wholesome curiosity and willingness to experiment, to test, and to try. But, in addition to flexibility and ability to adjust to new circumstances, all individuals need a measure of security, a feeling of being able to cope with new situations. In a changing society that security resides chiefly in working in a way that deals effectively with problems, in knowing and being able to use resources, in being able to apply appropriately and test basic generalizations previously arrived at through work in other related but different situations.

The democratic value of freedom to initiate change suggests questions such as the following when teachers and others consider how the curriculum shall be designed . . .

What are the essential characteristics of the process by which social change comes about?

How can learners be helped to see that ours is a dynamic society which requires new patterns of action? To believe that rules, regulations, and laws are the expression of the people and can be changed by them?

How can learners be helped to examine our traditions for the purpose of determining those that are worth keeping and those that should be discarded or modified?

How can learners develop fearlessness in dealing with issues of importance to society—crowded housing, sordidness of cities, meagerness of rural culture, the limited environment of many in a world of abundance?

How can children and youth be helped to use a problem-solving approach in dealing with situations?

How can a commitment to active participation rather than an apathetic attitude toward the community and larger society be developed?

EQUALITY UNDER THE LAW

In a democracy, rights accorded to one should be accorded to all. The right to be treated under the law equally with all others, regardless of economic, social, or political status, is one such right. Democracy protects every individual against exploitation by special privilege, power, or the law. It guarantees a legal assumption of innocence until guilt is proved; definite charges before arrest and detention; open and speedy trial by a jury of peers; and protection of rights by the court through a competent counsel. It precludes guilt by association. If society is to be a guide to curriculum development, this basic principle of democracy raises such questions as . . .

How can learners be helped to understand the full meaning of the principle of equality under the law?

How can all aspects of school life be organized and administered so as to give learners a feeling of security and confidence that all are treated equally?

How can learners be helped to a sound understanding of their rights, and of ways to protect and use them for the good of all?

FREEDOM TO PARTICIPATE IN THE RELIGION OF ONE'S CHOICE

American democracy guarantees to each individual the right to worship according to the dictates of his own conscience and recognizes the importance of complete separation of church and state. Spiritual and moral values in a democracy have no demarcation in terms of religious creeds or denominations. Rather, they provide the basis for understanding and respecting all religious doctrines. As such, they should permeate the actions of all who believe in the total welfare of individuals in society. When considering how these values can become a part of curriculum experiences, such questions as the following need to be examined . . .

How can the school become an important influence in developing individuals with respect for those who worship or believe differently from themselves?

How can moral and spiritual values be made a part of the educative process without involving doctrines, creeds, and other religious differences?

How can learners become aware of the importance of separation of church and state?

FREEDOM TO EXPRESS POINTS OF VIEW THAT CONFLICT WITH THOSE OF THE MAJORITY

Democracy guarantees the right of individuals to explore and voice opinions about new ideas, to use various media of communication to disseminate ideas, and to use peaceful means to have these accepted. To keep one from exploring ideas or to forbid their dissemination is a first step toward totalitarianism. This principle also recognizes and protects the right of individuals to work together to promote their own ideas and interests if these are compatible with the general welfare. Many of the great advances of mankind began with a minority. If the minority had been thwarted in its attempts to express its ideas, to organize groups to disseminate these ideas, and to influence public opinion to accept them, much of the progress of mankind would have been blocked. This principle, as it relates to curriculum development, raises such questions as . . .

What attitudes, skills, and understandings are basic to listening thoughtfully to developing ideas, to knowing when it is important to fight for an idea and when a difference of opinion is not crucial, to disagreeing with a point of view without personal antagonism?

How shall learners be encouraged to explore new ideas? To voice conflicting ideas or unpopular beliefs?

How can children and youth be helped to think clearly while exploring ideas so that they will have a sound basis for action?

FREEDOM TO CHOOSE AN OCCUPATION, TO FOLLOW IT, AND TO PROGRESS IN IT

Basic to a democratic way of life is the responsibility of the individual to share in the work of the world. Democracy guarantees to each individual the right to choose an occupation that is not contrary to society's best interests and to enjoy the fruits of his labor after paying his just share of the costs of government which operates for the benefit of all. This freedom assumes that individual and private enterprise will be encouraged in so far as they are compatible with the general welfare. It also recognizes that human rights are more important than property rights and that both are guaranteed in a democracy.

Inherent in the right to choose an occupation is the individual's responsibility to render an honest day's work for a day's pay and his obligation to negotiate problems that confront the employer and the employed. Negotiation, compromise, agreement—these are basic to democracy whether they occur in the field of work, of government, or of social relations.

Modern youth should see the challenge of the work to be done in a world of machines. The attitudes and understandings young people are helped to build will play a significant part in determining whether they, as adults, will help solve social and economic problems of society. To help them make positive contributions, the curriculum worker needs to answer such questions as . . .

How can the school experiences of children and youth be effective in truly making them free to enter the occupations of their choice?

How can what is known about building attitudes be applied to developing a sense of social obligation to share in the work of the world, to respect all labor, to make full use of one's talents, to work with a sense of service?

How can the school contribute to these attitudes needed in a society that recognizes both the right to free enterprise and the obligation to negotiate?

How can children and youth be helped to develop and maintain effective standards of workmanship?

FREEDOM OF MINORITIES TO PARTICIPATE FULLY AND WITHOUT PREJUDICE IN ALL ASPECTS OF LIFE AND GOVERNMENT

A democratic society guarantees to minority groups the same rights and privileges that are accorded to majorities. This principle is based on the recognition that in a democracy the will of the majority, as expressed in laws, elections, and other activities, governs all. The minority has a right to be heard, to exercise all peaceful means to change the will of the majority, and to be respected so long as its actions are compatible with the general welfare. Only when minorities are respected and given freedom to participate fully in the life and activities of the society can democracy really exist and flourish. Whether the minority is in terms of race, religion, occupation, or point of view, the principle is the same. At the same time, minorities have an obligation to deport themselves in a manner consistent with the society in which they live, respecting the rights of the majority.

The individual is a minority of one, and as such has the right to all privileges of the larger group. His welfare is of primary importance in a democratic society. Each individual is considered to be of essential worth. Each individual is believed to have within himself resources for creative expression which he has a right and responsibility to develop. The greatest resource of any nation resides in the potentialities of all its people. This means the recognition and appreciation of the worth of every individual at each stage of his growth and development. Equal men, each having opportunity to assume the rights and responsibilities that are his, are a first essential in a democratic society.

Educators interested in developing a total school environment which implements this basic concern with the rights of minorities—individuals or groups—and in helping children and youth grow in understanding, ability, and willingness to use this basic value as a guide to action, will reflect on questions like these . . .

How can the school establish a climate of acceptance of those who differ from the majority in point of view, color, religion, or occupation?

How can the school situation be organized so that minority groups may feel free to discuss their problems, find solutions to these problems, and feel they themselves are important in the total situation?

How can the school develop in the thinking of a member of a minority understanding that he, too, must respect the rights of others and their points of view?

How can children and youth be provided a vital and respected place in society in keeping with their maturity?

What is involved in assuring to every child and youth the maximum realization of his intellectual power and special abilities?

What is involved in helping children and youth appreciate the uniqueness of others?

FREEDOM TO PROMOTE THE CAUSE OF PEACE THROUGHOUT THE WORLD

In the years since World War II, there has been an affirmative and frightening response to the inquiry as to whether man could devise the means for destroying civilization as we know it. Nuclear and thermonuclear weapons leave no alternative to cooperation among all nations. Our present world has become a "little neighborhood" with no area beyond the round-trip nonstop range of aircraft. Alien ideas can challenge national assumptions. World communication systems expose youth and adults to every form of political theory. Lust for power in a few countries can endanger the world, for war in an age of atomic power recognizes no boundaries in its contagion and destruction. The same technological changes which have been affecting and changing relationships within a particular country have been changing them throughout the world. Ours has become an interrelated, interdependent world, despite great differences in history and language, wealth and national or cultural genius, attitudes and ideas, political ideologies and national aspirations.

A framework for peace has been established with the founding of the United Nations but its success will depend on more than lofty visions of peace and freedom for all nations. There is need for men with ability to work out plans for the proper distribution and conservation of the world's resources and skills and to establish methods of sharing the cultures of many nations. Every nation has a grave responsibility in keeping the peace. Each is neighbor to those called foreigners, or natives, or strangers, or just different kind of folk. The destiny of nations is linked together and the new relationships demand intelligent acquaintance.

But understanding alone is not enough. The problems of group cooperation will not be solved until those involved have learned to plan and work together. Experimentation in new forms of interaction is needed. Some of the United Nations agencies have opened up new and promising possibilities of international cooperation. The means for thinking together as well as for working together are multiplying as fast or faster than the means for more widespread industrial production. Effective ways of using these means must be found. Techniques that were adequate for the town meeting will not suffice in a conference of nations. As groups become larger and intergroup relationships more complex, new ways must be found for overcoming ideological barriers and for securing democratic participation of group members.

Schools must play their part by helping children become world-minded. Yesterday's stereotypes of other peoples must be replaced by realistic pictures of life in foreign lands; the values and attitudes held by these peoples must be emphasized; and fair consideration must be given to the reasons for conflicts. Schools must help children and youth understand the nature and promise of international cooperation, and ways in which nations can work together for the good of all. But most of all, children and youth should have opportunities to appraise local, national, and international issues in the light of their effect upon other peoples in the world. More specifically, there is need to give thought to such questions as . . .

How can school experiences help children and youth to sense the value of and the appropriate time for subordinating the smaller to the greater good, the personal to the social goal?

What is basic to building understanding and appreciation of the values and attitudes of others—those within the group and those representing other groups?

What types of experiences will be most effective in helping children and youth gain sound understanding and appreciation of people in other lands?

In what ways can the school provide for children and youth to share in community activities which are of concern to them and within their range of effective action?

What does the need to understand cooperative action mean by way of providing opportunity for children and youth to share in the planning of their experiences—to sense the responsibility of the individual in a group enterprise?

America—A Machine-Powered and Industrial Civilization

Coloring all aspects of society in America is the industrial age into which the whole world has moved or is rapidly moving. Wherever a community may be located, whatever the material conditions and the composition of its people, there are signs of the vast changes brought about by this industrialization and the problems which inevitably accompany such changes. Factory smokestacks, power plants, power-driven agricultural machinery, and many other evidences of technological development are everywhere. And now the possibilities of using nuclear energy for peaceful purposes open up areas for unbelievable advances in human welfare. The world of today is committed to science and technology. Society is being reshaped in an age of power. Tomorrow's youth must be able to control a machine era as effectively as the pioneer conquered the wilderness.

The values which are the foundations of our society provide one set of directives for the curriculum worker. It is also important to envision the world in which children and youth are to live, and the understandings and competencies they must have. No attempt is made in the pages which follow to include all the aspects of our industrial society. Rather, some of the crucial problems facing learners are pointed out as a basis for curriculum development.

INDUSTRIAL CIVILIZATION HAS ALTERED THE TRADITIONAL PATTERN AND CONCEPT OF OUR ECONOMY

The pattern of American and world economies is changing as a result of the machine and power age. New goods, materials, and processes are being developed, and at the same time new patterns of living are emerging. The home handcraftsman gave way to the small business which in turn is being replaced in many instances by the large industrial corporation. Although small business enterprises still exist in great numbers, economic power today tends to be concentrated in large organizations. As industries grew, organized labor also increased in power. The philosophy of laissez faire gave way to varying degrees of government regulation. With a great depression, a great war, and a persisting cold war, government regulation of the nation's economy continued. Yet there remain divided opinion and heated controversy regarding the extent and kind of government participation and regulation in our economic life.

In the last hundred years technology has plunged far ahead of social and economic thinking. Man learned to manipulate machines, to build factories, to construct bridges, and to conquer space. He conceived the idea of mass production and of the assembly line, and is moving rapidly toward automation. But he failed, in general, to use these instruments and forces in ways which would bring security to all men. Depressions recurred with increased intensity. Doubts were expressed as to whether minds which could conceive television or build supersonic aircraft or design nuclear reactors would also be capable of designing an economy wherein men could produce and consume far more than the economists of previous decades thought possible. But the goal of sixty million jobs, thought impossible in the mid-1940's, has long since been surpassed. For at least a decade and a half, however, military preparedness has been an important basis of the nation's economy. These years have shown that it takes the vision, skill, and ingenuity of all people planning and working cooperatively in terms of a common purpose to do the job. An equally compelling peacetime goal to unify the efforts of all is needed.

Notwithstanding technological advance and overt prosperity, there are still problems related to economic values and structures. A large section of our population is still poorly housed and ill-fed. A migrant-worker population moves from area to area, their children inadequately cared for and poorly educated. The move from the small family-sized farm to village and city continues. As retirement ages are lowered and the aged live longer, problems concerning the care and happiness of older people increase. The morning paper may tell of a bumper wheat crop in this country and of starvation in other parts of the world; of a Congressional dispute over civil rights legislation; of new proposals for aiding underdeveloped countries; of a nuclear-powered submarine able to circle the globe several times without replenishing its fuel supply; of a proposal to reduce surpluses through a soil bank; of an increase in juvenile delinquency and the incidence of adult crime; of negotiations with neighboring countries regarding trade. To cope with these and other problems requires men and women with far greater civic and economic competence than that possessed by the average person today. The school has an important role to play in helping to develop the needed understandings, values, and skills which are basic to these competencies.

Children and youth come to our schools with vital personal concerns and tensions created by this industrial society. In Baldwin, fathers are talking about the pending strike in the steel foundry; in Darby, the textile mill is about to move to a different location; in Suffolk, the nearby Air Force Base is replacing its propeller-driven planes with jet aircraft, increasing the noise level over the homes; in Belleville, the union and the corporation on which the community's workers depend are beginning to negotiate a new contract; in Broad Acres, a new housing development will add hundreds of homes to the village; in Oxford, a dispute with nearby Jackson threatens the source of water supply. These problems are part of the environment of the children and youth. Their families discuss the impact of these events on daily living.

Problems and tensions such as these must find their appropriate place in school activities; the task of curriculum planners is to decide what that appropriate place should be. Teachers and others who carry leadership roles need to consider such underlying questions as . . .

What are the fundamental and recurring problems in our industrial economy with which children and youth, men and women, are dealing and must deal?

What competencies—concepts, understandings, and skills—are needed to deal with these persistent problems?

What understandings and skills are needed to use the basic machines and instruments of our technological development?

How can the school most effectively develop attitudes needed to insure that industrial advance will be used for maximum social good, and in keeping with social values?

INDUSTRIAL CIVILIZATION HAS BROUGHT NEW MODES OF LIVELIHOOD

Technological changes have also created new types of work and modified the nature and kind of work to be done. New industries have sprung into existence and mushroomed in size. For example, there is now a vast airlines network which hardly existed thirty years ago. This expansion has not only created a need for additional persons who can build planes and parts but also for individuals who can service aircraft. A need for accurate long-range weather forecasting increased the demands for meteorologists and a whole new communications industry was developed for this transportation medium. Pilots, engineers, designers, mechanics, clerks, teletype operators, radio and radar technicians, and dozens of other service and technical workers were required by the development of the airlines industry. Whole new industries have grown up around the processing of foods and the development of plastic materials. Farming has become an occupation requiring sound scientific background. New machinery and new ways of processing foods, a virtual revolution in the textile industry, modern appliances of all kinds, are changing the activities of the housewife. Even in such established businesses as restaurants, cotton mills, and the building trades there have been marked shifts in the kinds of work required. With each new discovery have come new needs and demands for new abilities. New kinds of work, new substances, and new resources are found everywhere. Specialization breeds more specialization.

Industrialization also is bringing about a new occupational structure marked by a reduction in the proportion of workers engaged in the production of material goods and an increase in the number engaged in service occupations. More persons are being freed to enter service occupations directly related to the welfare of many individuals, such as teaching, social service, nursing, medicine, guidance, and recreation. These occupations demand highly developed techniques for working with others, as well as willingness to give service and a genuine desire to contribute to human welfare.

New industrial structures from time to time cause disorientation in the field of work. Power machines are constantly taking the place of labor. But, despite increased automation and temporary interruptions, industry the world over currently employs more men than ever before. Automation reduces the need for physical labor but at the same time it increases the need for intellectual and technical skills; it reduces the need for some kinds of workers and increases the need for others. There will be displacements and replacements in the labor force which will pose basic problems. To fulfill education's role in preparing children and youth to understand and deal with these problems, those planning the curriculum need to answer such questions as . . .

What are the problems and concerns of children and youth in the area of work and how are they related to the larger community problems arising out of rapid changes in ways of earning a living?

What is the place of direct work experience—in industry, on the farm, in the professions—in the curriculum for children? for youth? What must characterize the nature and quality of those experiences?

How can the school help individuals to determine vocational interests and aptitudes? How can the school facilitate occupational education at the time when it is most appropriate in terms of the capacities of the learner?

TECHNOLOGICAL DEVELOPMENTS HAVE BROUGHT A NEW STATUS FOR WORKERS

New recognition has been given to the dignity of labor. To handle tools, to work in overalls, to be part of the complex organization of men, each contributing his part to the production of automobile, radio, food freezer, an atomic reactor, has become an accepted work pattern of life. The worker has achieved a new status in American society. Increasingly, workers own their own homes, are active and respected community members, drive their own automobiles, have summer vacation spots, and live as relatively few persons could in earlier times. Automation has put a premium on different kinds of skills and intensified the need for trained manpower of many varieties—technical, scientific, and professional. In those areas in which automation is already established, the need for highly skilled individuals in ever-larger numbers has become a major problem. The unskilled laborer of yesterday has become the semiskilled operator of today and must become the highly skilled technician of tomorrow.

Manpower shortages in areas of specialized talents have turned attention to the conservation of human resources. While education in a democracy is inevitably committed to the cultivation of all the abilities of all its people, at the same time technological and population changes in a period of international tension have given impetus to a new search for human talent and to a more urgent need for developing educational programs that will insure the optimum growth of individual potential. The full development of high-level abilities becomes ever more urgent during a period of vast industrial and social change.

The right of every individual to work has been identified as a basic democratic value. This value and the status being realized by all workers pose a number of questions which must be faced. What length of working day, in various fields of endeavor, will give full employment? The five-day, forty-hour week has been widely accepted; will a twenty-four-, a thirty-, or a thirty-five-hour week be next? What is the responsibility of government to provide employment? How can we determine and guarantee adequate preparation of needed personnel in the various occupations, safguarding against both undersupply and oversupply? Shortages of engineers and scientists have led to strenuous recruitment efforts in these areas; how can these needs be met without depleting other areas? What is the place of women in industry? How can the rights of older workers be assured? What is indicated in the way of retirement programs?

Children and youth may not face these problems directly, but they come in contact with them through the vocational experiences of their families and communities. Those responsible for the educational programs schools should develop must consider such questions as . . .

> How can children and youth be helped to understand problems relating to the conservation of human resources, such as working conditions, length of the work day, governmental provision for unemployment, retirement plans, and the contributions of older workers?
>
> How can the school help individuals to relate their capacities, interests, and desires to national work needs in choosing from the large number of occupational fields?
>
> What experiences will help learners to understand and respect the contributions of various workers to the ongoing life of the school—cafeteria workers, secretaries, custodians, administrators, teachers, community workers?
>
> What experiences in the ongoing life of the school can help children and youth to use and respect the machines which facilitate the work they do—typewriter, mimeograph, television, projector, cafeteria steam table, shop tools?

INCREASED INDUSTRIALIZATION HAS BROUGHT INCREASED LEISURE

Technological advances have assured an ever-increasing leisure for all. The productivity of labor has been increased as working hours have decreased. The twelve-hour day has been reduced to eight, the sixty- and eighty-hour week to forty and less. Further reductions are quite probable. Paid vacations and holidays have become part of the labor scene. Retirement ages are being set earlier, and man is living longer. Indications are that increased use of power will continue to give man more time to develop his interests, talents, and abilities. Time and energy released for leisure activities and interests present a real challenge to school and community.

What are the questions to be raised and the problems to be faced by elementary and secondary schools which meet the challenge of helping children and youth to develop the skills and attitudes needed for creative use of leisure? Among them are such questions as the following . . .

What sources of creative outlet—music, drama, hobbies, sports, art—should the school help learners to explore? When should the emphasis be placed on participation and when on spectator activities?

Should the school help develop special talents that will make for creative use of leisure? What talents? For all pupils or for those otherwise unable to develop their talents?

Where in the school program should provision be made for creative use of leisure—as an integral part of the curriculum or as a tangential or co-curricular part?

Should periods of free or unassigned time be a part of every learner's program to provide opportunity to learn how to use his own time creatively and to take an interest in the way other people use theirs?

What part should the school play in fostering positive out-of-school leisure activities—bringing new resources to the community, working with the community library to help young people explore recreational reading, working with the home to help children make effective use of the radio, television, the press, and motion pictures?

INDUSTRIAL CIVILIZATION HAS CHANGED THE PATTERN OF FAMILY LIFE

Social units as well as economic structures are being affected by industrialization. This is particularly true of the home and the community. When families were larger, when they were more nearly self-sufficient, children and youth played an important part in carrying on the work of the home. Members of the family were intimately associated, and work and play experiences were shared. Each family unit had an important role in the social and educational development of its members. Although the family is still the primary social unit, its responsibilities and relationships are changing, especially in the urban and suburban areas.

Industrialization has greatly changed family functions. Work is no longer done in common; many work responsibilities of the household of an earlier day are not present. As the family unit does less to supply its own needs and becomes less self-contained, other persons and community enterprises share in teaching responsibilities. Much of the teaching formerly done by the home in the normal course of family living is now shared by other agencies—the school, the church, the press, the library, the motion picture, the radio, and television. Quality of materials is learned by helping mother shop, rather than by helping her with cooking and sewing. Standards of workmanship are learned through appraising the work of home and community helpers as well as by sharing in home responsibilities.

As the closely knit family pattern disappeared, the neighborly and intimate community of the past altered. No longer do the values of the self-contained family group go relatively unquestioned. Spiritual values and morals are increasingly being conditioned by influences outside the immediate family group. Both positive and negative community elements make their contribution—the church and the dance hall, the youth organization and the gang, the block party and the gang war.

Sources of recreation and leisure are being sought in the community rather than in the home. In some cases where family size has been reduced, the possibilities for a variety of cooperative recreational activities within the home have decreased. Slums, crowded city apartments, lack of adequate play space, all throw burdens upon the community which were formerly assumed by the family group. On the other hand, the fact that community resources are often easily available is causing some families to use these resources to the exclusion of activities in which only members of the family share.

Changed occupational patterns are taking women out of the home. More mothers are working in full-time jobs than ever before. What was viewed as an emergency wartime measure has become a permanently accepted pattern. Love and affection are still present in the home, but they do not necessarily appear in the earlier symbolism of the woman of the house cooking, sewing, and caring for her family. In many cases, children and youth are getting their own meals, are locked out of homes after school hours, or are left with heavy responsibilities for younger members of the family. In urban areas, the all-day child-care center has expanded greatly. This trend toward mothers working has raised many problems. How are parental responsibilities to children being fulfilled if a "second income" is necessary to meet budget needs? What responsibilities should the various members of the family undertake if there is to be family unity?

An increasingly high broken-home rate has raised the number of children and youth who face problems of insecurity. Sometimes living with one parent only, at other times shuttling between two homes, or adjusting to "new" parents—these youngsters may well turn to the school for some of the security and affection they need. Certainly the anxieties and tensions of such children and youth affect the quality of their learning and may even influence the climate of learning for others in the classroom.

Although frontiers have long since disappeared, people still continue to move across the country, and from country to country, in endless streams. Migrations of individuals and groups add up to staggering totals and pose major problems of readjustment. From farms to villages and cities; from mountains to plains; from southern farms to northern cities; from one harvest area to another; from old northern mill towns to new southern factories; from Old-World countries to New-World homes; from city to suburb; from East to West—families have followed wage earners and youth have left home to secure employment, or to improve their lot, or to seek new fortunes. The sudden removal of families or youth from one type of life to another means new school relationships.

Many schools have recognized the importance of cooperative relationships with the home, and changing family patterns have given added significance to the quality of these relationships. Home and school may need to work together even more closely to provide for the all-round growth of learners. Teachers and others who recognize the significance of the family in our society, and the changing pattern of family life, will want to give consideration to problems such as these . . .

For what areas of child growth should the home assume major responsibility? For what areas may the school rightly be expected to take a leadership role?

Does the school have a child-care responsibility during school hours? after school hours? If so, under what conditions?

Does the school have an obligation to provide special counseling or assistance for children and youth from broken homes? In what ways can and should the school work with special child-care agencies?

When should the school supplement family health services or provide recreational activities?

What leadership should the school give in helping both children and parents deal with problems growing out of changing family patterns?

What constitutes real security for children at different levels of maturity? When not gained through the home, what can the school do to provide this security?

How can school and home work together in understanding children and youth—their needs and their growth patterns?

How can home and school work together to support and supplement each other's efforts and to avoid working in ways that will minimize the efforts of either?

Should the school provide education for marriage and family life for all children and youth?

Interdependence—A Characteristic of Today's Civilization

The spread of industrial civilization has tended to obliterate the boundaries of local communities, and has materially reduced the functional meaning of state and national lines. It is a movement touching every part of the world and, even before the individual is wholly aware, drawing him into new national and world relationships. It has made the world a seemingly small planet. Already it has been demonstrated that man can leave California in the morning, lunch in Washington, D.C., and return to California for dinner. There is a functioning network of communication through post offices, through telegraph and telephone, through radio and television in millions of homes, through daily deliveries of newspapers and magazines, through less expensive books and more libraries, through museums and libraries on wheels for the more inaccessible communities. An event in one part of the country can be seen simultaneously by millions of individuals—sometimes more clearly than by persons on the scene. Cultural events, previously limited to relatively few individuals, can now be seen by millions. When a motion picture of a Shakespearean play was shown on television, it was estimated that more persons watched the performance than had seen the play in all its previous stagings. Never before have children and youth come to school from environments which provide so many stimulations or opportunities for understanding the social world in which they live.

TECHNOLOGICAL ADVANCE IS BUILDING A WORLD THAT REQUIRES COOPERATIVE ACTION

Failure of any part of our closely knit economy to function effectively influences the fates and fortunes of others. National groups—geographic or economic—face the problem of working together so that our industrial economy will function. A strike by steelworkers can cause hundreds of other industries to grind to a halt; an increase in the price of steel tonnage is soon reflected in a general price rise in other products. A sagging farm economy lowers prosperity in other areas; a temporary business slump slows new automobile purchases, causing layoffs in assembly plants. The future depends on how closely North and South, East and West, farm area and industrial center, work together and understand each other. Labor and management are developing new ways of working together as indicated by a marked reduction in major strikes. Problems of full employment are intimately linked with the well-being of both groups and "guaranteed annual wages" have already been incorporated into some labor–management contracts. Complex as the process of collective bargaining may be, recent years have shown that some means of intergroup cooperation must be established if our economy is to survive and continue its growth.

Within each community a variety of organizations has been established to make for closer cooperation between economic and social groups. Depending on the location, a chamber of commerce, a manufacturers' association, one or more labor unions, a consumers' cooperative, a grange, a bankers' association, a farm bureau or a farmers' union, a council of churches, and many others may be found. These organizations directly touch the lives of children and youth. Parents may belong to them and the policies established may affect the welfare of the community in many ways. Long before they are of legal voting age, young people are participating actively in organizations whose primary concern is community welfare—Junior Red Cross, the Community Chest, junior service clubs, and numerous church groups.

Racial and religious groups must also learn to live and work together. Even though loyalty to the principles of equality and freedom is professed, full "first-class citizenship" has not yet been extended to all citizens. Frequently members of certain races and creeds are excluded from particular fields of work and from various aspects of community life. Different treatment is given to various socio-economic classes, and there is much concern about social status. Notwithstanding Supreme Court rulings, segregation still exists in some schools and progress toward its elimination is slow. Discrimination against any group of individuals affects both the discriminating group and those treated unjustly. One of the causes of manpower shortages is the inadequate development of talents of some minority groups.

Growing interdependence is also reflected in an increase in the provisions for social welfare and in the development of institutions partially or wholly devoted to meeting social needs. Both our democratic ideal of respecting the worth of the individual and our closely knit social and economic structures make the welfare of each individual the concern of all. Constructive proposals are being worked out through social security measures, unemployment and sickness benefits, housing projects, community recreational programs, fair employment practices, and varied provisions for adequate medical care for all. Much remains to be done and many problems still need to be solved. Care of the aged and chronically ill poses major problems. How can every individual be assured the maximum realization of his health potential? To what extent is the individual employer responsible, through working conditions, recreation, and medical facilities, for the health of those employed? How can the contributions of service groups—medical, legal, teaching, and the like—be used for the welfare of all without sacrificing the right of individuals in service occupations to free enterprise? How is it possible to insure to every individual the maximum realization of his intellectual powers and special abilities? How can adequate financial support be provided to equalize educational opportunities for children and youth in all sections of our country?

As larger groups have become interdependent, more situations have arisen in which the welfare of each group is dependent on cooperative action through the processes of government. These situations have raised fundamental questions about the function of government in planning and coordinating. What should be the role of government in state and national planning? How far should government action go in the problems of labor and management? What types of responsibility should government assume for social welfare, for education? The relationship of the citizen to and his responsibilities for active participation in government are still in need of clarification.

Each individual, moreover, is facing what he may never have realized before—perhaps what he has refused to recognize—that he can no longer measure his life in terms of his own family or neighborhood, or that part of the world he calls his home. He has interwoven responsibilities to his fellow man which extend far beyond his immediate community. These responsibilities cross national boundaries and barriers until finally they dictate concern for the world community. The problems arising from living close to lands and people hitherto labeled remote are new, and it is our duty to participate in their adequate solution.

What are the best means of helping children and youth understand the technological advances which have, in effect, reduced the size of the earth and the events which bring all peoples together? How can the school develop greater understanding of community, regional, national, and world problems today and greater patience to find the common purposes and values necessary for working them out together? While the school cannot provide exact and complete answers to these problems, it can help learners to study them and to appraise sources of help. Those charged with this responsibility must answer questions such as these . . .

> What are the critical problems of today's world society? How can the school develop the understandings, concepts, and skills required to deal with these fundamental problems?
>
> How can historical backgrounds be used most effectively in helping children and youth to see today's happenings in perspective?
>
> How can children and youth be helped to interpret and appraise the range of resources dealing with social problems and issues—newspapers, television and radio, books, advertising, and the wealth of other materials that acquaint learners with their world?
>
> How can learners become acquainted with economic organizations and social groups; be helped to understand their functioning and appraise their activities; and be taught how to work through them and when to call on them for aid?
>
> How can the school in its own "behavior" lead in the practice of sound cooperative action?

DECISIONS AND ACTION CALL FOR A RATIONAL STUDY OF PROBLEMS

People in a democracy believe in the use of reason, of untrammeled investigation, of encouragement of all creative ability. They are committed to the methods of science. The world demands men who have developed a way of living which tests new ideas, explores new concepts, and rethinks the application of principles in new situations. Not what an individual knows, but how he uses what he knows as he faces problems of daily living, is a fundamental consideration in developing a curriculum for children and youth in our society.

As a method of work, a scientific approach implies the habit of seeking reliable information, of distinguishing between fact and fiction, data and opinion; of coming to reasoned conclusions on the basis of careful study of all available data; of evaluating conclusions in the light of new evidence; of judging the effectiveness of each decision and forming a basis for more satisfactory future decisions. The learner's method of work as he solves his problems, and his understanding of the process by which social change comes about, must be as important in curriculum designing as the actual content of his experiences, for he must understand and relate both process and ends. Thinking men, willing and able to use a scientific approach to the solution of individual and social problems, are essential in a democratic society. Disciplined intelligence is required for effective individual and cooperative decision-making and action-taking.

In implementing this way of working, there is need to give thought to such questions as . . .

What is involved in fostering intellectual curiosity—an interest in finding out, in exploring ideas and their use in action, in creating?

How can the school provide experiences that will develop the skills needed in a rational study of problems and situations?

How can children and youth be helped to base action upon the values they hold?

FAITH IN COOPERATIVE INTELLIGENCE AS A MEANS OF IMPROVING LIFE IS A BASIC COMMITMENT

Even though local, national, and world problems are increasing in complexity and magnitude, there is still a firm belief in the ultimate betterment of men and institutions, confidence in the possibility of progress, and conviction that something can be done about social problems. This faith is reflected in a system of government which guarantees to each individual the right to help make decisions regarding the laws under which he will live and the services he desires. It appears in the belief that abundant living for all is within the realm of possibility and is a goal worth striving for. It lies back of the concept of a just and enduring peace. As a nation, Americans have confidence in the collective wisdom of the people and believe that better solutions to social problems will come when each individual shares with others the results of his efforts, discoveries, and thinking. They recognize that true freedom in a closely knit world is attained only as men use their intelligence collectively and creatively to gain increasing control over their problems of daily living.

Americans have faith in a society in which the right and the responsibility of the individual to develop and use his talents and abilities in his own interests and in those of society are recognized. They believe in a nation in which each individual feels an obligation to develop his potential ability to a point where he can realize optimum self-fulfillment and make a maximum contribution to society. This is the basis for the American common school system which has already extended through the secondary level and is gradually going beyond. This belief and faith mean a world in which each individual feels obliged to use his powers for social ends and to help others make a similar contribution. Cooperative men, using disciplined intelligence and democratic processes to secure the maximum contribution of all, are another essential in a democratic society.

In addition to the questions faced in developing cooperative ways of working because our society is characterized by interdependence, faith in cooperative intelligence also means consideration of such points of inquiry as . . .

> How can the school provide for the interrelatedness of the interests and concerns of the individual and those of society? How help the individual to meet his needs through channels making for the greatest social contribution?
>
> What school experiences will help children and youth develop a sense of commitment and dedication to the constructive use of individual powers for the general welfare?
>
> How can the school work with children and youth to develop commitment to working with others for the common good?

DEMOCRATIC VALUES MUST BE TRANSLATED INTO ACTION IN AN INTERDEPENDENT WORLD

"Equal men," "thinking men," "cooperative men"—this can be a fighting faith. With national and individual commitment to this faith, the most serious problems can be approached with confidence. Democratic values give direction to human living and their implications widen and deepen as new situations are faced and new problems are solved. They have little meaning in isolation. The test of an individual's commitment to these values is his willingness and ability to put them into action. Willingness to put values into action can be built only when they are an integral part of every experience. Almost every choice faced by men and women, by children and youth, as they deal with their problems of everyday living, demands a value judgment. Every aspect of life can make a potential contribution to building sound judgments.

It is the responsibility of the school to help build the bases which give direction to these judgments and to help develop deeper insights as the maturity and experiences of learners permit. If that contribution is to be positive, democratic values must be in operation in all human relationships. The school is not alone in its desire for action based on democratic values, but it is one social institution in which there can be no room for wavering with respect to this commitment. Our democratic values must be reaffirmed and translated into action. The school can contribute to this end by helping children in their day-by-day activities to decide when to subordinate individual desires to social goals; by helping them to see the true worth of each individual; by teaching them to appraise their work with honesty and integrity; by showing them the satisfaction that can come with unselfish living. The school must be a place where children and youth can learn how to bring scientific methods to bear in adjusting to change and where they can develop the flexibility of mind imperative to successful living in the twentieth century. In this work there is need to give consideration to such questions as . . .

How can each aspect of the curriculum—the ways in which teacher and learners work together, the working relationships of teachers and administrators, the cooperative efforts of school, home, and community—be directed toward the development of democratic values? toward their translation in action?

How can children and youth be helped to develop consistent ways of behaving where there are opposing sets of values—to sense the dichotomy and deal with the conflict?

What responsibility should the school take as a social force in the community to promote action based on democratic values?

In the character of a democratic society and its resources lie the means for as good a life as man can build. While democracy asks much of each human being, it gives much in return. It defines its goal in terms of every citizen's best contribution out of his full creative development. It aims for the best life the men within it can conceive and build.

Related Readings

ALLEN, FREDERICK L. *The Big Change.* New York: Harper & Brothers, 1952.

ASSOCIATION FOR SUPERVISION AND CURRICULUM DEVELOPMENT. *Forces Affecting American Education.* 1953 Yearbook. Washington, D.C.: The Association, 1953.

ASSOCIATION FOR SUPERVISION AND CURRICULUM DEVELOPMENT. *Growing Up in an Anxious Age.* 1952 Yearbook. Washington, D.C.: The Association, 1952.

BRUBACHER, JOHN, editor. *The Public Schools and Spiritual Values.* Seventh Yearbook, John Dewey Society. New York: Harper & Brothers, 1944.

Bryson, Lyman. *The Next America.* New York: Harper & Brothers, 1952.

Butts, R. Freeman, and Lawrence A. Cremin. *A History of Education in American Culture.* New York: Henry Holt and Company, Inc., 1953.

Conant, James B. *Education in a Divided World.* Cambridge, Mass.: Harvard University Press, 1948.

Counts, George S. *Education and American Civilization.* New York: Bureau of Publications, Teachers College, Columbia University, 1952.

Havighurst, Robert J. *Society and Education,* Boston: Allyn & Bacon, 1957.

Linton, Ralph. *The Cultural Background of Personality.* New York: Appleton-Century-Crofts, 1945.

Mercer, Blaine, and E. R. Carr. *Education and the Social Order.* New York: Rinehart & Company, Inc., 1956.

Rugg, Harold O., and William Withers. *Social Foundations of Education.* Englewood Cliffs, N.J.: Prentice-Hall, Inc., 1955.

Stanley, William O., B. Othanel Smith, Kenneth D. Benne, and Archibald W. Anderson. *Social Foundations of Education.* New York: The Dryden Press, Inc., 1956.

3

CHILDREN AND YOUTH A GUIDE TO CURRICULUM DEVELOPMENT

Every proposal for designing the curriculum must take into account the capacities of the individual, how he matures, and the way he learns. Not to do so risks wasting valuable hours of child and teacher time on concepts or skills that could be acquired much more effectively at a later stage of development. Perhaps more serious is the possibility of teaching skills, concepts, and facts that do not make their anticipated contribution to effective living.

Research, particularly in the biological sciences and in the field of psychology, makes a direct contribution to decisions of when and how to teach. Such decisions relate to sequence, organization, and methodology—what experiences are most appropriate for different stages of development; what grouping of experiences will lead to the most effective learning; what teaching methods are most likely to provide the needed guidance. Equally important is the sometimes forgotten contribution which psychological research can make to educational goals, and therefore to decisions regarding the scope of the curriculum. For example, research regarding the transfer of learning and the nature of concept development is significant in determining the school experiences that are most likely to be effective in achieving any given educational goal. Psychologists and psychiatrists have important contributions to make in indicating the specific goals involved in achieving such a general objective as the maximum development of each individual. Social-psychological explorations of the area of interpersonal and group relationships have helped to define the behaviors and understandings needed for effective participation in the processes basic to living and working in a democratic society. What is known about learners, as well as what is known about society, should underlie every aspect of curriculum development—scope, sequence, organization, and methodology.

Many of the new developments and shifts in emphasis that have characterized the growth of psychology as a science have occurred within the lifetimes of persons now giving active leadership in curriculum construction. Because early research interests have continued to flourish while new emphases appeared, the impression gained is sometimes one of confusion and conflict in the field. True, no completely satisfactory over-all theory of behavior has as yet been evolved. Nevertheless, psychologists are in essential agreement on the practical implications of many specific research studies. The early 1930's marked the peak of the attempts to classify psychologists as belonging to particular theoretical schools. For the last twenty years, the trend has been toward using research applicable to specific problems, regardless of the "school" from which it stemmed. This is not eclecticism in the sense of an uncritical attempt to adopt all points of view but, rather, an effort to interpret research in terms of its particular setting and focus. For example, the work of the Behaviorists, relating to conditioned responses in the area of emotions, is drawn upon in problems centering around desirable classroom atmosphere; some of Thorndike's research in learning throws light on situations involving the planning of effective practice; the research of the Gestalt and organismic psychologists is of particular help on questions of motivation and problem-solving; and mental hygiene inquiries and psychoanalytical interpretations have provided many insights into the dynamics of human behavior.

Because the history of psychology as a science covers little more than fifty years, there are gaps in knowledge. There are more investigations which provide norms for separate phases of development, for example, than there are studies of the ways in which the interrelationships among these aspects influence behavior. It has been known for some time that the very young child develops according to a time schedule peculiarly his own. Explorations of the implications of this concept for the tasks which development itself poses for the maturing individual are just beginning. Discoveries regarding the influence of the learner's self-concept on his behavior, his learning, and his aspirations are just emerging. Because early learning experiments tended to be in settings in which motivation was extrinsic, and repetition rather than problem-solving the key to the task to be learned, relatively more is known about planning for drill and spacing repetition than about using intrinsic motivation or developing concepts and problem-solving techniques.

Relatively few of the studies over the past fifty years have examined the complicated classroom setting in which the teacher and learners work. As a consequence, most proposals for the classroom are still based largely on research done in laboratory and experimental child-study settings. Even though there are gaps, teachers and other curriculum planners cannot afford to treat as inconsequential the vast accumulation of basic research about individuals, about groups, and about the learning process.

The Maturing Learner—A Guide to Curriculum Development

Maturation and learning [1] are so interrelated in the over-all development of the individual that it is difficult to consider the one without the other. However, for the purposes of this volume, the maturing learner is discussed first and then the learning process. There are specific curriculum implications in the fact that the learner brings to the classroom his own unique combination of strengths and weaknesses and grows according to principles inherent in the developmental process itself.

EACH LEARNER IS UNIQUE

Perhaps nothing is as clearly established in psychological research as the fact of individual differences. Each learner has his own unique pattern of capacities. Research indicates that the intellectually able child is likely to be somewhat better developed physically, to have a better academic record, and to have fewer physical handicaps than the average. Nevertheless, the actual pattern in any particular class is one of diversity. Tommy, who has the highest IQ in the room, could be one of the smallest children and socially very immature. He could be the best reader in the class, or he could (though the chances, statistically, are against it)

[1] **Maturation** is a concept used to explain phenomena which are the result of an innate growth process rather than the product of direct teaching–learning. Maturation, then, involves organic and structural changes which emerge from the process of living and growing. **Learning** has been variously defined by theorists but generally refers to behavioral changes which result from an interaction of the individual and his environment.

be one of the worst. In arithmetic he might be slightly above the class average, in handwriting and general coordination very immature. Dividing sixty children on the basis of intelligence could, conceivably, place some of the best and the poorest readers in the same class. Grouping these same children on the basis of reading test scores could well put a child with high intellectual ability and another with very limited ability in the same section. Neither of these ways of grouping would necessarily result in much reduction in the range in arithmetic skills or in the variety of social and emotional needs. Judicious selection on the basis of many factors, often cutting across age lines, can reduce the heterogeneity of a group somewhat. Regardless of the organization of the school, a range of abilities within each class and a variation of ability levels within each individual must be assumed and planned for.

Not only does each learner have a unique combination of capacities, but he also has his own growth pattern. Susan's height, plotted at three-month intervals, will be very different from the typical smooth curve that results when thousands of youngsters are measured. At times, her mother will find it difficult to keep her dress hems adjusted to her rapid growth. At others, Susan will seem to stand still. There is limited evidence to suggest that learning spurts may possibly parallel celerity in physical growth and that, in the cases of some children, school achievement may be related to general growth patterns. Thus, curriculum workers must plan not only for the range and the diverse patterns of abilities within a group, but also for varying paces in growth. There will be some youngsters who display the typical needs and face the normal problems of adolescence as early as ten and some who will not begin to mature until fourteen. There will be times when individuals seem to grow slowly and times when they apparently spurt ahead.

Each learner is also unique in the experience background he brings to school. About half of our children live in rural areas—on farms, in scattered houses, or in small villages. Some of these will be living in homes with earthen floors, screenless windows, back-porch washbasins, and outdoor toilets. Some will be in comfortable homes situated on good highways that lead to neighbor and town, in touch with the world through radio and television. In a typical large city, one child in three is likely to be living in slum conditions which involve one or more of such experiences as playing in the streets, contact with adolescent gangs and agencies of law enforcement, with adult drinking and use of narcotics—experiences quite beyond the comprehension of learners in typical middle-class homes and often even beyond the comprehension of teachers.[2] There

[2] See J. Frederic Dewhurst and Associates, *America's Needs and Resources* (New York: Twentieth Century Fund, 1955).

are different experiential backgrounds even in a relatively homogeneous community. Bobby's parents may plan week-end trips and vacations with him in mind; Bertha's may leave her in the charge of a governess. Winona may live in an atmosphere of books; Peter may spend his time in front of a television set. Adolescent Linda may be involved in lively political discussions at the dinner table; Sandra's intellectual fare may consist of fashions and beauty aids. Even if it were possible to devise a plan to reduce markedly the diversity of capacities and skills among the learners in a given class, these experiential factors still call for curriculum planning that takes the uniqueness of each learner into account.

In recent years, the attention of psychologists and curriculum workers has been focused on still another way in which each learner is unique. This is in his own concept of himself—his evaluation of his capacities; his feeling of personal worth; his own ways of maintaining his feelings of self-respect; his interpretation of the value of the school, the role of the teacher, and the importance of learning, as they relate to his aspirations and needs. Even for two learners, seemingly very similar in capacities, growth patterns, and experience backgrounds, a learning situation has its own particular elements because of the way in which each regards it. The problem of meeting individual differences still exists.

The psychological evidence regarding the uniqueness of each learner poses several fundamental questions for those concerned with curriculum development. Thoughtful proposals and research in the classroom setting are needed to answer such questions as . . .

What techniques will best aid the teacher in studying the capacities, rates of growth, and experiential backgrounds of individual learners?

How can the range of differences be dealt with?

- How can experiences be selected and guided so as to contribute to maximum development of the potential of each individual?
- What procedures will allow for differing rates of growth?
- How can the curriculum provide the most effective adjustment to each learner's experience background?

What does the fact that each learner is unique mean for flexibility in curriculum development? What should be the nature of the planning done in advance of work with learners?

What does the uniqueness of each learner mean for grouping of pupils?

What recognition should be given to the learner's concept of self in guiding school experiences?

EACH LEARNER FACES THE SAME DEVELOPMENTAL TASKS IN THE SAME GENERAL SEQUENCE

Although each learner grows according to his own pattern, his development follows a recognizable sequence. Children sit before they walk. They use concrete terms before they make extensive use of abstract ones. They understand the present and near-at-hand before they comprehend the past or future in time and the remote in space. And they operate socially in clubs or "gangs" before they do much dating as couples.

Each new stage of development seems to bring with it its own developmental tasks. This is most easily seen in the area of physical growth. When a baby arrives at the point where he can grasp objects, he reaches for everything in sight. When he is capable of walking, he exercises this skill by the hour. At adolescence, he changes—sometimes to the amazement of his parents—from a carelessly clad member of an all-boy "gang" to a well-groomed usurper of the telephone and the family car.

Increasing intellectual maturity brings its developmental tasks. Nothing is safe from small Ricky's investigation now that he is toddling. Six-year-old Don asks "Why?" fifteen times in half as many minutes. John's room is cluttered with the beetle collections, chemical sets, and other evidences typical of a ten-year-old's concern with the hows and whys of his expanding environment. Sandra's interest in her youth group at church reflects, in part, the adolescent's struggle with the abstractions related to his developing philosophy of life.

Attempts to look beyond physical and intellectual growth sequences to the social and emotional tasks faced by children and youth growing up in our industrial, interdependent society have been of particular value to curriculum workers. The list of major developmental tasks proposed by Havighurst [3] is given below. Such lists suggest the areas in which learners must develop understandings and skills if they are to lead effective lives as children, youth, and adults.

Developmental Tasks of Infancy and Early Childhood

1. Learning to walk
2. Learning to take solid foods
3. Learning to talk
4. Learning to control the elimination of body wastes
5. Learning sex differences and sexual modesty
6. Achieving physiological stability
7. Forming simple concepts of social and physical reality

[3] Robert J. Havighurst, *Human Development and Education, passim* (New York: Longmans, Green & Company, 1953).

8. Learning to relate oneself emotionally to parents, siblings, and other people
9. Learning to distinguish right and wrong and developing a conscience

DEVELOPMENTAL TASKS OF MIDDLE CHILDHOOD

1. Learning physical skills necessary for ordinary games
2. Building wholesome attitudes toward oneself as a growing organism
3. Learning to get along with age-mates
4. Learning an appropriate masculine or feminine social role
5. Developing fundamental skills in reading, writing, and calculating
6. Developing concepts necessary for everyday living
7. Developing conscience, morality, and a scale of values
8. Achieving personal independence
9. Developing attitudes toward social groups and institutions

DEVELOPMENTAL TASKS OF ADOLESCENCE

1. Achieving new and more mature relations with age-mates of both sexes
2. Achieving a masculine or feminine social role
3. Accepting one's physique and using the body effectively
4. Achieving emotional independence of parents and other adults
5. Achieving assurance of economic independence
6. Selecting and preparing for an occupation
7. Preparing for marriage and family life
8. Developing intellectual skills and concepts necessary for civic competence
9. Desiring and achieving socially responsible behavior
10. Acquiring a set of values and an ethical system as a guide to behavior

DEVELOPMENTAL TASKS OF EARLY ADULTHOOD

1. Selecting a mate
2. Learning to live with a marriage partner
3. Starting a family
4. Rearing children
5. Managing a home
6. Getting started in an occupation
7. Taking on civic responsibility
8. Finding a congenial social group

Physiological growth patterns influence the sequence in which developmental tasks such as these emerge. It is the culture, however, that determines the specific demands made upon the learner as he faces these tasks. Because he is growing up in a western industrial society, the problems of the maturing individual in the satisfaction of his needs are different from those he would face in a primitive culture or in an oriental society. Adolescent social patterns, for example, are very different in modern America from those in a culture where puberty is a sign that the maturing individual is ready for marriage. These patterns also vary within the various strata of western society. Almost since birth Jessica's life has been pointed toward the social obligations of a debutante. She will be graduated from a private girls' school. Allen and Janice are wearing small hearts, the symbol in their high school that they are "going steady." Maria's parents will not allow her to go on dates unchaperoned. Geraldine has grown up in a neighborhood where sexual immorality is not uncommon.[4]

The individual's own capacities also make a difference in the ways in which he faces developmental tasks. The adolescent with an IQ between sixty and seventy-five will have the same needs as the more able youth —developing more mature relations with his age-mates, preparing for a vocation, preparing for marriage and family life. But he will be trying to achieve these goals with more limited insights, less ability to make decisions about complex problems, and greater need to be taught through planned experiences specific adjustments to his culture that the more able youth tends to acquire in the normal process of daily living.

Studies of developmental tasks have at least three implications for the curriculum worker: they suggest the types of problems to which learners will be actively seeking solutions, with or without the help of the school; they indicate the areas in which learners must achieve competence to live effectively in modern society; and the developmental sequence provides an important key to the sequence of school activities. All youngsters, of course, do not reach the same stage of development at exactly the same time. Nevertheless, growth patterns are enough alike to allow for general proposals regarding the kinds of experiences most appropriate for early childhood, later childhood, and youth.

Curriculum workers should plan with the learner's growth sequences and needs in mind. Just how these factors are to be given recognition in proposals of scope and sequence poses several questions . . .

How can proposals of curriculum sequence best reflect what is known about developmental patterns?

What place should the developmental tasks of learners be accorded in the curriculum?

What curriculum adjustments are needed because of the ways in which both cultural background and individual growth patterns condition when and how a new task is faced?

[4] For more detailed discussion of cultural influences on the ways in which learners face developmental tasks, see Havighurst, *op. cit.*

What curriculum adjustments are needed to give help both to the learner of limited intellectual ability and to the individual who is intellectually gifted?

What kind of research in the classroom setting can contribute to a more accurate identification of specific developmental tasks as they are faced in varied cultural settings?

EACH LEARNER GROWS AT HIS OWN PACE

Research regarding the rate of development has contributed another principle of importance to the curriculum worker. Attempts to speed up the normal maturation process by special experiences or practice have typically resulted in little permanent gain. In almost all studies of physical development in early childhood, the youngster allowed to mature at his own rate caught up with the one given special practice within a short period after the latter's training was stopped. Each child apparently develops according to his own timetable and special practice has little permanence unless given when he is at a point of sufficient maturation to profit from it.

Studies of ways in which a child's growth pattern affects the facility with which he learns at school are not made as easily as those focused on his early stages of physical growth. Many factors complicate the picture. First, readiness for school activities does not depend on maturation alone; experience background also influences learning. Second, teaching methods affect the ease with which something is learned; the more slowly the teacher proceeds, the more concrete the experience provided, and the more meaningful the repetition planned, the more likely it is that the immature learner will make progress. Third, differences in motivation will lead some children to face a task with much more zeal than will others. Research regarding readiness for school experiences must take these complicating factors into account.

In spite of difficulties in securing the evidence, the implications of research on readiness suggest that learning is less laborious, less time-consuming, less likely to lead to negative attitudes, and more likely to lead to satisfactory progress when it is geared effectively to the learner's stage of maturity. Time is not absolute in learning. Months devoted to giving Jill, a kindergartner, formal practice in reading, in the name of a "head start," may equal a time expenditure of minutes in the first grade. The arithmetic computation that Don takes an hour to master in spite of Miss Johnson's vigorous drill may be learned in twenty minutes when he is six months older. Anne struggles hopelessly with the more complex aspects of English grammar in the sixth grade, and grasps the same principles with ease in grade eight, provided her sixth-grade experiences have not built up negative attitudes about grammar and her ability to understand it. An effective proposal of scope and sequence should help the teacher provide for activities at the points at which learning is likely to be most efficient. Because rates of development differ, this will require flexibility from class to class and from individual to individual within each class.

There is still another side to the problem of adjusting activities to the learner's own growth rate. While attempts to speed up the normal developmental processes have not typically had much success, there is considerable evidence that a limited environment can be retarding. If it does not actually delay the time at which new powers develop, it can restrict disastrously the uses to which these are put. Ronnie, at six, may not have the coordination, the sense of team play, or the interest to become a good baseball player. By the time he is nine or ten, he is likely to be physically and socially mature enough to develop considerable skill. If he has not yet learned to handle a ball and bat by the age of twelve, he may refuse to try rather than risk his status in a group by parading his inadequacy. It is inefficient use of time to provide an experience at a point where a learner is able to profit from it only to a limited extent and with painful effort. It is equally inefficient to allow the point to pass when an experience could make its most effective contribution.

It is important to provide the environment and the guidance that will allow each learner maximum opportunity to exercise his developing capacities and skills. For some youngsters the school may act as the main safeguard against a severely limiting environment. Thousands of children are members of families that move about from place to place in search of seasonal employment. From severely underprivileged homes in a large city children may come to school wise in their knowledge of life in a congested area, but limited in vocabulary, experiences with reading, skill in oral expression. In an isolated rural area, it may be the teacher who is the one to raise problems of crop rotation and conservation, make available media for creative expression, build acquaintance with other parts of the country through films, pictures, and stories. Full use of developing capacities will not be made unless the environment challenges that use.

Present insights into the complexity of human development and the continuity of growth suggest that research on the role of maturation in readiness probably never will result in precise recommendations of a grade-by-grade sequence of learning experiences. The problem is more complex than the researchers responsible for the word counts and error studies of the 1920's foresaw. A number of questions suggest the need for further research in the classroom setting and for the thoughtful re-appraisal of present practices in terms of what we now know . . .

What adjustments are needed in what is taught and in how it is taught in order to take maximum advantage of learners' levels of maturation?

Are there teaching methods particularly effective for differing maturity levels?

What activities best contribute to readiness for beginning reading, work with numbers, written language skills?

When is the best time to introduce learners to the remote in time and space?

What contributes to ability to learn through vicarious experiences?

How can proposals of scope and sequence allow for differing maturation rates—for the child whose development is accelerated as well as the one whose maturation is slow, for different rates of maturation in the same child?

What characterizes an environment which provides maximum opportunity to exercise developing capacities and allows for experience when and as needed?

THE LEARNER IS A DYNAMIC, GOAL-SEEKING ORGANISM

Research, stemming particularly from the work of Gestalt and organismic psychologists, has changed markedly the conception held in the 1920's of the learner as a relatively passive organism responding mainly to stimulation from his environment. He has been revealed as active and dynamic, responding vigorously to his environment from his own inner motives. This emphasis on the learner as a dynamic organism has two important implications for the curriculum worker. First, the learner will respond selectively to his experiences in terms of his own purposes and his particular background of experience. Second, he will seek actively to satisfy his own basic needs.

Need is used in many ways in educational literature. At one extreme, terms such as **felt needs** or **expressed needs** are used to refer to those needs of which the learner himself is conscious or to his requests for help in solving problems or meeting situations. Curriculum proposals that stress learners' needs are sometimes interpreted (usually quite erroneously) to include in school experiences only those things the individual says he wants to learn. At the other extreme, there are those who put the stress on **societal needs**—those attitudes, knowledges, and skills that society demands of its citizens whether or not learners are aware of these demands. Neither definition alone provides an adequate interpretation of the concept of needs for the purposes of curriculum development.

The curriculum worker must be aware of three kinds of needs. First, the learner has needs in the sense of **purposes** which he accepts as his own and pursues. This is similar to the concept of felt needs, but more inclusive. Learners can be helped to identify and to accept goals of the importance of which they have not been aware. Second, the learner has needs in the sense of **developmental tasks** which are set by his own developmental stage in relation to the society in which he is growing up. Third, there are so-called **basic needs** or **psycho-social needs** within the individual that cause him to seek certain goals related to his biological nature.[5]

Societal needs are not excluded from the above. One of the developmental tasks of adolescence listed in the preceding section is to acquire the intellectual skills and concepts necessary for civic competence. Because a learner is in democratic, industrial America, the intellectual skills and concepts he will require will differ from those he would be learning in the schools of Communist China. Even to meet a physiological need for food the maturing learner must acquire tastes and amenities unique to his own cultural group. The problem facing the curriculum worker is to bring the needs of the learner and the demands of his society into relationship.

Because purpose is so integral a part of learning, it is discussed separately in the section on learning that follows. As will be indicated in that later section, two major questions face the curriculum worker: how to make most effective use of the purposes the learner identifies in any given situation and how to help him clarify new purposes and identify needs of which he is not aware.

Needs, in the sense of developmental tasks, have been discussed in an earlier section. How these tasks serve as motivating forces and the extent to which they are culturally determined were discussed at that time. A more detailed analysis of the problems faced by learners in our society is contained in the charts on pages 169 to 321 of this volume.

Attempts to develop lists of basic needs have not resulted in unanimity. The concept implies that the needs exist in some form in all human beings. Identifying them through research is a difficult problem, particu-

[5] See David A. Prescott, *Emotion and the Educative Process* (Washington, D.C.: American Council on Education, 1938); Robert J. Havighurst, *op. cit.;* Donald C. Doan, *The Needs of Youth: An Evaluation for Curriculum Purposes* (New York: Bureau of Publications, Teachers College, Columbia University, 1942).

larly if they are innate. Since the child is in contact with other human beings and is learning from the time of birth, any effort to identify needs, other than those that are physiological, as clearly innate and not learned seems doomed to failure. Existing lists of basic needs have come largely from analyses of case studies and observations of the behavior of children, youth, and adults, rather than from observations of infants. While a single universally accepted list does not exist, there are many practical analyses of help to teachers.

There is considerable agreement on basic needs that are **physiological** in origin. The individual must eat, drink, breathe, maintain appropriate body temperature, secure a reasonable balance between rest and activity, eliminate waste, and make a successful adjustment to sex needs. At first glance, this list may seem to have implications for the school only in terms of such problems as ventilation, sanitation, and lunchroom service. However, as the maturing individual takes increased responsibility for meeting his own physiological needs, he must acquire many skills and understandings. Problems of learning how to select an appropriate diet, of deciding when and how to use modern air conditioning, of choosing appropriate clothing, of cooperating with sanitary regulations, of developing wholesome attitudes toward the opposite sex, are all related to the satisfaction of physiological needs.

Because he has an active nervous system, the learner will seek to satisfy his **intellectual curiosity.** This basic need, on which there is rather widespread agreement, has been variously entitled the need for new experiences, for mastery, for exploration. It is one of the most frequent and strongest motives to which the school appeals. For the purpose of curriculum development, what constitutes a legitimate appeal to intellectual curiosity merits careful analysis. The skillful teacher who says that he can "interest" children in almost anything is reasonably accurate, for curiosity about the new and unusual can be readily aroused. This certainly does not mean that all areas to which the learner's intellectual curiosity could be directed are equally valuable educationally. Interest alone, then, is not an adequate guide for the selection of curriculum experiences. Other bases must be used to determine which, of the multitude of experiences in which the learner can be interested, are the most worth while.

Attempts to identify basic needs that are **psychological** or **personal-social** have led to many types of analyses. As a working hypothesis, the classification offered a good many years ago by Prescott[6] is still one of the simplest and most helpful. This analysis suggests that in his social relationships every person needs affection—a feeling of being loved and

[6] Prescott, *op. cit.,* pp. 116–125.

wanted for himself alone. He needs to feel likeness to others in the group —to be accepted as one who fits in, who is similar to others in the group in factors such as dress, economic status, social background, intellectual and physical capacities. He needs a feeling of belongingness—of acceptance as a contributing group member, of gaining the status that comes from a group job to do or an accepted role to play.

There is rather widespread acceptance of the idea that each individual also has a need to respect himself. Prescott used the term ego, or integrative need, to express this idea. In recent years, as concept of self it has received increasing attention. Among other things, the need to respect oneself implies a need to feel reasonably adequate in meeting the problems of daily living and to have a set of values by which one is willing to stand. It suggests, also, the need to have experienced sufficient successes and failures to be able to make a realistic appraisal of one's strengths and weaknesses.

Regardless of the particular curriculum design, what we know about psychological needs has many implications for effective teacher–pupil and peer–group relationships. No proposal for scope and sequence is likely to be effective if basic personality needs are not met—if learners do not feel secure, accepted by their teachers and peers, adequate in their own eyes. Studies of psychological needs also contribute to curriculum content in so far as they provide insights into ways of developing the skills in interpersonal relationships important in our democratic society.

What does this total concept of learners' needs mean for the curriculum worker? Certainly the implications are much broader than the terms felt needs or expressed needs would imply. While the preceding discussion has indicated that the learner is dynamic and active, seeking his own goals and responding to experience in terms of these goals, there is nothing to imply that the school should withhold guidance until the individual is conscious of or has expressed his need. On the contrary, there is the definite implication that teachers have an obligation to study learners, to give help in meeting needs of which they are not conscious, and to help them become more sharply aware of other goals.

What questions does knowledge of learners' needs pose for those who are concerned that the school contribute to the maximum growth of each individual? Among others might be . . .

> How should proposals of curriculum scope, sequence, and organization reflect what is known about basic needs?
>
> To what extent should proposals of scope and sequence help learners deal with the problems they are facing in the ever-expanding worlds to which their maturity is introducing them? What recognition should be given to developmental tasks?

What should be the relative importance of purpose (a need expressed or unexpressed) and of interest (intellectual curiosity) in the selection and guidance of learning activities?

What effect do aspects of the school organization—grouping, reporting, administrative procedures—have on the satisfaction of basic needs?

What are desirable teacher–child and pupil–pupil relationships if basic needs are to be met?

EACH LEARNER GROWS AS A WHOLE

Much has been written in educational literature about teaching "the whole child," sometimes using the term in a derogatory sense. The implied criticism usually is that schools are taking on too much; that many aspects of development might better be left to the home; that in a concern for all aspects of development, schools are doing less well the job of developing skills and knowledge. Actually, the teacher must be concerned, to some extent, with the whole learner, even though he considers his major aim to be to teach the pupil to calculate or to spell. Melissa, who suffers from recurring colds, is not as likely to function intellectually as effectively as Allen who is seldom ill. The poor academic achievement of Jill, a new student, may reflect her social need for her high school group. Randy, who suddenly finds himself much taller than his classmates, may change from an outgoing youngster, actively participating in his classes, to a retiring one. Even goals that represent the most limited conception of the role of the school are less likely to be achieved if teachers completely disregard aspects of development other than the intellectual. When goals are stated and the role of the school is defined in terms of maximum individual development, it follows that all aspects of growth must necessarily be taken into account in planning even though several different institutions may contribute to this total growth.

The learner not only develops but he also learns as a whole. Peter reacts to the intellectual task of the arithmetic problem before him, but he reacts also to the social climate of the room, the color of his teacher's dress, his own feelings of success or failure in dealing with previous arithmetic experiences, perhaps his discomfort from sitting still too long. These are not specific learnings, but feelings of pleasure or discomfort regarding one aspect of a situation frequently become attached to another. Peter may be quite successful in arithmetic and yet learn to dislike it thoroughly because assignments geared to the majority in the class offer him no challenge. Whether high school students think of the classics with pleasure or with dislike may well depend on feelings arising from their first introduction to these books. In an elementary school classroom where great stress is put on the Friday spelling test, but where children are encouraged to guess at unfamiliar words in other writing situations, there may develop the attitude that correct spelling is important only when taking a test. Even more important, every specific learning experience also contributes to generalized attitudes regarding the importance of accurate information, the place of authority, the value of education.

The written course of study does not tell the story of what is learned as the whole child responds to his total school environment. If the learning experiences recommended actually achieve the goals foreseen, attention should be given to the setting in which the learning takes place . . .

To what aspects of growth should the school give primary attention?

How can the school program be developed to achieve its major functions and at the same time recognize that the whole child comes to school?

What techniques can the teacher use to become acquainted with and understand the "whole" learner? To gain insights into the special problems of each child or youth?

What type of environment and classroom atmosphere is most conducive to maximum total growth?

The Learning Process—A Guide to Curriculum Development

Decision-making regarding the scope, sequence, and organization of school experiences involves more than considering the capacities of the learner, his maturity, and his needs. There are literally thousands of activities appropriate for the general maturity of any given learner, suitable for his particular capacities, and potentially of interest to him. Choices still have to be made. In part, these choices are made in terms of ultimate goals—the types of adult problems a pupil eventually should be able to handle, and the skills, attitudes, and knowledge toward which his present experiences should build. To give intelligent guidance in selecting experiences that will best achieve these goals, the curriculum worker must understand how learning takes place. Ideally, those activities in which the learner engages should result in maximum progress toward the stated goals and in maximum retention and carry-over to his life outside of school. An activity cannot be justified solely on the basis that "the children are interested," or "they enjoy it so." Interest and enjoyment are important factors in motivation, it is true, but the curriculum worker must also ask, "Is this the best possible use of the time available?"

Since Dashiell's pioneer article in the 1930's [7] there has been a trend toward seeking the common elements in various learning theories. In 1955, in a survey of the discussions of learning in psychology texts in common use, Snygg [8] pointed out that much practical agreement exists, even though theoretical differences have not been resolved. The learning process, as typically described, is as follows . . .

FIRST: **The learner** (possessed of specific capacities, experience background, and maturity) **is motivated to seek a given goal.**

SECOND: As he progresses toward his goal, **he encounters a new problem** (because he lacks necessary skills, knowledge, or generalizations needed to reach his goal or because he does not see how what he knows can be applied).

THIRD: As he explores the problem, **he hits on a solution in line with his goal** (through a process of trial and error, with varying degrees of insight, with varying types of guidance from his teacher).

FOURTH: **He refines and perfects his solution** (through repetition and reduction of incorrect responses, through increasingly accurate insights, through analysis of his errors).

FIFTH: **He makes his solution his own** (through repetition, practice, use in daily life).

At each step in the process, the teacher has a vital part to play. What is known about the details of how learning takes place guides the teacher in playing this part effectively.

THE INDIVIDUAL LEARNS IN TERMS OF HIS MATURITY AND EXPERIENCE BACKGROUND

A first step in selecting any learning experience is to appraise the maturity, the present skills and understandings, and the general experience background of the learner. Determining readiness for learning involves consideration of all these factors. In part, readiness is related to

[7] J. F. Dashiell, "A Survey and Synthesis of Learning Theories," *Psychological Bulletin:* 32 (April, 1935), 261–275.
[8] Donald Snygg, "Some Recent Texts in Educational Psychology," *Psychological Bulletin:* 52 (November, 1955), 510–517.

the developmental process, as discussed previously. However, the teacher does much more than merely wait for increased maturity. Developing readiness is also a matter of helping the learner, at his present stage of maturity, to acquire the skills and the experience background needed for undertaking the new activity. Louise, in grade one, five years old mentally and with a limited vocabulary, is not ready to read. She needs time to develop the maturity required to distinguish quickly and accurately among the configurations of words. She also needs many informal contacts with words and other types of enriching language activities. Sammy, in the same grade, seven years old mentally, but from a home where books and stories have not been part of his background, may not be ready to read. He has the maturity that will enable him to plunge successfully into beginning reading activities, but he may need prereading experiences with words in print in books, classroom notices, and other settings to develop interest in reading and awareness of the purposes this skill can serve. He may also need to develop some of the preliminary skills of interpreting pictures and responding accurately to word configurations that many children who have picture and story books at home teach themselves. Because Sammy's general intellectual development has reached the point where he can profit more readily from classroom prereading experiences than can Louise, he is likely to progress more quickly toward success in beginning reading.

The richness or meagerness of a learner's environment has much to do with his readiness for a new experience. Andrew, in a junior high school general science class, who came from an elementary school program which gave relatively little time to science, may not be ready for the same kinds of experiences as Arthur, who not only had a rich elementary school experience, but who, in addition, has a hobby in this area and has been collecting, preparing, and reading about biological specimens of various kinds. Jim's parents have taken him to the community drama theater since he was in junior high school while John has never seen a play except for performances viewed infrequently on his neighbor's television. In studying play production in the core class, their readiness for experiences are quite different. Marie, who has traveled widely and has had contacts with French-speaking people, is far more ready to deal with first-year French than her classmates who have not had this opportunity.

To what extent can vicarious experience provide the background that builds readiness for study of a country remote in time and space or for science concepts beyond the experiences of the immediate environment? The answer to this question seems to depend in part on the maturity of the learner, and in part on whether his life has provided him with any parallels upon which to draw. For most students, actually to go to see, or to have the real object in the classroom, provides the most meaningful experience. Pictures are one step removed. Words alone represent a second level of abstraction. Much can be done with comparisons. "It would be hot all year like our summer." "That would be just about as tall as our new department store." "How much room would they have in a boat like that? Let's mark off a plan on the floor and see." In general, however, the younger the child, the more important the concrete experience is. Even at the adult level, concepts are less accurate when experience background is meager. Witness the difference between seeing pictures of substandard living conditions and actually visiting the homes, between reciting the number of square yards in an acre and stepping one off, between estimating the size of the Sphinx from pictures and actually standing in front of it.

The many-sidedness of the concept of readiness for learning poses curriculum problems related to the flexibility of the program, the source of school experience, and the richness of the classroom and school environment . . .

How can the teacher determine the learner's level of maturation and readiness for learning in any given area?

What is involved in building and using the experience background needed for effective learning in any area?

How can the teacher determine when direct experience is a necessary part of learning? When vicarious experience alone can give adequate meaning?

What bases for selecting and guiding curriculum experiences will allow for flexible adjustment to a range of maturities and experience backgrounds?

What determines the school environment needed to supplement and enrich learners' out-of-school experiences?

THE INDIVIDUAL LEARNS IN TERMS OF HIS PURPOSES

Although the learner reacts as a whole and tends to respond to the total learning situation—including the classroom atmosphere—the exact nature of his learning will be determined by his purpose. Learning is always, to some extent, selective. John sets somewhat different standards for the paragraph that he sees as an assignment that will be corrected by the teacher than he does for the one he wishes to submit to the editorial board of the school paper. Depending on his family patterns and the attitudes built at school, his standards may change again if the teacher announces that the paragraph is to be graded as well as corrected. Adolescent Sarah, whose grandparents came from Czechoslovakia, will see in her study of world history values that may not be seen by Andrea, for whom the course is simply a graduation requirement. Walter, who reads about Greece with great interest in the unusual and bizarre ways of living in an ancient culture, may come up with a different set of facts than will Rudy, who reads the same chapter to find which elements in the ancient Greek civilization have parallels in our lives today.

Every goal—whether a good grade, a name on the honor roll, the recognition that comes from having an article in the school paper, the intellectual satisfaction of acquiring interesting information or solving a challenging set of arithmetic problems, or the praise of parents—relates to some need. By achieving his goal the learner gains status or self-respect, satisfies intellectual curiosity, wins affection.

When there is a close relationship between the task to be learned—the teacher's goal—and the goal of the learner, the motivation is called **intrinsic.** The pupils who achieve status in the school by securing finances for their school newspaper, for example, and whose opportunity to publish a second one depends on how accurately they keep their accounts, have strong intrinsic motivation to develop whatever arithmetic skills they lack. Here, the teacher's purpose—to develop new arithmetic skills—and the children's purpose—to be able to keep accurate accounts—are very much alike. In attaining their goal, the children will also achieve the teacher's goal. Even one careless mistake may make a difference. The children with sufficient skill to act as treasurers and accountants have a job to do that benefits the whole group. There is little temptation to "get by." The learning is likely to be thorough, meaningful, and effective.

If the same children face similar kinds of arithmetic problems in the next chapter of the text and are to be tested, motivation is still present—to gain approval from the teacher, to receive a good grade, to have the intellectual satisfaction of learning a new skill, to achieve status in the group. Depending on the importance attached to grades and the extent to which classroom competition is a basis for group status, the motivation may be very strong. But there are more opportunities in this situation to achieve the above goals without as consistent attention to arithmetic. For Andy, whose parents are concerned only that he be promoted, just enough accuracy for a passing grade may be sufficient. There may even be motivation not to do well in a particular group of friends, where good work only earns the dubious nickname of "teacher's pet." For Bob who is very able in arithmetic, a sloppy job may be good enough until the Friday test. In such situations the motivation is **extrinsic**—the task to be learned bears no close and necessary relationship to the learner's goal. Under both extrinsic and intrinsic motivation learning does take place, but the type of motivation affects the nature and quality of the learning. Sometimes in the same situation the motivation may be extrinsic for one learner and intrinsic for another. Realistically, intrinsic motivation for all children in all activities is an ideal goal but one infrequently attained.

Motives are usually complex and seldom exactly the same for any two learners. In Miss Sampson's English class, Joan may get much aesthetic satisfaction in writing for the school paper. The recognition of her work in class may give her some needed group status. Her father, a newspaperman, may take great pride in her work and she may find intellectual satisfactions in identifying word origins and in acquiring an effective vocabulary. At the same time she may be earning the grades needed to justify majoring in English in college. On the other hand, John, the managing editor of the same paper, may find satisfaction in the status his work provides, develop important feelings of self-respect through his activities, write a reasonably effective editorial mainly to hold his job, and not care how good his English grades are as long as he does passing work. How nearly these two editorial staff members achieve the learnings that represent Miss Sampson's purposes in sponsoring the paper depends on how similar the sets of purposes are, on how skillful Miss Sampson is in achieving her goals through the purposes that are real to the two students, and on how well, as the experience unfolds, she can help them see new purposes. John, for example, may find his reputation as an editor tied up with his ability to judge the quality of an article and turn back to his English studies with renewed interest and sharper purpose.

Although what is learned is determined by the meaning the learner sees in a situation in the light of his purposes, this does not imply that an effective learning experience must be restricted to the purposes students can identify unaided or to the needs they express. Purposes can also be developed jointly by teacher and learners in a planning session. Here the teacher has a responsibility to add suggestions to those of the group, bringing to consciousness needs of which the learners have not been aware. Not to take such responsibility is to restrict learning experiences to the immature insights of the group.

In helping learners develop new purposes, teachers should realize that learners are not always going to sense immediately and to accept all the goals an adult foresees in an activity. It is often desirable to start with the purposes that learners do see, and to help them identify and clarify new purposes as problems arise during the progress of the activity. "You've all been talking about space ships," a fifth-grade teacher says, "but do you know how far it really is to Mars, and how long people think it would take to get there?" "You all have had opinions about the election," comments the eleventh-grade social studies teacher. "Have you been gathering any facts or have you just been listening to one side? Take the matter of the park site. Who knows, for sure, what the issues are?"

It is also part of the school's responsibility to provide a stimulating environment in which purposes can develop. A class with a genuine responsibility for some aspect of its school life—operating a lost-and-found department, publishing a school paper—has been provided with an excellent source of intrinsic motivation. A classroom, or even the hallway, lunchroom, or auditorium, can be an environment that stimulates intellectual curiosity. Nor do sources of stimulation all reside within the school. The entire community can serve as a laboratory. In providing the environment in which new purposes can arise, teachers should be aware also of trends in the larger national and world community and should take responsibility for helping learners become aware of the ways in which these trends touch their lives. Mr. Jones posts on his science bulletin boards articles regarding the needs for qualified scientists. Miss Larsen takes advantage of a broadcast of sessions of the United Nations to discuss with her world history class the problems of living in a world any part of which can be reached by plane in a matter of hours. Miss Smiley uses an adolescent craze over a new television star to raise with her English class the problems of effectively using mass media of communication.

There is a fundamental difference, however, in what is learned when the individual recognizes as worthwhile and accepts as his own goal one which the teacher originally suggested and when he "goes along" with a purpose he does not see as meaningful. In the latter case, the learner's major goal may be that of reading the teacher's mind, and his activities limited to whatever seems to achieve this end. There is a difference also, when the learner's purpose is largely one of simply amassing interesting facts and when his purpose is to apply these facts to a personal problem or interest. As stated earlier, a skillful teacher can interest a child in almost anything within his maturity level. Such a teacher can also inspire many in a group to engage in the activities that will bring them his favor or approval. There is, however, a real difference between manipulating a group to accept certain purposes, at least on the surface, and having a class cooperatively plan activities for goals it recognizes. "Motivating the class" has deeper meanings than inspiring or interesting learners. For the most efficient learning, it involves helping them set purposes that they recognize as worthwhile—purposes that are directly related to that which is to be learned.

What is known about the role of purpose in learning suggests that ways must be found for recognizing and capitalizing on the learner's purposes if learning is to be most efficient. Curriculum proposals must reflect answers to such questions as . . .

How can teachers use what is known about ways of identifying the purposes of learners? Of modifying purposes and clarifying new purposes?

To what extent can school experiences capitalize upon those problems, needs, and real-life activities which are the genuine concerns of learners and which are among the most readily available sources of intrinsic motivation?

What constitutes effective pupil–teacher planning—planning that makes maximum use of both the purposes of learners and the insights of the teacher?

How can the purposes stated in a course of study or in other curriculum materials be related meaningfully to the lives of learners?

MAXIMUM TRANSFER COMES WITH OPPORTUNITIES TO GENERALIZE

Among the earliest studies in educational psychology and among the most consistent in terms of their implications for educators are those in the area of transfer of learning. Perhaps few problems are of more importance to curriculum workers. Every suggestion for school experiences is based, after all, on the assumption that what is learned will carry over effectively to life outside of school. Although an over-all theory has not yet been proposed that offers a completely satisfying explanation of how transfer occurs, the implications from many specific studies provide definite suggestions for school practice.

The mental discipline theory—that the mind can be exercised in a fashion similar to the way in which one exercises a muscle and will therefore be strengthened by any "tough" subject—was one of the earliest to be challenged. Research attempts to demonstrate that one subject area, regardless of how it is taught, is intrinsically "better" than another in teaching learners to think, develop vocabulary, or achieve any other generalized goal have not been successful. Whether or not the study of geometry leads to better problem-solving ability seems to depend upon whether geometry is taught with problem-solving skills in mind. The technicalities of grammar are helpful in developing good English usage if the learner is assisted in discovering how to use them as a guide to correct speaking and writing. Knowledge of grammar contributes relatively little to correct usage if it is taught as an end in itself. If Latin is taught so that its relation to English roots, prefixes, and suffixes is a point of focus, it will help to build English vocabulary. However, studies indicate that six months of Latin so directed will make a less significant contribution to vocabulary than the same amount of time spent in direct study of the structure and history of the English language, providing that the teaching is equally effective. Each learning experience must be appraised in the light of the use that the learner is expected to make of it and developed so that its potential contribution to this use is realized. The value of any particular subject area depends on exactly what it is and how it is taught, not on any general virtue inherent in the subject itself.

What is known about how to teach for maximum carry-over to life outside of school? From the work of Thorndike and his followers, whose experiments tended to call for a minimum of insight or generalization from the learner, comes the principle that the chances for carry-over are greater when there are similar elements in the two situations. If Billy actually makes change and helps to count the lunch money he is likely to be more efficient with money in other situations than Bob who only works out a series of money problems in his arithmetic notebook. Sam, who applies the principles of ratio and proportion to the bookcase he is making in the shop, is more likely to be able to use this mathematical understanding in daily life than George who has merely worked through similar principles in problems in his algebra text. The pupils who participate frequently in classroom experiences where officers are elected and responsibilities delegated have certain understandings about democracy not possessed by those whose concepts of our American heritage are derived solely from reading and discussion. The successful football team has had practice in scrimmage situations. Individuals learn through doing.

Planning school experiences similar to those out-of-school situations in which learning will be used is not a simple task. It involves more than setting up a classroom post office or simulating a market place. Since the pupil learns in terms of his purposes, much depends on whether or not he sees that the problem he is facing outside of school is similar to the school situation. Learning at times is discouragingly specific. The play store in which Allen so efficiently calculates change may seem an interesting game to him, quite unrelated to his spending problems outside of school. John, who argues for more representation on the student council in the name of democracy, may be quite arbitrary as chairman of a class committee. Conscious efforts are needed to help learners draw parallels between what they are doing in school and related out-of-school experiences. It would seem to be desirable, also, to teach by using the situations learners actually are facing in their out-of-school lives whenever this is practicable. Repeated contacts with varied aspects of a problem are important if learners are to adjust effectively to new situations. Problems of how the learner's perception alters an experience for him, how to understand what he sees in an experience, and how to work with his perceptions in order to achieve maximum transfer are among the most intriguing problems related to learning that face psychologists and educators today.

Research in the field of transfer has suggested another general principle which perhaps helps to explain why learning does not always carry over, even though the situations are seemingly very similar. The learner operates more effectively in a new situation when he has reached generalizations about the old one. Stress on the learner's perception of the situation came originally from the research of Judd and more recently from Gestalt psychology. A tune is recognized, for example, even though it is transposed. Having learned to read the legend of one map, individuals have little difficulty with a second. Once the basic laboratory techniques have been mastered, new arrangements of the equipment can easily be set up. Response is made to a new situation in terms of the general conclusions reached in an old one.

Examples of transfer through generalizations are all around us. The mechanic who understands the principles of one engine adjusts to a new make of car without much trouble. The layman who knows only the names of specific parts of his car is baffled when he lifts the hood of next year's model. Sharon, momentarily stumped by 9×8, explains, "I took ten eights and then took away eight." Faced with the same problem, Sandy, who has merely memorized the multiplication tables without reaching any generalizations, can only resort to guessing. Bill explains, "It's because your verb and subject have to agree. If you say 'the boy and his dog' you have to say 'are'." Alec, lacking the generalization, may say, " 'Is' sounds better," unaware that he is relying on an incorrect but familiar speech pattern from home.

Generalizations are arrived at through experience. Teachers can help at the point where learners' insights have almost been achieved, but presenting the generalization in verbal form to be memorized does not automatically provide a guide on which learners can act. "All through high school I heard about the need for doing something about my speech habits," says the recent graduate after being interviewed for several jobs. "Now I know what was meant." Teaching that leads to generalizations encourages pupils to experiment, to discuss, to reach conclusions. It means experiences that help to make relationships clear and that help learners to analyze new situations in terms of generalizations they now possess. "Let's take a look at all these. Can you see any rule that would help us?" "Think back to last week when we were experimenting with electric bells. Would anything you learned then be of use?" "You've talked before about the effect of a country's economy on its international relations. Does any of that apply here?" Generalizations take on greater depth and added meaning as they are used appropriately in new and varied situations.

There are differences both in learners' ability to generalize and in the quality of the generalizations likely to be arrived at by youngsters of various maturity levels. Other things being equal, younger children and children with limited intellectual ability will not generalize as readily nor will their generalizations be as comprehensive as those of older and more mature learners. The child who has the partial generalization that hands must be washed before eating may not see the need to wash before preparing food for others. Billy, in the slow-learning group, who has learned to respect others' property rights in the classroom may not realize that he should turn in the pencil he found in the hall. All learners need recurring experiences if generalizations are to become more inclusive. Those who learn slowly need many concrete and specific experiences before a generalization is firmly established.

Individuals who have found intellectual stimulation and satisfaction in the study of a particular subject sometimes read into discussions regarding the transfer of learning the implication that school experiences should be selected entirely on the basis of their utilitarian value. "What about knowledge for its own sake?" they ask. Actually, the satisfaction of intellectual curiosity is an important basic need, and it would be a limited school environment that failed to provide children and youth with opportunities to develop deep and lasting interests. However, the problem of transfer still remains. If the goal is to develop learners disposed to pursue in their adult lives a strong interest in history, a concern about astronomy, a love of Shakespeare, these subjects must be taught in a way that will guarantee a desire to continue learning. The question of how to achieve maximum transfer to life outside of school still must be answered. Furthermore, those who argue for teaching a subject "for its own sake" betray a limited orientation to the subject. Geometry, Latin, algebra, grammar, to mention a few that are most frequently associated with the mental discipline concept of transfer, have values in human living far beyond the intellectual satisfactions they offer. Learners' contacts with them should be planned so that these values are achieved.

The principles governing effective transfer have direct implications for the selection and organization of school experiences. They suggest that children and youth should learn through experiences that lead as directly as possible to the generalizations and ways of behaving defined by the school as its goals—goals predicated on what the learner will be expected to be and do in our society. This calls for the translation of these goals into specific behaviors and the consideration of such questions as . . .

> What are the basic generalizations most needed in dealing with the situations of concern to all individuals? What command of fundamental skills is needed—critical reading ability, problem-solving skills, skills in social relationships?
>
> What classroom and other experiences, and what use of subject matter, will lead most directly to the above goals?
>
> How can the curriculum be designed to include the situations and problems with which all individuals need to deal?
>
> What guidance of experiences will be needed to help learners of various maturity levels to reach generalizations most effectively?

THE INDIVIDUAL HAS AN ACTIVE, DYNAMIC APPROACH TO LEARNING

The picture of the learner drawn in preceding sections is that of an active, dynamic organism—he seeks actively to satisfy his own needs; he responds to a situation selectively in terms of his purposes; out of his experiences he tends to draw generalizations, to come to conclusions; and he sees patterns, has insights, senses relationships.

In modern schools the dynamic aspects of learning are capitalized upon in many ways. First, teachers plan with the learner—seeking to identify his needs and to help him clarify his purposes. Through cooperative planning teachers also try to share with learners the school's objectives, so that, in so far as possible, learners' goals and those of the school coincide.

Second, teachers organize learning experiences so that it is easy to see relationships and to draw conclusions. In arithmetic, for example, a teacher helps his group develop a multiplication table to aid in identifying the relationship between addition and multiplication. Pupils look at 2×2, 3×2, 4×2, in sequence. They talk about how $2 + 2 + 2$ can be added if the child has forgotten 3×2. They regroup concrete objects to see the relationship between 3×2 and 2×3. In reading, a child learns the phonetic equivalents for letters and phonograms, but he does so by comparing words he knows. He looks at "cat" and "sat" and discovers the rhyming elements and the beginning sounds. As he adds to his stock of sounds he also develops the generalizations that allow him to use word patterns to discover new sounds on his own. In social studies, a group raises questions and then focuses upon these through reading and discussion so that facts are seen in relation to broader issues.

Third, because of the learner's need to arrive at his own generalizations, as discussed in the preceding section, teachers provide active learning experiences. The learner is encouraged to compare, to discuss, to draw conclusions, to try out what he has learned. A first-grade room has a science corner; sixth-graders go to visit the city waterworks; tenth-graders spend an afternoon with the city council. In a third grade, children report on their observations about the seeds they are growing; in a fifth grade they pull together facts culled from many books; in an eleventh grade, they keep an up-to-date bulletin board of current events against which to view their study of world history.

Capitalizing on the learner's capacity to draw conclusions for himself does not mean that drill is frowned upon or considered old-fashioned. A boy does not become an outstanding shot in basketball merely because he has reached a generalization about the relation that must exist between the place where he is standing and the angle at which his basketball should hit the backboard. A third- or fourth-grader does not add or multiply with ease merely because he understands how addition and multiplication are related, and how both of these are connected with counting. Nor does a youngster whose cultural background has taught him to say "we was" speak correctly because he understands that verbs and subjects should agree. Practice and drill are important.

What is known about planning for drill? It seems most effective when it takes place after the learner has a clear idea of what he is trying to achieve. It seems more useful after certain understandings have been developed than it does as a first step in the learning sequence. Speed with multiplication facts should be achieved after the process is understood. A child needs to have a feeling for a poem as a unit before he starts to memorize it. A player will develop accuracy in basketball more quickly if he knows his mistakes and what he is working for.

Many of the ways of working with children and youth discussed in this section have, to a considerable extent, been adopted regardless of the curriculum design under which a school is operating. Irrespective of the particular goals, there is a general movement away from dealing with separate facts toward procedures that will achieve maximum understanding of facts in relationship. Schools have not ignored the funded knowledge already accumulated through study and investigation but have aimed at balancing "knowing how" with "knowing that." There is also a trend away from a passive approach to learning, directed step by step by the teacher or the textbooks, toward an approach in which the learner is active, creative, and self-propelled. In terms of their particular teaching interests, teachers need to answer such questions as . . .

How can learners be involved in planning, carrying out, and evaluating their experiences?

How can experiences be guided so that learners are helped to see relationships and reach generalizations?

What constitutes purposeful practice?

LEARNINGS NOT USED TEND TO BE FORGOTTEN

One of the most exasperating phenomena with which teachers struggle is that of forgetting. How rapidly this takes place seems to depend in part on how thorough the learning was in the first place, and in part on how dramatic and how meaningful it was. Under certain circumstances a single fact, a particularly apt turn of a phrase, or the details of a special event may remain sharp and clear over long periods of time. However, many of the specific facts and skills learned in day-to-day school activities become dim as time goes on and they are no longer used.

The phenomenon of forgetting often causes confusion among those in the professional ranks. High school chemistry teachers are disconcerted because tables of weights and measures, supposedly learned in the sixth grade, are not recalled readily by their students. College history teachers are concerned by the seeming lack of high school preparation in their freshman classes. "Why didn't their teachers do a better job?" is a common plaint. "This should have been taught before these learners reached me." Even prospective teachers, faced with answering the questions of eager ten-year-olds, are appalled by the number of times they, themselves, have to review facts studied in a college geography course just two years earlier.

What can be done to hold forgetting to a minimum? No matter how strenuous the efforts are, there will never be perfect retention. While most adults have overlearned a few things—the alphabet, the national anthem, a childhood prayer, certain arithmetic combinations—it would place an impossible burden on schools to expect that all facts and skills could be given the amount of use needed to achieve the same degree of overlearning. In part, teachers will have to console themselves with the knowledge that relearning takes much less time than the original learning.

There are procedures, however, that can help to reduce forgetting. The meaningfulness of the situation in which the learning took place seems to make a difference. Nonsense syllables typically prove much harder to recall than lists of words. Nine words in a list are harder to recall than the same nine words in a sentence. Thus, the many means used today to heighten insights and meaningful relationships also tend to contribute to the permanence of the learning.

Retention also implies repetition. If facts, skills, and generalizations are important in the learner's daily life and he continues to use them, his retention is likely to be quite high. The youngster who loves to read practices for hours each week beyond what is planned for him in school. The child who carries home an interest in birds, builds his own feeder, and keeps his own list of new birds, maintains his classroom learnings about birds at a high level. The adolescent who brings his problems in constructing an amateur radio to school and takes his science learnings home to his work on a radio set is not going to sound vague and confused in this particular area, at least, when he enters a new class next fall.

It follows that the less related to life the learnings are, the greater will be the chance of forgetting. The child who knows the number of pints in a quart and quarts in a gallon, because he has used these concepts frequently, may be at a loss when asked the number of ounces in a pint even though this fact was learned in the same table and appeared in the same number of textbook problems. Similarly, the high school graduate who can give dates for the discovery of America, the American Revolution, and the beginning of the Civil War may have trouble telling when Washington was inaugurated. Such lapses do not necessarily mean poor teaching or inattention to details. Often they demonstrate the phenomenon of forgetting and the problem of retention.

Good curriculum planning does not count on life out of school alone to provide the repetition that aids in retention. In varying ways, depending on the curriculum design, there must be plans for repetition . . .

> To what extent can what is learned in school be related to learners' out-of-school experiences so that there will be retention through use?
>
> What plans for sequence or continuity of experience will guarantee repetition under the guidance of the school?
>
> How can teachers work in terms of learners' purposes so that the contributions to memory of a meaningful situation can be capitalized upon?

Because psychology is an independent discipline and science, it is not the handmaiden of any particular philosophical position regarding the role of the school. In so far as the research is available—and new evidence may cause established research findings to be looked at in entirely different lights—it is not possible for a curriculum worker to pick and choose, to say, "This I believe because it fits my philosophy; this I reject."

Whether the school is in a democracy or in a totalitarian state, whether the role of the school is considered to be preservation of the cultural heritage or preparation for change, individuals learn and grow in the same way. All proposals for designing the curriculum delineate the scope of school experiences, the sequence in which these experiences are to be met by learners, and the organization of these experiences around topics, in units, in subjects, or in subject groups. In so far as goals differ, proposals regarding scope, sequence, and organization will differ. Whatever the proposed design, it will be effective only as it takes into account established principles regarding the nature of the learner and the learning process.

Related Readings

ALMY, MILLIE. *Child Development.* New York: Henry Holt and Company, Inc., 1955.

CANTOR, NATHANIEL. *Dynamics of Learning.* Third edition. Buffalo, N.Y.: Henry Stewart, Inc., 1956.

CRONBACH, LEE J. *Educational Psychology.* New York: Harcourt, Brace & Company, Inc., 1954.

CUNNINGHAM, RUTH, AND ASSOCIATES. *Understanding Group Behavior of Boys and Girls.* New York: Bureau of Publications, Teachers College, Columbia University, 1951.

EELLS, KENNETH W., AND OTHERS. *Intelligence and Cultural Differences.* Chicago: University of Chicago Press, 1951.

GESELL, ARNOLD, FRANCES L. ILG, AND LOUISE B. AMES. *Youth: The Years from Ten to Sixteen.* New York: Harper & Brothers, 1956.

HAVIGHURST, ROBERT. *Human Development and Education.* New York: Longmans, Green & Company, 1953.

HILGARD, ERNEST R. *Theories of Learning.* Second edition. New York: Appleton-Century-Crofts, 1956.

HURLOCK, ELIZABETH. *Developmental Psychology.* Second edition. New York: McGraw-Hill Book Company, Inc., 1953.

JERSILD, ARTHUR. *The Psychology of Adolescence.* New York: The Macmillan Company, 1957.

LINDGREN, HENRY C. *Educational Psychology in the Classroom.* New York: John Wiley & Sons, Inc., 1956.

NATIONAL SOCIETY FOR THE STUDY OF EDUCATION. *Learning and Instruction.* Forty-ninth Yearbook, Part 1. Chicago: University of Chicago Press, 1950.

NATIONAL SOCIETY FOR THE STUDY OF EDUCATION. *The Psychology of Learning.* Forty-first Yearbook, Part 2. Chicago: University of Chicago Press, 1942.

OLSON, WILLARD C. *Child Development.* Boston: D. C. Heath & Company, 1949.

PRESCOTT, DANIEL A. *Emotion and the Educative Process.* Washington, D.C.: American Council on Education, 1938.

RASEY, MARIE I., AND J. W. MENGE. *What We Learn from Children.* New York: Harper & Brothers, 1956.

RUSSELL, DAVID. *Children's Thinking.* Boston: Ginn and Company, 1956.

SNYGG, DONALD, AND ARTHUR COMBS. *Individual Behavior.* New York: Harper & Brothers, 1949.

TROW, WILLIAM C. *The Learning Process.* What Research Says to the Teacher Series, No. 6. Washington, D.C.: Department of Classroom Teachers, American Educational Research Association of the National Education Association, 1954.

Part II

A CURRICULUM FOR LEARNERS IN OUR TIMES

4

AN ANALYSIS OF MAJOR APPROACHES TO DESIGNING THE CURRICULUM

The proposal that indicates the basis for the selection and organization of knowledge, concepts, and skills stressed in any given school system is its **curriculum design.** Three types of questions need to be answered. First, what shall be the scope of the proposed curriculum? What areas of knowledge, facts, skills, and generalizations should be encompassed by school experiences? Second, how shall this knowledge and these skills and generalizations be organized for classroom instruction? Third, in what order shall the proposed learnings be developed—which are appropriate for a younger child, which for adolescents? What shall be the sequence or grade placement of experiences?

As indicated in Chapter 1, the widely varied answers to curriculum issues result in significantly divergent proposals of scope, sequence, and organization. The range is from designs developed around the framework of the traditional subjects to those in which the details of scope, sequence, and organization emerge as teacher and learners work together.

Throughout much of the past quarter century those concerned with curriculum research have stressed the need for studies to test the effectiveness of various proposals for curriculum design. How to conduct such studies is still one of the most baffling problems facing educators today. Any curriculum design stems from a set of values—fundamental beliefs relating to the type of citizen desired and the part to be played by the school in his development. Since each design is proposed to achieve its own particular goals, demonstrating that one design is "better" than another becomes a problem of comparing goals—of weighing one set of values against another—and of showing that the goals realized are a result of the particular design. It might be possible to identify certain common values that all designs aim to achieve and to attempt to discover which design actually attains these values most effectively. However, ultimate goals are not realized until learners are out of school in adult life. Long-term studies are needed and researchers will have to solve the complicated problem of assessing the influence of the school and of other educative agencies on the child. In addition, there is the equally difficult problem of sorting out the effects of the design itself and the contribution that would have been made by the teacher, regardless of the curriculum under which he worked.

Even if it is not readily possible to develop research procedures that will provide positive answers to the question of whether a better curriculum design exists, at least it is possible for the personnel in a given school to know why they prefer the one they do. This calls for a clear picture of what values are sought, how the role of the school is defined, and why the proposed scope, sequence, and organization are patterned as they are. It also means knowing the points of difference in goals, and in convictions as to how these goals are best achieved, that cause some educators to advocate other designs. Such understanding is important for the effective interpretation of the work of the school to the public. It is necessary if teachers are not to be confused (and possibly stampeded) by proposals that seem to challenge their present ways of working. Such insights are also vital for cooperation and forward movement in the total field of curriculum planning. Genuine and thoughtful differences in values held—and therefore differences in opinion as to what and how to teach—should be recognized and respected for what they are.

Varied Proposals of Scope, Sequence, and Organization

The curriculum worker attempting to locate analyses of the varied types of curriculum design currently in use in our schools finds himself in a verbal jungle. Subject-centered, experience-centered; correlated, integrated, fused; broad fields, major social functions, centers of interest;

core, unit, problem—in many combinations and under as many logics—these are among the terms used to describe modern curriculum designs.

One of the simplest systems of classification, and one that tends to make clear-cut distinctions, is to look at the design itself—the basic organization governing the grouping of facts, generalizations, and skills to be taught. Under this system, four major types of organization can be identified.[1] First is the organization by **separate subjects** in which the scope and organization of school experiences are designated in terms of the subjects to be studied. Sequence is determined with reference to what is most appropriate for different maturity levels. Second is the organization by **subject fields** or **groups of related subjects**—history and geography as social studies; physics, chemistry, and biology as the natural sciences. Related fields of knowledge become the bases for organization; scope and sequence are determined in much the same way as in the case of separate subjects. Third, and in contrast to the two preceding bases of curriculum design, are the patterns where scope and sequence are still designated from grade to grade but in terms of **broad areas that cut across subject fields.** In some designs these are areas of living or major social functions, so organized as to include every major aspect of life; in others they are broad preplanned units, some of which relate to pupils' personal needs and some to the world in which they live, but which do not necessarily contribute to all major areas of living in any one year. Aspects of life in which the learner must function effectively—communication, development and conservation of human and material resources, home and family life—are used to determine scope and organization, while sequence rests upon adjudged optimum placement in terms of the maturity of the learners as in the two preceding positions. Fourth are the designs in which choice of subject matter for any pupil group, how it is organized, and how it flows in sequence from grade to grade emerge from the **needs or problems faced by the group,** broadly interpreted. This organization is distinct from the other three in that neither scope, organization, nor sequence is specifically outlined and preplanned grade by grade.

Each of these types of design is planned to achieve certain specific values. Because of its point of primary focus, each gives only secondary emphasis to other goals and values. The typical characteristics of the scope, sequence, and organization of each proposal, the values sought

[1] A similar organization is used in Hollis L. Caswell and Arthur W. Foshay, *Education in the Elementary School,* Third Edition, pp. 257–268 (New York: American Book Company, 1951), and with slightly different terminology in J. Galen Saylor and William M. Alexander, *Curriculum Planning for Better Teaching and Learning,* pp. 245–304 (New York: Rinehart & Company, Inc., 1954). The writers of the present volume are indebted to the insightful analyses of these authors.

and those least likely to be achieved, and the practical problems which may arise in putting the design into operation are discussed in the material which follows.

SOME DESIGNS ARE PREPLANNED IN TERMS OF SEPARATE SUBJECTS

The most traditional design, and still the most popular, designates scope, sequence, and organization in terms of separate subjects. This pattern is particularly widespread at the high school and college levels. History, geography, physics, chemistry, art, algebra, geometry are separate areas of study, often taught by different teachers. Scope, in this type of design, is determined by the range of subjects included and the content of each subject. Organization is in terms of what is seen as the inherent logic of the subject. Sequence is outlined in terms of available studies of maturity. Spiral patterns typically provide for the repetition that leads to retention. Thus, first-graders begin to learn about their nation through study of family, school, and immediate community. In the third grade, understandings may be expanded through historical events connected with Thanksgiving Day, Columbus Day, Washington's Birthday. In the fifth grade there may be more intensive covering of American history, with particular stress on explorers, pioneer ways of life, and other of the more dramatic and colorful aspects of our tradition. The eighth grade may find learners concerned with the more complex political and economic aspects of our history. The senior high school may provide a deeper look at these same aspects. An undergraduate college course may cover the same territory still more intensively. Graduate courses treat in more detail such areas as the Civil War, the Reconstruction years, and twentieth-century America.

Those who favor separate subjects as a basis for curriculum design see, as major values, the preservation of the cultural heritage; the systematic acquainting of learners with the resources and the ways of thinking that are the special contributions of the separate subject; and, at more advanced levels, the opportunity to reconstruct the discipline in the light of research and new evidence. While it is seldom safe to attribute positions regarding curriculum design to particular philosophies of education, this point of view is frequently held by those classified as neohumanists and as essentialists. Although choices still have to be made from all the cultural heritage as to what to include or omit, what to stress heavily or touch lightly, learners are at least exposed systematically to an agreed-upon selection of subject matter. It is often argued that such a plan assures that each learner has worked with certain "basic" areas and provides the pupil who will later specialize with the background knowledge he needs. In a sense, this is true. The student who comes to the typical college science program from high school courses in physics and chemistry, organized in much the same fashion as his college work, may have somewhat fewer adjustments to make than the student who brings a general science background.

While one of the values held by those who favor separate subjects as the basis for curriculum design is to acquaint children and youth systematically with their cultural heritage, this does not mean that the stress is on facts for their own sake. The geography course in which the major learnings consist of such items as the capitals of Europe and the products of its countries is not as common today as formerly. Rather there is concern with helping learners develop basic understandings, concepts, and generalizations applicable to their problems of daily living. There is equal commitment to teach those ways of thinking that are the particular contribution of the subject. The teacher of chemistry sees one of his important functions to be that of helping learners acquire a scientific method of working; the teacher of history works for fundamental respect for the methods of historical research. Sound factual information is also considered important, but the approach is not encyclopedic. The facts stressed are those most useful to the learner in today's world, and most important in concept-building. This has been the trend since the concern with social utility of curriculum research of the early 1900's. It is a trend that is sometimes not given the recognition it deserves by those who see in this type of design the danger that there will be preoccupation with many relatively isolated facts.

There are other advantages attributed to the separate subjects approach. First, because it is the design most frequently used at the college level, teachers feel at home with it. It allows for the maximum direct use of their college work and provides the security that comes with a feeling of competence. Second, it is a traditional pattern and consequently tends to satisfy the public conception of the school's role. Parents feel secure that areas of knowledge which their own schooling impressed upon them as important are not being neglected. Third, textbooks and reference materials are typically organized in this way. Thus, it is possible to add to the important feeling of security of both teacher and pupils by providing specific and clearly laid out material to be studied. It is too superficial a view of the separate subject approach to brush it aside as "traditional" or "subject-centered" rather than "child-centered."

What has led some school systems to move away from designs built around separate subjects? This is the organization under which it is most difficult to teach learners to bring to bear on a problem facts and generalizations from several subjects. True, every effective teacher of a subject brings in illustrations from life and draws upon other fields as the opportunity offers. The very nature of this design, however, tends to focus learnings on the relationships inherent within the subject rather than on interrelationships among subjects. Even when the over-all design is developed so that related topics parallel each other—the history of prehistoric man concurrent with a study of prehistoric animals in science—these relationships may not be drawn. There is the added problem, when the teaching is departmentalized, that the teacher of one subject usually does not know what points are being stressed in another and thus does not always sense opportunities for developing relationships. The result is that the learner himself must cut across subject lines in search of related understandings.

The separate subjects organization also makes it difficult to work with problems of genuine concern to the learner. Certainly, effective teachers will do as much as possible to make learning purposeful. Pupil–teacher planning and unit activities are not foreign to classrooms operating under this organization. Time is often set aside for discussions of special concern to the group. However, the systematic acquaintance with the cultural heritage, a major goal for curriculum designs built around separate subjects, would not be achieved if the class moved away from designated topics too frequently. The prescription of a systematic sequence from grade to grade raises some doubt as to the wisdom of taking a fifth grade, for example, into an area that the sixth-grade teacher expects to cover.

Designs built around separate subjects raise additional problems in adjusting to individual differences. By the very values considered to be most worthwhile under this type of design, each child should have contact with each recommended aspect of his cultural heritage. What is the teacher to do with the slow learner for whom the concepts recommended for his grade are too difficult? What should be done for the pupil who lacks the experience background to make a subject meaningful? What are the teacher's obligations to the learner who has the capabilities to go well beyond the subject matter suggested for his grade?

There are other problems, perhaps not as fundamental as those just discussed, but nevertheless important. One is the tendency of subjects to proliferate. To the high school's earlier offerings of history and geography, for example, economics, sociology, and psychology have been added. One may ask whether such subjects as homemaking, driver training, typewriting, do not have a place in the program of every youth. Sometimes there are demands for special courses on the dangers of alcohol, or the history of a given state. Some five hundred courses are now offered in the secondary schools of America. As the offerings have increased, various proposals have developed for the introduction and use of electives, particularly at the high school level. This raises another type of problem, for what is meant to be a wide acquaintance with the cultural heritage actually may not be so. While a general science course might acquaint a student broadly with the field, the heritage in science transmitted to the student who has to choose between physics, chemistry, and biology may actually be quite limited.

The only acceptable basis for appraising any proposed design is to assume that it will be carried out with the best possible teaching. However, in practice, every design by its very nature may lead to certain kinds of poor teaching. Even with the most effective pupil–teacher planning, it is sometimes difficult to secure intrinsic motivation when the concerns of children and youth have to be channeled within subject organizations. Actual practice may rely on extrinsic motivation, or on intellectual curiosity about the odd and interesting aspects of the subject. There is also the possibility that there will be an overconcern with facts rather than generalizations, and a preoccupation with making sure that the prescribed text or the course of study outline is thoroughly covered. The result may be an overuse of recitation and memorization, although this is not a necessary corollary. But the fact that the values inherent in a proposed design may not be achieved because of such teaching is not a valid reason for discarding it. Those who feel that separate subjects do not offer the most suitable design for children and youth in today's schools should base their arguments on fundamental differences in values and goals which emerge from the most effective teaching possible.

SOME DESIGNS ARE PREPLANNED IN TERMS OF GROUPS OF RELATED SUBJECTS

Designs in which related subjects are grouped illustrate attempts to achieve many of the values of patterns in which subjects are separate while overcoming some of the potential weaknesses. History, geography, and civics become the social studies; reading, writing, spelling, speaking, and listening are combined as the language arts; work in general science encompasses selected facts and concepts from such separate subjects as physics, physiology, chemistry, bacteriology, zoology, and botany. The scope of the curriculum is still determined by the traditional subjects, but the organization brings together content of related subjects. Specific topics or concepts within the broad area indicate the sequence from grade to grade. The same general research regarding maturation that guides the designation of sequence in designs where subjects are separate is used in this organizational pattern.

Designs in which related subjects are grouped are more widespread at the elementary than at the secondary or college levels. Steps in the direction of grouping subjects are found in high schools in courses in general science, problems of democracy, communication arts, and in certain types of "core" combining two or more specific subjects. Although less common, similar groupings exist in some college courses—survey of mathematics, development of western civilization, introduction to education.

What do advocates of designs which group related subjects see as values? Basically, like organizations built around separate subjects, this type of design also provides systematic acquaintance with the cultural heritage. Scope is determined by the knowledge and concepts of this heritage. While two or more subjects are studied in relationship, the organization tends to keep subject fields as entities. The possibilities for helping learners see relationships among separate subjects is usually considered the special contribution of this curriculum design. As the learner studies this or some other country, for example, he brings to bear both historical and geographical concepts on the single problem or topic. When this is done, the teaching of interrelationships among fields is facilitated. The following set of content goals [2] shows how these interrelationships might be stated in the social studies.

LIVING IN EGYPT

GEOGRAPHY AND RELATED FIELDS	HISTORY, CIVICS, AND RELATED FIELDS
Egypt today occupies an important place because of the Suez Canal. (See Major Concept D.)	The Pharaoh and his court exerted great influence on the lives of the people in ancient times. (See Major Concepts A, E, and F.)
The mild climate and the waters of the Nile make it possible for farmers to derive a substantial yield from their limited farmlands. (See Major Concepts C and D.)	Ancient Egypt widely influenced her contemporaries. (See Major Concepts D, F, and G.)
Large areas of desert limit the development of Egypt. (See Major Concepts C and D.)	Ancient Egypt contributed to the present in art, written language, mathematics, religion, medicine, law, and science. (See Major Concepts A, E, G, and H.)

[2] Cincinnati Public Schools, *New Intermediate Manual,* Board of Education, Cincinnati, Ohio, Curriculum Bulletin 400, 1954, p. 251.

GEOGRAPHY AND RELATED FIELDS	HISTORY, CIVICS, AND RELATED FIELDS
Egypt exports mostly farm products, chiefly cotton. (See Major Concepts C and F.)	The people of Egypt have experienced many changes through the centuries. (See Major Concept G.)
Egypt imports many products. (See Major Concepts C, D, and F.)	Egypt is a land of contrasts between the old and the new; the have and the have-nots. (See Major Concepts A, G, and I.)
The growth of the city of Cairo was influenced by the millions of farmers located along the Nile. (See Major Concepts C and D.)	Ancient Egypt was able to develop art, medicine, and science because the primary needs of food, clothing, and shelter were easily met. (See Major Concepts C and D.)

Because the focus is upon helping children and youth to see relationships among various subjects, over-all goals are often stated in terms of broad generalizations. An example of such basic concepts are those suggested as the focus of the work of the intermediate grades in social studies in the course of study just quoted.

MAJOR CONCEPTS

A. Democratic ideals and practices have evolved through time and must be understood, cherished, and extended.

B. Basically all people are very much alike, although they differ in their ways of living because of geographic and historical factors.

C. Man meets his needs through the use of natural and human resources.

D. Man influences his environment and is influenced by it.

E. Many people have contributed to our present civilization.

F. Men and nations are dependent upon each other.

G. Man lives in a continually changing world.

H. Man has evolved social institutions to meet his needs.

I. Society improves most rapidly when every individual assumes his share of responsibility.[3]

Because there is concern about opportunities for learners to develop relationships, the work in a given subject field for any one grade is often outlined in terms of possible units of work. In the course of study just described, there is suggested a list of units from which choices would be made for the fifth-grade social studies program which focuses on the

[3] *Ibid.*, p. 193.

growth of our country. Understandings related to the units marked with an asterisk are considered essential, but teachers are free to develop these understandings as they see fit, as well as to select from among the other units suggested.

Living in the Ohio Valley and the Great Lakes Area, Today and Yesterday

* Cincinnati, Today and Yesterday
  Living Along the Wilderness Trail
* How the Pioneer Lived in Early Ohio
  Living in a Farming Community, Yesterday and Today
  Living in a Coal-Mining Community
  Living in a Metropolitan Community Based on the Development of One Industry: Akron, Detroit
* Men and Women Who Have Made Worthy Contributions to Our Culture

Living in the South

* Living on a Cotton Plantation before the Civil War
* Living in a Farming Community Today
  Living in a City of Historical Significance: New Orleans, Mobile, Atlanta
  Living in a Vacation Community: Miami, Asheville
  Living in an Oil Community
  Living in an Industrial Area
* Men and Women Who Have Made Worthy Contributions to Our Culture

Living in the Northeast, Today and Yesterday

* Living in Colonial Times
  Living in a Big City: New York, Philadelphia, Boston
  Living in a Fishing Community
  Living in a Manufacturing Community
  Living in a Vacation Community
* Men and Women Who Have Made Worthy Contributions to Our Culture

Living in the West

* Living on Trails to the West, Today and Yesterday
  Living in a Mining Community
  Living in a Salmon-Fishing Community
  Living in an Oil Town
  Living in a Vacation Community
  Living on a Sheep or Cattle Ranch

Living on a Fruit Ranch
* Men and Women Who Have Made Worthy Contributions to Our Culture [4]

In achieving additional opportunities to help children and youth see relationships among subjects, the curriculum design in which subjects are grouped is likely to include subject matter from more areas, but not always to go into any one area as deeply as would those designs where subjects are separate. John, spending four periods a week in a science survey course, will have contact with more varied science concepts than will Eddie who spends four periods a week in chemistry. But, assuming equally skillful teaching, Eddie may know more chemistry. John's insight into the total science field is seen as a strength gained from grouping subjects by those who conceive the role of the school to be the provision of broad general education appropriate for everyday living. It is seen as a weakness by those who feel that considerable opportunity for specialization should be offered, particularly at the secondary school level. It is also seen as a weakness by those who value knowledge for its own sake and who fear that less intensive contacts with a subject area will lead to a smattering of learning and a disposition to be satisfied with superficial answers.

There are other advantages attributed to designs in which subjects are grouped—advantages very similar to those of designs in which they are separate. The organization is sufficiently similar to typical college courses to give a feeling of security to teachers. The availability of a number of textbooks also provides security. While the public at large may not always feel that history and geography are really being taught under the nomenclature of social studies, or physics, chemistry, and biology under the general science label, the plan does not pose undue problems of interpretation to laymen.

What values are difficult to secure under designs in which related subjects are grouped? As just suggested, persons most concerned about equipping learners with essentials of specific subject areas tend to fear that the learning will be more dispersed and less thorough in any given area. At the high school level, this concern resolves into a problem of achieving balance between the desired breadth of understanding that the grouping of subjects is intended to provide and the experience of exploring deeply that should be part of the intellectual challenge to the maturing learner. In an effort to solve this problem some school systems group subjects at the elementary level but return to separate subjects for their secondary schools.

[4] *Ibid.*, p. 229.

Not all the doubts regarding designs in which subjects are grouped are expressed by those who wish to preserve the contributions of separate subjects. Educators concerned with equipping the learner with generalizations that he can use in daily life and teaching him how to bring all needed data to bear on a problem, point out that out-of-school problems are rarely restricted to a single subject field. Following intelligently the newspaper accounts of the negotiations for a new state turnpike, for example, may involve concepts from political science, geography, economics, physics, and perhaps something of the history of why the main thoroughfares run where they do. Even the simple problems faced by third-graders who are operating a classroom store may involve arithmetic, language skills, concepts of sizes and measures, information about which foods need refrigeration and which do not, and a number of human relations skills. When subjects are grouped, skillful teachers often feel freer to digress in terms of the concern of a particular group than they would were they working within a specific subject. Nevertheless, the primary focus is upon the subject field, and if the values of this focus are to be realized the majority of the generalizations developed will need to reflect it.

Many of the questions noted earlier regarding how to give help with problems of concern to a given group, when they are not designated as part of the sequence for the grade, can be raised again in appraising designs built around subject fields. While the semidissolution of subject lines may remove some of the feeling of pressure of work to be covered, there are still questions as to how far to digress from the general recommendations for a given grade. Thus, the genuine concern of a fourth-grade group to learn more about fossils and prehistoric animals may be only partially satisfied because this is a sixth-grade science topic.

How well a design built around subject fields will meet the needs of children with either limited or unusually high intellectual ability, or how well it will allow for adjustments for groups of different experience background is also questioned. These problems arise whenever a specific series of topics is assigned to a particular grade. The generally greater flexibility allowed when subjects are grouped gives the teacher more freedom than might be the case under a separate subjects design, both to simplify activities for the slower-learning child and to make a wealth of related material available to those who need additional challenge.

In a curriculum built around groups of related subjects inadequate learnings may result unless teachers see relationships and are broadly prepared in the subject fields. Skills in helping children set up and solve problems are also necessary. Units can become stereotyped, and, if not well developed, may yield neither the generalizations intended by combining subjects nor the thorough grounding in facts and information that adherence to a textbook in a single subject may achieve. And there are other problems. A teacher who is so overawed by the breadth and importance of his area may take students far beyond their depth in advanced-level facts rather than develop the generalizations and understandings appropriate for his group. On the other hand, because textbooks in such fields as general science or social studies are readily available, a teacher may concentrate on helping children acquire the facts in the book through a combination of recitation and drill.

SOME DESIGNS ARE PREPLANNED IN TERMS OF BROAD AREAS THAT CUT ACROSS SUBJECT FIELDS

If the grouping of subjects does not allow for focusing sufficient data on a particular problem, what organization might do so? One answer is found in designs developed around broad areas and problems that cut across subject fields. Two major patterns have emerged within this general approach—the first is a curriculum designed to deal with all major areas of human activity (commonly referred to as areas of living or major social functions), and the second is a design focused on selected problem areas relating to personal and social concerns of children and youth. In each of these patterns, subjects are drawn upon whenever and wherever they contribute the needed facts, understandings, and concepts.

Both approaches make specific proposals for curriculum scope, organization, and sequence in advance of the teacher's work with learners. Both attempt to define scope and to organize learnings in terms of areas in which problems and situations of life seem to group themselves. Sequence is usually designated by assigning specific points of focus to different grade levels, using psychological studies of the maturing learner to determine placement. Just what this approach to designing the curriculum really means can be seen more clearly through an illustration or two.

Pioneer efforts to develop an areas of living or social functions design were made in several states in the mid-1930's. Although the concept has exerted significant influence on curriculum organization, it has not been extensively applied in systematic and comprehensive form. Where the pattern has been proposed, it usually extends through both elementary and secondary schools. This was true of one program where the major functions of social life were identified as follows: [5]

[5] Virginia State Board of Education, *Tentative Course of Study for Virginia Public Schools,* 1934. Now withdrawn from use.

Protection and conservation of life, property, and natural resources
Production of goods and services and distribution of the returns of production
Consumption of goods and services
Communication and transportation of goods and people
Recreation
Expression of aesthetic impulses
Expression of religious impulses
Education
Extension of freedom
Integration of the individual
Exploration

These eleven areas suggested the scope of the curriculum for both elementary and secondary schools, with the exception that the last three were to be included only in the secondary program (eighth grade on through high school).

Sequence in this program was indicated by designating a specific center of interest for each grade and selecting for emphasis a particular aspect of each of the social functions. The following chart shows the selected emphasis at each grade level for two of the eleven social functions.

Grade	Center of Interest	Consumption of Goods and Services	Expression of Aesthetic Impulses
I	Home and school	How does our family provide itself with food, clothing, and shelter?	What can we do to make our home and school more beautiful and pleasant?
II	Community life	How do we use the goods and services provided in our community?	What do we do to make our community attractive?
III	Adaptation of life to environmental forces of nature	Why can communities markedly different from ours furnish us with goods we cannot produce?	How do people in communities markedly different from ours express their artistic impulses?
IV	Adaptation of life to advancing physical frontiers	How does frontier living restrict the consumption of goods and services?	How are music, literature, and art affected by frontier living?
V	Effects of machine production upon our living	How is the consumption of goods and services influenced by discoveries and inventions?	How do inventions and discoveries affect our art, music, and literature?

Grade	Center of Interest	Consumption of Goods and Services	Expression of Aesthetic Impulses
VI	Effects of machine production upon our living	How does machine production of standardized goods influence the choice and use of goods?	How does machine production modify art, literature, music, and architecture?
VII	Social provision for cooperative living	How do social agencies influence the consumer in his choice and use of goods?	How do social organizations provide opportunities for expression of aesthetic impulses?
VIII	Adaptation of our living through nature, social and mechanical inventions, and discoveries	How do inventions and discoveries affect the well-being of the consumer?	How do man's natural environment and his inventions provide worthwhile opportunities for the cultivation of aesthetic expression?
IX	Agrarianism and industrialism, and their effects upon our living	How and why do standards of living vary in agrarian and industrialized societies?	How do agrarianism and industrialism influence the development of our artistic resources and the adjustment of all individuals to their use?
X	Effects of changing culture and changing social institutions upon our living	How does the advancement of science affect the thinking and the welfare of the consumer?	How do culture areas and changing social institutions influence the development of the fine arts?
XI	Effects of a continuously planning social order upon our living	How can nations plan for the establishment of proper economic interdependence by apportioning the production of goods and services and by distributing these more equitably to the consumer?	How can a planning society improve the quality of living for all by utilizing man's desire for beauty?

Educators who propose that the curriculum be built around personal and social concerns of children and youth, rather than encompass all areas of living, have not agreed upon any list of these areas of problems. Alberty,[6] dealing with the secondary school curriculum, places emphasis

[6] Harold Alberty, "A Proposal for Reorganizing the High-School Curriculum on the Basis of a Core Program," *Progressive Education,* XXVIII: 57–61 (November, 1950); quoted in Alberty, *Reorganizing the High School Curriculum,* Revised Edition, pp. 177–180 (New York: The Macmillan Company, 1953).

upon "the common needs, problems, and interests of adolescents selected from established problem areas," and identifies the latter as:

Orientation to the School	Personal Value Systems
Home and Family Life	World Religions
Community Life	Communication
Contemporary Cultures	Human Relations
Science and Technology	Planning
Public Opinion	War and Peace
Hobbies and Interests	Education
Physical and Mental Health	Vocational Orientation

Resource Development, Conservation, and Use
Contemporary America Among the Nations
Competing Political, Social, and Economic Ideologies

The problem areas here stated, without any implications for sequence, are proposed as the scope of the curriculum designed for meeting the common needs of adolescents. The sequence in which these problems would be studied and the number covered in any one year would be decided by the staff of the particular school. Alberty illustrates a possible sequence from the Garrett County, Maryland, core program: [7]

7th Grade

School Living
Health and Safety
Transportation
Communicating Ideas

8th Grade

Knowing Garrett County
Natural Environment
Leisure and Recreation

9th Grade

Making a Living
Establishing Beliefs
Consumer Problems
Personal Development
American Heritage

10th Grade

Intercultural Relations
Living in One World
Leisure and Recreation
Communicating Ideas

11th Grade

American Heritage
Personal Development
Establishing Beliefs

12th Grade

Family Living
Role of Education
Making a Living
Health and Safety
Consumer Problems
Technology of Living

In designs where the organizing elements cut across subject fields, it is usually assumed that teacher and learners will engage in unit activities as they explore problems in each area. Courses of study typically suggest

[7] Alberty, *Reorganizing the High School Curriculum,* p. 184.

lists of possible problems and types of activities but the problems faced by the learners are generally considered more important in actual planning. Teacher and learners are given considerable freedom to approach a problem area from an angle of special interest or to move from a recommended area to a concern judged more valuable for the group.

Those who see major values in curriculum designs planned in terms of broad areas that cut across subject fields refer to the greater opportunity to help learners draw upon all needed subject-matter areas to develop generalizations that bear directly upon the problems of living they actually face. For example, in the area of communication, the learner under a separate subjects organization may learn many facts, but he may learn them in isolated parts of his school day or year. He may study about the telephone in a seventh-grade science class, and about radio or television several years later. He may touch on the invention of printing in sixth-grade history, the use of papyrus in a fourth-grade study of Egypt, and the effect of propaganda in an eleventh-grade study of World War II. He may work with the daily papers as part of a current events program in grade five, help to put out a classroom paper the following year, and publish the high school journal in a twelfth-grade English class. Whether these experiences are, or are not, related in the learner's thinking is more or less left to chance. When the focus is upon areas in which problems of living actually fall, the isolated facts may be brought together in a series of units on communication. The learner may discuss the invention of printing, trace its effect on the world of its time, and use all this to gain understanding of the power of the modern press. As he builds his own amateur radio he may be studying the effect of modern methods of communication on his life, the degree to which people secure status by their appearance on television, and the effect radio and television have on advertising or on the changing pattern of election campaigns.

Such a reorganization of knowledge does not mean that fewer facts are taught but rather that the focus is changed. Under this type of design the direct bearing of many subjects upon actual problems of life is considered too important to leave to chance. The chronological history sequence, or the time-honored order of topics in physics or chemistry is considered of secondary importance to using subject matter where needed. Of course, time lines or other devices would be used to develop a sense of historical perspective. Certainly, too, rather extensive study of a single subject area will be needed from time to time if the full contribution of the subject to the problem at hand is to be realized. But the basic orientation is toward the interrelation of subjects as they bear on an actual problem of living, not toward the internal structure of the subjects themselves.

Typically, in a design organized around areas that cut across subject fields there is much greater freedom to use class concerns as the basis of work. The feeling of pressure on the teacher to cover the textbook or to touch on every point suggested by the course of study tends to be somewhat relieved. As a consequence intrinsic motives can be capitalized upon much more easily and adjustments to individual differences made more readily. Further, the individual learns what is taught in the way that he is most likely to use it in meeting situations of everyday living.

What values are least likely to be achieved in this type of design? The concerns of those who see the role of the school as acquainting learners with the traditional cultural heritage are indicated in the preceding discussion. This curriculum pattern does not provide an orientation to facts in ways that have come to be accepted as "logical" both by tradition and by virtue of the interrelationships inherent within subjects themselves. These concerns often become more acute when considering the secondary school program. "How, out of this pattern," ask both subject specialists and many laymen, "will come the scientists and the historians of the future? How will pupils even orient themselves to the typical college course, let alone bring the solid foundation and the love of the subject that they will need for success?"

Other persons, very much concerned about enhancing the capacities of children and youth to use whatever parts of their cultural heritage are needed in the solution of a problem, argue that because a specific sequence is designated, artificiality may still exist. It is just as unlikely, they point out, that a ten-year-old fifth-grader will face a genuine problem requiring him to find out how the consumption of goods and services is influenced by invention and discovery [8] as it is that he will have a real need to become acquainted with the early explorers—a topic commonly found in fifth-grade social studies curricula. Thus, while the designation of curriculum scope by problems and areas of living is seen by these critics to focus desirably on the areas about which skills, concepts, and generalizations need to be built, they fear much of this is negated by too great specificity as to how each area is to be faced by each grade.

There are other, perhaps less basic, problems which often act as deterrents when school personnel think about adopting this type of design—textbooks and other teaching aids are not available in any abundance, and this is not the pattern that the typical college program has followed. Thus the teacher has few experiences that will transfer to the new situation and often has definite feelings of insecurity when he thinks about working in this way.

[8] See the emphasis for Grade 5 in the course of study cited on page 98.

Curriculum designs developed around broad areas and problems can foster their own particular type of poor teaching. If a teacher develops certain units that have "worked well" and manipulates the situation so that each new group is "motivated" to undertake much the same study, the entire pattern can become stereotyped. When this happens, many of the potential values of working within areas close to the lives of a given group of learners will not be achieved. Under a curriculum designed so that facts from many areas will be brought to bear on a problem, it is possible, too, that a teacher with limited insight may fail to sense the concepts that could be developed and may allow a group to spend too much time on a particular aspect of a problem or may stress too heavily construction, dramatics, art, or some other activity related to a unit. Under the poorest conditions, the result could be a series of very limited and isolated experiences, with little provision for arriving at generalizations and few of the virtues of thorough or systematic exposure to an organized body of subject matter.

SOME DESIGNS GROW OUT OF THE NEEDS AND PURPOSES OF LEARNERS

In each of the preceding types of curriculum design, scope and sequence are outlined grade by grade, although more flexibility is allowed when areas of study cut across subjects. Whenever there is a specific grade-by-grade recommendation of areas or problems to be covered or focal points to be stressed, at least three questions can be raised. Will not the choice of subject matter according to any preconceived plan, no matter what that plan may be, tend to result in certain experiences that have relatively little meaning to the learner? Will not such a design, no matter how flexible, make it necessary to set aside or to treat lightly problems of vital concern to the group and of high educative potential in favor of areas designated in the course of study? How will it be possible to meet the needs of individuals, or of groups, whose abilities and experience backgrounds differ markedly from those of the "typical" child?

Educators concerned with these questions—with helping children and youth learn to draw upon all needed subject-matter areas to solve their problems of daily living, while still capitalizing on pupil purposes, backgrounds, and capacities—advocate a curriculum design that frees each teacher to develop experiences in terms of the purposes and needs of his particular class. Examples of this curriculum design, the details of which emerge as teacher and pupils work together, can be located more readily in the literature than they can in practice. Suggestions for scope vary from statements that leave this entirely to the teacher's judgment to rather careful analyses of the needs of children and youth, and of problems with which they are likely to have to deal in our modern world, to be used as vantage points from which each teacher can study his own class. Guides for the teacher range from those that are aids in studying children to rather detailed discussion of the maturation process with suggestions as to how learners of different maturity may face problems related to the same general area. The organization for a particular group depends on the ways in which problems become focal with them, and sequence is a matter of starting with learners where they are and taking them as far as the new problem or situation demands.

The major values seen in designs which free teachers to work with the purposes and needs of a specific group have already been suggested. Facts, generalizations, and skills are considered important, but the bases for their selection are the problems meaningful to children and youth because they are actually faced in daily life. Educators favoring a curriculum design preplanned around areas that cut across subject fields also value learnings selected and grouped around actual problems of living. However, those who would free the teacher to work with problems faced by his pupils believe that the intrinsic motivation provided by specific concerns of individuals and groups will, in the long run, result in a more effective selection of learnings than will any preplanned structure. This type of design is also one that provides the greatest opportunity to adjust to the special capacities, problems, and purposes of individuals. To these values must be added another—a major concern with equipping boys and girls with the problem-solving techniques needed to live effectively in a changing world. This implies a willingness to sacrifice, if necessary, the acquisition of some specific facts (which will perhaps need to be reinterpreted anyway in the light of research and new findings) in order to give the time needed to develop the ability to locate information, to think logically and critically, to use a scientific approach in problem solution.

A curriculum growing out of the needs and concerns of learners, by the very nature of the values it stresses, cannot give equal weight to other values. This is the design least likely to guarantee that extended acquaintance with subject matter as specific bodies of knowledge will be part of all learners' experiences. Many facts will undoubtedly be stressed and many generalizations developed, but which facts and generalizations will be determined by the way in which particular learners face the problems of their world. There will be many understandings and skills needed in common because children and youth are living in an interdependent world. However, this does not satisfy those who feel that there are specific elements in the cultural heritage with which every learner should have contact.

At the secondary school level many of the questions raised in connection with the preplanned organizations that cut across subject lines can be asked again. Will there be ways of securing the needed depth of knowledge, of interest in special subjects? How will the youth who has grown up under this type of design adjust to college?

There is also a very genuine concern on the part of some as to whether research in the areas of psychological and social foundations has yet provided the techniques needed by teachers to identify the purposes of children and youth. Certainly the experiences provided under this design must be more extensive and insightful than the concerns expressed by learners, or the problems that arise fortuitously. Do educators know enough about the problems learners face to guarantee wise selections?

There are related questions of textbooks and other teaching aids. This is probably the proposal that requires the classroom with the richest equipment. It also demands the most varied equipment, as there is no way of assigning certain texts to certain grades. Many teachers feel at a loss when they consider the possibility of having to provide the wealth of resources to satisfy the varied needs and interests of children and youth in a class where scope and sequence are so flexible.

This curriculum design is one that demands a very high quality of teacher preparation. It calls for expert understanding of learners and for breadth of knowledge, as well as for ability to help children and youth focus facts from many sources on a single problem. Since this broad and deep orientation to problems of human living is not typical of the majority of college courses today, teachers may not have the necessary preparation. Under inexpert guidance, or in the classroom of a teacher who develops certain stereotyped units into which he leads his group year after year, the learnings could be meager and inconsequential.

Even in the hands of an expert teacher, will there be the understanding and insight to guarantee the breadth of experiences learners need? Will there not be gaps, superficial learnings, overstress in terms of the teacher's particular judgment as to what is important? Is it possible to provide a guide against which the teacher can check his judgment without imposing a pattern that will make it difficult to capitalize upon the purposes, needs, and problems of the particular group? These types of questions are raised even by those desiring to take maximum advantage of the sources of intrinsic motivation from learners' concerns.

Common Goals and Points of Difference

In the preceding sections differing emphases in values have been examined. Discussions of various proposals for curriculum design sometimes give the impression that many dichotomies exist, that stress on one point completely prevents attention to another. The terminology used in professional writing often serves to heighten this impression. We read of the subject-centered curriculum or the experience curriculum; of teaching subjects or teaching children; of learnings that are useful or learnings that are cultural.

Actually, such dichotomies do not exist. Educative experiences cannot be provided without drawing information from subject areas. A subject cannot be well taught if one ignores the learner, nor can one teach a child well without teaching him something—knowledge, generalizations, skills. It is impossible to teach useful information that is not part of the cultural heritage, or to explore the cultural heritage without teaching facts that are useful. The differences are those of focus and of emphasis.

THERE ARE MANY AREAS OF COMMON CONCERN

While differences in emphasis make for varied proposals of scope, sequence, and organization, there are a number of common concerns. In appraising today's programs for children and youth, it is important to recognize these common elements.

FIRST: All proposals for curriculum designs recognize and strive to develop basic democratic values. There are differences in whether democracy is seen as a way of life rather than as a type of political organization which legally guarantees certain rights and privileges to each individual. As a consequence there are some differences in beliefs as to exactly what kinds of experiences have greatest worth in developing these democratic values. But many areas of agreement exist—the need to help citizens understand and act upon their rights, privileges, and obligations; the importance of being able to bring to bear on current problems pertinent facts regarding the history of the development of democratic institutions; the development of basic respect for others; and a willingness to engage in the cooperative solution of problems.

SECOND: All proposals are seeking ways to help the learner to become effective in his daily life. While the meaning of effectiveness differs, there is essentially no conflict between teaching what is useful and developing a sense of the cultural heritage. The aim of the study of history or physics is to provide the learner with understandings he can use just as truly as is a study of a city's recreational facilities. However, as indicated in the preceding discussion, there is a marked difference of opinion as to what basis for selecting knowledge, generalizations, and skills will make for the most effective transfer to daily life—as to what way of organizing knowledge is likely to be the most useful to the learner as he faces his problems of daily living.

THIRD: All proposals would develop to a high level of competence the skills needed for effective membership in a democratic society. There is common concern that the learner be able to read, to express himself effectively and accurately in speech and writing, to calculate, to solve problems. At times, discussions of the curriculum designs that are not subject organizations give the impression that the traditional tool subjects have also been lost. This is not the case. Actually, it might be argued that the designs calling for the highest level of skill are those that take the learner away from his textbook into a series of reference activities. It is important, also, to realize that modern methods of teaching the so-called fundamental skills do not vary greatly from one design to another. In areas such as arithmetic and spelling, there is a tendency on the part of those favoring a specific delimitation of sequence to outline goals grade by grade. There is, however, increasing recognition of the need to start where the learner is, to make his learning meaningful by using his real-life problems, to challenge him with new activities he is capable of taking on whether or not they are designated for his grade level.

There is somewhat more concern about problem-solving and human relations skills under curriculum designs where democracy is seen as a way of life. The teacher of history or of a science is concerned with helping the learner to sense the rigors of historical research or to approach problems scientifically. However, with his prescribed field to cover, he may not always devote, with as clear a conscience, a period or more to solve a personal relations problem in the classroom or to discuss student council responsibilities.

FOURTH: All proposals are equally concerned with a high level of scholarship, with accurate use of facts, with rich and deep exploration into the wealth of knowledge that today's world provides. To the person who uses "knowledge" and "subjects" synonymously, it sometimes seems that much of the cultural heritage is being neglected if areas such as transportation, communication, conservation, are the basic organizing centers in the curriculum design. It can be argued that the most challenging teacher working with a class on some aspect of history will not be able to stimulate his learners to explore any more widely and deeply than an equally able teacher helping a group understand the controversy about the new community swimming pool. The difference is in the organization and purpose of the exploration, not in the quality of the scholarship developed.

FIFTH: All proposals for curriculum designs recognize the value of helping learners not only to see interrelationships among fields of knowledge but also to understand how to bring many fields to bear on a problem. The difference lies in whether these are primary or secondary aims. The teacher working under a subject-organized design tends to make interrelationships secondary to relationships within the subject itself. Under organizations around problems that cut across subject fields interrelationships among subjects are primary.

SIXTH: All proposals are concerned with making the most effective use of available research regarding the learner and the learning process to achieve their varied goals. All designs, for example, are concerned with adjusting to the learner's general maturity. Kindergarten and first-grade activities, particularly, look remarkably alike under the various designs that have been discussed. Individual differences are given attention under all designs, although the flexibility possible within a particular one sometimes forces choices as to whether to adjust a program to the child or to fit the child into the program either by acceleration or retardation. All recognize that the learner's purpose determines what he learns. Whether the technique is to help learners see values in the recommended learnings or to help them clarify their own purposes, skillful teachers under all designs work toward intrinsic motivation. Whether such motivation can be readily achieved when sequence, scope, and organization are prescribed, and what the effect will be on the value of the learnings are the points at issue. All proposals recognize that the learner must be active, that generalizations come from experience, that the memorizing of facts does not necessarily result in the ability to use them. The most effective teaching, then, under all designs, involves pupil–teacher planning and active problem-solving. All recognize that the learner grows as a whole. Under the most effective teaching, regardless of the design, there is concern for mental hygiene, attention to health factors, concern with the development of values.

Some designs, however, by their very nature make it more difficult to implement certain of these psychological principles. In this sense some can be said to be more subject-centered—concerned with assuring systematic acquaintance with subjects, even though this poses difficulties in making the most effective adjustment to the nature of learners. Some can be said to be more child-centered—concerned with using what is known about the learner, even though this poses certain difficulties in providing systematic contacts with subjects.

THERE ARE POINTS OF FUNDAMENTAL DIFFERENCE

If there are so many values held in common, what are the differences which curriculum committees should consider in making decisions regarding the design for their school system? Why, in particular, is there so much interest in proposing plans that depart from traditional subject organizations? Why not stay with the familiar patterns with which teachers feel secure, perhaps being somewhat eclectic when isolated suggestions from other types of design seem to offer better motivation or better adjustment to individual differences? Will not good teaching, after all, achieve many of the same goals regardless of the design?

Whether or not a skillful teacher, equipped with a rich cultural background and a sensitivity to its bearing on modern problems, is the complete answer to effective learning is a challenging question, which extensive research might answer. Without evidence to the contrary, it would seem that the most effective teacher will be even more effective if the curriculum design facilitates his efforts. The minutes in the school day are limited; time spent on one concept cannot be spent on another.

Those who support prestructured designs, whatever the basis for that structure may be, essentially are asking for two safeguards in the selection of the knowledge, generalizations, and skills to be taught. They want assurance that competent adults have surveyed the potential learnings and selected those of most worth. They also want to be sure that those learnings considered to be of most worth will actually be taught. This, they believe, is achieved by designating a definite scope and sequence.

Those who would not prestructure the curriculum have a basically different viewpoint regarding how to identify learnings of most worth to children and youth. This is not a position that merely acquiesces to the urgencies of immaturity or to the demands of the immediate world. Underlying the decision that the best starting point is the concerns and needs of learners, expressed or unexpressed, are certain basic assumptions regarding the quality of the resulting learnings.

FIRST: No predetermined selection of facts is believed to be intrinsically better than some other possible choice. Facts will be taught, and there is a conviction that by the very nature of our highly interdependent culture many will be common to the experiences of most learners. However, there is a firm belief that, for any one individual or for a particular group, the most effective basis for selecting what is to be taught is found in the problems actually faced in daily living. There is also a firm conviction that experiences so chosen will acquaint children and youth with broad cultural resources and help them become skilled in using these in meeting life situations.

SECOND: There is a firm belief that no one organization of facts is intrinsically better than any other organization. There is a conviction, for example, that insights into history can be developed without a strict chronological sequence; that aspects of the sciences can be the subject of intensive study without following the sequence in a typical textbook. The critical factor is that the organization be meaningful for the learner and one that he can use.

THIRD: There is the conviction that concepts and generalizations are the crucial learnings if the goal is to develop the learner's ability to act effectively in his world. With this is a belief that these concepts can come in many ways—that learners in California and learners in Norway can be helped to develop many of the same concepts regarding the contributions of agriculture to the economy by studying problems peculiar to their own localities.

FOURTH: There is a conviction that in this changing world it is important to educate for change. This carries with it a willingness, if necessary, to treat some of the past in less detail to make room for a look at the present. There is also a belief that it is important to devote some of the learner's time to the techniques of problem-solving, through experiences in group and individual problem-solving and through opportunities to study how issues are resolved.

The Proposal of the Writers of This Volume

The writers of this volume support substantially the position that the needs and purposes of learners must be central in designing a curriculum, and the choice and organization of learning experiences should grow out of situations of home, school, and community life as they are faced by the particular pupils. In general, we hold the basic assumptions just outlined regarding the quality of the learnings that will result when the starting point is the learner and his needs. However, we recognize some critical problems when no safeguards balance the needs of society against the needs of children and youth. In proposing a curriculum design we see the need for examining the following as fundamental questions for which safeguards must be provided.

1. How can balanced development be assured? What guarantees can there be that important areas of life in which students or teacher are insensitive to problems will not be neglected?

2. How can there be continuous growth from year to year without undesirable repetition or undesirable gaps in learning?

3. How can desirable depth of knowledge be assured? How is it possible to prevent learners from ending up with a smattering of superficial knowledge about many areas and little of the depth they need for genuine understanding?

4. How will the depth of command of special subject areas important to individual learners be assured? Where will the persons with specialized talents come from—the scientists, historians, linguists, artists, teachers, statesmen, philosophers of the future?

5. How can it be guaranteed that children and youth will become acquainted with the broad cultural resources which are a part of our heritage and become skilled in drawing upon and using these resources in meeting life situations?

6. How can there be guarantees that choices of problems are not trivial and do not represent transitory interests rather than basic concerns?

7. How can there be genuine group problems? Will there not actually be many times when extrinsic motivation will be needed if group study is desired? Does the point of view not logically lead to work that is completely individualized?

Working with learners in terms of their concerns demands depth of understanding—of how to identify learners' real needs, of the world in which they live, of the ways in which they can best be helped to acquire new understandings and skills. The chapters that follow spell out a proposal for a curriculum design which attempts to provide some of the essential safeguards that will free teachers to develop experiences in terms of the situations most meaningful to their groups.

Related Readings

ALBERTY, HAROLD B. *Reorganizing the High School Curriculum.* Revised edition. New York: The Macmillan Company, 1953.

CASWELL, HOLLIS L., AND ARTHUR W. FOSHAY. *Education in the Elementary School.* Third edition. New York: American Book Company, 1957.

FAUNCE, ROLAND, AND NELSON BOSSING. *Developing the Core Curriculum.* Englewood Cliffs, N.J.: Prentice-Hall, Inc., 1951.

FEATHERSTONE, WILLIAM B. *A Functional Curriculum for Youth.* New York: American Book Company, 1950.

GWYNN, J. MINOR. *Curriculum Principles and Social Trends.* Revised edition. New York: The Macmillan Company, 1950.

HOPKINS, L. THOMAS. *Interaction: The Democratic Process.* Boston: D. C. Heath & Company, 1941.

LEONARD, J. P. *Developing the Secondary School Curriculum.* Revised edition. New York: Rinehart & Company, Inc., 1953.

NATIONAL SOCIETY FOR THE STUDY OF EDUCATION. *Adapting the Secondary School Program to the Needs of Youth.* Fifty-second Yearbook, Part 1. Chicago: University of Chicago Press, 1953.

SAYLOR, J. GALEN, AND WILLIAM M. ALEXANDER. *Curriculum Planning for Better Teaching and Learning.* New York: Rinehart & Company, Inc., 1954.

SHANE, HAROLD G., editor. *The American Elementary School.* Thirteenth Yearbook, John Dewey Society. New York: Harper & Brothers, 1953.

SMITH, B. OTHANEL, WILLIAM O. STANLEY, AND J. HARLAN SHORES. *Fundamentals of Curriculum Development.* Revised edition. Yonkers-on-Hudson, N.Y.: World Book Company, 1957.

5

A PROPOSAL FOR DESIGNING A CURRICULUM FOR LIVING IN OUR TIMES

The values anticipated when teacher and pupils are free to develop the curriculum will only be achieved with careful planning. The design cannot be written down as a series of problems to be studied grade by grade. Nevertheless, there must be a design, and the teacher must be able to work with as real a sense of this plan as does one for whom the curriculum essentials are spelled out in a course of study. Such a plan is needed so that the precious time of the children and youth in our schools will be expended on important learnings. It is essential if the needs of individuals with special talents or limitations are to be met.

As indicated in Chapter 4, every curriculum design poses certain kinds of problems in achieving the basic values or goals sought by those who propose it. The problems listed at the end of the chapter are the major ones to which answers must be given by those who would give each teacher maximum freedom to work with his learners in terms of the immediate situations they face. This chapter describes the general nature of the curriculum design proposed in this volume and indicates the answers it provides to these problems. Subsequent chapters spell out in detail the implications of this proposal for classroom practice.

A Proposal for a Curriculum for Learners in Our Times

Chapters 2 and 3 pointed to the need to consider the nature of society and of the learner as critical factors in curriculum development. On one hand, there must be recognition of what has meaning for the learner, and on the other, there must be concern for society's basic values. Further, the work of the school must be seen in relation to the experiences of the learner in his home and in his community.

THE EVERYDAY CONCERNS OF THE LEARNER ARE THE STARTING POINT

Children and youth develop at different rates, have widely differing backgrounds, and come to school with varying interests. Their concerns are many—how to make a model airplane fly, what to feed a pet turtle, whom to elect as captain of the baseball team, why paints dry out, how to interpret the headlines in the daily paper, how to get a bicycle license, what it means to fly faster than sound, whether to complete a committee assignment or go out with the "gang," how to build a "ham" radio station, which college to attend, what part to take in a community clean-up campaign.

In some cases the problems and interests are those of individuals; in others they are group concerns. In some situations the learners have clearly formulated purposes; in others they are inarticulate. In some cases learners may be unaware of situations in the immediate community or the larger national or world setting that could have much meaning if only their attention were drawn to them. They may not sense sources of aesthetic expression in which they could find lasting satisfactions if they were given opportunity to explore. They may not respond to wonders in the natural or technological world in which deep and abiding interests might develop if these worlds were opened to them.

These everyday concerns of learners are the sources of situations which have meaning for them in the light of their maturity and experience and which provide strong motivation for learning. Expressed or unexpressed, these immediate problems, concerns, and interests need to be the starting points around which classroom experiences are developed. This is a concept of the curriculum which . . .

> recognizes the worth of each individual and allows for his uniqueness—in needs, concerns, talents, interests

helps the learner face the world at his level of understanding

recognizes the nature of his growth and utilizes the meanings experiences have for him

values the learner's daily living at any stage of his development as important to the society of which he is a member

relates his in-school and out-of-school experiences

A curriculum which has maximum meaning for learners develops as learners and their teacher work together on the problems and interests of everyday living.

EVERYDAY CONCERNS ARE RELATED TO PERSISTENT LIFE SITUATIONS

If the starting points are to be the learners' everyday concerns, within what framework can the teacher view these concerns so that the resulting experiences will have maximum educative value for individuals and for the class as a whole? The foundation of the proposed design is a blend of the genuine concerns of learners with society's needs and values. Learning to meet problems at their level of maturity, growing more able to face and handle the problems of tomorrow—this goal can be achieved when the situations of everyday living are seen in the light of **persistent life situations,** those situations that recur in the life of the individual in many different ways as he grows from infancy to maturity.

Every individual is concerned to some degree with such fundamentals as keeping well, understanding himself, making a living, getting along with others, adjusting to the natural environment, dealing with social and political structures and forces, developing a sustaining philosophy or set of values. These and other concerns tend to persist throughout life, although the circumstances through which they are met vary with the individual's background and maturity. The little child faces persistent life situations in the area of HEALTH,[1] primarily in adjusting to family and school health patterns, and develops simple understandings which serve as a basis for his actions. The adolescent assumes a much larger responsibility for his own health. His concerns and activities include such prob-

[1] Throughout this and Chapter 6, the major areas in which the persistent life situations have been grouped in the analysis made by the authors appear in CAPITALS. Major categories within these areas appear in CAPITALS AND SMALL CAPITALS. Persistent situations, whether large problems or the subproblems into which some of these have been divided, appear in SMALL CAPITALS. The complete list is given in Chapter 6 on pp. 155–165. The ways in which these life situations might be faced by children and youth are contained in the charts on pp. 169–321. For clarity, the wording of the charts is used in this chapter.

lems as those of his weight and skin condition which are important to attractive appearance, of the routines required for membership on the athletic team, of whether or not to begin to smoke. He needs more knowledge as well as more fully developed concepts of the relationship of good health to effective living. The adult takes on a wide variety of family responsibilities and, at times, his health activities may relate to the national and world scene.

Such illustrations can be multiplied for every aspect of life. Establishing effective PERSON–TO–PERSON RELATIONSHIPS is an area involving many persistent life situations. They are met in coping with a schoolmate's teasing; in inviting a friend to the high school dance; in acting on committees; in working in the councils of nations. The area of NATURAL PHENOMENA as it relates to DEALING WITH TOPOGRAPHIC FEATURES is explored by the young child as he identifies points to which his family goes for picnics or vacations. The slightly older child plans the route for a scout hike, examines pictures of mountains, oceans, or other features unfamiliar in his locale, or traces the travels of a brother with the armed forces. The adolescent seeks to understand international disputes or joins in discussions about soil erosion or the location of a new highway affecting his community. The adult votes on the site for a new school, reacts to plans for new power projects, expresses his opinion on an international issue regarding boundaries or territorial rights.

Persistent life situations, as learners face them, become the fabric from which the curriculum develops. First-grade Billy learning that plants will die without water; tenth-grade Jane sharing her talent with the committee building stage sets; Dorothy in grade four discovering that she cannot serve as treasurer unless she is a better mathematician; Jim and a committee of eighth-graders talking with officials about a school bank; Grace in the tenth grade struggling with the conflict between the values held by her family and those governing the activities of her crowd—these are situations central in living in our society as they are reflected in the activities of learners.

In the range of the persistent life situations with which all learners must deal, the teacher finds his guides for balanced development. In the ways in which they recur from childhood through adulthood he finds his cues for deciding how to help his group explore their concerns and assures continuous growth. This is a concept of the curriculum in which . . .

the basic problems and situations which are central in life itself are central in education

the **content** and **organization** of learning experiences are determined by the experiences of learners as they deal with their everyday concerns and the persistent life situations which are a part of them (these situations of everyday living take the place of "subjects" and the varied other ways of focusing the curriculum)

the **scope** lies in the range of persistent life situations with which, to some extent, every individual deals

the **sequence** and **continuity** are determined by the changing aspects of persistent life situations as the learner moves from childhood into the full responsibilities of adulthood

school and community experiences are related because the same persistent life situations are faced in the home, at school, in the neighborhood, at church, and everywhere the learner works and plays

the nature of the learner's daily living at any stage of his development is recognized as important to the society of which he is a member

A curriculum in which the learner and society are brought into relationship is one in which the daily life concerns of children and youth are seen as aspects of persistent life situations with which all members of society must be able to deal.

THE PROPOSED CURRICULUM REPRESENTS A PROCESS OF DESIGNING, NEVER A FIXED DESIGN

Since it grows out of the experiences of learners, the curriculum will always be developing and flexible. Persistent life situations recur in many combinations in the learner's daily living. Exact predictions as to how or when a given group of learners will face a particular problem or as to which persistent life situations may be interwoven in an immediate concern, are not possible. To differences occasioned by variations in individual maturation rates must be added those resulting from the experiences learners have had and from the homes and communities in which they are growing up. The choice, organization, and guidance of the experiences for any group, therefore, will grow out of the situations of home, school, and community the particular group faces.

The situations selected for study within any one year will vary both for groups and for individuals within groups. The learners' own needs and interests, coupled with local, national, or world events with which they are capable of dealing at their maturity levels, will provide more situations of potentially high educative value than can be encompassed in the course of one year. The teacher's function is to help identify those which are of greatest importance to the group and to its individual members. He also guides decisions as to whether to explore situations fully or briefly, whether to focus the attention of the entire class on the situation, or to refer it to individuals or to smaller groups.

One basis of choice will be the degree of concern to learners.[2] For example, the consideration of vocational problems may be an important part of the curriculum of the upper grades in those schools where many pupils go to work at the close of the ninth grade. If, however, most youth in a school are college bound, vocational problems may not be real concerns of learners until late high school or even college years. New insight into persistent life situations is developed at the time when daily life experiences demand increased competence and understanding.

When two problems are of equal concern to a group, the choice may be made on the basis of which has a greater potential contribution to make to balanced development. A fifth-grade group interested in their community's plans to exterminate flies and mosquitoes were also concerned with the appearance of their classroom. About the same time, other classes told them that they were too noisy as they went through the halls. This class had already carefully studied many aspects of the problem of fly control in relation to screening the school lunchroom; hence the first concern was dealt with very quickly. Up to this time they had had little opportunity to do anything about their immediate surroundings and in the ensuing weeks they spent considerable time carrying out plans for redecorating their room. Although they were not especially concerned about quiet in the halls, this was a problem well within their maturity and of which they needed to be aware if they were to be responsible members of the school community. This problem also became part of their curriculum although it did not call for extended study. After a discussion to clarify reasons, coping with the problem of noise became a matter of daily practice. Decisions regarding how to help learners with their concerns are made in the light of growth needed to deal with the range of persistent life situations.

Since the group's activities grow out of the situations they face, the manner in which persistent situations are dealt with in one group may be very different from the experiences in another group. The activities and experiences of a class whose concern about SAFEGUARDING RIGHTS AND RESPONSIBILITIES OF RACIAL, RELIGIOUS, AND NATIONAL GROUPS has arisen through contacts with members of another race will be different from those of a class disturbed about instances of religious intolerance. With children in a metropolitan area the problems of living with members of a minority group may arise early and keep arising at frequent intervals.

[2] For a more complete set of guides for selecting curriculum experiences, see Chapter 7, page 344.

In a farm community learners may have no firsthand contact with minority-group situations until they enter a large high school, but may meet situations vicariously through family discussions, radio and television, newspapers, and books about persons with other backgrounds, customs, and beliefs. Further, the child who is a member of a minority faces the experiences in a different way from those who belong to the majority. While many of the same values and basic understandings may result in each case, the actual experiences are determined by the situation faced by the particular class. Part of the teacher's role is to identify the experiences through which values and understandings can be most clearly and meaningfully developed for given learners.

The entire class will not necessarily work together on all problems. In the situation described earlier where some ninth-graders are seriously considering vocations, those whose plans include higher education may not participate, or may spend the same amount of time considering the educational experiences most suitable for them in terms of the colleges they plan to attend. At another point during the year, when everyone in the class is concerned with situations within the general area of AESTHETIC EXPRESSION AND APPRECIATION, the creative activity undertaken may be almost entirely individual. At other times, individual interests may be made subsidiary to those of the group. The entire class, for example, might investigate the nature of propaganda in order to solve a problem arising from a discussion about the reliability of news articles.

How intensively each of the several persistent life situations that are part of an immediate concern are to be studied will vary with individuals and groups. The abilities and maturity of the learners condition the meaning situations can have, both for individuals and for the group, and suggest experiences on which they are able and ready to work intensively and those with which they can do little at the given time. For example, a first grade and a sixth may both be intrigued by the new power plant being built on the nearby river. While some attention would be given to this interest in both groups, not much more would be done with first-graders than acquaint them with a source of energy. Sixth-graders, however, might be helped to gain more understanding of the problems of USING SOURCES OF ENERGY to supplement human power and, in addition, might explore aspects of the persistent life situation of CONSERVING AND USING NATURAL RESOURCES. Depending on their maturity and experiential background, the group might also gain some understanding of what is involved in USING TECHNOLOGICAL RESOURCES FOR MAXIMUM SOCIAL GOOD.

Since persistent life situations recur in many ways, and more than one may be a part of the immediate concern, a group may face in a new experience problems for which they have considerable background. This influences the amount of exploration desirable and needed. A class which has previously had little reason to keep accounts might spend several weeks on such persistent life situations as MAKING EXACT COMPUTATIONS and MANAGING MONEY as they learn the techniques and skills needed for the school store. On the other hand, children who have managed the store might shift to work in the school bank without spending much extra time on these persistent life situations as they deal with the accounting aspect of their new responsibilities. However, as they acquire banking experience, the latter group might work on persistent life situations in the general area of ECONOMIC–SOCIAL–POLITICAL STRUCTURES AND FORCES as they consider the functions of banks in our economy, the nature and types of investments, and basic practices in the exchange of money. The potential educative values of all the persistent life situations in a particular immediate situation should be appraised by the teacher. All, however, will not require extended study. Some may not even be considered because they have little meaning for the learners at their stage of development.

When the curriculum deals with situations of everyday living, it includes problems and concerns to which home and community are also contributing. One class, for example, may profitably spend considerable time on problems related to nutrition which arise from the lack of school lunchroom facilities. Another group may gain the same understandings in a much shorter period because of experiences they have had in homes where these problems are considered as they arise. More typical still, the range of pupil backgrounds will create a need for school help on nutritional problems that is much greater with some children than with others. The school should be responsive to the total growth needs of learners and should vary its contributions in the light of those of other agencies.

Underlying the preceding discussion is the implication that learners will share in the selection and development of the experiences which make up their curriculum. Learners are the source of the experience; the actual situations they face and the varied backgrounds they bring indicate the general nature of the exploration that seems to be most appropriate. The specific experiences through which situations are studied are determined as teacher and learners together investigate the immediate problem. This is a concept of the curriculum which . . .

recognizes that the same concepts and understandings can be developed through many different immediate situations and experiences

recognizes that concepts, skills, and understandings are more likely to be maintained at high competence when they are developed in situations which the learner can identify as being related to those faced in daily life

recognizes the importance of adjusting to individual differences in capacities and in experience background if maximum growth is to be achieved

A curriculum that develops maximum effectiveness in meeting the problems of modern living makes use of the immediate situations learners face as a basis for developing competencies and understandings for future action.

The Persistent Life Situations Concept and the Essentials of Curriculum Development

The sense of curriculum design in which each teacher develops experiences with learners comes from the scope of persistent life situations, the ways in which they recur in the lives of individuals of varied maturities and backgrounds, and the resulting concepts, informations, and skills needed for competent living. What answers does this proposal suggest to the problems raised in Chapter 4? Will it guarantee that balanced growth will result? Can it assure that there will be continuous growth from year to year without undesirable repetition or major gaps? If there is no definite allotment of topics or bodies of subject matter to specific grades, how can depth of learning be assured? How can teachers be helped to appraise the immediate concerns of learners—will there not be unwise choices, groups going off on tangents, valuable time expended on something that turns out to be trivial and transitory? Will all citizens have the familiarity with the cultural heritage that is their right—will needed acquaintance with organized bodies of subject matter be developed? What about classroom organization—will there be a place for group problems and for individual concerns? Will there be opportunity for specialized as well as for general education—what of the youth whose education terminates in the high school, of the one who is headed for college?

THE SCOPE OF PERSISTENT LIFE SITUATIONS PROVIDES THE GUIDE TO BALANCED DEVELOPMENT

Even with a curriculum design where scope and sequence are delineated specifically from grade to grade and where time allotments are recommended, the teacher must guard against giving undue weight to an aspect of the program which his own talents, preparation, or interests have led him to consider very important. He must be equally careful that he does not neglect aspects in which he himself has little ability, is not interested, or which he may consider inconsequential. These dangers are multiplied many times over when the experiences of a group of learners develop around the situations of concern to them. Here the teacher plays a major part in determining what will be the focus of the year's work, what situations to expand and what to deal with briefly in the course of daily classroom living, what new experiences to provide.

The safeguard against omitting or slighting important aspects of growth lies in the range and variety of persistent life situations with which all persons inevitably deal. When the members of a school faculty have worked together to prepare an analysis of the persistent problems of living, such as that presented in the next chapter, each teacher has an objective basis against which to study the growth of his group. This does not mean that every persistent life situation identified in this analysis as important need have a place in the daily work of each group. The teacher would use such an analysis as a check, not a prescription. Do the immediate situations these children and youth face reflect persistent life situations with which they need experience? Does the analysis reveal areas in which society is facing new needs of which learners should become aware? Are there areas in which home, school, and community are all failing to provide help—areas for which the school should take more responsibility? Such an analysis can also help the teacher identify areas in which his own competence is limited and those which he is likely to slight. This conscientious effort to understand the breadth of the life situations in which children and youth must eventually become competent is one basic guarantee that provision will be made for balanced development.

The fact that persistent life situations may be met through very different experiences is another safeguard in providing for balanced development in a curriculum designed to deal with situations when and as learners face them. The same concepts can be arrived at through many avenues of exploration as the following illustrations point out.

USING TOOLS, MACHINES, AND EQUIPMENT is a persistent life situation met under varied conditions in different communities . . .

In a **tenement home** where cooking is done on a small plate, where illumination comes from one central outlet, where there is no mechanical refrigeration, children and youth may "use tools, machines, and equipment" in regulating the gas burner while preparing a meal, and in building a window box for keeping food cool. These children may use simple tools in mending or building furniture, rigging a pulley clothesline, repairing toys, or carving wooden figures as a hobby.

In a **suburban home,** equipped with central heating, home freezer, numerous electrical outlets, vacuum cleaner and washing machine, and having lawn and garden plots, children and youth may use different tools and equipment as they read the heating thermostat, care for the bicycles which take them to and from school, manage a part of the family garden, mow the lawn, or rake leaves. But they use some of the same tools as children of the tenement area as they put up screens, repair toys, build birdhouses, or carve wooden figures as a hobby.

CONSERVING AND USING NATURAL RESOURCES is another persistent life situation that learners meet in a variety of ways . . .

In a **rural community** problems may relate to soil erosion, crop rotation, protection of wild flowers. Needs to conserve animal life may become apparent through fishing regulations and hunting seasons. There may be questions of whether to destroy or to protect birds of prey.

In an **urban community** problems regarding soil conservation may relate to fertilizing gardens or to the work of gardeners in city parks. The animal life to be protected will consist largely of songbirds. There may be requests to conserve water. Picnics, motor trips, and hikes along nature trails in local parks may result in experiences relating to prevention of forest fires, protection of wild flowers, purposes of local, state, and national parks.

In both examples the two groups have different orientations and will learn through different experiences. Yet many similar understandings and skills will result. Because of differences in family and community backgrounds, in ability, interests, and associations, learners of essentially the same maturity may grow in ability to cope with the same persistent life situations through widely varied everyday experiences. Balanced growth does not mean identical learning experiences.

Balanced development grows out of the teacher's best insight into the real problems with which the learner is trying to deal, not simply his "expressed" needs and interests. What of the shy child whose need is to learn to work as a cooperative group member, but who repeatedly slips into a corner to read? What of the youth who accepts without question community or parental attitudes on social issues? The city child may face problems of restricted play space without realizing that steps can be taken to remedy the situation. The learner seriously handicapped through lack of reading skill does not necessarily see his need. These problems are just as important for total development as those about which learners may be articulate.

Similarly, providing balanced development requires consideration of ways to acquaint children with new experiences which will enrich the total pattern of their living. It is not sufficient to deal only with that which is "immediate," "crucial," or "focal" with the individual or group.

An important function of the teacher is to guide learners in going beyond the immediate situation—helping them to become aware of related situations with which they are ready to deal, to see further meaningful implications of the immediate situation, and to grow in ability to deal with the persistent life situations in ways that provide for meeting the new and changing as well as the present.

Both vicarious and firsthand experiences are needed to provide balanced development. The radio, the newspaper, the rapid increase of informational materials in many areas, have opened for children and youth a world far wider than that which firsthand experience allows. Situations vividly described in print, materials made real through dramatization and the use of audio-visual aids, can as truly concern learners as those which occur in the immediate environment. This does not, of course, justify adult-imposed experiences or bodies of information. Rather, it suggests that the boundaries of the learner's exploration into vicarious living be set by the meanings those situations can have for him. The proposed curriculum design would not limit the learner's experiences to the near-at-hand and to the here-and-now. There will be as much breadth and depth of experience as the learner can accept as worthwhile, are within his maturation level, and promise vital learnings for him. For the intellectually able learner, this may mean extensive opportunities to explore many areas; for the pupil with more limited ability, a firm grasp on essentials of daily living.

To help each learner grow maximally, balanced development must also be viewed in the light of out-of-school experiences. Persistent life situations are faced at home, at school, in the neighborhood, at church, at the movies, at camp, and in the host of other places where children and youth work and play.

USING SAFETY MEASURES is a persistent life situation that occurs . . .

In the **home,** when deciding where to keep playthings and tools, when using tools and machines, when using matches or caring for fires, when repairing household appliances, when deciding where to play, when deciding where to keep medicines.

In the **school,** when using tools and equipment, when deciding where to keep tools and how to use them, when participating in fire drills, when working with traffic patrol, when participating in active sports.

In the **community,** when riding a bicycle or driving a car, when crossing streets, when swimming, when picnicking in woods, when taking action on legislation regarding safety measures.

DEALING WITH SUCCESS AND FAILURE is a persistent life situation that occurs . . .

In the **home,** when a favorite toy breaks or a pet dies, when parental restrictions upset plans, when brothers or sisters tease, when parents praise a job well done, when report cards come home, when constructing a playhouse or taking on a paper route.

In the **school,** when representing a class in making an announcement in assembly, when making a report, responding to a question, taking an examination, when participating in a class play, playing on the basketball team, acting as a member of the newspaper staff, serving on the student council, nutrition committee, or safety patrol.

In the **community,** when participating in such social gatherings as dances at the community center and birthday parties, when taking part in such recreational activities as playing ball, tennis, and card games, when participating in club activities through voluntary effort—serving as chairman, officer, or committee member.

The fact that persistent life situations are a part of all aspects of the learner's daily life suggests the need for coordination among the agencies guiding the learner. To assure balanced development the school must examine its work in relation to other educative groups. The school, as an institution delegated by society to help children and youth achieve maximum continuous development, has certain unique responsibilities for envisioning the total educational program needed in the given community and for providing resources in those aspects of growth not otherwise available. In developing the curriculum the teacher considers the learner's whole life and what other agencies are helping him to learn. This may mean undertaking responsibility for personal cleanliness in some schools, for meals in other schools, for clubs and recreational opportunities for families in still others, for none of these where home and community life provide adequately. Fundamentally, it means that the school will vary its own leadership functions to make the best use of community resources, recognizing that at some points the school will institute and carry full responsibility, at others it will be a coordinating agent, and at still others it will contribute only in an advisory capacity as study of the learner indicates the need for cooperative efforts.

THE RECURRING NATURE OF PERSISTENT LIFE SITUATIONS PROVIDES THE BASIS FOR CONTINUITY

Persistent life situations are continuing threads through life, appearing again and again in the everyday concerns of the individual. Continuity is achieved as the learner deals with new aspects of these situations at different stages of his development. As they move from childhood into the full responsibilities of adulthood, children and youth are helped to deal with varied aspects of the same situations over a number of years.

MANAGING MONEY, for example, is a recurring life situation . . .

> A **five- or six-year-old** manages money as he goes on an errand to a neighborhood store and decides how much of his allowance to spend on candy, put aside for Sunday school, or save in his bank.
>
> At **eight or ten** the child meets the same persistent life situation when he buys at the store, shares in decisions about spending family funds, puts money in the local or school bank, repays money borrowed from parents.
>
> At **fifteen** the young person also buys at the store. He decides where to buy so that he can get the best merchandise for his money, what the price differences are on similar materials, what labels on materials mean. His everyday concerns may include budgeting his allowance, deciding whether to ask for a larger allowance, seeking jobs to supplement his allowance so that he can satisfy his needs.
>
> The **adult** deals with problems of money management in making purchases and he meets many of the same everyday concerns faced by the adolescent. He deals with larger amounts of money and more complicated situations—deciding when to purchase commodities wholesale, getting information from various agencies for consumer protection, financing a home or a business, providing funds for the education of his children, providing security for later life.

Will there not be breaks in the continuity? Should there not be deliberate plans to prepare the learner for situations that he will have to face two or three years hence? The answer lies, in part, in the concept of persisting situations and in the fact that life itself has continuity. It is virtually impossible for a pupil to reach adolescence, for example, without having faced situations calling for responses to the opposite sex, without having had to deal with forces in his natural environment, without having made moral choices, without having contacts with social institutions. If the teacher has been sensitive to the problems children and youth have been facing, he recognizes that the pupil does not come to each new situation completely unprepared—except perhaps in the sense that the entire world faces a substantial readjustment when confronted with such a major development as the atomic age.

Is there not a danger that a class will engage in the same activities year after year? Duplication will not occur if each new activity begins with an appraisal of present knowledge and an identification of new problems and new needs. If this is done, repetition is not likely except in cases where present competencies are inadequate in dealing with situations studied previously. In these cases repetition of some activities may be needed to develop the desired level of competence. More often, both in the development of skills and of understandings, there would be study of an aspect of the same persistent life situation as it arises in a more complex form. It is through the identification in learners' everyday living of the new aspect of the problem or situation and the new interrelations with other situations not made previously, that continuity of learning is assured without undesirable repetition.

Continuity also lies in the extension and widening of concepts as new aspects of persistent life situations are dealt with. The child who learns to care for his wraps may be developing some understanding of the processes of conservation. Earning money for birthday gifts can build toward economic competence. Electing a student council representative is a forerunner to electing a president. Learning is guided to help children and youth use previously developed concepts in meeting new situations and to extend these concepts as needed in dealing with the new aspects of persistent problems. This is a continuing process of reflecting on experiences, identifying basic understandings and generalizations, and using these understandings in meeting new immediate situations in which the persistent problems recur.

THE INCREASING COMPLEXITY OF PERSISTENT LIFE SITUATIONS PROVIDES THE GUARANTEE OF DEPTH OF LEARNING

Because persistent life situations take on wider meaning as the individual matures and his interests and needs change, depth of learning, as well as continuity of development, is guaranteed. As the situation recurs in a new and more complex setting, it is the responsibility of the teacher to help pupils acquire new insights.

ACHIEVING STATUS IN GROUPS is a persistent life situation that all individuals face, but acceptance has different meanings at different ages . . .

For the **six-year-old,** being accepted in a group may mean getting others to play with him, knowing when and how to share his toys and other possessions, being allowed to use the toys of other children, being chosen by his group to do certain jobs. The six-year-old wants everyone to like him, but on his own terms.

The **ten-year-old** has some understanding of the feelings and wishes of others. He is willing that others be considered, provided his wishes are not neglected. He will accept his friend being made captain if he himself is chosen to be on the team. Special problems of acceptance arise in working on teams or committees with members of the opposite sex.

For a **fifteen-year-old** both social customs and taboos must be carefully observed to gain acceptance in a peer group. Acceptance for the adolescent also means maintaining the security of close family ties while achieving acceptance by the new groups that are part of his developing independence. Among the everyday situations that he faces as he seeks to establish himself in his group are deciding when to break with community customs, resolving conflicts between the values of family and of friends, and deciding how long to observe a code not accepted by others in the group.

An **adult** faces similar problems of acceptance. He must learn how to make a constructive contribution to a community group; how to develop satisfactory group membership in church, club, or business when there are differences in race, religious affiliation, socio-economic status; how to relate himself to his family group; how to help his children make a positive contribution to the family group.

The meaning of an aspect of the persistent life situation for the learner, at his level of maturity, sets the limits of depth of study at that time. The problem and the learner's maturity together dictate the knowledge and skills needed and provide the drive to work until the required competence is achieved. Those who accept this approach to curriculum development are committed to deal with each situation as precisely and thoroughly as the maturity of the pupils permits.

It is unnecessary to study all aspects of a problem when it is first considered. To do so might well mean dealing with concepts beyond both the concern and the ability of the learner. Because it is a persistent life situation, it will be met again. When it is, the learner's increased maturity will provide readiness for looking at it in new ways and with greater depth. The very fact that the situation will recur in more complex settings as the learner matures, together with the fact that the maturing individual will be able to see its new facets even in the same everyday experiences, provides a fundamental safeguard against a curriculum which leads to a smattering of knowledge or a meager understanding of many things.

THE RELATION BETWEEN THE IMMEDIATE CONCERN AND THE PERSISTENT LIFE SITUATION PROVIDES THE SAFEGUARD AGAINST TRIVIAL PROBLEMS AND UNWISE USE OF TIME

What safeguards does this concept of curriculum design provide against undue expenditure of time on experiences which make a limited contribution to learners' growth? This proposal does not advocate simply bringing into learners' lives that which they themselves mention. Neither does it mean that each casual show of intellectual curiosity must lead to an extended exploration. The teacher has an obligation to appraise the potential value of each new experience in terms of possible contribution to growth in dealing with persistent life situations. In addition the teacher must help learners become aware of needs and purposes about which they are not articulate.

When an immediate situation is examined in terms of its contribution to persistent life situations, an essential precaution has been taken against unwise use of time. For example, Bobby's preoccupation with making paper airplanes may indeed be trivial unless he is helped to experiment to find answers to such questions as: Does it fly better when the airplane is small or large? Does it fly better in different parts of the room, in the room or out of doors? Why does the cardboard cut-out airplane from the store stay in the air longer? In finding answers to questions such as these Bobby can be helped to deal with such persistent problems as ADJUSTING USE OF MATERIALS TO THEIR PROPERTIES and ADJUSTING TO ATMOSPHERIC CONDITIONS. He will again deal with aspects of the same problems when he chooses clothing suitable for various kinds of wear and service, decides whether certain materials will shrink, determines the kind of wood to use in making a toy boat, finds how to pour hot liquids into china or glass, or flies a kite. Bobby's paper airplanes, of course, would not become the center for weeks of class activity. Bobby alone might be involved, and new understandings could be developed through a few short discussions with his teacher, together with the time and encouragement to experiment.

Take another illustration—the interest of the tenth grade in plans for their first formal party or dance might be considered transitory and not worthy of much class time. This important event in the lives of teen-agers may be a significant learning experience as they are helped to cope with such persistent problems as DETERMINING THE ABILITIES NEEDED BY AND CHOOSING LEADERS when decisions are made regarding hosts and hostesses, extending invitations to selected patrons, and assigning special responsibilities to committees; USING APPROPRIATE AMENITIES as the group learns how to introduce parents, and boy and girl friends, and decides whether there should be a receiving line; MANAGING MONEY as class funds are considered in making choices regarding music, foods, decorations, and the like; PROVIDING ARTISTIC LIVING CONDITIONS as attention is given to room arrangement and decorations, and the use of music; RESPONDING TO AUTHORITY and MODIFYING PERSONAL DESIRES IN THE INTERESTS OF OTHERS as proposals are made regarding length of the occasion, the kind of beverage to be served, how best to integrate parental and community social customs and mores with the desires of the group.

In some cases, the nature of the growth desired will dictate repeated short contacts with some persistent life situations. An aspect of classroom living need not be considered trivial or inconsequential simply because it makes its contribution to learners' growth in a matter of minutes. For a group of slow learners, for example, very vital growth in ability to meet health needs could come from the routine activity of spending a few minutes daily washing after strenuous play. The fact that one or many persistent life situations are a part of every immediate situation means that no concern or interest need be trivial. Each situation included in the curriculum will be so guided that its contribution to growth in dealing with persistent life situations is realized.

PERSISTENT LIFE SITUATIONS PROVIDE THE GUIDE TO SELECTION OF LEARNINGS FROM THE VAST CULTURAL HERITAGE

In every curriculum design choices of subject matter must be made. Even in a high school history course on twentieth-century America, time will not permit all possible facts and relationships to be studied. In the very designation of what to include in the subject-focused curriculum designs, choices are made both among and within subjects. Some aspects of our cultural heritage are given heavy weight while others, of necessity, are either treated lightly or completely omitted.

In Chapter 4 it was pointed out that in each of the various types of curriculum designs pre-eminent attention is given to a particular set of values. Under the proposed curriculum design learners will not have the same kind of acquaintance with organized bodies of subject matter that would be provided in a curriculum where the organizing elements are subjects or groups of subjects. Rather, they will draw upon the cultural heritage as needed to develop the understandings, skills, attitudes, and appreciations required in dealing with persistent life situations. In appraising the actual grasp of subject matter that learners will have, it is important to keep in mind the values desired and the assumptions made regarding the learning process inherent in the proposed design. Seven basic beliefs are discussed in the following pages.

FIRST: There is an assumption that in meeting new situations individuals draw most heavily upon the generalizations and understandings which have emerged from previous experience. Sound generalizations are made as the learner sees the various elements in his experiences in relationship, as he combines facts and brings them to bear on the new situation. Understanding of the basic principles and processes in science, for example, does not come alone from the acquisition of a number of facts —no matter how closely related—but from a conscious generalizing and conceptualizing of the processes and meanings. Insights, generalizations, and meanings derived from relating facts, rather than the facts themselves, are the goals sought. Children and youth of any age can become interested in a wide range of facts if these are presented in a way that suggests something new or different. The small child and the adult tourist alike are interested in the unique and novel about the American Indian or a foreign people. When the concern or interest, however, is mainly to satisfy curiosity about the unusual, the generalizations which result are likely to be centered primarily on the new or different elements. To foster generalizing that will be of maximum value in meeting new aspects of persistent life situations, teachers need to ask what pupils see as their goal—to solve a problem or to meet a situation recognized as worth while, to collect some odd and interesting facts, to satisfy the teacher's demands with a minimum of effort, to gain prestige among their classmates? The learner's purpose, not merely his interest, is the key to the type of generalization that will result.

SECOND: There is a conviction that the organization of the learner's knowledge and generalizations around persistent problems of living has values for him for effective living which are superior to those of the traditional subject designs. Twelfth-grade John may have fewer opportunities to study economics as a field of knowledge than he would were he under a curriculum design organized by subjects. However, through exploration of the economic problems he has faced over the years, he may actually bring to DECIDING WHAT WORK TO DO and MANAGING MONEY more comprehensive generalizations. These might include insights into the factors that make for salary differences, the role of government in securing better working conditions, the history and present status of organized labor, the regulations under which banks operate and the reasons why, the purposes of insurance, the basis for tax and social security payroll deductions, the values and hazards in setting up his own independent enterprise. John's understandings, skills, and insights are learned in the ways in which he is likely to use them.

THIRD: There is a belief that the attitudes learners develop regarding the importance of accurate information, together with their skills in locating and evaluating needed resources and in solving problems, will provide a guarantee that they can and will locate new information as they need it. Significance is attached to preparing learners to operate effectively in a world in which previously accepted facts are constantly being challenged and where discoveries are providing new information. What is now known about nutrition may need to be completely re-examined in the light of new medical discoveries. This, of course, does not mean that the teacher would fail to help learners understand present concepts of good nutrition. Rather, the teacher must also stress how such concepts were derived, where to turn for the best available information, how to evaluate newspaper columns on diets, what problems are still unsolved, and similar learnings. Education for a changing world must develop learners with high competence in problem-solving methods.

FOURTH: The conviction that learners who have both the disposition and the skills to locate new information will do so is coupled with the belief that the greater maturity the learner brings to the problem the more readily the new learnings from traditionally organized bodies of knowledge will be grasped and functionally used. An American college student who elects a course in English history, for example, does not have difficulty acquiring the same information about the sequence of royal houses which an English child may have drilled on in the elementary grades. Nor does the college student come to this study completely unprepared because he has not taken earlier courses in English history. Newspaper accounts of the present royal family have provided some information. He has studied the American Revolution, and he knows the history of the Pilgrims and the Puritans. In his study of the American Bill of Rights he has learned about the Magna Charta. His writing interest may have led to a study of French and Latin roots of the English language. Through his interest in international relations he has built some understanding of the British Commonwealth of Nations. He has watched productions of Shakespeare's *King Richard III* on television. When he brings the maturity of a young adult to the college course in English history, the pieces fall together quite readily and with greater meaning. However, the fact that more mature learners can grasp information more readily is not itself an argument for putting off or neglecting areas of knowledge. It does suggest that learners can safely approach areas of knowledge when needed for problems which are meaningful to them at their maturity levels without jeopardizing the ability to grasp competently the interrelations within a traditional subject field.

FIFTH: There is a strong feeling that learners can acquire a sense of the logic of a subject without detailed experience under a traditional organization. For example, a fifth-grader can have a clear sense of chronology as he studies the story of the Pilgrim landing without knowing the details of each of the earlier voyages to the continent. What a ninth-grader must know to understand magnetism does not depend upon his grasp of all the other material typically related to this topic in the usual ninth-grade science course. And a sixth-grader, studying parallel and series circuits for hooking up Christmas tree lights, does not need a course in the fundamentals of electricity. Further, there is no one inherent logic in a discipline. Concepts, processes, and relationships, even in a discipline as logical as mathematics, can and have been arranged in many hierarchies. That subjects can be approached in many ways is evidenced by the variations in the textbooks and courses of study in which areas of knowledge form the basic organization. All chemistry texts do not put the same topic first. Some history courses start from the present, some with the remote past, and others are organized around themes or problems rather than in chronological order. In the curriculum design proposed here, learners work carefully and thoroughly with whatever block of knowledge serves their purposes. They do as much with its relationship to the total subject field as is required for clear understanding, but they do not necessarily explore the complete field at that time.

SIXTH: While there is a conviction that the various subject fields can best serve the learner as resources, the systematic study of organized bodies of knowledge at times is certainly not precluded. The need for such contacts will arise in several ways and will partially determine the intensity of the study. For example, while many problems call for information from several areas, there are occasions when a single field can make an important contribution. A twelfth grade, interested in following international relations intelligently, may need to make an extensive study of world history. A fourth grade's interest in the Indian mound being excavated near their village may lead to a study of early America, while a sixth grade's concern with space travel may be extended to a study of the solar system. In addition there will be individuals with special interests and abilities. In a world in which an understanding of other peoples is vitally important, some youth will need to acquire proficiency in one or more foreign languages and insights into these cultures. The high school boy who is planning eventually to assume responsibility for the management of his father's farm may find needs and interests developing that make it desirable for him to undertake a systematic study of chemistry. There may also be learners with special aptitude in music or art, amateur radio operators, budding engineers or machinists who must be given opportunity for more extensive experiences in their particular talent area.

The criteria for deciding the appropriateness of systematic study of a subject as part of the curriculum for a particular learner or group of learners are twofold: Is his need or purpose one that can best be met through such a study? Will his maturity make it possible for him to grasp the concepts as developed, to select those pertinent to his needs, to relate them directly or in reorganized form to his problem, and to use them in subsequent situations? These criteria apply equally to the study of higher mathematics by a student interested in engineering as a vocation or by one whose interest is purely recreational and personal. They apply to both the elementary and secondary school—in fact, to the college level as well. The point at which individuals will have explored relationships sufficiently to make the systematized organization of a subject or discipline meaningful varies. In all probability, if these criteria are met, such systematic study should come much later in the curriculum for most learners than is now common practice. For slow-learning children and youth, for example, there may be little need in either elementary or secondary school to deal with subject matter as logically organized bodies of knowledge. This, of course, does not mean that because of their ability the intellectually able should engage in a total program of such study early in their school work. While ability to see and to understand relationships is a characteristic of individuals with higher intelligence, ideas must have real meaning and concepts should be put to work functionally for these learners as well. Gifted children and high school and college youth are more likely to need and to benefit from such experiences than are slow-learning and younger children. Typically there should be more opportunities to explore intensively within a subject area as learners become more mature. As high school youth progress from seventh through twelfth grade, such opportunities should increase. This calls for a careful guidance program, elective courses, and the provision of laboratories in which individuals with talents or needs for intensive activities can work for relatively large blocks of time under the guidance of teachers with special competencies.

The curriculum design, however, cannot rightly be one that moves from the study of life situations to the study of subjects in their traditional forms of organization. Readiness comes at different points in the lives of learners. While an increasing amount of time may appropriately be given to systematic study of organized bodies of knowledge in areas of specialization, it must be remembered that the high school student is also growing in his powers to see new aspects of continuing life situations, to understand their complexities, and to see their more subtle implications. The learner needs help in developing these powers and in making use of his learnings.

SEVENTH: There is belief that sound development of skills results from seeing the need for the skill in life situations, engaging in practice, and then using the skill appropriately in a variety of situations in which it is needed. Skills are as much a part of our vast cultural heritage as are facts and are equally needed in dealing with life situations. READING, USING

LANGUAGE TO COMMUNICATE IDEAS, LISTENING, COMPUTING, USING A SCIENTIFIC APPROACH TO THE STUDY OF SITUATIONS are among many persistent life situations faced by children and youth which clearly involve the development of skills. They differ from other persistent life situations in that they are usually not faced in isolation. Computation is necessary to balance a bank account, to count change when shopping, to estimate how much time it will take to complete an assignment, to approximate the cost of a purchase. Individuals read for information or pleasure, and discuss in order to influence a group decision, to share information with a friend, to persuade another to change his mind.

Mastery of a skill for its own sake is not the aim, but rather the appropriate and efficient use in any daily life experience in which it is needed. This does not suggest less attention to the basic skills, but rather that techniques be developed in relation to the situations in which they are used. Emphasis would be on experience in using the skill in practical situations and on providing prompt and effective help when the learner faces a situation in which the skill is needed. Meaningful drill—that is, drill which is concrete and related to the situation in which the skills actually function—has a very real place in helping learners to develop these skills to needed levels of proficiency. The objective is to help learners make flexible adaptations of skills to suit the needs of the situations in which they are trying to use them.

As indicated in Chapter 4, persons advocating curriculum designs that focus on helping learners to solve problems tend to stress high competence in a wide range of skills. Proficiencies commonly associated with the three R's are not enough. Required for effective living in a democracy, and sometimes neglected in the curriculum, are such skills as the use of a scientific approach to problems, conference and discussion techniques, and the various abilities needed for sound leadership or for effective group membership. Provision must be made for the development of these skills as integral parts of the curriculum.

Just as situations appearing in increasingly complex form call for expanding understandings and generalizations, so the situations involving use of the skills grow more complex. Skills previously mastered may not be adequate to the demands of new situations. Individuals must develop new skills appropriate to new purposes. As the learner matures and situations calling for the use of a given skill change, his competencies will have to be developed and extended. For example, the reading skills acquired by the elementary school child will have to be greatly extended by the time he undertakes independent research in college. The skills needed by a ten-year-old participating in committee discussion are very different from those needed by the chairman of the senior high school student council. All needed competence in basic skills cannot be developed in the elementary school alone. High schools, colleges, and even graduate schools have their share to do in skill development.

THE VARIETY OF EXPERIENCES IN WHICH PERSISTENT LIFE SITUATIONS ARE MET PROVIDES THE KEY TO BALANCE BETWEEN GROUP AND INDIVIDUAL ACTIVITY

The proposed curriculum design is based on a concept that values the unique qualities of each individual and that seeks to provide for his optimum development. If individual needs and concerns are to be met, time must be allotted for appropriate learning experiences. Relatively more time may be devoted to the needs of individuals and small groups in the proposed curriculum than might be apportioned under a design where specific bodies of content and activities are designated for each grade. Some concerns will be those of individuals, others of small groups—two children who wish to construct a radio, a small group enthusiastic about learning more of Stephen Foster's songs, one child with special artistic talent trying out a variety of media, a budding scientist reading all he can find about the myacins, a youth deep in the chemistry of photography.

Other concerns will be shared by the entire class. A curriculum organized with reference to persistent life situations as they are faced by learners does not call for a program that is entirely individualized. Pupils who live in the same community, share the same work and play facilities, read the same newspapers, and face the same developmental tasks will certainly have problems in common—participation in all-school activities, concern about community enterprises, interest in local or national events, the selection of new books for the school library, decisions as to convenient arrangement of classroom furniture. Such problems of genuine concern to the group become the organizing centers for all-class activities. How much of the total day should encompass such activities will depend on their potential contribution to growth in ability to cope with persistent life situations as compared with the possible learnings that seem likely from dealing with individual and small-group concerns.

Work on all-class problems can itself yield differentiated learnings. The number of persistent life situations that can be dealt with will vary from one immediate concern to another, and from one learner to another, depending on insights and abilities. Whatever the number, since the immediate situation learners actually face is usually complex, it is possible to contribute to individual interests and abilities while focusing on total group problems. For example, in a class sharing in the community drive for fly and mosquito control there may be some pupils whose interests and needs for further understanding result in their readiness to work on persistent life situations relating to MAKING AND ENFORCING LAWS and SECURING EFFECTIVE GOVERNMENT ORGANIZATION. Others may deal with basic problems of PROVIDING FOR DISEASE CONTROL and CONTROLLING AND USING INSECT AND RELATED FORMS OF LIFE as they consider aspects of the drive. A third group with a strong desire to know more about the modern machines to be used in the drive may give attention to such situations as USING TOOLS, MACHINES, AND EQUIPMENT and USING TECHNOLOGICAL RESOURCES FOR MAXIMUM SOCIAL GOOD. Individual activities are not always required to meet the different needs of group members working on a common problem. In fact, to develop the understandings and skills for dealing with a persistent situation such as WORKING ON A COMMON ENTERPRISE requires group effort.

Individual needs and interests are provided for through work on different aspects of a situation, through varied approaches and activities, through recognition of the right of individuals to bring diverse purposes to a common experience, through "free" and unassigned time for following individual pursuits, through provision for both individual and group experiences in scheduled class work. These methods for individualization take into account differences in interests and concerns, provide for diverse working rates, and enable individuals to pursue interests to a depth and breadth appropriate to their ability.

PERSISTENT LIFE SITUATIONS RELATE BOTH TO GENERAL AND TO SPECIALIZED EDUCATION AT ALL EDUCATIONAL LEVELS

Does the proposed curriculum design provide answers to problems of specialized as well as general education? Is it a workable guide for experiences beyond the elementary school and the general education experiences of high school students? What help does it offer in planning the curriculum needed for specialized and vocational education in high school, for professional school in college?

As a guide to needed general education, the concept of persistent life situations can make a major contribution. In the situations with which all individuals must deal with reasonable competence lies the scope of general education. In the knowledge, generalizations, and skills needed by people as they meet everyday problems of living lies the key to what of the vast cultural heritage should be stressed or omitted. As pointed out earlier, the degree of competence to be acquired in those areas classified as general education will vary with the capacities of the learner. The adult of limited intellectual ability faces many of the same decisions in purchasing a house as does the person with high intelligence. The former may act on a number of generalizations—one should consider the neighborhood to which he moves; it is important to consider such items as number of rooms, basement space, and heating facilities, as well as an attractive exterior; it is wise to consult a lawyer before signing papers; contracting to buy a house involves setting aside a definite part of one's salary each month. In addition to the above generalizations, the more able individual may bring to this same problem much more extensive economic information and a greater awareness of the related factors involved. Similarly, one adult may find aesthetic satisfactions through a minimum of self-expression skills and high appreciative talent, whereas another may be a talented musician or artist whose satisfactions come from performing. Again, the general education experiences provided for the learner in a rural community will not be exactly the same as those provided for the child or youth in an urban community, although many of the same generalizations will result. Under this concept of curriculum design, general education is not defined in terms of specific bodies of subject matter. The problems, as seen in the light of the talents, needs, and experience background of the particular learner or group of learners, set the goals of general education.

In addition, each individual will face situations in which, because of special talent, interest, or vocational choice, a different or greater degree of competence is demanded. These are the situations calling for specialized education.

> In a sense, every vocation has its own professional persistent life situations . . .
>
> > The **parent** draws upon general competencies in many persistent life situations related to maintaining a home, planning meals, avoiding illness. There may also be problems which are, in a sense, the professional problems of parenthood, such as preparing the correct foods for young children, providing necessary clothing, meeting children's rest and relaxation needs, helping them to develop bases for moral choices, providing a safe environment, and providing essential securities in person-to-person relationships.
> >
> > The **pediatrician** draws upon general competencies in many of these same areas. But he faces such persistent professional problems as diagnosing illnesses, applying accurate standards in appraising a young child's

> development, advising on diets to meet special deficiencies, dealing sympathetically with parents, locating reports of recent research, deciding when to call for the advice of other specialists.
>
> The **teacher** also draws on general competencies in providing midmorning snacks or supervising noon lunch hours, planning for an effective balance between work and relaxation, helping children wear appropriate clothes for outdoor play. But the teacher faces such persistent professional problems as adjusting to individual differences, identifying special talents and weaknesses, providing effectively for readiness, developing essential securities in a classroom with thirty or more children, guiding activities so that there will be maximum learning.
>
> The **psychiatrist** draws on many of the same general competencies but must also deal with persistent professional problems related to those of the pediatrician and also those of determining basic needs, identifying sources of insecurity, deciding what help to provide to children or parents who show extreme emotional deviations.

Clearly, the two—general and specialized education—are not mutually exclusive. Learning to use tools which are regular household equipment—hammer, saw, screw driver—may also be a part of learning the tools of a trade, which is specialized education for some learners. Developing a sense of responsibility to other people is an objective of general education, and it is also a necessary attitude in many vocations. For the slow learner, particularly, experiences that develop this attitude could be an important part of vocational competence. Specialized education provides for greater depth of understanding of certain aspects of general education and for the development of particular understandings and skills needed by the individual because of his vocational interests or special concerns and abilities.

The fact that any persistent life situation may be faced under circumstances calling for special competence means that the work of elementary and secondary schools will include both general and specialized education. The situations of everyday living met by the elementary school child call primarily for general education experiences. However, even at this level, the school must provide some specialized education in areas of unusual ability and talent, in hobbies, in unique interests, and occasionally in some preliminary vocational experiences. As the high school youth becomes concerned about securing a position, managing a home, or deciding what profession to enter as he makes plans for college, his curriculum may include supervised work experience, special vocational preparation, or experience in home management. As such areas of specialized education assume greater importance in the lives of learners, it is appropriate that a larger share of their school activities be devoted to them. This may call for certain types of guidance not needed earlier and for adjustments in scheduling the school day.

The persistent problems approach can provide useful insights into the specialized education needs of any profession or vocation. For example, an analysis of the persistent problems of the teacher can illustrate the nature of the specialized experiences needed. From such an analysis might come guides in developing professional experiences that could serve the same function for teacher education as the analysis presented in Chapter 6 serves for elementary and secondary school programs. The persistent life situations concept has universal application—in kindergarten as well as in graduate school, in the general problems of everyday living that all must face and equally in the specialized experiences that develop high competence in a particular area. The difference lies in the organization of experiences, the learning activities, the schedules, the guidance needed to work effectively with learners of differing maturities, abilities, and aspirations.

A Summary Look

In the curriculum design under discussion, the focus is upon building understandings, values, generalizations, and skills through experiences arising out of daily situations that learners actually face. The persistent life situations, the recurring situations which are the constants in a changing society, give the clue to the direction in which the experience should be guided.

In summary, what are the premises underlying this concept? What characteristics of persistent life situations should teachers developing this type of curriculum design keep in mind? What kind of teacher, of school organization and administration, of school–community relationships are needed?

A CURRICULUM THAT RELATES IMMEDIATE AND PERSISTENT LIFE SITUATIONS BUILDS ON KNOWLEDGE OF THE LEARNER AND THE LEARNING PROCESS

To what extent does the proposed approach to curriculum design take into account what is known about learners and the learning process? Will working in terms of persistent life situations facilitate or hinder the teacher in using sound learning principles as he develops the curriculum? A curriculum which helps learners to deal with varied aspects of the same persistent life situation and with the range of these recurring situations is based on a recognition of four major principles.

Children and youth learn those things that are related to their purposes. The proposed curriculum, therefore, . . .

starts with the everyday concerns and experiences of learners

deals with those aspects of persistent life situations appropriate to the learners' background and maturity

helps learners deal with the one or more persistent situations which are a part of the immediate situation and most closely related to their needs

provides opportunities for learners to share in the selection and development of experiences

Individuals differ in interests, needs, abilities, and growth patterns. The proposed curriculum, therefore, . . .

provides varied experiences for individuals and for groups from one year to another

helps individuals work on different aspects of the same persistent life situation which is a part of a group concern

helps individuals work on different persistent life situations which are a part of the group's immediate problem

gives recognition to the right of individuals to bring different purposes to a common experience and to use different ways of working

takes into account the fact that learners will attain different levels of growth in dealing with a given situation, growth that will be further developed as the persistent situations recur

Physical, mental, emotional, and social development are related and take place simultaneously; learning is affected by the interrelations among these areas of growth. Therefore, the proposed curriculum . . .

helps learners deal with the several persistent life situations that make up an immediate situation

helps learners see interrelationships among areas of experience as they deal with the various persistent life situations which must be considered in dealing with the immediate concern

provides for rounded and balanced development through helping children and youth deal with the range of persistent life situations

fosters growth in individual capacities, social relationships, and control of environmental factors and forces needed in dealing with persistent life situations

Something is learned only when the individual can and will act on his new insights, skills, and understandings. Thus, the proposed curriculum . . .

helps learners deal with persistent life situations as they appear at home, in the neighborhood, at church, at work, at play helps individuals use their learnings—understandings, generalizations, skills—as guides in dealing with the same persistent life situations when they recur

helps learners develop consistent ways of behaving as learnings gained in one situation are used in another

THE CONCEPT OF PERSISTENT LIFE SITUATIONS PROVIDES THE KEY TO RELATING THE LEARNER AND SOCIETY

As is true in any other approach to the curriculum, the degree to which the above learning principles are implemented depends upon the teacher's insight and skill. He is the one who, with the help of parents and others acquainted with the children, brings the greatest insight into the ramifications of the situations learners face. It is his awareness of persistent life situations as they appear in the lives of his pupils that determines how rich their experiences will be. Five major characteristics of persistent life situations provide the guides for the teacher's work.

Because persistent life situations are a part of all aspects of life . . .

balanced or rounded development can be defined by the range and variety of situations with which all persons inevitably deal and in which all need to develop competence

no experience, however transitory or specific, need be trivial if the learner is helped to see and deal with the recurring situations or problems which are a part of that experience

children and youth can be helped to see the same persistent life situation in everyday activities in home, school, and community

children and youth can be helped to develop consistent ways of behaving by using learnings from one situation in another

children and youth will find in-school learnings functionally useful out of school and vice versa

Because persistent life situations recur and take on new meaning as the individual matures . . .

the child or youth who is helped to see that similar situations recur in his everyday living can apply what he has learned in one situation to another and can test in experience the worth of his former learning

the child or youth who is helped to deal with these problems as they appear in more complex form grows in the ability to meet the problems he faces and extends his understandings, insights, and skills maximum opportunity is provided for the learner to organize facts, concepts, and generalizations which are his cultural heritage for use in coping with the actual problems of life

continuity lies within the learner, not in external logic, and is achieved because life itself has continuity

Because the same persistent life situation may be a part of very different experiences . . .

the curriculum can be responsive to the interests and abilities of individual learners through all-class, small-group, and individual activities

the curriculum can be developed in terms of the particular situations of most concern to individuals and still enable them to grow in skills, understandings, and competencies needed by all persons

both a flexible curriculum and one which provides for growth in ability to deal with common and universal problems can be provided

Because many persistent life situations may be involved in an immediate situation . . .

such situations can be used to develop a variety of skills and competencies

individual needs and interests can be provided for through work on group problems

emphases can be adjusted so that the needs and abilities of the individual learner will determine which of the several persistent life situations will receive the greatest attention

children and youth can be helped to understand interrelationships among persistent life situations

Because dealing with persistent life situations calls for action based on understanding . . .

maximum opportunity can be afforded to generalize and to use basic understandings and accepted values in new situations

learners can be helped to acquire knowledge, concepts, and skills under circumstances which provide optimum encouragement to use these learnings

learnings tend to remain at a high level of competence, since recurring situations call for their repeated use

learners can be helped to acquire problem-solving skills essential in a world of change

A CURRICULUM DESIGN IN TERMS OF PERSISTENT LIFE SITUATIONS MAKES NEW DEMANDS ON TEACHERS AND SCHOOLS

The degree to which any proposed design achieves desired goals depends, to a great measure, both on the teachers who guide learning experiences and on the conditions under which they work. This curriculum proposal, like all others, implies certain conditions in our schools. To implement and translate this proposal into practice requires that attention be directed to at least four factors which have a major effect on the educational program.

The role proposed for the teacher intensifies the need for teachers who . . .

- are broadly prepared, particularly through activities that have helped them relate and use their cultural heritage in their own daily lives
- are students of human nature, able to sense the problems of each learner and to propose sound goals in terms of individual strengths and weaknesses
- are students of society, alert to new problems, sensitive to trends, open-minded to new developments, intellectually curious
- are adept in human relations skills, able to give others the essential security they need, skilled in the arts of democratic leadership
- are skilled in problem-solving techniques and able to apply these both in meeting their own professional problems and in helping learners meet persistent life situations
- have been helped to meet their persistent professional problems, have developed insights into the learning process, and act with a clear sense of purpose and sound understanding of the reasons why they guide children as they do

New types of instructional materials are needed which . . .

- will aid learners in bringing our vast cultural heritage to bear on the problems of daily living
- can be used flexibly, and are readily available to groups when they are needed
- are geared to many levels of ability and maturity so that appropriate help is available whenever a problem is met—by first-graders or high school seniors, slow learners or gifted children, rural or urban children

Traditional patterns of school organization need to be examined to ascertain the modifications which . . .

- will provide for individual needs of the gifted child as well as the slow learner, the child with special talent or special handicap will make available the services of the specialist, so greatly needed if depth of learning is to result, on a basis sufficiently flexible to make a maximum contribution to learners' growth

will provide the combination of specialized and general education needed at the high school level on a basis sufficiently flexible to allow genuine problems to arise and genuine needs to be met

will facilitate articulation among various parts of the educational system that makes for maximum continuity of development

will gear the school's program to the educational needs of the community

New demands being made upon administrators call for leaders who . . .

can help teachers to develop common goals and consistent ways of working within a flexible structure

can help teachers use effective problem-solving techniques in meeting new professional problems

can coordinate the efforts of lay and professional groups in establishing and carrying out the school's appropriate functions in the community

can interpret to the community the ways in which the school is working to promote effective learning for all

The curriculum resides, after all, in the actual experiences of boys and girls, not in the course of study written for teachers and filed on library shelves. The foregoing discussion outlines the conditions that must be met if this concept of curriculum design is to be implemented. The chapters that follow suggest, in more detail, what these conditions may mean for teaching methods, classroom organization, and administration of the whole school.

6

THE SCOPE OF PERSISTENT LIFE SITUATIONS AND WAYS IN WHICH LEARNERS FACE THEM

Underlying the proposal oι a curriculum designed around persistent life situations as learners face them has been the assumption that an analysis of the scope of these situations can be made. The charts contained in this chapter indicate the analysis made by the authors. This represents only one of many ways of grouping and classifying the situations which recur in daily living and with which all persons should be able to deal competently. School faculties can work out other organizations with which they feel more comfortable and effective. The important point is that such an analysis exist, and that it serve as a guide to teachers in studying the day-to-day concerns of learners. Such a guide also provides the means of evaluating learners' growth and insures against neglecting important aspects of growth.

The Scope of Persistent Life Situations

Some method of grouping persistent life situations is essential to a useful analysis. Whatever classification system is developed, care must be taken to assure that it is inclusive. No major aspect of living can be omitted. The diagram which follows indicates the general classification system the authors have used. It attempts to bring into relationship the

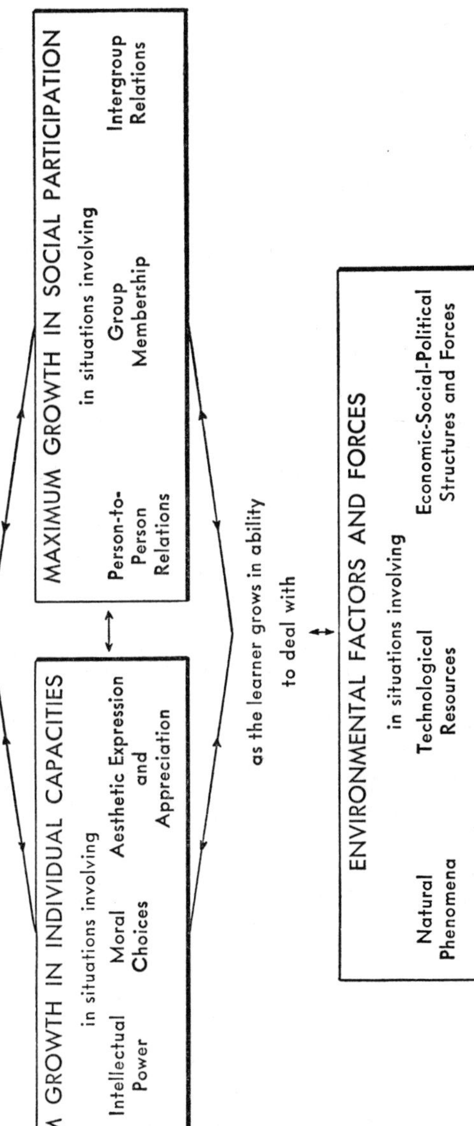
EDUCATION IN OUR DEMOCRACY
means
development of individual understanding and responsibility in dealing with
INDIVIDUAL AND GROUP SITUATIONS OF EVERYDAY LIVING
in
The Family—Civic, Social Activities—Work—Leisure—Spiritual Life
by providing
MAXIMUM GROWTH IN INDIVIDUAL CAPACITIES
in situations involving
Health
Intellectual Power
Moral Choices
Aesthetic Expression and Appreciation
MAXIMUM GROWTH IN SOCIAL PARTICIPATION
in situations involving
Person-to-Person Relations
Group Membership
Intergroup Relations
as the learner grows in ability
to deal with
ENVIRONMENTAL FACTORS AND FORCES
in situations involving
Natural Phenomena
Technological Resources
Economic-Social-Political Structures and Forces

sources of the situations of daily living the learners actually face, the areas in which the persistent life situations recurring in these daily life experiences have been grouped, and the relationships which are seen among them.

THE SOURCES OF PERSISTENT LIFE SITUATIONS ARE IN EVERYDAY LIVING

The situations of everyday living, as indicated in the diagram on page 147, are seen as residing in five major aspects of human life—in the home, as a member of a family; in the community, as a participant in civic and social activities; in work, as a member of an occupational group; in leisure time; and in spiritual activities, whether or not connected with an organized religious group. From these five sources come the problems and situations which learners face and with which the school curriculum must be concerned.

Most learners, as members of family groups, face a wide variety of situations with which they must deal—situations ranging from putting clothes away or sharing toys to helping to plan the family budget, preparing meals, caring for younger children, or taking care of persons who are ill.

Learners are also members of civic and social groups, not only in the school which is itself a complex and vital community, but in the local and national community as well. From the three-year-old interested in the policeman's uniform to the adolescent trying to understand the headlines in the daily paper, learners are bringing their community problems to the school and asking for help.

Work life—those activities which have for their purpose the performing of tasks which society wants done—is an integral part of the life of almost everyone. Caring for the third-grade aquarium or selling tickets for the high school basketball game is no less a work obligation than is the parent's job in the local factory.

Leisure time—those periods of time when one feels under obligation to no one but oneself—is also a vital part of the lives of both young and old. "What shall I do now?" is a recurring question. From the answers emerge hobbies; lasting interests in music, art, or good books; ability to paint, draw, carve, or write; and those social skills which make one a good host or a pleasant companion.

Most people also spend time seeking to identify, express allegiance to, and draw upon meaningful spiritual sources. Whatever he places at the center of his universe, every man identifies values which he endeavors to make central in his life. From the small child asking questions about the stars, deciding whether or not to share his toys with his friends, or going with his parents to church, to the adolescent struggling with his personal philosophy of life and his orientation to the world around him, learners are spending some of their time thinking about spiritual aspects of living.

PERSISTENT LIFE SITUATIONS ARE GROUPED IN THREE MAJOR AREAS

Increased understanding and responsibility in dealing with the problems and situations arising in family, civic-social, or spiritual life, or through work or leisure-time activities, will be built as these problems are explored in terms of persistent life situations. As indicated in the diagram, the authors see individual and group situations of everyday living calling for three kinds of growth: in individual capacities, in social participation, and in ability to deal with environmental factors and forces. These three divisions provide an inclusive basis for grouping the persistent life situations with which the learner is dealing and must continue to deal as he faces them in various combinations in his daily experiences. The categories of situations within each of these three divisions provide the framework for the analysis made in this volume.

Growth in individual capacities. A major value of our society is that the maximum development of each individual is essential to the well-being of all. In this concept is a recognition that the learner must be concerned with the physical and emotional aspects of growth, HEALTH in its widest sense. He also faces situations in which INTELLECTUAL POWER is of great importance—situations where he is called upon to use language and number, to apply the techniques of problem-solving, to use adequate methods of work and effective techniques for bringing about change. The many situations which call for individual capacity for AESTHETIC EXPRESSION AND APPRECIATION must likewise be recognized—great music to be enjoyed; clay, weaving, finger paint to be experimented with; classrooms, homes, and communities to be made beautiful as well as convenient. Nor can this concept of individual development neglect the fact that every person faces a number of situations which have moral implications—establishing personal values, identifying spiritual resources to which he is willing to give allegiance, and taking responsibility for the MORAL CHOICES he makes.

Growth in social participation. Another basic value of our society is that optimum individual and group welfare can be attained only when there is maximum growth in each individual's ability to work with others. Thus it becomes important to identify those situations in which the individual is called upon to work with others and to assist him in building understandings and abilities needed for effective group membership. Situations in this division have been grouped under three areas. There are those involving PERSON–TO–PERSON RELATIONSHIPS —friends, the doctor, the local storekeeper, individual members of the family, and many others. There are other situations for which the individual must have skills in GROUP MEMBERSHIP—the family, the class, the club, the city council, Congress—in which he faces problems of deciding on appropriate action as a group member, of leadership choice and responsibility, and of obligation to delegated authority. There are also situations in which he is involved in INTERGROUP RELATIONSHIPS—the minority group, the pressure group, the union, the nation.

Growth in ability to deal with environmental factors and forces. As the individual grows in ability to use his capacities and in ability to work effectively with others he is constantly dealing with environmental factors and forces. NATURAL PHENOMENA—weather, chemical and physical phenomena, biological forces—are always present. Where complete control is impossible, intelligent adaptation is necessary. TECHNOLOGICAL RESOURCES have created a series of new situations in which American citizens must have competence. The combine has replaced the harvesting and threshing gang; the research laboratory is a vital part of every industrial concern; information now comes by way of the newspaper, radio, television, telegraph, or telephone rather than the town meeting or the local post office. And in our increasingly complex world, ECONOMIC–SOCIAL–POLITICAL STRUCTURES AND FORCES are powerful environmental factors with which all persons are dealing—the United Nations organization has been established, government is concerned with raising standards of living, collective bargaining is a recognized instrument, cooperatives and credit unions are being organized, to mention only a few.

PERSISTENT LIFE SITUATIONS AND THE IMMEDIATE SITUATIONS OF DAILY LIVING ARE INTERRELATED

In almost every situation of daily living—in family, civic-social, or spiritual life, in work and leisure-time activities—individual capacities are called into play, social relationships are present, and the surrounding environment—natural, technological, or socio-economic-political—must be dealt with. The girl who prepares a family meal, for example, should have some knowledge of health needs and of aesthetic arrangement of food and table. She also uses certain intellectual abilities in reading recipes, measuring, and the like. If she is working with anyone else she must establish cooperative working relationships. In shopping for food she deals with aspects of the economic structure, and in preparing it she uses scientific and technological resources. Lack of adequate competence in any one of these areas may result in a less satisfactory meal than it otherwise would be. Similarly, getting a job—whether persuading the class to place one in charge of the lost-and-found department or convincing the factory's employment director to hire one—may demand pleasing personal appearance, adequate self-expression, techniques for establishing person-to-person relationships, and ability to handle the tools of the job.

The three major divisions in which the persistent life situations are grouped, as well as the subgroups within them, are interrelated. The quality of development in one may influence the competence that can be attained in another. Poor health, for example, may make certain kinds of social relationships difficult to achieve or may alter vocational aspirations. Inadequate methods of work may impede growth in ability to deal with environmental factors and forces. Inability to establish adequate person-to-person relationships may make it impossible for an individual to be an effective group member. Inaccurate information about environmental factors and forces may cause unwise decisions regarding ways of cooperating with community, national, and international groups.

Competence in the use of intellectual power, ability to make moral choices, certain aspects of mental or emotional health, and ability to work with others are called for in almost every situation. Out of repeated experiences contributing not only to specific understandings but also to development of these constantly needed competencies, come some of the general values and ways of behaving so important in a democracy. Respect for the unique worth of the individual, desire to preserve the values inherent in the democratic way of life, determination to use technological resources for the welfare of all, ability to use a scientific approach to problems, and willingness to assume responsibility for actions can be built through almost every experience with which an individual is helped to deal.

The Analysis of Persistent Life Situations

The over-all analysis presented in the preceding section lacks the detail needed by teachers for identifying persistent life situations in the day-to-day experiences of children and youth. Teaching must focus on a specific problem as it recurs in the lives of learners, rather than on a general area. Just as three or four areas of problems were identified within each of the three inclusive divisions in the preceding section, so specific persistent life situations can be identified within each area. This section contains the list of specific situations identified by the writers.

SOME PROBLEMS MUST BE KEPT IN MIND IN ANALYZING PERSISTENT LIFE SITUATIONS

Curriculum committees preparing their own analyses of persistent life situations will find it a most challenging but perplexing enterprise. Since several major problems will inevitably be faced, it is important to have these noted. These same problems should be kept in mind when studying the analysis prepared by the authors.

What will be the classification scheme? The first step is to determine some inclusive classification system. The over-all scheme discussed in the preceding section—to look at the individual's growth in relation to himself, to other people, and to the world around him—is not the only one. Another possibility might be to look directly at the areas in which an individual's daily activities fall—he acts as a homemaker, communicates with others, works at his job, transports himself from place to place.[1] Whatever areas are chosen, they must cover every major aspect of living if they are to be effective as a basis for the more detailed identification of situations.

How detailed should the analysis be? Once the general scheme for determining major problem areas has been established, specific persistent life situations within each area must then be identified. In doing this the question of the amount of detail necessary is raised. Any persistent situation suggests a series of more specific situations calling for certain competencies needed to deal successfully with the larger situation. It is possible to stop with a rather gross analysis, giving three or four major situations within each area, or to subdivide to the most minute detail. The area of HEALTH, for example, calls for eating appropriate foods. This involves knowing what foods are appropriate for what meals, what are acceptable substitutes within one's budget, how to prepare foods so as to preserve nutritional qualities, how to store foods, and a host of other problems. Where should the detailed analysis stop? There is no single answer to this question. In general, however, the persistent life situations should be identified in sufficient detail to enable the teacher to see these situations recurring in the day-to-day problems

[1] A preliminary draft of such an analysis, made by teachers of slow-learning children, can be found on pages 450 ff.

and concerns of his learners, but not so detailed that the very weight of the analysis hinders its use. For example, in the analysis in this volume, MEETING FOOD NEEDS is identified as one persistent life situation in the general area of HEALTH. This situation is further subdivided into BALANCING MEALS, KNOWING AND SAFEGUARDING NUTRITIONAL VALUES, and CONSERVING FOOD SUPPLY. More specific situations are subsumed under these three. Some planning groups might prefer to use only the large category, MEETING FOOD NEEDS; others would want more detail.

In which category should a specific situation go? Perhaps even more difficult than the problem of deciding how much detail is needed is that of classifying the situations identified. Even when the major categories seem clear and mutually exclusive, most specific situations usually can be seen as relating to a number of categories. BALANCING MEALS is a persistent life situation that seems readily classifiable as one aspect of the larger situation of MEETING FOOD NEEDS. However, food needs cannot be met effectively without attention to some of the persistent problems listed in the paragraph above—budgeting one's income, preparing food, using refrigeration or other storage systems. Under which category should a situation be placed? Should a specific item be repeated in relation to every area upon which it has a bearing?

Part of the difficulty of classifying persistent situations is resolved once it is recognized that the interrelationships among them are inevitable, for this is a characteristic of life itself. In any problem faced in daily life, no matter how simple, several persistent life situations can usually be identified. No matter what wording describes a persistent life situation, the fact that it is expressed in terms of behavior needed to solve a problem will mean that other persistent situations can be identified within it. They are all threads in a complex plaid, so to speak. Even in a single thread, the zealous analyst will be able to find fibers. Consequently, if they are to make progress, committees attempting to identify and categorize specific persistent life situations must establish their own "ground rules" and hold firmly to them.

One "ground rule" regarding the amount of desirable detail has already been suggested. The rule governing the category in which to place a specific problem and whether to repeat it comes from the purpose to be served by the analysis. The objective is to identify a workable series of situations that will serve as guides in helping learners to develop competencies needed in coping with the situations of everyday living. If its potential contribution to developing particular concepts or skills is used as the major factor in deciding in which category a situation is to be placed, some of the problems of overlapping tend to be resolved. For example, there are some learnings regarding the nutritional values of foods that clearly contribute to good health. These extend from such specific habits developed by the young child as drinking milk or eating some of each kind of food on his plate, to the understanding the adult brings to deciding whether the day's meals have been balanced or knowing what food pattern adjustments are needed for small children, invalids, and elderly people. The persistent life situations related to balancing meals, then, can be placed under the more general problem of MEETING FOOD NEEDS. On the other hand, the problem of purchasing food wisely contributes to the development of concepts and skills needed in MANAGING MONEY and could be listed as a subproblem related to this persistent life situation. Or, as is actually done in the analysis which follows, this problem might be seen as one of many daily life problems contributing to the development of sound concepts regarding DECIDING WHERE TO BUY OR SELL and DETERMINING A FAIR PRICE.

The same kind of problems will be faced whatever the over-all organizational frame and the same rules can be applied. For example, a committee working with an analysis in which "learning to keep healthy" and "learning to be a homemaker" were two of their major categories, faced the problem of where to include the persistent life situations centering around food. This group decided to include food-related problems in both categories. In the section on keeping healthy, problems dealing with nutritional concepts were listed, leading to such adult situations as planning balanced meals and knowing how to diet safely. In the homemaking category, they placed situations leading to adult skills in purchasing food economically for a family and being able to use sanitary measures in handling and preparing foods. A cross reference indicating that the section on food in both categories was to be consulted was added to make clear the interrelatedness of the two areas. Here the persistent situation of planning balanced meals is clearly related to both areas.

Some organizations may involve fewer overlapping areas than others. However, the critical factor is the ease with which the analysis can be used by the teachers involved as a guide to studying the needs of learners. In actual practice, children and youth cope with persistent situations in whatever combinations they appear in the immediate situation under consideration.

AN ANALYSIS OF PERSISTENT LIFE SITUATIONS IS PROPOSED

The authors of this volume have chosen to analyze persistent life situations in considerable detail. This is done in the belief that the quality of guidance provided learners depends to a large extent on the teacher's insight into the persistent life situations tnat appear in their day-to-day experiences.

In the analysis which is given on pages 155 to 165, the major divisions are the three listed earlier—situations calling for growth in individual capacities, in social participation, and in ability to deal with economic-social-political structures and forces. The large areas under each of these were also discussed earlier—HEALTH, INTELLECTUAL POWER, and so on. Each of these has been divided into several categories, which are further subdivided into a number of situations. The divisions were judged to be large enough to keep the teacher's problem in studying the learner's progress in each area from being hopelessly complicated, but small enough to indicate specific situations in which there should be growth. In terms of "ground rules," previously suggested, the general procedure is to group situations contributing to a closely related series of concepts, information, and skills, and to indicate the larger situation of which they are a part. The items in the left column of the Master List are the larger situations, those on the right a more detailed breakdown. While an analysis of learnings needed to deal competently with any of the situations will reveal relationships with other areas in the list, the situation is placed under the area to which the authors felt its major contribution is made.

The following analysis is intended as an aid to teachers in studying learners and, for curriculum committees embarked on similar projects, as a suggestion of one way this job might be done. While the analyses made by other groups may be quite dissimilar in general organization, the fact that the persistent problems of living have been the focus should make this list a useful reference against which to check other plans.

MASTER LIST OF PERSISTENT LIFE SITUATIONS

Situations Calling for Growth in Individual Capacities

HEALTH

A. Satisfying Physiological Needs

MEETING FOOD NEEDS	Balancing meals (p. 174) [2]
	Knowing and safeguarding nutritional values (p. 174)
	Conserving food supply (p. 174)

[2] Page numbers refer to sections of the detailed charts showing typical experiences in which learners of different maturity levels might face the given persistent life situation in their everyday living.

MEETING NEEDS FOR AIR AND LIGHT	Regulating ventilation and lighting (p. 176) Adjusting to or controlling air conditions or sunlight in community (p. 176)
MAINTAINING COMFORTABLE BODY TEMPERATURE	Selecting appropriate clothing (p. 176) Adjusting activity to temperature (p. 176) Regulating building temperature (p. 178) Securing housing conditions for achievement of desired temperature (p. 178)
SECURING NEEDED REST AND ACTIVITY	Balancing rest and activity (p. 178) Developing needed skills for relaxation and activity (p. 178) Securing facilities for relaxation and activity (p. 180)
MEETING SEX NEEDS	Establishing appropriate relationships with opposite sex (p. 180) Obtaining constructive social regulations (p. 180)
GETTING RID OF BODY WASTES	Establishing individual routines (p. 180) Securing adequate sanitary facilities (p. 182)

B. Satisfying Emotional and Social Needs

ACHIEVING SECURE RELATIONS WITH OTHERS	Establishing affectionate relationships (p. 182) Achieving status in groups (p. 182)
MAKING CONSTRUCTIVE USE OF EMOTIONS	Achieving constructive expression of emotions (p. 184) Securing balanced satisfactions (p. 184)
ACHIEVING SELF-DIRECTION	Adjusting to personal strengths and weaknesses (p. 184) Dealing with success and failure (p. 186) Making choices and resolving conflict situations (p. 186)

C. Avoiding and Caring for Illness and Injury

AVOIDING ILLNESS	Practicing desirable health routines (p. 186)
	Providing for disease control (p. 188)
AVOIDING ACCIDENTS	Using safety measures (p. 188)
	Providing needed safety measures (p. 188)
CARING FOR PHYSICAL DEFECTS	Correcting or adjusting to defects (p. 190)
CARING FOR ILLNESS OR INJURY	Providing first aid (p. 190)
	Providing care in time of illness (p. 190)

INTELLECTUAL POWER

A. Making Ideas Clear

USING LANGUAGE TO COMMUNICATE IDEAS	Contributing to informal discussions and conversations (p. 194)
	Making oral presentations (p. 194)
	Expressing ideas in written form (p. 196)
USING MEDIA OTHER THAN LANGUAGE TO EXPRESS IDEAS	Using graphic forms to express ideas (p. 196)
	Using aesthetic forms to express ideas (p. 198)

B. Understanding the Ideas of Others

READING	Using appropriate reading approach (p. 198)
	Using source materials (p. 200)
	Interpreting graphic presentations (p. 200)
LISTENING	Following and evaluating informal discussions and conversations (p. 202)
	Following and evaluating oral presentations (p. 202)
	Understanding musical and dramatic forms of expression (p. 202)
OBSERVING	Interpreting environmental surroundings (p. 204)

C. Dealing with Quantitative Relationships

INTERPRETING NUMBER VALUES AND SYMBOLS	Understanding symbols and relationships (p. 204)
COMPUTING	Estimating amounts (p. 206)
	Making exact computations (p. 206)
	Using measuring instruments (p. 208)

D. Using Effective Methods of Work

PLANNING	Deciding on and clarifying purpose (p. 208)
	Determining sequence of steps to achieve purpose (p. 208)
	Budgeting time and energy (p. 210)
	Evaluating steps taken (p. 210)
USING APPROPRIATE RESOURCES	Locating and evaluating resources (p. 212)
USING A SCIENTIFIC APPROACH TO THE STUDY OF SITUATIONS	Solving practical problems (p. 212)
	Testing beliefs and attitudes (p. 212)

MORAL CHOICES

A. Determining the Nature and Extent of Individual Freedom

RESPONDING TO AUTHORITY	Meeting legal regulations (p. 216)
	Deciding on obligations to constituted authority (p. 216)
	Reacting to group mores, traditions (p. 218)
ACTING UPON A PERSONAL SET OF VALUES	Formulating guides for action (p. 218)

B. Determining Responsibility to Self and Others

PRESERVING INTEGRITY IN HUMAN RELATIONSHIPS	Carrying out commitments (p. 218)
	Respecting property rights (p. 220)
	Being intellectually honest (p. 220)

MEETING THE NEEDS OF OTHERS

- Respecting individual differences (p. 220)
- Modifying personal desires in the interests of others (p. 222)

DEVELOPING AND USING POTENTIAL ABILITIES OF SELF AND OTHERS

- Developing individual capacities for social ends (p. 222)
- Securing contribution of all concerned with a problem (p. 222)

AESTHETIC EXPRESSION AND APPRECIATION

A. Finding Sources of Aesthetic Satisfactions in Oneself

EXPRESSING THE SELF THROUGH VARIED MEDIA

- Providing resources for aesthetic expression (p. 226)
- Experimenting with varied media (p. 226)
- Developing special interests and abilities (p. 228)

ACHIEVING ARTISTRY IN DAILY WORK

- Finding means of creative expression in work (p. 228)

ACHIEVING ATTRACTIVE PERSONAL APPEARANCE

- Achieving good grooming (p. 228)
- Selecting attractive clothing (p. 230)
- Using voice, manner, and posture effectively (p. 230)

B. Achieving Aesthetic Satisfactions Through the Environment

PROVIDING ARTISTIC LIVING CONDITIONS

- Achieving satisfying space relations (p. 230)
- Selecting furnishings appropriate to use (p. 232)
- Using color effectively (p. 232)

SECURING BEAUTY THROUGH COMMUNITY PLANNING

- Planning community architecture and landscaping (p. 232)
- Providing care to keep community attractive (p. 234)

SECURING AESTHETIC SATISFACTION IN THE NATURAL ENVIRONMENT

- Appreciating natural beauty (p. 234)

Situations Calling for Growth in Social Participation

PERSON–TO–PERSON RELATIONSHIPS

A. Establishing Effective Social Relations with Others

DEVELOPING FRIENDSHIPS AND AFFECTIONATE RELATIONSHIPS	Interpreting responses of others (p. 240) Making appropriate responses to family and friends (p. 240) Deciding on rights and responsibilities in relationships (p. 242)
RESPONDING TO CASUAL SOCIAL CONTACTS	Making appropriate responses (p. 242)
PARTICIPATING IN SOCIAL ACTIVITIES	Determining kind of social activity (p. 242) Using appropriate amenities (p. 244)

B. Establishing Effective Working Relations with Others

WORKING ON A COMMON ENTERPRISE	Adjusting working relationships to capacities and needs (p. 244)
WORKING IN SERVICE GROUP RELATIONSHIPS	Deciding on services to expect or give (p. 246)
WORKING IN GUIDANCE RELATIONSHIPS	Deciding on guidance to give or secure (p. 246)

GROUP MEMBERSHIP

A. Deciding When to Join a Group

DECIDING WHEN GROUP ACTIVITY IS DESIRABLE	Deciding what existing groups to join (p. 250) Determining membership obligations (p. 250) Deciding when to organize new groups or disband old ones (p. 250)
DECIDING ON NATURE OF GROUP PARTICIPATION	Determining how actively to participate (p. 252)

B. Participating as a Group Member

HELPING TO FORMULATE GROUP POLICY	Keeping informed about group activity (p. 252) Expressing opinions regarding group activity (p. 252) Coming to joint decisions (p. 254)
SELECTING LEADERS	Determining the abilities needed by and choosing leaders (p. 254)
HELPING CARRY OUT GROUP POLICIES	Determining needed organization and personnel (p. 256) Evaluating the work of those to whom responsibility is delegated (p. 256) Executing group decisions (p. 256)

C. Taking Leadership Responsibilities

OUTLINING PRELIMINARY PLANS	Projecting activities and needed personnel and materials (p. 258)
SECURING PARTICIPATION OF GROUP MEMBERS	Keeping group members informed (p. 258) Securing cooperative action (p. 258)

INTERGROUP RELATIONSHIPS

A. Working with Racial, Religious, and National Groups

UNDERSTANDING THE BASIC CHARACTERISTICS AND PURPOSES OF A GROUP	Securing reliable information about other groups (p. 262)
SAFEGUARDING RIGHTS AND RESPONSIBILITIES OF RACIAL, RELIGIOUS, AND NATIONAL GROUPS	Acting on legal and personal obligations to racial, religious, and national groups (p. 262)

B. Working with Socio-Economic Groups

DETERMINING VALIDITY OF SOCIO-ECONOMIC DISTINCTIONS	Understanding basic characteristics of other groups (p. 264)
SAFEGUARDING RIGHTS AND RESPONSIBILITIES	Assuring economic, political, and social opportunities (p. 264)

C. Dealing with Groups Organized for Specific Action

DECIDING WHEN GROUP ACTION IS JUSTIFIED	Deciding when to support organized group action (p. 266)
SECURING COOPERATIVE INTER-ACTION	Securing effective intergroup cooperation (p. 266)

Situations Calling for Growth in Ability to Deal with Environmental Factors and Forces

NATURAL PHENOMENA

A. Dealing with Physical Phenomena

ADJUSTING TO ATMOSPHERIC CONDITIONS	Adjusting to weather conditions (p. 272)
	Adjusting to conditions of air, moisture, sun-light (p. 272)
USING THE EARTH'S SURFACE AND CONTENTS	Dealing with topographic features (p. 274)
	Conserving and using natural resources (p. 274)
ADJUSTING TO FACTORS CON-DITIONED BY THE STRUCTURE OF THE UNIVERSE	Understanding factors conditioned by relative motion in solar system (p. 276)
	Exploring the nature of the universe (p. 276)

B. Dealing with Plant, Animal, and Insect Life

PRODUCING AND USING ANIMAL LIFE	Producing, caring for, and controlling animal life (p. 276)
	Using animal products for human welfare (p. 278)
CONTROLLING AND USING INSECT AND RELATED FORMS OF LIFE	Controlling and using insect life for human welfare (p. 278)
PRODUCING AND USING PLANT LIFE	Producing, protecting, and controlling plant life (p. 278)
	Using plant products for human welfare (p. 280)

CONTROLLING AND USING BACTERIA AND OTHER MICROSCOPIC ORGANISMS	Providing immunity to and the positive use of microscopic organisms (p. 280)

C. Using Physical and Chemical Forces

PRODUCING NEW FORMS THROUGH PHYSICAL AND CHEMICAL CHANGE	Using physical and chemical change (p. 280)
CONSERVING MATERIALS	Adjusting use of materials to their properties (p. 282) Preserving materials (p. 282)
USING PHYSICAL FORCES	Adjusting to physical forces (p. 282) Using sources of energy (p. 284) Using and adjusting to light and sound (p. 284)

TECHNOLOGICAL RESOURCES

A. Using Technological Resources

USING TOOLS, MACHINES, AND EQUIPMENT	Using common tools (p. 288) Selecting and using the tools and machines of a trade (p. 288)
USING HOUSEHOLD AND OFFICE APPLIANCES	Using equipment to conserve human energy (p. 290)
USING INSTRUMENTS OF COMMUNICATION	Using effective means of communicating with individuals or groups (p. 290)
USING MEANS OF TRANSPORTATION	Using effective means of transporting people and materials (p. 290)

B. Contributing to Technological Advance

ENCOURAGING TECHNOLOGICAL ADVANCE	Supporting experimentation (p. 292)
USING TECHNOLOGICAL RESOURCES FOR MAXIMUM SOCIAL GOOD	Using resources in keeping with social values (p. 292)

ECONOMIC–SOCIAL–POLITICAL STRUCTURES AND FORCES

A. Earning a Living

PROVIDING FOR WORK NEEDS OF SOCIETY	Assuring that needed work will be done (p. 296)
	Deciding what work to do (p. 296)
ACHIEVING EFFECTIVE WORKMANSHIP	Assuring adequate work standards (p. 298)
	Providing good working conditions (p. 298)
ASSURING THE RIGHTS AND RESPONSIBILITIES OF WORKERS	Securing adequate remuneration (p. 298)
	Assuring other benefits, rights, and responsibilities (p. 300)
MANAGING MONEY	Budgeting income (p. 300)
	Saving and investing (p. 300)
	Borrowing money (p. 302)

B. Securing Goods and Services

MAKING GOODS AND SERVICES AVAILABLE	Securing effective distribution (p. 302)
BUYING AND SELLING GOODS AND SERVICES	Deciding where to buy or sell (p. 302)
	Determining quality (p. 304)
	Determining a fair price (p. 304)
	Deciding on means of payment (p. 304)

C. Providing for Social Welfare

WORKING IN THE FAMILY GROUP	Providing secure relations (p. 306)
	Sharing family responsibilities (p. 306)
PARTICIPATING IN COMMUNITY WELFARE PROVISIONS	Sharing in protective measures (p. 306)
	Sharing in community welfare efforts (p. 308)
USING GOVERNMENT TO GUARANTEE WELFARE	Providing and using public services (p. 308)
	Providing and using legal protections (p. 308)
	Controlling use of natural resources (p. 310)

D. Molding Public Opinion

PROVIDING ADEQUATE EDUCATIONAL OPPORTUNITIES	Participating in organized education (p. 310)
	Providing and supporting other educational agencies (p. 312)
USING INSTRUMENTS FOR DISSEMINATING INFORMATION	Interpreting information (p. 312)
	Using appropriate means of presenting a point of view (p. 314)
	Acting on issues involving freedom of press (p. 314)

E. Participating in Local and National Government

ELECTING GOVERNMENT REPRESENTATIVES	Nominating and electing candidates (p. 316)
SECURING EFFECTIVE GOVERNMENT ORGANIZATION	Considering effectiveness of existing organization (p. 316)
	Appraising work of representatives (p. 318)
MAKING AND ENFORCING LAWS	Taking responsibility in making and changing laws (p. 318)
	Cooperating in enforcing laws (p. 320)
PROVIDING FINANCIAL SUPPORT FOR GOVERNMENT	Determining amount and sources of income (p. 320)
	Determining use of government income (p. 320)

PRECAUTIONS MUST BE TAKEN IN USING THE ANALYSIS

Curriculum planners should use the foregoing analysis with some caution. The persistent life situations just listed are in no sense a basis for fixed curriculum units; nor are they the only ones at which a school faculty might arrive. Normally every area, and practically every persistent situation within that area, will be faced in some form at each grade level. As suggested in Chapter 5, the intensity of study of a specific life situation, as well as the way in which it will be approached, depends on the needs of the particular pupil group. The above list should never be used to prescribe the order in which learners should face these persistent life situations or the grade levels at which they should be focal.

Nor are these persistent situations intended to serve as specific educational goals or objectives. Rather they are listed here to indicate the nature and scope of the problems faced by learners. Teachers and other curriculum planners wishing to use the situations as a basis for determining goals must first study each situation in terms of the understandings and competencies needed by citizens in a democratic society if they are to deal adequately with the recurring problems and situations of daily living. However, because the analysis indicates the types of situations with which all persons must deal, the list can certainly be used as a guide to the areas in which specific goals are needed. Some curriculum committees working on similar analyses of their own may well include specific goals in the statements they prepare.

Competencies and understandings needed in dealing with persistent life situations develop gradually, not all at one time. The small child with only a few pennies may be on his way toward developing concepts of money management which will eventually make him competent to handle a family income. The slightly older child may be concerned only about sharing a playground with a neighboring group, yet he is building a basis for later insights into international cooperation. Understandings are enlarged a step at a time as situations which call for them recur. The understandings and abilities needed to meet satisfactorily the situations with which the learner is dealing will determine the accomplishment level he will attain. The small child, for example, evaluating his boat-building efforts, sets up workmanship standards in keeping with his maturity. For the very young child these are relatively simple—does the object actually float and does it look like a boat to him? Standards of workmanship are raised for the high school student who may want the boat he is building or repairing to actually carry passengers. His standards may include not only a better product than that of the younger child, but may also encompass problems of carrying out obligations to others and determining the relative importance of several jobs. As persistent life situations are dealt with in their changing and more complex forms through the situations of everyday living significant to maturing learners, understandings are enlarged and abilities are extended.

While indicating the scope of situations learners face, these persistent life situations serve only as guides for curriculum planners. They cannot be used to determine how or through what experiences an individual or group of learners can secure needed competence. They do not, in and of themselves, indicate what competencies are needed. They present the recurring problems with which all citizens must be able to deal and furnish guidance as to the nature of balanced and rounded development for the learner.

Typical Situations of Everyday Living in Which Persistent Life Situations Appear

To recognize the persistent life situations learners are meeting is but one aspect of the teacher's work in guiding learning experiences. Equally significant is his sensitivity to the meaning everyday situations have for particular learners and to the ways in which persistent situations recur. The section which follows illustrates some typical experiences in which each of the persistent life situations might appear in the everyday lives of learners.

The detailed charts are offered as a guide to the teacher in studying his own class. They indicate situations of daily living that are typical of those faced by children, youth, and adults of varying maturities and backgrounds. In so far as possible, situations arising in the home, in the school, and in the community have been included, although the list does not necessarily identify the source.

In order to provide maximum help to teachers working with learners of different ages, experiences have been grouped under **early childhood, later childhood, youth,** and **adulthood.** Even so, situations similar to those listed under one heading may appear for the first time with some children who are younger or with many who are older. These four divisions are not meant to indicate grade levels. A third-grade child, for example, may be involved in many experiences similar to those listed under "later childhood." Similarly, a sixth-grader may be having experiences more characteristic of "youth," or he may be struggling for the first time with some which are typical problems of "early childhood." The type of family, community, and society in which a child lives, as well as his own development rate, all affect the situations with which he will be trying to deal.

No attempt has been made in the charts to cover all possible experiences relating to each persistent life situation. Rather, the emphasis has been on identifying a sufficient number which are typical of rural and urban groups, of various economic levels, and of various cultural patterns so that the teacher will be able to see his learners in the analysis. Certainly no one learner will deal with all the experiences listed. In fact, a particular learner may not meet any of them exactly as described.

The grouping of several experiences around a persistent life problem shows how the everyday situations from early childhood to adulthood contribute to and call for growing competence. Although a variety of typical daily life situations has been listed for each persistent problem, there is no intent that the learner shall have experience in dealing with each separate situation. To attempt to have the learner experience what is involved in each separate situation would be a flagrant misuse of the charts, for it would ignore individual differences in needs, concerns, and ways in which persistent life situations are met. In addition, it would fail to take into account all the help that home and community may provide in relation to certain situations and would result in a great deal of unnecessary repetition of experience.

Because daily life experiences are complex, each one listed as calling for growth in a particular persistent life situation may also make a contribution to others. More than one persistent life situation may appear in a single experience. Thus the teacher, dealing with the complex problems faced by learners, will not work within the area of a single chart. A high school group concerned with the issues involved in union efforts to provide better working conditions in local factories may well find themselves face to face with situations in the major categories of EARNING A LIVING, CONTRIBUTING TO TECHNOLOGICAL ADVANCE, and AVOIDING AND CARING FOR ILLNESS AND INJURY—categories found respectively in the charts on ECONOMIC–SOCIAL–POLITICAL STRUCTURES AND FORCES, TECHNOLOGICAL RESOURCES, and HEALTH. A single experience, therefore, may be repeated in more than one section of the same chart, or in several charts, as its varied aspects contribute to or draw upon several persistent life situations. For example, sharing in the planning of activities appears in varied forms at all age levels. Specific experiences involving planning will be found listed under such categories as USING EFFECTIVE METHODS OF WORK, MAKING IDEAS CLEAR, and UNDERSTANDING THE IDEAS OF OTHERS, which are parts of the chart giving typical situations calling for growth in ability to use INTELLECTUAL POWER. Experiences in which individuals learn to plan together contribute to ability to deal with persistent situations in these three categories, and in some cases to still others. The teacher, guiding the specific learning activities, will help his learners deal with as many persistent situations as are significant for them. The experiences indicated in the following charts serve only as guides to what these situations might be.

PERSISTENT LIFE SITUATIONS AS LEARNERS FACE THEM

Pages 170 to 321 contain the charts which give illustrations of typical situations of daily living through which children, youth, and adults face persistent life situations. They suggest the changing nature and complexity of situations of everyday living as learners move through childhood toward adulthood. They are presented as a guide to teachers, parents, and others seeking (1) to identify the everyday situations faced by those with whom they are working and (2) to understand the persistent life problems involved in these everyday activities.

As shown in the Master List on pages 155 to 165, the authors have grouped the situations into three major divisions—Growth in Individual Capacities (pages 170 to 235), Growth in Social Participation (pages 236 to 267), and Growth in Ability to Deal with Environmental Factors and Forces (pages 268 to 321). Again it should be emphasized that these charts represent one kind of analysis. Faculty study groups may develop other categories or assign specific examples to different categories.

Growth in Individual Capacities

Into every experience each person takes himself—his capacities and limitations, his values and attitudes. This first group of charts illustrates the persistent life situations which each learner faces as he is called upon to develop and use his individual capacities in the experiences of daily living.

Society's general welfare depends, ultimately, upon the degree to which each citizen is helped to live appropriately in his culture. Maximum self-realization of the individual is closely linked with societal welfare. Helping each individual develop maximum use of his own powers is a fundamental democratic value. Attaining this goal involves the individual's total development. To meet the demands of daily living, persons with optimum physical health and emotional stability are needed. These individuals must be persons who can think clearly, who have learned the techniques of a scientific approach to problems, and who have developed the intellectual tools with which to work effectively. If individuals are to draw upon the full resources which make for richness and balanced satisfactions in living, their needs for aesthetic expression and appreciation must be met. In addition, if they are to make consistent and effective judgments in the wide variety of situations they face, individuals must establish their own sets of values, come to decisions regarding the spiritual resources to which they are willing to give allegiance, and learn to use their values as guides in decisions involving moral choice and responsibility.

Some or all of these individual capacities—physical, emotional, intellectual, aesthetic, spiritual—are needed in every experience with which an individual must deal. They are interrelated in many ways. The young child who learns to use recreational reading as a source of enjoyment is satisfying certain physical and emotional health needs. At the same time he is calling upon intellectual skills, finding aesthetic satisfactions in the story and the illustrations, and perhaps making some moral judgments as he identifies with the characters about whom he is reading. At the adult level, the person making decisions on international issues brings a complicated combination of intellectual, emotional, and moral factors into play. Failure to develop fully capacities in any of these areas leads to less effective self-realization and, as a result, to a less adequate contribution to social welfare than is desirable and possible.

To see the total range of persistent problems with which all persons must deal, the recurring life situations involving growth in individual capacities should be studied in relation to those in the two sections which follow—situations involving social participation and those calling for ability to deal with environmental factors and forces. Actually, daily life experiences call for competence in all three areas. Each individual brings to the situations he faces in dealing with his environment the intellectual skills in problem-solving he has been helped to develop, the values he has learned to live by, his own physical and emotional stamina, and his sense of aesthetic appreciation. He also brings his competencies in working with other people. The division of the charts into three major groupings should serve to highlight the variety of problems faced, not to deny the interrelationships. While the actual situation a learner faces is almost always complex, the teacher must be aware of the specific area or areas in which competence and understanding are lacking. As each separate chart in this, and in later sections, is discussed, some of the more important interrelationships with other sections will be pointed out.

Merely achieving a high degree of competence is not enough in developing individual capacities. Each person should understand the processes through which his growth came about so that he will be able to maintain and continue to increase his competence. To be physically well, for example, is only half the problem. A person must know how to maintain his health, be able to act intelligently to recover from an illness, and know what to do to safeguard the health of others. Excellent ability to read must be supplemented with knowledge of how to go about developing the techniques needed in reading new types of materials. High moral standards, acquired through absolute acceptance of the values of others, may not stand the strain of continued pressures unless the individual has been helped to make intelligent appraisal of the bases upon which these standards rest. The desired goal is a person who has effectively developed his individual capacities and who has established sound bases for intelligent action in meeting his own growth needs.

GROWTH IN ABILITY TO MEET HEALTH NEEDS

Health needs involve both individual welfare and the welfare of others —in the family, in other immediate social groups, and in national and world relationships. Even the young child faces situations in which he is called upon to safeguard the health of others. As an adult he faces questions regarding the feeding, clothing, and housing of the peoples of his own and other lands, the provision of adequate medical care for all, the support which should be given to facilitate research in the prevention and control of disease. Today the world implications of human health needs are increasingly clear—peace cannot be maintained in a world in which large groups of people are starving, or are lacking the barest clothing and shelter necessities and drugs for controlling disease. Nor can peace be maintained if people cannot find the good will and the sources of balanced satisfactions in living which make for security in relationships with others.

In the chart which follows, physical and mental health are treated separately. While this may help focus more clearly on specific situations, it should not obscure the interrelationships between the two aspects of the total problem. Physical well-being definitely affects ability to satisfy emotional and social needs. On the other hand, severe emotional tensions, unresolved conflict situations, unsatisfied needs for status in the group or for affectionate relationships with others affect physical functions. Health, in its full meaning, calls for ability to meet both types of situations. Many of the everyday experiences which people face involve persistent problems of both physical and mental health.

Persistent situations calling primarily for ability to meet physiological needs have been grouped separately from those centered around avoiding or caring for illness or injury. There are obviously many interrelationships. Daily life experiences which require using health routines frequently call directly for ability to deal with the persistent problems of meeting food needs, maintaining body temperature, and others related to satisfying physiological needs. The teacher, helping learners face the complex situations of daily life which call for a variety of health routines, identifies and helps to build the understandings demanded by whatever problems related to the meeting of physiological needs are involved in the particular immediate situation. At the same time, he builds such other concepts as the importance of knowing the routines suited to individual needs and the desirability of practicing them regularly. Some overlapping is inevitable when showing a single persistent problem in relation to the immediate activities of daily life in which many other persistent situations are also involved.

The daily life experiences given in this particular chart are related to and involve many persistent situations appearing in other parts of this analysis. For example, experiences with such situations as securing adequate housing and clothing for self or family draw upon several persistent problems in the health area and also upon certain aspects of aesthetic expression and appreciation as well as problems of securing goods and services, providing for social welfare, and using technological resources. Some situations involving ability to meet physiological needs also call for understandings important in dealing with physical phenomena, plant and animal life, physical and chemical forces. Many of the experiences in which the individual strives to satisfy emotional and social needs also call for competence in person-to-person relationships, in group membership, and in intergroup relationships, and at times may even include problems of moral choice and responsibility and of aesthetic expression and appreciation.

The young child faces many situations in which the problem is mainly one of adapting to family and school patterns. Some of the most important learnings at this level come as habits are formed through repeated opportunities to use good health practices. Simple explanations are generally all that are necessary at first. In later childhood and adolescence, many more of the "reasons why" are needed and a much larger measure of understanding of both physiological and psychological processes can be given as the problem demands it and the maturity of the learner makes the information meaningful to him. In later childhood, and more definitely in youth and adulthood, understandings should be expanded beyond individual needs to those basic to safeguarding the health of social groups ranging from the immediate family to the world.

Teachers who must work within rather restricted subject boundaries will still find this chart useful in selecting experiences. The typical situations calling for growth in meeting health needs suggest many problems learners face that require learnings for which teachers of science, health, physical education, and home economics usually strive. When the health needs of individuals involve others, the situations have meaning for the kinds of learnings normally included in social studies. This chart can help the teacher to improve the quality of learning regardless of the curriculum design under which he works.

Some typical situations calling for growth in ability to meet health needs

	EARLY CHILDHOOD	LATER CHILDHOOD
	A. Satisfying Physiological Needs	
MEETING FOOD NEEDS Balancing meals	**Adjusting to family food patterns—** Trying new foods; learning to eat standard family dishes; understanding general reasons for differences in foods eaten by various members of family; discovering general reasons for varied food patterns among one's friends; accepting parental choices in restaurant meals; sharing in mid-morning lunch at school . . .	**Making choices which satisfy individual tastes within family patterns—** Suggesting alternative dishes in family meals; choosing from among kinds of foods in cafeteria; finding reason for school lunchroom regulations regarding choice of food; selecting food for school lunch box; suggesting foods for special occasions; deciding what to eat between meals; choosing candy or other food on which to spend allowance . . .
Knowing and safeguarding nutritional values	**Adjusting to family patterns which safeguard maximum contribution of nutritional elements in foods—**Finding why parents urge drinking milk and eating the varied foods on one's plate; taking adequate amount of time for meals; chewing food well; acting on parent requests to make mealtimes pleasant; helping prepare food on occasion at home or school . . .	**Understanding major nutritional contributions of common foods and helping conserve them—**Asking about meaning of common terms such as vitamin, calorie; finding out about new foods seen in grocery store; selecting items on family grocery list; finding major nutritional contributions of such foods as milk, common vegetables; finding differences in nutritional values of soft drinks and fruit juices; helping to store foods . . .
Conserving food supply	**Sharing in family and school efforts to guard against waste of food—** Taking small helpings and asking for seconds; taking small portions of unfamiliar foods; helping grow vegetable garden; helping apportion mid-morning lunch . . .	**Understanding family and community concerns about food shortages—** Helping grow garden or raise fowl; sharing in school lunchroom plans to prevent food waste; finding what is done to provide food for victims of flood and famine; finding how money collected in local Community Chest or Red Cross drives is used to provide food for needy; discussing measures for assuring quality of foods such as pasteurization, inspection of stores . . .

YOUTH | **ADULTHOOD**

A. Satisfying Physiological Needs

YOUTH

Selecting food to achieve definite physical results—Planning and preparing occasional family meals; preparing meals for young children; helping prepare meals for invalids; following special athletes' diets; considering problems of dieting to maintain attractive personal appearance; deciding whether to adopt food fads of "gang"; selecting refreshments for parties, school banquets . . .

Sharing in family responsibility for identifying nutritional quality of foods and preserving it in food preparation—Interpreting labels of common brands and accepted standards; analyzing advertisements about foods; shopping for fresh fruits or vegetables; finding how to use information from food research and promotional agencies; taking partial responsibility for preparing meals to preserve nutritional values in foods; investigating nutritional differences between canned, frozen, and fresh products; investigating effects of various nutritional elements on health; storing foods . . .

Understanding the issues involved and taking action when possible to safeguard the quality and quantity of food supply—Growing garden; finding how to care for plant and animal life to insure most satisfactory yield; cooperating in emergency food measures for victims of flood and famine; helping preserve foods; discussing purpose of pure-food laws; discussing international plans to provide for nutritional needs of underfed peoples; discussing issues involved in proposals to raise national standards of living . . .

ADULTHOOD

Providing balanced meals in terms of individual needs of those who consume them—Adjusting food choices to personal needs; preparing meals to meet varied family needs; feeding invalids; selecting refreshments for special occasions; deciding when to supplement diet with special nutritional products . . .

Selecting and preparing foods which meet desired nutritional standards—Interpreting brands and labels; interpreting advertising; deciding between fresh, frozen, or canned vegetables; choosing meats; deciding whether to buy products which have vitamins added; deciding whether to buy prepared mixes and other prepared foods; using information from food research and promotional agencies; preparing meals so as to conserve nutritional elements; helping achieve conditions at mealtimes that allow body to make use of full nutritional qualities of foods; arranging appropriate means of storing foods . . .

Acting to safeguard the quantity and quality of national and world food supply—Raising garden or livestock for family or community needs; preserving foods needed for family; cooperating in relief, famine, flood emergencies; studying and voting on pure-food laws; acting upon international plans to provide for nutritional needs of underfed peoples; acting upon proposals to raise national standards of living; taking action on national plans to increase supply of raw foods through subsidies, crop control, experimental farms and the like . . .

	EARLY CHILDHOOD	LATER CHILDHOOD
MEETING NEEDS FOR AIR AND LIGHT Regulating ventilation and lighting	**Carrying out adult decisions as to needs for fresh air and light**—Finding why parents ventilate home; helping regulate ventilation in classroom or home; helping decide when lights are needed; pulling shades when needed; holding book or placing work to secure adequate light . . .	**Finding how and when to provide fresh air and adequate light in situations where personally concerned**—Helping air house or classroom; regulating ventilation in own bedroom; finding how to ventilate room properly; finding why people feel drowsy in poorly ventilated rooms; operating air conditioners in rooms; turning on lights when needed; securing good light for reading; protecting eyes from glare . . .
Adjusting to or controlling air conditions or sunlight in community	**Sharing in home and community provisions for fresh air and sunlight**—Playing out of doors during recess or after school when choice of outdoor activities is desirable; sharing in family picnics, trips; accepting family recommendations to prevent sunburn . . .	**Understanding significant community measures for controlling air conditions and providing sunlight**—Discussing community plans for smoke control; investigating local measures to control air conditions in industrial areas; discussing city planning projects which affect one's family or neighborhood; following city regulations for burning trash; finding how to prevent sunburn; studying or participating in planning park areas, selecting shade trees . . .
MAINTAINING COMFORTABLE BODY TEMPERATURE Selecting appropriate clothing	**Telling when different amounts or kinds of clothing are needed**—Understanding when discomfort is caused by too much or too little clothing; selecting, under guidance, special clothing for rain, cold weather, very warm days; deciding what to wear out to play at recess . . .	**Selecting clothing with regard to activity and temperature conditions**—Selecting appropriate clothing for various types of activities, outdoor play, rainy days; deciding on amount of covering needed when sleeping; finding how and why weight of clothing is adjusted to activity and temperature; finding why parents insist on special clothing after illness, on sweaters after being overheated . . .
Adjusting activity to temperature	**Making simple adjustments to temperature conditions**—Taking adult advice about games on hot days; finding how to keep hands and feet warm on cold days; following adult advice about cooling off after strenuous play . . .	**Choosing activities which take account of temperature conditions, with minimum adult supervision**—Deciding what games to play on very warm days; deciding how to keep warm when outdoors on very cold days; finding how to use cool drinks; bathing appropriately to cool off . . .

YOUTH

Taking responsibility for regulating ventilation and lighting in situations where personally involved—Securing proper ventilation and lighting in home or school rooms; assuming responsibility for ventilation in school auditorium, other places where large crowds are gathered; finding what is involved in building house to assure proper ventilation and light; discovering methods and purposes of air conditioning; investigating new methods of lighting; arranging adequate lighting for reading or work . . .

Understanding issues involved in community measures for control of air and sunlight and cooperating where possible—Investigating slum conditions; understanding issues involved in community measures to provide smoke control, parks and playgrounds, adequate housing; cooperating in community plans to safeguard community needs for fresh air and sunshine; taking responsibility for own welfare in situations when under a hot sun . . .

ADULTHOOD

Regulating ventilation and lighting in home or place of work to meet needs of self and others—Selecting or building house to insure proper ventilation and light; deciding whether to air-condition place of business or home; regulating ventilation and lighting to meet needs of self and members of family when sleeping, at play, at work; helping children learn how to meet their needs for light and air . . .

Acting to safeguard an adequate supply of fresh air and sunlight for self and others—Taking action on community provisions for smoke control; securing adequate play space for children; helping provide summer camp experiences for children; taking action on city planning to separate housing and industrial areas . . .

YOUTH

Selecting clothing in terms of individual needs and social demands—Selecting clothing which will gain social approval and still meet temperature needs—following peer fad in sweaters, socks, while still keeping warm; selecting clothing in terms of weather and projected activities; dressing younger children for various activities and weather conditions; deciding how much bedding is needed for self or younger children; sharing in efforts of local welfare agencies to provide clothing for underprivileged or victims of disaster . . .

Adjusting activity, without supervision, to temperature conditions—Deciding where to take vacation; deciding what time of day to play active sports; planning group activities with reference to temperature; finding how to cool off after strenuous sports . . .

ADULTHOOD

Providing clothing suited to the needs of self and others—Deciding on amount and warmth of clothing for self or children in the light of such factors as kind of activity, temperature, weather, physical condition; deciding how much bedding is needed for various family members; helping children learn to make sound choice of clothing; sharing in community and national plans to supply clothing to those in special need . . .

Adjusting or helping others adjust activity to temperature conditions—Deciding when to plan vacations for self or others; deciding where to take vacation; helping children plan activities for very warm or cold weather; adjusting personal activities to weather conditions . . .

	EARLY CHILDHOOD	LATER CHILDHOOD
Regulating building temperature	**Finding ways of avoiding discomfort caused by room being too warm or too cold**—Knowing when room is too warm or too cool; helping regulate heat in room; reading thermometers; helping decide when classroom temperatures need changing; regulating opening of doors and windows; helping in keeping doors closed, shades lowered, other measures for maintaining room temperature . . .	**Adjusting temperature in rooms where one is at work or at play**—Finding how to tell how warm room should be; reading thermometers; helping parents regulate heating system at home; helping control temperature in classroom; finding how to control drafts in adjusting room temperatures; understanding factors that affect room temperature . . .
Securing housing conditions for achievement of desired temperature	**Observing family and community efforts to provide housing conditions that contribute to desirable temperature**—Watching house in neighborhood being built; watching father put up storm windows; finding how school ventilation system is operated by custodian and when classroom windows must be kept closed . . .	**Helping with family efforts to provide housing conditions which contribute to desirable temperature**—Finding purpose served by systems of insulation in home—helping put on storm windows, weatherstrip doors; finding differences between heating systems of home and school; understanding general principles of air-conditioning systems in use in home or local buildings; finding how community housing projects contribute tc better heating and ventilation . . .
SECURING NEEDED REST AND ACTIVITY Balancing rest and activity	**Securing rest and exercise within family and school facilities**—Seeking physical activity or rest as needed; knowing when tired and in need of rest; taking afternoon nap; following parents' instructions about going to bed; sharing in school rest periods; participating in school play periods; deciding what to play at school and at home . . .	**Selecting activities which meet individual interests within family and school facilities**—Sharing in decisions as to hour of going to bed; helping plan schedule of school day; taking advantage of opportunities in school schedule for relaxation, for activity; finding why parents and others insist on adequate rest and activity; making independent decisions in regard to fatigue and need to rest; planning out-of-school time to secure both active play and quiet activities . . .
Developing needed skills for relaxation and activity	**Experimenting with a variety of ways of securing relaxation and activity**—Throwing and catching balls; running, skipping, jumping; skating; sharing in rhythmic activities; playing in water; learning to find satisfaction in quiet activities such as reading, music, painting, watching television, or listening to radio . . .	**Developing skills basic to meeting needs for rest and activity**—Playing baseball; skating, swimming, skiing; riding bicycle; developing hobbies; experimenting with reading, clay, construction, sewing, music for pleasure and relaxation; learning to play quiet games; discovering when television and radio are relaxing . . .

YOUTH	ADULTHOOD
Helping control temperature in buildings to meet the needs of those using them—Adjusting temperature of room to given activity; taking charge of heating system at home or of measures to keep home cool in summer; deciding on needed temperature of school gymnasium for dances or games; deciding on temperature of classrooms . . .	**Adjusting building temperatures to the needs of those who use them**—Adjusting temperature of home and place of business to purposes for which they are to be used; taking responsibility for heating system in home; adjusting temperatures by means which avoid drafts, other undesirable conditions . . .
Cooperating in home and community actions to secure housing conditions which facilitate the maintaining of desired temperature—Helping insulate home; discussing issues involved in proposed housing projects; investigating methods and purposes of air conditioning; helping parents decide on adequate heating or air-conditioning system for home; discussing possible repercussions of threatened fuel shortage . . .	**Securing housing conditions which facilitate maintaining desired temperature**—Securing necessary construction for adequate control of temperature in home; evaluating proposed housing projects; deciding whether to install air conditioning in home or office; deciding what heating system to use in house or place of business; regulating heating to take account of local and national fuel shortages; deciding whether to support plans that provide for raising housing standards in other nations . . .
Meeting individual rest and activity needs and understanding issues involved in assuring the same to others—Deciding amount of sleep needed, number of nights out; taking responsibility for training routines as member of school team; adjusting routines to unusual demands—securing extra rest when facing unusually active days; discussing purpose of legislation relating to shorter working week . . .	**Providing for balance of rest and activity to meet needs of self and others**—Adjusting amounts of rest and relaxation to physical demands; planning vacations; seeing that children in family secure adequate rest and activity; acting on labor laws regarding shorter working week . . .
Adjusting forms of relaxation and activity in the light of personal and social considerations—Learning to dance; developing increased skills in sports—swimming, sailing, fishing, skating, camping; deciding what school teams to play on; deciding what other active individual and social enterprises to take part in; developing hobbies; extending interests in reading, in forms of aesthetic expression; watching sports . . .	**Adjusting activity and relaxation to age and energy**—Deciding on channels through which to secure exercise—golf, hiking, tennis, fishing; teaching children how to play games; pursuing hobbies; enjoying and helping children to enjoy forms of aesthetic expression; deciding when to use or to help children use radio and television as means of relaxation . . .

	EARLY CHILDHOOD	LATER CHILDHOOD
Securing facilities for relaxation and activity	**Finding sources for play and relaxation within the environment**—Deciding where to keep playthings; using school play facilities; using community playgrounds; finding sources of activity in environment—playing with pets, climbing, playing in sand piles . . .	**Sharing in home and community facilities for relaxation and activity**—Taking responsibility for toys and playroom at home; taking responsible share in using and caring for equipment in community playgrounds; helping equip playground at school or play space at home; deciding which teams or clubs to join; adjusting games to space and numbers playing; making a garden . . .
MEETING SEX NEEDS Establishing appropriate relationships with opposite sex	**Learning to work and play with both sexes**—Helping care for new baby in family; finding where babies come from; asking about physical differences of boys and girls; playing with children of own and opposite sex; adopting role of own sex in games and imitative play; discovering differences in behavior expected of boys and of girls in some situations . . .	**Establishing friendships and working relationships with members of own and opposite sex**—Finding how babies are born; finding reasons for physical differences between boys and girls; deciding when to include members of opposite sex in activities; observing accepted mores regarding behavior of one's own sex . . .
Obtaining constructive social regulations		**Finding implications of parental or press references to social problems**—Asking about reasons for divorce; asking why older brothers or sisters are subject to certain regulations regarding time to be home, places they may go; following parental instructions not to speak to or accompany strangers; asking questions about tabloid reports . . .
GETTING RID OF BODY WASTES Establishing individual routines	**Practicing good habits under adult supervision**—Attending to toileting; helping with baths; bathing and changing clothing after hard play; washing hands after going to toilet, before meals; cooperating with parents when shampooing hair; cleaning nails; brushing teeth regularly . . .	**Taking responsibility for health routines**—Attending to toileting, bathing without supervision; keeping nails and hair clean; finding why body perspires; finding ways in which waste products are eliminated; finding why laxatives are given, why parents insist upon regular bathing . . .

YOUTH	ADULTHOOD
Finding what is involved in making adequate provisions for relaxation and activity and taking responsible share where possible—Helping make school facilities available to other groups; sharing in plans for community playgrounds; organizing or sharing in hiking clubs, teams; discussing plans for community parks; helping with club or church groups for younger children; cooperating with other members of family to provide atmosphere conducive to rest and relaxation; adjusting type of activity to needs of others for rest; helping equip family rumpus room . . .	**Acting to secure home and community facilities for relaxation and activity**—Providing community facilities for recreation for children and adults; organizing clubs and community recreational groups; providing home and community resources for aesthetic expression and appreciation; making playroom or playground at home for children; providing atmosphere conducive to rest and relaxation; providing adequate sleeping quarters for self and children; deciding on beds and other facilities which will give most effective rest . . .
Understanding and dealing with changes in bodily structure and their resulting social implications—Understanding and adjusting to physical changes which occur in one's own and opposite sex; finding what personal hygiene is needed; attracting and holding interest and friendship of opposite sex; deciding on desirable characteristics of a mate; deciding on degree of physical contact with opposite sex acceptable in social situations; deciding whether to marry before going to college or establishing one's own business; finding sources of reliable information when facing problems in this area . . .	**Making socially acceptable adjustments to adult sex roles and needs**—Choosing and making adequate adjustments to mate; making decisions regarding establishment of family; helping children develop wholesome attitudes toward sex; finding reliable sources of help and information in marriage counseling . . .
Understanding general issues regarding social controls of sex relations—Discussing curfews and other laws affecting activities of youth; discussing place of married women in vocational world; discussing implications of divorce laws, birth control, proposals for control of venereal disease; discussing parental and community attitudes toward sex . . .	**Obtaining constructive social regulations**—Deciding whether wife should work; providing socially acceptable outlets for youth—supervised dances, home as center for activities; deciding on dissemination of birth control information; making decisions regarding adequacy of divorce laws, care of unmarried mothers, control of prostitution; working for effective control of venereal disease . . .
Understanding the relation of elimination of wastes to other physiological factors—Taking responsibility for bathing, shampooing hair, manicuring; finding how regular cleansing routines can help prevent acne; using deodorants appropriately; choosing food which helps keep elimination regular; finding what harm may result from too free use of laxatives . . .	**Helping self and others for whom one is responsible to maintain regular and adequate routines**—Maintaining body cleanliness habitually; helping young children develop appropriate habits; finding diets which help maintain regularity; knowing when to consult physician; knowing properties of and when to use various laxatives . . .

	EARLY CHILDHOOD	LATER CHILDHOOD
Securing adequate sanitary facilities	**Learning how to use sanitary facilities properly**—Helping clean bathtub; learning how to flush toilet; learning how to use school sanitary facilities . . .	**Taking full responsibility for proper use of sanitary facilities**—Keeping facilities at home and school clean; helping set up dressing table, mirror in classroom; finding how community provides for sewage disposal . . .

B. Satisfying Emotional and Social Needs

ACHIEVING SECURE RELATIONS WITH OTHERS Establishing affectionate relationships	**Finding sources of affection in family and friends**—Expressing affection for parents; reacting to expressions of affection from parents; establishing affectionate relationships with relatives living in home or with other children in family; making friends in school and neighborhood; sharing parents' affection with new baby, with older children in family . . .	**Building friendships and satisfying need for affectionate relationships**—Distinguishing between ways parents express affection for younger children and those used with oneself; building affectionate relationships with brothers and sisters; establishing friendships with members of peer group; identifying expressions of affection in friends, adults outside of family; establishing friendly relations with teachers and other school personnel; finding sources of affection when home is broken; sharing parents' affection with other children . . .
Achieving status in groups	**Finding ways of contributing to group activities**—Sharing in family activities; sharing in class discussions; taking leadership responsibilities in games; finding ways of using special reading ability, artistic talent, musical ability in interest of group; sharing personal things, interests with group; locating smaller groups within class who have like interests . . .	**Learning ways of taking appropriate responsibility in group situations**—Sharing in family activities and responsibilities; finding ways through which to make contribution to class activities; deciding what share to take in carrying out class project; taking leadership responsibilities in class group; sharing in club or "gang" activities; becoming part of group if physically much larger or smaller; making up for physical defects . . .

YOUTH	ADULTHOOD
Understanding issues involved in and taking action where possible to secure adequate sanitary facilities—Helping parents make needed changes in home facilities; discussing community housing projects; investigating proposed community plans for more adequate sewage disposal . . .	**Acting to secure adequate sanitary facilities for self and others**—Deciding what bathing and toileting facilities are needed in home, schools, places of business; taking action on proposed housing projects designed to provide adequate facilities; taking action on community plans for sewage disposal . . .

B. Satisfying Emotional and Social Needs

YOUTH	ADULTHOOD
Extending the range and quality of friendships and affectionate relationships—Establishing mature patterns in giving and demanding affection from parents; maintaining affectionate relationships with younger members of family; establishing friendships with members of opposite sex; building close friendships with members of one's own sex; deciding what to demand of and offer to "best" friends; establishing new sources of friendship when in college, in new job; deciding what expression of affection to seek from or give to teachers, other adults on whom "crushes" are formed . . .	**Establishing mature and satisfying friendships and affectionate relationships**—Establishing patterns of mutual affection with husband or wife; establishing secure affectionate relationships with children in family; deciding on degree of friendship to expect from friends; deciding whether to share an apartment or living quarters if unmarried; determining what degree of friendship to expect in business relations; determining what degree of friendship to expect from or give to persons in service relationships . . .
Extending ability to use individual capacities to secure group status—Sharing in responsibilities and decisions of family group; deciding whether to seek class office; finding means of participating in all-school activities; making constructive contribution to community groups; adjusting to social, economic, racial, religious, or other factors placing one in minority group; accepting and playing one's appropriate sex role; helping members of minority groups achieve status . . .	**Helping self and others to secure status in a variety of groups**—Playing satisfying role in family group; making constructive contribution to community group; finding status satisfactions in one's job; adjusting and helping children adjust to minority group problems; helping colleagues or other group members achieve status needs; helping children find means through which to make positive contribution to family group, to school group, to church and social groups . . .

	EARLY CHILDHOOD	LATER CHILDHOOD
MAKING CONSTRUCTIVE USE OF EMOTIONS Achieving constructive expression of emotions	**Exploring acceptable ways of expressing emotions**—Finding ways to express anger, annoyance without hurting self or others; expressing pleasure, sorrow, anger, or fear in words so that others can understand; finding ways to express affection for family and friends; learning to take positive steps to control a situation—making new plans instead of crying if disappointed, getting acquainted with objects of which one is afraid . . .	**Developing constructive channels through which to express emotions**—Using words instead of actions to express emotions; knowing what to do when teased; finding what steps to take to get help when worried, afraid; making positive proposals when plans are upset; expressing friendship, affection, and pleasure in ways that are satisfying to oneself and acceptable to others; deciding when to express and when to inhibit emotions . . .
Securing balanced satisfactions	**Finding sources of emotional satisfaction in daily activities**—Sharing exciting stories, pictures with others; finding sources of pleasure in games, other social activities; exploring paint, clay, wood, and other media; finding sources of interest in the natural environment; enjoying friends and family; sharing musical experiences—songs, singing games, records, rhythms, toy instruments . . .	**Learning to use varied sources of emotional satisfaction**—Finding satisfying games to play with friends; choosing radio, television, and motion-picture programs; exploring sources of pleasure in books; collecting things; satisfying intellectual curiosity through reading, experimenting; helping make classrooms or clubrooms pleasant places in which to work; exploring sources of satisfaction in forms of aesthetic expression; getting satisfaction out of work well done . . .
ACHIEVING SELF-DIRECTION Adjusting to personal strengths and weaknesses	**Becoming aware of individual strengths and weaknesses**—Finding activities one does well, others in which skills are needed; learning how to respond in situations in which one excels, is less able; finding that other children differ in the kinds of work they do, the way they react; learning to tell when tired and needing rest; finding what activities can be engaged in if one has a physical defect; accepting help from parents or others in situations difficult to master . . .	**Finding ways of using or adjusting to individual capacities**—Making effective use of special abilities—skill in sports, use of hands in construction; evaluating effectiveness of one's contribution to class group; identifying activities in which one can give leadership, those in which to follow or accept help; planning for special help in school work; deciding whether to volunteer athletic, musical, artistic ability to group; finding ways of sharing in activities in spite of poor vision, hearing, very small size, overly large size, other difficulties . . .

YOUTH	ADULTHOOD
Extending ability to control and direct emotions—Disagreeing with parents and others without becoming annoyed or upset; finding ways of achieving constructive solutions in situations which cause anger, worry; expressing joy, affection, friendship in more mature fashion; appraising group mores for expressing emotions; establishing mature patterns in giving and demanding affection from parents; judging when to express and when to inhibit emotions; discovering dangers of alcohol or drugs as temporary escape from a problem . . .	**Achieving constructive and mature expression of emotions**—Achieving satisfying emotional relationships with husband or wife and children; deciding what expressions of affection to give and expect from others, including children; taking constructive positive action when emotionally disturbed; helping children overcome fears; helping children achieve satisfying and acceptable expressions of emotions; appraising social issues involved in use of alcohol and drugs as means of emotional release; knowing when to seek professional help in attaining emotional balance . . .
Extending the range of constructive sources of emotional satisfaction—Learning how to dance, participate in other social activities; pursuing hobbies; appraising sources of spiritual expression offered by churches; finding aesthetic satisfactions in decorating own room, in helping family decorate home; exploring school and community resources for aesthetic expression; discovering wider uses of reading as source of emotional satisfaction; discovering emotional satisfactions in doing a job well; exploring sources of emotional satisfaction in the natural environment; deciding whether to seek excitement through disobeying parents, through "illegal" activities with friends . . .	**Using constructive sources of emotional satisfaction**—Providing sources of emotional satisfaction for self and family; identifying emotional satisfactions in a vocation, in activities with social groups; finding sources of emotional satisfaction in books, television, radio, motion pictures; establishing mature sources of spiritual and aesthetic satisfaction; pursuing hobbies; helping children establish hobbies and special interests; securing and helping children secure time for individual activities; establishing satisfying personal contacts with colleagues, community groups; using and helping children to use recreational facilities in community . . .
Growing in ability to use individual capacities—Choosing vocation which will provide best use of one's ability; deciding whether academic records indicate ability to succeed in college; planning high school course to develop academic strengths or care for weaknesses; deciding whether to attempt special musical, literary, artistic, athletic career; deciding which activities of student council to help with; finding ways of social participation in spite of physical or intellectual defects; finding ways of dressing to minimize physical peculiarities; recognizing and adjusting to limitations in health and strength; helping those who have disabilities to participate in activities . . .	**Making constructive use of individual capacities**—Deciding what vocation will make best use of one's capacities; deciding which special talents to use for personal and group satisfactions; deciding what level of perfection to demand of oneself in special fields; identifying areas in which special help from others should be sought; deciding what level of perfection to expect from children; adjusting balance of rest and activity to capacities; adjusting to other persons whose capacities are different from one's own; selecting activities which allow for physical, intellectual, or other shortcomings; helping children make constructive use of strengths and weaknesses . . .

	EARLY CHILDHOOD	LATER CHILDHOOD
Dealing with success and failure	**Finding ways of meeting successes and disappointments**—Deciding what to do when favorite doll or toy breaks; reacting when parents or others praise, compliment, or criticize one; deciding what to do if an object being made does not turn out right; reacting to parental restrictions, school regulations; being helped to understand death of parent, friend, pet; making other plans if bad weather spoils class picnic . . .	**Learning how to plan next steps after meeting success and failure**—Responding to commendation and criticism; reacting in situations where leadership responsibility or other special recognition is given; deciding what steps to take if special plans do not work out; deciding how to proceed when someone destroys partially completed job; deciding what to do when plan fails because of lack of skills; adjusting to death of member of immediate family . . .
Making choices and resolving conflict situations	**Learning what is involved in making simple choices**—Choosing between two toys; deciding whether to spend allowance now or save it until end of week; deciding whether to save candy for oneself or give part of it to friend; deciding whether or not to touch cookie jar when mother is away; deciding free-time activities to undertake in school; finding how parents or others can help think through a problem . . .	**Finding how to identify major issues in a situation and what sources of help to use**—Choosing between two things one wants very much; deciding what to do in situation when one is afraid or worried; choosing between activities which the "gang" wants to do and those which parent wants; deciding when to seek parental or other adult help; finding how to analyze elements in problem when additional information is needed before making decision . . .

C. Avoiding and Caring for Illness and Injury

AVOIDING ILLNESS Practicing desirable health routines	**Practicing simple routines under adult guidance**—Eating the variety of foods set before one; adjusting to parent requests for unhurried and pleasant meals; taking responsibility under supervision for bathing, washing hands; going to bed on time; adjusting amount of clothing as needed; moving to better light, holding book at proper angle when reading; cooperating with school nurse or physician during physical examination . . .	**Practicing and finding reasons back of health routines**—Deciding what and how much to eat; finding why parents and others insist on adequate rest and activity; being responsible for bathing, other regular routines; finding why parents insist on sweaters after active play; taking responsibility for appropriate clothing; finding what lighting is needed for reading; finding why different kinds of shoes are recommended for various activities; measuring growth in height and weight; discussing results of physical examination . . .

YOUTH	ADULTHOOD
Extending ability to make constructive plans in situations involving success and failure—Reacting after losing or winning school election; deciding what to say to opposing team after winning or losing game; planning next steps when plans have not worked; deciding what to do if girl or boy friend goes off with someone else; reacting when classmates or others compliment or criticize one on job done; reacting when special talents bring popular acclaim; balancing personal standards and group approval in evaluating success or failure; setting realistic levels of aspiration . . .	**Making constructive use of success and failure**—Establishing bases for judging success and failure; evaluating progress toward one's goal; deciding what steps to take after losing job, business deal, after other plans fail; reacting when circumstances or talent bring unusual success; adjusting and helping children adjust to death in family; helping children set realistic levels of aspiration . . .
Developing increased ability to identify issues and use appropriate sources in making choices—Appraising one's bases in making a moral decision; examining bases on which decisions regarding other racial and religious groups are made; discussing how propaganda influences decisions; appraising family and community mores as guides for making decisions; locating and evaluating sources of guidance outside of home—church, youth groups, citizens in community . . .	**Using reasoned decisions to determine action in conflict situations**—Identifying personal goals and values that are inherent in a choice situation; finding which issues have to be faced before making decision; deciding how one's personal philosophy and values influence one's decision; deciding when to ask someone for assistance; deciding whether to act upon advice given; helping children determine bases on which they are making decisions . . .

C. Avoiding and Caring for Illness and Injury

YOUTH	ADULTHOOD
Taking responsibility for personal health practices—Choosing diets that will maintain proper weight, improve complexion; choosing cosmetics with regard for effects on health; taking responsibility for shampooing, manicuring, regular bathing; choosing clothing appropriate to health needs; planning amounts of exercise; adjusting lighting to activity; choosing shoes appropriate to various activities; acting upon results of physical examination; examining health problems involved in use of alcohol, tobacco; discussing effects of narcotics, alcohol, tobacco . . .	**Taking responsibility for health practices of self and others under one's care**—Choosing balanced diets for self and others; choosing proper shoes for children; helping children select proper clothing; providing adequate lighting in home; providing adequate heating, ventilation, bathing facilities in home; having periodic medical examination, providing for health examination of children; deciding on extent of use of alcohol, tobacco; taking action on legislation regarding narcotics . . .

	EARLY CHILDHOOD	LATER CHILDHOOD
Providing for disease control	**Discovering personal and general community provision for disease control**—Remembering to wash hands before meals; using handkerchief; covering coughs and sneezes; helping keep toilets and washrooms clean; co-operating with doctor in being vaccinated and given other inoculations; finding why one cannot play with child who has contagious disease, why school nurse examines those who have been exposed to a disease; helping kill flies; keeping screen doors closed . . .	**Finding how germs and viruses are carried and sharing responsibility for the control of disease**—Finding why hands should be washed before meals, why fingers and pencils should not be put in mouth, why other children's handkerchiefs should not be borrowed; finding general purposes of disinfectants, other common means of destroying germs; discussing purposes of vaccination, inoculation, quarantine, or isolation; finding why raw fruits and vegetables are washed before being eaten, why some foods must be well cooked, why some foods in stores are covered; finding why parents buy pasteurized milk; disposing of garbage properly in home or on picnics; helping eliminate breeding places of flies and mosquitoes . . .
AVOIDING ACCIDENTS Using safety measures	**Finding how to use simple safety controls in home and community**—Following adults' advice on how to use matches, knives, hammers, saws; finding safe places to play; following adult restrictions regarding stoves, electric cords; taking precautions in approaching strange animals; finding why one cannot handle contents of medicine chest; playing and working with other children safely; handling scissors, pencil, chair properly; obeying traffic regulations . . .	**Using safety controls in situations where personally involved**—Using tools; riding bicycle in traffic; using other means of transportation safely; taking precautions around stove, in helping serve hot dishes, in replacing lights; finding safe place to play; taking care of younger children; finding what precautions to take when swimming, skating, walking on slippery streets; recognizing poisonous plants; practicing reasonable precautions in active games . . .
Providing needed safety measures	**Helping parents and others take needed safety measures**—Picking up toys, helping decide where to keep playthings; putting away tools in proper place; helping to decide where to keep scissors, other sharp objects; understanding what fire department does; participating in fire drills . . .	**Understanding purpose of home and community safety measures**—Helping eliminate common hazards in home and school; finding why various community regulations are enforced; helping plan steps to take in school and home in case of fire; helping family plan ways of protecting younger children from accident; acting as safety guard; finding where to get help in time of emergency . . .

YOUTH	ADULTHOOD
Understanding and cooperating in home and community efforts toward germ control—Taking precautions to keep from spreading a cold; helping with family precautions in case of contagious disease; finding why regular medical examinations are recommended; helping keep home clean—sterilizing dishes, disposing of garbage; preparing and caring for food; helping keep school and public buildings clean; helping enforce community measures to insure unadulterated food supply; discussing reasons for government regulations on foods; cooperating in drives to control flies and mosquitoes; discussing reasons for laws requiring health examinations for certain types of workers; investigating news reports of work of local health department and similar state and national agencies to protect health . . .	**Taking responsibility for germ control for self and others in home and community**—Deciding when to have children vaccinated or inoculated; teaching children proper health routines; maintaining adequate operation of septic tanks and drinking wells; taking appropriate precautions in cases of contagious diseases; providing for community garbage and sewage disposal; using proper precautions in preparing and caring for food; evaluating work of public health officials; supporting government regulations to insure unadulterated food supplies . . .
Taking responsibility for safety controls in situations where personally involved—Driving car; obeying traffic regulations; driving tractor, using other farm implements; finding how to keep injury to minimum in active sports; providing precautions needed in caring for young children at home, on community playgrounds, at camp; obeying safety regulations relating to activities on part-time job; using tools and machines at home and school . . .	**Taking responsibility for using safety controls in home and community**—Taking needed precautions when driving car; deciding where to keep tools; using kerosene, gasoline with proper safeguards; deciding where to keep poisons; teaching children how to use tools, to play safely; helping children develop needed precautions with fire, boiling water, gas, electricity; using safety measures needed in occupation; using and helping children use adequate precautions in swimming, skating . . .
Taking proportionate responsibility in providing needed safety measures in home and community—Removing hazards in home or school; finding what is involved in community efforts to lower occupational hazards, provide fire protection, provide safe play space for children; understanding need for traffic enforcement; understanding how to contact appropriate community agencies in time of emergency; cooperating in civil defense plans . . .	**Providing needed safety measures in home and community**—Surveying home to eliminate common sources of accident; taking adequate precautions with articles in medicine chest; providing adequate fire protection in home; providing safe play space for children; considering adequacy of community fire, flood protection; taking action on legislation to provide safety measures in community, in industry; sharing in civil defense efforts . . .

	EARLY CHILDHOOD	LATER CHILDHOOD
CARING FOR PHYSICAL DEFECTS Correcting or adjusting to defects	**Adjusting to family and school requirements in caring for defects—** Understanding why some people wear glasses, hearing aids, braces; remembering to wear glasses; cooperating with dentist, physician, physiotherapists, persons giving special help with speech; following mother's advice as to amount and kind of activity after illnesses; learning to share in family or school activities in spite of physical handicaps . . .	**Understanding reasons for and cooperating in correction of defects—** Taking responsibility for wearing glasses if needed; adjusting position in classroom to need for better vision or hearing; adjusting to and accepting need for braces on teeth or limbs; finding why parents insist on visits to dentist; working with correctionists to remedy speech defect, physical disability; finding why different kinds of shoes are recommended to correct foot weaknesses; finding why some kinds of activities are not allowed after certain illnesses; contributing to group activities despite serious handicaps; learning how to be helpful to other children who have defects . . .
CARING FOR ILLNESS OR INJURY Providing first aid	**Getting help for self or others when injured—**Going to teacher, parents, or school nurse with cuts, burns, bruises; going for help when others are injured . . .	**Giving first aid for simple injuries—** Finding general methods of treating cuts; finding what to do for burns; caring for insect bites; understanding general uses of disinfectants; finding how to treat poison ivy; caring for frostbite; knowing when and where to go for help; telling others what kind of help is likely to be needed . . .
Providing care in time of illness	**Cooperating when self or members of family are ill—**Learning to tell mother or teacher when feeling ill; adjusting to routines of illness; playing quietly when someone in home is ill . . .	**Finding what kind of cooperation is needed when self or members of family are ill—**Finding how to behave in sickroom; helping prepare meals for sick person; finding why one is not allowed certain foods when ill; carrying out physician's recommendations; finding why certain medicines must be taken; finding why special precautions are taken with contagious diseases; finding what kinds of care are provided in hospital and clinic . . .

YOUTH	ADULTHOOD
Making necessary correction of or adjustments to physical defects in ways which are socially acceptable—Securing popular style of glasses; buying shoes that are corrective, yet attractive; taking responsibility for regular visits to dentist; taking responsibility for continued practice for speech correction, physiotherapy; finding what community provisions are made for correcting defects of children; buying clothing which minimizes physical defects; finding channels through which to become accepted in social group in face of physical defects which cannot be corrected; helping handicapped person gain group acceptance . . .	**Securing adequate correction of or adjustment to physical defects for self and others**—Securing needed corrections for personal defects; providing for correction of physical defects in young children; helping children adjust to serious defects; helping children learn to accept and make the best of corrective measures—wear glasses, use hearing aid; acting on proposals to provide additional medical or dental care in schools, for other community groups; helping secure adequate school provisions for children with special handicaps, community provisions for older handicapped persons . . .
Giving adequate first aid when needed—Treating self or others when injured in home or in games; treating insect bites, poison ivy; giving emergency care to serious cuts; caring for persons who faint; packing first-aid kit for camp or hikes; finding what major precautions should be taken in giving preliminary care to person who is seriously injured; securing training needed to give first aid at camp, on hikes, in other emergencies . . .	**Giving or providing for adequate first aid for self or others**—Giving emergency care to children; providing first-aid equipment in home, school, or car; giving emergency help in traffic accidents; knowing ways of meeting emergencies likely to arise in one's home, in one's occupation; acting on measures to provide adequate emergency care in one's occupation, for others in community . . .
Sharing in providing care in time of illness—Recognizing symptoms of illness; giving home care in minor illnesses; taking temperatures; preparing meals for persons who are ill; using medical care provided in school as needed; sharing in drive to build new hospital; discussing newspaper reports of needs to make medical care more widely available in community; considering work of doctor or nurse as a vocation; finding how to evaluate patent medicines; knowing when and how to take drugs without prescriptions; evaluating advertising related to health and medicines . . .	**Securing or providing adequate care for self and others in time of illness**—Recognizing symptoms of illness in self or others; deciding when to call doctor; using various community health services; following doctor's orders in caring for self or children during minor illnesses; voting on proposals to increase school medical services, to provide for medical care of workmen, to increase amount of medical service in community; participating in plans to provide adequate hospitalization; knowing what drugs to use without prescription; knowing how to evaluate patent medicines and articles about health . . .

GROWTH IN ABILITY TO USE INTELLECTUAL POWER

Persistent life situations calling for growth in ability to use fundamental intellectual skills are present in every daily life activity. This can be clearly seen in the numerous times when skill in making ideas clear or in understanding the ideas of others is needed. Effective methods of work are required at every point in carrying out individual or group activities. Quantitative relationships also are involved in many situations. Almost every daily life experience listed elsewhere in this analysis could have been repeated here. In selecting items for this chart, emphasis is on those which would most clearly identify the variety of techniques and skills involved in using intellectual power.

In a world where cooperative relationships are essential, ability to present a point of view clearly, to take part in discussions, to understand and evaluate the ideas of others becomes crucial. Use of quantitative relationships is important, not only in many immediate situations where effective living requires ability to balance a budget or to understand the benefits from insurance or annuity plans, but also in world relationships involving international loans, the relation of tariffs to international trade, and many other situations. Effective methods of work—planning, using appropriate resources to set up satisfactory working conditions, using a scientific approach to the study of situations—are basic if sound solutions to problems are to be reached, whether they are local, national, or world-wide in scope.

The situations which follow point up the close relationship between the daily life experiences calling for ability to make ideas clear and those calling for understanding the ideas of others. However, the skills needed do not necessarily develop together. A child may clearly understand what an author has written or what an adult tells him, yet be unable to explain it to others. An equally close relationship exists among the several situations within the category of dealing with quantitative relationships and among those in the category of using effective methods of work, although each situation listed for the given category calls for a different set of skills. The persistent situations calling for distinct skills have been considered separately, therefore, even though many of the same problems of daily living may be repeated in identifying the experiences in which these skills are needed.

Two interrelationships with other charts should be noted here. The problems of determining standards adequate for the job to be done and of providing working conditions which make for the greatest efficiency belong both under the general heading of using effective methods of work in this chart and under the section on achieving effective workmanship under earning a living in the chart on economic-social-political structures and forces. Because of their importance in the latter area, they are placed there and are not included in this chart. Certain daily experiences under participating in organized education also are closely related to the present section, but are not included here.

The complexity of the immediate situation faced is the teacher's clue to the nature and degree of skill that must be developed. For example, the young child needs mainly the techniques basic to expressing his own opinion in informal group discussions. Somewhat older children face situations where it is important to keep to the point, to give others a turn, to evaluate the suggestions of others. Here, and more particularly at adolescence, it becomes important to know how to conduct a meeting, to secure the contributions of all members in the group, to resolve differences and reach conclusions. The adult must be effective in a still wider variety of discussion situations—in the family group, the club, the political meeting, Congress. In helping the learner develop his ability to meet persistent problems in this area, the teacher builds in terms of the demands of the new situation.

Here again, teachers working under a curriculum organized by subjects can find help, although growth in ability to use intellectual power actually involves all teachers regardless of subjects. The skills and understandings indicated in the situations in this chart have particular meaning for the English or language arts, business education, and mathematics teachers. Such typical situations as those under making oral presentations, expressing ideas in written form, or expressing ideas in graphic form can be helpful to all teachers who are concerned with communicating ideas and are of particular value to those who teach English. While the typical situations illustrating the use of quantitative relationships do not specify topics as they are found in the usual textbooks, the skills and understandings required are those which mathematics teachers try to develop. Business education and science teachers will find leads in such problems as making exact computations and solving practical problems. At the elementary school level, the situations in this chart have direct implications for the so-called fundamental skills. However, many of the daily life activities will be identified as arising during other activities, especially those related to social studies, science, or health.

Some typical situations calling for growth in ability to use intellectual power

A. Making Ideas Clear

	EARLY CHILDHOOD	LATER CHILDHOOD
USING LANGUAGE TO COMMUNICATE IDEAS Contributing to informal discussions and conversations	**Telling ideas and simple experiences to informal groups**—Sharing experiences with class members; expressing opinion in class discussions; planning how to carry out a project with three or four other children; talking over plans for work with teacher; taking message to principal or to another teacher; telling members of family about school, special interests; persuading parents to allow favors; persuading other children to share toys, participate in games; conversing with visitors in home or classroom; acquiring more effective vocabulary and basic habits of grammatical correctness; acquiring basic understanding of need to take turns, to listen to others . . .	**Building techniques of give-and-take in discussion and conversation**—Contributing to a variety of class discussions; leading or participating in class committee work; presenting own or class point of view to student council, to all-school committees; sharing experiences and interests with peers and adults; asking for what one wants in shopping; serving as member of panel; sharing in family discussions; sharing in conversation at family dinner table; talking with visitors; making introductions; telephoning friends; telephoning for information; acquiring standard forms of grammatical correctness; acquiring basic skills of effective give-and-take in discussion . . .
Making oral presentations	**Making simple announcements and reports**—Telling class group about interesting experiences; presenting proposals for activities to group; telling class what a special committee has done; making an announcement to another class; explaining new game to friends; explaining class plans to parents, visitors; telling a story; reading notices or favorite books to others; learning to speak clearly and distinctly in informal class situations . . .	**Building basic techniques of simple oral presentations**—Presenting results of special study to class; explaining procedures and results of science experiment or some other activity requiring clear directions; reviewing a new book; presenting class proposal to student council; reporting committee or student council plans; making announcements to other classes; announcing cast and scenes of class play; making short speeches as candidate for school office; reading minutes of meeting; giving clear directions; preparing notes for use in oral presentation; reading factual material aloud; reading or telling stories to own class or to other groups; learning to speak with pleasing voice and manner before small audience . . .

YOUTH	ADULTHOOD

A. Making Ideas Clear

Extending techniques for participating in a variety of situations involving discussion and conversation—Taking part in class discussions; sharing in student council discussions; acting as discussion chairman; chairing or participating in formal meetings; chairing or acting as panel member; acting as member of debating team; using telephone appropriately for variety of purposes; interviewing school visitors; being interviewed for job; acting as salesman in part-time job; acting as host at class tea, dinner, parties at home; adjusting conversation to varied situations and age levels; acquiring insights into more complex problems of grammatical usage; acquiring techniques needed to play a variety of roles in group discussion effectively; acquiring techniques needed to meet many of these same problems when conversing in another language . . .

Using techniques of discussion and conversation appropriate to the situation—Discussing family problems; helping children share in family discussions; taking appropriate share in conversation at social events; acting as host in varied situations; guiding conversation at family dinner table; selling or conversing with salesmen; acting as counselor or guidance worker for friends, children; taking part in town meetings; chairing or participating in meetings requiring parliamentary order; interviewing or being interviewed for positions, other purposes; participating in committee work; leading forum or panel discussion; conversing with reasonable efficiency in another language . . .

Extending ability to use oral presentation effectively for a variety of purposes—Reporting results of research or reading done independently or by committee; taking part in school speakers' bureau; making campaign speeches in school elections; presenting council proposal to younger children in school; reading minutes of class or council meeting; chairing or participating in all-school assemblies; taking part in a youth service in church; representing school as panel member on television or radio presentation, or at meeting of local organization; telling stories to younger members of family, camp, or church school groups; reading materials aloud effectively for wide variety of purposes; acquiring poise, manner, and methods of presentation appropriate for a variety of audience situations . . .

Adjusting the nature of oral presentations to a variety of situations—Making political speeches; presenting reports of delegated responsibilities to clubs, committees; giving lectures; making formal reports of work at end of term of office; presenting papers to social group, literary society; talking to children's groups, to clubs, to special vocational groups; helping launch Red Cross, Community Chest drives; taking part in radio or television programs; giving needed explanations or directions as teacher, supervisor, floor manager; telling stories to children; reading aloud to children and others . . .

	EARLY CHILDHOOD	LATER CHILDHOOD
Expressing ideas in written form	**Using simple forms of written expression**—Writing letters or get-well cards to child who is ill; writing thank-you letters to friends, relatives; sharing in writing variety of records of class experiences; helping make simple class newspaper; writing simple stories or poems; helping write announcements for class bulletin board; writing captions to pictures and needed classroom signs; labeling an exhibit; finding how to write manuscript, cursive styles; learning basic punctuation and capitalization skills; developing basic spelling skills . . .	**Developing techniques basic to common forms of written expression**—Writing committee reports, announcements for bulletin board, summary for notebook; helping keep class records of rules, safety precautions, others; making notes on materials read; writing book report; making simple bibliography; writing directions for a game, for special use of science equipment, for care of library books; writing business letters for information, other purposes; writing friendly letters, thank-you notes, invitations; taking minutes for class or council meeting; writing stories, poems; helping publish school paper; making simple outline of plans for a report, a story; learning to use advanced rules of punctuation, paragraphing, and other appropriate instruments of expression . . .
USING MEDIA OTHER THAN LANGUAGE TO EXPRESS IDEAS Using graphic forms to express ideas	**Using pictorial forms of expression**—Drawing pictures to illustrate a story; illustrating records of class activities; writing rebus stories or letters; making simple weather chart; doing cartoons to illustrate safety or other rules; drawing get-well cards, other greeting cards; making simple bar graphs, other diagrams to show results of science experiments, number of books read, other information about class activities . . .	**Understanding the uses of common forms of graphic expression**—Presenting facts in simple tabular, graph, or chart form; using postcards, pictures, photographs as illustrative materials; using opaque projector as aid in committee report; developing simple classroom exhibit; using dioramas to illustrate report; making historical time lines; making and using maps; making frieze or mural; making posters or cartoons to advertise class project; keeping weather map; developing basic understanding of how to make graphic forms effective . . .

YOUTH	ADULTHOOD
Extending the range and variety of uses of written expression—Writing more extensive papers or committee reports based on reading; taking notes from a variety of sources to solve problem; outlining in detail plans for a paper or committee report; making an extensive and accurate bibliography; writing friendly and business letters appropriate to wide variety of situations; filling in forms requesting personal data; writing an order, letters of application; developing more effective style in writing stories, poetry; writing announcements, reports, stories for school paper, magazine; acquiring skill with correct forms of usage, manuscript style appropriate for advanced writing problems; using knowledge of grammar and rules of usage to proofread . . .	**Using forms of written expression appropriate to a variety of situations**—Writing informal letters to friends; writing appropriate business letters; replying to letters asking for specific information; writing letters to paper, to congressmen; writing papers for a professional group; writing announcements of group activities to be posted or published in paper; filling in applications, other forms; choosing appropriate language in writing directions for young children; reporting research; writing short stories; acting as newspaper correspondent; using effectively those forms of correct usage appropriate to writing task at hand; using effectively such aspects of format and organization as paragraph heads, summaries, special type, or spacing; using footnotes and quotations accurately in technical writing . . .
Extending the range of uses and variety of forms of graphic expression—Illustrating class paper, school magazine; using cartoons to express an opinion; using diagrams to explain a game; preparing appropriate tables, graphs, or charts to express factual data; using murals or friezes to summarize information; using a variety of projections of maps; using film or slides as aids in a presentation; developing more complex time lines or other devices for summarizing related facts; developing bulletin-board displays to advance school projects; planning advertising campaign for school projects; developing increased skill in selecting and using forms of graphic presentation for maximum effectiveness . . .	**Using forms of graphic expression appropriate to a variety of purposes**—Using cartoons, diagrams, chalk talks to clarify presentation; using appropriate graphs or tables in presenting factual reports; using appropriate maps to illustrate geographical relationships; developing floor plans and architectural blueprints; helping plan and use documentary motion pictures; collecting and using color slides to illustrate talks about trips or hobbies; planning appropriate advertising . . .

	EARLY CHILDHOOD	LATER CHILDHOOD
Using aesthetic forms to express ideas	**Experimenting with a variety of aesthetic forms of expression**—Expressing ideas through singing and rhythmic activities; dramatizing favorite story; saying favorite rhymes in chorus; putting on puppet show; setting favorite poems to music; choosing music to accompany rhythms, dramatization; experimenting with variety of musical instruments . . .	**Exploring a wide variety of uses of aesthetic forms of expression**—Using hands, facial expressions to help make point clear; securing effective scenery, costuming for a play; planning sequence of dance activities to express a story; experimenting with pantomime, shadow plays, as forms of expression; developing dramatizations with puppets; finding which musical instruments and what type of music are appropriate to various kinds of expression; making models; experimenting with choral speaking; developing basic skills in judging forms of expression appropriate for specific purposes . . .

B. Understanding the Ideas of Others

READING Using appropriate reading approach	**Interpreting simple stories and informational materials**—Enjoying simple stories in readers or library books; reading bulletin-board notices, class records, other classroom informational materials; reading simple informational books; following directions for use of library corner, class plans, other types of directions; reading traffic signs and other school and community notices; enjoying stories and information in children's magazines or newspapers; developing skills in word analysis that increase ability to read independently; developing ability to read independently; developing ability to read increasingly complex materials with comprehension; reading at adequate rate for material being read; developing ability to make simple evaluations of materials read; using oral reading to share stories or information; developing understanding of need to vary reading techniques with purposes . . .	**Developing the reading techniques necessary for varied purposes and materials**—Enjoying library books, children's magazines, wide variety of fictional and factual materials for recreational reading; reading precise directions when carrying out science experiments, cooking, following class plans; making independent use of textbooks and a variety of reference books to locate information; reading children's newspapers and magazines; following news and special features in daily paper; skimming to locate desired information; taking notes on reading for special project; developing stock of word meanings and word-analysis skills necessary for independent reading of technical vocabulary of informational materials; developing increased skill in adjusting reading techniques flexibly to problem at hand; reading effectively in audience situations; evaluating reading materials critically in terms of specific purposes . . .

YOUTH	ADULTHOOD
Making appropriate use of a variety of aesthetic forms of expression—Experimenting with dance as a form of expression; increasing in ability to use manner and gestures to assist voice in oral presentations; acting in plays; using music, drama in school assembly program to launch a special cause; taking part in community rallies, celebration of national holidays; helping select appropriate music for variety of school occasions; dramatizing group efforts at creative writing; using choral speaking as a form of presentation; developing greater insight into when and how to use various forms of expression for maximum effectiveness . . .	**Selecting, combining, and adjusting a variety of aesthetic forms of expression appropriate to a given situation**—Sharing in dramatic productions; deciding what gestures, facial expressions will most appropriately convey sense of a story, other oral presentation; helping with church services, club or other uses of ritual; planning pageants or use of music and drama at community meetings; arranging entertainment for children or friends; considering appropriateness of motion pictures, plays, for various age levels . . .

B. Understanding the Ideas of Others

YOUTH	ADULTHOOD
Building the techniques needed to read a wide variety of materials critically—Becoming acquainted with a variety of literary styles—classics, modern prose, many types of poetry, biography, scientific writing—as sources of recreational reading; using variety of resources for information on a single problem; making independent use of variety of textbooks as reference aids; locating accurate information in daily paper; interpreting editorials, other articles representing personal opinions; following complex written directions; interpreting advertising; adjusting silent reading techniques effectively for purpose; reading to appreciate cadence and rhythm of poetry and prose; adjusting reading rate to secure accuracy in reading directions, figures, details; using effective standards in evaluating informational material; acquiring advanced technical vocabulary of special subject fields; participating through oral reading in variety of audience situations; acquiring ability to read another language . . .	**Adjusting reading approach to a variety of purposes and materials**—Enjoying a wide range of recreational reading materials; reading technical information in trade or professional magazines; evaluating information in daily paper and other current news publications; doing independent reading needed as background for an extensive piece of research; evaluating advertising; evaluating materials produced for propaganda purposes; evaluating editorials and other statements of personal opinions; reading instructions for completing income tax blanks, filling in other complex forms; helping children select appropriate recreational reading; building home library . . .

	EARLY CHILDHOOD	LATER CHILDHOOD
Using source materials	**Using simple source materials**—Using tables of contents to help locate story; using indexes to locate information; discovering purposes of children's encyclopedia; using picture or simple dictionary for word meanings; using several books, under guidance, to locate information on single problem; using textbooks in skill areas or in subject fields as resource materials; becoming acquainted with school or public library; investigating types of resource materials in classroom library; developing skill with alphabetical order; finding purposes of chapter titles, other aspects of format of materials read; discovering how to use pictures or simple diagrams to help interpret accompanying reading material . . .	**Building techniques for independent use of common source materials**—Using catalog system in school or local library; using dictionary efficiently; locating information efficiently in children's or adult encyclopedia; using atlas; using one or more standard textbooks as resources for specific problem; understanding special contributions of wide variety of other types of resource materials—almanacs, special types of magazines, government pamphlets, industrial and labor organization bulletins; using such reference aids as table of contents and index efficiently; using such standard aids to readers as chapter summaries, section and paragraph headings, illustrations or rules in heavy print; reading special symbols of various subject fields—arithmetic signs, diacritical marks; using maps, tables, graphs, and other visual aids in interpreting content; reading telephone directories, store directories; timetables; evaluating accuracy of information located and its appropriateness to problem at hand . . .
Interpreting graphic presentations	**Interpreting simple pictorial forms of expression**—Interpreting pictures which accompany stories; using pictures as aid in word recognition; reading traffic signs; interpreting pictures drawn by self and others; interpreting simple diagrams used with informational material; interpreting posters; reading classroom weather charts, helpers' charts, other graphic records; becoming acquainted with purposes of maps, globes; getting information from simple illustrated books; watching simple motion pictures, filmstrips, television programs . . .	**Developing ability to interpret common forms of graphic expression**—Getting detailed information from pictures in reference books; reading common forms of maps; using globe; reading weather maps; reading diagrams accompanying articles to be constructed; reading simple pictograms, graphs accompanying informational material; interpreting illustrative examples in textbooks; getting information from slides, motion pictures, filmstrips, bulletin-board displays; using selected television programs for information . . .

YOUTH	ADULTHOOD
Extending the range and variety of uses of source materials—Deciding which of a variety of adult resource materials will be most appropriate for given problem; using library card catalog independently; using *Readers' Guide* or other indexes; using atlas, other resources with special graphic or pictorial aids; interpreting wide variety of tables, maps, and graphic presentations in relation to content of article; making effective use of headlines, other aspects of format of daily paper; evaluating accuracy of information from various current sources; preparing bibliography on special topic; using such aspects of format as chapter headings and summaries as aids to rapid and accurate reading . . .	**Using source materials appropriate to a wide variety of needs**—Using library card catalog effectively; using published indexes and sets of abstracts to locate needed publications; using formats of variety of technical materials as aids to skillful reading; deciding which professional or trade magazines to subscribe to; using consumer guides; deciding what reference books to add to home library for self and for children; determining validity of source materials . . .
Extending techniques for interpreting a wide variety of forms of graphic expression—Interpreting cartoons; reading more complex maps, globes; reading diagrams accompanying directions for setting up household or office gadgets; interpreting tables or graphs accompanying information in text or source books; interpreting items of national or local interest, or trends, presented in daily paper in graphic form; appraising advertising; using wide variety of documentary films, television and radio programs for information . . .	**Interpreting forms of graphic presentation accurately**—Interpreting cartoons; reading variety of maps; reading weather charts; interpreting budgetary and economic statements of national or local groups; interpreting charts or statistical tables relating to vocation; reading blueprints or floor plan of house; interpreting charts giving local or national trends in items of common interest; interpreting documentary motion pictures, television programs . . .

	EARLY CHILDHOOD	LATER CHILDHOOD
LISTENING Following and evaluating informal discussions and conversations	**Understanding ideas and simple experiences told by others**—Listening to suggestions made by other members of class in making plans; following proposals made by members of small committee; understanding teacher's suggestions; listening to conversations in home, at school; interpreting questions asked by peers and adults; understanding telephone conversations; talking informally with friends and visitors; acting upon parents' requests at home; developing willingness to take turns in discussion . . .	**Building techniques for following the give-and-take of discussion and conversation**—Interpreting suggestions of others regarding proposed class plans; listening to proposals for activities in club meeting; following trend of conversation with friends or visitors; following reasoning in group attempts to solve class problem; interpreting teacher's or parent's comments; listening to telephone conversations; following and taking appropriate share in panel discussion; developing those attitudes of respect for others' opinions basic to effective discussion . . .
Following and evaluating oral presentations	**Understanding simple stories, announcements, and reports**—Listening to stories or poetry read or told by another person; listening to teacher's explanation of work to be done or another child's explanation of game; listening to report of class committee; understanding announcements made in class; listening to occasional special speakers in assembly; listening to experiences related by other children; developing basic understanding that it is important to give a speaker full attention . . .	**Interpreting common forms of oral presentation**—Following stories, poetry read or told by others; following the commentator on documentary film or television program; listening to stories over radio and television; evaluating and taking notes on reports made by other class members; checking on accuracy of minutes of meeting; understanding directions or explanations regarding class activities; listening to announcements or speakers in assembly; developing advanced skills in evaluating adequacy of information and accuracy of reasoning in speaker's report . . .
Understanding musical and dramatic forms of expression	**Enjoying musical and dramatic forms of expression**—Listening to music; interpreting music through rhythmic activities; listening to rhythms on drums, other percussion instruments; learning to know common musical instruments; listening to favorite songs; enjoying dramatizations of new or favorite stories; enjoying favorite poems; enjoying puppet shows; sharing in school celebration of special holidays . . .	**Exploring a variety of musical and dramatic forms of expression**—Listening to good music; enjoying folk songs, ballads, popular music, others; following plot of motion picture or dramatic production; enjoying a variety of school dramatizations, pantomimes, pageants; sharing in school celebration of special holidays, other school traditions; sharing in ritual of church; listening to choral speaking; developing some awareness of how to judge quality of a production . . .

YOUTH

Extending techniques for interpreting discussion and conversation in a variety of situations—Following gist of conversations at variety of social gatherings, with group of friends; following panel discussion or debate; identifying and evaluating proposals made in class discussion, committee meeting; interpreting questions asked when being interviewed for job; responding to requests or suggestions from parents, teachers, others; listening to panels on television; developing more mature ability to evaluate logical reasoning, sense propaganda or emotional appeals; developing ability to sense need for roles such as leader, compromiser, others in following discussion; developing advanced skills as leader to identify issues, to keep discussions to point . . .

Extending ability to interpret a variety of oral presentations—Listening to monologues, choral speaking presentations, following presentation of assembly speaker; listening to radio and television programs; taking notes on college lectures; judging adequacy of committee report, minutes of a meeting; evaluating speeches of candidates for student offices; listening to sermon in church; developing deeper insights into accuracy of a speaker's facts and reasoning; developing increased sensitivity to means of swaying audience opinion . . .

Growing in capacity to get meaning from forms of musical and dramatic expression—Interpreting such musical forms as symphony, opera, folk music, popular music; interpreting modern dance, ballet, other dance forms; appraising plot and effectiveness of dramatic productions; understanding and responding to symbolism and ritual in churches, in clubs, on special holidays; helping to decide techniques to be used for effectiveness in a dramatic production, school rally, pageant; developing increased ability to recognize techniques through which appeals are made in music and drama . . .

ADULTHOOD

Making accurate interpretations in situations involving discussion and conversation—Following gist of conversations in social gatherings; evaluating proposals made by other members of committee; following panel discussion or interview on radio or television; following gist of discussion as panel or committee member; responding effectively to interviewer's questions; understanding children's requests and contributions to conversation . . .

Making accurate interpretations of a variety of oral presentations—Evaluating lectures; interpreting remarks of commentators; following details of a proposal in club or council meeting; following committee report presented orally; evaluating political speeches; evaluating community appeals; appreciating oral reading of a play or presentation of poetry . . .

Making discerning interpretations of a variety of dramatic and musical forms of expression—Attending opera, symphony concerts, plays; appraising quality of a variety of musical and dramatic productions; helping children interpret music and drama; appraising values of a variety of radio and television productions for self and for children; reacting to rituals of church, club; deciding how to respond to community or national appeals presented through dramatic forms; responding to dramatic aspects of political rallies . . .

	EARLY CHILDHOOD	LATER CHILDHOOD
OBSERVING Interpreting environmental surroundings	**Finding how to get needed information by observing objects of interest—** Examining objects brought to class by other children; watching plant and animal life in classroom aquarium; distinguishing foods and other objects by odors, tastes; distinguishing the feel of common objects; finding how to use touch, smell, sound, and taste to supplement vision; interpreting expressions of parents and friends . . .	**Extending techniques for securing information through observation—** Identifying distinguishing characteristics of common birds, animals, plants, flowers; discovering ways of making general weather predictions; interpreting exhibits in museums, local libraries, school display cases; making accurate observations in science experiment; making distinctions between weights and distances without using scales and measures; using expression and tone of voice as aids in interpreting reaction of adults, friends, committees; observing in sufficient detail for accurate description . . .

C. Dealing With Quantitative Relationships

INTERPRETING NUMBER VALUES AND SYMBOLS Understanding symbols and relationships	**Expressing concrete number relationships in symbols and interpreting symbols—**Counting; identifying numbers representing small quantities—pupils in class, crayons needed for group; understanding ordinal numerals—telling who is to go first, second; understanding the meaning of small sums of money written in numerical form; knowing approximate value of common coins, stamps; understanding price of candy, pencils, other purchases; interpreting half, quarter, other simple fractions in common use; telling time; finding important dates on calendar; finding pages in book; using numbers to locate other classrooms; finding street numbers; understanding common terms for number groups—dozen, pair, crowd; understanding simple size relationships; understanding such common measurement terms as inch, foot, quart . . .	**Interpreting commonly used number values and symbols—**Knowing money value of common coins and bills; interpreting distances, amounts, weights, heights of objects of interest; interpreting percentages as expressed in advertisements, batting averages; interpreting large numbers expressing populations of countries, distances beyond immediate travel; reading simple scales on maps; interpreting speeds; reading Roman numerals in common use; interpreting directional numbers—above and below zero on thermometer; understanding measurements needed in daily activities; interpreting time relationships and dates; reading telephone books, timetables; interpreting symbolism of fundamental operations; interpreting basic aspects of number system—place values, zero as place holder, decimals; interpreting size relationships expressed in fractional form; using simple geometrical relationships—circle, square, rectangle . . .

YOUTH

Increasing in variety and precision of observation—Using local exhibits as sources of information; planning how best to supplement class study with firsthand study of community; determining what factors to observe for accurate judgments—in examining soil, selecting foodstuffs, purchasing clothes; increasing in sensitivity to differences in personal expressions; finding how to tell reactions of an audience; using variety of instruments to make observations more accurate—scales, color charts, other tests . . .

ADULTHOOD

Making accurate observations needed in course of daily activities—Using observation techniques of needed accuracy in experimentation; establishing accurate means of testing products, grading raw materials; using local museum, other exhibits as sources of information; helping children notice items of major importance in their environment; interpreting moods and expressions of friends and business associates; knowing what signs indicate that young children are ill or upset, friends pleased or discouraged, audiences friendly or hostile . . .

C. Dealing With Quantitative Relationships

Extending the range and variety of symbolism used and interpreted—Reading tables, graphs, more complex scales in maps, complex weather maps; understanding percentages; understanding figures indicating large sums of money; interpreting more complex concepts of area—acre, quarter section, township; interpreting reports of speeds attained by planes, cars; interpreting distance and time relations reported in connection with travel, speed of light, radio; reading large numbers in newspaper reports; understanding simple statistical concepts, such as average; understanding fractional or decimal concepts used to report sizes of germs, molecules, other infinitely small objects; interpreting infinitely large distances or sizes; developing increased understanding of special measurement terms—carat, light year, calorie; making more accurate interpretations of dates relating to distant past or future; interpreting signed numbers—budgets in the red, temperatures, latitudes above and below equator; understanding geometrical forms and relations; understanding basic mathematical concepts underlying insurance, pensions, interest, profit and loss, taxation; reading algebraic formulas, formulas used in chemistry and physics . . .

Making accurate interpretation of number values and symbols met in adult life—Interpreting figures giving state and national debts, other large sums; reading tables, graphs, charts, maps accompanying news reports or technical discussions; understanding statistical concepts back of public-opinion polls; understanding distances as related to proposed air, transportation lines; interpreting reported velocities; understanding reports of weights, sizes referred to in news articles; understanding geometric forms used in construction, landscaping, gardening; reading blueprints; understanding insurance policies, taxation plans; reading tables for calculating income tax, annuity, social security benefits; interpreting correctly business practices such as discounts, credit sales; reading financial statements of a vocational group, club, church; reading formulas related to one's profession—statistical formulas, codes for making reports . . .

	EARLY CHILDHOOD	LATER CHILDHOOD
COMPUTING Estimating amounts	**Making gross estimates in situations involving simple quantity and price relationships**—Getting pencils or paper for class group; determining how many chairs are needed for reading group; deciding about how many people will be needed to finish job; deciding amount of paper needed for mural for given wall space; choosing boards about right length for construction or approximate number of blocks needed for building purposes; putting a picture in center of bulletin board; breaking candy bar in halves or thirds to share it; deciding whether article can be purchased with amount of money at hand; deciding how much time is left to finish play or work . . .	**Establishing effective techniques of using estimates to supplement exact computations**—Deciding how much change to expect after making purchase; estimating approximate distances and space relations in moving furniture in classroom, in putting up pictures, posters on bulletin board; getting out pencils, paper for class without counting; estimating how many cookies to order for class party; estimating time needed for a given job or to reach a given place; judging volumes—amount of water needed to fill aquarium, space needed for books; discovering how to use round numbers in making estimates; discovering value of estimates as check on precise calculations . . .
Making exact computations	**Making simple computations**—Figuring how much candies, other purchases will cost; getting right amount of change from purchases; deciding how many articles can be purchased for amount of money at hand; adding lunch money for class; getting right number of pieces of paper for members of one's group; adding scores in games; figuring cost of class excursion; finding how many members of class are absent; deciding how many cookies are needed for class party; using fractional amounts in simple recipes; developing understanding of number groupings needed for efficient computation . . .	**Developing understandings and skills needed for effective and accurate computation**—Keeping accounts in school store; acting as clerk in school store; checking on accuracy of change from purchases; deciding on number of yards needed to curtain classroom windows; drawing map to scale; keeping score in games; keeping one's batting average; finding cost of needed amounts of material; deciding how much must be saved weekly to make desired purchase; deciding what to charge at class sale to make needed profit; developing computational skills needed for efficient and rapid calculations; using an abacus to demonstrate number relationships . . .

YOUTH

Extending ability to use estimation effectively in a wide range of situations—Deciding how much food to order for school party; estimating how much of total allowance the purchase of a desired article will leave; estimating cost of class party, approximate profit from a sale; deciding about how much more time will be needed to finish project; approximating amount of top soil needed for garden; estimating time needed to drive to given destination; estimating approximate amounts when comparisons are stated in fractions, percentages . . .

Extending ability to apply understandings and skills in computing to more varied and complex situations—Balancing bank account; accounting for expenditure of funds for class party; acting as treasurer for school or community club; helping keep family accounts; helping run school bank; checking on change after purchases; doubling or tripling recipes; expanding or reducing size of maps, graphs; translating percentages given in news reports or advertising into ratios; making floor plan for workshop or clubroom; experimenting with geometric forms in design; calculating averages; computing cost of running car; figuring discounts at sales; sharing expenses with others; discovering principles underlying computing machine, slide rule; using algebraic principles as aids in rapid computing; using effective short-cut devices in making calculations . . .

ADULTHOOD

Using estimates appropriately and accurately in situations of adult life—Estimating amounts in cooking; estimating approximate effect of price increases on income; checking on government estimates of tax returns; judging weight of letters, packages to be mailed; judging approximate cost of moving furniture; making estimates of cost of building new house; deciding whether budget will allow for added purchases; estimating area to be covered when painting house, varnishing floor; estimating lumber needed for home construction project; estimating cost of heating home; estimating amount of material needed for specific piece of work; estimating crop yields . . .

Making the exact computations needed for efficient handling of the range of adult situations of everyday living—Figuring income taxes; balancing bank accounts; figuring budgets; keeping accurate expense accounts; sharing expenses with other persons; adjusting directions in knitting, crocheting, cooking, sewing to varying needs; figuring profit and loss on business deals; figuring discounts; calculating construction costs; figuring insurance costs and benefits; calculating calories in diet; calculating acreage under cultivation on farm; determining most economical way of purchasing household supplies; making mathematical computations needed in one's vocation; using computing machine, slide rule, logarithmic tables, tables of square roots or percentages . . .

	EARLY CHILDHOOD	LATER CHILDHOOD
Using measuring instruments	**Becoming acquainted with common measuring instruments**—Using ruler to measure paper, wood for construction; measuring curtains, wallpaper for playhouse; measuring paper for mural; helping fill aquarium; telling time; reading thermometer; finding dates on calendar; figuring how many more days before special holiday or excursion; keeping chart of weight or height; using such measures as cupful, spoonful, pint, quart, in following recipes; learning to tell time . . .	**Using common measuring instruments effectively**—Using yardstick, ruler effectively; deciding whether ruler, tape measure, or yardstick is most suitable to measure given distances; finding how to use stop watch; investigating uses of compass in telling direction; finding how to use pints, quarts, other measuring instruments in the home; using scales to weigh self, other objects; reading speedometer; reading thermometer, barometer; making charts, maps, scale drawings; developing simple time chart in social studies . . .

D. Using Effective Methods of Work

PLANNING Deciding on and clarifying purpose	**Identifying immediate purposes in general terms**—Deciding what kind of object to construct, paint, or draw; helping in class decision as to questions which need answering to solve special problem; considering how best to share classroom equipment; considering what kind of record is needed to tell about class activity; deciding how best to entertain another class; deciding what kind of letter would be enjoyed by sick friend; deciding what kind of gift to make for parents . . .	**Determining major issues involved in achieving purposes**—Deciding exactly what responsibilities have been delegated to one's committee; determining what next steps are needed to move an activity forward; deciding what questions will have to be answered to solve problem raised in class; determining what form final report of class activities will take; deciding what type of gifts are most likely to please other members of family; determining specifications of model airplane, birdhouse, other objects to be constructed . . .
Determining sequence of steps to achieve purpose	**Planning immediate next steps**—Laying plans to complete articles being constructed, a drawing; deciding what to do during independent work period; helping decide how best to organize class activity; deciding on most effective order in which to carry out activities proposed in class plans; helping to plan daily class schedule; deciding what equipment is needed to carry out job . . .	**Making longer-range plans**—Deciding on steps to collect information needed by committee; deciding in which order to carry out household responsibilities; outlining what needs to be done to prepare class assembly program; helping outline steps needed to achieve better skill in tool subject; helping make daily class schedule; helping outline plans for class project—school store, science experiment, study of community problem . . .

YOUTH	ADULTHOOD
Extending the range and variety of measuring instruments used—Using stop watch; using efficiently protractor or compass; using kitchen utensils to measure ingredients; laying out basketball court; using a T square for construction activities; using transit, angle mirror, or other instruments for measuring heights or distances; using fine scales in experimental work; reading gasoline gauge, speedometer, and other indicators on car; reading directions from compass; using color charts; adjusting shutter and lens speed on camera; reading barometer; interpreting different types of thermometers, metric and other scales . . .	**Using instruments of measurement appropriately in a variety of situations of adult life**—Using precise instruments appropriate to one's vocation; recognizing when inaccurate instruments might throw measurements off, when more accurate instruments are needed; interpreting statements about industrial processes requiring precision measures; using surveying instruments; using scales in grocery store, scales to weigh self, children; reading utility meters; reading clinical thermometer; using barometer and thermometer to make weather predictions; using scale on light meter, other photographic equipment; reading automobile gauges . . .

D. Using Effective Methods of Work

YOUTH	ADULTHOOD
Extending ability to identify aspects and long-time implications affecting purposes—Deciding what must be taken into account in selecting a college; identifying issues involved in choosing a vocation or in deciding between two part-time jobs; delimiting a problem involving several weeks of special study; deciding what issues must be considered in exploring community or national problem of interest; deciding what special questions to ask school counselor in getting advice on personal problem; considering what group interests and preferences should be taken into account in planning a party; deciding what equipment is needed in pursuing a hobby . . .	**Making the clarification of purposes needed to give effective direction in a variety of situations**—Identifying issues to be taken into account in changing jobs, moving to another part of country, building a home; deciding what kind of report would be appropriate to make to board of directors; considering what is involved in helping children answer scientific questions; helping children or others clarify issues involved in personal problems; deciding when to seek help of others in clarifying a situation; determining what issues must be faced in solving a professional problem . . .
Extending range and details of planning—Projecting steps needed to secure a college education, desired vocational training; outlining plans for high school work for next several years; projecting steps to secure advanced training in area of special concern; cooperating in planning various aspects of school program—assemblies for year, student activities, school paper; deciding what needs to be done to secure information for class report; outlining tasks to be done and personnel needed to carry out individual or class plans; making individual work schedule . . .	**Projecting appropriate sequence of steps to achieve a variety of purposes**—Deciding what steps to take to secure needed information about new job; projecting sequence of activities most effective in completing job; helping children plan ways of carrying out household activities; laying plans for education of children; determining steps to be taken toward building a home, securing desired vocational promotions, extending a business, retiring; helping guide policies and procedures as member of board of directors, as committee member, in church, club, or other group . . .

	EARLY CHILDHOOD	LATER CHILDHOOD
Budgeting time and energy	**Planning time allotments with the help of others**—Helping plan day's activities in class; completing activities within allotted stretches of time; learning to use clock in following simple schedule; helping decide how many activities should be undertaken in period of time; understanding purposes of clean-up period and warning bell; learning to abide by family schedule for meals, bedtime; choosing among activities when time does not allow for all . . .	**Developing the ability to make independent decisions as to use of time**—Helping plan class daily schedule; helping decide how to adjust class schedule for special events; helping decide how much time to spend on one activity in terms of other things to be done; planning individual schedule so as to meet deadline for special piece of work; deciding how much time it will take to finish given job; deciding how much time should be allotted to various steps in a plan; taking responsibility for stopping in time to clean up, responding to warning bells; acting as timekeeper for class or committee; scheduling home responsibilities to allow time for play . . .
Evaluating steps taken	**Deciding on the success of immediate steps**—Deciding what more needs to be done to complete class project; considering how much was accomplished in free-work period; determining what caused difficulty on playground; helping decide what practice in reading, numbers, spelling is needed; helping suggest standards for behavior, class contributions . . .	**Considering the effectiveness of progress toward longer-range plans**—Evaluating present status of group plans; deciding what skills most need improvement if class activity is to be successful; helping set standards against which to appraise various classroom projects; helping evaluate needs of self and others in learning to read, spell, other skills; helping decide when committee is ready to report to whole class, when more information is needed; deciding what will make for better excursion, series of committee reports; deciding on relative effectiveness of contributions of various group members; helping decide what should be included in cumulative records or reports to parents . . .

YOUTH

Budgeting time in terms of a greater number of activities and a longer time span—Planning individual schedule of class work and home study; planning how to complete home responsibilities to allow for club meetings, social events; deciding how much time to allow for completion of various aspects of class problem; budgeting time needed to complete special paper or project on time; setting up college study program; apportioning work on extended project over series of weeks; deciding how much time to spend in perfecting a piece of work in relation to values in other activities; balancing school work, home and community activities, and part-time job; deciding how many school or community leadership responsibilities time and strength will allow . . .

Taking increased responsibility for evaluating progress toward goals—Helping evaluate potentialities for success in college or vocation; deciding whether a piece of independent work has met desired standards or merits more attention; deciding whether information collected for a report is adequate and appropriate; judging effectiveness of recent student council proposal; deciding whether to seek special help in reading, spelling, other skills; deciding whether talent or interests merit electing advanced classes in a given area . . .

ADULTHOOD

Making the time allotments needed to carry out desired activities and to secure balance in activities—Balancing daily activities so as to get time for leisure, hobbies, participation in family activities, community service; apportioning time in vocational activities; setting up schedule for community drive, committee responsibility; deciding how much time should be given to one piece of work or interest in terms of other values and needs; helping children learn to use time wisely, to set up study schedule; setting up family schedule for responsibilities, study, recreation . . .

Using evaluation effectively and independently as an aid in planning—Deciding what additional training is needed for new job; weighing satisfactions and frustrations in deciding whether to change jobs; appraising effectiveness of family budget, other aspects of home management; deciding additional experiences needed to become more proficient in hobby; appraising children's progress in school, growth at home . . .

	EARLY CHILDHOOD	LATER CHILDHOOD
USING APPROPRIATE RESOURCES Locating and evaluating resources	**Finding how people, books, and materials provide needed information**—Finding which teachers can help on special problems; using pictures to secure desired information; becoming acquainted with simple reference books; finding how parents and community members can give special help; going to see how house is built, road constructed, store operated; finding what one can see in museum, zoo, park . . .	**Learning how to use the more common resources effectively**—Finding what reference books and other materials are available in library; exploring exhibits, special collections in school; exploring resources of community; deciding when to ask advice of teacher, of other adults; deciding when firsthand observation and experience or direct experimentation will provide needed information; appraising newspaper, radio, television as sources of information . . .
USING A SCIENTIFIC APPROACH TO THE STUDY OF SITUATIONS Solving practical problems	**Applying simple tests in the solution of practical problems**—Experimenting with methods of keeping paints and clay moist; testing to find which kind of paper is best for painting or drawing; finding when books or pictures can help solve a problem; finding that conclusions from firsthand experiences do not always agree—that one child may think dogs are fierce and another may think they are friendly; being helped to see when to withhold judgment until more information is secured; reasoning from several concrete experiences to simple generalization; giving concrete evidence rather than opinions as to why class plans did not work out, why an argument arose . . .	**Finding when and how to use simple research techniques**—Finding how to test differences of opinion by experimentation—setting up experiments with animals, testing two methods of planting seeds; gathering needed facts to verify point of view, conclusion reached; making simple surveys—children using given street crossing, food wasted in school cafeteria; discussing why historical research might lead to conflicting dates or figures; discussing general procedures back of an important scientific discovery; discussing in general terms fact that individual behavior has to be interpreted in light of motives; deciding whether generalizations are based on sufficient evidence . . .
Testing beliefs and attitudes	**Learning to distinguish facts from opinions in situations of concern to one**—Being helped to test incomplete generalizations through actual experience—having satisfying experiences with children of other races, becoming more familiar with animals feared, being helped to explore dark rooms; knowing when one is telling or reading an imaginative story, when giving or getting factual information; becoming acquainted with work of policeman, other persons around whom stereotypes have been built . . .	**Finding how to use facts to test opinions**—Testing superstitions—deciding whether it is unlucky to break mirrors, walk under ladders; deciding when to get additional firsthand information to test an opinion; deciding what to take as fact, what fiction, in historical novels; appraising opinions about racial, religious, socio-economic groups in the light of experiences and facts available; withholding judgment regarding behavior of friends until evidence is secured; learning to identify rumors . . .

YOUTH	ADULTHOOD
Making increasingly critical use of resources— Exploring more broadly resources of local library; identifying a wide variety of community industries, utilities as resources; exploring more intensively resources of local museum, zoo, historical society; deciding which persons to ask to speak at school assembly; finding what materials can be secured from state departments, government agencies of this and of other countries; evaluating news reports, personal opinion columns as sources of information; interpreting advertising; deciding which commentators to listen to; interpreting films . . .	**Making discriminating use of available resources—**Considering what sources of firsthand information to use; using appropriate reference books as sources of information; deciding which of several authors to use as a resource; deciding on adequacy of available firsthand information; deciding whether public speaker brings needed competence to his subject; using appropriate state or national resources for information on specific problem; appraising research bearing on one's job; appraising news releases; interpreting advertising; helping children explore library, museums, parks . . .
Extending ability to use scientific methods appropriate to situations—Finding how to use scientific tests to verify observations—quality of cloth, foods, tools and machines, others; following results of medical, other research; helping conduct school or community survey; using historical research methods to give needed perspective on problem; using logical reasoning to evaluate advice regarding a personal problem, to test logic of speaker or writer; deciding what steps are appropriate in resolving conflicting opinions; discovering importance of evaluating present generalizations in terms of new evidence; discovering influences that must be considered in analyzing personal behavior—realizing that illness, worry, fatigue, need for affection can influence actions . . .	**Using a scientific approach effectively in the situations of daily living—**Using appropriate methods to decide on selection of materials and equipment—testing new garden seeds, experimenting with new methods of insulation in housing, trying out new household or office equipment; making surveys needed as guides to business procedures; evaluating popular or professional articles quoting research; helping children resolve differences on basis of sound evidence; helping children arrive at sound generalizations; using generalizations about research techniques to evaluate new business and governmental proposals; supporting social and scientific experimentation; deciding when to encourage business firm to adopt new methods which are subject to experimentation; using case-study approaches in understanding problems of adjustment . . .
Extending ability and inclination to examine beliefs and attitudes in the light of available evidence—Deciding whether to hold beliefs in face of scientific evidence; discussing adequacy of existing evidence regarding racial equality, prejudices regarding economic or religious groups; building some bases for evaluating policies of other nations; withholding judgment regarding persons and situations until satisfactory evidence is obtained; getting information needed to support or deny rumor; finding how to take positive steps to deal with fears and worries; finding place of value judgments in making decisions . . .	**Making unbiased use of available evidence to test present beliefs and attitudes—**Deciding when scientific evidence is sufficient to warrant change in point of view or policy; considering implications of technological advances for attitudes toward world cooperation; evaluating new methods in education; identifying how basic values influence decisions; exploring and helping children explore evidence regarding other racial, religious, and socio-economic groups; taking positive action to stop rumors; taking positive action to eliminate prejudices . . .

GROWTH IN ABILITY TO TAKE RESPONSIBILITY FOR MORAL CHOICES

Ability to deal with persistent life situations in the area of moral choice emphasizes the development of values and attitudes basic to our democratic society. Under determining the nature and extent of individual freedom there are experiences calling for development of a democratic point of view toward authority and toward one's obligations in a society which trusts its people's judgments as to the laws needed for their welfare. Group mores and traditions sometimes exert a powerful influence over the behavior of those who hold them dear. Duly constituted authorities represent another distinct type of control. Legal regulations agreed upon by the total group to safeguard its welfare are still another. Because these various authorities sometimes conflict, social values which will serve as guides to action are needed.

If the individual is to make sound social judgments he must acquire insights into his own values. All questions related to the identification of sources of spiritual allegiance and those related to social values ultimately go back to the individual's personal philosophy. The personal values which condition respect for the unique worth of individuals and willingness to work cooperatively with others can be identified as underlying the persistent situations grouped under determining responsibility to self and others.

These persistent life problems appear constantly in combination with others in the situations of everyday living. Many of the experiences listed in this chart also contribute to growth in social participation and many involve decisions calling for growth in ability to deal with economic, social, and political structures and forces. Questions of meeting health problems require decisions about sharing food resources and medical care and thus demand moral as well as economic judgments and information about how to maintain physical well-being. Again, many of the experiences listed in other parts of the analysis could have been repeated in this section and vice versa. The selection, in so far as possible, was made to indicate the variety of situations faced, and the experiences were stated so as to show the kind of choice involved.

Chapter 2 indicated the importance of reaffirming democratic values in the light of present demands. Today, questions of responding to authority clearly stretch to situations calling for willingness on the part of all nations to substitute common agreements for force as the final authority. This in turn demands willingness to preserve integrity in human relationships, to meet the needs of others, and to use the potential abilities of self and others for the welfare of all. The full implications of the values to which the democratic society expresses allegiance are far from being realized even in America. Children, youth, and adults, each at their own level of maturity, must be helped to see the issues more sharply and must have opportunities to work together toward solutions more satisfying than any now reached.

A changing world is no place in which to build rigid patterns of behavior or to give children absolute answers. Expanding insights into the principles of democratic behavior and the implications of values, are needed, together with a willingness to study their meanings as new problems emerge. As new national and world relationships draw the lives of many peoples closer together, decisions involving moral responsibility become infinitely complex. Learners will grow in these insights as they discover the elements involved in the daily situations they face, identify the bases upon which they make judgments, and appraise decisions made in the light of effects on their own welfare and that of the group.

The illustrations of typical situations in this area, also, can be helpful to the teacher who must work within subject boundaries. Every teacher works toward growth in responsibility for moral choices both through the way he works with learners and through his interpretation of his subject field. The scientist is concerned with the uses to be made of new advances. The mathematician faces problems regarding the honest use of statistics. Because democratic values are the focus of this section, the social studies teacher will find situations that suggest ways of moving beyond historical facts and topological features. Particularly in the adolescent and adult columns in this chart, where problems of moral choice stretch to the national and international fields, will implications for specific subject fields be found. However, responsibility for moral choices begins to be built long before children come to school. Those who work in kindergarten and primary grades will find problems similar to those indicated in the chart recurring in every aspect of the day's work. In a sense, every school activity contributes to growth in this area.

Some typical situations calling for growth in ability to take responsibility for moral choices

	EARLY CHILDHOOD	LATER CHILDHOOD
	A. Determining the Nature and Extent of Individual Freedom	
RESPONDING TO AUTHORITY Meeting legal regulations	**Becoming acquainted with legal regulations which one must obey**—Obeying traffic regulations; becoming acquainted with work of the policeman; becoming acquainted with legal restrictions related to one's daily living—finding why dog must be kept on leash, asking about quarantine or isolation regulations, regulations regarding covering refuse, burning leaves; obeying school fire or civil defense regulations; obeying school regulations regarding time school opens, attendance . . .	**Understanding the major purposes of legal regulations**—Obeying traffic regulations; serving as traffic guard in school building, at school crossings; finding how laws protect property rights—picking flowers in park, defacing public buildings, taking store merchandise; having police help in finding stolen bicycle; learning about city fire regulations; discussing purpose and origin of laws one hears most about—who makes laws, responsibility of individual and police for their enforcement, how laws protect individuals and groups . . .
Deciding on obligations to constituted authority	**Identifying major obligations to the constituted authorities in one's life**—Finding in which situations parents expect obedience, in which one can make up one's own mind; finding what school requirements must be met and why—fire regulations, regulations regarding use of playground, behavior in halls; discovering areas in which teacher's authority must be recognized; finding obvious reasons for requests of parents, teacher, other adults; finding one's obligations to safety guards, other children who are school helpers; being helped to know when to follow suggestions of adults, other than parents, in home or community . . .	**Distinguishing the functions of the various constituted authorities which affect one**—Identifying areas in which parents or other adults have greater experience, those in which personal judgment can be relied on; finding what regulations of summer camp, recreation center, church club, must be followed; determining obligations to principal, other teachers, school secretarial, custodial, or cafeteria staff; discovering responsibility of umpire in games; deciding obligations to school safety guards, to age-mates in positions of responsibility; determining what authority is vested in owner of store, of property near which one plays, in parents of other children, and why . . .

YOUTH | ADULTHOOD

A. Determining the Nature and Extent of Individual Freedom

YOUTH

Increasing in understanding of man's responsibility for governing himself—Following legal regulations governing school attendance, holding jobs; deciding one's responsibility for obeying laws, helping to enforce laws; discussing effectiveness of present regulations for punishing criminals; discussing value and probable effects of proposed legislation—curfews, building or traffic ordinances, regulations regarding teen-age voting; cooperating in community efforts to change unwise legislation; recognizing differences in ways in which laws in a democracy and in a totalitarian state are used to govern behavior of individuals; discussing proposals for international laws and law enforcement . . .

Establishing more discerning basis for evaluating functions of constituted authorities—Weighing parental advice in light of standards of other groups and individuals; determining bases for obligations to employer, to other pupils as chairmen of school committees, editors of school paper; developing mature relations with teachers, other school personnel; acting as umpire in games; helping supervise classes, lunch hours of younger children; evaluating advice of homeroom teacher or counselor before acting upon it; determining areas in which guidance of parents and teachers or other adults must be recognized, those in which one should be exercising independence . . .

ADULTHOOD

Taking a responsible share in making, changing, and enforcing legal regulations in terms of human needs and values—Assuring that legal regulations are met in one's home, driving, other community relations; taking action to secure improved legislation; acting to secure constructive penal regulations, constructive administration of justice, and enforcing of laws in local community; helping children build constructive attitudes toward legal regulations; considering proposals for international laws and law enforcement; discussing rights of nations to use force to secure their ends . . .

Appraising the functions of constituted authorities in the light of individual freedom to act on values—Deciding on obligations to one's employer, supervisor, or responsibilities as employer or supervisor; determining one's obligation to leaders in lodge, union; determining in what areas to exercise authority over children and how to explain it; testing basis upon which a religious, social, or family group exercises authority; helping children resolve conflicts with parental, social, church authority; evaluating leadership exercised by school, church . . .

	EARLY CHILDHOOD	LATER CHILDHOOD
Reacting to group mores, traditions	**Becoming acquainted with common group mores and traditions which influence one's actions**—Learning to follow home and school patterns—walking to right, excusing oneself, greeting others, taking turns, using other common social amenities . . .	**Reacting to group mores, customs, and traditions**—Trying to resolve conflicts between parents' standards and those of some members of peer group; finding reasons for community mores; finding what social amenities make one acceptable to others; discovering what behavior results in acceptance in club, team, other peer groups . . .
ACTING UPON A PERSONAL SET OF VALUES Formulating guides for action	**Understanding the general nature of the values of one's family and school group**—Finding how family expects one to treat other people; understanding family and school standards of honesty; finding what is expected of one in using property of others; being helped to evaluate results of thinking of others in home and school; finding what is expected in carrying out promises; finding why rules cannot be changed in middle of game; accepting consequences of unwise decisions; being helped to analyze unwise decisions; accepting judgment of trusted persons . . .	**Finding how personal values guide the lives of people**—Being helped to identify what is involved in choices one makes—keeping promises, meeting group responsibilities, changing plans to meet needs of others; helping set up rules for games; discussing standards of behavior needed in school for group welfare; finding general reasons for family standards; understanding codes of Boy Scouts and other groups to which one belongs; evaluating consequences of one's acts; clarifying areas in which advice of other persons should help govern behavior . . .

B. Determining Responsibility to Self and Others

PRESERVING INTEGRITY IN HUMAN RELATIONSHIPS Carrying out commitments	**Finding what it means to carry out a commitment**—Finding what it means to make a promise to parents or friends; meeting obligations in household tasks; carrying out committee assignments and other school obligations; finding importance of meeting time obligations when other people are involved—coming to meals on time, being ready for special group activities . . .	**Identifying bases for determining the importance of commitments**—Deciding what must be done to fulfill special school responsibilities; discovering what members of group owe to each other and to their chairman; setting standards for job no one is going to inspect; deciding standards to be met in home responsibilities; considering whether to keep to promise if another interest interferes; deciding how important it is to be on time . . .

YOUTH	ADULTHOOD
Developing bases for evaluating group mores, customs, and traditions—Deciding whether to abide by standards of a social group which conflict with those of family; considering whether one's family should make special sacrifices to help one meet standards of peer group; discovering bases of community, religious, or family traditions; evaluating prevailing community attitudes toward minority groups; discussing how to deal with conflicts created by differences in patterns of youth and mores of "older generation"; deciding to what extent to follow or ignore community expectations regarding social amenities . . .	**Appraising group mores, customs, and traditions in the light of individual freedom to act on values**—Deciding when to oppose community traditions; determining when and how far to permit children to move away from traditional family patterns; deciding what social amenities children should be helped to learn; deciding how far mores of one's social group shall set values; helping children and youth resolve conflicts between family patterns and community mores . . .
Becoming articulate about a philosophy of life—Making clearer identification of bases governing choice of action; trying to resolve conflicts between scientific discoveries and religious teachings; comparing one's spiritual and ethical concepts with those of friends; clarifying understanding of how concepts of a religious group influence their actions; deciding what one's understanding of man's place and destiny means in terms of obligations toward others, toward oneself; finding resources—people, books, other means—for continued exploration of one's values . . .	**Acting upon an integrated philosophy of life**—Formulating a satisfying concept of man's place and destiny; using one's philosophy as a guide in weighing values in conflict situations; determining whether to act on values in face of opposition; helping children begin to develop guides for action; helping children understand role of religion as a guide to action; establishing methods through which to continue to study and test one's values; evaluating bases for prevailing national values; discussing international implications of conflicting bases of values among national groups . . .

B. Determining Responsibility to Self and Others

YOUTH	ADULTHOOD
Establishing deeper understanding of the meaning of integrity in individual and group commitments—Setting standards for one's school work; deciding what sacrifice of personal interests to make in order to meet school or class responsibility; deciding what standards of work to achieve in part-time job; deciding whether to live up to full implications of commitments; discussing proposals to eliminate forms of corruption in local community; considering importance of guaranteeing integrity of international treaties . . .	**Acting to assure that commitments made by self or others are met with due regard for human values**—Determining standards of workmanship on job; determining extent of obligations in church or club responsibilities; keeping promises to children; helping children decide whether to carry out an obligation assumed; taking action in eliminating forms of corruption in community; discussing proposals to guarantee integrity of international treaties; deciding how exacting to be in holding others to commitments . . .

	EARLY CHILDHOOD	LATER CHILDHOOD
Respecting property rights	**Learning to distinguish own possessions from those of others**—Finding when other people's property should not be touched; distinguishing between parent's money and one's own; taking proper care of borrowed materials; reporting articles found; returning borrowed articles; taking care of other children's toys; finding why flowers in park cannot be picked; helping care for school building; helping protect neighborhood trees, flowers, shrubs . . .	**Investigating the purpose and values of respecting property rights**—Helping manage school lost-and-found department; discussing importance of protecting lawns, gardens, trees of school neighbors; respecting play space and equipment of younger children; deciding whether to give fare to ticket collector if he doesn't ask for it; helping to replace or repair property one has damaged; cooperating in care of school, other public buildings, parks; finding the importance of keeping accurate accounts of class or committee funds . . .
Being intellectually honest	**Finding what it means to tell the truth**—Telling exactly what happened in reporting a quarrel; reporting trip or other exciting experience accurately; distinguishing between informational books and fiction; deciding whether to report to parents when one has broken a household article; deciding whether to "tell on" other children . . .	**Extending insights into the implications of being honest**—Giving credit to others who have helped on a job; deciding whether to tell parents when one has disobeyed them; learning what is involved when one cheats in class work; deciding when to tell unfavorable things about another; deciding when to make and when to withhold comments; reporting facts of situation accurately; distinguishing between fact and opinion . . .
MEETING THE NEEDS OF OTHERS Respecting individual differences	**Identifying differences in the capacities and needs of others in the immediate environment**—Adjusting games to children of other ages; adjusting behavior or activities to a member of family who is ill, to playmate who is physically or intellectually handicapped; helping classmates in areas in which one has special abilities; accepting help of those having special abilities; accepting advice and help of parents . . .	**Developing techniques of adjusting to the abilities and backgrounds of others**—Finding ways of including younger children in games; deciding whether to include new child, an unliked child, in "gang"; finding why special consideration is sometimes needed by older persons in family, by very young children; finding reasons for differences in school achievement of classmates; discussing how class can help a new child, child with poor social adjustment; beginning to appreciate why some individuals dress or act differently; finding reasons for differences in customs of racial and religious groups . . .

YOUTH

Developing more discriminating bases to govern action regarding property rights—Taking responsibility for care of home and school property; understanding issues involved in cooperative responsibility for public property; deciding precautions needed in safeguarding entrusted funds; discussing issues involved in sharing nuclear energy research; discussing national demands for air bases; discussing proposals for public ownership of natural resources . . .

Increasing sensitivity to the meaning of reactions that are intellectually honest—Deciding whether to express disapproval when peer group engages in activities contrary to one's standards; determining when one has explored a problem sufficiently to be justified in supporting a position; withholding judgments or criticisms of people until evidence is available; giving credit to those cooperating on a piece of work; providing adequate references in using quoted material or ideas of others; phrasing critical reactions with regard for needs of person to whom they are addressed; refusing to pass on rumors . . .

Extending insights and skill in adjusting to the backgrounds and abilities of others—Adjusting to members of family of different ages and interests than one's own; acting as church school teacher or leader for younger children; deciding how to include members of other socio-economic, racial, religious groups in social activities; helping pupil with handicap to fit into school; discussing community provisions for maximum development of handicapped; discussing whether honor students should be selected and on what basis; considering merits and problems of fraternities and other selective clubs; exploring more deeply basic similarities and differences in religious groups . . .

ADULTHOOD

Acting with due regard for property rights—Safeguarding public property; reporting income accurately in figuring income tax; helping children understand need to respect property rights; respecting possessions of children; discussing proposals to adjust international boundaries; discussing justice of demands of other nations for right to share of certain raw materials; taking action on proposals to control monopolies, trusts, to release inventions for use of all . . .

Preserving respect for other individuals in giving reactions which are intellectually honest—Deciding whether to act on one's values in face of opposition; giving an honest evaluation of work submitted; refusing to gossip; giving criticisms directly to persons involved in terms they can understand; deciding whether to take action when one's group acts on policy with which one does not agree; designating credit appropriately in cooperative work; helping children develop standards of intellectual honesty . . .

Acting to assure respect for the unique background and abilities of each individual—Adjusting demands upon others to their age, maturity, and ability; helping handicapped child find a respected place in family and school groups; helping members of family adjust plans to needs of each other; taking action to assure rights and responsibilities to minority groups; helping to provide for participation in community affairs of varied ability groups; helping children and youth find a place in community affairs; respecting and helping children respect contributions of persons in other social classes . . .

	EARLY CHILDHOOD	LATER CHILDHOOD
Modifying personal desires in the interests of others	**Adjusting to the interests and needs of parents and friends**—Deciding which piece of cake or candy to give to friend; sharing toys, school equipment with other children; deciding which children shall have crackers left over at morning lunch; sharing family radio or television; deciding how to amuse oneself so that other members of family may rest, complete work; saving allowance to purchase birthday gifts; giving up personal plans to fit in with group suggestions; allowing other children to participate in deciding what game to play; rearranging games so that more can play . . .	**Extending ability to adjust personal desires to the needs of those in the wider community**—Deciding whether to offer to do extra jobs for other members of family, friends; deciding whether to give money to church group or to make a personal purchase; deciding whether to give up personal plans in order to help at home, to do favor for friend; planning games for party so that all may share; finding what work is done by Red Cross, March of Dimes, Community Chest; deciding when to withdraw one's suggestions for class activities in favor of group desires; sharing materials with classmates and friends . . .
DEVELOPING AND USING POTENTIAL ABILITIES OF SELF AND OTHERS		
Developing individual capacities for social ends	**Finding how one's contribution can make for group welfare**—Finding the difference that one's contribution makes to class activity; being willing to undertake special jobs that one can do well; contributing to group through doing routine jobs; assuming special responsibilities at home . . .	**Deciding what individual contribution to make to the group**—Practicing so as to be able to make a useful contribution in games, in class project; deciding what contribution one can best make to class project; meeting requests to play or sing or use other special talents; planning group responsibilities so that less able members of group have turn; helping plan so that all will get needed help on skills important to group welfare . . .
Securing contribution of all concerned with a problem	**Finding how other people can contribute to a group undertaking**—Learning how to plan with others; finding how others' ideas can help in planning class enterprise; discussing what allotment of responsibility will let each member of group do his best work; finding how members of family can help each other; finding contribution to one's life made by well-known community helpers . . .	**Finding ways of helping others make a contribution to group activities**—Helping to involve others in class or committee in planning an activity; deciding when other classes in school should be consulted on plans; helping to allocate activities so as to draw on potential ability of each person in the group; helping younger children share in family plans . . .

YOUTH	ADULTHOOD
Developing more discriminating bases for the modification of personal desires in terms of the needs of others—Deciding when one has right to ask parents, other members of family to do special favors; sharing family car, living room, television; deciding when to give up personal plans for sake of friends, members of family; deciding how much time to give to voluntary school or community project; discussing issues involved in indulging in any excess which affects others; discussing proposals to assure adequate standard of living to all; deciding how much of allowance to spend on others, to give to relief or charitable organizations; discussing proposals to provide relief or financial assistance to other nations; discussing issues involved in assuring sovereignty of other peoples . . .	**Modifying personal desires in terms of the interests and needs of individuals and social groups**—Deciding how salary demands, demands for time off, should be adjusted to needs of others; adjusting personal plans for sake of friends, children; deciding which relief or charitable organizations to support; taking action on proposals to assure adequate standard of living for all; deciding whether to indulge in excessive behavior which affects others; deciding whether to support proposals to provide relief or financial assistance to other nations; budgeting time between family group and voluntary community activities . . .
Establishing more adequate bases for determining what is the most effective contribution to the group—Deciding which vocation to prepare for; deciding how to use artistic, musical abilities to entertain others; deciding what is involved in breaking training while on school team; deciding one's obligation to participate in decisions of any group of which one is a member; determining best direction of one's efforts—number of clubs to belong to, committees to serve on, course load to undertake; discussing proposals to equalize educational opportunities; helping establish community centers where people can develop special talents . . .	**Making a maximum contribution of individual abilities for the good of the group**—Deciding which of one's abilities can be developed for greatest social usefulness; deciding how far to develop special talents; deciding what responsibility to undertake in community problems; taking action on proposals to equalize educational opportunities, to provide for greater financial support of schools; deciding whether to share new ideas, inventions with others; helping children and youth develop and use special abilities . . .
Establishing more adequate basis for securing the most effective contribution of other members of the group—Securing opinions of all concerned in school project; making provision as committee chairman for all members to contribute; helping students with special talents to find ways of sharing them; discussing state or national proposals to guarantee right to vote to all citizens; discussing situations in which individuals or groups are barred from participation; discussing right of an individual to withhold contribution needed by group . . .	**Acting to secure the maximum contribution of others for the good of the group**—Acting to open educational, work opportunities to members of other socio-economic, racial, religious groups; sharing in provision of special opportunities for talented youth; acting to secure best thinking of all concerned in problem; helping children share in joint family decision; acting to secure right to vote, to participate in democratic decisions, to all persons concerned; taking action to give youth proportionate share in community activities . . .

GROWTH IN ABILITY TO MEET NEEDS FOR AESTHETIC EXPRESSION AND APPRECIATION

Every individual has resources for creative expression and for securing satisfaction from the creative expression of others. Growth in capacity for aesthetic expression and appreciation is as much a part of total growth as is the meeting of health needs. An important contribution to the learner's ability to meet the persistent life situations of achieving constructive expression of emotions and of securing balanced satisfactions in living is made when he is helped to explore the resources for aesthetic expression and appreciation which lie within himself and in the world around him.

In the chart which follows, situations calling for aesthetic expression and appreciation have been listed together because the sources of satisfaction for a particular individual may lie in either direction. One person plays a musical instrument, a second listens; one attempts to express himself through writing stories or poetry, a second finds great satisfaction in reading; one paints, whittles, or knits, another purchases beautiful paintings for his home or collects fine handiwork.

Situations calling for different forms of expression have not been separated. The mode of expression for one person might be clay, for a second music, for a third painting, for many, combinations of these and other media. The persistent problems identified in this subsection relate to providing resources, experimenting with varied media, and developing special interests and talents. A second subsection gives situations providing for creative expression through daily work, through achieving an attractive personal appearance, through providing artistic living conditions, through community planning, through coming to know the aesthetic satisfactions in the natural environment.

The persistent life situations calling for aesthetic appreciation and expression, although demanding certain distinct competencies and understandings, appear as do situations in other areas in this section in almost every situation of everyday living. The satisfactions of a creative response and one which shows sensitive appreciation are possible in almost every daily life experience. The close connection between the situations in this chart and those calling for satisfying emotional and social needs has already been pointed out. Aesthetic forms can also be used to express ideas to others, and must be interpreted in understanding the ideas of others—persistent life situations found in the chart dealing with growth in intellectual power. Economic factors affect many of the everyday situations given in this chart. Purchasing a new dress which is aesthetically satisfying also raises such persistent problems as budgeting income and determining the quality of goods. Many of the situations calling for ability to deal with the natural environment contribute to aesthetic appreciation of it.

Children and youth need to grow both in their ability to face life situations with creativity and zest and in their knowledge of resources for aesthetic expression and how to use them. In addition to developing techniques for effective and satisfying use of media, help is also needed in increasing the sensitivity and judgment required for depth of appreciation. With younger children much of the emphasis will be on becoming acquainted with media and other sources of aesthetic satisfaction. As they grow older the problem is one of adding techniques and deepening insight without destroying the creativity basic to all aesthetic expression. At all ages there is the problem of extending sensitivity to the countless possibilities for creative expression and satisfaction in the day-to-day activities in which everyone engages.

Creativity and aesthetic satisfaction too often are seen as relating to music and the arts rather than as aspects of all living. Typical situations in the chart which follows have many implications for teachers who must keep within subject boundaries as well as for those teachers free to develop programs around the problems of learners. The contribution of the chart to the work of teachers of such subjects as art, graphic arts, and music will be readily apparent. Teachers of home economics will find many of the situations listed under providing artistic living conditions applicable. Science teachers help learners appreciate natural beauty. Many aspects of the language arts involve creative expression. The problem of achieving artistry in daily work may suggest to the teacher of business education some of the satisfactions to be found in neat and attractive work. In all subjects there is increasing concern with the use of a variety of media as means of expression. Students summarize their study through a play, a mural, a well-planned bulletin board, creative writing, choral speaking. In this sense, all subject areas have a contribution to make to growth in ability to meet needs for aesthetic expression and appreciation, and all teachers are concerned with problems of achieving artistry in daily living.

Some typical situations calling for growth in ability to meet needs for aesthetic expression and appreciation

A. Finding Sources of Aesthetic Satisfactions in Oneself

	EARLY CHILDHOOD	LATER CHILDHOOD
EXPRESSING THE SELF THROUGH VARIED MEDIA		
Providing resources for aesthetic expression	**Securing materials needed for a given activity**—Asking for special crayons, pencils; asking for blackboard; asking for colors needed in painting; getting out materials needed to work with clay; sharing favorite books with class; helping select pictures and books for home or classroom; finding materials to use for dolls' dresses; making puppets and puppet theater . . .	**Sharing in home and school decisions regarding resources for aesthetic expression**—Deciding whether to purchase musical instrument; making recommendations for home or school collections of records; purchasing favorite books; recommending needed books for school library; selecting pictures for classroom or room at home; helping order supplies for workshop or crafts; helping set up hobby clubs; helping equip workbench; locating suggestions for new ways of making puppets, paints, looms, and the like . . .
Experimenting with varied media	**Becoming acquainted with a variety of media**—Exploring use of paints, crayons, other sources of color; reading stories; listening to stories, poetry; saying favorite poems in choric style; using clay; singing with group; trying musical instruments; expressing ideas through rhythmic activities; learning to play phonograph; using blocks, wood for construction purposes; experimenting with other simple craft material; making clothes for dolls; deciding what television programs to watch; discovering favorite radio programs; experimenting with the "feel" of different kinds of materials . . .	**Exploring the uses of varied media**—Finding which media are most appropriate for various kinds of expression—discovering potential uses of clay, paint, wood, cloth, paper; discovering potentialities of a variety of musical instruments; singing with class chorus or school choir; going to children's concerts; taking part in class play; finding which radio or television programs, motion pictures are most enjoyable; extending range of reading materials enjoyed; joining school orchestra; finding uses for common and discarded materials—tin foil, cloth, cans, yarn; exploring ways of producing various textural effects with paint, paper, cloth; using home workbench to build birdhouses, articles for room . . .

YOUTH | **ADULTHOOD**

A. Finding Sources of Aesthetic Satisfactions in Oneself

Taking greater responsibility in providing home and community resources for aesthetic expression—Building a collection of records; helping select school's collection of records; purchasing sheet music or songbooks for home or club; helping in plans to open school art studio, shops to more students; working with "little theater" group; helping plan a series of school assemblies, special school concert; selecting pictures for one's own room; co-operating in drives to establish a public library; helping build better school library; participating in plans to set up art exhibit in school; taking action to secure choral or orchestral group, dramatic club, hobby clubs; participating in plans to share school resources with parents or other townspeople; equipping home workshop or studio . . .

Developing increasingly effective techniques in using varied media—Playing in school band or orchestra; cooperating in production of school play—acting, making costumes, constructing scenery, arranging lighting, providing effective advertising; writing stories, poetry for personal enjoyment, for school paper; listening to opera, symphony recordings; exploring the variety of resources offered by radio, television, various types of motion pictures; experimenting with modern dance, folk dancing, other dance forms; continuing to explore sources of aesthetic satisfaction in good books; working with metals, wood, plastics, leather; experimenting with photography; attending local concerts, exhibits, art galleries, museums; attending special exhibits of photography, paintings . . .

Providing adequate home and community resources for aesthetic expression—Deciding what musical instruments to have in home; deciding what records to add to collection; helping children decide which musical instruments to learn to play; selecting books for home library; equipping home workbench or workshop; helping establish a community library; deciding on proposals to bring concerts, theater groups to town; helping establish community recreation center or open schools for further work with arts and crafts; taking steps to bring high quality films to local theater and better television and radio programs into home; helping support local museum, art gallery; acting on proposals to add art, music specialists to school staff; helping to encourage local handicrafts . . .

Securing aesthetic satisfaction through creative use of varied media—Joining music, art groups; selecting reading matter to suit a variety of needs; writing poetry, short stories; telling stories to children; expanding interests in dance, crafts, music, others; using photography as hobby; refinishing furniture or building home furnishings; pursuing interests in sewing, knitting, crocheting, weaving; attending local concerts; attending productions of local theater guilds; taking children to museums, art galleries; helping children and youth select worthwhile reading, movies, television programs . . .

	EARLY CHILDHOOD	LATER CHILDHOOD
Developing special interests and abilities	**Identifying media that have special appeal**—Choosing which activity to undertake during free periods; finding ways in which expression is most satisfying; having others express appreciation of efforts . . .	**Developing basic techniques for using media of special interest**—Helping plan music lessons; deciding whether to spend extra school time on aesthetic interests; deciding which of a variety of media one finds most enjoyable, can use most effectively; deciding how to spend leisure time at home; choosing special materials to work with at home; finding people to whom to go for special help; pursuing a hobby . . .
ACHIEVING ARTISTRY IN DAILY WORK Finding means of creative expression in work	**Finding what satisfactions can accompany work well done**—Helping arrange toys, books, magazines so that house or classroom looks neat and attractive; helping keep own desk, locker, closet, drawers neat; finding satisfaction in helping to clean up after work, putting tools and materials away in order; carrying out class responsibilities to dust, arrange books, keep room attractive in other ways; helping wash and press doll clothes, curtains for play corner; painting library corner furniture; helping make decisions on satisfying standards in class work—how papers should be arranged, why legible handwriting is important, what makes for a pleasing oral report . . .	**Growing in ability to work in ways that bring aesthetic satisfaction**—Finding satisfaction in well-done household responsibilities; keeping own room neat and attractive; arranging displays attractively on bulletin board; taking satisfaction in thorough job in committee report; setting up standards for class activities—quality of handwriting, accuracy of reporting, neatness of papers, and the like; developing skills needed to find satisfaction in a game, in group activities; being helped to develop adequate standards in part-time job—giving service, meeting time schedules, keeping accurate accounts . . .
ACHIEVING ATTRACTIVE PERSONAL APPEARANCE Achieving good grooming	**Carrying out accepted routines under adult supervision**—Helping with bath; cooperating with barber in having hair cut; combing hair; washing hands, face before meals; cleaning up after hard play; helping keep nails clean; helping decide when fresh dress or shirt is needed; wearing apron when painting; asking to have rips stitched, buttons sewn on; helping clean own shoes . . .	**Taking responsibility for major practices in good grooming**—Taking responsibility for getting haircuts, deciding on hair style, helping shampoo hair; being responsible for neat and attractive appearance for meals, church, other occasions; dressing for special parties; taking responsibility for baths, for washing hands and face properly, cleaning nails; taking responsibility for hanging up clothes, sewing buttons; protecting clothing when doing "messy" jobs; polishing own shoes . . .

YOUTH	ADULTHOOD
Taking steps to secure further guidance needed in developing special interests and abilities— Deciding whether to elect special classes in art; deciding whether to join club or interest group experimenting with a special medium; deciding whether to continue with music, other lessons; deciding whether to try out for school play; determining whether one has talent to make special interest a vocation; deciding how much time and money to spend on a hobby; determining how much to spend on special equipment . . .	**Providing opportunities for self and others to develop special abilities and interests—**Deciding how intensively to develop creative ability in art, music, other areas; budgeting time to allow for special interests; deciding whether to equip special shop for woodwork, ceramics, other forms of expression; deciding how best to encourage children to experiment with new media; determining whether children have special talents which should be encouraged . . .
Extending satisfying work techniques to new activities undertaken—Achieving artistic layout of school paper, yearbook; helping set standards for articles to go into school paper; planning decorations for party; taking responsibility for neatness and attractiveness of one's room, clothing; finding how to serve an attractive meal; keeping car in good condition; finding how to keep notebook in orderly and functional form; discovering ways of carrying out part-time job as effectively as possible; setting own standards for study, reports, papers in school . . .	**Achieving the quality of work that brings aesthetic satisfaction—**Finding sources of aesthetic satisfaction in one's vocation; finding opportunities for creative expression in cooking, sewing, knitting; expressing creative tendencies in making garden; constructing furniture or other articles for home; deciding standards in making home attractive and clean; helping children share in keeping home, clothing attractive; finding how to blend color, taste, other qualities to secure artistry in meals; judging what constitutes craftsmanship in work of others . . .
Achieving appropriate grooming which makes for individual satisfaction and social approval—Finding which type of cosmetics is most appropriate; applying cosmetics attractively; manicuring nails; learning to shave; deciding on appropriate haircut and style; caring for hair; deciding when and how often to bathe; finding how to use perfumes, toilet waters, bath preparations; finding how and when to use deodorants; taking responsibility for sending clothes to cleaners, washing, pressing; taking responsibility for clean linen, hems of dresses, buttons in place. . .	**Taking full responsibility for good grooming—** Deciding on appropriate hair style; keeping hair in good condition; adjusting cosmetics to a variety of situations; taking proper care of hands; using deodorants, toilet water, bath preparations appropriately; taking responsibility for helping children build appropriate personal hygiene techniques; keeping clothing of self and children clean and neat . . .

	EARLY CHILDHOOD	LATER CHILDHOOD
Selecting attractive clothing	**Sharing in selection of clothing—** Helping decide clothing appropriate for special occasion; appreciating teacher's and mother's dresses; helping choose colors which match in sweaters, socks, skirts; helping decide on purchase of clothing . . .	**Finding how to select clothing appropriate to varied situations**—Selecting clothing for parties, church, other occasions; helping purchase clothing; appreciating clothing of peers; selecting clothing which follows fashion of peers; discussing what jewelry to wear; choosing harmonizing colors . . .
Using voice, manner, and posture effectively	**Finding what behavior is acceptable to others in situations in which one finds oneself**—Learning how to keep voice controlled in working and playing with others; finding how to make requests pleasantly; using appropriate table manners, using common amenities in other situations; remembering to sit and stand with good posture . . .	**Adjusting voice and manner to the major demands of situations**—Finding how to adjust voice to needs of specific situation—speaking in assembly, lowering voice when someone is ill at home; making suggestions pleasantly and effectively in class discussions; standing or sitting with good posture in varied situations; developing poise in walking before an audience, into room with strangers; helping serve at class party; greeting friends graciously at home or school; participating in conversation at table . . .

B. Achieving Aesthetic Satisfactions Through the Environment

PROVIDING ARTISTIC LIVING CONDITIONS Achieving satisfying space relations	**Making suggestions about the arrangement of furniture**—Arranging furniture in library corner, playhouse; helping arrange desks and tables in classroom; deciding best place for workbench, museum table; helping put up pictures, arrange bulletin board; setting places for midmorning lunch; discovering that neatness is important in attractive room . . .	**Understanding major factors to be considered in achieving space relations that are both satisfying and efficient**—Helping arrange classroom furniture to get most satisfying working conditions; arranging furniture in one's bedroom; arranging classroom for party; helping set table at home; arranging an effective bulletin board; deciding where to put pictures; placing and arranging exhibit case; displaying a collection; taking responsibility for keeping places in which one works and plays neat . . .

YOUTH	ADULTHOOD
Selecting clothing suited to personal characteristics and social needs—Selecting clothing suited to figure and coloring; deciding what clothing is appropriate to given occasion; deciding when coat and tie are appropriate; deciding when and how to follow fads of crowd; finding how to adjust clothing fads to suit individual needs; finding when and how much jewelry is appropriate; choosing accessories to combine with chosen costume; finding how to extend wardrobe through use of accessories . . .	**Selecting attractive and appropriate clothing for self and others**—Deciding on appropriate style of clothing; choosing and combining colors appropriately; selecting appropriate costume jewelry and other accessories; helping children select clothing which is both practical and attractive; renovating own or children's clothing to achieve recent style, better fit . . .
Growing in ability to use voice and manner appropriate to the needs of the situation—Finding how to secure needed effect through voice and manner in making announcements, talking to friends; taking responsibility for practicing to correct speech defects; discussing importance of good posture to personal attractiveness; learning to carry adolescent height gracefully; learning to dance; acting as host or hostess at school function, acting as guest; helping people of different ages and backgrounds feel at home in a social situation; being considerate in situations involving other members of family . . .	**Adjusting voice, manner, posture effectively to the varied aspects of a situation**—Modulating voice in variety of situations; being sensitive to needs of others in variety of situations; developing poise in large audience situations; helping children develop sensitivity to appropriate voice and manner for variety of situations; helping people feel at ease as host, committee chairman, discussion leader; recognizing and knowing when to use accepted social amenities; helping children develop appropriate amenities . . .

B. Achieving Aesthetic Satisfactions Through the Environment

YOUTH	ADULTHOOD
Extending ability to apply basic principles in achieving satisfying space relations in situations for which one has responsibility—Helping arrange household furniture; arranging chairs, table in home for party or special entertainment; helping hang pictures; deciding on appropriate frames for pictures; setting up conference room for council meeting; setting up classroom bulletin board, class exhibits; arranging auditorium for school dance; setting tea table; assuming responsibility for keeping home neat and clean; helping parents appraise floor plan for new house; sharing in plans for building new clubhouse . . .	**Achieving satisfying space relations in home and place of work**—Securing satisfying and functional arrangement of furniture in home; arranging chairs, tables at dinner party, at tea; deciding how best to frame and where to hang pictures; deciding what type of furniture, length of drapes are most appropriate to size of room; making plans for new house; choosing between two apartments; considering arrangements in new office building; helping children develop skill in achieving attractive home surroundings; helping children realize that neatness is important to attractive surroundings . . .

	EARLY CHILDHOOD	LATER CHILDHOOD
Selecting furnishings appropriate to use	**Making suggestions for furnishings in situations in which one works or plays**—Choosing bowl for flowers; deciding which picture to hang over one's table; choosing textile to be placed under piece of clay modelling; deciding what furnishings are needed in playhouse; helping decide what furniture is to be in one's room . . .	**Helping to select furnishings for one's own use**—Helping select fittings appropriate for own room; sharing in family discussions of choice of home furnishings; helping decide furnishings for class library corner; helping decide whether to have curtains in classroom; helping decide what kind of storage or shelf space will meet needs of group . . .
Using color effectively	**Enjoying and making suggestions about colors used in home and school**—Painting classroom furniture; helping decide on curtains for classroom; helping decide which pictures should be put up in one's room; helping place special pottery, prints, other decorative materials in classroom; making place mats, place cards for special occasions; painting wallpaper for playhouse; planning scenery for a play; helping choose color of paint or paper for one's own room; making decorative gifts . . .	**Identifying major factors which must be considered in using color in interior decoration**—Painting or helping select colors for furniture in one's room; deciding what sort of mural, special pictures would be appropriate in classroom or school lunchroom; arranging border or other decoration for bulletin board; helping select drapes, furniture for one's own room; decorating classroom for special party; helping decorate the school for special event or holiday; arranging flowers . . .
SECURING BEAUTY THROUGH COMMUNITY PLANNING Planning community architecture and landscaping	**Helping parents and others to carry out plans to beautify home and community**—Helping water garden; helping plant garden; assisting father in mowing lawn, trimming hedges; sharing in developing plans for walks, borders, gardens, trees on school grounds . . .	**Sharing in home and school efforts to beautify the community**—Cooperating in plans to provide attractive school building and grounds; planning where walks are most needed on school grounds; helping parents plan garden; taking responsibility for watering and weeding garden; helping plant trees in local park, on school grounds; cooperating in school efforts to develop local park; discussing proposed local housing project . . .

YOUTH	ADULTHOOD
Developing understandings basic to appropriate selection of furnishings—Selecting furniture for one's own room; deciding what style of furnishings is most suitable for clubroom; helping parents decide what is most suitable in adding new furniture; making drapes and accessories for one's room; deciding what china and silver to use for dinner party . . .	**Selecting furnishings appropriate to use and aesthetically satisfying**—Choosing furniture for home; selecting appropriate furniture for child's room; choosing kitchenware which has both beauty and utilitarian value; deciding what porch furniture best suits needs; deciding what dishes, glassware are appropriate; choosing style of silver . . .
Extending ability to use color to include more of the elements involved in securing attractive living conditions—Selecting colors to be used in redecorating one's own room; selecting drapes, pictures most suitable for clubroom; deciding how to use color in arranging bulletin boards, displays; achieving satisfying color effects in table linen, dishes, flowers in setting tables; decorating school gymnasium for class party; finding how to adjust color to size of room; using solid colors, figured materials, contrasting colors appropriately . . .	**Using color effectively to achieve satisfying living and working conditions**—Deciding how to secure satisfying harmony or contrast in walls or furniture; decorating baby's room, room for young children, kitchen, other special room; choosing rugs, furniture covers, drapes for special rooms; achieving satisfying effects with pottery, textiles, knickknacks; helping decide on color schemes to be used in office, factory, store, or other place of business; giving children a share in deciding how color is to be used in their rooms and furnishings . . .
Cooperating in plans for beautifying the community—Discussing plans for new public buildings; helping provide attractive school buildings and grounds; discussing proposed actions to remove slum areas, unsightly buildings; discussing proposals for planned housing projects; discovering beauty in bridges, factories; helping in campaigns to control advertising in industrial areas, along city highways; helping establish camp site for local youth groups; discussing proposals to preserve local beauty spots . . .	**Securing beauty in community architecture and landscaping**—Taking action to remove slum areas, unsightly buildings, untidy vacant lots; voting on proposals to use community funds for boulevards, parks, planting of trees; reacting to proposed architecture and landscaping of new public buildings, highways, bridges; acting on proposals to remove or control advertising on city highways, in industrial areas; taking action to have local beauty spots preserved . . .

	EARLY CHILDHOOD	LATER CHILDHOOD
Providing care to keep community attractive	**Sharing in the care of community resources which one uses**—Helping keep city streets clean; helping keep papers off classroom and hall floors, city boulevards, sidewalks; helping keep parks clean; using receptacles for refuse; putting outdoor playthings away when through with them; helping keep school grounds attractive; taking part in all-school clean-up campaign; obeying "keep off the grass" signs; helping weed garden . . .	**Cooperating in general community upkeep**—Cooperating in city clean-up campaigns; helping to clean up vacant lots; helping keep own home and garden looking attractive; cooperating in plans to keep school rooms, halls, and grounds attractive; helping keep parks clean; keeping lawn mowed, hedges clipped; helping paint screens; becoming acquainted with work of departments of sanitation and parks and highways; making simple repairs on house, school buildings . . .
SECURING AESTHETIC SATISFACTION IN THE NATURAL ENVIRONMENT Appreciating natural beauty	**Becoming acquainted with natural beauty**—Asking about the stars, moon; watching bird and animal life; becoming acquainted with common flowers; watching cocoons hatch; enjoying pets; noting changes in foliage; enjoying flowering trees; examining shells, pebbles; noting colors of insects, birds, animals; enjoying park beauty; noting pleasant odors in flowers; discovering differences in texture in objects one touches . . .	**Extending acquaintance with natural beauty**—Recognizing color and beauty of bird life, of flowers, trees typical of one's locality; making a collection of shells, unusual stones; noting changes in surroundings with different seasons; studying the stars; finding sources of beauty in local lakes, hills; examining snowflakes, frost patterns on windows, hoarfrost; identifying beauty in weather changes—rain, lightning, unusual clouds; cooperating in efforts to preserve wild life, wild flowers; developing more sensitivity to odors—flowers, pine trees, garden after rain; helping set up bird feeding station . . .

YOUTH

Cooperating in the development of plans for improved community upkeep—Discussing measures to secure better community upkeep; helping family decide how to keep home and garden attractive; cooperating in plans to provide waste containers, other means of keeping community attractive; helping clean up untidy vacant lots; cooperating in antilittering campaign; evaluating work of municipal departments concerned with community upkeep; evaluating effectiveness with which school grounds and buildings are kept clean and in good repair . . .

ADULTHOOD

Securing satisfying community appearance through adequate care and upkeep—Acting to secure cleanliness of city streets; keeping hedges in yard clipped, garden attractive; helping keep boulevards attractive; painting house; keeping house, other buildings for which one is responsible in good repair; helping children learn to take responsibility for keeping home and garden neat and attractive; voting on budgeting proposals for municipal departments of sanitation and upkeep; evaluating work of such departments . . .

YOUTH

Increasing the range of satisfactions found in natural beauty—Finding beauty in sunsets, skylines, lakes at night, snow; appreciating mysteries and majesty of the universe; discovering sources of beauty in trees, flowers; sharing in community or state plans to establish sanctuaries or state parks; planning entertainments which will allow for appreciation of natural beauties; studying reasons back of state game laws; exploring beauty spots of various parts of country in person or through films . . .

ADULTHOOD

Helping self and others find aesthetic satisfaction in natural phenomena—Visiting natural beauties of this and other countries; helping children appreciate beauties of their natural surroundings; finding sources of aesthetic satisfaction in mysteries of universe, in mystery of plant and animal life; taking action to prevent commercializing of natural beauties; voting on game laws, laws to preserve trees, wild flowers; providing opportunities for family travel . . .

Growth in Social Participation

The area of social participation is being recognized by educators and laymen alike as important to the growth of children and youth. Techniques for achieving adequate interpersonal and group relationships are important both for the individual and for society.

From the standpoint of the individual, problems of achieving secure relations with other people are vital aspects of satisfying emotional and social needs. From society's standpoint, techniques of working with others and of establishing bases upon which organized groups can cooperate are fundamental to the survival of democracy. Problems range from maintaining adequate family relationships to every phase of international cooperation. Situations calling for effective social participation deserve a place in the school curriculum as important as any other persistent life situations.

The emphasis in the charts in this section is on necessary techniques in social relationships. The illustrative situations show these techniques and indicate some of the experiences in which they are called into play. Other aspects of social participation are located in charts in other sections. In the charts concerned with control of environmental factors and forces are persistent situations having to do with ability to deal with social, economic, and political structures, another aspect of the total problem of learning to live in social groups. Persistent situations calling for value judgments in relationships with others are grouped with other problems having to do with moral choice and responsibility. Among the health situations calling for meeting social and emotional needs there are some related to satisfying needs for affection and for security in group relationships. This is a fourth major aspect of the problem of learning to live and work with others.

One daily life experience often involves all four kinds of social problems—ability to use effective techniques in social relationships, to deal with social structures, to make value judgments in social relationships, to meet social and emotional needs. The youth with responsibility to a student council committee must establish effective working relationships with those on his committee and must take his appropriate part in its activities. He must also understand the structure and organization of the group. He faces the problems of deciding how important it is to carry out his commitments to others and how to make maximum use of his own abilities and those of others. And he must be able to satisfy his own need for status in a group without making unwholesome demands on others. The teacher needs to identify which type of growth is most needed. If the problem is mainly one of organizing a committee for effective work, further help would be in terms of many other cooperative group experiences coupled with study of what makes for effective cooperation. If it is lack of understanding of the structure and functioning of an organized group, additional help might involve study of the constitution of the student council and of other organized groups—the city government, the state legislature, and the like. Neglect of duties through lack of a sense of responsibility to others requires experiences in other situations where the primary question is one's obligation to other people. Excessive demands for attention, withdrawing, or other evidences of insecurity and lack of status in group relationships may lead to many kinds of individual guidance and group responsibility where the teacher is primarily concerned with helping the individual develop a feeling of at-homeness with the group. Once the teacher has identified the persistent problem or problems with which the learner most needs to be helped, he may supplement the immediate experience with a variety of others calling for similar competencies as suggested in the appropriate chart.

Every situation in which other persons are involved calls for skills in social participation. Therefore, opportunities to observe needs in this area and to give help are always present. The teacher concerned about social growth builds an informal classroom atmosphere in which pupils have opportunities to work together, to visit with each other, to explore common interests, and to share reactions to situations. Such procedures are appropriate for all grade levels and for all subject areas. While the demands of the particular situation must be the deciding factor in the class organization, teachers of all subjects have, throughout the school year, many opportunities to help children and youth develop skills in human relationships. Needs for growth in social participation are not quite as apparent, nor does as much growth take place, in the situation where learners must always work quietly at their own desks, where individual rather than group enterprises are the heart of the program, where teacher guidance is in the form of paternalistic authority or direction rather than democratic leadership.

GROWTH IN ABILITY TO ACT IN PERSON-TO-PERSON RELATIONSHIPS

Person-to-person relationships, the focus of the first of the three charts in this division, include the situations in which the techniques are primarily those needed to work, play, and live successfully with other individuals. Techniques for making friends, for showing appropriate affection to family and friends, for establishing the personal relationships which make for ease in working with others, for giving or receiving help in guidance relationships—these are basic to the well-being of every individual. At all ages these situations demand the capacity both to give and to receive. One must know how to accept affection from family and friends and, in turn, how and when to express it. In work relationships the enterprise is at times cooperative, while at other times the individual may be leader or follower; in more complex work relationships many other roles are played. Guidance is both given and received—one is at times asking for help from others and at times striving to give help to others. Basic democratic values calling for respect of the unique worth of each individual, and modification of desires in terms of the needs of others, also call for effective person-to-person relationships if these values are to be put into action.

The most desirable method of grouping the persistent life situations within this area seemed to be in terms of the kind of relationship—social or work; friendship or casual contact; cooperative, service, or guidance. Some common techniques are needed in meeting the situations in all these categories. To be able to understand the other person, to sense his capacities and limitations, to adjust one's response to another's needs, are important whether the relationship is social or work, close or casual. To show some of the differences in the demands made and the situations faced as the kind and degree of the relationship change, as well as the interrelatedness, some of the daily life experiences demanding these common techniques have been given in connection with each kind of person-to-person relationship.

As was true of the charts in preceding sections, there are many interrelationships between the situations in the area of person-to-person relationships and those in the areas of group membership and intergroup cooperation. The importance of effective techniques in person-to-person relationships to meeting problems successfully in these other areas is obvious. Therefore, the aspects of situations which call primarily for understanding and responding to others as individuals are given in this chart and are not repeated in either of the other charts. There are also many interrelationships between the situations listed in this area and those listed under the persistent situation of working in and through the family group included in the area of economic-social-political structures and forces and between this chart and the earlier one focused on mental health problems of achieving secure relationships with others. In general, the emphasis in this chart is upon the techniques through which these other ends may be achieved.

Many of the techniques of adequate person-to-person relationships will be built through day-to-day guidance as activities proceed which involve other persons. Many times during the day learners of all ages face decisions in this area—to criticize or to be silent, to express approval or to withhold it; to use common amenities in expressing thanks, asking to be excused, and greeting others, or not to do so; to decide if the other person has spoken in anger or is joking, whether a friend is annoyed or merely tired, whether or not a friend is pleased when no outward expression of pleasure is given. Teachers alert to the need to grow in person-to-person relationships identify situations such as these and provide necessary guidance for learners. There also will be times when an individual or a group may give extended consideration to a particular problem. What to do when one is teased, how to treat the clerk in the corner store, how to answer the telephone, how to behave when on a date, how to reply to criticism, how much to demand of friends, what to do to show sympathy to a friend—these situations and others like them may at times become important direct concerns of learners. When they do, time spent in discussing the particular situation or providing the needed help in other ways is an important contribution to growth. These problems requiring extended direct study arise in most class groups and under all types of curriculum design.

Certain of the subject fields relate closely to the problems in this chart. Teachers of home economics and home and family living usually devote time to many of the day-to-day situations involving social amenities and to the problems of family relationships listed here. The area of health has expanded in recent years to include many problems of person-to-person relationships as they bear on social and emotional needs. Teachers of English and language arts work with situations in this area as they help learners analyze drama and other forms of literature for the meanings of person-to-person relationships and for an understanding of how these interpersonal relations affect the course of events. Likewise, teachers concerned with the social sciences guide children and youth in exploring the social scene for increasing insights into ways in which individuals and groups relate to one another. The daily life situations listed may have particular value for teachers working in these fields.

Some typical situations calling for growth in ability to act in person-to-person relationships

	EARLY CHILDHOOD	LATER CHILDHOOD
	A. Establishing Effective Social Relations with Others	
DEVELOPING FRIENDSHIPS AND AFFECTIONATE RELATIONSHIPS Interpreting responses of others	**Making gross interpretations of the responses of those with whom one has contact**—Responding to smiles, tears, anger of other persons; knowing when other children are pleased with one's suggestions; knowing when one is being teased; identifying evidences of displeasure or disturbance in other children—pushing, calling names, hitting back; selecting children who seem friendly and congenial to share in special activities; interpreting changes in tone of voice and manner on part of parents, teachers, other adults . . .	**Discovering ways of making finer discriminations in interpreting the responses of family and friends**—Telling when friends are happy, when bored, annoyed, or angry; developing some understanding that causes of behavior are not always apparent—that disappointment at home can cause one to be difficult to get along with in class, that a child who is disturbed does not always mean what he says; telling when child is bluffing or boasting; telling when teacher is pleased, worried, annoyed; knowing when parents or others are issuing a command, when making a suggestion; knowing when one is being teased; finding which children are most congenial, have like interests, can be counted on; discovering the different ways in which people express the same feeling . . .
Making appropriate responses to family and friends	**Exploring ways of expressing feelings to family and friends**—Developing acceptable ways of showing friends that one likes them; deciding what expressions of affection are appropriate at home, in school; teasing others and responding to teasing; finding effective ways of expressing displeasure or dissatisfaction—learning to substitute discussion for action, deciding when to withdraw from a situation; deciding which children to invite home, to a party; finding ways of expressing interest in new child in school or neighborhood; responding to offers of friendship; learning to thank people . . .	**Finding ways of adapting expressions of feeling to reactions of friends and family**—Explaining activities to younger children; adjusting expressions of affection to different age levels; developing ways of responding to members of opposite sex; responding when very much disappointed; deciding what action to take in a quarrel; knowing what to do when teased; knowing what is involved in teasing others; knowing what to say or do when scolded, when critical suggestions are made about one's activities; discovering ways of expressing criticism helpfully; learning what types of gifts are appropriate; using appropriate ways of thanking others . . .

YOUTH | ADULTHOOD

A. Establishing Effective Social Relations with Others

YOUTH

Developing increased sensitivity to the reactions of others—Knowing how to interpret subtle reactions of members of family—when parents are becoming disturbed, worried, what younger children are feeling; understanding ways in which a close friend is likely to show pleasure or concern; telling whether member of the opposite sex likes one; knowing when to interpret teasing or disparaging remarks as forms of affection; telling real from unintentional slights; developing increased sensitivity to multiple causation of behavior; distinguishing flattery from genuine approval; deciding when and how far such external factors as personal appearance, manners, socio-economic background should influence one's friendships; deciding which friends to entrust with confidences . . .

ADULTHOOD

Using available knowledge of family and friends appropriately in interpreting behavior—Knowing when members of family are pleased, discouraged, disturbed; sensing weariness, pleasure, excitement in close friends; "reading between the lines" of letters from friends; knowing when an argument is causing others to become irritated; deciding when others are joking, when serious; interpreting behavior of small children—what crying means, what is meant by expressions of affection, by pouting; knowing when children are becoming tired; distinguishing between situations when anger is directed against one personally and when one is merely a symbol—realizing that children kept from trip by rain may show hostility to teacher, that child who says "I hate you" does not always mean this; deciding importance of mutual interests, similarity of backgrounds, age differences, in developing friendships . . .

YOUTH

Developing increased sensitivity in expressing feelings to family and friends—Developing friendships with members of opposite sex; determining frequency and type of dating; learning what is involved in "going steady"; expressing friendship to one's own sex—deciding what confidences to share, what activities to undertake together; learning what is involved when one gets a "crush" on a friend; pressing one's point in argument without showing annoyance or anger; deciding how to respond to criticism or reprimand; deciding how best to express criticism or disapproval; deciding how best to "make up" after a quarrel, what to do when friend loses his temper; adjusting expressions of sympathy, congratulations, apology, appreciation to needs and ages of different individuals . . .

ADULTHOOD

Establishing mature patterns of expressing feelings to family and friends—Adjusting expressions of affection to different members of family; deciding when and how to show displeasure, disagreement, or disappointment to others in family or to friends; deciding when and how to express interest in friend's affairs; showing appropriate interest in affairs of children and youth; expressing sympathy in variety of situations; judging when to joke with or tease others; using appropriate expressions of thanks for children, close friends, others; responding in evaluative conferences with supervisor or superior; knowing when and what form of apology is needed; choosing persons with whom to share close friendship . . .

	EARLY CHILDHOOD	LATER CHILDHOOD
Deciding on rights and responsibilities in relationships	**Learning to give and take in relationships with others**—Finding what it means to mother to be asked to do special things for one; giving up special desires when others in family are too busy to accede to them; finding what special adjustments should be made for those who are sick; deciding whether to share toys with other members of family, with other children in school; learning how to take turns; finding what classroom behavior best helps work of all to move ahead; writing letter to classmate who is ill . . .	**Finding how to consider the needs of others in making demands or undertaking obligations**—Deciding when to ask special favors of parents; deciding what one's responsibilities should be in home; deciding when to assume home responsibilities, when to ask others in family to carry one's duties; finding ways of adjusting activities to interests of friends—taking turns in choosing games, deciding where to play; deciding what acquiescence to expect of "best" friend; sharing books, toys, play space with others; adjusting requests for use of family television to needs of others . . .
RESPONDING TO CASUAL SOCIAL CONTACTS Making appropriate responses	**Exploring ways of responding to casual social contacts**—Talking to adult visitors in home; talking with friends' parents when visiting in their homes; taking care of visitors in classroom; using common courtesies; getting acquainted with new children in class; taking message to principal or to another teacher; helping strangers who ask directions in school . . .	**Finding ways of adapting responses to the reactions of persons met in casual social contacts**—Using appropriate expressions or means of thanking others; responding to persons who express thanks; finding why and what means of showing respect are used in contacts with women, with elderly persons, with other adults; making introductions; responding when introduced to visitors; talking with adults visiting in home, school; using good telephone manners . . .
PARTICIPATING IN SOCIAL ACTIVITIES Determining kind of social activity	**Helping make plans for entertaining friends**—Deciding how to entertain friends invited to party, to lunch, or to play after school; helping decide how to entertain another class; deciding when and how to entertain parents at school; suggesting games to play at party; helping make decorations for party; deciding what refreshments to have when entertaining parents; making suggestions for luncheon menus . . .	**Finding ways of adjusting social activities to the general interests of guests**—Entertaining parents or others at school events; deciding on games for class; planning club program that meets varied interests; entertaining friends at home; planning refreshments for birthday party; helping plan hikes, picnics; deciding what movie to attend with friend; deciding what activities would be appropriate for a party . . .

YOUTH	ADULTHOOD
Developing increased sensitivity to the needs of others in making demands and undertaking obligations—Deciding what personal services to ask of family and when; adjusting requests for use of family property to needs of others—car, television, telephone; determining what responsibilities one has to parents—in sharing household tasks, in informing them about activities, in demands on family funds; deciding what favors to ask of or grant "best" friends—borrowing money, borrowing clothes, help on special jobs; deciding how exclusive a given friendship should be—whether to "go steady" with one person, whether "best" friend should have other close friendships; considering when to ask friends to adjust activities to one's interests, when one should do what friends demand . . .	**Adjusting demands and obligations undertaken to the abilities and needs of others**—Deciding what responsibilities to take with regard to members of the family; deciding how far and when to make sacrifices for children; deciding what considerations to ask from children in family; determining what represents real consideration and affection from husband or wife; deciding what responsibility to assume with regard to personal friends—how much time to spend with them, what help to give on personal problems, when to assume financial obligations; deciding what activities to share with different friends; deciding when and what confidences to share with friends; deciding when to ask special favors from friends . . .
Gaining increased ability to adjust responses in a variety of casual social situations—Getting acquainted with new pupils; helping visitors from another school feel at home; visiting with parents of friends; adjusting introduction to particular situation; deciding what special consideration to give to women, to elderly persons, to other adults; acting as host or hostess at school affair; learning how to initiate and carry conversation with persons whom one meets casually . . .	**Using appropriate form of expression in a variety of casual social situations**—Calling on new families in town; adjusting conversation to person and situation—talking with shy persons, with persons who are very outgoing, with children, with persons having special interests; deciding when to offer or expect traditional deference to women; helping children understand use of common courtesies in casual social contacts; helping children learn appropriate use of telephone . . .
Extending ability to plan social activities appropriate to a variety of situations—Deciding what activities to plan for a date; determining the number and kind of all-school functions to have during year; deciding what activities at class party will best meet the needs of all; deciding whether to plan class function in which expenses and kind of clothing demanded will bar some members; planning how one's club can entertain another group; helping plan school affair to entertain parents; acting on program committee of club or church youth group; entertaining friends at home . . .	**Providing social activities appropriate to the needs and interests of those concerned**—Planning a variety of means of entertaining guests in home—teas, coffee hours, dinners, card parties; considering how formal a function to plan; deciding which friends and how many to bring together at a given occasion; planning congenial seating arrangement of guests; planning church or benefit tea; helping plan formal banquet, community dance, club dinner; planning party for children . . .

	EARLY CHILDHOOD	LATER CHILDHOOD
Using appropriate amenities	**Exploring family and school patterns of behavior in social situations**—Greeting guests in home or at school; finding how and when to excuse oneself; finding how to act at dinner table and how to use table service customary in family group; participating in conversation at meals; greeting guests at a party; thanking one's hostess; writing thank-you notes for gifts; sending invitations and thank-you notes to other classes; writing invitations to parents; answering telephone . . .	**Using amenities appropriate to the social situations met**—Introducing friends at home or in school; greeting guests in home, visitors at school; using common courtesies appropriately; acting as hosts to or guests of another class; helping determine appropriate manners for school lunchroom; using appropriate table manners at home and in homes of friends; deciding what to wear to a party; finding how to make guests feel at home; carrying one's share of conversation; writing friendly letters, thank-you notes; using appropriate telephone courtesies . . .

B. Establishing Effective Working Relations with Others

WORKING ON A COMMON ENTERPRISE Adjusting working relationships to capacities and needs	**Exploring ways of working happily with others**—Helping decide which child should take special responsibilities in class; helping decide how to divide task among several children; finding how to make suggestions to friend working with one, how to adjust work in terms of his suggestions; knowing when to let friend finish his part of the job even when he uses a different method; sharing tools and equipment with others . . .	**Finding ways of taking individual interests and needs into account in working relationships**—Helping plan work so as to make best use of individual abilities; setting standards against which to choose person who would make best editor of class paper, store manager; helping decide how to give less able children opportunity to learn how to do a job; giving advice to others about their part of job, and taking suggestions; developing more effective personal and group work habits; considering what obligations are part of job one has accepted . . .

YOUTH	ADULTHOOD
Learning amenities appropriate to a wide variety of situations—Learning amenities appropriate to formal dance, tea, concert, formal dinner, others; deciding what kind of invitation to use for various occasions; helping set formal dinner table; arranging table decorations at tea; helping serve at tea; deciding what courtesies should be extended to patrons at class function; deciding what refreshments are appropriate for a variety of social functions; participating in church supper, community dance; finding what courtesies should be extended to escort; selecting clothing appropriate to occasion; writing thank-you notes, friendly letters, cheer messages; adjusting telephone conversations to a variety of needs . . .	**Adjusting the use of social amenities to the needs of particular situations**—Adapting behavior in social groups to kind of occasion; deciding what clothing is appropriate for a social event; issuing appropriate kinds of invitations for a variety of social events; adjusting activities as host or hostess to a variety of situations; engaging in a variety of social correspondence —friendly letters, notes of sympathy, thank-you notes, cheer cards; helping children and youth understand and use amenities appropriate to most common situations . . .

B. Establishing Effective Working Relations with Others

YOUTH	ADULTHOOD
Increasing in ability to make effective adjustments to individual capacities of those working together—Adjusting work responsibilities to make maximum use of abilities and interests of individuals; deciding how and when to assign leadership responsibilities; working with younger children in school on joint projects; considering what obligations one has assumed in working with others on class enterprises; considering whether personal interests should be allowed to interfere with accepted responsibility; adjusting time and method of work to capacities and plans of others . . .	**Adjusting working relationships to the abilities and needs of those working together**—Deciding how abilities or interests of associates can best be utilized; adjusting leadership–follower relations to abilities needed in particular aspect of job; adjusting to physical stamina and work habits of those involved in a piece of work; deciding in whom to place trust and responsibility; considering when to share personal problems with coworker, to what extent to take on personal problems of others; determining nature and extent of social contacts with coworkers; advising with children regarding their work responsibilities . . .

	EARLY CHILDHOOD	LATER CHILDHOOD
WORKING IN SERVICE GROUP RELATIONSHIPS Deciding on services to expect or give	**Finding how to give and ask for services**—Finding how to ask storekeeper for what is wanted; talking with school custodian, policeman, other adults who help in school; finding how much and what kind of service to expect from school custodian, maid, personnel in the school cafeteria, others; finding what services are rendered by policeman, postman, others; learning when and how to thank people for services rendered; carrying out one's share of home or class housekeeping responsibilities . . .	**Finding ways of adjusting responses to those involved in service situations**—Learning how to make requests of service groups—to place order at store, to make request of school custodian; adjusting requests to other demands being made upon service personnel; finding how to telephone for special information; expressing appreciation for services rendered; deciding what obligations one has taken toward subscribers on one's paper route, what is involved in being an errand boy; responding to criticism or appreciation from employer, from parents, classmates, or teacher who have assigned a job . . .
WORKING IN GUIDANCE RELATIONSHIPS Deciding on guidance to give or secure	**Finding how others can give help in problem situations**—Learning when to turn to teacher or parent for special help; finding which friends can give best advice on different problems; finding what kind of help is given by doctor, dentist, nurse; finding why parents insist on following doctor's advice; helping younger children with simple problems—showing how toy works, opening door . . .	**Becoming better able to ask for and give help in terms of the needs of the situation**—Stating clearly one's request for help; deciding to which teacher to go for help on a particular problem; finding what competence is brought by doctor, nurse, others with special training; helping parents carry out doctor's orders; deciding when to turn to older brother or sister, to one's peers for advice; helping younger children with school work, with advice about games or toys . . .

YOUTH	ADULTHOOD
Developing increased ability to make appropriate adjustments of responses in service situations—Adjusting requests in terms of ability of person giving service and other demands being made upon him; deciding when to ask one's employer for special privileges; discovering amenities appropriate on a part-time job—manners, courtesies, sense of humor, others; deciding what expression of appreciation is appropriate—when to tip, when to give gifts, when to express thanks verbally; responding to expressions of appreciation; responding to just and unjust criticism . . .	**Establishing effective and harmonious relationships in service situations**—Evaluating services and adjusting requests for service to ability and responsibilities of person involved; adjusting services to particular demands of job; deciding what positions of trust to ask service personnel to assume; considering what positions of trust to accept, if an employee; expressing appreciation or criticism in terms which will be understood and acceptable to those for whom it is intended; interpreting expressions of approval or disapproval; deciding how to act upon criticism; considering what personal associations to give or accept from employees or fellow workers . . .
Extending ability to identify the elements in the situation in which guidance is asked for or given—Finding which persons in school or community are best able to give advice on a personal problem; learning how to identify aspects of a personal problem for counselor; evaluating advice given by different people—parents, friends, clergyman, school counselor; deciding when to ask for further help or another point of view on problem; acting upon advice of physician; deciding when to advise friends, when they should be encouraged to seek advice from more competent or better informed persons; acting as leader and counselor in camp, in church-school class . . .	**Securing or giving guidance appropriate to the demands of the situation**—Determining what factors to consider in selecting physician, lawyer, other person giving professional advice; deciding when to take advice of colleague on a professional problem; giving advice in terms of needs and capacities of other person—deciding what explanation to give, what terms to use, what technical information to provide; giving guidance to children in family, to youth seeking advice . . .

GROWTH IN ABILITY TO PARTICIPATE AS A RESPONSIBLE GROUP MEMBER

The experiences faced and the techniques needed by an active member of a cooperative group are included in the following chart. Deciding when group activity is desirable, determining what groups best serve existing needs, taking a responsible share in formulating and carrying out group policy, and taking appropriate leadership responsibility as a group leader or one to whom special responsibility has been delegated, are some of the problems the individual faces.

Democratic procedures are based on the belief that all will profit when each individual takes a responsible share in the decisions which affect his welfare. As more complex intergroup relationships direct living in today's world, it becomes increasingly important that each individual be able to contribute to the formulation and execution of the policies of the groups to which he belongs. Sound techniques for coming to joint decisions, selecting leaders, evaluating the work of delegates or of experts, and executing group decisions are essential.

In more and more situations, the individual's effectiveness is coming to be contingent upon the effectiveness of the groups through which he works. In turn, the strength of group action depends upon the soundness of the leadership given. Children and youth require opportunities to discover how individual power can be extended through a group, to learn the importance of considering the membership requirements and appraising the policies of the groups they join, to understand the obligations assumed with the acceptance of group leadership responsibilities. With the young child it is mainly a question of taking part in a small group working on a special problem. With the adult, the situations of daily living range from sharing in the work of local social or service groups to making oneself felt when crucial national and international policies are being reviewed or formulated by his government.

The fact that everyday experiences involving the techniques of cooperative group membership often include the persistent situations of working with economic and social structures has already been indicated. The close relationship with persistent situations calling for moral choice and responsibility in using the potential abilities of self and others for the good of all has also been pointed out. Understanding of the structures and organization within which one is working, and the ability to exercise value judgments about the importance of cooperation and one's obligation to work with others in a democratic setting, must accompany skills of cooperation.

With little children the social group is small, flexible, and shifting in membership. Leadership responsibilities move easily from one child to another and group solidarity is not strong. Guidance at this level comes through help in sharing opinions, listening to others, coming to simple conclusions, carrying out what one has promised to do, and abiding by group decisions. The intermediate-grade child has a much more highly developed sense of group responsibility. This is the age of secret clubs and "gangs," of devotion to leaders, and of loyalty to the group. In a democratically organized classroom much can be done to increase ability to plan, to come to joint decisions, to make wise choices in delegating responsibility, to evaluate the effectiveness of delegates, and to carry out responsibility. At adolescence interest in parliamentary techniques and the precise mechanics of arriving at group decisions becomes strong. If growth has been consistent, there will be steady increase in ability to discuss, to plan, to work cooperatively, to carry through responsibilities, and to make wise choice of leaders. Democratic values require such growth of all citizens. The complexity of the social interrelationships in today's world adds new meaning and urgency to this demand.

The techniques and situations described in the following chart involve learnings important at all levels and in all subject areas. Developing ability to participate as a responsible group member is usually an important goal, regardless of curriculum design. Whenever children or youth are involved in group activities the situations suggested in this chart are likely to arise. However, teachers of English and social studies in the upper elementary and high school grades will find particular help in this chart. While all teachers work on group membership skills, it is often the teacher of language arts who takes special time to develop skills in chairing meetings, making motions, taking minutes, writing or giving orally committee reports. Those who teach social studies will find that the situations faced by adolescents and adults extend to problems of government—the responsibility of the individual in keeping informed about government action, in participating in community groups, in selecting local and national leaders, in deciding when to seek or to accept office, in appraising the work of public officials. Teachers in both these areas may have special interest in helping learners find how to secure and to give accurate information about group activities—using appropriate methods to report such activities, evaluating oral and written reports of activities, appraising the way in which a delegated responsibility or the duties of a public office are discharged, deciding how to secure additional information when reports are conflicting, interpreting propaganda. Teachers who must focus on experiences within a particular subject area will find leads in the illustrations to guide their planning. Developing ability to participate as a responsible group member is usually an important goal in these areas regardless of curriculum design.

Some typical situations calling for growth in ability to participate as a responsible group member

	EARLY CHILDHOOD	LATER CHILDHOOD
	A. Deciding When to Join a Group	
DECIDING WHEN GROUP ACTIVITY IS DESIRABLE Deciding what existing groups to join	**Deciding in which informal group activities to take part**—Deciding which games to join on playground or street; choosing children to cooperate in a group project; helping decide what classroom committees are needed; deciding whether to join Cub Scouts, Brownies, other community groups . . .	**Deciding which of a number of peer groups to join**—Deciding whether to join Boy Scouts or other community youth groups; finding neighborhood group with which to play; deciding which school team to join in playing games; deciding which group to work with in carrying out class project; discussing what it means to belong to a church, political party, labor union, or other group to which one's parents belong; choosing which of a number of school interest groups to join . . .
Determining membership obligations	**Finding what it means to offer to work with a group**—Finding what responsibilities must be carried out if one has offered to share in a project; finding what it means to be part of class committee; finding what is entailed in being a representative to student council; discovering what is expected of one in a church school group; finding what one will have to do to become Cub Scout, Brownie . . .	**Finding what membership obligations accompany the joining of various peer groups**—Investigating membership requirements of various community groups in which one is interested; gaining more insight into responsibilities of class committees; discussing what the job of school helper or student council representative should be; deciding whether membership obligations of group are those one can undertake . . .
Deciding when to organize new groups or disband old ones	**Helping decide when other groups are needed to carry out class activities**—Deciding when another class committee is needed to do a special job; helping plan for group with special interests to work together; deciding when committee's job is done; asking parents to provide play space or equipment for neighborhood group . . .	**Taking an active part in organizing desired informal groups**—Helping organize hobby clubs, "secret" clubs, special-interest groups; organizing group of classmates to do special job; sharing in organization of desired school teams; helping organize neighborhood groups for play; deciding when club has served its purpose; deciding when class committee is no longer needed . . .

YOUTH | ADULTHOOD

A. Deciding When to Join a Group

YOUTH

Determining more discriminating bases for appraising the value of various kinds of group membership—Deciding which high school clubs to join; deciding whether to try out for a high school team; deciding whether to join a sorority or fraternity; deciding whether to join a church; finding what work is done by churches and other service groups; deciding which community youth organizations to join; discussing work of political parties and what it means to become a member of one; discussing work of management associations, labor unions, other community groups . . .

Appraising membership requirements in terms of one's abilities and interests—Appraising and adjusting to demands of a social peer group; considering whether one can develop abilities needed by school team, band, chorus; finding what obligations are involved in church membership; discussing what is involved in joining a labor union, political party; deciding whether activities of community youth groups justify undertaking their membership obligations; deciding whether satisfactions from college fraternity or sorority justify meeting requirements . . .

Organizing peer groups to achieve definite ends—Helping to organize special youth service group; deciding which persons to include in high school or college social crowds; helping decide whether student council is needed; appraising effectiveness of existing council organization of committees; helping decide needed high school club program; sharing in organization of needed community group; discussing issues involved in proposed organization of new political party . . .

ADULTHOOD

Deciding upon the groups through which to engage in economic, social, and political activities—Deciding whether to join a political party; deciding whether to join a labor union, professional group; deciding what kinds of social groups best satisfy leisure-time needs; considering whether to affiliate with lodges or other service groups; considering desirability of church membership, whether to help children become affiliated with a church, attend church school; helping children and youth evaluate membership in various groups . . .

Appraising ability and willingness to meet the membership obligations of a given group—Deciding whether to undertake obligations of lodges or other service groups; deciding which friendship groups to affiliate with most closely; considering what obligations are necessary to effective church membership; deciding whether values to be derived from membership in a professional organization are commensurate with investment of time and money; deciding whether to work actively for political party . . .

Taking action to secure the groups needed to carry on social, service, economic, and political activities—Deciding which community projects can best be carried out by group action; deciding when special group for community action has served its purpose; organizing neighborhood groups to carry out special projects; adjusting structure and purpose of social groups to new interests; deciding whether to help organize a professional group; helping set up better recreational groups for young people; deciding whether to help establish a knot-hole baseball team; considering desirable kinds of international organizations . . .

	EARLY CHILDHOOD	LATER CHILDHOOD
DECIDING ON NATURE OF GROUP PARTICIPATION Determining how actively to participate	**Finding what part to take in class and play groups**—Deciding whether to stay with group until job is finished; deciding whether to share toys with children playing in neighborhood, when to take toys home; finding what happens if a promised task is not done; being asked to give help on something one does especially well . . .	**Deciding what group obligations to undertake**—Deciding whether to volunteer for special committee responsibilities; deciding how to apportion time among various group activities; determining which of a number of services to a group is best use of effort—which part to try for in school play, which position to ask for on team; discovering what happens to group project if one does not complete one's share . . .

B. Participating as a Group Member

	EARLY CHILDHOOD	LATER CHILDHOOD
HELPING TO FORMULATE GROUP POLICY Keeping informed about group activity	**Keeping in touch with the plans of one's immediate group**—Deciding how to keep a record of group plans; using class records as guides to next plans; deciding when to ask others what plans are; watching bulletin-board announcements; sharing in group discussion which reviews plans; learning how to confer with teacher about plans . . .	**Finding a variety of ways through which one can get information about the activities of a group**—Deciding which of a variety of records will best inform group of next steps; using classroom bulletin board appropriately to record group plans; deciding what means should be used to place student council decisions before others in school; studying exhibits or displays of group's work as guide to their activities; using minutes of a meeting . . .
Expressing opinions regarding group activity	**Taking part in informal small-group discussion**—Contributing to class plans; listening while other members make their contribution; taking part in family discussions; finding how leader of group helps various group members contribute; making plans with other children in informal group situations—deciding what games to play, who is to take first turn on swing . . .	**Exploring various ways through which one can express an idea in a group**—Sharing in class planning; deciding when and how much to say in meeting; finding how to be recognized by chairman; finding how one reports class opinions to student council and vice versa; finding how to participate in informal planning of small-group projects; preparing written report to present to group; deciding what information is needed before expressing an opinion; using cartoons or pictures to make point clear to group; deciding how and when dramatization might be used to present an idea . . .

YOUTH	ADULTHOOD
Establishing more critical bases for determining extent of group activity—Deciding how many school activities can be participated in effectively, how many special responsibilities to accept; deciding what committee responsibilities to undertake in community youth groups; determining when participation calls for ability which one does not have, when for a contribution which one is specially fitted to make; determining when time schedules or other obligations make effective participation in project impossible . . .	**Bringing all appropriate factors to bear in deciding on the nature and extent of active group participation**—Deciding how actively to work in political party; deciding on nature and extent of active church participation; deciding when financial support of group represents adequate participation; considering whether to join bridge club or other social group that meets regularly; deciding whether to accept responsibilities in community group—being a member of school board, community council, accepting other leadership responsibilities . . .

B. Participating as a Group Member

YOUTH	ADULTHOOD
Appraising various methods of becoming informed as to group activities—Reading school newspaper; reading financial report of group; helping keep minutes of group activity; considering adequacy of reporting by various school groups through bulletin boards, exhibits, advertising; discussing adequacy of press, magazines, and other sources of information about activities of national groups; becoming acquainted with *Congressional Record;* considering what constitutes adequate report from student council representative; evaluating radio and television reporting; appraising use of propaganda in reporting . . .	**Using appropriate means of becoming informed about the activities of groups**—Studying written reports to be discussed in group meeting; keeping track of notices of special activities; serving as group secretary or treasurer; deciding which magazines or papers best give picture of activities of national group; deciding how to get additional information when conflicting reports appear in papers; deciding what agencies best help interpret propaganda . . .
Evaluating the appropriateness and effectiveness of the variety of means through which opinions can be expressed—Learning how to use parliamentary procedures; gaining insight into group roles operating in classroom or club group; developing increased skill in adjusting one's contribution so as to facilitate group progress; deciding when and how to use bulletin board to put a proposal before group; using graphs, pictures, charts in making ideas clear to group; appraising value of writing letters to newspaper, congressman; finding what procedures are used in congressional debates and reasons for them; finding how chairman leads discussion in large groups—attending town meetings, or meetings of other community groups . . .	**Expressing opinions through means appropriate to a variety of group situations**—Determining when and what parliamentary procedures in discussion are appropriate to size and purpose of group; deciding when written report rather than verbal one should be used as starting point for group discussions; deciding when and how to write to senator or congressman; deciding whether to write letters to newspapers or magazines; deciding whether to vote in election primaries; understanding reasons for procedures in legislative or congressional debates; taking active part in discussions of community councils, town meetings, social and service groups . . .

	EARLY CHILDHOOD	LATER CHILDHOOD
Coming to joint decisions	**Finding how one comes to informal agreement with other members of a group**—Finding what saying "yes" to a proposal commits one to; deciding which of two or three suggestions made in class to support; helping adjust plans when there are disagreements; referring back to previous plans when disagreements arise; considering whether plans should be changed in light of new demands and problems . . .	**Applying simple techniques of securing group agreement on problems of immediate interest**—Deciding when to secure group vote; finding what majority vote means; discussing why secret ballots are used in elections; understanding how to vote by ballot; deciding when advice of a specialist should be used to guide group decisions; identifying when a problem centers around facts or school regulations which group decisions cannot alter; evaluating alternative proposals and considering ways of resolving conflicting opinions; finding ways of getting alternatives or compromises clearly before all concerned . . .
SELECTING LEADERS Determining the abilities needed by and choosing leaders	**Choosing persons to lead in immediate tasks**—Planning with others in group jobs that need to be done to carry out class project; deciding what kind of person should be delegated to carry out special tasks; deciding when a teacher can give special help; finding when school nurse or others on school staff can give expert advice; deciding which classmates should be given committee responsibilities or special jobs; deciding which parts should be taken by various children in producing a play; deciding which child to ask to announce assembly program . . .	**Deciding what general ability is possessed by various candidates for a job**—Deciding what ability is needed in captain of team; considering what class delegate to student council should be able to do; deciding what special responsibilities those appointed to class committees are to undertake; deciding when leader needs special ability in getting along with other people; deciding which teacher or club leader to ask for special help on project; determining whether job can be delegated to classmate who has not met previous obligations; deciding to what degree popularity of classmate should influence his appointment; finding how parents and others decide among political candidates . . .

YOUTH	ADULTHOOD
Understanding and using a variety of techniques in coming to group decisions—Developing skill in evaluating alternative proposals made in council or class meetings; deciding what voting procedures are appropriate to a variety of school or club activities; finding when a motion is appropriate, how to make or to amend a motion; deciding when opinion of an expert instead of majority vote should be the basis of decision; deciding how to use report of delegated committee; discussing methods through which congressional votes are arrived at; discussing what is involved in voting in local and national elections; studying procedures used to come to agreements on international questions; analyzing differences from nation to nation in ways of coming to decisions . . .	**Adjusting techniques of coming to joint decisions to a variety of group situations**—Deciding which methods of securing expressions of opinion are suitable in a variety of situations—when to call for vote, when informal agreement is sufficient; deciding when to use ballot, show of hands, or other methods of showing agreement; using appropriate methods of making, amending motions in groups where formal procedures are used; determining what kind of summary is needed in discussion at a large town meeting, a committee, an informal social group; deciding how conflicting proposals will affect ultimate action taken by group; deciding whether group approval needs to be unanimous or majority vote; considering whether local voting procedure by proportional representation or other special system should be revised; evaluating existing machinery for achieving international agreements . . .
Extending ability to make critical appraisal of the competence of individuals who are being considered for positions of leadership—Determining qualifications for various officers of student council; learning to distinguish those leadership positions where ability to inspire followers is needed from those where skill in group leadership is important; deciding how far special talent is important in choosing a team, club president; deciding what expert advice is needed in order to complete class project; discussing qualifications demanded by major community and national offices; deciding when to offer to do special job; deciding whether to accept position of leadership responsibility when it is offered; deciding how many leadership responsibilities should be delegated to one person; making a critical review of previous evidence of leadership abilities of a candidate; weighing popularity of candidate against evidence of needed ability; discovering how one learns about records and abilities of political candidates; discussing ways other nations select their leaders . . .	**Applying appropriate techniques for determining the competence of candidates for positions of leadership**—Deciding what qualifications should be looked for in selecting president of service or social club; determining what qualifications to consider in nominating or electing city mayor, President, other public officials; deciding on abilities needed in chairmen of selected committees; evaluating training and experience of persons from whom technical competence is demanded; securing information about previous work of political candidates; deciding how to interpret references of candidate for position for which one is the employer; deciding how well candidate for club presidency will be able to work with other people; deciding when to run for office or accept nomination in local or national groups . . .

	EARLY CHILDHOOD	LATER CHILDHOOD
HELPING CARRY OUT GROUP POLICIES Determining needed organization and personnel	**Finding how various members of the group can share in carrying out responsibilities**—Deciding when to choose one or two persons to carry out job for group; helping to delegate class responsibilities to committees; deciding when specialists should be called in to help; considering how many people will be needed to finish job; helping decide how long an individual should hold special responsibility . . .	**Organizing class or other group to carry out class decisions**—Determining number and size of committees needed to carry out class projects; deciding what officers and committees are needed in student council; deciding what officers and committees are needed in class or community club; planning for help of specialist; finding what work is done by prominent local and national officials; helping plan how members of family can best work together . . .
Evaluating the work of those to whom responsibility is delegated	**Deciding how well tasks nave been carried out**—Deciding how well work of committee has been done; discussing how well various classmates have contributed to a joint enterprise; deciding how to revise plans in order to have work better done next time; helping children who have failed to carry out responsibilities plan for their next jobs . . .	**Determining bases on which to judge whether individuals have carried out their responsibilities**—Deciding whether report of committee provides needed information or should be questioned; judging work of delegates on given projects; appraising effectiveness of cooperative work of several committees putting on class party; deciding whether class representative to student council has represented class point of view fairly . . .
Executing group decisions	**Finaing how groups of which one is a member carry out their decisions**—Finding when it is important for members of class to stand by their agreements; giving up individual plans for group plans; applying rules in playing games; helping revise group plans to provide for individual or small-group interests; carrying out one's part in a plan; taking one's share in common problems such as cleaning up; being ready for next activity in program at time agreed upon . . .	**Developing a variety of methods of expressing and executing group decisions**—Deciding when members of group have the right to withdraw from majority decisions; deciding what to do if member of group refuses to participate; revising plans as new problems demand change; keeping members informed of group decisions; setting up and enforcing rules of a game; finding how local and state systems of law enforcement operate . . .

YOUTH	ADULTHOOD
Understanding and using a variety of methods to carry out the plans of a group—Building effective constitution for student council or club; planning for adequate representation on student council; deciding when special committees should be asked to undertake responsibilities; apportioning responsibilities so as to include all members who have contributions to make; deciding when to call for expert help; discussing organization through which local or national government functions; discussing existing organizations for international cooperation . . .	**Selecting appropriate organization and personnel for carrying out plans in a variety of groups**—Deciding what officers are needed to carry out activities of groups of various sizes; deciding when and what committees are needed in lodge, club, school staff, social group; considering effectiveness of constitution of club, local or national organization; deciding when to delegate responsibility to an expert or specialist; considering place of bureaus and commissions in local or national government; considering effectiveness of present organizations for international cooperation . . .
Building more adequate bases on which to evaluate a variety of delegated responsibilities—Deciding how long special committees should be given to bring reports back to class; appraising work of class committee before making second-term appointments; considering how well class chairman helps others to participate; deciding when to request financial statement from those handling class budget; developing more mature bases for evaluating recommendations of a committee; finding how one keeps informed about activities of congressional representative, community council . . .	**Evaluating the work of those to whom responsibility has been delegated**—Determining bases for evaluating proposals of an expert or committee delegated to do special job; evaluating report from a delegate; deciding how long it should take to test a new program in operation, what is best evidence of progress; deciding how far a committee decision represents joint thinking of all members of group; reviewing budgets, financial statements, reports of year's work; helping children evaluate how well each helped in family plan; appraising work of congressmen, other public officials; considering reports of work of delegates to international groups . . .
Taking responsibility for evaluating and helping carry out group decisions in groups in which one is involved—Deciding what controls student council should exercise; planning next steps when group disagrees on procedures; deciding whether to oppose what rest of group wishes to do; using effective methods in keeping group informed; discussing principles on which local and national systems of law enforcement function; discussing use of force as an international proposal; investigating critical function of minorities in government . . .	**Deciding when and through what means to uphold the joint decisions of a variety of groups**—Considering degree to which unanimous action is important in club or other group; helping children build bases for deciding when to support family plans, when to act independently; deciding how to deal with minority group demands; deciding whether to disagree with a majority decision; helping enforce state or national laws; deciding when it is appropriate to try to change a law; evaluating proposals for enforcing international agreements . . .

	EARLY CHILDHOOD	LATER CHILDHOOD
	C. Taking Leadership Responsibilities	
OUTLINING PRELIMINARY PLANS Projecting activities and needed personnel and materials	**Deciding on the steps to be taken to carry out delegated tasks**—Finding what is involved in specific tasks delegated by group; deciding best time for carrying out a special responsibility; checking with teacher or class record about plans for which one is responsible; choosing people one would like on committee; helping decide when aid from other class members will be needed; getting out materials and tools needed for job . . .	**Finding what is needed to lay plans for class activities for which one is responsible**—Deciding how much planning to do before committee meets; planning what should be considered at class, committee, or student council meetings; making rough estimate of time needed for an activity; thinking of possible ways in which work might be carried forward; making tentative decisions of what tasks might be done by individuals in group; deciding whether special books or materials are needed . . .
SECURING PARTICIPATION OF GROUP MEMBERS Keeping group members informed	**Helping others remember group plans**—Helping remind others of previous decisions; explaining plans to others; helping write class plans on board or experience chart; reporting progress and needs in class planning period . . .	**Becoming acquainted with various ways of keeping a group informed**—Deciding whether to report to class orally or to use written reports; keeping minutes of meeting; deciding what detailed information is needed by class; deciding how best to summarize reasoning behind plans . . .
Securing cooperative action	**Helping others to share in plans which one is proposing**—Presenting plans to class groups so that others have chance to share ideas; deciding when others should be allowed to change one's plans; calling on different members of group to make suggestions; listening to suggestions others make . . .	**Taking responsibility for securing cooperative action in situations where one is a leader**—Securing opinions from other members of committee; making sure that class members with differing opinions are heard; giving others credit for work done; planning how often to have group meetings to report progress and revise plans . . .

YOUTH | ADULTHOOD

C. Taking Leadership Responsibilities

Youth

Doing independent planning in delegated leadership situations—Making an outline of order of business when chairman of meeting; deciding what possible activities might be proposed in class meeting; considering implications of responsibilities delegated to committee one is asked to head; estimating time needed for various phases of work; estimating persons needed to carry out work; appraising special abilities of committee in terms of assignment; deciding what expert help is most likely to be needed; studying details of job to be done in order to determine possible needed equipment; providing needed materials for committee meeting . . .

Adulthood

Projecting preliminary plans in a variety of situations calling for leadership or expert responsibilities—Making preliminary slate of order of business when conducting meetings; coming to preliminary decisions as to responsibilities delegated to committee one is heading; deciding what information to bring if called as an expert; deciding how detailed a report to bring back to group; setting up tentative time schedule; considering whether subcommittees are likely to be needed and most effective distribution of personnel, whether specialists will be needed; securing estimates of costs of needed materials and services; providing equipment needed for effective committee work—securing adequate meeting room, blackboard, paper, and other materials . . .

Youth

Developing further ability to select appropriate methods of keeping group members informed—Deciding kind of minutes to keep; preparing detailed written report of proposed plans; using school paper to present various proposals and student council decisions; using school bulletin boards to get plans before group; deciding how detailed a report should be; deciding whether to make a progress report; considering how often reports are needed . . .

Adulthood

Adjusting methods of reporting to the nature of the group and the problem—Deciding whether to read minutes of executive board to total group; considering when and how printed reports should be used; planning how to make budgets meaningful; deciding when and how to get technical information before a group; considering when to use radio or television to disseminate information; deciding what visual aids to use . . .

Youth

Adjusting techniques of securing cooperative action to the nature and purposes of the group—Developing means of securing opinions from each group member in groups of varying sizes and personnel; deciding how complete to make plans before asking for group approval; using questionnaires, ballots, interviews, or other devices to secure all-school opinion; deciding when to summarize progress and agreements for group; becoming acquainted with ways in which local and national leaders secure cooperation of legislative bodies . . .

Adulthood

Securing cooperative planning and activity in a variety of group situations—Securing representative group opinions on joint problem; deciding when and how often to call for a vote on ongoing plans; deciding how detailed report should be to group who have asked for expert advice; deciding when and how to take children into family plans; adjusting procedures, when chairman, to needs of such varied groups as town meeting, club, small social group; deciding when written report should be used to present ideas to group . . .

GROWTH IN ABILITY TO ACT IN INTERGROUP RELATIONS

The persistent life situations in this chart are arranged somewhat arbitrarily by the kind of group represented. Racial, religious, and national groups—persons who because of birth or viewpoint have similar customs, traditions, backgrounds, or beliefs, whether or not they actually work as organized groups—are classified in one large category. Socio-economic groups—even less clearly identifiable on the basis of distinguishing characteristics and no more likely to work as definitely organized bodies—are placed in a second category. Groups organized for specific action—welfare, service, pressure, labor, management, government, and many others—are in a third category.

Clearly all individuals find some place in these three categories. Any one category may contain persons drawn from a cross section of the groups in each of the others. Also, one group may be listed under two categories, depending on the focus of its activities. Members of any religious denomination, for example, form a religious group. Their church, acting upon a positive social policy, is also a group organized for action.

The persistent problems faced and the goals desired are sufficiently clear-cut to warrant using these categories to identify the variety of groups who must learn to live together. Under the problems of working with racial, religious, social, and economic groups are found many of the life situations involving the place to be accorded to members of a minority. On local, national, and international levels there are problems of how to secure reliable information about other peoples, how to interpret their mores, and how to accord them the respect for their unique worth as individuals which democratic values presuppose. Under the problems of dealing with groups organized for specific action are the situations calling for effective techniques of intergroup cooperation—securing reliable information about policies; deciding when to support a group organized for specific action; using appropriate cooperative skills in groups that range from a community council, through the relationships of labor and management, to groups organized on an international basis.

Each person faces two kinds of situations: as an individual representing a group he must decide on his personal relationships with others representing different groups, and as a member of a particular group he must take responsibility for determining the policy of his group toward others.

The child faces problems of how to treat members of other groups from the first time he meets persons who differ from him in some respect. For some children this will come through contact with members of a group discriminated against by others in the community. In other cases, the child himself will be a member of a minority. Even before he attends school, the child has begun to develop attitudes toward other individuals in his immediate vicinity and sometimes toward those from other nations. Often his tolerant or intolerant responses are the result of adopting the attitudes of adults. The school has a responsibility to help the child as he matures to evaluate his information, secure better understanding, and appraise the bases on which he is acting.

In working in class committees, in sharing school responsibilities with other classes, and in coordinating various groups to which they belong, children begin to sense the similarities of techniques of intergroup cooperation to those which they use as individuals. As they become more mature, learners need help in studying the functioning of local, national, and international groups with which they have acquaintance—a local youth council, the labor and management relationships in local industries, the coordination of welfare efforts through a community chest, the problems of nations striving to establish the techniques and build the understandings that will allow them to live and work together.

As with all other charts in this division, these situations should be seen as contributing to the development of democratic values. The smaller the world becomes, the less a nation can afford to be barred from full cooperation with others of good will by prejudice, misunderstanding, and lack of techniques which would enable people to work together. Children and youth must grow not only in world-mindedness, but in depth of understanding of the complex problems that must be solved in the course of achieving effective cooperation among groups with divergent interests and viewpoints that are working toward democracy as a way of life.

Understanding the basic characteristics and purposes of groups, safeguarding rights and responsibilities, securing cooperative interaction—these are persistent problems. They are also essential goals which many subject specialists aim at attaining. The illustrations in the following chart should be particularly helpful to teachers of subject fields such as social studies, language arts, and vocational education, where many of the desired generalizations are related to problems of understanding or being able to work with groups. At both the elementary and the high school levels, growth in this area will be attained through direct experience as a member of a group working with other groups in school and community situations, as well as through study of the problems faced in intergroup relations.

Some typical situations calling for growth in ability to act in intergroup relations

A. Working with Racial, Religious, and National Groups

	EARLY CHILDHOOD	LATER CHILDHOOD
UNDERSTANDING THE BASIC CHARACTERISTICS AND PURPOSES OF A GROUP Securing reliable information about other groups	**Noting that other persons express the same meanings through different customs, appearance, and behavior—**Noting differences in appearance among school friends—asking about differences of hair, eyes, skin; visiting another church school with one's friends; asking about special garments of members of religious orders; asking about differences in accents among friends or their parents; tasting strange foods when visiting in homes of children of other racial backgrounds; asking about pictures and stories of other peoples; asking about discrepancies between stories and personal experiences . . .	**Finding what other groups mean by their customs, behavior, and appearance—**Discussing reasons for customs of other persons with whom one has immediate contact; asking why one's own or other families eat special foods, keep special holidays; helping to explain major celebrations in one's church to others in class; learning songs and enjoying an exhibit of crafts of another country, of a special group in this country; discussing why adults in community express varied attitudes toward one's own or other groups; comparing pictures of folkways and those showing modern living in other lands; talking with persons from other countries who visit one's home or school . . .
SAFEGUARDING RIGHTS AND RESPONSIBILITIES OF RACIAL, RELIGIOUS, AND NATIONAL GROUPS Acting on legal and personal obligations to racial, religious, and national groups	**Identifying major family and community relationships with other racial, religious, and national groups—**Attending or having one's friends attend parochial schools; leaving school for religious instruction; asking about comments one hears in family group regarding desegregation; finding that one's own or other parents may restrict places to play, friends one may play with; asking about prejudice directed toward oneself or one's parents as members of a special group . . .	**Discovering the major legal rights and responsibilities of racial, religious, and national groups—**Finding why some children attend religious schools, are excused from school for religious instruction or religious holidays; discussing reported steps taken by groups to assure legal protection; discovering major differences between the support one's own or other parents give to legal rights of other groups and degree of social interaction they will foster or tolerate; being helped to understand some major reasons for prejudices one meets as a member of a special group; finding how a person from another country becomes an American citizen; discovering what legal regulations one must meet in traveling to another country . . .

YOUTH

ADULTHOOD

A. Working with Racial, Religious, and National Groups

Extending ability to make accurate interpretations of existing attitudes toward other groups—Considering evidence for classing all members of another group as having inferior or superior intellectual ability, as exhibiting common personality traits; finding how to detect propaganda for or against special groups; exploring special contributions of national groups—crafts, folklore, music, social or scientific advances; examining current news accounts referring to national characteristics of other countries; understanding in more depth similarities and points of difference in church services other than one's own; considering whether to abandon or to persuade parents to abandon customs that make one stand out as different . . .

Dealing with other groups with adequate understanding of basic factors governing their mores—Finding what resources are available to give unbiased information about another group; appraising propaganda directed toward special groups; deciding whether to ask for or to provide for the celebration of special religious holidays or beliefs; discussing basic differences in tenets of religious groups; deciding how far to require children to maintain the mores of one's special group; helping children appraise statements regarding other groups; helping children understand reasons back of customs of other groups; interpreting news reports discussing national groups; finding what customs to observe in traveling in another country . . .

Extending ability to make critical appraisal of existing legal and social commitments to racial, religious, and national groups—Discovering place and function of parochial schools; deciding how far to make vocational plans in terms of discrimination against or special opportunities for group of which one is a member; discussing issues involved in intermarriage; analyzing issues implied by current news releases on problems of desegregation; deciding whether to allow restrictions on membership in club or social group; deciding whether to maintain personal friendships with members of other racial or religious groups in face of home or community opposition; deciding whether to choose a college where one's racial or religious group predominates; discovering reasons for immigration quotas, restrictions in granting citizenship to certain groups; discussing wisdom of steps taken by groups to bring about desirable social relationships . . .

Using democratic values as a guide to legal and personal commitments in racial, religious, and national groups—Deciding whether to have children attend parochial school; taking a stand on issues of financial support to parochial schools; deciding whether to accept local social patterns that result in restrictions on housing; deciding whether to support regulations restricting membership in clubs, participation in community activities; considering whether to work actively with groups striving for better intergroup relations; deciding whether to employ a person of another racial or religious background in one's home; deciding what position to support on proposed immigration quotas, on restrictions in granting citizenship to certain groups . . .

B. Working with Socio-Economic Groups

	EARLY CHILDHOOD	LATER CHILDHOOD
DETERMINING VALIDITY OF SOCIO-ECONOMIC DISTINCTIONS Understanding basic characteristics of other groups	**Identifying similarities and differences in standards of living and patterns of work of families of one's acquaintance**—Helping with household tasks; finding what work is done by members of community with whom one has contact; asking why mother is at work when other mothers are not, or vice versa; comparing work activities of parents and those of friends; asking about differences in homes of friends; finding why playmates have more or less toys than oneself, why their clothing is different . . .	**Understanding contributions of the various socio-economic groups in the community**—Discussing how one's parents and those of one's classmates earn their living; finding what contributions various service groups make to one's well-being; sharing in work of service groups in home and school; finding why one cannot have as much spending money as other children, why others have less to spend than oneself; visiting homes which represent different socio-economic levels from one's own . . .
SAFEGUARDING RIGHTS AND RESPONSIBILITIES Assuring economic, political, and social opportunities	**Working and playing with members of other socio-economic groups**—Helping maid, custodian, other members of service groups with which one has contact; asking why parents, or friends' parents, object to certain playmates, why one is not allowed to play in certain parts of town; finding why other children are not allowed to play with certain individuals when one is allowed to play with them; asking why one is not invited to certain homes . . .	**Understanding general community patterns regarding economic, political, and social opportunities for socio-economic groups**—Finding reasons for picket lines; discussing implications of local strike; discussing local proposals for eliminating slum conditions, housing projects; discussing what responsibility one's class has in cooperating with school custodian; discovering what responsibility one has in helping maid, cook, other helpers in family; sharing in or discussing special community plans for Thanksgiving baskets, Christmas stockings . . .

YOUTH

ADULTHOOD

B. Working with Socio-Economic Groups

Appraising community mores regarding distinctions among socio-economic groups—Discussing relationship of economic factors to vocational choices—deciding whether it is important to hold a white-collar job; discussing effects of living in undesirable sections of town; investigating causes of slum conditions, poverty in one's community—discovering whether such conditions are a true reflection of desires and abilities of those who live under them; discovering bases on which special status is accorded members of social or economic groups of one's acquaintance; examining group attitudes toward status and leadership of persons whose status comes from stage, screen, athletics, or some other entertainment field . . .

Applying adequate understanding of basic issues in making distinctions between socio-economic groups—Helping children build desirable attitudes toward those who work—deciding what attitudes to help children build toward custodian, maid, members of other service groups; weighing social and economic values in deciding on vocation; helping children identify factors to consider in making vocational choices; helping children understand and appraise relative importance of socio-economic status; helping children examine attitudes toward persons achieving status through entertainment media . . .

Developing more critical insights into national and community provisions and customs related to socio-economic groups—Considering rights and responsibilities inherent in collective bargaining; discussing government regulations regarding right to bargain collectively; discussing implications of proposed minimum wage laws, laws governing length of day and week, provisions for employment insurance and social security; investigating strengths and weaknesses of present tax systems; considering reasons for and merit of proposals to provide needed educational opportunities for all; considering how far parents' occupation should make a difference in choosing friends; studying reasons for parental restrictions in choice of friends; considering whether to plan class activities that are financially impossible for certain members of group; deciding whether or not to entertain in one's home if living at "wrong end of town" . . .

Using democratic values in safeguarding the rights and responsibilities of socio-economic groups—Taking action on proposals to secure minimum salaries for groups; taking action on extension of social security benefits, medical and hospitalization plans; deciding when processes of collective bargaining are justified; appraising adequacy of proposed tax regulations; considering how far to extend equal opportunities to women; voting on community proposals regarding housing projects; considering proposals to equalize educational opportunities; taking action to secure cooperative participation of various socio-economic groups in a community enterprise; deciding which children to encourage as companions for one's own; deciding whether to send children to private school . . .

	EARLY CHILDHOOD	LATER CHILDHOOD
	C. Dealing with Groups Organized for Specific Action	
DECIDING WHEN GROUP ACTION IS JUSTIFIED Deciding when to support organized group action	**Becoming acquainted with important community groups touching one's life**—Sharing in school collection for March of Dimes, Junior Red Cross; finding what activities Brownies, Cub Scouts, other such groups undertake; sending a representative to student council . . .	**Identifying the purposes of major groups active in school or local community**—Discovering purposes served by contributions to March of Dimes, Junior Red Cross, other groups; discussing purpose of national or community groups organized to meet special emergencies—collections for flood relief, for aiding refugees; deciding whether to join community or children's church groups; identifying service clubs that have helped with school projects, with provision of playground facilities; deciding which of several school services one's class should undertake; discussing obligations of one's class to cooperate with plans of others; finding what parents mean when they talk about Democrats and Republicans; discussing major news reports of policies of other nations . . .
SECURING COOPERATIVE INTERACTION Securing effective intergroup cooperation	**Finding how one's class can work with others on school enterprises**—Helping plan joint assembly program; contributing to school paper; deciding which of several school services one's class will undertake; deciding how best to share equipment and playground space with other groups; finding how other classes can help one's group carry out special project . . .	**Developing simple techniques for intergroup cooperation**—Discussing reports of school cooperation with community groups to secure play facilities; cooperating with other classes in clean-up drives, Red Cross drive, and other community projects; deciding how class may best contribute to school enterprise; deciding how to allocate parts of an all-school enterprise to get most effective contributions from children of various age groups; discussing general aspects of news reports of international efforts toward cooperative activity . . .

YOUTH | ADULTHOOD

C. Dealing with Groups Organized for Specific Action

Gaining increased insight into the issues involved in using group action to secure desired ends—Discussing youth "gangs"—what motivates them and how they can be used effectively; investigating functions of political parties in American government, in other nations; investigating government regulations regarding cartels, trusts, monopolies; considering issues involved in collective bargaining; deciding what community groups to join, whether to participate actively in fund raising, other drives; discussing news reports of means used to influence policies of other nations; identifying major issues involved in foreign policy of this, of other nations . . .

Using democratic principles in deciding when and how to support the activities of organized groups—Deciding whether to work actively with a political party; deciding whether to join community group established to work for specific reforms; becoming informed about policies and techniques used by one's professional organization; evaluating existing policies and procedures of labor and management groups; identifying bias or propaganda from pressure groups as expressed through various media of communication; securing information and evaluating foreign policies of this, of other nations . . .

Extending techniques and appraising methods for securing effective intergroup cooperation—Coordinating work of several committees working on a school enterprise; discussing whether present school organization makes for effective cooperation among class groups; discussing techniques used in cooperative efforts of local community groups; acting as a member of a community youth council; deciding what responsibilities youth groups should share in community life; considering proposals to facilitate cooperation of labor and management; discussing proposals to give government a share in national planning; discussing proposals for international cooperation . . .

Acting to secure effective intergroup cooperation—Helping organize or share in a community council; helping to coordinate work of community service groups, youth groups; serving on interfaith council; suggesting methods through which school and community can work together; considering national proposals to facilitate cooperation of labor and management; planning effective means through which labor and management in a given vocation can work together; considering function of government in national planning; considering effectiveness of present techniques of international cooperation . . .

Growth in Ability to Deal with Environmental Factors and Forces

Environmental factors and forces represent the third large grouping of the persistent life situations with which all persons must deal. Just as the individual draws on his own capacities and his skill in working with others in almost every daily life experience, he also draws on his ability to handle the world which surrounds him.

The recurring problems in each of the three charts which follow are stated in terms of practical situations with which people seem to be trying to deal. Daily life experiences which call for related competencies and understandings are grouped together without giving such a detailed breakdown as to make functional use of the charts difficult. Under each persistent problem, several subproblems which recur in the lives of people can also be identified.

To focus on immediate situations does not deny the need to understand the past and to look toward the future. Nor does attention to the present problem calling for action deny the need for understandings upon which to base that action. Children, youth, and adults can manage their world effectively only when they have the knowledge that frees them for intelligent action. However, the charts in this area and the grouping of situations do not follow the usual lines of organized bodies of subject matter. The understandings needed for competence in any one situation may draw on understandings from several branches of knowledge. The learner faced with a specific question, such as the need for reforestation, may explore aspects of such subjects as the natural sciences, geography, history, political economy, and government, as he tries to discover what trees are required, what the effect on nearby land and water resources might be, how the timber in the area came to be destroyed, what economic value the reforestry project will have for the community or the nation, and what responsibility government should take in the matter. According to the maturity of the class and the demands of the problem, teacher and learner will draw upon whatever subject matter is needed.

The interrelationships among the three charts in this section are many. In the above example one can identify the persistent situations of producing, protecting, and controlling plant life, of conserving natural resources, of using government to guarantee the control of natural resources, and of using technological resources in keeping with social values. Through experiences with gardening or tree planting, the learner may have already developed considerable ability to provide the conditions necessary for the growth of trees without having much understanding of the need for and the problems of safeguarding the natural resources of the land. He may have had many experiences which helped him to become conscious of the need for conservation without much conception of the function of government in conserving human and natural resources. And he may have considerable background in all of these areas and lack the understanding of the tools and equipment which must be provided for an efficient job. Which of these problems, or of others that might be involved, will be carefully investigated will depend on the needs of the particular individual or group. What supplementary daily life experiences are used to build toward similar concepts and understandings will depend on the persistent problem or problems in which growth is most needed.

Immediate situations which call, in part, for ability to meet health needs or those of aesthetic expression and appreciation relate to the persistent problems in this area. Securing adequate housing, for example, calls for certain knowledge of health needs, and also for information about where and how to buy, what appliances to provide to conserve human energy, how to budget funds, and the like. Such interrelationships were pointed out as the charts in the two preceding sections were discussed. The focus in those charts was primarily on problems the individual has to solve to achieve maximum individual growth and maximum effectiveness in social relationships. In this section, in relation to many of the same situations of daily living, the recurring problems demanding competencies and understandings related to environmental factors and forces are stressed.

While the charts in earlier sections also have special implications for teachers working in subject fields, those in this section suggest, perhaps even more clearly, the daily experiences to which subjects make their special contribution. While, as pointed out previously, many of the problems listed cut across subject fields, teachers of natural sciences may find particular points of focus in the charts dealing with the natural environment and technological resources. The chart concerned with economic, social and political structures and forces may be of special help to teachers whose subjects are related to the social science area. More specific suggestions to subject specialists will be found in the introductions to the separate charts.

GROWTH IN ABILITY TO DEAL WITH NATURAL PHENOMENA

Great progress has been made in the effective use of natural phenomena for human welfare. Synthetic materials of all kinds are replacing or supplementing natural products. Many sources of power have been harnessed to replace human energy. Methods of conserving foods have made marked changes in the work in many homes. Nuclear energy research has opened a new area, many of the results of which are still unimagined.

All persons face innumerable situations where effective action depends on understanding natural phenomena. Growing a garden, caring for a pet, deciding what kind of clothing is best for a warm day, using electricity, running a motor, protecting metals from rust, removing stains, cooking—these are but a few. Many of these simple, day-by-day activities are done less effectively than they otherwise would be because individuals do not have functional knowledge of natural phenomena. But this area has even more far-reaching implications. Beyond the immediate activities of the present are many situations with fundamental implications for human welfare which have as their base better understanding of natural phenomena. Should there be any concern about the rapidity with which certain irreplaceable natural resources are being used? Is it necessary to safeguard trade relations with countries producing certain essential raw materials or can we rely on synthetic products? Can nuclear energy research be safely shared? These questions involve not only fundamental social and economic concepts but sound judgments dependent partly on an understanding of natural phenomena. Where progress in scientific research is as rapid as it is today, no absolute answers can be given. Nor can lay persons be expected to grasp fully the complex concepts developed by experts. Nevertheless, it is important that children and youth know the processes through which change comes about, that they gain some understanding of present knowledge in relation to the issues they now face, and that they learn how to keep abreast of new developments. It is also important that youth have opportunities to explore deeply enough so that genuine interests and talent in the field of science can be fostered.

The situations in the chart dealing with natural phenomena are closely related to those calling for ability to deal with technological resources. Technological change has its base in increasingly effective control of natural phenomena. No attempt has been made to repeat the problems which bear upon both areas. Rather, the situations identified in this first chart are those which relate to the development of technological resources through effective control of natural phenomena. The chart which follows supplements this with the situations calling for effective use of these resources.

In daily living many of the persistent life situations in this area will be faced in combination with those related to health needs. The actual problem faced by the learner usually involves knowledge both of human needs and of the natural phenomena required to meet those needs. The person who knows the purpose he wishes to achieve through a special diet must also know enough about food chemistry to be sure he is properly nourished. The citizen who feels that world health is important must know enough about the causes of disease to foresee some of the major steps involved. In order to make the chart on aesthetic appreciation and expression complete, the persistent life situation of finding beauty in the natural environment is listed there. But as the learner becomes better acquainted with natural phenomena he should also grow in appreciation of their beauties. Many of the daily life situations in this chart can also contribute to growth in relation to aesthetic appreciation.

For many learners the problems faced will center mainly in learning how to use natural phenomena to meet daily problems effectively and in gaining the understanding necessary to make judgments in situations which have at their base control of natural phenomena. For some, with special avocational interests in this field, much more extended knowledge may be required. Others, whose vocational choices take them into industrial research, engineering, agriculture, home economics, nursing, and the like, will also need more opportunities to explore problems thoroughly under guidance.

At the high school level, teachers who are specialists in subject areas that relate to the vocational fields just mentioned, should find in this chart helpful leads to the types of problems for which their fields should be developing special understanding and competence. Problems involving advanced mathematical concepts can also be readily identified by teachers working in this area. Teachers concerned with the social studies will note many implications for their fields in such situations as those dealing with topographical features, conserving and using natural resources, and using physical forces.

At both elementary and secondary school levels, teachers of the natural sciences may find particular help in the types of daily situations suggested as those normally faced by children and youth. Understanding weather conditions, conserving and using natural resources, dealing with plant, animal, or insect life, using sources of energy—these represent only a few of the persistent life situations that are directly related to the natural science field.

Some typical situations calling for growth in ability to deal with natural phenomena

A. Dealing with Physical Phenomena

	EARLY CHILDHOOD	LATER CHILDHOOD
ADJUSTING TO ATMOSPHERIC CONDITIONS Adjusting to weather conditions	**Finding how changes in weather affect one's activities**—Reading thermometer; finding how to protect hands when playing in snow; finding what snow, rain, hail, sleet, clouds are like; helping decide whether it is likely to rain; watching weather reports on television; finding what clothing is appropriate to a variety of weather conditions; inquiring about frost or steam on window pane; keeping simple weather charts; finding how animals protect themselves in winter . . .	**Developing bases for judging and adjusting to weather conditions**—Reading thermometer, barometer; making simple weather station; finding how to interpret reports from weather bureau; testing superstitions about weather; finding what causes thunder, lightning, hail, rain, snow, fog, dew, hurricanes, cyclones; finding why trees grow heavily in some areas, why there are deserts, prairies; finding why sheltered parts of garden do not freeze; finding why places near large bodies of water often have more temperate climates; choosing clothing appropriate for weather; finding what it means to say "a plane rides a jet stream"; finding out about differences in and adjustments to climate as reported in articles about other countries . . .
Adjusting to conditions of air, moisture, sunlight	**Noting effects of different atmospheric conditions**—Helping ventilate rooms; providing adequate ventilation when pet is taken on trip; finding why strong winds make it hard to walk; finding why balloons burst, why they are so light; asking where winds come from; asking how birds, airplanes can stay up in the air; finding how toy pinwheel works; finding when it is necessary to protect oneself from sunburn; inquiring about frost or steam on window pane . . .	**Finding out about phenomena associated with the atmosphere and reasons for common adjustments**—Finding how to avoid drafts in ventilating room; finding why humidifiers are used at home, in school; finding what weatherman means in reporting that humidity is high; finding what makes clothes dry faster; finding why windows steam up when mother is cooking; discussing why forests are closed during a long drought; using basic principles in flying kite, toy airplanes; finding why tires blow out; discussing how fresh air is supplied to submarines, deep-sea divers; discovering why protections against sunburn are more necessary when near water . . .

YOUTH

ADULTHOOD

A. Dealing with Physical Phenomena

Understanding climatic and weather conditions and making appropriate adjustments—Understanding principles on which barometers, other such instruments operate; reading weather maps; discussing reasons for regular occurrence of hurricanes, cyclones, floods in specific parts of country; discussing adequacy of community provisions against these disasters; helping parents decide on crops, plants, trees, which will thrive in the prevailing climate; finding how houses are built to take account of different weather conditions; discussing reports of effects of drought, excessive rains on nation's food supply; discovering effect on national economy of prevailing weather of regions; discussing possible effect of prevailing weather conditions on location and use of international air lines . . .

Making effective adjustment to weather and climatic conditions—Using appropriate instruments to predict weather—thermometer, barometer, weather bureau; deciding on appropriate clothing for self, children; deciding whether prevailing conditions make hail, wind, flood insurance or special protections desirable; adjusting style of house to prevailing climatic conditions; adjusting kind of crop and garden to length and nature of season; deciding where and when to take vacations; considering possible effect on price and availability of raw materials of unusual weather conditions in this or other countries; using knowledge of prevailing weather and soil conditions to interpret national policies . . .

Acting on basic principles to make needed adjustments to atmospheric conditions—Ventilating home, schoolroom; discussing issues involved in proposed measures to assure smog control in industrial cities; discussing new discoveries which prolong the time man can stay in rare atmospheres, under water; discussing problems involved in travel to outer space; finding how air conditioning can control heat and humidity; finding why dry warm climates are recommended for certain illnesses . . .

Making effective adjustments to atmospheric conditions—Deciding how best to ventilate home, office; deciding when humidifier is needed; considering whether to install air conditioning; voting on proposals to control smog in industrial cities; finding what adjustments to make in moving to different altitudes; taking action on measures to rid atmosphere of pollen; adjusting and helping children adjust activities in hot, humid weather; providing protection from sunburn for self and children . . .

	EARLY CHILDHOOD	LATER CHILDHOOD
USING THE EARTH'S SURFACE AND CONTENTS Dealing with topographic features	**Becoming acquainted with surface features in the local environment**—Exploring with parents parks, lakes, rivers, other special aspects of one's locale; asking about mountains, glaciers, deserts, other features pictured in books but not in one's locale; asking about China, England, other countries mentioned by adults, in books; finding how currents carry objects downstream; asking about dams on local rivers; finding why some soil is fine, some rocky; asking what caused sand on lake shore; helping make simple map of schoolyard or neighborhood . . .	**Extending acquaintance with the earth's surface and its effect upon life**—Exploring geological features of one's locale—finding about high river banks, evidence of glaciers, evidence of early oceans; asking about fossils found in neighborhood; asking how mountains, volcanoes, deserts, other features not in one's locale came to be; asking about formation of oceans, islands, rivers; finding why some water is salty, some fresh; making a rock collection; asking about ocean currents; finding how to locate places on map, globe; finding how one would travel to other parts of this country or countries in other parts of world; finding why canals have been built on strategic routes; finding how topographic features influence ways of living of other nations, of people in different parts of same country . . .
Conserving and using natural resources	**Identifying the common uses of natural resources with which one has contact**—Asking about mines, oil wells, logging, other industries in one's community tapping natural resources; asking names of precious stones with which one has contact; learning names of common minerals used in household appliances—iron, tin, nickel, aluminum; finding uses of oil, coal, wood in home or school; asking why father fertilizes garden, gets special top soil; asking about community regulations regarding watering gardens during dry spell . . .	**Extending knowledge of the nature and value of national and world resources**—Discussing local plans for preventing soil erosion, plans for reforestation, irrigation in locality; finding why gardeners and farmers use fertilizers; helping preserve wild flowers and trees in parks and local resorts; discovering why there are bird sanctuaries, game preserves, national parks; helping protect birds' nests in one's neighborhood; cooperating with regulations to prevent forest fires; asking why certain minerals are very rare; asking about uses of special minerals reported in the news; discussing reports of trade agreements with other countries for purchase of raw materials . . .

YOUTH

Expanding ability to apply knowledge of topographic features to human problems—Finding how national surface features affect transportation, location of industries; discovering geological explanations for location and difference in size of various mountain ranges; reading greater variety of maps; finding why different types of stone are used for varied building purposes; becoming better acquainted with nation's sources of natural beauty; discussing proposals to redeem sections of land by irrigation; discussing issues involved in establishing power projects on large rivers; discussing reported international agreements regarding location of airlines; discussing issues involved in other nations' demands for seaports, for island bases, for protection of trade routes . . .

Developing increased understanding of the issues involved in national and world use of natural resources—Discussing kinds of fertilizer recommended for local soils; studying relationship between temperature, rainfall, and loss of soil fertility; helping community workers, parents take action to prevent erosion; helping with plans for crop rotation; discussing implications for conservation in discoveries of new uses of natural resources; considering issues involved in proposals to conserve natural resources; cooperating in local plans to preserve local beauty spot as state park, to establish bird sanctuary, other plans for conservation; discussing proposed trade agreements guaranteeing supply of needed raw materials from other countries; considering issues involved in other nations' demands for sources of oil, minerals . . .

ADULTHOOD

Making effective use of knowledge of the earth's surface to solve human problems—Deciding which route to take when traveling; deciding what places of natural beauty to visit on vacation trip; deciding where to locate summer cottage; helping decide where to locate community airport; voting on proposals to establish power projects; deciding what flood protections are needed in given localities; considering demands of nations for island bases, seaports; discussing justice of demands for changes in national boundaries . . .

Taking action to secure appropriate use of natural resources for the good of all—Deciding on system of crop rotation; cooperating in local plans to prevent erosion; taking action to preserve places of natural beauty; taking action on proposals to conserve national supplies of oil, coal, lumber, other raw materials; helping children learn to protect wild life, rare plants; considering needs of other nations for sources of oil, minerals; discussing proposed international trade agreements for purchase of raw materials . . .

	EARLY CHILDHOOD	LATER CHILDHOOD
ADJUSTING TO FACTORS CONDITIONED BY THE STRUCTURE OF THE UNIVERSE Understanding factors conditioned by relative motion in solar system	**Identifying changes in time and season**—Asking why it gets dark early in winter; asking what causes night; finding that sun and moon rise in the east; asking why one's shadow differs at different times of day; asking why moon looks different at different times of the month; identifying characteristics of seasons in one's locality; asking about reported differences in seasons in other parts of country; finding why sun is hotter in some seasons than in others . . .	**Finding simple explanations of time and season**—Finding why there are differences in time in broadcasts from other parts of the earth; finding what it means to go on daylight saving time; finding how a sundial works; discussing reports of ways people in different zones of the earth adjust to prevailing climate; finding why different parts of country have different growing seasons; understanding parent or press comments on equinox, longest day in year; discussing reasons for differences in climate on different parts of the earth's surface . . .
Exploring the nature of the universe	**Becoming acquainted with the heavenly bodies**—Asking simple questions about stars; finding stars can be grouped to make pictures; asking what sun, moon are made of; asking why positions of sun and moon change in sky; finding why an object feels warm when it has been in the sun . . .	**Finding simple explanations of the movements of heavenly bodies**—Discussing how people know that the earth is round; finding why positions of sun, moon, and stars change; finding simple explanations of nature of solar system; discussing nature of comets, eclipses, other phenomena which one sees or about which one reads; identifying Big Dipper, Milky Way, major constellations; locating information about the nature of planets—what they are made of, whether there is thought to be life on them . . .

B. Dealing with Plant, Animal, and Insect Life

	EARLY CHILDHOOD	LATER CHILDHOOD
PRODUCING AND USING ANIMAL LIFE Producing, caring for, and controlling animal life	**Becoming acquainted with animal life and helping care for pets**—Helping care for pets; helping feed animals on farm; finding names of common birds; watching birds build nests; finding kinds of homes of common animals; asking about habits of common birds and animals; learning about animals that do special work for man; watching tadpoles grow; finding how a snake travels; asking about squirrels, other animals in immediate environment; visiting animals in zoo . . .	**Using common methods of controlling and caring for animal life**—Taking complete charge of pets; helping care for animals on farm; putting up bird feeding stations; helping care for class aquarium; finding why game laws prevent shooting or fishing at certain times of year; finding out about habits and uses of animals from other countries seen in zoo or read about in books; obtaining information on prehistoric animals about which one reads or sees pictures, fossils one finds; finding which reptiles are harmful . . .

YOUTH

Understanding and adjusting to factors conditioned by the relative motion of bodies in the solar system—Discussing purposes of daylight saving time; finding how to calculate time changes in this and other countries; discussing principles underlying proposals to utilize the sun for heating; discussing scientific reports about nature of ultraviolet, infrared rays and their effect upon people; discussing effects of differences in length of season on products of different parts of country; exploring scientific explanations of proposals for space satellites . . .

Making more detailed exploration of facts and hypotheses regarding the structure of the universe—Investigating soundness of popular articles about planets, of predictions that man will be able to travel to other planets; testing common superstitions about heavenly bodies; following reports of discovery of new stars, further information on the nature of stars and planets; considering implications of current theories about nature and origin of the universe . . .

ADULTHOOD

Making effective adjustments to factors conditioned by the relative motion of bodies in the solar system—Choosing crops, garden produce appropriate to season in particular locale; deciding what clothing to take if traveling north, south; considering proposals for orientation of houses to utilize sun's heat; understanding and cooperating with physician's recommendation of treatment by ultraviolet, other rays . . .

Continuing to explore new facts and hypotheses regarding the structure of the universe—Answering children's questions regarding solar system; reading popular articles on nature of the sun, earth, stars; considering implications of new theories regarding nature of the universe; identifying ways in which change in knowledge about the universe has influenced ways of thinking; deciding to support fundamental research . . .

B. Dealing with Plant, Animal, and Insect Life

Developing increased ability to secure effective production, control, and care of animal life—Raising or caring for one's own animals on farm; raising tropical fish; breeding special varieties of birds or animals; interpreting articles about prehistoric animals; having dog vaccinated against distemper; discussing new developments in breeding of livestock for specific purposes; taking part in projects to increase and conserve wild life; discussing adequacy of existing game laws; finding which wild birds should be destroyed as pests, which preserved; finding how to use first aid when bitten by poisonous reptiles . . .

Using effective means of producing, controlling, and caring for animal life—Deciding on kind of pet for children; answering children's questions about animals, birds, reptiles; deciding what protection from reptiles is needed in given section of country; keeping informed of new methods of controlling contagious diseases among livestock; deciding whether to join cooperative ventures to assure pure-bred stock; experimenting with methods of increasing production of eggs, of speeding growth of animals; taking action on proposals to conserve and increase wild life; deciding whether to join local Audubon society, fish and game league . . .

	EARLY CHILDHOOD	LATER CHILDHOOD
Using animal products for human welfare	**Becoming acquainted with common uses of animal products**—Helping gather eggs; finding where eggs, milk come from; learning to drink milk, eat eggs, cheese; asking about furs worn by one's mother, other adults; asking how leather is made; identifying different kinds of meat . . .	**Exploring a variety of uses of animal products**—Finding how milk is pasteurized; interpreting labels such as "Grade A homogenized milk"; finding what milk, eggs, meat contribute to diet; discussing why father likes earthworms in garden, why animal products are used as fertilizer; visiting local dairy; finding how leather is made; finding how animal fibers are used to produce clothing one wears . . .
CONTROLLING AND USING INSECT AND RELATED FORMS OF LIFE Controlling and using insect life for human welfare	**Becoming acquainted with common insects**—Finding names of common insects; watching butterfly emerge from its cocoon; helping keep doors shut, taking other measures to control flies; learning not to touch powders put out for insect control; finding why mother kills clothes moths, why she uses moth repellents in storing woolens; watching ants, bees at work; asking where honey comes from . . .	**Using common methods of controlling and caring for insect life**—Finding how communities control flies, mosquitoes; finding out habits of ants, bees, other insects; finding how some insects help in pollination; finding why communities try to control Japanese beetles, grasshoppers, other local pests; helping care for hive of bees; learning to tell common, harmless insects from those which are harmful; discovering more detail about life cycles of insects that interest one—moths and butterflies, bees . . .
PRODUCING AND USING PLANT LIFE Producing, protecting, and controlling plant life	**Becoming acquainted with common plants and their care**—Helping parents plant garden; helping water house plants, garden; asking why father takes up bulbs in fall, covers special plants for winter; asking what fertilizer is for; finding why parents tell one not to touch poisonous plants; helping father dig up dandelions, weeds; finding how to pick flowers without destroying buds, roots; finding names of common plants and trees . . .	**Using common methods of producing and controlling plant life**—Helping care for terrarium, for plants in classroom; planting and caring for garden; discussing why different parts of country grow different crops; finding reasons for special methods used by farmers of one's acquaintance; examining fruits, grains at state experimental farms; helping plant trees; finding how to identify poisonous plants . . .

YOUTH	ADULTHOOD
Understanding factors involved in effective use of animal products for human welfare—Finding how to order meats; finding how to prepare animal products for meals; helping preserve meats on farm; exploring reports of underwater resources in oysters, fish, seal; discussing new developments in use of animal products for synthetic materials; considering reasons for government inspection of meat, herds; finding how to interpret labels on clothing; considering problems involved in securing a greater supply of special products to meet changed needs . . .	**Using animal products appropriately for human welfare**—Deciding what cuts of meat or fish to serve; preparing animal products to conserve nutritional qualities; preserving meats on farm; following new developments in use of animal products to produce synthetics; considering adequacy of regulations regarding inspection of meat, herds; considering proposals to shift focus of production to meet changed needs . . .
Expanding ability to secure effective control and use of insect life—Finding which insects in any given community should be destroyed, which protected; discussing implications of destroying natural balance by destroying one kind of insect; discussing values of insects in cross-fertilization of plants; cooperating in drives to control flies, mosquitoes; taking responsibility for hive of bees; discussing measures to control influx of insect pests from other countries . . .	**Using effective means of controlling, using, and producing insect life**—Taking action on proposals to control insect pests, to control influx of insect pests from other states, countries; taking appropriate measures to protect one's house from moths, termites, ants, other insects; knowing which insects to destroy as garden pests; finding which methods of control are most effective; cooperating in community plans to eliminate breeding places; raising bees for home or commercial purposes, for pollination purposes . . .
Expanding ability to secure effective production and control of plant life—Helping parents decide on appropriate crops, garden products; helping make plans to irrigate, fertilize, take other needed steps to assure a good yield; discussing reports of new plants appropriate for particular locality; helping plant experimental plot on farm; discussing agricultural experimentation needed in one's district; finding how to save a variety of seeds, bulbs from family garden; discussing issues involved in achieving adequate protection for national forests; finding what protections for wild flowers exist; cooperating in weed control in farming districts . . .	**Using effective means of producing, protecting, and controlling plant life**—Deciding what kinds of crops are best suited for given types of soil; deciding when and how to use fertilizer; planning necessary irrigation; deciding when to plant crops, set out gardens; setting up needed protections against frost, winds; experimenting with cross-fertilization; helping establish state laboratories and experimental stations; assisting in reforestation projects; considering adequacy of existing protection against forest fires; considering adequacy of existing protection for wild plants . . .

	EARLY CHILDHOOD	LATER CHILDHOOD
Using plant products for human welfare	**Becoming acquainted with common uses of plant life**—Finding names of flowers and vegetables used in home; finding which berries to eat and which not to touch; finding how different garden products taste; finding why parents insist on one's eating vegetables and fruits; watching mother preserve fruits and vegetables . . .	**Exploring a variety of uses of plant life**—Finding what uses are made of local crops; finding how cotton, linen cloth is produced; discussing meaning of parental comments about crop failures; reading about uses pioneers and early peoples made of plants; asking about plywood, other types of wood; investigating reports of new products coming from plants—cloths, plastics, oils, paper; finding what grains are in breads and breakfast foods used in one's home . . .
CONTROLLING AND USING BACTERIA AND OTHER MICROSCOPIC ORGANISMS Providing immunity to and the positive use of microscopic organisms	**Becoming acquainted with home and community measures to control bacteria**—Asking why dishes are sterilized when person is ill; finding why one is not allowed to drink from local streams; asking why one cannot play with child who has a cold, one who is quarantined; finding why food is covered, why flies are killed, why refuse is wrapped or covered; finding why disinfectant is put on cut or scratch . . .	**Discovering common actions of bacteria**—Finding how community purifies its water supply; finding what turns milk sour, why milk is pasteurized; finding why one is inoculated or vaccinated; finding how and when disinfectants are used at school or in one's home; finding how to keep articles from molding, mildewing; finding the part played by bacteria in making cheese, vinegar, in yeast; discussing articles reporting use of molds in producing drugs . . .

C. Using Physical and Chemical Forces

PRODUCING NEW FORMS THROUGH CHEMICAL AND PHYSICAL CHANGE Using physical and chemical change	**Finding how materials change in form**—Finding how to get suds for soap bubbles; asking why paints get dry; asking about steam from teakettle; finding how sugar, salt melt in water; finding why streets and walks are salted on icy days; helping make ice cream; watching paper or wood turn to ash, candles melt; finding cause of rust on toys left out of doors; learning to avoid handles of pans, spoons, and other objects which have been in contact with hot stove . . .	**Acting upon simple understandings of physical and chemical causes of change**—Asking about major function of common ingredients in cooking—baking powder, eggs, flour; finding why pop fizzes when top comes off bottle; finding why some substances dissolve, others do not; asking about shape of snowflakes, other crystals; finding why care must be taken in using gasoline; discovering how odors are produced; finding out about cloth made from glass, other synthetic materials; finding how camera film works; finding why rope may burn skin when sliding . . .

YOUTH	ADULTHOOD
Understanding factors involved in effective use of plant life for human welfare—Discovering nutritional values in various vegetables; finding how to arrange flowers for special purposes; finding how local industries make use of plant products; discussing issues involved in maintaining adequate national and world sources of food; discussing importance of proposed trade agreements guaranteeing supplies of timber, coffee, others . . .	**Using plant life for good of self and others**—Deciding what vegetables and flowers to plant in garden; trying new ways of preparing fruits and vegetables; adjusting crops in terms of market demands; considering proposals to shift focus of production to meet change in needs; following new developments in use of plant products for production of synthetic materials; considering obligation of this country to contribute to world market needs; discussing trade agreements which assure supplies of foods and materials . . .
Developing increased understanding of the factors involved in the control of bacteria—Discussing proposed measures to assure adequate water supply for community; considering purpose of local regulations safeguarding purity of water supply; discussing techniques used to develop and purposes of vaccines; following popular reports of medical research on germ control; using disinfectants appropriately; discussing principles upon which foods are kept from souring, fermenting; investigating uses of mold in production of new drugs . . .	**Using effective means of controlling bacteria in home and community**—Acting on proposals to locate city reservoir; securing a pure supply of drinking water; deciding when and against what diseases to have children inoculated; using appropriate precautions in caring for and preparing foods, in general household sanitation, in appraising community health safeguards; using proper safeguards in caring for cuts, burns, other injuries; deciding how much state support should go to medical research . . .

C. Using Physical and Chemical Forces

YOUTH	ADULTHOOD
Extending understanding of and ability to use chemical and physical principles to produce desired changes—Knowing what results to expect in cooking when using baking powder, applying heat, mixing variety of ingredients; knowing what to do when acid is spilled; finding what must be considered in removing ink, iodine, other stains; following reports of work of research chemists in experimenting with production of new materials; investigating variety of by-products resulting from preparation of a given substance; operating photographer's darkroom; finding reasons for recommended methods of caring for burns, poisoning; finding effect of and precautions to take against carbon monoxide gas poisoning . . .	**Applying chemical and physical principles appropriately in producing change**—Using knowledge of chemical change effectively in cooking; using heat properly in cooking; selecting soaps, detergents, and cleaning fluids with regard for their effect upon materials; removing inks, iodine, other stains; discussing industrial implications of new alloys, of plastics and synthetic materials; interpreting medical advice—meaning of metabolism reports, purpose of special diets, methods of caring for burns, antidotes to poisons; taking adequate precautions in installing gas heaters, starting car in garage; considering effect on international trade of production of synthetic materials . . .

	EARLY CHILDHOOD	LATER CHILDHOOD
CONSERVING MATERIALS Adjusting use of materials to their properties	**Finding how to use different kinds of materials**—Finding which type of doll is most likely to break; finding how to carry and use dishes without breaking them; finding why nails, screws, saws are made of metal; finding which kinds of paper, cloth will cut or tear easily; finding why paper tears when wet; finding which toys can be washed, which clothing safely worn in rain . . .	**Applying basic understanding of the properties of materials in their use**—Choosing clothing suitable for rough play; finding how raincoats are treated to repel moisture; finding what makes materials shrink; deciding what kind of wood to use in making toy boat; investigating types of material that go into building of new house; finding which kitchen utensils can be used over heat; finding what care must be taken in heating or cooling china or glass . . .
Preserving materials	**Helping care for one's possessions**—Finding how to hang up clothing; finding what to do with damp clothing, wet shoes; helping care for books which have been out in rain; asking why mother protects table from hot dishes; asking why certain foods are kept in refrigerator; protecting clothing and table when using paints or clay; protecting toys from weather . . .	**Discovering and using general understandings about the preservation of materials**—Caring for tennis racket, violin; finding why woodwork and furniture in home are kept painted, waxed, varnished; helping store garden tools; understanding why iron fences, equipment are painted; finding why certain materials are protected from sunlight; caring for wet shoes, clothing; helping put food away; helping mother polish silver; becoming acquainted with materials that stain, helping remove stains . . .
USING PHYSICAL FORCES Adjusting to physical forces	**Identifying the effects of physical forces on one's activities**—Playing in water, learning to keep afloat, to swim; asking why one's boat floats; noticing that some soaps float, others do not; identifying other materials that float; asking about balloons that float, why airplanes stay up in the air; finding how to use simple lever to help move heavy articles; asking why air seems to be moving above hot radiator, why balloon bursts; asking why mother's teakettle whistles . . .	**Using simple understandings of the principles underlying physical forces**—Developing more effective swimming skills; finding why it is easier to float in salt water; investigating general principles on which aircraft operate; finding how siphon operates; finding how fountain pen works, how to prime a pump; finding how high and how fast airplanes can go; finding why cream rises, ice floats; finding how to throw ball accurately; asking why people don't fall off on other side of the earth; learning to ski, skate . . .

YOUTH

Extending ability to adjust the care and use of materials to their properties—Testing materials for shrinkage, colorfastness; discovering which commercial labels indicate that materials have been treated to prevent shrinking, fading; discussing reported discoveries which have made wood and glass stronger, have removed disadvantages from other materials; discussing local or national laws regarding quality of materials to be put into airplanes, other equipment where public safety is involved; discussing reports of new uses of materials—lighter trains, longer-wearing products . . .

Understanding and using principles underlying various conservation techniques—Finding what purpose is served by waxes, paints applied to wood; helping close up camp site; finding how to wash sweaters, other personal property; finding how to treat stains, spots; taking care of leather goods; finding how to clean silver, polish other metals; discussing uses of refrigeration in storing and shipping foods; helping can foods; finding how to prevent rust on household equipment and farm machinery . . .

ADULTHOOD

Adjusting choice, care, and use of materials appropriately to their properties—Helping children select playthings of appropriate durability; deciding on quality of materials to be used in building house—what kind of pipes, insulation to use; appraising building codes with respect to restrictions on building materials; taking action on measures to assure use of adequate quality of materials in machines and equipment where public safety is involved; following research reporting on new uses for common materials . . .

Using appropriate methods of preserving materials—Deciding what kind of wax or paint to apply to furniture, woodwork, frame house, car; preventing metals from rusting; caring for tools and farm machinery; removing stains; washing a variety of materials; deciding what kinds of polish to apply to leathers; deciding when furniture, materials should be protected from sunshine; protecting clothing against moths; knowing when to keep foods cool, dry, airtight; canning garden produce, meats; testing methods of dehydrating and freezing foods . . .

YOUTH

Extending understanding and ability to apply principles underlying physical forces—Finding how to adjust to tides, waves, undertow, currents when swimming; learning to load a boat; securing technical information about flying an airplane; throwing a ball, discus; discussing technical problems of travel to other planets; investigating principles operating in a vacuum cleaner, or other devices in common use that depend on air pressure; finding how ramps, levers help in moving heavy objects . . .

ADULTHOOD

Adjusting effectively to physical forces in situations of daily living—Teaching children to swim, handle boats; loading a boat; aiming gun accurately; planning irrigation system for farm or garden; following developments in lighter-than-air transportation; fixing vacuum cleaner; installing pump for private water system; using gravity, principles of leverage, to best advantage in work, at home . . .

	EARLY CHILDHOOD	LATER CHILDHOOD
Using sources of energy	**Becoming acquainted with common sources of energy**—Finding how to turn on electricity; playing with toy electric trains; finding which materials magnets will attract; flying kite; making toy pinwheels; floating boats in current; finding how wind affects toy sailboat; asking questions about running family car; finding that some persons use horses, other animals as sources of energy; asking why window sill, floor on which sun shines is warm . . .	**Applying general principles underlying the use of energy in daily activities**—Finding how winds keep kite aloft; finding what purposes can be served by magnets, how compass works; finding how electrical household equipment operates—vacuum cleaner, washing machine, doorbell, iron; asking about Diesel engines, jet planes, relative power in car engines; finding why mercury rises in thermometer when it is warm; finding why certain foods are recommended for energy; asking about local power projects; asking how explosives are used in dynamiting tree stumps, firing guns, blasting rock; asking about adult references to atom bomb, hydrogen bomb . . .
Using and adjusting to light and sound	**Responding to changes in light and sound in one's environment**—Testing sound of various musical instruments; finding different sounds that can be produced by various objects—glasses filled with water, bowls, metal pipes; asking about echoes; learning how to whistle; asking what causes a rainbow; investigating shadows and sunbeams . . .	**Finding how to use light and sound for one's purposes**—Finding how to make a whistle; making musical instruments, tuning them; discovering basic principles upon which the eye, ear operate; finding how recordings are made, how telephone transmits sound, how radio operates; finding how to mix paints to get desired colors; finding what causes a rainbow; reflecting sunlight with mirrors, finding how simple camera works; finding how mirrors can distort images; finding how to adjust light o kind of work being done; finding why some animals see in the dark; finding what it means to say an airplane can travel faster than sound . . .

YOUTH

Extending ability to use sources of energy effectively in a variety of situations—Repairing simple electrical appliances; constructing a radio; overhauling engine of a "hot rod"; discussing relative merits for heating and cooking of gas, wood, electricity; discussing advantages of electrification of rural districts; discussing proposals to use sun as main source of heat in house, as source of energy in industry; discussing significance of national power projects; discussing principles upon which jet propulsion operates; using propellers and windmills as sources of power; discussing current references to uses of nuclear energy as source of energy . . .

Extending ability to apply basic understandings governing effective use of light and sound—Applying knowledge of speech mechanisms to voice control; investigating new methods of recording; finding what is involved in soundproofing, providing for good acoustics in auditorium; finding how to use color effectively in home planning; using light meter to measure adequacy of light in home or school; investigating principles involved in television, radio, motion pictures; adjusting lens and light of camera or projector; using microscope, telescope; investigating causes of various visual or hearing defects, how glasses or hearing aids help to correct them . . .

ADULTHOOD

Using sources of energy effectively to supplement human power—Deciding what sources of heat to use for cooking, heating house; deciding what electrical equipment to use; repairing an engine; deciding how powerful new car should be; using windmills, propellers as sources of energy; considering proposals for rural electrification; taking action on power projects; establishing private power plant in camp or on farm; discussing needed controls of nuclear energy for human welfare . . .

Making effective use of the principles of light and sound in everyday living—Interpreting medical reports on hearing or visual difficulties of self and children; providing adequate lighting in home; helping plan for effective acoustics and soundproofing of office or public building; planning effective color in home; taking color films, using variety of lenses and filters in camera; operating a recording machine; deciding what kind of radio or television to buy . . .

GROWTH IN ABILITY TO DEAL WITH TECHNOLOGICAL RESOURCES

The industrial age was identified in Chapter 2 as a basic characteristic of present society. The changes which it has brought about have colored every aspect of human living. The chart which follows contains only those persistent life situations related to two areas: the problems of using technological resources in the practical situations of daily life and the problems of contributing to technological advance. The preceding chart contains those situations which have to do with the development of technological resources through increasingly effective control over natural phenomena. And the chart in the area which follows, dealing with economic, social, and political structures and forces, reflects, both in the persistent situations and in the everyday experiences, the effect of the industrial age upon the ways in which people must learn to live and work together.

Several closely related situations, included in this chart and in others, show the difference in emphasis. The problems of making effective use of instruments of communication and transportation, in so far as they are concerned with such questions as choice of instruments and how to manipulate them, are in this chart. Another phase of transportation as it affects the problems of trade relationships appears in the problem of securing effective distribution of goods in the next chart. Similarly, another phase of communication as a question of how to use the press, radio, and television in disseminating information is listed as part of the problem of molding public opinion. As a technique of group participation, communication appears also in the earlier section on social relationships as a part of keeping group members informed. Using the tools of the trade in this chart is closely related to the economic problems of providing good working conditions included in the next chart.

In relation to many of the persistent problems in preceding charts, situations have been listed requiring decisions as to how to solve the problem to benefit the people of all the world. Questions of securing adequate food, clothing, and housing for all, of extending medical care, of increasing means of disease control, are re-emphasized in this chart under the heading of using technological resources for maximum social good. The relationship of this problem to the situations calling for moral choice and responsibility is obvious. Higher standards of living for all have never seemed more certain or at least more possible, but many problems must be faced before the promise is achieved. What constitutes adequate financing and encouragement of medical research, research in education, or the social sciences? How far should technological advance be accompanied by wage adjustments which will bring new discoveries within the reach of all? What is the responsibility of one nation toward the welfare of peoples beyond its own boundaries? How can the benefits of nuclear energy research be provided for all while the possibilities of its misuse are prevented? These are not simple problems and children and youth cannot solve them. Even the accumulated wisdom of adults has not solved them. Yet our young people can be alerted to the problems, to the factors which make solutions difficult, and to the training needed by those who will contribute to the solutions. Today's youth will have a very real share in the way such problems are met tomorrow.

Children and youth must come to know the industrial world in which they live. On farms, they are as close to the tractor and the combine as they are to horses and cattle. In cities and towns, they are near factories, cars, radios, power plants, and the like. Through the daily papers they become acquainted with inventions which promise to change their lives radically. Many will enter vocations where use of technological resources is a basic skill. All will use these resources in their own daily living and will share in decisions as to how they can be used best in the service of mankind. Learners must be helped early to begin to make discoveries and draw conclusions as to both the potentialities for abundant living which have been made possible and the responsibilities they entail.

As with other areas, every teacher working in a subject field will find among the situations listed in this chart many which relate to his subject. No subject has been untouched by the technological advances of our times. Even those working in fields which focus on the past do so with different emphases because of modern inventions facilitating their research. At the elementary as well as the secondary school level, many daily life situations related both to the field of science and to that of social studies can readily be identified. Teachers of English will find in these charts problems related to the effective use of the new means of communication technological change has made available. In addition, high school teachers of vocational education can find specific problems related to their fields.

Some typical situations calling for growth in ability to deal with technological resources

	EARLY CHILDHOOD	LATER CHILDHOOD
	A. Using Technological Resources	
USING TOOLS, MACHINES, AND EQUIPMENT Using common tools	**Finding how to use a few common tools with safety**—Finding names of common tools; learning how to use hammer, saw, scissors with safety; using pencil; experimenting with mechanical pencil; sewing; building toys; raking leaves; learning to use other garden tools; finding how to care for tools one uses . . .	**Finding how to use the tools necessary to complete successfully desired repairs and construction**—Using appropriate instruments to measure angles correctly in building birdhouse, bookcase; deciding on best nail or screw for particular job; finding how to use screw driver; using hammer as lever to remove nails; using pliers and wrenches in repairing bicycle; doing simple repairs around house; using simple camera; using common garden tools; becoming more skilled in using sewing equipment, knitting needles, crochet hook . . .
Selecting and using the tools and machines of a trade	**Finding that different workmen use a variety of tools**—Watching plumber at work; asking what dentist or doctor is using; finding what tools one's father uses at work; finding purpose of machines used on farms; watching construction gang at work; watching building of house in neighborhood; watching street being resurfaced; visiting firehouse and examining special equipment; examining equipment in school cafeteria . . .	**Finding how a variety of tools helps a workman or professional person on his job**—Finding purposes of major implements used by one's dentist, doctor, school nurse; observing and asking about industrial equipment in local factories; finding how a garageman repairs a car; asking about articles describing earlier methods of farming, manufacturing; finding out about operation of machines used by building and construction gangs at work in one's community—road scraper, steam shovel, steam roller, pneumatic drill, acetylene torch; using machines to duplicate school paper; using typewriter; finding how local paper is produced . . .

YOUTH | **ADULTHOOD**

A. Using Technological Resources

YOUTH

Using correctly the tools appropriate to the job to be done—Making emergency repairs on automobile; helping make household repairs—fixing faucets, putting up screens, mending furniture; using appropriate tools for gardening; using knives, hatchets, other tools in camping; using inclined plane to load a truck; discovering purposes of various sorts of pulleys; helping equip workbench or tool chest; developing increased skill in making fine repairs—framing a picture, working with small screw driver; making clothes, knitting; developing skill with more complex photographic equipment; helping care for tools—sharpening tools, preventing rust, knowing when to oil . . .

Understanding the general nature of the tools and machines used by various occupations—Learning how to use tools and equipment needed for part-time jobs; discovering skills needed for work in selected divisions of local factory; finding what machines must be operated by a secretary; finding what equipment is used in beauty salon; helping decide whether to install new machines on farm; gaining increased understanding of tools used by various professional groups—helping surveyors on summer job, assisting in local hospital, others; finding how local newspaper is printed; finding out about machines used in administrative offices of school; discussing implications of articles regarding automation; discussing effects of competitive production from countries that use hand labor . . .

ADULTHOOD

Using common tools correctly in a variety of situations—Caring for tools; selecting adequate garden tools; stocking tool kit of car; equipping tool chest or workshop for the home; making ordinary household repairs; using most efficient tools in making emergency repairs on car; rigging pulley clothesline; mending, sewing, and knitting for self and family; using tools needed in simple carpentry jobs about home or farm; pursuing photography as a hobby; carving, building household fixtures or finishing furniture as a hobby; using new kinds of kitchen equipment; teaching children to use tools efficiently and safely . . .

Using machines and tools of one's trade efficiently—Developing skill in using tools of one's vocation; securing needed equipment for effective work in one's vocation; securing information about new technological developments in a given field; testing new devices; becoming expert in judging whether tools or machines with which one works are in need of repair; securing or making necessary repairs; keeping tools or machines of one's vocation in good condition; helping youth make vocational choices in light of new industrial equipment and production trends . . .

	EARLY CHILDHOOD	LATER CHILDHOOD
USING HOUSEHOLD AND OFFICE APPLIANCES Using equipment to conserve human energy	**Finding how to manipulate simple household appliances**—Finding how to put lights on and off; finding how mother uses various kitchen appliances; using pencil sharpener; adjusting blinds; adjusting radiator; using bathroom appliances; finding how to operate drinking fountain; manipulating zippers, buttons, buckles, overshoe fasteners; finding what mother does with vacuum cleaner, sewing machine . . .	**Using a variety of common appliances**—Setting up proper lighting arrangement in room; finding how to run gas, electric, wood stove; using common kitchen gadgets; fixing blinds; finding how to fill and use fountain pens; helping run washing machine, dryer; doing simple pressing; comparing descriptions of old-time kitchen equipment with that of today; finding how mother uses electric mixer, pressure cooker; helping run mimeographing machine; learning to use typewriter . . .
USING INSTRUMENTS OF COMMUNICATION Using effective means of communicating with individuals or groups	**Becoming acquainted with the common instruments of communication**—Finding how to talk over telephone; finding how to call people by telephone; asking what telegram is; watching school mimeograph machine at work; trying to write with typewriter; finding favorite program on radio or television; watching teacher or older children set up motion-picture projector, slide projector . . .	**Understanding the general nature of a variety of means of communication**—Telephoning for a variety of purposes; finding how telegraph works; setting up electric bells, amateur telegraph sets; sending Morse code messages on home-made set; finding how and when cables are sent; speaking over school amplifying system; managing family radio and television; using typewriter; helping run school duplicating machines; discussing stories of pony express, other early means of sending messages; visiting local paper . . .
USING MEANS OF TRANSPORTATION Using effective means of transporting people and materials	**Exploring common means of transportation**—Finding what safety measures are necessary in traveling by bus, trolley, car, boat; finding how to pay fare on bus, trolley; learning how to behave on school bus; learning to ride bicycle; finding what different kinds of stamps are for; finding what express man does; asking about packages, letters which come by mail; finding purposes served by trucks seen in one's locality; traveling by train or plane, or asking friends or parents about such travel . . .	**Understanding the general nature of a variety of means of transportation and using common ones with safety**—Traveling alone by bus or trolley; riding bicycle with safety; deciding which way to send a package; finding various ways that mail can be sent; finding how locks are used to send boat through canal; inquiring about reported improvements in boats, trains, airplanes; comparing present means of transportation with those described in stories about pioneer days; finding how various states and nations transport produce . . .

YOUTH	ADULTHOOD
Using and adjusting household appliances for convenience of self and others—Replacing fuses; mending electric cords; using kitchen equipment in preparing meals; discussing descriptions of forthcoming new inventions for home and industry; using family vacuum cleaner, washing machine, sewing machine, refrigerator; pressing one's clothes, ironing family laundry; using pressure cooker, electric mixer; running school duplicating equipment; discussing nature and purpose of a dictaphone; working with filing system at school or in part-time job; using a typewriter; finding how to appraise quality of new equipment . . .	**Selecting and using household or office machines appropriately as labor-saving devices**—Deciding whether to purchase vacuum cleaner, washing machine, refrigerator, sewing machine; using effectively appliances which accompany household equipment; discussing new household equipment seen in advertisements; deciding what kind of heating, lighting, air-conditioning equipment to install in home or office; setting up office filing system; considering what tests to use in deciding which brand of equipment to buy; finding how to repair equipment; helping children learn to manage common household equipment . . .
Extending ability to select and use appropriate instruments of communication—Using telephone appropriately in personal and business situations; running telephone switchboard; finding how to send telegrams; using a microphone, tape recorder effectively; running school duplicating equipment; running school projectors; taking movies; helping edit youth column in local paper; planning with printer for publication of bulletin or yearbook; becoming acquainted with means through which news reports reach local paper; helping decide on most effective means of publicizing school campaign—local paper, local radio, mimeographed announcement, posters . . .	**Using effective means of communicating with individuals and groups**—Deciding when to use long-distance phone or telegraph; setting up amplifying system; establishing intercommunication system in office, school; helping plan broadcast for a special campaign; recording own or other voices; deciding which kind of duplicating machine to use for a given job; deciding which make and style of typewriter to purchase; choosing type and format of material to be printed; deciding on most appropriate medium for desired advertising . . .
Extending ability to select and use appropriate means of transportation—Driving car, tractor; running motorboat; discussing potential developments of air transportation; deciding which means of transportation to use in traveling; discussing relative advantages of different ways of shipping merchandise; discussing implications of improved means of transportation on international trade relations, on availability of goods for all people . . .	**Using effective means of transportation for persons and materials**—Deciding whether to buy a car; using appropriate means to insure or provide special handling for articles mailed; deciding how to have furniture moved; choosing appropriate method of travel—what kind of train accommodation, when to travel by airplane; considering proposals to lower or raise travel, freight rates; voting on state plans for new highways, city plans for expressways; considering national demands or needs for development of trade routes in light of new developments in transportation; helping children to use appropriate means of transportation . . .

B. Contributing to Technological Advance

	EARLY CHILDHOOD	LATER CHILDHOOD
ENCOURAGING TECHNOLOGICAL ADVANCE Supporting experimentation	**Examining the new discoveries which come into one's world**—Trying out new mechanical toys; watching strange and different machines; asking about parents' comments on atom bombs, other inventions frequently mentioned; examining interesting articles found in school . . .	**Becoming acquainted with widely known technological discoveries**—Asking about new technological developments reported in the paper and work that went into them; investigating effects of new developments in cars, farm machinery, trains, other machines in neighborhood; finding how new types of engines, airplanes are planned and tested; asking about new developments causing changes in local factories; experimenting with new equipment for bicycle, new kinds of mechanical pencils, other gadgets . . .
USING TECHNOLOGICAL RESOURCES FOR MAXIMUM SOCIAL GOOD Using resources in keeping with social values	**Appreciating how technological resources with which one is familiar make life pleasant**—Finding how rapidly father cuts grass with power mower; appreciating cold drinks from refrigerator; being given a ride on brother's bicycle; hearing mother comment on effectiveness of new stove, other labor-saving equipment . . .	**Finding how human needs are served by technological resources**—Discussing improvements in living conditions that might come about with prefabricated houses, through improved household equipment; discussing possible uses of plastics; considering how machine production increases quantity and quality of goods available for oneself and one's family; finding how modern cranes, steam shovels are used to save man's energy . . .

YOUTH	ADULTHOOD

B. Contributing to Technological Advance

Understanding general methods by which technological advance comes about—Discussing reported work of a variety of research laboratories; discussing nature of work and kinds of specialization needed in various research areas; following the use of new developments in local enterprises; discussing processes through which synthetic materials are developed; trying out new tools and methods of work in personal life; testing out new household equipment . . .

Supporting experimentation which contributes to the development of technological resources—Deciding what technical publications to subscribe to in a given field; testing new developments in one's field of work; deciding whether to include research work in one's business; helping test proposals of the research laboratory where one works; considering whether research in a given field is meeting public needs; considering how to encourage needed research; considering effectiveness of proposed legislation to foster research . . .

Understanding issues involved in assuring the use of existing technological resources for social good—Discussing potentialities of new inventions reported in press or magazines; discussing possible means of making farmers financially able to purchase new equipment; discussing issues involved in proposals to assure better working conditions in factories; discussing issues involved in reassigning workmen as automation increases; considering the effect of existing patent laws on availability of new inventions; determining what issues are involved in control of monopolies, trusts, cartels; discussing issues involved in controlling inventions which are potentially destructive; considering potentialities of nuclear energy research . . .

Taking action to assure the use of existing technological resources for social good—Taking action to make significant inventions available for general use; considering means of enabling farmers to purchase or share needed equipment; considering laws assuring adequate working conditions in factories; considering needed action to solve problems of dislocation of employment due to technological advance; considering adequacy of funds spent on medical or social research as against those used for technological research; considering adequacy of community provisions for increased leisure brought about by technological advance; taking action to provide needed controls over potentially destructive inventions; considering safeguards needed as new instruments of communication make for increased influence over man's thinking . . .

GROWTH IN ABILITY TO DEAL WITH ECONOMIC, SOCIAL, AND POLITICAL STRUCTURES AND FORCES

This final chart focuses on the individual in relation to the structures through which society maintains its existence and the forces which impinge upon it. These include the structures through which the individual carries on his vocation; the complex organization which assures that goods and services are made freely available; structures through which personal and community welfare are safeguarded; and the means through which public opinion is modified. Finally, the individual must be intelligent about the forms of local and national government in which he shares.

The importance of working toward solutions to economic, social, and political problems which will guarantee that people can work and live together in such a way as to make a maximum contribution to the well-being of all was stressed in Chapter 2. This emphasizes the need for children and youth to develop understandings and sound ways of working in and through the structures of society and of changing these structures when it becomes necessary.

The interrelationships among the various parts of this chart are many. The situations faced in assuring that the work of the world will be done cannot be solved without taking action in regard to such recurring problems as determining adequate work standards, providing good working conditions, and assuring trade relations. Problems of electing government representatives, securing effective government organization, and making and enforcing laws are closely tied to those of molding public opinion. Decisions as to the function of government in the various aspects of our society are related to the problems of earning a living, securing goods and services, providing for social welfare, and molding public opinion. Depending on whether the concern of learners involves mainly understanding the kind of provision needed to meet a problem or how this provision is to be secured through the existing structures of government, the teacher will work in other parts of the chart or spend more time on the problems suggested by the section on government.

As the other charts were discussed, the interrelationships with this area were pointed out. Effective action in dealing with economic, social, and political structures and forces frequently calls for basic understanding of natural phenomena or technological resources. Understanding of the functioning of social structures is closely related to understanding of the techniques of social participation. Health problems requiring social channels through which well-being can be assured and needs for aesthetic satisfaction, as they require cooperative community efforts, draw upon understandings of economic and social structures and forces.

From birth, children are building concepts of the nature and function of the family group. Very early they are spending their pennies in the neighborhood store, coming to know various community workers, learning traffic laws, playing in public parks. By adolescence there should be both the maturity and the need to go deeply into some of the issues and underlying problems with which the nation and the world must come to grips.

Ideas as well as structures must be considered among the social forces with which our young people deal. They face communism, fascism, socialism, democracy as opposing social philosophies. They read statements about "free enterprise," "the capitalistic system," "laissez faire." They talk about "the freedom of the press," "the right of the individual." While younger children cannot gain much fundamental understanding of such complex concepts, teachers must help youth, whose maturity allows it, to expand their ability to think clearly about these and other concepts. The perspective of the past as it throws light on present problems, and a consideration of the solutions that have been achieved in other lands, are both needed. Adolescents, particularly, may well face problems calling for extensive study of historical backgrounds or of the social structures of other lands. The chart in this area does not outline historical sequences or blocks of work that could be classified as economics, political science, or sociology, but teachers of social studies will find in the situations listed many which suggest the types of everyday problems to which their fields should contribute understandings and skills.

Solutions to problems involving economic, social, and political structures and forces are not static. Even as learners are being helped to appraise the factors involved in a controversial area, school and community should be working together toward more adequate solutions to the same problems. The function of the school is to help learners investigate the facts which are within their comprehension and appraise present solutions. They should be helped to identify unresolved problems, to understand the processes through which social change comes about, and to gain in ability to envision the possible results of change.

In considering any social problem the importance of helping learners appraise the issues in the light of democratic values cannot be overstressed. Every effective solution to a social problem demands consideration of the degree to which democratic values have been put into operation. Children and youth, through concrete experiences in their school and local community and through discussion of the same issues as they appear in the larger world, must be helped to develop an attitude and an inclination to appraise social trends in the light of democratic values.

Some typical situations calling for growth in ability to deal with economic, social, and political structures and forces

A. Earning a Living

	EARLY CHILDHOOD	LATER CHILDHOOD
PROVIDING FOR WORK NEEDS OF SOCIETY Assuring that needed work will be done	**Finding what work is done by other persons with whom one has immediate contact**—Eating meals prepared by mother or cook; having school nurse bandage cut finger; watching custodian, other members of school staff at work; finding what all-school services are performed by other classes; talking with members of fire department, police force about their work, having postman deliver letter; watching a farmer plant crops; going to a concert; learning what happens in family when father or mother is ill; finding what happens to flowers or animals when they are not watered or fed . . .	**Extending acquaintance with the work of individuals and community agencies**—Becoming better acquainted with the occupations in one's locality—bank employees, hospital staff, mechanics, retailers; helping one's class carry out all-school services; asking about occupational groups about which one reads, or whom one sees on guided tours; finding what workers contributed to goods one purchases; discovering work opportunities for children and youth in community—errand boy, newspaper boy, baby sitter; discussing the strike in a local factory; inquiring about unemployment of parent or friends; finding why parents have to work overtime . . .
Deciding what work to do	**Assuming responsibility for simple tasks at home or at school**—Keeping room, toys, and clothes in order; gathering eggs; helping plant garden; arranging chairs and tables in classroom; watering plants; running errands; decorating library corner; deciding which class committee to work with; helping decide what must be done to carry out class project . . .	**Deciding on work responsibilities with or without remuneration**—Deciding whether to take job as errand boy, newspaper boy, baby sitter; mowing lawn; raising farm animals; constructing toys or furniture; helping to construct and care for playground or clubhouse; acting in various capacities in school store, other all-school projects; deciding which of several class responsibilities to offer to help with; sharing in family work responsibilities . . .

YOUTH	ADULTHOOD

A. Earning a Living

Understanding the range of occupations, the nature of specialization, and proposals for assuring that the needed work of the world will be carried out—Discussing new occupations created by technological changes; considering the importance of occupations which provide essential raw materials; discovering what is done by various workers in a factory; discussing the purpose of civil service; noting kinds of specialization within professions; discussing subsidies, minimum wage laws, work of labor unions, and other ways of assuring that needed work will be done; finding why child labor laws in one's state prevent one from taking certain jobs; considering function of government projects in providing work; considering purposes of unions, government subsidies, retirement plans; discussing implications of major strikes or lockouts reported in news releases; considering problems posed by increasing automation . . .

Participating in decisions that assure that the needed work of the world will be carried out—Considering function of and personal relationship to labor unions; voting on minimum wage laws; finding methods of assuring needed income to producers of raw materials—subsidies, soil banks, tariffs; dignifying "menial" jobs of the world; considering needed steps to encourage adequate numbers to join service occupations, become scientists, select other vocations where shortages exist; investigating unemployment insurance, health and accident insurance, retirement plans, tenure; taking action regarding child labor laws; deciding when union action is justified; considering how to adjust to probable effects of automation; helping youth appraise occupational trends in choosing vocation . . .

Studying vocational possibilities and making vocational choice—Deciding whether to take part-time job; joining youth group engaged in a special industrial enterprise; examining vocational trends—areas where workers will be in great demand, areas where machines are replacing workers; determining competencies needed in various vocations; appraising other factors important in making vocational choices—financial and other compensations, tenure, hours of work; appraising one's interests and aptitudes for specific vocations; deciding for which school service jobs to volunteer; seeking opportunities to explore vocations firsthand; deciding whether to accept job for sake of immediate financial independence or to go to college . . .

Selecting and/or carrying forward chosen vocation—Deciding on specific occupation with reference to such factors as supply and demand, advancement on job, social status, social security, financial and other compensations; securing preparation needed to bring desired competence to job, to advance on job; working through a variety of channels in securing job—placement office in college, ads in paper, employment agencies, personal efforts; determining when to change position; discussing vocational choice with children . . .

	EARLY CHILDHOOD	LATER CHILDHOOD
ACHIEVING EFFECTIVE WORKMANSHIP Assuring adequate work standards	**Noting differences between jobs well done and jobs poorly done**—Planning with class what is needed to carry out special assignment effectively; changing class plans when one or more members fail to carry out appointed tasks; finding why parents set certain standards in household tasks; making plans to get help with needed skills . . .	**Discovering bases for standards of workmanship**—Setting standards to be achieved before class project is begun; appraising results of job done; making plans to give needed help to those who failed to do job; finding what obligations one has assumed in promising to mow lawn regularly, in taking on paper route, in serving as member of school patrol, helper in lunchroom; appreciating fine performances in music, beauty of line and color in art . . .
Providing good working conditions	**Securing and replacing tools and materials needed for work**—Helping put away school supplies and toys; being responsible for helping keep library corner, some other work location tidy; deciding what is needed for special job; assembling and organizing equipment before beginning work; helping mother put away household appliances, put toys away; deciding how many people in class can work conveniently in one place, on one job; donning proper clothing for special jobs . . .	**Understanding relation of adequate working conditions to efficiency, adjusting immediate environment to work needs**—Planning and securing needed equipment for special committee assignment; planning where to keep needed materials in classroom or home; helping rearrange classroom furniture for special job; replacing equipment which is lost or broken; finding how careful plans and records help with work; finding how lighting, fresh air, rest, affect ability to work . . .
ASSURING THE RIGHTS AND RESPONSIBILITIES OF WORKERS Securing adequate remuneration	**Becoming aware that there are differences in the ways in which people live**—Finding why one's friends have different amounts of spending money; asking for toys like one's friends; noting differences in clothes and homes of one's friends; finding why oneself or one's friends have to wear made-over clothes; being paid for running special errand . . .	**Understanding the general nature of salary differences among persons of one's acquaintance**—Finding why one's family lives on smaller, greater income than one's friends; finding why father is taking advanced training, how mother helps stretch income in home; asking why some people, like baseball players, President, movie stars, get large salaries; discussing reasons for community plans to provide Thanksgiving, Christmas donations to some families; discovering effect of increased prices or subsidies on family's income, if in farming community . . .

YOUTH

Gaining increased insight into personal and legal obligations to maintain adequate work standards—Discovering legal requirements of part-time job—having health examination, keeping hair covered, others; appraising efficiency of work of class committees, persons with all-school responsibilities; discussing importance of manners, grooming in securing positions; discussing legislation requiring minimum building standards, certification of professional workers, testing of machinery, pure foods; discovering accepted standards in job one takes; laying plans to get education needed to do job well; discovering what demands for advanced specialization are likely to be needed in a profession . . .

Developing further understanding of personal and legal importance of good working conditions—Planning steps which will complete job most easily; finding why teachers in shop, home economics classes insist on specific ways of organizing, storing equipment; setting up efficient study conditions; experimenting with better tools or methods; securing proper ventilation and lighting; deciding how long to stay at job when tired; discussing articles about efficiency experts; investigating legislation regarding safety measures, length of working week; discussing effect of withholding labor-saving devices from market . . .

ADULTHOOD

Securing or applying standards of workmanship adequate for the job to be done—Developing competencies needed for effective work, advancement in one's vocation; taking action to secure adequate legal regulations in vocations where human lives may be endangered by low standards; adjusting and helping children adjust standards and materials in work situations at home to purposes job is to serve; deciding as an employer what provisions to make for those who lack skill or standards to do given job well; voting on legislation which provides for minimum standards, methods of testing products, and means of informing public as to standards met; discussing implications of competing with products of poorer quality . . .

Securing working conditions for greatest efficiency for oneself or others—Making time and motion studies; keeping up with latest trends in professional field; securing proper lighting and ventilation, effective safety measures, rest and relaxation—reasonable hours of work; reacting to legislative measures concerned with these conditions; keeping effectively records and plans needed for job; planning how best to adjust to conditions that cannot be changed; helping children build orderly work habits . . .

Understanding factors affecting income differentiation—Understanding what constitutes a living wage; considering adequacy of part-time salary in relation to one's competence, hours of work, working conditions; considering reasons for low salaries of some service groups and unskilled workers; finding what financial obligations accompany wages—union dues, income taxes, retirement plans, social security deductions; finding how to increase value of allowance through wise spending; considering purposes of collective bargaining, and other action of labor unions; helping decide what crops will produce best farm income; discussing values of extended preparation, specialization in the professions . . .

Assuring adequate remuneration for a given job for self or for others—Appraising income in light of such factors as risks, working conditions, hours of work, standards of living, personal satisfactions, living costs, health insurance, tenure, company dividends or bonuses, investment in preparation; deciding how to vote on minimum wage laws; deciding what action to take regarding salaries of public employees; considering problems of taxation as related to distribution of wealth, excess profits; deciding how to increase income in private business; stretching income by repairing and constructing household appliances, clothing, furniture; appraising effectiveness of collective bargaining procedures . . .

	EARLY CHILDHOOD	LATER CHILDHOOD
Assuring other benefits, rights, and responsibilities	**Understanding responsibilities of workers in home or in school**—Finding what one's job is as member of class committee, person with special responsibility; discovering how members of one's family share their work; finding why father does not have to work over week end, or why friends' fathers do not have to work when one's father does . . .	**Discovering some of the major rights and responsibilities guaranteed to workers**—Finding why parents attend union meetings, professional meetings; sharing in camps, outings, other services provided by companies, or by vocational groups; discussing purposes unions serve; finding what one's parents mean by unemployment insurance, by social security; finding what makes it possible for grandfather to retire . . .
MANAGING MONEY		
Budgeting income	**Spending small allowance on immediate needs**—Deciding how much to spend on candy; putting aside part of allowance for church; sharing in class decisions as to how to spend petty cash; making gift lists to estimate expenses; balancing simple class accounts; accounting for personal spending . . .	**Allotting personal allowance and sharing in family budgeting problems**—Deciding how much to save and how much to spend on candy, amusements, church, gifts; deciding whether to spend allowance on something that will soon be consumed, on something that will last; being wholly responsible for some part of wardrobe; sharing in decisions as to expenditure of family funds which involve one; sharing in decisions about club funds, class funds; helping balance simple class accounts; reimbursing others in case of carelessness with money or property . . .
Saving and investing	**Saving funds for special purposes**—Accumulating money in "piggy bank"; having parents or teacher hold money for one until it is needed; deciding when it is important to save money in order to get something that is badly wanted; depositing money in school bank; having bank account started for one . . .	**Understanding main purposes of investments with which one has direct contact**—Putting money in local or school bank; joining Christmas saving club; buying defense stamps; being given a bond; buying shares in school cooperative; investing part of income in paper route or equipment for some other job; finding reasons for fire, hail, life insurance . . .

YOUTH

Gaining increased insights into the methods through which benefits, rights, and responsibilities are assured to workers—Deciding whether to take part-time job involving union membership; finding how one applies for social security coverage; finding how professional groups protect and supervise members; discussing what it means for high school or college to be accredited; finding how professional groups work to secure higher standards for the profession; exploring health, retirement, and other benefits offered by one's chosen profession; discovering what educational services vocational groups offer to members . . .

ADULTHOOD

Acting to assure that rights and responsibilities of self and others as workers are guaranteed—Deciding whether to join business associations, grange, other organizations of special vocational groups; deciding how actively to participate in union activities; finding what associations within profession can give help in disputes regarding better working conditions, higher standards; finding how to obtain social security coverage for domestic workers; deciding whether to participate in retirement systems, hospitalization plans available to vocational groups . . .

Budgeting personal allowance or group funds and sharing in decisions regarding family budget—Apportioning allowance among activities and needs for which one is responsible; helping decide what proportion of family income should be used for personal needs; helping decide on family expenditures; planning ways to finance and present budget for class newspaper, class parties; understanding reasons for publishing town, church, or business budgets; understanding issues involved in sales tax, income tax, national debt; deciding how much of first earnings belong to self and to family; planning how to set aside funds for college expenses . . .

Apportioning total income for needs of self or group—Budgeting income for self or family in light of present and future needs; preparing written budgets for civic or social groups; reading financial statements from organization of which one is a member; voting on proposed budget or financial statement of town council, school board; helping children in family learn how to keep a simple budget; considering issues involved in legislative action such as sales tax, income tax, national debt . . .

Understanding major economic provisions for investment—Having life insured; keeping savings account; finding why it is important to give and keep receipts, to keep canceled checks; discovering how cooperatives in community operate; finding what it means to be bonded if responsible for funds; owning bonds purchased to insure education; balancing material against educational and other cultural investments; understanding principles on which fire, hail, life insurance operate; finding how stock market operates, what people mean by market slumps and rises . . .

Understanding and using existing economic structures in saving and investing money for self or others—Deciding on annuities or bonds; insuring self or others; purchasing stocks; knowing what is involved in speculation; deciding whether to invest in projected business; helping to establish cooperatives; deciding on wise investment of trust funds or funds owned by lodge or club; determining soundness of investments bearing different rates of interest; deciding whether to buy or rent home, farm; deciding how much to invest in cultural advantages for family; developing ways of balancing accounts, keeping receipts . . .

	EARLY CHILDHOOD	LATER CHILDHOOD
Borrowing money	**Understanding why money borrowed must be paid back**—Returning borrowed money to parents or teachers; understanding difference between parents' or other children's funds and one's own . . .	**Understanding the general obligations assumed in borrowing money**—Giving IOU when borrowing money; paying back when borrowing from friends or being paid back; finding what pawnshops are for; finding meaning of words like "mortgage," "interest," "loan," as one reads about them or hears members of family use them; finding how banks can pay interest on savings accounts . . .

B. Securing Goods and Services

MAKING GOODS AND SERVICES AVAILABLE Securing effective distribution	**Finding how some of the products one uses reach one**—Receiving gifts from other places; asking about strange fruits or vegetables in store; asking about trucking fleets that pass one's home; finding how milk is delivered; helping parents pick toys, clothing from mail-order catalogue; asking about persons who sell flowers or garden produce on streets; going with parents to purchase produce from nearby farm; going with father to deliver produce to town if living on farm; finding where milk comes from . . .	**Discovering some of the major ways in which people and nations achieve the distribution of goods**—Finding out about individuals and groups of people who have handled produce that one uses; finding how mail-order house distributes goods; asking about characteristic products from other parts of country, from other nations; asking about news releases discussing importance of raw materials from other countries to economy of this society . . .
BUYING AND SELLING GOODS AND SERVICES Deciding where to buy or sell	**Finding which stores are the most likely sources of goods one desires**—Finding what is sold in drugstore; finding which stores sell candy or ice cream; finding where to buy school supplies; looking at a mail-order catalogue; shopping for groceries with mother; going to markets with parents . . .	**Building bases for deciding where to buy or sell**—Finding why wholesale and retail prices are different; finding why farm products in store are more expensive than when bought on farm; finding why stores ask different prices for similar materials; discovering local stores in which prices more often fit one's budget . . .

YOUTH	ADULTHOOD
Understanding basic principles of borrowing money, and relationships between borrowing and investing—Securing loan for educational purposes; finding nature of legal securities needed when getting loans; finding what kinds of collateral are accepted for loan; investigating relation between paying interest on a loan and receiving interest on an investment; taking personal responsibility for individual or group financial obligation; discussing current proposals for guaranteeing financial security of nations . . .	**Understanding and using existing economic structures in borrowing money for self and others**—Deciding to mortgage house or property; voting on city plans for bond issue; deciding on reliability of company from which loan is secured; considering fairness of given rate of interest; deciding whether to sign a note for another person; knowing what legal protections are needed to make a loan valid; understanding import of "tight money" policies; assuming responsibility for individual or group financial obligation; considering how important it is to guarantee financial security of other nations . . .

B. Securing Goods and Services

YOUTH	ADULTHOOD
Increasing insight into the major economic structures governing world, national, interstate, or local trade—Discussing major issues relating to tariffs, interstate commerce reported in current news; investigating regulations regarding monopolies, cartels, trusts, interlocking directorates as reported in current news; discussing articles regarding proposed government control of sources of production or distribution; finding how to interpret what one reads about effects of rich or poor natural resources, of much or limited industrialization on development of given area or country . . .	**Dealing with the major national and international structures which control the distribution of goods**—Deciding what stand to take on government proposals regarding tariffs, reciprocal trade agreements, interstate commerce; interpreting press and other references to needs of other countries for markets, trade routes, sources of raw materials; taking position regarding government ownership, rural electrification; deciding what channels to use to get produce on market—to sell with a cooperative group, to wholesaler, on local market; taking action on proposals to make medical or other services more readily available, to attract youth to given professions . . .
Developing increased insight into principles governing where to buy or sell—Deciding whether to join school cooperative; finding reasons for price differences from one store to another on similar materials; studying function of wholesaler and middleman and effects on price; deciding whether to patronize an exclusive shop; sharing in parents' decisions regarding where to sell farm or garden produce . . .	**Applying sound principles in deciding where to buy or sell**—Determining neighborhood retailers which seem to offer most satisfactory purchases; identifying reason for higher prices in specialty shops; deciding when to purchase wholesale; deciding whether to purchase where discounts for cash payments are given; helping children learn how to make purchases at local stores . . .

	EARLY CHILDHOOD	LATER CHILDHOOD
Determining quality	**Learning the names and some of the characteristics of common products**—Finding differences in feel of wool, silk, cotton; discovering that rubber keeps one dry; finding differences in materials in toys, furniture; distinguishing colors; finding that leather mittens protect hands from wet, that wool lining keeps hands warm; helping select cookies for party or lunch at school . . .	**Understanding the characteristics of different products**—Finding why wool is warmer than cotton, rubber is used for overshoes; reading about new synthetic materials; helping choose clothing, select gifts; sharing in choosing certain school equipment; finding what labels on materials mean; understanding purposes of government regulations—why eggs are graded, butter fat is recorded; making choices while shopping for mother . . .
Determining a fair price	**Finding that articles have different prices**—Finding why various kinds of candy are priced differently; choosing between two editions of same book priced differently; choosing between two toys; finding that large articles or highly decorated ones do not always cost most; buying gifts; helping buy boxes of paints, special paper, other equipment needed by class . . .	**Identifying common factors influencing price**—Comparing commercial advertising with product itself; deciding whether article one ordered from an advertisement is worth money paid; helping parents decide between two articles of clothing; finding why one's mother or mothers of one's friends sometimes make clothes, knit sweaters; helping operate school store; deciding whether to make nominal charge for school paper; finding why mother talks about not buying out-of-season foods; finding how prices for wheat, other produce are determined if living on farm; setting prices on items for class sale; determining profits from newspaper route, magazines, or Christmas cards . . .
Deciding on means of payment	**Knowing the value of coins and small bills**—Telling real from imaginary money, giving right amount of money for purchases; counting change; finding how much money is in bank account . . .	**Using currency and other common means of payment**—Giving right amount of money for purchases; acting as cashier in class sales; cashing checks or money orders sent as gifts; finding how to send money order; writing checks on bank account; finding why family charges purchases; arranging for charge account in school store; finding what it means to buy goods on installment plan . . .

YOUTH

Using increased insights into quality differences as a guide to purchasing—Choosing clothing in relation to suitability of material and style; selecting fresh vegetables or fruits; interpreting common brands and labels; using information from educational, research, and promotional agencies; interpreting advertising; discussing need for government control of standards; finding purpose of better business bureaus; testing products in school laboratories; learning how parents and others determine differences in quality of services—medical, educational, domestic, governmental, others . . .

Purchasing or selling in the light of major factors affecting price—Deciding whether or not to pay more to get article which is "different" from those owned by "gang"; planning advertising campaign to sell school yearbook; evaluating commercial advertising; understanding reasons for making or not making things at home; interpreting news articles reporting effect of scarcity or abundance of raw materials; running class project to insure profit; discussing effects of cartels, monopolies, or trusts on prices; investigating implications of government controls to assure low prices of essential goods or to tax luxuries . . .

Using variety of means in paying for goods—Writing checks on personal account; purchasing money orders; purchasing postal notes; gaining general understanding of relationship of currency in this country to that of other nations; investigating reports of inflation in certain countries; using parents' charge accounts; discussing advantages and disadvantages of installment buying; discussing purposes and values of cooperatives and credit unions; finding why discounts are sometimes given for cash purchases . . .

ADULTHOOD

Using appropriate sources and tests to tell quality of products—Getting information from various agencies for consumer protection; knowing government tests; interpreting labels and brands; recognizing quality of goods from inspection; applying adequate tests for quality of workmanship; deciding how to appraise style as an aspect of quality; interpreting advertising; evaluating quality of works of art, of entertainment, decorative quality of furniture and craft materials; appraising quality of services —medical, educational, domestic, governmental, others . . .

Evaluating prices in the light of sound economic principles—Understanding relation of supply and demand to price—deciding whether or not to purchase foods out of season, planning or taking advantage of bargain sales; appraising style as factor in quality; interpreting advertising; understanding skilled workmanship and production costs as factors in price—deciding whether to purchase handmade products; understanding transportation costs as a factor in price; deciding what should be paid for services; setting prices in one's own business in order to assure profit; securing adequate information about antitrust laws, cartels, monopolies, relation of subsidies or government control of prices to production of essential materials . . .

Selecting medium and means of payment appropriate to the need—Using checking account; choosing appropriate ways of transferring various amounts of money to other people; deciding when to use bank drafts; using currency of other countries appropriately; deciding how many charge accounts to open; deciding whether to purchase on installment plan; deciding whether to capitalize on discounts offered for cash purchases; investigating legal protection for those purchasing homes, for farmers purchasing land . . .

	EARLY CHILDHOOD	LATER CHILDHOOD

C. Providing for Social Welfare

	EARLY CHILDHOOD	LATER CHILDHOOD
WORKING IN THE FAMILY GROUP Providing secure relations	**Finding sources of affection and guidance in members of the family—** Responding to affection from members of family; finding why it is necessary to obey parents; finding when one can make independent decisions or disagree with parents; finding why and when it is necessary to obey older brothers and sisters; adjusting to younger brother or sister in home; finding what relationships exist between various relatives of one's acquaintance; visiting other families and finding what members live in them . . .	**Finding how members of family groups depend on each other—**Finding when and how far it is possible to discuss a problem with parents; deciding when to go to parents for advice; deciding what to do when parents will not let one do what "gang" wants; finding what courtesy and obedience one owes grandparents, older brothers or sisters; taking care of younger brothers and sisters; discussing what it means to have parents separated . . .
Sharing family responsibilities	**Finding how members of the family share responsibilities—**Finding how family members share in household responsibilities; helping with dishes, sweeping, errands; helping keep room tidy; helping other children put toys away; taking care of pets; finding that parents earn the money that goes into one's allowance, that money is not always available for special purchases; asking why mother does or does not go to work, why other children's mothers go to work or not . . .	**Assuming responsible membership in the family group—**Helping decide what responsibilities to assume in home; finding why it is important to carry out household tasks as planned; helping mother or brothers and sisters do special jobs when needed; finding how much family budget can allow for special requests for clothing, movies, candy; finding what father does to support family; identifying mother's role as a worker, as homemaker; finding how parents share family funds . . .
PARTICIPATING IN COMMUNITY WELFARE PROVISIONS Sharing in protective measures	**Finding out about provisions for protection—**Asking why playgrounds are fenced, why cars are not parked in front of schools, why traffic controls are provided near schools; visiting school nurse . . .	**Finding the general purposes served by insurance and other protective measures—**Finding why parents take out life insurance; discussing purposes of hail, fire insurance; using playgrounds provided for employees of local factories . . .

C. Providing for Social Welfare

YOUTH	ADULTHOOD
Understanding the nature of family groups and the source of their leadership—Finding spheres in which independent decisions are possible; negotiating changes in parental regulations; taking responsibility for conduct and well-being of younger children; helping parents make grandparents, relatives feel members of family group; deciding whether to go to a college that will make it necessary to live away from home; deciding whether to take position which makes it necessary to leave home; discussing what divorce does to family groups; considering what causes divorce, what restrictions should be imposed by divorce laws . . .	**Taking responsibility for secure relationships among members of the family group**—Assuming leadership responsibilities as parent; deciding how much freedom to give to children and in what areas; planning recreation activities that include children; deciding whether to take parents or relatives into family group; considering whether divorce or separation is justified; deciding whether to accept position which takes one away from family group; deciding whether mother should be at home when children return from school; deciding how far older children should be made responsible for younger ones; deciding what relations to maintain when children have set up their own homes; helping children develop affectionate relationships with other members of family . . .
Finding what leadership is necessary in maintaining a family group—Deciding what salary is needed before marriage; deciding whether to marry while still securing education; considering whether to live at parents' home if married; determining how much of part-time salary to contribute to support of parents' home; deciding whether to ask parents to be responsible for bills, for caring for clothes; deciding whether to ask younger members of family to do special favors; assuming responsibility for share of household tasks . . .	**Taking responsible leadership in the family**—Deciding whether both husband and wife should work; deciding how far children should contribute to support of family; deciding how much allowance to give children; deciding whether to pay children for carrying out household tasks; assigning share in household responsibilities to various members of family; helping children establish appropriate relationships with service members of family; taking joint responsibility in decisions regarding purchasing home, sending children to college . . .
Understanding the nature of insurance and other protective measures—Investigating various types of life insurance, annuities, accident and hospital insurance; deciding whether to share in hospitalization plans; finding general principles on which insurance operates; helping parents decide whether to take out fire, hail insurance; finding what benefits are provided for employees in the industry in which one has part-time job; discussing nature and purpose of retirement plans and who pays for them . . .	**Participating in group insurance and other protective measures**—Deciding how much and what kind of insurance to take out; helping decide what a union or other vocational group should do for members; deciding what benefits to provide for employees, if an independent owner; deciding whether to share in hospitalization plan; taking action to provide adequate health and recreation facilities for vocational group; taking action to provide adequate community recreation facilities for children and youth . . .

	EARLY CHILDHOOD	LATER CHILDHOOD
Sharing in community welfare efforts	**Understanding the general purposes of home and school contributions toward social welfare**—Finding what is done by Junior Red Cross; taking part in school efforts to share in welfare activities; asking about tag days, advertisements, other prominent evidence of community welfare activities; making church contributions; visiting community library, museum, art collection; participating in activities in community recreation center . . .	**Taking proportionate share in prominent community efforts toward social welfare**—Taking part in Junior Red Cross; helping organize school drives to support national Red Cross, local community chest, other organizations; finding what general services are performed by various agencies to which money has been contributed; helping service club establish a local playground; finding how local library, museum, zoo are maintained; discussing how money, clothing contributed to international relief agencies will be used . . .
USING GOVERNMENT TO GUARANTEE WELFARE Providing and using public services	**Finding what is done by various service groups**—Finding what is done by local policeman; visiting local fire department; going with parents to health clinic; finding what public health nurse does; talking with park caretaker; asking about city sanitation workers, road repairmen . . .	**Finding the nature and purpose of major public services**—Discovering variety of services undertaken by police, fire, and sanitation departments; discovering variety of personnel in such departments; finding how post office is organized; discussing work of various public health officials in office or clinic visited . . .
Providing and using legal protections	**Obeying laws which safeguard the welfare of all**—Obeying quarantine regulations; helping with sanitary disposal of garbage; taking part in fire and civil defense drills; finding what other regulations exist for fire prevention; finding what traffic laws to obey in coming to school . . .	**Finding what major legal protections safeguard the welfare of all**—Finding purpose of quarantine and isolation regulations; finding what legal regulations exist for fire prevention, why one must not play with fire signals; finding what laws must be obeyed in garbage disposal; finding purpose of various traffic laws; finding why special brands and labels are placed on foods . . .

YOUTH	ADULTHOOD
Understanding the nature and purposes of various community efforts toward social welfare— Discussing purposes served by local housing projects; deciding which of several welfare agencies to give individual or school support; finding what kind of help is provided by family welfare associations, other guidance groups; helping establish community recreation center; deciding whether to devote part of club time to service activities; participating in special classes offered by school, art museum, adult education council; helping supervise recreational opportunities made available by school or other community services; discussing function of international relief, labor, religious groups; becoming acquainted with welfare services performed by one's church; turning to community groups for assistance in individual or school need . . .	**Supporting and using desirable community efforts toward social welfare—**Deciding whether to support or share in housing projects; deciding how much to contribute to community chest, other agencies; deciding what support to give to church welfare activities; considering whether to get help from family service group; engaging in or helping plan adult education program; deciding whether to join a service club; sharing in setting policies of welfare agencies; helping sponsor movements to meet community cultural needs; considering how the school can best serve community needs; discussing activities of international relief agencies; helping children discover functions of major community welfare groups . . .
Considering the nature and variety of public services desirable—Discussing local proposals to secure better fire or police protection; considering proposals to increase health services for all; discussing responsibility of government groups in securing better housing; identifying means whereby one's community supports schools, role of school board, superintendent, other officials; helping establish community recreation center; investigating proposals for international cooperation on health projects; identifying issues involved in establishing an international police force . . .	**Providing and drawing upon public services for the welfare of self and others—**Deciding whether to go to health clinic or to consult private physician; considering adequacy of service provided by local police, sanitation, fire departments; deciding whether to support measures for increased government participation in housing, other welfare projects; sharing in local provisions for recreation; considering effectiveness of local administration of schools; considering proposals for an international health commission, for an international office of education; deciding whether to support proposals for an international police force . . .
Understanding the bases for and nature of legal protections—Discussing nature and effectiveness of health, traffic, and other laws protecting community welfare; discovering nature and purpose of pure food and drug laws; discussing existing safeguards of property rights; exploring work of juvenile court, other legal groups established to help children and youth; considering nature and purpose of social security measures; discussing nature of legal protections for collective bargaining . . .	**Assuring adequate legal protections for the security of self and others—**Considering adequacy of health, traffic, fire, other laws governing community life; considering adequacy of legal restrictions on amount of interest, regulations on foreclosure of mortgages and on safeguarding of other property rights; considering adequacy of community juvenile court, other services to youth; voting on proposals for social security; considering adequacy of legal protections for collective bargaining; helping children develop understanding and ability to abide by community legal protections . . .

	EARLY CHILDHOOD	LATER CHILDHOOD
Controlling use of natural resources	**Sharing in family and community efforts to preserve natural resources—** Finding why one should not destroy birds' nests, throw stones at birds; learning how to care for matches on picnics; finding why some wild flowers are not to be picked; helping clean up after picnic in park . . .	**Finding ways of cooperating in the preservation of national resources—** Finding what game laws are to be obeyed in given community; finding what local regulations exist regarding camp fires; cooperating in reforesting projects; helping in special projects for weed or insect control; discussing proposals to establish local or state park; participating in local or state plans to establish summer camp; visiting local fish hatchery; discussing proposed projects to build new power plants . . .

D. Molding Public Opinion

PROVIDING ADEQUATE EDUCATIONAL OPPORTUNITIES Participating in organized education	**Finding how oneself and others share in providing school experiences—** Finding what kinds of things are done in school; finding what brothers and sisters are learning in other classes; finding what teachers and equipment are available to help one; helping plan daily class activities; finding how mother and teacher plan together; helping explain class experiences to visitors; discovering one's responsibility in helping care for school building and property . . .	**Finding how parents and others share in planning and providing for education—**Finding why parents and teachers insist on regular attendance at school; finding why other children, or oneself, attend private or parochial schools; helping plan class activities, share books or hobbies with classmates; sharing in three-way parent–teacher–child conferences; helping plan how class work can best be explained to parents during "open house" or special visiting day; finding how parent–teacher association shares in school activities; finding how parents help pay for organized education; helping conserve books and other materials provided by school . . .

YOUTH	ADULTHOOD
Understanding major issues in the preservation and use of national resources—Discussing purposes of game laws; considering what needs to be done to restock game; obeying legal regulations to prevent forest fires; cooperating in local, state, and national plans to stop erosion; considering work of game wardens or forest rangers as possible vocation; cooperating in plans to control insects, spread of weeds; considering issues involved in safeguarding world supplies of oil, other crucial products; considering problems involved in sharing oil, nickel, other products with other nations . . .	**Cooperating in the preservation and use of national resources for the good of self and others**—Planning farming procedures so as to prevent erosion or depletion of soil; cooperating in efforts to reforest, to restock game; taking action to secure and enforce adequate game laws; taking action on proposals to increase forest ranger, game warden service; deciding whether to support plans to establish national or state park; participating in government plans for insect, weed control; deciding whether to support power projects; considering government proposals to safeguard world food supply . . .

D. Molding Public Opinion

YOUTH	ADULTHOOD
Developing increased insight into the function of organized education in a community—Deciding whether to leave school for a job, to combine schooling with part-time job; deciding whether to attend a state university or private college; deciding between an academic and vocational high school program; discussing proposals to organize a municipal junior college; participating in a school–community curriculum council; examining reasons for reported differences in educational programs from community to community; discussing articles about modern schools, proposals from school board or community groups that touch one's program; asking exchange teacher about schools in other countries; discussing articles regarding educational programs for semi-illiterate peoples . . .	**Assuming appropriate responsibility for assuring an adequate program of organized education for community and family**—Considering proposals to extend amount of free education; deciding whether to send children to public, private, or parochial school, to state or private college; deciding whether to enter young children in nursery school; helping adolescents decide between vocational and academic high school programs; attending meetings of local school board; discussing adequacy of present programs for exceptional youth; appraising proposals to start foreign language instruction in earlier grades; discussing proposals to guarantee adequate teacher supply, adequate classrooms; evaluating popular articles about schools; evaluating proposals to equalize educational opportunities among communities; deciding whether to support educational experimentation in schools . . .

	EARLY CHILDHOOD	LATER CHILDHOOD
Providing and supporting other educational agencies	**Sharing in the activities of other educational agencies**—Going with parents or class to museum; borrowing books from local library; visiting zoo; discovering what plants, birds, and animals can be seen in local park; helping care for community places one visits; finding what provisions one's church makes for children; visiting children's programs in churches of other children; taking part in Cubs, Brownies, or other national youth groups; going to summer camps; joining puppetry group in local art museum; sharing in program of community recreation center . . .	**Using community educational resources**—Finding how to use public library, museum; visiting points of historic interest in local community, in state; sharing in musical program, plays, motion pictures brought to community; joining interest groups in local recreation center; taking responsibility for caring for community resources one uses; deciding whether to join one or more of national youth groups; exploring programs offered by one's church; finding why some children are in parochial schools or spend added time in religious schools; exploring activities offered by YMCA, YMHA, CYO; joining in activities of settlement houses or other community recreational groups . . .
USING INSTRUMENTS FOR DISSEMINATING INFORMATION Interpreting information	**Becoming acquainted with a variety of sources of information**—Reading comics; asking what headlines in paper mean; finding what kinds of information one can get from books; finding how to distinguish between imaginative stories and factual information; finding what children's magazines to use for factual information; finding how to tell real photographs from imaginative pictures; talking about information secured in motion pictures, television shows . . .	**Discovering bases for testing the soundness of information**—Learning how to distinguish editorial comment in newspaper from news reporting; finding which magazines to use for factual information; finding how and when to use such sources as encyclopedia; identifying the variety of information made available by radio and television; deciding whether a motion picture or television program has given a true picture of American life; deciding how to interpret advertising in newspaper, on radio and television . . .

YOUTH

Gaining increased insight into the educational resources a community provides for its members—Helping equip town library, local museum; sharing in or sponsoring traveling libraries for rural districts; sharing in little theater group; sharing in adult education programs; helping provide special evening or after-school activities for younger children; deciding whether to join a church; considering value of participation in national youth groups; investigating work of unions, of various professional groups, in providing educational facilities for members; attending local town meetings, other groups on current affairs; deciding what activities in local Y to share in; helping determine youth program of local Y; deciding whether to work with an active political group; discussing right of religious or racial minorities to provide special instruction for their children . . .

ADULTHOOD

Taking responsibility for provision of community educational resources for all—Helping children use library; planning for children's museum; deciding whether to support community proposal to establish zoo in local park; helping identify and preserve local points of historic interest; deciding whether to open school buildings for special evening activities; deciding what adult education programs to sponsor; deciding whether to join groups providing information about national and international events; deciding whether to teach a children's class in church, whether to have children excused from school to receive religious instruction; deciding whether to encourage children to join Scouts or other youth groups; sharing in activities of music, drama, or art groups; deciding whether to take part in educational activities provided by one's union, attend conferences of one's professional group . . .

YOUTH

Extending ability to evaluate the soundness of sources of information—Discussing how to tell what influences are most likely to be reflected in policy of a paper, magazine, radio or television program; evaluating editorials, news commentaries; appraising authenticity of documentary film, historical movie; discovering sources of reliable information about other countries; developing effective techniques for interpreting advertising; finding how to interpret propaganda; finding how to use publications of agencies of consumer information; identifying available sources of adequate scientific information . . .

ADULTHOOD

Using sound bases for interpreting information—Determining what policy is represented by daily papers or magazines; interpreting news coming from press of another nation; finding what factors might influence policy of radio and television reporting, of newspapers, of motion pictures; evaluating experience and reliability of author of a book; using materials from various agencies of consumer research; identifying government sources which provide reliable factual information; deciding whether to act on medical or other scientific advice given in popular magazines, radio and television programs, pamphlets . . .

	EARLY CHILDHOOD	LATER CHILDHOOD
Using appropriate means of presenting a point of view	**Finding ways of communicating with other school groups**—Advertising class sale; sending notice to school paper; writing class record to tell parents about activities; writing announcement to be read to other classes; posting notice on bulletin board; deciding when a picture will make a communication more attractive . . .	**Finding what sources may be used to influence group thinking**—Writing editorials or letters to school paper; discussing letters which appear in local paper or in magazines; choosing pictures or films to present information to one's class; deciding when to make announcement over school amplifying system; helping plan for one's class to appear on an educational television program; helping plan for series of pictures of class activity in local paper . . .
Acting on issues involving freedom of press	**Finding that parents exert controls over what one reads and sees**—Finding that parents disapprove of certain comic books; finding there are television programs one is not allowed to watch . . .	**Finding ways through which sources of information are supervised**—Discussing work of censor in some countries; finding why some nations control their news services; finding why some books are banned; asking why parents will not allow certain newspapers to be read; asking why some movies are listed as "for adults only" . . .

YOUTH	ADULTHOOD
Understanding how and when to use various sources of public information—Helping plan editorial policy of high school or college paper; considering which local papers to use to interpret a school project to the public; considering what audiences are reached by various kinds of national magazines; deciding when advertisements might be used to put across a point of view; deciding what type of all-school assembly to use in presenting student council proposal; helping plan for school participation in television or radio program . . .	**Using appropriate agencies through which to present a point of view to the local or national group**—Deciding when to write to newspaper or magazine; deciding which newspaper or magazine to ask to publish letter or article; considering use of television and radio to present plans to a community group; helping plan documentary film; planning political advertisement; taking part in public forums and town meetings . . .
Understanding the issues involved in granting freedom of speech—Discussing principles underlying censorship of news in time of emergency; discussing right of college board to suppress college paper whose editorials have disagreed with public opinion in general; discussing regulations which prevent or protect publication of seditious points of view; considering purpose and adequacy of post office regulations with regard to obscene literature; identifying bases on which some books are banned; discussing purposes of standards for motion-picture, television, and radio productions; discussing controls on advertising; sharing in community efforts to control sale of comic books . . .	**Taking action in keeping with democratic values in situations involving control or supervision of sources of information**—Considering adequacy of censorship of news in time of emergency; considering proposals designed to keep nondemocratic points of view from being published or circulated; deciding whether to support action which bans books; appraising legal restrictions on printing of scandal; considering adequacy of government regulations on mailing of obscene literature; considering effectiveness of Motion Picture Board of Review; taking steps to secure needed controls of advertising; deciding whether to allow children to read comics, reports of criminal acts, watch crimes enacted in motion pictures and on television; cooperating in community efforts to control sale of comic books . . .

E. Participating in Local and National Government

	EARLY CHILDHOOD	LATER CHILDHOOD
ELECTING GOVERNMENT REPRESENTATIVES Nominating and electing candidates	**Sharing in the selection of classmates for special responsibilities—**Voting for class committees; sending delegates to student council; choosing delegate to meet with assembly committee; helping decide which persons should be trusted with special responsibilities in class; discussing what one should take into account in suggesting people for special jobs . . .	**Using appropriate procedures in nominating and electing candidates—**Nominating and electing candidates for student council; considering special qualifications needed for particular jobs—electing captain of baseball team, editor of school paper; discussing whether secret ballot should be used to elect class officers; planning campaign speech as candidate for student council office; discussing qualifications of prominent candidates for local or national elections; finding how parents get information about candidates; finding why adults must register to vote; finding what voting machines are like, how parents cast their votes . . .
SECURING EFFECTIVE GOVERNMENT ORGANIZATION Considering effectiveness of existing organization	**Identifying the prominent members of local and national government—**Finding how class representatives take part in student council; asking what is done by President, governor, mayor; asking about prominent officials discussed by family or friends; asking about pictures of Capitol, White House . . .	**Finding how government groups are organized—**Deciding how long class officers should remain in office; appraising effectiveness of present structure of student council, staff of school paper; finding what kind of work is done by mayor, governor, President, other prominent local and national officials; finding how Constitution of this country came to be; visiting state legislature, meeting of city council; studying differences between Senate and House of Representatives; finding how school board, park commission, other local groups change or improve opportunities to go to school, to work or play; discussing work of ambassadors and other members of Department of State mentioned in the news; finding what it means for a country to have a king or queen; discussing relation of Canada, Australia, to British Commonwealth of Nations . . .

YOUTH | ADULTHOOD

E. Participating in Local and National Government

Understanding and applying the principles involved in nominating and electing candidates— Helping nominate and elect representatives to student council; acting as member of nominating committee for club officers; discussing process through which political candidates are selected; following procedure of national political rally to nominate presidential candidate; discussing qualifications of candidates for local or national offices; considering local procedures which regulate registration for voting; taking part in local drives to get all voters to register, to cast their votes; discussing how ballots are cast, how votes are counted; comparing election procedures with those of other countries prominent in the news . . .

Taking an active part in the selection, nomination, and election of government candidates— Deciding what qualifications a candidate for office should have; considering respective qualifications of several nominees for office; deciding whether to work actively in political party; holding office in local branch of political party; taking part in nomination of candidates; considering efficacy of local procedures to register voters; deciding what action to take on measures which restrict the right to vote; evaluating proportional representation or other election procedures unique to the given community; deciding whether to electioneer for a candidate; helping plan methods of securing large turnout to vote at elections; considering what points of view are represented by various parties . . .

Understanding major issues involved in securing an effective organization of government personnel—Helping set up constitution of student council or class organization; considering needed changes in existing council organization; discussing organization of local and national governments; finding how present structure of the national government came to be; discussing news releases on appointments of cabinet members; discovering what municipal positions exist in local community; finding how to proceed to get driving license; deciding which government departments to write to for special information; working with members of Department of Agriculture on demonstration farms; finding how the government is organized to work with those of other countries; securing information about the organization of governments of other nations prominent in the press; tracing the history of democratic forms of government . . .

Acting to secure and maintain an effective government organization—Discussing how long local officials should remain in office; discussing effectiveness of local organization of mayor and council; taking action on proposals to hire a city manager; evaluating presidential appointments to government posts; discussing effectiveness of the work of Department of State in international problems; appraising proposals to put emergency powers in hands of President; considering specific proposals to increase government efficiency; taking action on measures to secure continuity of personnel in government departments; deciding which department to go to for assistance on special problems; deciding what measures should be taken to assist other countries desiring democratic forms of government . . .

	EARLY CHILDHOOD	LATER CHILDHOOD
Appraising work of representatives	**Making informal appraisal of the work of classmates to whom responsibilities have been assigned**—Deciding whether special committee has done its work well; discussing how to tell if special jobs are well done; deciding whether a special delegate has spoken well in assembly; discussing appropriateness of proposals of lunchroom committee, other special committee; considering how well persons responsible for an all-school service did their jobs the previous week . . .	**Finding how local and national groups may follow the work of their representatives**—Discussing reports of student council representatives; making suggestions for new committees on basis of work of those retiring; discussing press and parent comments on work of prominent political representatives; following congressional vote on a major issue of local or national significance; following actions of town council or school board in providing new playground or other special provisions for young people . . .
MAKING AND ENFORCING LAWS Taking responsibility in making and changing laws	**Sharing in agreements necessary to effective home and school living**—Helping decide desirable conduct in halls; setting up policies for use of room library table; helping set up lunchroom regulations; coming to agreements as to how many people can share in one kind of work; discussing fire regulations; helping formulate and post important classroom rules; reaching family agreements about playtime, care of toys, time for going to bed . . .	**Finding what general procedures are followed in making laws**—Helping set up regulations necessary for effective class living, family living; visiting state legislature; discussing how Congress votes on bills; finding what it means when President vetoes a bill; following vote of city or town council on proposal in which one is interested; discussing parent, press, or radio comments on prominent national bills; learning how regulations of school are developed . . .

YOUTH	ADULTHOOD
Understanding what is involved in evaluating the work of representatives—Discussing effectiveness of work of student council or other selected group in school or college; following activities of political representatives as reported in the press, magazines; finding how to follow voting records of representatives; discussing state or national legislative action on prominent bills; discussing value of the *Congressional Record* in providing full reports of debates . . .	**Taking active part in appraising the activities of local and national representatives**—Following records of representatives; interpreting press reports of speeches, of activity by representatives on committees; deciding when to write to congressional representative urging special action; deciding when to expect representative to support interests of a local group; deciding what congressional action should be expected from minority and majority representatives in Congress; considering effectiveness of local government; following publications of local and national groups in which appraisals are made of work of representatives . . .
Understanding the procedures through which laws are made—Following progress of an important bill through Congress; discussing importance of public action in securing support for a bill; discussing effect of amendments or riders on bills of public concern; considering purpose and importance of presidential vetoes; discussing press or radio reports of methods through which controversial bills are held up; studying proposed reforms of Congress; discussing methods through which the Constitution can be revised; discussing methods through which treaties are ratified; participating in establishing school rules and regulations; comparing methods by which democratic and totalitarian governments achieve their ends; comparing actions of dictators with those of democratic leaders . . .	**Taking a responsible part in the making and changing of laws**—Following progress of a bill through Congress; deciding when to write to representatives urging that a bill be passed; considering effect of proposed amendments or riders; considering wisdom of presidential vetoes; discussing action of House and Senate committees in revising bills; discussing proposals to amend the Constitution; discussing proposed changes to harmonize divorce laws, traffic laws, other laws under control of states; taking an interest in legislation which has no immediate relation to one's personal or economic interests; discussing effectiveness of present methods of ratifying treaties . . .

	EARLY CHILDHOOD	LATER CHILDHOOD
Cooperating in enforcing laws	**Obeying the laws which affect one's immediate conduct**—Cooperating in carrying out class, school, or home agreements and regulations; respecting property rights; learning to obey traffic laws; finding what to do on streets with stop and go signs; asking about work of local policeman; finding what is done by traffic policeman; understanding school fire regulations . . .	**Cooperating in and finding what general organization exists for law enforcement**—Finding what adults mean by "Bill of Rights"; investigating game, traffic, other laws which affect one's immediate conduct; serving as member of safety patrol; taking responsibility for self and others in carrying out school policies; finding what work is done by FBI, state and local police; discussing current methods of punishing criminals; finding what function is served by judge and jury in court . . .
PROVIDING FINANCIAL SUPPORT FOR GOVERNMENT		
Determining amount and sources of income		**Identifying the main kinds of taxes with which one has personal contact**—Finding what is meant by income tax; finding purpose of local or national sales or luxury taxes which one pays; owning a savings bond, postal savings certificate . . .
Determining use of government income		**Finding the general use of taxes with which one has contact**—Finding what is being done with special sales tax which one pays; finding who pays for public buildings, parks, teachers' salaries, free school supplies; finding how policeman, mailman, fireman are paid . . .

YOUTH	ADULTHOOD
Understanding the general principles and organization through which laws are enforced and cooperating with agencies of law enforcement—Investigating traffic, curfew, marriage, and other laws directly affecting one's conduct; finding what laws exist for protection of life and property of all; investigating history and present implications of Bill of Rights; discussing progress of a case of national importance or local interest through Supreme Court; discussing proposed appointments to Supreme Court; considering proposals for reform in penal institutions; discovering way in which local juvenile or domestic relations court functions; investigating respective responsibilities of state and federal police, district attorney, local and state courts; discussing proposals for an international court, international police force . . .	**Cooperating with agencies of law enforcement for the protection of self and others**—Finding what laws protect property rights; learning local and state traffic laws; obeying current income tax laws; deciding what steps to take to appeal to courts in case of dispute; discussing effectiveness of work of grand jury, district attorney; taking action to secure constructive treatment of juvenile delinquents; performing jury duty; deciding what action to take on proposals for an international court, an international police force . . .
Identifying major issues regarding the sources of government income—Discussing effects of sales, luxury taxes on various income groups; discussing issues involved in determining rate of income taxes; considering purposes of corporation, excess-profits taxes; considering relation of tax load to widening functions of government . . .	**Taking action in determining policies regarding the sources of government income**—Deciding whether to support proposed sales tax; considering value of proposed luxury taxes; discussing national proposals to vary rate of income tax; deciding whether to support proposed state or local income tax; considering means of enforcing excess-profits and corporation taxes; discussing rate of proposed property taxes . . .
Understanding major issues involved in decisions as to government expenditures—Discussing reported salaries of various government officials; investigating proportion of government income devoted to police and fire protection, to education; sharing in community efforts to finance better roads, parks, improved sanitation; helping publicize school bond issue or tax levy; discussing issues involved in national proposals for expenditure of funds on public works, unemployment insurance . . .	**Sharing in setting policy regarding the use of government income**—Taking action regarding salaries of government officials, of government employees, of teachers; discussing proposals to limit the national debt; deciding whether to purchase a house in a community where there is a high tax for community improvements; deciding whether to support an increased tax levy, bond issue, for schools; deciding whether to support proposals for unemployment insurance, for national medical care . . .

Using the Charts of Persistent Life Situations as Learners Face Them

The charts illustrating typical situations which learners of various maturity levels might face, and the persistent life situations with which they would need to cope, can serve the teacher in several ways. They can help him to identify the major persistent situations which are a part of the various everyday situations with which children or youth may be dealing. Conversely, the teacher who recognizes persistent situations with which individuals and groups need help may find in the charts beginning points for planning needed learning experiences. The charts may serve as a guide to balanced growth and the direction of growth, and also to selection of subject matter and materials. Finally, they can serve as a prototype for school faculties making their own analyses.

THE CHARTS CAN BE USED TO GAIN INSIGHT INTO THE IMMEDIATE CONCERNS OF LEARNERS AND THE PERSISTENT LIFE SITUATIONS INVOLVED

"Jane bought one just like it, but hers cost . . ." The ninth-grade group were talking about new sweaters. They had been involved in a study of how to read advertisements effectively. As often happens when learners explore situations of genuine concern, they began to apply what they had been learning to their own purchasing problems. From these discussions came related problems of potentially high educative value. The continued references to experiences in buying clothes caused their homeroom teacher, Miss Dearborn, to ask herself questions like these. What should Jane have taken into account in making her purchase? With what persistent life situations did she have to deal? What help may Jane and others in the group need from the school?

The charts help to identify a combination of persistent life situations that are a part of the problem faced by learners. Buying clothing was a new and important problem for Jane and the other ninth-graders. Up to this year, the allowances of most of the group were sufficient only for incidental purchases. Buying clothes under parent guidance had provided opportunity to make only limited judgments of their own. Now, as greater maturity heightened interest, many families were allowing increasing freedom in the choice of clothes. Their teacher saw in this new interest and increase of responsibility opportunities for many kinds of growth.

Miss Dearborn first checked her thinking about the immediate problem against the Master List of persistent life situations on pages 155 to 165. Then, having listed a series of problems that seemed likely to be related to the selection and use of clothing, she used the page numbers indicated in the list to locate illustrations of typical everyday situations.

Looking particularly under the column headed "youth," Miss Dearborn was able to identify related situations which in turn suggested other persistent life situations which her group might need to consider. For example, she recognized the importance of health factors in the selection of a clothing item such as a sweater. In the list under HEALTH she found the recurring problem of SELECTING APPROPRIATE CLOTHING [3] for temperature conditions and the reference to page 176 of the charts of typical situations faced by learners. Looking in the "youth" column she noted "selecting clothing which will gain social approval and still meet temperature conditions—following the peer fad. . . ." This brought into focus an idea she had that, in the problem of choosing clothing, some of the youngsters might need to cope with the persistent life situation of ACHIEVING STATUS IN GROUPS.[4] Again using the Master List to locate the problem and then the detailed chart she turned to page 183 and noted "adjusting to social, economic, . . . or other factors placing one in a minority group." In her own initial planning she had also identified other possible persistent life situations such as ACHIEVING ATTRACTIVE PERSONAL APPEARANCE. Turning to page 231 she found in the "youth" column a number of immediate situations that seemed likely to be faced by the members of her group as they began to purchase their own clothing—"selecting clothing suited to figure and coloring; deciding when and how to follow the fads of the crowd; finding how to adjust clothing fads to suit individual needs. . . ."

Miss Dearborn continued to use the charts both to test her thinking and to locate new suggestions. Eventually her plans listed the following as persistent life situations and possible specific concepts with which these students might need help as they assumed increasing responsibility for selecting and purchasing their own clothing: aesthetic decisions—selecting attractive clothing (style, color, line, fabric); economic problems—managing money (budgeting allowances), determining a fair price for goods, determining the quality of goods, deciding where to buy; social relationships—working with others in service relationships (transacting business with clerks), reacting to group mores (group fads); health—selecting clothing suited to temperature conditions.

The charts suggest possible immediate situations, not the exact experi-

[3] See page 156.
[4] *Ibid.*

ences desirable for particular learners. Just how to work with Jane and her peers with reference to these persistent life situations is something no chart can indicate. Only the teacher and his group, developing the specific learning experiences, can determine which persistent life situations should be explored in greatest detail and how this can best be done. The teacher helps learners to deal with as many persistent life situations as are significant for them and in which they need to develop further competence.

Jane and her friends knew a great deal about the phases of budgeting needed to plan wisely for the clothing they wanted to buy. The increased responsibility they were now being given did not raise completely new budgeting problems since most of them had handled small allowances for several years. The amount of guidance they had received in deciding on the quality of the goods they bought had been much less than in budgeting. Here was the beginning of a series of new experiences including, among others, the testing of materials in the chemistry laboratory, discussions as to the nature of good workmanship in making one's own clothes, visits to the local factory to see how clothing is produced in quantity, and investigation of the meaning of various labels. At the same time, the group explored the question of color in clothing—in the art studio there was a display of French prints; in one of the stores visited, the shopping consultant talked about color as related to complexion, hair, and eyes. The boys became equally involved in matters of style as they paid a special visit to a men's clothing shop and talked with a tailor. Several of the girls in the group struggled with the problem of the wisdom of purchasing school costumes in very delicate colors. Most of the activities were carried out with Miss Dearborn as leader during the time scheduled for the core program, but other teachers were involved for short periods when laboratories were open for special help. Several group members, pursuing special interests in chemistry on an elective basis, carried the problem of testing materials into considerable detail.[5]

With another group of young people, not used to managing their own allowances, the matter of wise budgeting might have been primary and the question of color and style in clothing might not have been explored so intensively. In still another group with limited finances, the emphasis might have been upon the durability and suitability of clothing, the proper care of clothes, and techniques for dyeing, mending, and remaking clothing. Decisions as to emphasis, direction, and activities can be made only as the teacher identifies the particular needs of his group. The charts merely suggest possible situations faced by learners; they do not indicate the exact nature or extent of the experiences considered desirable for a particular individual or group.

[5] For a more detailed description of a tenth grade at work, see Chapter 13.

The charts suggest related experiences with which learners should be helped to deal. Jane and her group did not end their exploration of the meaning of labels with their discussion of clothing. Miss Dearborn, in examining the persistent life situation of DETERMINING QUALITY as outlined in the chart on page 305, had noted the following immediate situations often faced by youth: "choosing clothing in relation to suitability of material and style; selecting fresh vegetables or fruits; interpreting common brands and labels, interpreting advertising. . . ." These helped to sharpen her thinking about a related problem of the class—their concern with the refreshments for a party. Under Miss Dearborn's guidance, the group discussed the question of quality and consumer protection in the purchase of food. Here they faced an aspect of budgeting for which previous learnings had not provided since very few had ever helped to apportion and use group funds. Solving this problem added to competence in budgeting and also increased understanding of the issues involved in purchasing in quantity. In building toward competence and understanding through one experience, a basis for the solution of problems in related areas is being provided. Growth in ability to deal with one of the situations often results in increased competencies important in many others.

The charts suggest situations in home and community which also contribute to the immediate problem. Miss Dearborn's group did not develop their understanding of the quality of goods in the school alone. Home and community also contributed. Understandings about good workmanship, for example, had already been built by some mothers who sewed for their families and by others who had taken these young people shopping. The factory owner and the department store buyer contributed through talking with the class on their visits. In studying the charts, the teacher will note typical situations in home, school, and community. In working with learners, the teacher must capitalize on, and build in terms of, the contributions of other persons and agencies to pupil learnings.

THE CHARTS CAN BE USED AS A GUIDE TO BALANCED DEVELOPMENT

Because of the recurring nature of persistent situations, children and youth will undoubtedly have experiences calling for competence in dealing with a wide range of situations. However, it is quite possible for home, school, and community agencies all to fail to give the needed help. As indicated in previous chapters, the proposed curriculum design places great responsibility on the teacher for assuring that children and youth achieve maximum growth and balanced development.

The charts suggest the range of situations against which growth should be evaluated. The teacher will find his guide to balanced development in the scope of the persistent life situations found in the Master List on pages 155 to 165. This list should not be studied for the purpose of providing experience in each area every year or of planning a schedule where problem areas appear regularly, as courses might on the schedule of a curriculum organized by subjects. Rather, the list should serve as a guide to areas in which adequate competence seems to be lacking. It can serve this last purpose in at least two ways.

First, the list can be scanned by the teacher to sensitize himself to areas in which children and youth are displaying inadequate competence as they try to deal with persistent life situations. Mr. Marsden, whose own experiences have failed to develop a depth of sensitivity to artistic surroundings, may be reminded by the situations in the area of AESTHETIC EXPRESSION AND APPRECIATION that he has not capitalized upon opportunities to help his group develop more pleasant living and working arrangements in their classroom. Miss Jones, who has had little opportunity to work with tools and equipment, may recognize on checking the area on TECHNOLOGICAL RESOURCES that many youngsters have inadequate work skills. She may realize that many needed understandings about their technological world are suggested by the clippings the children are bringing for the bulletin board to which she is giving only cursory attention.

Second, the list of persistent life situations can suggest areas in which learners' experiences need to be enriched. This may be because neither the home, school, nor community is providing opportunities within a given area, or because of trends in the wider social or national scene which learners have the maturity to understand and of which they should be aware. The Master List can be used as a guide to studying both the richness or poverty of the learners' environments and social trends.

As teachers appraise the growth of learners in the light of the scope suggested by the Master List, sometimes they will decide to enrich the environment or provide special help for an individual or a small group rather than for the class as a whole. For example, if all the children find unusual satisfaction in creative expression except Jerry, what other opportunities might be offered to him? Most pupils in Miss Fox's group have shopped for their mothers for years and have unusually good judgment about money values, but Joanne has never had such experiences. The list of persistent problems can help a teacher take a thoughtful look at the needs of individuals as well as of groups.

The charts suggest daily life situations as starting points where learners need help. Identifying learners' lack of experience in a given area is only a first step in identifying meaningful situations which might serve as starting points. How might the charts help a teacher who realizes that her fourth-graders have never had much guided experience with CONSERVING AND USING NATURAL RESOURCES or CONSERVING MATERIALS, and who is seeking situations in their daily lives in which they are actually facing these problems? Miss Clark, working in a rural consolidated school, looks at the charts on pages 274 and 282 and notes the following illustrations: "discussing local plans for preventing soil erosion, plans for reforestation, irrigation in locality; finding why gardeners and farmers use fertilization; . . . helping store garden tools; understanding why iron fences, equipment are painted; caring for wet shoes, clothing. . . ." These items suggest conservation problems relating to natural resources and to personal property. They remind Miss Clark of current happenings in the community and at school and suggest the following as situations which can have meaning for the particular pupil group—the special project to prevent soil erosion being demonstrated by Farm Bureau agents at the farms of some of the parents (do the children need help in understanding what is taking place), the children's interest in their own gardens, the need for improved and more cheerful living conditions in many homes, and how such materials as feed sacks might be used to make curtains and table runners. Then, too, there are the immediate situations relating to conservation of materials used in schools, especially paper. One or more of these might appropriately become a part of the curriculum of children attending this rural school.

Miss Harrison's fourth-graders also have had little experience in dealing with the same persistent situations as the group above, but her pupils live in a small city. What do the same charts suggest to her as possible starting points for work in this area? She, too, recognizes the need for conservation as it relates to wasteful use of paper and careless handling of books and other school equipment. For Miss Harrison the charts also suggest some quite different pupil interests and concerns—interest in the impending water shortage and the urgings in the press and on the radio to conserve the water supply, the recent request of a school neighbor at the PTA meeting that her lawn not be used as a path to the interesting construction project near by, the problem of food wastage in the cafeteria, the observed carelessness of many of the children in leaving scooters and other toys on porches and in yards unprotected from the weather and rust. Any one of these immediate situations can have meaning for this fourth grade.

For both teachers the charts suggested everyday situations which might be the starting points of experiences with the persistent situations of conserving materials and resources. Further study of the groups might reveal high competence in certain of these daily situations, distinct lacks in others, and strong interests and concerns that have previously not found their way into the classroom. Final decisions as to how to work from the situations identified come from observations such as these. When the teacher adds personal knowledge of his learners to the typical situations described in the charts, the value of the analysis for planning experiences is increased.

THE CHARTS CAN BE USED AS AN AID IN ACHIEVING DESIRED DIRECTION OF GROWTH

Teachers who are free to work from the everyday experiences of learners assume much greater responsibility for the direction and continuity of growth than do those for whom school experiences are specified grade by grade. In the charts that give the sweep of daily life experiences from early childhood to adulthood, there can be found a number of aids in assuring desirable direction and continuity in growth.

The charts provide insights into desirable continuity of growth. Continuity involves identifying the level of competence a learner brings to a new situation and the growth in ability needed to meet it effectively. The teacher builds upon the present and toward providing a sound basis for dealing effectively with the more complex situations of the future. Grouping of typical experiences under four maturity levels shows the interrelationships among the problems now faced, the types of previous experience learners may have had, and ways in which the situation might be faced again as learners grow older. For example, the experiences in budgeting funds typical of "early childhood" include such activities as purchasing candy, saving for Christmas gifts, and helping to decide how to spend class funds for books. In "later childhood" there are the more complex experiences of taking responsibility for purchasing part of one's own wardrobe, helping to spend club funds, balancing class accounts in the school store, making decisions as to the use of an allowance. To these experiences "youth" adds problems such as handling the earnings from a part-time job, sharing in more complicated decisions as to the use of family funds, exploring the issues involved in taxes and in the spending of government funds. At the "adult" level, the problems of family income, the finances of organizations of which one is a member, the expenditures of local and national government are faced. In the sweep of typical situations from "early childhood" to "adulthood," illustrated in the charts, the teacher should find help in recognizing normal and continuous development. The way in which persistent life situations are faced by learners at different maturity levels gives a basis for judging continuity of development.

The charts provide the basis for deciding which concepts, information, and skills to stress. As the teacher guides learning he must decide which concepts are likely to be of most value, which skills need to be stressed, which subject matter should be drawn upon most heavily. Questions concerning emphasis and selection are answered in part by the nature of the problem or situation faced by the learners, but the teacher has a responsibility to widen horizons, deepen insights, and point to interrelationships of which learners are not aware.

The growing complexity of the situations with which a learner deals as he matures provides a guide to the desired direction of growth. While helping the learner with the problem he is facing at the time, the teacher who is aware of the expanding nature of persistent life situations can guide learning in such a way as to build bases for coping with related but more complex experiences. Growth in ability to deal with life situations depends on how clearly teachers and learners see the relationship between present problems and those which demand similar competencies. The youth who does not realize, for example, that some of the same principles which he applied when he experimented with various dyes also operate when he tries to remove stains, is not making full use of basic understandings he possesses about chemical properties.

When the teacher helps learners to see relationships, insights into new situations are often achieved with comparatively little additional study. In the sweep of the situations from "early childhood" to "adulthood" the teacher of any age level should be able to identify the concepts appropriate for the immediate situation that are likely also to be of major value in meeting a more complex problem. He can also find what types of concepts from past experiences he may be able to draw upon in helping learners deal with a present situation. The teacher thus reinforces the past, helps the learner make wider application of the past to the present, and builds as soundly toward the future as the learners' present maturity and insights allow.

In the detailed charts the listing of some of the same experiences in connection with several persistent situations may help the teacher to see other implications for extending growth. For example, the youth's job as an errand boy is listed as an experience through which he learns something about what comprises the world of work. It also appears as contributing to his ability to decide what work he shall do, to his understanding of the relation of income to occupation, to his ability to work effectively with others, and to his understanding of standards of work. When the teacher sees the need and possibilities for such related competencies, he faces experiences with heightened insight into the various ramifications which may be involved for the learners.

The direction of learners' growth should be toward democratic values and the facts and understandings necessary for reasoned decisions in terms of these values. While the analysis in the charts implies but does not state the desired values or the specific facts and activities, it does supply two sources of help. Specifically, those charts suggesting situations faced in the area of MORAL CHOICES and in establishing effective PERSON–TO–PERSON RELATIONSHIPS give some indication of the variety of value judgments which must be made. In addition, the concern for basic democratic values is found in all charts in the suggested experiences which stretch out to the problems of national and world responsibility. Built in terms of the situations faced by learners, the analysis is a guide to the direction of growth through implications for values, concepts, understandings, and skills.

THE CHARTS CAN BE USED AS A GUIDE TO SELECTION OF SUBJECT MATTER AND THE INTERRELATIONS AMONG SUBJECTS

Preceding chapters have stressed the fact that the proposed curriculum design does not deny learners as deep and as extensive contacts with subject matter and with subject fields as their maturity and the situations they face allow and require. Many of these contacts, however, will not come through the traditional subject organizations. The charts provide help in determining the nature of the contacts with the cultural heritage and the contributions that logically organized bodies of subject matter can make.

The charts suggest new bases for organizing the cultural heritage. Learners cannot deal with persistent life situations without knowledge. As they relate facts in terms of meaningful situations, concepts emerge. In the widening concepts needed as persistent situations expand from childhood to adulthood lies a major challenge for the reorganization of subject matter. What knowledge is needed, for example, as children and youth grow in their concepts of CONSERVING MATERIALS? What facts are needed as concepts of USING GOVERNMENT TO GUARANTEE WELFARE expand? What hierarchy of mathematical understandings is basic to the persistent situation of SAVING AND INVESTING as it stretches from the five-year-old's piggy bank to the adult's problems of deciding where to invest, whether to buy insurance or annuities, how much insurance to purchase? The charts can be used as an aid in developing new organizations of knowledge, functional in terms of the situations learners face and the concepts they need.

The charts suggest ways in which traditional subject areas contribute to learners' problems of everyday living. Even within the boundaries of a subject curriculum the charts can serve a useful purpose. The high school science teacher, for example, must make his subject matter vital, meaningful, and of real use to his students. This involves presenting the material so that it contributes to the learners' ability to deal with practical situations, and using, for illustrative purposes, situations which they can identify. The analysis provides help on both problems. While no area is labeled "physics" or "chemistry," the teacher of these subjects will find in the typical situations faced by learners in the areas of NATURAL PHENOMENA and TECHNOLOGICAL RESOURCES, as well as in those of HEALTH and ECONOMIC–SOCIAL–POLITICAL STRUCTURES AND FORCES, a number of situations to which the content of his special field can make a major contribution. Similarly, the teacher of history or the social studies can find real situations centered around the learners' endeavors to deal with the same areas of persistent life situations. The persistent situations suggest major areas of growing competence and understanding to which a particular subject may contribute, while the daily life experiences give concrete examples of typical concerns around which classroom experiences may be developed.

Since each subject has a potential contribution to make to many persistent life situations, the various subject areas must be seen in relationship. For example, many of the situations faced in USING TECHNOLOGICAL RESOURCES FOR MAXIMUM SOCIAL GOOD call for scientific knowledge, understanding of social problems, and mathematical ability sufficient to grasp the major implications of price levels, taxes, tariffs, and the like. As learners are helped to deal with such situations there are opportunities for cooperative teaching by representatives of several subjects. Teachers in high schools moving toward core programs have realized this, and are making a variety of provisions for cooperative teaching to build work around situations of genuine concern to learners and to draw upon various subjects and specialists as needed.

THE CHARTS CAN HELP TO IDENTIFY NEEDED INSTRUCTIONAL MATERIALS

A curriculum developed around the situations learners face requires that a wide range of instructional material be readily available. When the concerns of daily living are the source of school experiences it is not possible to select a set of textbooks for each grade and to count on these texts, together with some supplementary materials, meeting the learners' needs. At the present time the wealth of informational material needed to work on situations of everyday living with learners is not available. Simpler materials are needed for children in the lower grades and greater amounts of materials related to present problems are required in every grade. A wide range of other than printed materials—pictures, documentary films, radio transcriptions—is important.

Analyses such as the one in this chapter give persons concerned with preparing new materials a picture of the types of situations with which learners need help, and should prove useful in creating the source material needed for effective teaching. The charts have implications not only for the preparation of new materials, but for the choice of materials for school and classroom libraries. In addition, they raise questions about the amount and variety of the visual aids available, and suggest the use of community resources as well. Those who are aware of the range and kind of problems which learners may face can plan to use firsthand community resources.

THE CHARTS CAN BE USED AS A GUIDE TO CONTINUOUS CURRICULUM IMPROVEMENT

Ours is a changing world, and the everyday experiences in which persistent situations appear today are not the same as the experiences in which they will appear five or ten years from now. While the persistent life situations continue, the immediate situations of daily life vary over the years and from one school–community to another. No guide to curriculum development centered in the persistent problems of everyday living can be static. One of the contributions of analyses such as that presented in this chapter is the challenge to teachers to engage in the cooperative study of learners that will result in guides of their own. Curriculum improvement is a continuous process. Those most closely associated with learners should continually study them to add new insights into the ways in which they face persistent life situations.

Part III

DEVELOPING THE CURRICULUM WITH LEARNERS

7

SELECTING CURRICULUM EXPERIENCES

Not all the situations faced by children and youth can become part of their school curriculum. Even if this were possible, it would not be profitable. The teacher has a crucial part to play in identifying the needs and concerns of learners; in sensing how these concerns can contribute to growth in terms of the meanings they have, or can have, for learners; and in guiding decisions regarding the balance of activities appropriate for a school day, a month, a year.

How can the teacher accurately identify concerns of learners? What should guide his decisions as to which of the concerns identified should be part of the school curriculum and the weight each should be accorded? What should be the pattern of a day's or a week's activities at the elementary school level? In planning the pattern of activities what adjustments will teachers working with high school youth have to make? What first steps can be taken by teachers now working under other curriculum designs? This chapter focuses on these basic professional problems relating to the selection of curriculum experiences, and makes specific suggestions for taking this step in designing the educational program. The chapters which follow elaborate upon other problems of the teacher in developing the proposed curriculum with learners—guiding learning activities, meeting individual needs, scheduling, making the services of specialists available, and evaluating pupil growth.

Identifying the Concerns of Learners

In the selection of the experiences which are to be part of the curriculum, perhaps no area of the teacher's work is more significant than the identification and interpretation of the everyday concerns of learners. Since they are the starting points for curriculum experiences, the teacher's insight into these concerns and needs in essence determines the quality of the learning that will result.

While this section focuses on the kinds of insights needed by teachers who are free to develop experiences in terms of the problems learners face, sensitive understanding of pupils is no less important to the teacher working in a prestructured curriculum design. The science teacher will be more effective if he knows what interests in natural phenomena his pupils bring to class. An eleventh-grade history class's study of immigration trends can be more meaningful to the pupils if their interests in their own ancestors are capitalized upon. Insightful understanding of learners is the foundation of all good teaching and learning. Through what avenues can learners' interests and concerns be identified?

THE INTERESTS LEARNERS BRING TO SCHOOL GIVE CLUES TO CONCERNS

Much can be learned about the meaning situations have for children and youth through study of the interests they express. The teacher who takes time to talk with learners on the playground or to chat informally in the classroom, for example, can find out a great deal about their interests and the kinds of experiences for which they are ready. Comments about television programs, motion pictures, and comic books may suggest school cooperation in improving or extending the range of recreational activities. Questions about the natural and technological environments or about projects—such as gardens, pets, construction of a soap-box derby entry, repair of a "hot rod"—suggest needs to explore the world of science. Discussions about clothes for certain occasions, or about dates and relationships with the opposite sex, may point to the need for guidance in these areas and to the group's readiness for such help. Arguments about local and national events may highlight the kind of problems which have meaning for different ages and may reveal misinformation and inadequate reasoning which require attention.

The objects brought to school offer another source of information about concerns. Cocoons, insects, bunches of berries, unusual leaves, stones, and many other items indicate curiosity about the natural environment. Other leads may come from mechanical toys, half-finished constructions, various types of handwork, or parts of collections. Books being read outside of school, newspaper pictures and clippings which the learner thinks important to show to the group, indicate the trend of interests.

On the playground it is possible to gain further insight by noting the games learners play, what they stop to watch, how they work out problems of interpersonal relationships. In high schools, the teachers can learn much from the clubs learners join, the nonclass activities in which they engage, the responsibilities for which they volunteer.

In short, an important step in knowing learners' concerns is to be aware of what they reveal about themselves by the voluntary choices they make and the experiences they seek. All such interests, of course, will not become part of classroom experiences. Many represent needs which are being met quite adequately through other channels, but those which are finding no other fruitful outlet may provide sources for school activities.

COMMUNITY RELATIONSHIPS SUGGEST NEEDS AND INTERESTS

Understanding learners also means coming to know the social settings in which they live. On entering school the child has already had many learning experiences and is a product of all the forces that have affected him up to that time. The teacher must understand the nature and strength of the impact of these forces in the learner's home, in his immediate neighborhood, and in the larger community surrounding him.

An important function of those who work in the school is to interpret the learner to his home and his community. Equally important, the school must provide opportunities for parents, youth leaders, policemen, storekeepers, and others to share their knowledge and understanding of learners. Much can be learned about children and youth through contacts with those in the community who meet them in out-of-school situations. Such persons can often point to important problems involving the learner. A family may be expanding its living quarters and giving the child or youth an opportunity to share in the plans. If financial problems are causing another family to restrict activities, all its members may be seeking ideas on how to stretch limited resources. In several homes high school girls may have responsibility for younger children and may be meeting many situations involving child care. A scout group may be mending old toys for hospitalized children. A church youth group may be taking major responsibility for the recreation program which involves sharing the parish house with other community groups. Mothers of nine- and ten-year-olds at a meeting may express concern about their children's carelessness with clothing. The quality of the Saturday afternoon motion pictures may suggest another problem area.

The teacher who wishes to gauge out-of-school influences on learners must have firsthand contacts with the home and the community. Discussing learners with adults visiting the school is not enough. Teachers must visit homes to sense family activities and relationships in each individual's home surroundings. In addition, the teacher should have some direct contact with the clubs and groups to which learners belong, with the neighborhoods in which they play, with the stores in which they shop or work. There is no adequate substitute for these activities which deepen insights into learners' needs.

Another obligation in identifying needs and concerns in the community setting involves the teacher being alert to social trends, even prior to the recognition of them by learners and some adults in the community. Such trends, which have been analyzed in detail in Chapter 2, touch on the lives of children and youth not only through daily papers and magazines but through changing local circumstances. This emphasis upon social awareness does not imply indoctrination. It does suggest, however, that children and youth should be helped to understand social movements and issues and that an important aspect of the teacher's study of the community setting is the identification of the impact of social trends.

Learners' interests and concerns centering in home and community—whether that community be the immediate neighborhood with which the learner has direct contact or the wider world whose trends influence his life in many ways—should be known by school personnel. As with learners' expressed interests, not all concerns will necessarily become part of the school curriculum. In some cases school activities may be planned to supplement the home or community program; in others they may be restricted in the light of experiences already being provided. In some cases the school may provide experiences which are not typically within its responsibility, in an effort to counteract negative home or community influences.

ONGOING ACTIVITIES IN THE CLASSROOM GIVE INDICATIONS OF CONCERNS

As classroom experiences develop, new competencies needed in dealing with life situations become apparent, and new problems arise. All teachers appraise these needs as bases for further school experiences. In such an area as developing language skills, for example, many new needs and problems can be identified merely by studying pupils' present modes of communication—their accuracy, clarity, coherence, and effectiveness. Further, in the course of locating the information needed to deal with one situation, learners may develop many new interests. Consider, for example, the areas that could be explored if the teacher were to follow up all the needs and interests apparent in one morning in this second-grade classroom.

Grouped about a large metal tank of water, several children are trying out newly fashioned, bright-colored boats. "Look! Mine floats!" exclaims Terry. Mary's sailboat stays afloat, but lists heavily. Tom watches anxiously as his ocean liner sinks to the bottom of the tank. "Why does Tom's boat sink?" "What makes a boat float?" Here is a growing awareness of one aspect of the natural environment. Although these children cannot be expected to grasp the physical principles involved, they can be given other experiences with buoyancy which will lay the foundation for more technical study later.

Nearby, a group of children are busily engaged in constructing an aircraft carrier from large blocks. Tony, obviously the leader of the enterprise, is deeply concerned with the problem of finding a way to lower the airplanes on to the deck. "Do you remember," says Bert, "when we built the elevator of our apartment house last month we used pulleys? Do you suppose that would work?" This is not the first time this group has brought tools and machines to their aid. The idea is eagerly seized upon, but many problems remain to be solved. The pulleys must be properly attached and the planes kept aloft. Here is an opportunity to develop further controls over common equipment.

Someone suggests lights and a bell for the carrier. Soon a group of children are transforming wire, dry cells, and other essential materials into workable shape. Frank, who thus far has assumed little leadership in the project, is called upon for help. Experiences in other projects have shown that he is good at this kind of thing. Further contacts with scientific and technological resources can come from this situation. In addition, the children are learning when to delegate and when to take leadership responsibilities and how to make use of the "expert."

Across the room, Nancy hovers before the box containing a family of white mice. She fondles one of the babies. Nancy lives in a city apartment. Her persistent craving for "a puppy all my own" has never been realized. This family of mice is serving to satisfy this longing to some degree. As the teacher passes by Nancy exclaims, "I never held anything so little and soft." John pauses for a moment to observe the scurrying feet and nibbling jaws, but his immediate concern is the building of a cage to house these pets and he has struck a snag. He is not quite sure how a mouse's home should be built. What to do about it? Then he remembers that Mr. Hill, the school custodian, usually can help a fellow with such things. John goes to enlist his aid. Emotional needs to establish affectionate relationships with others—pets as well as human beings—should find their place in the classroom. For Nancy the school is helping to meet a need which the home does not completely satisfy. Investigation of the satisfactions she is finding in her friendships might be a logical next step in meeting this concern. John and those who work with him are learning new ways in which people can serve as resources. These children are gaining certain concepts of the use and value of specialization and of the dignity of labor.

Several children are putting the finishing touches to the mural which they are painting. Ellen pauses, arrested by the color effect which has resulted when the blue paint she was using dripped accidentally on a bright, freshly painted red flower. Taking a sheet of paper she experiments with other color combinations, the mural momentarily forgotten. This is a new experience for her and very satisfying. Here, not only for Ellen but for others in the group, is an opportunity to expand both aesthetic appreciation and ability to use forms of aesthetic expression.

Jim is working alone, completely absorbed in trying out the recently acquired skill of writing. From a new pencil box he extracts one shiny pencil after another. The muscles of his mouth tighten as he practices with eager intensity. Through the day the children will be given help in learning to write, to read, to manage numbers, and to develop, as well as each one can, the skills necessary to meet the situations they face.

Every teacher has similar opportunities to study the ongoing activities of his group for clues to next steps. The classroom setting described above represents a rather informal primary work period with many opportunities for individuals and small groups to pursue special concerns. However, the questions raised by twelfth-grade history students whose teacher encourages them to think would offer as many helpful leads to further activities. Of course, other criteria than interest alone must be applied in deciding which of the many possibilities should receive more detailed attention, for how long, and by which learners. This is equally true both for the teacher working within the boundaries of a given subject and for the one who has major responsibility for deciding what the curriculum experiences for the year will be.

CONCERNS ARE REVEALED AS LEARNERS SHARE IN PLANNING

Out of learners' questions, their discussion of what they already know, their suggestions as to what they would like to know or to do and how to go about it, the alert teacher draws his conclusions relative to the areas in which experience is lacking, the skills needed, the understandings still to be developed, the related problems which might be explored, and the adjustments which should be made to meet individual needs.

The teacher who makes maximum use of cooperative planning to assist in identifying learners' concerns still retains leadership responsibilities. Learners' suggestions are not always followed exactly as given, nor are the purposes, problems, and needs which they express always accepted as setting the limits for exploration and study. The teacher, as guide, evaluates the problems faced and through questions and suggestions helps the group to see wider and deeper implications and possibilities. However, giving learners a share in planning is essential if the teacher is to know what situations mean to them and have any assurance that his guidance is effective.

NEW NEEDS AND INTERESTS DEVELOP FROM OPPORTUNITIES TO EXPLORE

The teacher has a responsibility to enrich learners' environments as well as to capitalize on the worlds they know already. Where a variety of classroom experiences is available, needs, interests, and concerns which might not otherwise appear can be identified. The child from a limited cultural environment probably will not evidence any particular need for musical or artistic experiences if he has had no taste of what they can mean for him. His potentialities in these areas can be identified only as he has opportunity, time, and material to explore a variety of experiences. The pupil from a crowded apartment in an underprivileged area may have little opportunity to discover the wonders of his natural environment or the satisfactions of leisure reading unless the school makes such experiences available to him. Where homes have provided little experience with attractive living quarters, the teacher may be the one to suggest bringing beauty into the classroom. Children who are not accustomed to reacting to community situations may need to have local papers where they can examine them.

Opportunities to explore should extend to every part of the school. Children and youth who stay within the walls of their own classrooms, however rich these may be, are not sharing fully in the educational opportunities the school has to offer. The playground, the library, the halls, the lunchroom, the principal's office, the health office, are all fruitful sources of information about learners' real needs and interests. Cooperative relationships are needed in the halls, on the playground, and elsewhere, when space must be shared with others. The assembly hall, the lunchroom, and the library are situations in which older and younger children must work together. Health concerns can often be identified more quickly in the lunchroom or in the nurse's office than in the classroom. The teacher who observes learners' relationships with the custodian or the secretary learns something of their respect for the dignity of labor and their awareness of the function of specialized workers. Much can be learned about ability to use safety regulations by watching children and youth on the playground, in the halls, or crossing streets to and from school. "Free" and unassigned time, at both the elementary and secondary levels, provides an opportunity for observing how students use leisure time and what their needs are in this area. What they do during such periods may also point to special interests and concerns.

Concerns which are the source of extended activities within the classroom often come from situations arising in other parts of the school. How many vital situations will arise depends on the freedom which children are allowed elsewhere in the school. The lunchroom can provide opportunities for identifying social needs, health problems, and aesthetic interests, or it can be so rigidly controlled that learners' real concerns do not appear on the surface. The playground can be a place where interests and abilities are evidenced, or one in which strict supervision drives natural tendencies underground. Freedom under supervision is needed in the whole school if the situations which have meaning for learners are to be identified.

AVAILABLE BACKGROUND DATA THROW LIGHT ON NEEDS AND CONCERNS

To anticipate needs and interests and to identify and interpret immediate concerns, the teacher must see learners in perspective—know what they are like, what their previous experiences have been, how they have met their problems, and what their backgrounds have had to offer. The child with a history of illness may need special adjustments in his program; the quiet youth who has shared in many family responsibilities is able to make a contribution to the problems of group living faced by the class; the child who in past years has spent much time on situations relating to control over natural resources may need to have his attention turned to questions related to social and economic structures and forces. Previous experiences are the bases on which teacher and learners plan next steps.

The teacher not only identifies the needs and concerns of learners through observing them in many settings; he also uses data from cumulative records and case studies, objective and informal classroom tests, and projective techniques. Under the impetus of the guidance movement, there has been a significant accumulation of methods by which teachers can study individual learners.

Cumulative records contributed to by all persons concerned with the learner's growth and development, including the learner himself, are a valuable resource. To be of greatest assistance to the teacher, records should contain a comprehensive picture of the learner's previous experiences—his share in group activities, individual interests and enterprises, significant home and community backgrounds and experiences. Statements should also be included indicating the learner's growth in sensitivity to the demands of situations, in ability to use effective methods of work, in the use of fundamental skills and basic understandings in new situations. As the year progresses new data should be added. An effective record not only provides information about past experiences but is a working tool for interpreting present activities and guiding future experiences.[1]

The teacher also should use available data regarding the individual's potentialities and achievement level, but should observe cautions warranted by normal limitations of tests. Undue faith should not be put in test scores simply because they are derived from commercially produced instruments. The intelligence quotient for a child with limited reading skill which is derived from a test where speed and comprehension count heavily, or a record secured on a day when a pupil was emotionally upset, should be re-examined. Standardized achievement test scores must be interpreted in terms of the objectives for the class. The lack of skill in using fractions, which lowers a class average on an arithmetic test, may be of little concern at the time because of the way in which children's number experiences are developing toward desired goals. When precautions are taken, standardized tests can provide general estimates of pupil achievement and diagnostic leads for further planning of experiences.

The teacher can also use various informal classroom procedures to examine pupil strengths and limitations. These may include classroom tests, observations of group use of specific skills, work-type activities which pupils and teacher analyze together, handwriting scales by means of which pupils evaluate their own progress, class diaries, lists of individual service on committees, reports of reading, and so on.

Other devices and techniques provide useful supplements to teachers' day-by-day observations of children and youth when information is needed regarding self-concepts and group relationships. Many of these

[1] See Chapter 11 for more specific and detailed suggestions on cumulative pupil records.

are of a projective nature—open-ended sentences, wishes, unfinished stories, creative writing on topics of personal concern, sociograms, and social distance scales. There are also some commercially prepared materials in the form of problem check lists, personality tests, "guess who" tests. The teacher, in seeking to know the concerns of an individual, tries to know the forces in his group which play upon him—the challenges he must meet, the acclaim he is getting, the prowess he is trying to defend, the sources of friendship he has found.

While each learner must be guided in terms of his own pattern of development, his growth can be better understood against the norms for other learners. The teacher who knows normal growth trends, not only for the age level with which he is dealing but also for younger and older children, brings to a particular group a depth of understanding which provides better insight into their development and concerns.

THE ANALYSIS OF TYPICAL SITUATIONS WHICH LEARNERS OF DIFFERENT MATURITIES ARE LIKELY TO FACE POINTS TO NEEDS AND CONCERNS

Help in understanding the needs of a particular learner or group can be found in statements of typical situations which learners are likely to face. Through study of the charts in the preceding chapter the teacher can identify situations with which learners are dealing but without help, locate areas in which competence and information are lacking and the kinds of experiences through which these might be gained, note related experiences with which learners should deal, and direct attention to experiences in which home, school, and community can supplement each other.

Determining the Place of an Experience in the Curriculum

In the sense that a pupil rarely, if ever, should be denied at least an answer to a question, all concerns actually expressed by a learner, and some that are equally significant but unexpressed, should find some place in his curriculum. This is true whether the concern is lasting or transitory, whether it is within the maturity level at which the learner can achieve definite growth or beyond his present stage of development. Purely from the mental hygiene standpoint, a learner struggling with something beyond his present controls, or engrossed in an interest of immediate and great concern, must have some recognition given to his problem in order to free him to deal with others.

However, the experiences in the proposed curriculum design must be much more than the meeting of emergencies and the immediate satisfaction of inquiries and interests. One problem that teachers face, regardless of curriculum design, is that of determining the place a particular experience should have in the curriculum. Even when a year's work in social studies, science, or mathematics is outlined for a given grade in considerable detail, there is usually still room for choice. How much time should be devoted to an area in which learners seem to have little background? What about a topic, usually treated lightly, but a source of much concern to this group? How much of the time allotted to this subject should be used to develop needed spelling, language, or study skills? Such questions must be answered by every teacher but they become crucial when there is no preplanned curriculum pattern to serve as a guide.

The discussion in Chapters 5 and 6 indicated criteria that help in deciding which situations should be the focus of school experiences and how to explore them. These guides or criteria are discussed in more detail in this section. Teachers working under other curriculum patterns will find that they offer help to them, too, in deciding when and where to plan for flexibility.

WHAT MEANING DOES THIS EXPERIENCE HAVE FOR THE LEARNER?

In deciding what recognition should be given to a specific concern, the teacher must consider the meaning the experience actually has or can have for the learner. At least three questions need to be answered. First, what maturity and insight does the learner bring to the situation that suggest that he will profit from a more extended study of his problem? There will be times when very vital concerns will be met adequately by a few general suggestions. In terms of his maturity and the meaning the situation has for him, the young child questioning the need for drinking milk is not ready to discuss food content and values in terms of carbohydrates, proteins, fats, and vitamins. A pupil with very limited intellectual ability may never be ready for more than a minimum of technical information. Although his mental maturity permits him to bring practically adult consideration to any situation, the adolescent should not be expected to reach solutions to problems for which society itself cannot find satisfactory answers. Study of the role of government in industry by an eleventh grade, for example, can supply a comprehensive factual background and an opportunity to examine issues, but it should not be expected to eventuate in conclusions regarding existing problems. In making preliminary decisions about the time that might be given to a problem and the way it can be explored, the teacher considers what learnings it can yield in terms of the maturities, backgrounds, and present insights of his group.

A second question which should be asked in considering the meaning which a situation has for learners is, how helpful will logical explanations and additional information be? For example, formal study will provide little help for the child who has lost a pet, who is lonesome for his father away on a business trip, who needs to share his excitement about a new bicycle for his birthday. Similarly, a unit on cloud formation will not reduce the frustrations of a class which has had to postpone a greatly anticipated trip because of rain. What is needed in these cases is security, understanding, reassurance, and suggestions as to how best to meet or live with the immediate situation—not further rational explanations.

The third question is, to what extent is the concern transitory or of more lasting interest? Anything which is different will cause elementary or high school students to cluster around asking questions. This does not mean that each such show of interest should be seized upon to involve learners in extensive activities. Many times the initial satisfaction of curiosity is sufficient. There will be times, however, when the searching questions and comments in response to a new interest indicate that further activity could make a contribution to learning. "Where did it come from and how did it grow like that?" "That's what we were reading last week!" "But it doesn't fit with what we tried in science lab." "That's one that belongs in our current events discussion." Questions and comments such as these, drawing upon and expanding present interests, give reassurance that the expressed concern represents an area worth further time. This is particularly likely to be true if interests persist. The obviously transitory interest, on the other hand, may be dealt with quickly by listening to what is said, and giving the requested help or answer.

These same three questions—what meaning does it have for learners, what kind of help is really needed, and how transitory is the interest—must be answered for the individuals within a class as well as for the class group. In a class of forty eleventh-graders trying to follow election issues intelligently, some will have the reading skills needed to do insightful analyses of newspaper reports; others with equal reading ability may have strong emotional needs to support their parents' positions, some may have limited reading skill and uncritical listening ability. Interests in the election could also vary greatly. Some in the group might be concerned with next steps in a local housing plan, several of the boys might be following statements regarding military training with great care. For some, academic interest could be secondary to a desire to sound informed in order to acquire status in the group. Whether these differences call for individual rather than group study suggests another criterion to be considered in the selection of experiences.[2] When group study seems appropriate, it is a part of both the art and the excitement of teaching to provide for these differences in meaning which a common experience may hold for the class members, to widen these meanings, and to foster new purposes.

WHAT CAN THE CONCERN CONTRIBUTE TO GROWTH IN DEALING WITH PERSISTENT LIFE SITUATIONS?

A second criterion in selecting learning experiences involves a judgment about the contribution which the concern can make to growth in ability to deal with persistent life situations. Problems are chosen or rejected, enlarged upon or treated briefly, used as the basis for extended study or dealt with in terms of immediate practical solutions, according to the teacher's judgment of their potential contribution to one or more persistent life situations. The teacher is always concerned with meeting present needs in the way that will make for the most effective growth in ability to meet new situations.

In determining the potential value of an immediate situation to understanding persistent life situations, it is important to realize that many valuable contributions to learners' growth are made through repeated short contacts with the same problem. Day-by-day experiences of sharing, none of them calling for very extended discussion, can result in important growth in little children's skills in cooperative living. For the adolescent, advanced reference skills and library techniques may be built through repeated needs to use the library, each of which alone makes only a small contribution to skill building. For a group of slow-learning nine-year-olds repeated experiences in caring for clothing—a coat dropped on the floor is hung on a hook, a tear is stitched before further play can do more harm, an apron or an old shirt is worn to protect clothing from paint—can contribute far more lasting understandings and habits than a four-week unit on clothing conservation. Experiences are given a place in the curriculum that will capitalize on the growth they can provide.

Situations requiring extended study should be part of the curriculum

[2] See also p. 349.

as well as those that contribute to slow but regular growth. In appraising the potential learnings in situations that seem to be good centers for more comprehensive study the teacher should estimate the degree to which they seem likely to extend the learners' ability to deal with one or more persistent problems of living. Contrast two interests of a sixth grade, one the scientific aspects of a space satellite, and the other learning more about an interstate trucking fleet recently routed through their town. While both concerns might be given some consideration, which offers more opportunity to deal with problems at the maturity level of the group? The extent to which the learners can grow with reference to the one or more persistent life situations and the degree to which the area of growth is significant for them at the time are equally important in selecting from possible experiences.

Experiences which contribute only to the immediate and in which little growth is needed to meet the situation successfully may have a place in the curriculum if they are a compelling interest, but the place accorded them must be in terms of the growth they provide. A class which has had many experiences in entertaining parents does not stop doing so simply because a fairly high degree of competence is attained. However, the third or fourth time this situation occurs all hands turn to the practical problem of doing it as effectively as possible, and the hours of planning which were appropriate the first time are no longer necessary. Teacher and learners are governed in their activities by the nature of the problem. Maintenance of present skills through repeated practice is an important aspect of growth, but intensive study of the problem is called for only when some new demand, hitherto not met by the learners, arises.

DOES THE INTEREST OR CONCERN CONTRIBUTE TO BALANCED GROWTH?

The need for educational experiences which provide for growth in dealing with all persistent problems has been mentioned in earlier discussions. The contribution of an experience to balanced development is a third criterion to be considered in selecting and developing curriculum experiences. For example, an eighth grade in a rural consolidated school may be equally eager to learn about new efforts for preventing soil erosion which are being tried out in their community and new developments in radio being used by the local station. If this group has already had extended exploration of the latter and, except for some time in the fourth grade studying regulations about destroying birds' nests and picking wild flowers, few experiences in conservation of resources, soil erosion may be judged the more important. Plans then could be made for this problem to be studied as intensively as the maturity of the group warrants. The recent events in the radio station would not be entirely neglected. Building on previous backgrounds, groups or individuals for whom radio is a special interest might explore developments and make periodic reports to the class. The choice between the two areas is based upon the competence already acquired. Understanding of both radio and soil erosion would be extended for this class, but the need for balanced growth places the emphasis on the situation which is most likely to extend competence to all major areas.

Balanced growth does not mean equal growth in all areas every year —individual differences in interests and abilities make this impossible as well as undesirable. Nor does provision for balanced growth necessarily mean including in the curriculum of a given year separate study of one or more problems in each of the major areas of persistent life situations. It is not essential, for example, to select one problem which includes study of ways in which people secure goods and services, a second on how people work together, and a third on individual health needs. A single situation—perhaps a study of existing health and safety provisions in a local factory or the problem of purchasing food for a class party—can contribute to all three aspects of growth.

IS THE CONCERN A MATTER FOR INDIVIDUAL OR FOR GROUP STUDY?

If individual needs are to be met the teacher must not, in selecting experiences, always seek situations in which all learners are equally concerned and on which they will work as a class. In determining the potential values of an experience, the teacher asks "for whom?" If it seems important for the class as a whole, it is explored as a total-group problem. But time is also scheduled for smaller groups or individuals to work on independent plans. Normally, among the ongoing activities of the class, there will be one or more centered around total-group interests, several which are the concerns of smaller groups, and some which reflect individual talents, needs, or interests.

Within the class there may be individuals with special interests who are not receiving sufficient encouragement in the home or community. The gifted need provision for work on interests and concerns growing from their special talents, as well as opportunities to pursue in greater depth some of the concerns of everyday living which these children and youth have in common with others. For those who are ready—both the gifted and those without special talents—provision should be made for intensive work in areas of particular interest. Individuals need opportunity to pursue special interests and to carry their study to depths that are appropriate to their purposes and maturity.

Even within total-class concerns which all share, the teacher should examine the potential contribution of various aspects of the problem to individual growth. Rarely, if ever, will a class of thirty-five or forty have exactly the same interests in an experience or exactly the same growth needs. Adjustments can be made for differences in concern, ability, and interest by making it possible for individuals to work on special phases of the situation. The child with a reading disability may be unable to use many resources other than pictorial materials; his contribution, for the present, may be in finding needed illustrative material. The child with limited intellectual ability in a class studying problems dealing with technological advance may explain the more simple machines. The high school youth especially interested in biography may participate in a unit on disease control through a careful study of men and women significantly involved in that advance. For some, the major contribution of the experience may lie in increased ability to work cooperatively and effectively with others. Separate experiences should not necessarily be selected in order to meet adequately the different needs of group members. Further, one of the basic persistent life situations in a democracy is that of working effectively as a group member. Some values can best be realized through common experiences.

IS THE CONCERN BEST DEALT WITH DIRECTLY OR INDIRECTLY?

The variety of persistent life situations and the number of immediate situations which make up everyday living may seem overwhelming until the teacher realizes the extent of interrelationship and how a few minutes' help with one problem may contribute to the learner's growth in that area and, at the same time, to growth in several others.

Some concerns can be effectively handled quite casually or indirectly. This may be through a passing comment such as when the teacher, remembering Sally's comment, "I wish Judy liked me more," suggests to Judy that Sally might be glad to help with the map that Judy feels she cannot finish on time. It may be through a change in the environment or materials made accessible—finger-painting materials provided as individuals show a need for increased freedom of movement and expression. It may be achieved through providing opportunity to re-experience a situation as was the case when Jane asked to serve again as chairman of the planning committee for a party.

Then, too, as indicated earlier, some growth comes most effectively by a gradual extension of a concept through frequent use in new situations. A long period of time would not be devoted to a unit on how to plan one's method of work since this is a daily concern and children and youth learn bit by bit as they solve new problems. It is possible, however, that a twelfth grade, interested in the preparation which precedes United Nations meetings, might take several weeks to consider what planning means in national and international settings. In this, all learnings from previous practical experience in their activities would be of value. Curriculum experiences should help learners gain maximum educative values from their day-to-day problems of living together and also provide for more extensive studies as situations demand them.

WHAT HELP CAN THE LEARNER RECEIVE THROUGH HOME OR COMMUNITY EXPERIENCES?

The close relationship between home, school, and community in guiding learners' experiences has already been stressed. Helping children and youth meet persistent problems of living does not mean that the school must duplicate life in the home and the community. Concerns and interests with which children and youth are already being given positive help in home, church, or other community agencies are not usually as important for the school program as those that do not receive such attention.

Many concerns require the cooperative efforts of two or more educational agencies—and one of these may be the school. For some learners correcting physical defects may be the joint responsibility of the school, the home, and community medical units. For some children, needed and consistent growth in caring for personal property—books, toys, and clothing, for example—requires supporting guidance from teachers and parents. The teacher is often the one to coordinate the efforts of different educational agencies in helping children and youth meet and deal with these situations of everyday life.

Traditionally, the school's role has been defined in terms of developing fundamental skills and assuring that learners have adequate contacts with the vast cultural heritage. Even in these areas, the interlocking relationships with home and community must be carefully considered. In a particular class, children who have home libraries and ample time to read will not need the same stimulation in school as those lacking these facilities and with no encouragement at home to reach the same high level of reading skills. This same condition would apply in a class where some children come from homes in which standard English is spoken and others have colloquial speech backgrounds. The teacher must become acquainted with home and community backgrounds in order to know what responsibility the school should take.

Providing Effective Experiences for Children in the Elementary School[3]

What will the activities in a school day or a school week look like in a design where the teacher is developing the curriculum with learners? The preceding discussion implied that effective learning can come in many ways. First, the mere process of living together in a class group with such attendant responsibilities as housekeeping, washing before lunch, deciding what to wear outdoors, drying out clothing on a rainy day, reacting to student council proposals, makes an important contribution to growth in ability to deal with persistent life situations. Second, brief discussions—before school, during sharing periods, during a weekly pooling of current events interests—have value in situations where concerns are transitory, where learners already have a strong background, or where their maturity does not permit extended study. Third, certain situations merit extended study by the entire class. Fourth, individualized and small-group activities are important to provide for differences in levels of ability, in experience backgrounds, and in talents and interests.

The resulting pattern is one of teacher and children living and planning together, growing through the day-to-day situations which are a part of living together, and through more extensive activities involving the whole class or parts of it. What would be the characteristics of the pattern of group living and working that should result in a self-contained elementary school classroom?

SEVERAL ACTIVITIES MOVE FORWARD AT THE SAME TIME

Just as the normal day in any person's life is made up of a variety of activities, so several areas of study are likely to be carried forward in the course of a school day. For example, a group may be carrying out its responsibilities for the school's lost-and-found department concurrently with studying the essentials of a good lunch, following the presidential election campaigns, and planning a book fair to share an extensive recreational reading experience with parents. During the same day,

[3] This section is a brief overview of the design that might result as teachers and learners in elementary schools select curriculum experiences. Readers are referred to Chapters 12 and 14 for descriptions of the year's work of a fifth and a first grade.

individuals may be dealing with such recurring problems of living together as taking turns writing to a classmate who is ill, completing articles for the school paper, caring for various housekeeping responsibilities in the room, collecting lunch money. Small groups may also be spending time practicing decimal fractions they need to calculate the nutritional qualities of various foods, working on advanced word-analysis techniques to master an increasingly technical reading and spelling vocabulary, or reviewing punctuation rules as they write original stories. In addition, a period set apart for special interests might find a group receiving help from the teacher in writing the music they have composed for a song, several others experimenting with art media, one or two writing contributions for the school paper, and a group of boys setting up a science exhibit.

SCHEDULING OF ACTIVITIES IS FLEXIBLE IN TERMS OF WHAT NEEDS TO BE DONE

The time devoted to the activities just described would vary with the stage of development of the class plans. The more extensive units seldom reach the same important stage on the same day. When the lost-and-found department is first undertaken, for example, a full hour of planning might precede another half hour spent in taking the proposed preliminary steps. At this time the children may do some of the recreational reading leading to the book fair at home, and reports on new election developments could be made during a regular sharing period. Later on, getting the book fair under way may take a good part of the morning while the lost-and-found department runs smoothly enough to take up very little time.

A period of an hour or more for independent individual or group work is often regularly scheduled to allow time for the teacher to work with individuals or groups needing special help with the so-called fundamental skills. This period, and perhaps two periods some days, would also allow time for individuals and groups to proceed with short-term responsibilities—to get the letter written to Susan, to proofread the story for the school paper, to change the water in the aquarium, to pursue a special interest or talent.

The day just described is, after all, not much more complex than a day in which the learner, following a fixed schedule, starts with a half-hour health class, goes on to a forty-minute period in social studies, has a fifteen-minute recess break; returns to write answers to questions outlined for his reading group; finishes the morning with arithmetic flash-card drills; spends the first period after lunch writing an assigned composition; works on a special project with his art teacher; and ends the day in a free work period, helping with housekeeping chores and writing to a classmate who is ill. The major difference is that in the latter schedule the periods do not usually vary as much from day to day, and more aspects and activities are likely to be planned by the teacher alone, rather than by teacher and pupils together.

PROBLEMS EXTEND FOR DIFFERING LENGTHS OF TIME

Choice of experiences in this elementary school classroom would not be made with a view to providing extended study of every situation selected. Nor would exploration of all experiences terminate after a specific period of time. Some problems—such as publishing the school paper—might extend throughout the entire school year with many persistent life situations considered during the project. Some will involve decisions taking only a few minutes; some will call for study lasting several days or longer. Needs for new skills will arise from time to time and these will be met in extended practice sessions.

Sometimes one problem will lead into another, and the result will be a series of short units. A group interested in local government may return to this topic at various times during the school year as situations of concern arise. This interest might lead to several weeks' exploration of the problems of community sanitation at one time, discussion of the proposed new traffic regulations at another, and study of the use of local taxes at still another. Occasionally at the elementary school level, and more frequently with high school youth, a problem may require a semester's intensive study in a given content field. The length of time given to each problem, as well as the number of problems studied at one time, will be determined by the demands of the situations themselves in terms of the meanings they can have for learners.

PUPIL–TEACHER PLANNING PROVIDES A NEEDED SENSE OF UNITY

When planning has been effective, teachers and learners work easily under the more flexible yet more complicated pattern of work. It is the plan of study which gives the experience unity and helps each individual see his part. It is also the cooperatively developed plan which gives the day unity, and allows learners and teacher to move from one experience to another without confusion.

At any grade level, when the number of significant concerns exceeds the number the group can handle satisfactorily at one time, a new problem is introduced—and this is persistent throughout life—the necessity for choosing which demands will be given a preferred place and for deciding when and how to deal with the others. Those not selected for immediate study may be deferred to a later time, referred to an individual or a small group, or developed just far enough to meet the immediate aspect of the concern.

A flexible but well-planned pattern of experiences at the elementary school level allows for using specialists when needed. The entire class might seek help on an area of common concern, or a group might ask for special assistance during a laboratory period, or an individual might schedule time for rather extensive exploration. The proposed curriculum design makes many special demands on the time schedules of specialists, on systems of grouping learners, on the availability of materials. The entire school must be responsive to the practical implications of the concepts developed in the two preceding chapters in terms of the demands placed on personnel and resources.

Providing Effective Experiences for High School Youth[4]

The interweaving of individual, small-group, and all-class activities, with their varied demands, challenges the teacher of the self-contained elementary school classroom. But what of high school youth? Here the learner's greater maturity means increased ability to profit from extended study and additional need for the help of specialists. Here, too, there must be more specialization—some youth heading toward college, others terminating formal education with the high school, and all needing opportunities to explore and to extend their special interests and abilities.

Adolescents, as well as younger learners, must increase their ability to cope with more complex aspects of persistent life situations. They require opportunities to delve deeply into specific areas and to become more effective in bringing the subject matter from many areas to bear on the problems they face in daily life. It was pointed out in Chapter 5 that many learners in high school and college will need extensive exploration of certain subject areas. The pattern at the secondary level must allow both for studies that cut across subject lines and for as intensive exploration of subject areas as the learners' needs, concerns, and maturities

[4] This section is a brief overview of the design as teachers and learners in the secondary school select curriculum experiences. A detailed description of a tenth-grade's work is given in Chapter 13.

demand and allow. Because persistent life situations in expanding form are a part of living at all ages, the curriculum cannot rightly move from the study of life situations to subjects—and a number of challenges to the traditional secondary school organization result. What would be the essential characteristics of the pattern of group living for high school youth?

TIME FOR A GENERAL EDUCATION CORE MUST BE PROVIDED

The growth in dealing with persistent life situations, foreseen under the curriculum design proposed, requires that each pupil be assigned to a class with learners of similar maturity for a period of time in which they are free to develop plans with a teacher who works closely with them. The result will be a program, usually described as a **core,** centered around the concerns of the group and the persistent life situations reflected in these concerns. The activities which make up this core would not be prescribed in advance and would cut across subject fields as the problems and concerns of the group demand. This conception of a core differs from the programs in the curriculum organized by subjects, where two or more subjects are usually assigned to the core—English and social studies, science and mathematics. In such a subject core, the pupils benefit from having more time under the guidance of one teacher and have greater opportunities to discover interrelationships within the combined subject areas. However, study of problems of group concern is restricted by the boundaries of the subjects assigned to the core. The type of core program proposed in this design differs also from the one in which a theme or topics are assigned to a given grade level—school living, knowing the community, health and safety, and communicating ideas, assigned to the seventh grade for example. While opportunities to cut across subject lines are provided, the exploration of pupil concerns is still limited by the themes assigned.

The experiences making up the proposed core would be of the same order as the all-class activities described for elementary pupils, adjusted, of course, to the greater maturity of adolescents. Teacher and pupils would cooperatively plan and work together on persistent life problems with which all individuals must deal with reasonable competence. The means of identifying the needs of learners and the criteria for deciding what weight to give a particular experience would be those described earlier in this chapter.

As in the elementary school, varied activities would demand total group attention as the year's work of the core class evolves. Some would be related to daily living in the school situation—requests from the student council, plans for an all-school carnival, plans for a class party, consideration of the membership requirements for school clubs. Some might be centered around special services to the school undertaken by a class, or by students of a given year working cooperatively—the appeal and publicity of a drive for quieter halls, one of several other responsibilities identified as important by the student council. These opportunities to serve the school community have many contributions to make to growth in ability to deal with persistent life situations.

One or more group problems arising from sources outside tne school community and demanding intensive study would also be a part of the core program. Depending on their nature, these studies may last several weeks or through the entire semester and may draw on one or many subject fields. The classroom organization for such studies would not be dissimilar to that found in the upper elementary grades. It might involve individual and small-group assignments as well as certain all-class responsibilities. In some cases opportunities might be found for individuals to push special interests to considerable depth. The services of specialists in subject fields other than those in which tne core teacher possesses competence should be available. Even at the elementary school level, it is impossible for one teacher to have adequate command of all the areas of knowledge to which students need to refer. Adolescents, with their increased intellectual maturity, have even greater need for the stimulation and challenge of contacts with specialists. Programing at all levels must facilitate the availability of specialists to groups requesting help with life situations that cut across subject lines as well as those requiring intensive study in a particular field.

The allotment of time to the core program and to the pursuit of special concerns would depend upon the learners' maturity, their needs for individualized experiences, and their readiness for work in areas of specialization. Some schools bridge the gap from the elementary school with a relatively large block of time assigned to the core at the seventh-grade level. As needs for specialization become more focal, the core is then decreased. With some groups of slow-learning students it has proved advantageous to continue to provide for large blocks of time under one teacher throughout the high school years. Special teacners would contribute in such areas as physical education, music, and art.

In some schools, the advantages from the consistent guidance and flexible activities possible within the larger time block of the core have been secured, without sacrificing opportunities for contacts with specialists, by arranging for two teachers with complementary specialties to work as a team with their classes. In these situations each teacher assumes major responsibility for planning with nis group, but he and nis class are free to include the other teacher as a resource person. Whatever the exact nature of the organization, teacher and students will need time to get to know each other, freedom to embark on projects most likely to contribute to growth in understanding and dealing with persistent life situations, and access to specialists when their help is needed.

OPPORTUNITIES TO WORK WITH SPECIALISTS SHOULD BE AVAILABLE

Core class activities occupy only part of the high school youth's day. The rest of the time he will have opportunities, under the guidance of specialists, to pursue interests, to strengthen areas of weakness, or to meet special needs. Because needs for specialization arising from the problems learners face cannot be easily pigeonholed, this would not be merely a matter of electing subjects.

Throughout the secondary school, but particularly at upper levels, students will need to spend relatively long periods of time working in areas of special concern with teachers having special interests and competencies in particular fields. There will be youth who have special concern with foreign languages; some who bring strong science interests; some who have special talents in music and art; some who have developed deep interests in literature, history, economics. **Service courses,** offering opportunities for extensive explorations into fields related to the students' interests or concerns, and under the guidance of specialists, must be available.

In addition, work in the core program will often lead to identification of subproblems requiring several weeks of study in a special field. These problems might concern the entire class or a small group. For example, several pupils may wish to pursue the science aspects of a particular problem, or engage in a more intensive study of the history of language, or delve into consumer education problems. If such developing interests are to be nurtured, special help must be available on a short-term basis when needed. This requires **service units** from specialists—blocks of activities shorter than a semester's duration but long enough to provide for the intensive exploration needed for sound understandings of the special concern.

There will also be individual needs such as those of an intellectually gifted student, for example, who requires time and guidance to pursue a concern which may be his alone. Such opportunities are important to a talented musician, a student with artistic ability, a youth whose forte is creative writing, or the individual who likes to work with machines.

There will also be learners who need special help—students who lack basic English skills, who have inadequate study habits, who are struggling with speech defects, who need to polish basic mathematical skills. At the elementary school level, time for such special needs and interests is often provided by scheduling individual activities for part of the day when specialists are available for individual guidance. An open period for the first part of the afternoon and a session for those with special interests for a half hour before school opens in the morning have been tried. At the high school level, more careful scheduling is required to meet such individual needs by having specialists available at stated times for **individual work in studio or laboratory.**

TRADITIONAL SCHEDULING PATTERNS MUST BE RE-EXAMINED

What do these varied needs for special help mean for the scheduling of activities for a typical group of high school learners? Certainly, traditional patterns for schedules must be critically re-examined. The usual pattern of the six- or seven-period day must be re-thought, with a possibility of substituting three time blocks. One block might be provided for core activities. At this time specialists could be available "on call" to give help with problems arising from the core activities. A second block of time might be devoted to opportunities for long-term activities relating to special interests and work in areas of specialization under the guidance of specialists. Students would enter these service courses after consultation with their counselor and core teacher. For a third block of time, laboratories and studios might be open for "free" or "special-help" activities during which individuals or groups, guided by counselors or core teachers in deciding what concerns or interests to pursue, could engage in short-term projects either of individual concern or relating to the general education core.

Implications for high school scheduling go beyond merely assigning different parts of the day to diverse types of offerings. As with the elementary pupil, the situations faced by the high school learner are not all resolved in a specified length of time. Certainly, all will not be resolved at the end of a report period or a semester. Students who complete one project need opportunities to move on to another under the guidance of the same or some other teacher. The traditional patterns of scheduled examinations and report periods must be replaced by more flexible means of evaluating and reporting progress. While balanced development would still be one criterion for the choice of activities, there might be times when a student with special interests would spend almost all his time for several weeks in intensive study of background information in science, in an integrated study of the history and language of a country, or in a broad social science exploration. Balance would be achieved, then, through counseling rather than through set requirements regarding basic courses and electives emanating from a central office.

TRADITIONAL ORGANIZATIONS OF SUBJECT FIELDS MUST BE RE-EXAMINED IN THE LIGHT OF THEIR CONTRIBUTION TO PERSISTENT LIFE SITUATIONS

Learners at the secondary school level will have contacts with subject areas in many ways. There will be times when knowledge from many fields will be brought together in the solution of a single problem and there will be times when a problem will demand either extended or short but intensive study of an aspect of a subject field. The traditional assumptions regarding subject fields must be reappraised in terms of the potential contribution of each field to growth in dealing with persistent life situations. What difference in learners' lives could the study of a given field make? How can its values be translated into terms more meaningful than "preparation for college work" or "important from a cultural point of view"? Even within a relatively inflexible secondary school schedule, the teacher who asks how his field actually touches the lives of learners can make a significant contribution to their growth in dealing with persistent life situations.

In addition, the traditional ways of organizing subjects should be reconsidered. Are there not units within larger wholes that can stand as independent entities? Is the step-by-step approach that appears in the textbook the only one? Have creative teachers and textbook writers suggested new ways of looking at subject fields? Often a new organization provides the clue for selecting smaller blocks of information for short-term studies. There is also need to consider how effective use can be made of learners' maturity in the organization of subject matter. Certainly the capacities to read, to grasp generalizations, to sense sequences from brief statements, to see relationships, suggest possibilities for starting with learners in terms of the problems they face. But the approach used to help a nine-year-old grasp a new field would not be the same as the one used when he is a sixteen-year-old.

It is important for teachers of various subject fields to study cooperatively the contributions of their fields to growth in dealing with persistent life situations. Through such interdisciplinary study will come clues to working more flexibly with learners' needs and concerns and, at the same time, to helping them explore their cultural heritage more widely and deeply.

CONTRIBUTIONS OF OUT-OF-CLASS ACTIVITIES TO GROWTH IN DEALING WITH PERSISTENT LIFE SITUATIONS SHOULD BE STUDIED

Just as all the group living experiences at the elementary school level need to be appraised in the light of their contribution to learners' growth in coping with persistent life situations, so do all those experiences in which high school learners engage. In a sense, the proposed curriculum concept makes terms like "extracurricular" or "co-curricular" obsolete. Every activity in which high school youth engage should contribute to growth in dealing with persistent life situations. Sharing in the preparation of stage sets can be an outlet for artistic talent, an excellent experience with blueprints for the learner responsible for scenery, and an exercise in using the techniques of historical research for the crew who are to advise on details. Acting as manager of the basketball team can provide many worthwhile experiences in interpersonal relationships. From such experiences come not only opportunities to put learnings into practice, but new needs and interests may be developed. The entire school contributes to the growth of adolescents in meeting persistent life situations.

CONSISTENT GUIDANCE OF LEARNERS IS NECESSARY

The fact that learners at the secondary school level will be spending relatively longer periods of time with specialists on schedules that have less flexibility than is possible at the elementary school level suggests that there must be one teacher who knows each student especially well. This is important if the concerns of individuals are to be sensed, their strengths and weaknesses given due attention, and the schedules on which individuals and groups are assigned to work with specialists are to meet their needs. Much of the flexibility suggested in preceding sections would not be possible without adequate guidance.

How to plan so that one teacher knows a group of learners well enough to approximate the type of sensitive understanding of individuals achieved by able teachers in the self-contained classrooms of the elementary school is a major problem. High schools have experimented with several possibilities. In some schools the counselor is also the core teacher, sometimes continuing with a group over several years. A teacher with particular talent in counseling might handle the core courses for the first year and then continue as counselor with his group through later years. Whatever the adjustment, such responsibility for counseling in a school of any size could not be assigned entirely to deans of students. Further, any homeroom system used must allow ample time for the types of cooperative activity that provide some of the opportunities to identify individual concerns discussed earlier.

Making a Start Toward the Proposed Design from More Traditional Types of Organization

The self-contained class group at the elementary level or a generous block of time for a core program at the secondary level provide the school organization most readily adapted to developing the proposed curriculum design. There must be a teacher who knows the members of the group well enough to provide guidance. Specialists must be available to help in terms of the particular contribution which their area of specialization can make to students' problems and concerns. However, many teachers and learners, at both the elementary and secondary school levels, are working within varied forms of departmentalization and within curriculum designs in which the organizing elements are subjects or subject fields. What steps toward helping learners meet persistent life situations can be taken when children and youth go to a different teacher for each of a series of subjects or when they work with one teacher for from a third to a half day and meet with different subject specialists for the remainder of the day? Can there still be selection of curriculum experiences that will contribute to growth in dealing with persistent life situations?

CONTRIBUTIONS OF SUBJECT FIELDS TO LEARNERS' NEEDS CAN BE IDENTIFIED

Even without freedom to select experiences in terms of learners' concerns and to work on flexible schedules, teachers who know learners and the problems they actually face can do much toward guiding them in terms of this point of view, regardless of the pattern of school organization. The teacher who meets a group for only one period a day and is responsible for acquainting them with a subject area can start by asking, "What situations do my learners face to which this field can make a significant contribution? How does this field touch the lives of my group?"

For instance, the science teacher does not need to start a study of electricity with abstract definitions of terms. Children and youth are handling electric wires, trying to set up stage lights, helping parents fix electrical appliances at home, building radios. These are life situations which can become the starting points for further study. The business education teacher, likewise, can draw upon the entire economic world with which his learners are dealing. The teacher of typewriting can ask, "Why do they want typewriting? What are their problems with which typing skills can help?" The shop teacher has as a resource all the kinds of construction at home or in the community in which learners are engaged. The foreign language teacher utilizes interest in the civilization of the country as reflected in its language form, in its literature, and in the news reports in the daily paper. The mathematics teacher has the many situations of everyday life in which computations are needed—housing, budgeting, surveying, estimating costs, deciding whether to purchase on a deferred payment plan, and the like. The chronological sequence of history can also make a contribution to present problems. Some of the questions raised by learners about modern Greece cannot be answered without going back to ancient times. The high school youth's concern about the function of government in the control of industry needs the perspective of the rise of our modern business structure. Young people who are interested in European royal families may need to go back into feudal days to understand the historical position of the monarchy. The teacher, knowing the background of his particular group, asks, "What is my point of contact with my learners?"

CONTRIBUTIONS OF SUBJECT FIELDS TO PERSISTENT LIFE SITUATIONS CAN BE IDENTIFIED

As suggested in Chapter 6, it is also possible to ask how subject fields contribute to the areas under which persistent life situations are grouped in the charts. What opportunities are there to help learners grow in such areas as health, intellectual power, moral choices, aesthetic expression and appreciation, social participation; to develop competence in dealing with situations involving natural phenomena, technological resources, economic-social-political structures and forces? Teachers who are aware of the full contributions their subject fields can make to human living will find many ways of sharing their insights with children and youth.

The classification of persistent life situations used in the charts in Chapter 6 is not the only way of grouping the problems which occur in the lives of learners. Teachers working within subject areas can cooperatively develop their own grouping of persistent life situations. These might be more useful for their purposes than the classifications included in the charts in this volume, and might reflect more directly the subject fields. For example, another way of looking at the problem might be to say that children are facing situations in such areas as . . .

Fundamental skills—reading, writing, computing, listening, evaluating, observing, problem-solving
Exploring the world in which they live—school, community, state, nation, world—and its historical heritage
Exploring the cultural aspects of their society—art, music, dancing, handcrafts
Exploring themselves—interests, talents, abilities, strengths and weaknesses
Exploring the world of science
Learning to live together—in school, at home, in the community
Building moral and spiritual values
Developing creative interests for personal and recreational purposes

For youth, approaching adult responsibilities in social problems and adult demands to establish themselves in homes and professions, the list might contain areas such as the following . . .

Fundamental skills—reading, writing, computing, listening, evaluating, observing, problem-solving
Dealing with the economic forces and instruments of society
Dealing with government and politics in the school, the community, the state, the nation
Dealing with problems of home and family life
Understanding the historical bases for present-day democracies and the forces that would seek to destroy democracy
Understanding one's self in terms of interests, abilities, aptitudes, weaknesses and strengths, health and physical fitness, and career possibilities
Understanding the world of science
Understanding and respecting all groups in society, and being able to participate in social and work groups
Building moral and spiritual values
Building leisure interests and values

These and similar areas represent the ways in which children and youth need to draw upon various subject fields. If his subject area is to make its contribution to the learner's growth, the teacher must ask, "How can my field extend the understandings and skills needed to act with competence in such areas? How are learners approaching these problems in their daily lives? Where do their present needs lie?" From answers to questions like these come decisions regarding where to start, what concrete illustrations to draw upon, how to select from among the many possible learnings those that are likely to be most important for this group of children or youth. The criteria are those suggested earlier: What contribution will this experience make to growth in ability to deal with persistent life situations? What degree of balanced development will result? What meaning can extended exploration of this problem have for children or youth? Is it a group or an individual concern?

NEW WAYS OF ORGANIZING SUBJECT FIELDS AND OF COMBINING RELATED FIELDS CAN BE EXPLORED

When the situations learners actually face are used as the starting points for study, there usually will be much greater flexibility in the ways in which children and youth are introduced to and encouraged to study a subject field. The sequence of their experiences will change from an organization in terms of the so-called logic of the subject to an organization based on the demands of their problems. It will mean that sometimes certain parts of a subject field will be omitted for a given group of children or youth and that subject lines will be crossed when needed. Teachers of different subject areas may coordinate their efforts so that learners are helped to bring the subject matter of several fields to bear on related aspects of one problem. This requires active cooperation on the part of subject specialists, both in pooling helpful and functional ways of approaching their own fields and in working with others to find fruitful ways of helping learners see relationships among fields. Teachers may experiment by cooperatively planning work in closely related areas, working as a team during a double class period, developing a subject around situations with which pupils are dealing, and many others that teachers will identify as important ways for them to take first steps toward the proposed design.

PUPILS CAN BE INVOLVED IN PLANNING AND TAUGHT PROBLEM-SOLVING SKILLS

The values that come from deciding which of two problem areas is more important for study, of clarifying a problem, and of working actively toward its solution need not be denied learners working under subject organizations. Much can be done to develop ability to work cooperatively, to take a scientific approach to problems, to use techniques of cooperative problem-solving, to relate facts and arrive at generalizations. Every teacher can provide children and youth with opportunities to share in the planning and the carrying out of experiences. Every teacher can encourage learners to collect information from many sources, to think through problems, to arrive at valid conclusions. Many of the competencies required to cope with persistent life situations included in the area of intellectual power will be developed by capable teachers, regardless of the curriculum design under which they work.

PLACE CAN BE FOUND FOR INDIVIDUAL NEEDS AND CONCERNS

Working within the boundaries of a subject field does not necessarily mean that learners must be denied opportunities to bring their interests to the classroom. Teachers of particular subjects have found a number of ways of providing for learners' everyday concerns. Some plan sharing periods when learners have opportunities to talk about events in their lives. In one classroom, a "Week-end News" bulletin board provided a way to share, in writing, home and community happenings. A current events bulletin board, a science table, a corner museum, or a mathematics bulletin board on "How We Use Large Numbers" or "Fractions and Decimals in Our Lives" can be means of recognizing learners' interests in their natural environment and in the economic-social-political world. In some rooms a period is set aside once a week for special interests within the subject area. A science club, a literary or a current events club may meet during such times, or these periods may be used by individuals to follow special interests under the teacher's guidance. During time scheduled for independent enterprises, pupils with special concerns can be encouraged to pursue them through home and community activities as well as in school.

Many teachers provide for discussion of major current events that touch their fields. The social studies class follows the local and national elections. The science class takes time to discuss the forthcoming eclipse of the moon. A consumer education group analyzes the values advertised in the sales of a local store. A world history class follows discussions in the United Nations. Many courses of study developed around subject fields include one or more units related to learners' lives. Illustrative of such units are "How Our City Grew," "Our National Parks," "How a City Feeds Its Millions." Creative teachers are sensitive to learners' worlds regardless of the curriculum design under which they operate.

Even within the boundaries of a forty-five-minute period, individuals and small groups can be allowed to take responsibility for special aspects of a problem or to work on different aspects of the subject. In one sixth-grade science class, for example, the boys who were interested in photography set up their own dark room. In the same class, most of the girls were interested in establishing a bird feeding station and in keeping an accurate record of the winter birds. One gifted third-grader, with the help of both teachers and parents, wrote his own book about astronomy. Students in a ninth-grade literature class formed groups to study various means of expression—short stories, poetry, radio, drama. Each group worked intensively on its area and shared its findings with the class. In a ninth-grade geometry class, the boys built a scale model of a log cabin. Some of the girls worked on scale models of kitchens, and one creative and talented group produced some good nonobjective art, using geometric forms. Working within a subject area does not require that all pupils read the same books, engage in the same activities, or even work intensively on the same aspects of the subject.

GOOD TEACHING IS NOT THE PREROGATIVE OF ANY ONE CURRICULUM DESIGN

The next four chapters focus on problems of how to teach—developing activities with learners, including cooperative planning, scheduling, providing resource materials, meeting individual needs, evaluating growth. These discussions are oriented to the proposed curriculum design in which experiences are developed with reference to the persistent problems of living reflected in the daily lives of children and youth. Nevertheless, teachers working under other curriculum patterns will not find the suggestions foreign to their ways of working. They, too, plan with learners, provide rich resources, evaluate. While the focus and organization of the actual classroom experiences will be different under various curriculum designs, as values and goals differ, much that is the essence of good teaching will be common, regardless of the curriculum design.

Related Readings

ANDERSON, VERNON. *Principles and Procedures of Curriculum Development.* New York: The Ronald Press Company, 1956.

ASSOCIATION FOR SUPERVISION AND CURRICULUM DEVELOPMENT. *What Shall the High Schools Teach?* 1956 Yearbook. Washington, D.C.: The Association, 1956.

CUNNINGHAM, RUTH, AND ASSOCIATES. *Understanding Group Behavior of Boys and Girls.* New York: Bureau of Publications, Teachers College, Columbia University, 1951.

GANS, R., C. B. STENDLER, AND M. ALMY. *Teaching Young Children.* Yonkers-on-Hudson, N.Y.: World Book Company, 1952.

HERRICK, VIRGIL E., JOHN GOODLAD, FRANK ESTVAN, AND PAUL EBERMAN. *The Elementary School.* Englewood Cliffs, N.J.: Prentice-Hall, Inc., 1956.

HILLIARD, PAULINE F. *Improving Social Learnings in the Elementary School* New York: Bureau of Publications, Teachers College, Columbia University, 1954.

HURLEY, BEATRICE D. *Curriculum for Elementary School Children.* New York: The Ronald Press Company, 1957.

KELLEY, JANET A. *Guidance and Curriculum.* Englewood Cliffs, N.J.: Prentice-Hall, Inc., 1955.

MIEL, ALICE, AND PEGGY BROGAN. *More Than Social Studies.* Englewood Cliffs, N.J.: Prentice-Hall, Inc., 1957.

NOAR, GERTRUDE. *The Junior High School Today and Tomorrow.* Englewood Cliffs, N.J.: Prentice-Hall, Inc., 1953.

OTTO, HENRY J. *Social Education in the Elementary School.* New York: Rinehart & Company, Inc., 1956.

PRESCOTT, DANIEL, editor. *Helping Teachers Understand Children.* Washington, D.C.: American Council on Education, Commission on Teacher Education, 1945.

8

GUIDING THE EXPERIENCES OF LEARNERS

Selecting centers of activity and experiences, as described in the preceding chapter, is but the beginning of the work of teacher and learners. Clearly, the job is much more complicated—and more alive and stimulating—than that facing a group whose year's work is already outlined in terms of specific subject matter found in a textbook or course of study. As stated earlier, some concerns will be common to the entire class, some will be problems of small groups, others will be individual. Some will call for cooperative efforts over the entire year, some will last a month, some will be solved in a matter of minutes. As a situation of concern to the whole class unfolds there will be differing experience backgrounds, needs, interests, talents of value to the group, and jobs to be done.

Is it possible for such complicated plans to unfold smoothly? How do teachers and learners together develop experiences; will there be units of work? What kinds of planning will be needed—by the teacher alone, by teacher and pupils together? What will the daily schedule look like? How will organized bodies of subject matter be used and skills developed? What types of materials will be needed? How do the teacher and class get started at the beginning of the year?

Because the experiences for any particular class should be based on the exact nature of the situations of greatest value and concern to that group, the above questions can never really be answered in detail apart from the actual teaching–learning situation. However, it is possible to suggest principles and procedures which can guide teachers and others in translating the proposed curriculum design into practice as they work with learners.

Developing Experiences with Learners

General principles governing such aspects of teaching as planning, scheduling, using subject matter, developing skills, and providing resource materials must be considered in the context of the total process of guiding experiences with learners. What will be the general pattern in which an experience will develop with a class, a small group, or an individual learner?

THE SITUATION LEARNERS FACE PROVIDES THE ESSENTIAL UNITY OF THE LEARNING EXPERIENCE

The particular situation with which learners are dealing at the time is the guide to the general pattern in which the learning experience will develop. In the sense that coping with the immediate concern or problem involves a number of closely related or unified activities, this pattern will be that of a unit of work. However, this term has many different meanings. As used in this volume, a unit of work is synonymous with a problem-solving approach to learning. Together, the teacher and learners clarify the nature of their problem. Together, they plan the steps needed to solve it—the specific questions to be answered or the skills to be acquired, the information needed, the activities that may help, the responsibilities to be assigned to various group members—and then carry out their plan. Depending on the complexity of the problem, there may be more planning sessions, new problems raised, new activities undertaken. Eventually the group shares its findings, decides whether the problem has been solved, and thinks about next steps. It is the underlying plan tying the series of activities into a meaningful whole for the learners that gives the experience the characteristics of a unit.

When a unit of work is defined in terms of activities that have unity for the learners, the phrase can be appropriately applied to a short series of arithmetic activities for six third-graders who are helped to see that their uncertainty in number combinations is making them poor storekeepers, who plan with the teacher for practice, and successfully pass a speed test. It is equally applicable to the activities of a twelfth grade which embarks on a two-month study of the development of European nations in order to be able to answer the questions raised by their reading of daily newspapers. This is a way of guiding learners that applies to all aspects of the curriculum and to all experiences in which learners engage. Basically, it is a way of working in which the following are considered the critical elements in dealing effectively with the situations of daily life:

1. Developing a healthy curiosity about day-to-day experiences
2. Planning a way of working on a problem of special concern
3. Identifying needed resources and competencies
4. Locating these resources or developing these competencies and using them appropriately
5. Thinking critically about data gathered
6. Making decisions based on evidence
7. Initiating and taking action on decisions made
8. Evaluating action taken and, if necessary, planning a new course of action

THE NATURE OF THE SITUATION DETERMINES THE ACTIVITIES AND THE WAYS OF WORKING

When a unit of work is defined as the series of related activities needed to carry out a plan or to solve a problem, the particular activities and ways of working will be determined by the nature of the problem or situation faced. Art or construction activities may be needed, extensive reading may be important, musical experiences could be included, trips might be taken, a dramatization or some other specific culminating activity might be used. None of these, however, is essential. Learners may work in committee groups, but this is not a necessary organization for work. If the learning experience is to be effective the activities and ways of working must be appropriate to the specific concern at hand.

The activities in which learners engage will vary from some that are very simple to some that are quite complex. How simple or how complex will depend, in part, on the insights of which learners seem capable and the experiences for which they are ready. For example, the difference in learners' insights is apparent in these two illustrations.

A group of **slow-learning children** might have experience with the persistent life situation of achieving attractive personal appearance through setting up a "dressing room" in one corner of the classroom. The only planning might involve the whole group's discussing what is needed—a dressing table, a mirror, a box of paper tissues, perhaps a soap tray, and a pile of paper towels. The only committee activity might be the work of two or three volunteers to help hang the mirror and cover an orange-crate dressing table, and a rotating group of helpers to keep the corner tidy. There might be a few discussions about why we like to look at well-groomed people and how being neat makes us feel. Most of the learning might come through the day-by-day practice of good habits as individuals use these facilities.

A group of **able ninth-graders** might explore extensively the same problem of achieving attractive personal appearance. They might be ready to think about principles of good design. Consideration of color values might be appropriate. Problems of the importance of good grooming in applying for jobs and in other personal relationships could be studied in detail. Applications to health factors could be considered. Day-by-day classroom practice for habit-building purposes might not be included at all for this class. The principles and generalizations evolved from the discussions could be sufficient for these students.

The skills possessed by the group could make a difference in the extensiveness of the unit and the complexity of the organization.

In a **second-grade** study of animals which was planned after discussions of trips to the zoo made by various individual members, the organization was a combination of all-class activity and individual work. The teacher read much of the information to the class as a whole, although some simple picture books were also used. The whole class took a trip to the zoo, with some mothers along to help so that smaller groups and individuals could spend more time with animals of particular interest. The information gained was drawn together largely through individual activities. Children drew pictures, told stories and wrote riddles about favorite animals. Their teacher mimeographed and stapled these into small books for all to read. Groups interested in the same animals shared their work but there was little cooperative group work.

In a **fifth grade,** a more complex committee organization was needed. This class made plans to interest the entire school in making more use of the local zoo over the vacation period. Several types of group activity were used. Committees volunteered to learn as much as they could about the major classifications of animals. Although some all-class help on note-taking was needed, these children possessed the requisite reading skills to locate most of the information they needed. After the information was gathered, the class planned to share it with the rest of the school by means of an assembly program. Here each child worked on two committees, one to plan a special part of the program about the animals he had studied, and the other to share in other jobs needed to make the assembly a success—invitations, ushers, hosts and hostesses, scenery makers, and stage hands committees.

A **tenth grade,** concerned with problems of conservation of wild life, made much independent use of the community. After general plans were laid by the class as a whole, committees undertook to explore existing community resources. This involved field trips by the separate committees, some on week ends, some during school time. Among the persons and places visited were the local game warden, a fish hatchery, a game farm, the president of the local fish and game league, a member of the park commission. In addition to serving on one of these committees each student took a special aspect of the national conservation problem as his special concern. There were some all-class experiences when films and speakers were brought to the school. In the end, the class turned its homeroom into an exhibit room. This required participation in a variety of ways. Jane, for example, arranged the materials she had received in response to her letters; helped her group to decide how to picture the decrease in the number of waterfowl over the past fifty years and the results of recent efforts at conservation, and then worked with a smaller group to prepare one of the graphs; shared in the class planning sessions to determine whom to invite and how to help them get the most out of the exhibits; and acted as chairman for the group of usherettes.

It should not be interpreted from the foregoing illustrations that increased maturity and ability always means increasing complexity in all the activities undertaken by a given group. There will be many times, with learners of all ages, when a very simple plan will result in the desired growth. The problem itself is a factor affecting the nature of the activities and the ways of working.

The **fifth grade** which completed the rather elaborate unit on the zoo also had a library club. This club met once a week to share new "finds" in recreational reading. The only organization was a plan for club officers to rotate once a month. Those ready to report on books signed for time on the program. Occasionally reading groups shared particularly good stories or poems. This uncomplicated plan which operated all year did much to stimulate more extensive reading.

As plans for the **tenth grade** conservation exhibit progressed, about half the class developed a short-term unit on the use of visual materials in communication in an effort to discover the most effective ways of developing greater school interest in conservation problems. This small unit consisted of a series of discussion sessions built around items suggested by the English and the art specialists to whom the group went for help.

For each new situation, the teacher asks: "What growth in meeting persistent life situations can appropriately come from this experience? What does the situation mean to these students? What insights can they be expected to develop? What activities will lead most easily and directly to the desired growth?"

THE SUBJECT MATTER SELECTED DEPENDS ON THE SITUATION OR PROBLEM

The specific situation of everyday living and the meaning it has and can have for the particular learners determine the exact content or subject matter to be used. For example, the subject matter for the second-graders responsible for managing the money for midmorning milk will include identifying money values, counting, and simple addition of money. The fifth-graders responsible for the school store also deal with the subject matter of arithmetic. The problems they meet in the store require competence in adding amounts (with the necessary practice and drill), determining prices based on figuring profit and loss, simple keeping of accounts, and possibly simple percentage involved in computing discounts on certain merchandise or periodic sales. Take another illustration: two junior high school groups—one in California and one in Minnesota—are interested in the problem of what proposed government policies regarding farm supports will mean to their families and communities. Both groups might consider some of the same problems of the relation of price to supply and demand, the importance of encouraging conservation, the history of government support to farmers, and the possible effects of various kinds of aid. However, the Minnesota group will study the problem as it relates to the growing of wheat and other grains while the learners in California will be interested in how it affects truck gardens and citrus groves. Many of the same basic concepts will be developed by both groups, but each will work with content appropriate to the way the problem is most real to it. The groups will use some similar sources of information but will find the actual content quite different when dealing with such problems as federal aid, government controls, technical aspects of growing, storing, transporting, and merchandising products, and securing labor. Although both groups are studying government policies on farm aid, the nature of the specific concern will necessitate their dealing with quite different subject matter in order to get the data needed to understand their particular problem.

THE EXTENSIVENESS OF THE UNIT DEPENDS ON THE SITUATION AS FACED AND UNDERSTOOD BY LEARNERS

The extensiveness of the unit will depend on the problem or situation actually faced and understood by the particular group of learners. The teacher and pupils will feel no compulsion to include all related subject-matter areas merely because they are related. For example, children planning a school garden would gather information and develop skills needed to carry out their plans effectively but would not necessarily study the citrus crops of California or grain growing in the Midwest. Similarly, a tenth grade concerned with understanding the problems of a modern colonial people seeking self-government would concentrate on the political and historical backgrounds required to comprehend this situation. They would feel no pressure to study other aspects of the particular culture—housing, occupations, the arts—although some classes might see a relation between these and the struggle for freedom, and engage in a detailed study of them. Nor would there be any requirement that they expand their concern to a world-wide study of the problems of all colonial peoples. Teacher and learners together determine what is relevant and what is extraneous to the specific situations at hand.

Several of the principles suggested in Chapter 7 as guides for deciding whether a situation is appropriate as part of the school program are also helpful in deciding how extensive a study of a given area should be. Information which does not actually contribute to the solution of the situation learners face, although important for closely related problems, may not be appropriate. Information beyond the maturity level of the group has no place. Understandings which learners have already acquired through previous experience will be used but not retaught—except where learning is inadequate.

UNDESIRABLE REPETITION IS AVOIDED THROUGH CAREFUL DELIMITATION OF THE SITUATION FACED

Is there a possibility that a group will work on the same unit year after year? What about the child who transfers to a new school—might he not be asked to engage in the same study a second time? As pointed out briefly in Chapter 5, these very real difficulties tend to be resolved once the specific situation of concern to the group is used as the key to content and activities. The situation or problem is never a "peg" on which to hang a predetermined body of subject matter or a previously planned "unit" that the teacher knows has "worked well" in the past and that he has been planning to "lead" the current group into doing. The problem is not a device used merely to arouse interest, but rather a guide to appropriate activities and necessary information. When a group returns to a problem area that was a center of study a year before, it is because new problems have arisen, or the learners' increased maturity has resulted in new insights, or discussion of a new situation has revealed that facts and generalizations supposedly developed last year are not clear. It is quite possible, for example, that strong interests in civic government developed in a ninth grade by a study of the problems the city council faces in planning better recreation facilities could continue to spark new studies all through high school. This would not mean a series of similar units on the structure of civic government. Rather, the facts learned would provide a background for interpreting council disputes, understanding why certain issues are referred to committees, realizing the purposes of public hearings.

The flexible organization of a unit of work provides another means of avoiding obviously undesirable repetition. A continuing interest in an area need not require the same depth and extensiveness in further study. The fifth-graders who, in the preceding year, made an extended study of the types of plants most suitable for a classroom and how to care for them may continue this interest. But their planning at this time may merely be for rotating responsibility in caring for the window boxes. Later in the year an entirely new problem may arise if a child brings to school a plant covered with aphids which infects the other plants. In this curriculum design learners share in decisions regarding the balance in their activities. Plans are not made without reason, and all interests expressed by a group do not necessarily become centers of study. It would be appropriate, therefore, to ask the sixth-graders who wish to continue a fifth-grade unit on rockets and space travel to consider what new areas they would like to explore and also to evaluate the potentialities of this learning experience in the light of other possible uses of their time. The continued interest may actually be secondary to a number of new concerns. Perhaps, after all, only a small group of boys have this major concern. Could they pursue this study as a small-group activity?

Flexible experiences for individuals are also anticipated in the kind of unit activities being discussed. The pupil from another class or school where a similar problem had already been studied would contribute his expert knowledge to the new group. He might undertake special research in an aspect of the problem of concern to him, or he might even put comparatively little time on this group activity in order to pursue a problem in some other area. While a transferee may have relatively more background in a particular area than the group to which he comes, there will inevitably be new aspects of the problem to engage his attention and concepts still vague to be sharpened. In the case of the slow learner, the repetition of several experiences with the same general problem may be quite desirable.

Because the exact nature of the situation or problem faced by the particular learners is the determiner of subject matter and activities, undesirable repetition can be avoided. Persistent life situations recur throughout the life of the individual but the specific immediate situations of which they are a part vary widely and the meanings expand as the individual matures. This change in the ramifications of persistent situations learners face decreases the possibility of undesirable repetition.

LEARNING IS GUIDED TOWARD DEVELOPING CONCEPTS AND GENERALIZATIONS

Factual information alone does not insure the kind of understanding needed in a world of continuous discovery and invention. Only as facts are seen in relationship and individuals think about and generalize from their experiences are understandings likely to be useful beyond the immediate situation in which they are learned. But what is known about the nature of learning indicates that generalizations can rarely be taught directly. The learner arrives at them for himself as he is helped to deal with situations in which he must draw conclusions. For example, to solve the problem of their paints drying out, the first-graders must understand the basic concept of evaporation. A beginning understanding can come as their teacher helps them discover that water changes form under certain conditions—a damp cloth on the radiator steams and a puddle on the walk vanishes in the sun. An eleventh grade concerned about the many problems of delinquency in one section of their city may be helped to discover significant facts about living conditions and recreational opportunities. The answer to the question "Why?" can bring understanding which may then be phrased thus: "People are not naturally bad. What they do, either good or bad, is caused by the conditions in their homes and community."

The learner also arrives at generalizations when he is helped to see interrelationships among the facts and factors in his experiences. Children in a second grade were curious about many things in their environment—what happened to the squirrels who no longer ran about a particular section of the school grounds, several large groups of birds "going south," Bobby's report of not seeing the bears on his last trip to the zoo.

As these observations were shared, the teacher began to raise with them the question "why?" As the children began to think about the many examples of physical adjustment of animal life, they acquired some insight into the basic generalization, "All life adjusts to a changing environment or else it perishes."

Generalizations take on added meaning when learners use and extend them in a variety of experiences. The physical adjustment of animal life observed by second-graders may later be extended to include physical adjustment of the human organism as the children note how they adjust to changes in weather conditions and the differences in the dress of peoples who live in other geographical areas. Many years later this generalization will be extended as the group considers problems of adjustment as individuals face failure, a great catastrophe, or forced changes in surroundings. For a ninth grade the generalization, "Real cooperation is based on ability as well as on willingness," may take on meaning as ability to speak Spanish is needed to interview two families in the district. It may have added meaning as special competence in art becomes an asset in making posters needed in the campaign to alert the community to the need for a new recreation center. The word "ability" may come to mean time and needed energy as well as special competence as the students observe that when Jim offered to take on too much he was unable to do his usual good job of preparation and often delayed committee work. Such expanded generalizations are not as likely to be developed unless teachers stimulate thinking. "We don't go to sleep or go away in the winter. What do we do when the weather gets cold?" "How could you tell from their clothing what kind of country they live in?" "Yes, some people won't try again if they've failed. What do you think of that as a way of solving a problem?" "Jim, we needed your help, but what about the job you were able to do? How could you have planned better?"

One generalization may be useful in a variety of situations. For the ninth grade mentioned above, the concept of cooperation based on ability as well as on willingness was useful as the group shared in the work of the student council, selected interview teams for a community poll, worked on committees suggesting kinds of building facilities for the proposed recreation center. Conversely, several generalizations may emerge from a single experience. An eleventh grade concerned with world security and peace visited the United Nations and followed developments in that group and in the news. Their experiences contributed to generalizations in several areas—fundamental principles of cooperation as they apply to nations as well as school groups, the place and use of propaganda, the use and evaluation of resource material, the effect of natural resources on the economy of a country.

Democratic values are basic generalizations to which many everyday situations contribute. When learners work together in a variety of situations they have experiences through which they can be helped to generalize about the worth of the individual and the values of cooperative intelligence. When solutions to everyday problems are approached through carefully planned action there are opportunities for growth in understanding of generalizations basic to problem-solving and to the use of a scientific method of work. Teachers can help learners develop these basic values as a part of ongoing experiences. To fail to do so is to neglect a major responsibility of every teacher.

Planning for and with Learners

Sometimes the decision on how to deal with an immediate situation must be made rather quickly and at the time the incident is introduced. This would be true of a reported "stolen" bicycle. Other areas may be thought through more carefully by the teacher before beginning work with children or youth, such as the activities of Book Week or the bond issue for better schools which is soon to be placed before the public. Still others may be partially dealt with at the time and considered more fully later. The growing concern about the proposed throughway and what it may mean for the homes of some of the pupils deserves consideration but probably at a specific later date if the schedule is already crowded. Recognition of the concern, identification of the particular questions of individuals, and the allocation of a definite time to deal with the problem may be all that is needed at this time. Whatever the circumstance, the teacher who effectively helps learners to deal with their concerns tries to give prior thought to guiding their learning experiences.

Units of work call for planning by both learners and teacher. For the teacher, involving learners in planning has two basic values. First, as mentioned in Chapter 7, it is the interaction between teacher and pupils that helps the teacher to identify strengths, needs, and concerns, to note insights, and to assist learners in becoming aware of gaps in their understanding and skills. Second, in planning ways of dealing with a concern or problem the teacher will find opportunities to help learners to clarify purposes, to consider related problems of which they may have been only partially aware, and to share thinking about ways of working.

For learners, sharing in planning offers a safeguard that experiences will be meaningful. Pupils who help to propose next steps are more likely to understand what they do, to recognize the relation of the proposed activity to their purposes, and to see their share and responsibilities in the proposed activity. Experiences in planning also contribute to problem-solving skills important for every individual in dealing with situations of living in a changing society. These include such learnings as how to appraise proposed solutions realistically, how to foresee needs for materials and equipment, how to budget time. Planning with others brings such additional values as skills in working cooperatively—understanding of steps that may be taken to resolve a disagreement, of the responsibilities of leaders and followers, of the rights of those in majority and minority positions.

BOTH LONG-TERM PLANNING AND DAILY PLANNING ARE NEEDED

As each new unit is undertaken, planning will be needed to block out—at least in general outline—the activities proposed for dealing with the specific concern or situation. This might be thought of as a long-term or unit plan. As the work unfolds more detailed consideration will be needed of the various aspects of the long-range plan that are to be carried out on a particular day. This plan will be used as a guide for the day's work along with the proposed schedule of activities—the time to be allotted to each and the optimum time in the day for work on them.

The first step in long-term or unit planning is for the class to clarify what is involved in working on the selected area of concern or the particular problem. What do we want to find out? What questions have to be answered? What do we already know? This aspect of the planning normally leads to a reasonably clear delimitation of the area of concern—a series of related questions or a clear-cut statement of the job to be done. Consideration should then be given to ways of accomplishing the desired goal—steps to be taken, possible sources of help, desirable ways of working, and perhaps tentative allocation of responsibilities to individuals and groups. If the situation to be studied is a complex one which requires work in unfamiliar areas, only a few steps may be outlined in the beginning. In some instances planning may go no further than the proposal, "Can't we read a little more first?" On the basis of seemingly appropriate first steps, the group begins to work. Later stages are blocked out as new insights are acquired and problems raise new demands. If new proposals contribute to the original situation or concern, or suggest an expansion that learners recognize as worthwhile, ways of working on them might be added to the original plan. If they appear to be extraneous, or if learners cannot see their appropriateness, such problems may either be set aside for later study or, if time is available, made the subject of separate investigations while the original problem is carried to its conclusion.

In the next pages the unit or long-range plans developed by four groups of learners and their teachers are outlined.[1] The first group—a first grade—was concerned with meeting a classroom situation resulting from the drying of paints over the week end. The fourth grade also dealt with a classroom situation, one created by the illness of a classmate. The ninth and twelfth grades were concerned respectively with problems suggested by a textbook and by their teacher. The text assignment in the field of community civics and the students' strong feeling that community planning was a theoretical matter in textbooks stimulated the group to enter into an intensive study of the possibility of their helping in creating interest in a community center for their section of the city. The twelfth grade, through a proposal made by their teacher, extended their study of radio and motion pictures as media for disseminating information and molding opinion to the field of advertising. Each group, in terms of its specific problem and its particular abilities and insights, developed the plans which follow. Steps in the cooperative planning of teacher and pupils are the same for young and old. The difference lies in the areas of concern, the speed of planning, the skills in seeing possibilities, the facility in generalizing, and the range of resources used. However skillful the planners may be, some change is usually needed as plans progress.

FIRST: **Learners and their teachers decide what concerns to explore in school.** Together they set up criteria to guide their selection . . .

Is it something that we need to do—a responsibility or obligation that must be met?

Can it be done with little or no additional exploration—have we done it previously?

Is it important enough to be studied carefully? Is it something that we shall meet again?

Should it be considered by the whole class or referred to one or more individuals?

Should it be considered now or deferred until a later time? Will our present work allow us to start it now?

[1] Adapted from F. B. Stratemeyer, M. G. McKim, and M. Sweet, *Guides to a Curriculum for Modern Living*, pp. 34–41 (New York: Bureau of Publications, Teachers College, Columbia University, 1952).

A first grade

considers a classroom situation

"Our paints get dry over the week end. We can't use them on Monday when we come to school."

"Can't you keep them wet, Miss Boston?"

"Why do they get dry?"

"We use paints over and over. We better learn how to take care of them."

The criteria were unconsciously applied as the children talked.

Painting was so important a part of the life of this first grade that it was decided to give time to the problem in the schedule for Monday "so that it won't happen next week end."

A fourth grade

expresses concern about a classmate ill at home

The possibility of catching measles because of their association with Joan had special meaning for these children in view of the part their class was to play in the coming spring festival.

"I certainly would like to know if some of us are likely to get them."

"We ought to do everything we can for protection."

"We don't know much about contagious diseases but that is something important to know."

"It's something we all ought to know about."

"Let's find out about it now. We don't have to give as much time to festival rehearsals and we could use that time beginning tomorrow."

These were the ways in which members of this fourth grade tested the proposal for finding out about contagious diseases—it is important now and at other times; it is important for all of us to work on the problem; we know little about it and work on it will take time; we can find a place for it in our present program.

A ninth grade

reacts to a text assignment in community civics

"Why study about community planning! You can't get anything in this community—not even a decent place to swim or play with your friends."

Was community planning merely the dream of textbook writers? Would it work? Here was an opportunity to find out, and Howard received much support for his point of view.

True, the group had no responsibility for the situation under discussion, but it certainly would mean a lot if they could do something toward getting a place to play and have fun.

"Our whole community needs a place to relax and have fun. What could we do to help get a community center like they have in Doville? It could serve grownups as well as kids and young people."

It would take time and careful study.

"Why not make it a class study to replace the work we are now doing with the text?" . . .

A twelfth grade

considers a proposal made by their teacher

As the members of the twelfth-grade social studies class were nearing the completion of their study of the radio, television, and motion pictures as media for disseminating information and molding opinion, Mr. Spence raised the question of advertisements: How many of the same appeals were used? In what way? Could the conclusions arrived at in the study of radio, television, and motion pictures be used in interpreting advertisements?

"We've touched on the problem of advertising from time to time in our study of radio and television—in a somewhat casual fashion. Why wouldn't it be a good idea to really consider the relationship between the programs and the commercials?"

Student reactions showed interest and readiness to consider advertising through commercials (as suggested by Mr. Spence) and in other forms.

"I don't know whether the same conclusions could be used in interpreting ads, but it sure would be a good idea to have some help in knowing what to believe."

"Advertising certainly must be a powerful influence on what people do—millions, maybe billions, of dollars are spent on it."

"Let's find out something about it, but let's not begin until we have completed plans for the Hallowe'en party." . . .

SECOND: **Teachers in their own planning identify persistent life situations** which are a part of the concern to be explored . . .

In the first grade	In the fourth grade
Miss Boston recognized the following persistent life situations:	The teacher's plan noted that learners would need to cope with:
Using physical and chemical change Preserving materials Using a scientific approach to the study of situations Using appropriate resources . . .	Practicing desirable health routines Providing for disease control Providing and using legal protections . . .
as well as	as well as
Planning Working on a common enterprise . . .	Planning Using appropriate resources Working on a common enterprise . . .

In the ninth grade	In the twelfth grade
Work on the community center might include such problems as:	Mr. Spence wanted especially to help this twelfth grade to deal with such problems as:
Securing facilities for relaxation and activity Meeting legal regulations Deciding on obligations to constituted authority Using government to guarantee welfare Using appropriate means of presenting a point of view Making exact computations Planning community architecture and landscaping . . .	Using appropriate means of presenting a point of view Interpreting information Meeting legal regulations Formulating guides for action Determining a fair price . . .
as well as	as well as
Planning Using appropriate resources Working on a common enterprise . . .	Planning Using appropriate resources Working on a common enterprise . . .

THIRD: **Learners and teacher clarify what is involved in working on the problem . . .**

What do we want to find out?

What questions have to be answered?

What do we already know?

In the first grade	In the fourth grade
What makes the paint get dry? Why does it get dry only over the week end? Why doesn't the green paint in the big jar dry out? What can we do to keep it from getting dry?	How long does it take for measles to show if you've been exposed? What does quarantine mean? Is a person who has measles quarantined? Some of us have had measles. Will we get them again? Why do some people get measles and others don't? How can people be protected so they won't get contagious diseases? How can we let Joan know what we are doing and help her to keep up with her work?

In the ninth grade	In the twelfth grade
What do the adults, young people, and children in our community like to do for recreation? What are they doing now? What can be done in a community center? Who runs it? Who pays for it? How can we get people interested in a community center? What persons and groups would need to be contacted? What facts would be needed to make a sound proposal? How can we present our facts and needs most effectively?	What types of appeal are used in advertising? Which are found to be most effective? What is the relationship between the programs and the commercials? What is the cost of different kinds of ads? How does cost of advertising affect the molding of opinion? Why aren't some important ideas put before the public? Are there any legal restrictions on advertising? How is advertising appeal determined?

FOURTH: **Learners and teacher plan ways of accomplishing their purposes . . .**

How shall we work on the problem?

How shall we begin?

What steps do we need to take?

What should be done by the class? by individuals? by small groups?

What materials do we need?

When shall we do our work? When shall we report?

In the first grade *

Jobs we need to do:	Responsibility of:
1. Ask Miss Cole (art specialist) what the paint is made of	Bobby, Mary, Janet (at 11 o'clock)
2. See what is different about the green paint jar and other paints	Sally, Sue, Gerald, Fred (during noon hour)
3. Think why paint might dry	
4. Test to find out if this is true	

In the fourth grade

Jobs we need to do:	Responsibility of:
1. Get facts about measles—period of development, symptoms, recurrence, degree of contagion	Sue to ask her father (a physician) Jim and Agnes to locate material in school library and either borrow or set up on special shelf
2. Get facts about causes of measles, protective measures, by	Mary, Sally, Bill to locate material available in branch public library
a. Asking responsible persons	Don, Fred to consult school nurse
b. Reading available materials	Class members to read available material
3. Write letters to Joan	Class members to volunteer

* This was as far as this group could go in projecting plans for dealing with the problem they faced. Miss Boston, in her long-term plan, had outlined other proposals. Some of these are a part of the further planning of the group as shown on page 389.

In the ninth grade

Plan of work:	Responsibility of:
1. Get information about community centers *a.* Location *b.* Activities provided *c.* Who has charge *d.* Cost, initial *e.* Cost, running	Mary, Ella, Margaret to write letter of inquiry to director of American City Community Center Class group of six to visit Doville Community Center over week end with Miss Nichols
2. Decide on ways of securing information on recreational needs and interests of community	
a. Essentials of a valid poll	Ralph to report on poll techniques Zella, Fred to ask "math" instructor to discuss sampling techniques
b. Questions to be asked	Class divided into committees—each committee to present questions for class criticism
c. Permission to administer the poll	Committee to confer with member of City Planning Commission Bill to contact Miss Ray, principal
3. Give and record results of poll	(To be determined in light of #2)
4. Outline plans for community center suggested by results of poll	
a. Prepare a statement of purposes and bases of use	Class discussion followed by statement prepared by a committee
b. Make scale drawings of suggested buildings	Individuals and committees—to be reviewed by class as a whole
c. Determine desired location (1) Accessibility to population needs (2) Zoning restrictions (3) Cost of likely property (4) Ways of securing property for public use—condemning property	Committee assignments, using *a.* Available literature *b.* Reliable persons as resources
d. Determine approximate cost of each center as designed (*b*) *e.* Study means of securing needed finance—taxes, fund drive, bonds, subscription	Each committee presenting a design to study costs and prepare questions to be discussed with Bill's father (an architect) at a class session
(Steps 5–8 omitted in illustration)	(Further assignments of responsibility to be determined later)
9. Present plans to Planning Commission	

In the twelfth grade

Working plans:	Responsibility of:
1. *a.* Part of class apply and test conclusions from study of radio, television, and motion pictures in molding opinion, in advertising field *b.* Other part of class start with ads and determine types of appeals used (After a beginning has been made by each group, share ways of working and findings with class as a whole—to check on soundness of work)	Individuals and committees to study various types of ads: *a.* Newspaper *b.* Popular magazines *c.* "Exclusive" magazines *d.* Billboards, posters *e.* Radio *f.* Television
2. Get information on: *a.* Cost of advertising of various types *b.* Legal restrictions *c.* Ways in which actual appeal is determined	Committees get information on each item for a particular type of ad: *a.* Newspaper *b.* Magazine *c.* Billboards *d.* Radio *e.* Television (Each committee to work out plans for getting information and have them checked by class as a whole)
3. Meet with individuals from an advertising firm, a broadcasting station, and a television studio to discuss unanswered questions.	(To be worked out later)
4. Combine work of committees in a set of statements to be used in judging and testing advertising.	

FIFTH: **Teacher and learners modify plans from time to time . . .**

What difficulties, if any, have we met?

What new problems and needs have arisen?

Do we need to make a change in our plans?

In the first grade

Plans are made more definite as work progresses:

4. Find why paint dries

a. Put same amount of water in four tall cans and in four shallow pans	Margaret, Ronald
b. Put one set of pans in sunshine	Mary, Sue
Put set of pans in darkest corner of room	Jean, Martin
Put set of pans on radiator	Jim, Charles
Put set of pans in refrigerator in home economics room	Billy, Rose, Jimmy
c. Watch and keep record of time when water disappears:	
Pans in sunshine	Jack, Tom
Pans in dark corner	Betty, Louise
Pans on radiator	Frank, Gladys
Pans in refrigerator	Dorothy, Howard

Further plans involved repeating the experiment to be sure there were no errors . . .

In the fourth grade

New plans emerge from inquiries arising from discussion of facts about measles:

1. Observe bacteria under microscope (from water used in washing hands)	Miss Jensen make arrangements
2. Report on use of microscope and way it works (a special-interest report)	Fred, Jim
3. See film on pasteurization and care of milk	Miss Jensen and committee to preview it and compare with findings from visit to local dairy
4. List common sources of infection	Each class member to share list made from readings
5. List recognized safety measures against infection	Each class member to share list made from readings
6. Observe safety measures that are or could be used: *a.* by the individual *b.* in the home *c.* in school *d.* in public places *e.* by the physician, dentist	Each class member to keep a week's log of observed use and nonuse of safety measures
7. Consider steps the group might take to improve conditions observed. (Development of this part of the plan of work after taking step 6)	(Assignments to be determined later)
8. Become acquainted with the work of community agencies in guarding against disease: *a.* Department of Sanitation (meaning of Grade A restaurant) *b.* Department of Health—quarantine, vaccination *c.* The Press—reporting health conditions, illnesses	Bob to ask his father to meet with the class to tell what is done at his restaurant and to answer questions regarding care of foods Maude, Frances, Virginia, Ellen to report on ways of protecting foods during transportation—foods sent into community, where from, means of transportation used, travel time, costs Class members to read available material

The new plans indicate the need to cope with other persistent life situations such as:

Controlling and using bacteria and other microscopic organisms

Using safety measures

Cooperating in enforcing laws

In the ninth grade	In the twelfth grade
Plans are changed and made more specific as work develops. An early change written into the class plan follows: 2. *d.* City Planning Commission to send poll throughout the city and tabulate results Class to poll school district by house-to-house interview and record results (1) Consider essentials of good interview (2) Study district and organize by teams (3) Send letter in advance of visit (a letter of introduction from principal) (4) Prepare "credentials" for each team City Planning Commission and class to share and compare findings	Proposals are made for applying findings to school situations: 1. Use conclusions reached in reviewing ads to be included in Senior Yearbook 2. Send suggestions to poster committee for all-school activities (relating to request for new ways of arousing interest) 3. Share findings with ninth grade (to help in creating public sentiment for new community center)

Long-range plans such as the foregoing may serve to block out tentative group activity for one or two days, as in the instance of the first grade deciding how to keep their paints from drying up, or require work over several months or more, as did the ninth grade's concern about the community center.

The daily planning related to the development of a unit helps both teacher and learners take an immediate look at next steps. How far along are we? How shall we carry out the next steps in our plans? What kinds of help do individuals or groups need? Are special materials needed? Sometimes the unit plan will be sufficiently detailed or the learners will be at such a stage in their activities that the daily planning will be simply a quick check. At other points it may be important to spend considerable time clarifying the details of the day's work.

As noted earlier, daily planning also involves thinking through the schedule of the day's work. "Will our normal time allotment serve for today or will we need to make some changes?" This does not mean that time must be taken each day to reconsider aspects of the schedule that are relatively fixed—a scheduled physical education period or a specific time when an art or music consultant is available. It may seem desirable to both teacher and learners to assign special activities to certain parts of the day. For instance, the time between the pupils' arrival and the official opening of school may be most profitably spent if the first period in the morning is given to independent and small-group work. Joint scheduling, then, is focused on clarifying details and talking through needed changes in the usual schedule. There may be an assembly program to fit in or a special time when a motion picture ordered in advance may need to be used. Whether or not a specially long work period will be required may be discussed in terms of the stage a particular unit has reached. Adjustments may be required to allow more time for individuals or small groups to carry out special responsibilities. Because scheduling the day's activities is a major teaching problem, this aspect of daily planning is considered more fully in a later section.

PREVIOUS PLANNING BY THE TEACHER IS ESSENTIAL TO EFFECTIVE PUPIL–TEACHER PLANNING

The teacher's role in developing experiences with learners is that of guide and leader. He neither foregoes the responsibility of planning in advance of his work with learners, nor does he use his plans in an authoritarian or subtly paternalistic manner. Both his long-range and his daily planning prior to working with learners are tentative. This planning makes it possible for a teacher to fulfill his appropriate role as a democratic group leader. It frees him, while teaching, to give added attention to individuals and to their thinking because he has already appraised the potentialities of the situation, blocked out alternative ways of working and their implications, and considered the probable needs of his group.

The teacher's responsibility for planning a unit of work has at least four aspects. The initial, and a continuing part of his planning, involves a study of the learners. What strengths have individuals developed? What weaknesses and needs are apparent? What problems are these learners facing? With what aspects of persistent life situations must they deal? Are their present activities raising new problems of significance in terms of over-all growth? Are there areas in which little or no experience has been provided this year? Such an evaluation alerts the teacher to new possibilities, to genuine problems of which the group may not be aware, and helps him avoid deciding to "lead" the class into an area of no real concern to them.

From all the possible experiences of concern or interest to a group, only a few can be selected for intensive study. Before teacher and learners together decide which experiences to explore in detail, which to treat lightly, which to delegate to small groups or to individuals, it is important for the teacher to have done some advance thinking. This is a second aspect of the teacher's planning responsibility—he must bring to the planning session with learners his own best judgment as to the possible values of an experience. This involves considering questions similar to those raised in Chapter 7 in connection with the choice of experiences: What balance of activities and experience will this problem area provide? Does it represent an area in which learners need added experience? What are the persistent life situations that seem to be involved? Is this a problem that should be of concern to the entire group or is it more appropriately a special project for one or two individuals? Is it an area in which home or community is already making strong contributions? What are its potential contributions to growth in the light of other needs?

Advance planning does not mean that the teacher decides ahead of time exactly how an experience is to be handled and then "guides" the members of his class to reach the same conclusion. Rather, it provides background for discussing the situation with them intelligently. Many of the questions just listed may be raised in more concrete terms with the group. "Many of your interests this year have been along health and science lines. If we volunteer to handle the folk music for the assembly we would branch into a different area. What do you think?" "John has wanted time for this problem for a long while, but Jane and Sarah have also been asking for time. Do we all need to work on each problem?" "I thought you might be having all the experience you need in this area at home, but you've indicated several possibilities that had not occurred to me."

For each experience that is to become the center of unit activities, whether for a few days or for several weeks or more, the teacher needs to engage in a third aspect of preplanning. This step includes thinking through how best to help the group plan. Careful analysis of possibilities —persistent life situations to which the unit could contribute, questions that should be considered, possible ways of working, materials and resources needed, difficulties that might be encountered—provides background for helping members of the group appraise their specific suggestions. The critical factor in this aspect of planning is for the teacher to be prepared to be specific and helpful without offering such definite conclusions that the learners are, in effect, led to agree with the teacher's plan. The safeguards lie in recognizing the need to use any plan flexibly and in planning how to involve learners rather than planning exactly what they are to decide or do. The teacher who has given thought to the potentialities in a situation brings more insight to pupils' suggestions and possesses sufficient security to allow greater freedom in counseling the learners as they plan to deal with the given problem or concern.

A fourth specific aspect of the teacher's planning should focus on how to handle discussion to get the group started. There is usually a need to sketch in detail the daily plan for the first day of work on the unit. While it is desirable when developing unit plans to block in many possibilities, planning for the initial discussion should be very precise. As leader and guide, the teacher is responsible for seeing that the problem is raised for the group. How will this be done—is it a problem arising from a previous experience; was it originally proposed by a pupil and should he be asked to raise it again; is it a problem sensed by the teacher or other staff members, and if so how can it be presented so that it has meaning for the group? The teacher should also be prepared to lead the discussion so that first steps are taken in working on the problem. What first steps should be considered—is it enough, today, to clarify the problem and to identify subproblems; should some thought be given to ways of working; will time allow for an extended discussion of possibilities? This thinking does not say what the decisions are to be; rather it indicates the areas in which decisions are desirable.

There are those who believe the amount of advance thinking suggested by the four aspects of preplanning is too time-consuming for the busy teacher. However, even when it becomes necessary in planning with learners to make major changes in the unit plan as originally developed, the teacher's work is not lost. As suggested earlier, the teacher who has given thought to the area will be more effective in judging the possibilities in the proposals made by learners, and in guiding their thinking. Further, a carefully worked out unit plan provides an essential guide for the teacher's daily planning. When the possibilities within the unit are clearly seen, the daily plan may consist of only a brief statement indicating suggestions for working on the particular phase of the study—what needs to be done and the order in which it can best be done—and a memorandum of any data needed by the teacher in guiding the learning experience.

EFFECTIVE PLANNING CALLS FOR UNDERSTANDING REASONS WHY

If learners share in the planning, won't they select the easiest activities? Suppose they vote to do something utterly foolish? These fears, frequently voiced when teachers discuss the implications of pupil–teacher planning, suggest a need to clarify understanding of the meaning of cooperative planning.

One of the major purposes of pupil–teacher planning is to discover the meaning learners see in an experience. In this sense, cooperative planning is a means of guaranteeing intrinsic motivation. Learners who know why they are engaging in an activity, and who realize that it contributes to purposes that are worthwhile to them, do not avoid it or treat it lightly. The evidence supporting this can be seen readily by studying pupils' out-of-school activities. What endless pains go into caring for a pet rabbit, planning for a boy scout week-end trip, getting ready for the high school senior prom!

Democratic planning is not simply a majority vote. In fact, more often than not there will be no voting. It is a process of securing the best thinking of all concerned in proposing an effective solution to a problem. This requires intelligent consideration of the reasons underlying various proposals and acknowledgment of the limits a democracy imposes on individuals in the interests of effective group living. "School regulations exist for the good of all the pupils in the school. Our class can discuss them with those in authority and we may even persuade them of the need to make changes, but we can't vote the regulations out of existence." "We must take into account in our planning time limits, available facilities, and needs of other classes, or of groups or individuals within a given class." "Time spent on one activity cannot be devoted to another; which is going to be most useful to us?" Criteria should be set up to help in making choices. A particular proposal may be of little value—even seemingly foolish—but the teacher's responsibility is to help the individual and the group to evaluate the suggestion. This the teacher is prepared to do if he, himself, has thought about many possibilities in his preplanning.

Must all activities be those that learners can propose without the teacher's help? If a teacher does not contribute his appropriate share to the planning session, this might happen. Can he make proposals without directing the planning process and, in effect, making the planning basically a matter of reading his mind? Much depends on whether learners have had enough experience in having their suggestions thoughtfully appraised and respected to develop an atmosphere of mutual respect. If they have, the teacher can advance suggestions, knowing that if class members cannot see the value of his proposals they will say so. In such an atmosphere, it does not matter whether a suggestion comes from learners or teacher as long as learners can recognize it as meaningful and worthwhile. Only when the learners' purposes become that of "going along" with an activity, the worth of which they do not see, does the motivation become extrinsic. Once a teacher is sure that a purpose he thinks is worthwhile cannot be seen as such by learners, he would give up this particular goal until a later occasion provides an opportunity to raise the problem again. When teachers have done the suggested kind of broad preplanning, they are equipped to see possibilities for achieving worthwhile goals in situations recognized as meaningful by learners without imposing their own.

SKILL IN PLANNING MUST BE TAUGHT

To be able to plan effectively in a group situation is a complex skill. It is important to listen to the ideas of others, to identify possibilities for compromise, to know when to support one's own ideas and when to yield to the majority. Learners must be taught these skills. They must also learn how to appraise the possible values in an experience and how to anticipate problems. Teachers themselves may have to develop new skills if their typical classroom roles have not led them to include learners in the planning process. Pupils who are not accustomed to sharing in planning their activities may, at first, even resent being involved. Often it helps if first planning sessions are built around situations where the need for pupil participation is obvious—how to decorate the room, where the best place for the museum corner would be, how to plan a class party.

Planning skills are taught primarily through the planning sessions themselves. When proposals that are beyond the realm of possibility are made, the reasons for their rejection are discussed. Sessions in which individuals have pleaded too hard for special interests are evaluated. Reasons for considering minority needs are examined. Failures of original plans are analyzed, and when new plans are laid care is taken that the same thing does not happen again. Planning sessions in which smaller groups operate with a member as chairman often offer excellent opportunities to discuss ways of working together effectively.

A variety of aids should be used to keep plans clear and to help learners carry through effectively. Daily planning and sessions to evaluate progress provide such means. Setting limits both for the time to be devoted to an activity during a single day and for its probable completion or termination can help. Written plans and check sheets—the schedule for the day, a list of individual activities to be started when other jobs are done, the major questions to be considered in a unit, a list of extra activities for a unit to be worked on by those who have time, a schedule for group reports as a unit nears completion, a committee list of specific jobs to be done, a check-off sheet for those who have attained certain number competencies and are ready for new practice activities, a list of those wishing to report on recreational reading, a "special-help" list of people who particularly need the teacher's assistance—may be useful. Planning has meaning in the classrooms that have been described because it serves important purposes and such aids help to keep these purposes clear.

SKILL IN PLANNING VARIES WITH THE MATURITY AND INTELLECTUAL ABILITY OF THE LEARNERS

The principles that have just been discussed underlie the planning process at any age level. However, skill in planning will vary with the maturity of learners and with their intellectual ability. A general statement of interest, together with a few proposals, may be the extent of the long-term planning of a group of slow-learning children. For these learners and for younger children, units will be shorter and less complex. Day-by-day planning will have an even more important role and the teacher will take relatively more responsibility for suggestions about scheduling, ways of working, and materials. Older children and youth, and those who are intellectually able, will block out plans for longer periods of time, will outline more extended and varied activities, and will take more responsibility in appraising their own progress. Participation in planning is equally important for the youngest learner and the college youth, for the slow learner and the intellectually gifted—but each will contribute according to his maturity and ability. The nature and quality of the planning will vary but all can develop some skill.

Scheduling the Day's Activities

As indicated in the preceding section, one important aspect of pupil–teacher planning is setting up the day's schedule. Learners need to be helped to consider a time schedule as both a guide and a definite commitment, to evaluate what is involved in changing plans, to determine ways of achieving their purposes without interfering with schedules that serve the purposes of many others. Through sharing in scheduling their activities learners grow in ability to estimate how much time will be needed for a given activity, to recognize the value of budgeting time, to meet emergencies, and to use time efficiently in carrying out plans. These are fundamental problems of living in our society.

LARGE TIME BLOCKS ARE A CHARACTERISTIC OF EFFECTIVE SCHEDULES

Large time blocks, rather than many short periods, characterize the program focused on experiences growing out of concerns of daily living. For example, a fourth grade making plans to visit the local airport needs a block of time long enough to include giving committee reports, planning for the visit in terms of these reports, and writing letters or calling to make the necessary arrangements. For another fourth grade, at a point where they need to learn the techniques of two-digit multiplication, it might be desirable to have sufficient time both to come to some understanding of the principles involved and also to have an ample practice session. Too short a period for either of these groups might waste time as momentum gained the first day would have to be built again on the second. A longer time block makes it possible to carry an activity through to a logical stopping point, or to undertake a variety of shorter tasks when this is desirable. Then, too, longer blocks provide for differences in the time individuals need to carry out activities and responsibilities common to the group as a whole, or to pursue special interests.

At the elementary school level it is sometimes convenient to think of the day as divided into four large time blocks with morning recess, noon lunch, and afternoon recess breaks serving as the dividers.

9:00–10:15	First large time block. (This might start with a planning session and perhaps proceed to individual or small-group work, or to the activities related to a unit of work.)
10:15–10:30	Recess break.
10:30–12:00	Second large time block. (A longer primary recess could be achieved by shortening this period somewhat. This block is also long enough to allow for shorter periods when needed.)
12:00– 1:00	Lunch.
1:00– 2:00	Third large time block. (This would allow for work on a unit in another area.)
2:00– 2:30	Recess, rhythms, physical education.
2:30– 3:30	Fourth large time block. (This block might provide time for still another unit, for a free and unassigned period, or for special work in music or art.)

The fact that this schedule shows only four time blocks, or "periods," does not mean only four areas of study in a given day. Within the large time blocks one or more activities would be planned, depending on the amount of time needed for each. The block from 10:30 to 12:00, for example, might be devoted to a variety of class and small-group activities related to skill development. Work on reading, arithmetic, and language skills could all be included in varying amounts for individuals and groups. Similarly, in a block set aside for work on a unit, several types of plans might be moving forward. One group might be receiving special help with reference techniques. Part of the time might be spent with the class as a whole sharing information, while another part might be devoted to the completion of an exhibit or to planning a mural. The purpose of the larger time block is to provide a means for securing flexibility, not to restrict the range and variety of activities included in any one day.

Secondary schools are also moving toward longer time blocks—particularly where a core program is scheduled for part of the pupil's day. The schedule for a typical ninth-grader, about half of whose day is devoted to a core program, might look as follows:

9:00–11:30	Core program devoted to units on social living (communication arts, literature, citizenship, social studies, and guidance). Period may begin with a planning session, followed by varied activities for total group, subgroups, and individuals.
11:30–12:30	Physical education and recreation (organized activities, free play, health, body conditioning).
12:30– 1:10	Lunch.
1:10– 2:00	Science and mathematics (units on number systems, symbolism, relationships, measuring, budgeting, for example, and others on interplanetary travel, collections, heredity, and the like).
2:00– 2:50	Art and music (units may be related to core experiences or may be developed separately).
2:50– 3:40	Exploratory period (devoted to industrial arts, general business, homemaking, or general language study—introduction to foreign languages and cultures).

As in the elementary school, fewer periods do not necessarily mean fewer activities or areas explored. Chapter 13 describes in more detail the year's work of a tenth grade. The numerous and varied units and activities under way concurrently are illustrated in that chapter, particularly in the section which describes the work of the core class.

FLEXIBILITY IN SCHEDULING IS IMPORTANT AS SPECIAL NEEDS ARISE

While there is security for learners in a reasonably regular schedule, having the flexibility needed to meet the demands of the developing situation or concern is equally important. There will be times when the series of related activities necessary to move a project forward will require a longer time block. These variations from the regular schedule would be planned by teacher and learners together. While the plans on the blackboard for such days may give the impression that learners are being asked to concentrate on a problem for a period that exceeds their capacity to give attention, the activities encompassed by the period are usually quite varied. The following report of the day's work for a fifth grade at the point at which they faced a variety of problems related to their responsibility for the school store is illustrative.

What Appeared on Classroom Blackboard	What Took Place
9:00–11:00 Discuss store problems *a.* Overdrawn accounts of customers *b.* Size of orders to place *c.* Inability to handle groups of customers quickly	This group was responsible for the store in which the entire school bought such supplies as paper, pencils, notebooks, crayons, erasers, and the like. The discussion considered such items as steps the store management could take to prevent checks being returned by the school bank, marked "No funds"; how the entire school population could be made aware of their responsibility in this matter; how to estimate, through the records of preceding years, the amount of merchandise likely to be needed and the value of ordering these supplies in quantity; the failure to serve people quickly due to inability to make out sales slips and lack of speed in adding sale amounts. After the discussion, which lasted about an hour, the class broke into several groups—the store management to study the records of sales for the past years, some members to practice on improving addition skills, others to work on speed of legible writing, others to draft a communication to be sent to all customers regarding overdrawn accounts, and still another group to continue posting store accounts.
11:00–11:30 Outdoor play	Some members of the group returned to their classroom for midmorning lunch at 11:20.
11:30–1:00 Individual work	This period was used in a variety of ways by individuals. John and Mary continued posting the store accounts. Sue worked in the school library on a special report she was to make to the class later in the week. Jim rewrote the story he was submitting to the school paper. Eight students worked with the teacher on improving their skills in outlining materials they read. Later in the period, six other students worked with the

What Appeared on Classroom Blackboard	What Took Place
	teacher on problems of note-taking. Five students spent most of this period on a mural. Several spent part of the time doing leisure reading. Bobby, who had just returned to school after an illness, spent an hour resting in an adjoining room.
1:00–2:00 Lunch	Most of the children went to the cafeteria for lunch. Since weather permitted, the group spent time after lunch out of doors. A few returned to their room to play games or rest.
2:00–3:30 Discuss use to make of money made at paper sale	The group had been considering the welfare agency to which they would contribute the money made at the paper sale. Such agencies as the following had been mentioned—March of Dimes, Red Cross, international relief agencies, local community chest. Individuals and small groups had volunteered to report on the work of each of these agencies in terms of specific questions which the group as a whole desired to have answered.
3:30–4:00 Plan for the next day	At this period the class discussed the areas which should be considered on the day following and the time that seemed to be needed for each.

Later in the year, these same children faced an emergency created by having to give their play in assembly a week in advance of the time originally planned. As the group discussed the problem it was agreed that it would be necessary to spend practically all day, other than time for lunch and some recreation, on painting stage sets. The program for the day was, accordingly, very different from their usual schedule. On the board the following memorandum was listed:

9:00–11:00	Stage sets
11:00–11:30	Outdoors and midmorning lunch
11:30– 1:00	Stage sets
1:00– 2:00	Lunch and rest
2:00– 3:30	Stage sets
3:30– 4:00	Planning

Tired but satisfied children came together at 3:30 to check on progress and make plans for next steps.

The schedules for these two days differ quite distinctly from normal schedules. Ordinarily one would not expect ten-year-olds to concentrate for such long periods on a single problem. Yet these are programs that met the needs of the group at a particular point in their work. Not to have allowed the time would have meant failing to help these children to reach satisfying solutions to their problems. However, these were deviations from typical scheduling guided by a teacher who knew the needs and capacities of his group and who, over the weeks and months, checked for balanced growth on the part of each individual.

The same qualities characterize the program of the secondary school working on the same basic principles of curriculum development. Although it is not possible to cut across time blocks as readily when the help of specialists needs to be made available in definitely scheduled service courses, considerable flexibility can be achieved in the way a period is used from day to day. The following suggests the variety of activities in the daily schedule of an eleventh-grade group.

8:30–11:30 Core program Continue discussion of evaluation of the soundness of sources of information	This was one of a series of discussions that grew out of widely divergent newspaper accounts reporting the same specific incident. Starting with consideration of how to tell what influences are most likely to be reflected in the policy of a paper and how to evaluate the suggestions in editorials, the group was extending its discussion to include propaganda, sources that provide reliable information, the use of materials from various agencies of consumer research, and the nature and authenticity of advertising. The three-hour period included group discussion, listening and reacting to two reports, and committee work on other reports and aspects of the problem yet to be considered.
11:30–12:30 Physical education	
12:30–1:30 Lunch	
1:30–3:30 Service courses and laboratories	During this two-hour period the class group divided into sections according to special interests and abilities. Members were to be found in the art studio, the science laboratory, the business department, the music studio, in foreign language and mathematics classes.

This is flexible but not haphazard programing. Planning is an integral part of the process of scheduling; but the responsibility for planning has been shifted from more or less remote administrative control to the persons most concerned with carrying out the program—children and youth, and teachers who are working with them.

EFFECTIVE SCHEDULING DEPENDS ON PUPIL–TEACHER PLANNING AND CONTRIBUTES TO SOUND WAYS OF WORKING

The schedule grows out of, and is a part of, pupil–teacher planning. This is a way of working which helps learners to become self-directive in their activities because they understand what they are doing and the goals they are trying to achieve. It is a very different classroom pattern from the one in which the teacher leads most discussions, teaches most lessons to the class as a whole, makes the assignments (and probably corrects and grades most of them). The increased independence and self-direction of learners, which comes from experiences in which they play a mature role in planning, make it possible for the teacher to work with individuals and small groups as special needs arise. He works with the class as a whole, too, but he is frequently found helping a group locate materials, talking over a gifted child's special plan, working with a group having difficulty with spelling, helping another group making an enlarged map to work out correct proportions. Learners are not receiving less help by this system of scheduling and planning. Rather, they are getting more intensive help directed toward their special problems. At the same time, they are developing work habits, initiative, and problem-solving abilities important in later life.

Using Organized Bodies of Subject Matter

If experiences are selected and developed in the manner that has been indicated, will there not be great gaps in learners' knowledge? While they delve deeply into information related to whatever problems they undertake, over the year many different areas may be involved. Will they stay with any one subject field sufficiently long to build comprehensive understanding? How can there be any sense of the chronology of history, of the interrelated aspects of chemistry as a field of knowledge? Will a young person who has grown up under this type of curriculum designing not be woefully handicapped when he goes on to college? How will logi cally organized bodies of subject matter be used?

LEARNERS MUST BE HELPED TO APPRECIATE THE WEALTH OF FACTUAL DATA AVAILABLE

One major safeguard against superficial knowledge is the fact that children and youth will be helped to draw, as deeply as their maturity allows, on the various areas of knowledge. As they work with the problems and situations of everyday living, learners must be helped to grow in appreciation of the wealth of factual data available to them. This, of course, will not happen by accident. Teachers have several responsibilities if learners are to develop wholesome respect for the vast accumulation of knowledge which comprises their cultural heritage. First, there is a responsibility to help learners develop wider and deeper insights by bringing new aspects of the problem to their attention and turning them to resources of which they have not been aware. No study stops at the level of the learners' first understanding. Second, teachers have a responsibility to make materials available and to suggest sources of information pertinent to the situations with which learners are dealing. Of all types of curriculum design, this is the one that demands the widest variety of resources and their most flexible use. Third, the teacher and, for that matter, the entire school faculty are responsible for providing the rich and stimulating environment that helps achieve balanced development, and for helping learners become aware of the many resources in their community. Fourth, and perhaps most crucial, the teacher is responsible for extending his own knowledge and information. It is particularly important for him to orient his knowledge so that what he doubtless learned as part of a subject field is seen in its relation to the many persistent problems of living. If there is any difference in learners' awareness of the wealth of information available to them and their feelings of responsibility for using it accurately and wisely to solve their problems, this curriculum design is likely to lead to heightened interest in broader areas of knowledge. No field of knowledge is closed at any time to learners who need to use it and can profit from it. No field remains untouched for long if teachers are helping learners deal with the range of situations which they face.

LEARNERS MUST BE TAUGHT THE SKILLS OF PROBLEM-SOLVING AND OF LOCATING RESOURCES

A basic premise underlying the proposed curriculum design is that there will be constant attention to the skills needed to locate and evaluate resources and to problem-solving techniques. From the beginning children are helped to clarify a problem, to decide what resources to tap to locate needed information, to be critical in deciding whether their problem has been solved or their goals have been reached. Learners who have the ability to secure necessary data and to appraise its accuracy and pertinence possess a skill that will help open new fields of knowledge and a fundamental safeguard against shallow thinking based on too little evidence.

As learners mature, the resources they use will change. The small child may turn more often to human resources—parents, teacher, others with special knowledge—and to the concrete evidence of his immediate environment. As he grows older he uses reference books, maps, exhibits, motion pictures, television, more complex community resources. The youth may consult more difficult and varied reference books, newspapers, magazines, scientific publications, and a wider range of community resources. He faces even more complex problems of authenticating his source, identifying propaganda techniques, distinguishing a proven fact from a theory.

In helping learners develop the skills needed to secure accurate information appropriate to their problem, the teacher has several responsibilities. First, he must practice in his teaching the problem-solving skills he is trying to develop. He must challenge inaccurate statements or vague generalizations, question the use of unreliable authority, refuse to allow a group to accept glibly-voiced opinion as a fact. Second, he must identify the problem-solving skills his learners need and provide whatever practice seems necessary. With some classes this might become a separate problem for group study—a fourth grade takes time to find how to use the encyclopedia accurately, a sixth grade learns to use techniques of historical research to find why the dates in two books differ, a tenth grade spends several weeks analyzing propaganda techniques. Third, the teacher himself must be aware, and help learners become aware, of the areas in which it is possible to come to conclusions and those in which it is not, and of the problems on which the specialist must be consulted. One does not reach an absolute conclusion on American foreign policy, for example. This is an area which demands specialization and in which, because of the complex human relations involved, even specialists disagree. Neither does one reach a conclusion on the best way to prevent a smallpox epidemic without consulting a specialist. Here, however, the scientific answer is not open to as much speculation. Fourth, the teacher must help learners become aware of the ways in which problem-solving techniques are used in the various subject disciplines—to appreciate the work of the scientist, the historian, the archeologist, the artist. Learners who have basic respect for problem-solving techniques have developed attitudes toward the importance of accurate information which are essential safeguards against inadequate solutions of problems.

The ways of working with learners described in this volume do not allow for a superficial approach to knowledge, for "snap" judgments, for majority decisions without information, for voting in situations where learners do not possess the information needed to make the vote meaningful. Accuracy, careful thinking, and a willingness to withhold judgment are required.

EACH NEW SITUATION MUST BE APPROACHED SO THAT KNOWLEDGE NEEDED FOR ACCURATE CONCEPTS IS ACQUIRED

Even if learners are helped to appreciate the wealth of information available and possess the skills to locate it, won't there be gaps in knowledge? Won't youth come to a problem in high school classes with so little background in some fields that they will accept a superficial answer without recognizing it as such? Isn't it necessary to anticipate what knowledge they will need and make sure it is acquired? Part of the answers to these questions lies in the concept of persistent life situations; part lies in the learners' ability to acquire knowledge more rapidly with increased maturity; part is in the teaching techniques considered an integral part of this curriculum design.

As suggested in Chapter 5, because teacher and learners are working with persistent life situations, it would be virtually impossible for a problem to arise for the first time during adolescence or adulthood. Over the years the learner faces the same problem in more complex settings. The new information and understanding he acquires is added to what he already possesses, and a more inclusive concept results. At six the child learns something about costs when he finds what he can buy for mother's birthday for twenty-five cents; at ten, he decides whether he wants to own the cheaper or more expensive baseball glove and relates the cost to the hours he must mow grass; at fifteen he is budgeting an allowance to cover many of his incidental expenses. Each of these experiences builds on previous concepts and information. It is the persisting or recurring nature of the problems which guarantees there will not be gaps.

The proposed curriculum design is based, however, on the assumption that knowledge need not be assigned bit by bit to each grade level in order to have continuity in growth. It would be a misuse of the charts in Chapter 6 to allot one group of situations to first grade, another to second, and so on. Increased maturity brings added problem-solving ability and greater power to derive understandings from information. Some groups may develop concepts in a specific area through a number of short experiences as slightly different aspects of the same problem recur frequently. Other groups may develop the same concepts through a single comprehensive study. For example, in a school system in which there is a fixed cafeteria lunch for elementary school pupils, the problem of selecting a balanced lunch may not be studied until the junior high school grades. In another school, problems of selecting an appropriate lunch may have been important from first grade on, and seventh-graders may merely learn to apply concepts already well developed to problems of dieting for purposes of keeping slim, athletic training, and care of the complexion.

The way learners are guided as they approach a new problem provides another guarantee that gaps in learning will not occur. Learners must be helped to explore background information required for the development of as accurate concepts as their maturity will allow. The youth mentioned above, who face the problem of selecting a balanced meal for the first time in the junior high school, might explore questions of good nutrition in considerable detail. This does not mean that all learners, regardless of maturity and intellectual ability, would be encouraged to explore every situation widely and deeply. How much background information they acquire will depend on their maturity. The teacher builds as far as his learners' present capacities will allow, and then assumes that when the situation recurs and learners are more mature, new areas of knowledge can be tapped. If the problem is complex, first-graders might be satisfied with a simple explanation by the teacher; slow-learning nine-year-olds might be shown concretely what to do with little technical information; able twelfth-graders might explore the scientific concepts in the situation in considerable detail.

AWARENESS OF THE VALUES OF TRADITIONAL SUBJECT AREAS AS A MEANS OF ORGANIZING KNOWLEDGE SHOULD BE DEVELOPED

The fact that children and youth under this curriculum design will study subject matter as traditionally organized in a subject field less frequently does not mean that they will be unaware that such fields exist, that they will fail to see the relation of aspects of their particular problem to these fields, or that they will know less about the subject.

It would be almost impossible for learners in today's world to remain ignorant of the fact that knowledge has been traditionally organized in subject fields. In their school there may be a science laboratory, an art studio, a music room. From first grade on they hear about the history of their country. They read about atomic physicists, historians, mathematicians, philosophers. Older brothers and sisters in college are majoring in history, chemistry, the classics.

The teacher does many things to help learners see how the information needed in dealing with their problem or concern relates to a subject field. Members of a class may develop a sense of historical sequence as they add items to a time line from such discussions as the history of Columbus Day, the origins of the fossils in the stream near their school, the history of the airplane. As they turn to special bodies of knowledge, they are helped to see that physicists, historians, or archeologists have contributed the research that helps to answer their questions. Older learners, in dealing with the complex problem of foreign relations, may discuss the relationships between various disciplines as they discover that part of the reason people feel so strongly on this question is found in history while part is a matter of present economic conditions.

As learners mature intellectually, their understanding of the importance of traditional subject fields in the solution of problems will increase. The high school youth concerned with the controversy over the building of public or private dams on a river in his state will find that the origins of the issue are historical, social, political, economic, scientific, and that if he is to avoid argumentation and polemics he must dig into some or all of these areas for knowledge and insights. The class visiting the local steel plant may need to know more than "steel is refined iron ore" and may have to explore the various chemical processes involved, the laboratory procedures used during these processes, the organization of the physical plant as well as something about management, sales, research, and labor relations. A unit on genetics should send youth to a number of sources for information. If they are to conduct their own experiments on heredity, then learners may need some direct teaching of necessary skills in order to set up their study in a way which will contribute to problem solution. The traditional subject areas become sources to be drawn on as needed. With maturity and increased insights, children and youth understand how to use these resources.

OPPORTUNITY SHOULD BE PROVIDED FOR STUDYING SUBJECT MATTER AS AN ORGANIZED BODY OF KNOWLEDGE WHEN THIS IS NEEDED

All learners will undoubtedly have contact with blocks of information within given subject fields and some will need extensive contacts with one or more fields. How is the teacher, developing experiences with learners, to decide when these contacts are appropriate? On what bases does the teacher–counselor make his recommendation that extended work in a given subject area be planned? Two criteria were suggested in Chapter 5. First, the learner's purpose or problem should be one that can best be solved through extended contact with a given field. Second, he should have the maturity required to grasp the concepts that are being developed, to see how they relate to his problem, and to use them in subsequent everyday situations.

It is important to remember that contacts with a given field can be long or short, simple or complicated, depending upon the problem and the maturity of the learner. As suggested in the discussion of the program for high school youth in Chapter 7, learners will need opportunities to work with specialists in given fields for short and for extended periods.

At just what point it would be appropriate to help pupils engage in a systematic exploration of a subject field, or of a logically organized block of information from within a total field, will depend on the group and on the individual learner. In some cases the teacher will help learners secure the needed background as one part of a unit activity through opportunities for individuals or small groups to pursue a particular problem in greater depth and breadth. While, for its particular purposes, a class may need to understand only the basic concept underlying an electric computer, there may be students who want to know more. With teacher guidance, such students may explore number theories as these set limits to such computers, or analyze circuits, or even design and build a small device for personal use or for demonstration. Gifted youth particularly tend to like activities which increase their insights and understandings of basic concepts, relationships, and processes. As a result, they are willing to dig more deeply into traditional subject areas for the new meanings they can acquire for problem solution.

In other cases individuals or groups might be referred to a subject specialist or, under the guidance of the core teacher, undertake a study of a subject field. The elementary school child who has read historical novels of early America over the years may turn to a systematic study of colonial years, the Revolution, and the westward movement with marked appreciation. The seventh-grader who for years has been experimenting with chemistry sets may be eager for a more systematic opportunity to explore. A gifted twelve-year-old may announce his ambition to become a nuclear physicist. There will also be individuals with special talents and interests who will be ready to work with systematically organized bodies of subject matter—those with special ability in art or music, a long-standing interest in archaeology, for example.

Developing Fundamental Skills

If one were to visit, in sequence, classrooms in which separate subjects, broad fields, areas of living, and the curriculum design proposed in this volume govern the selection and guidance of experiences for children and youth, the greatest similarity, both in selection of activities and in teaching methods, would undoubtedly be found in the teaching of the so-called fundamental skills—to express oneself effectively orally and in writing, to understand the communications of others by listening and reading, to calculate.

What is known about the learning process suggests some criteria desirable in a program for the development of skills. Skills should be developed through situations where learners can see the need for them. They should be developed through situations as much as possible like those in which the skill will be used again. Activities and experiences should be adjusted to the needs of individuals. Ample and carefully planned practice should be provided at those points where it is needed. Learners should be helped to grow in understanding the principles underlying effective development and use of the skill. And pupils should know what they are trying to learn to do, why it is important, and how it can best be learned. Meeting these criteria requires programs of skill development that are flexible in terms of individual abilities, that use every appropriate opportunity during the school day for skill development, that use basal texts and work-type materials flexibly in the light of the total classroom situation, and provide for planning with learners and treating a problem of skill development in a fashion similar to any other problem-solving situation.

In the proposed curriculum design, the criteria named above would, perhaps, be applied somewhat more consistently and completely than under other curriculum patterns. The sequence of activities in each skill area will be guided by the teacher's and learners' identification of needs rather than by the organization in a basal text or workbook. Texts will be used flexibly as resources for information and for special practice rather than followed lesson by lesson. Spelling lists, for example, will come from daily writing needs, not from a text. Material in a language text on how to write a business letter will be consulted when needed rather than taken up as a special lesson. Day-by-day classroom experiences will be guides to identifying needs and providing practice.

Nevertheless, systematic efforts to develop basic skills will be necessary, and the scope of the skills program will be broader than that encompassed by the traditional three R's. The chart relating to the development of intellectual power [2] suggests that such abilities as listening, observing, planning, using appropriate resources in solving problems, and using a scientific approach to the study of situations are as important in meeting the problems of daily living as are reading, using language to communicate ideas, and computing.

[2] See pp. 194 to 213.

THE WHOLE SCHOOL DAY CONTRIBUTES TO SKILL DEVELOPMENT

Every part of the school day can contribute to skill development. Children and youth use numbers in counting the cost of refreshments for their parties, in purchasing gifts, in buying books and other school supplies. Their work often calls for measuring, working with fractional amounts, estimating costs, and keeping accounts. They are learning something of number relationships, percentage, and proportion when they read graphs and charts relating to social questions such as the number of persons living in substandard housing or the proportion of travelers carried by train, ship, bus, or airplane. In planning the daily schedule and in carrying out their activities learners budget their time.

From the first grade on, children read notices on the bulletin board, directions on the library table, captions under pictures, names on possessions, letters to be sent home, and many other printed messages. As they mature, the demands of the situations they face broaden their reading experiences. They need to consult books to find what different authors have to say, to check an impression or an opinion. They need to take notes on readings to be shared with others. They read for recreation.

Individuals must express themselves clearly if others are to understand them and they, in turn, must listen critically. The group depending upon a pupil for one aspect of its study must be able to read his handwriting and understand his notes. Letters asking for information must be carefully phrased and properly spelled and punctuated. Discussion techniques are needed as groups explore problems together—how to ask good questions, how to give constructive criticism, when to contribute, the need to give others a chance to speak, how to evaluate varied opinions, when to hold decisions tentatively, how to discriminate between superficial verbalization and comments backed by understanding and information.

SKILL DEVELOPMENT NEEDS ARE IDENTIFIED AS DAILY WORK PROCEEDS

As the teacher works with his group he identifies the skills in which they lack needed proficiency. Learners, too, help in this process. This means determining specifically the techniques that are inadequate in the present situation. For example, it is not enough to note that Allen, struggling with the problem of drawing a map to scale, seems unable to get proportions right. What does he need to know in meeting this situation? What command of fractions is involved? What concepts of proportion does he have? How well can he interpret scales? How ably does he use the four fundamental processes? What measurement concepts does he have, and how sound are his concepts of distance? How well does he use a ruler or other simple instruments for measuring? Similarly, the conclusion that Janet in grade two and Jerry in grade ten do not express themselves well before a group is too general to be of much use. Have they the vocabulary needed for clear expression? Can they organize words into clear sentences? What errors in usage are getting in the way? Is there difficulty with pronunciation or diction? To what extent is the problem that of judging what an audience would like to hear?

The last illustration points to another factor important in determining needed skills. Lack of proficiency must be interpreted in terms of maturity—one would not hold the same standards for Janet that one would hold for Jerry. In deciding on next steps the teacher thinks about what the individual is capable of accomplishing as well as what is demanded by the situation. In some cases the decision may be that the degree of skill required to meet the situation adequately is beyond the ability of the individual or group, but that certain attitudes and concepts can be acquired. A primary teacher, for example, would not deny a pupil the use of the word "locomotive" in a letter to a friend. Nor would the child be expected to master the spelling of the word before using it. If the word is written where he can copy it, he can be helped to develop the attitude that correct spelling is desirable. Copying the word correctly can contribute to the ability to analyze a word visually. Both are important in learning to spell. Skills are developed as far as the learner's maturity will permit.

Decisions on what specific techniques can be developed at any one time must be made by the teacher as he works with his class. However, a source of help in identifying the nature of the skills needed day by day can be found in the charts in Chapter 6. The section on intellectual power [3] suggests an organization of the persistent life situations calling for fundamental skills and names typical daily situations in which they recur. This limited selection of illustrations could have been expanded to include practically every situation in every other chart since these skills are a part of almost all aspects of daily life. The teacher, therefore, can also turn to the daily life situations listed as typical of other areas and study them in the light of the fundamental skills which they may demand.

The charts in the section on intellectual power become more functional for a particular class when the teacher looks at them in relation to the

[3] See pp. 194 to 213.

actual situations his group is facing. Part of the planning with regard to each aspect of the learners' activities as work progresses should include consideration of the skills needed, the learners' present effectiveness in their use, and the points at which further help is needed.

PROVISION SHOULD BE MADE FOR THE ORDERLY DEVELOPMENT OF SKILLS

Working toward increased competence, as learners face situations demanding it, does not mean haphazard teaching. There must be provision for the orderly development of skills. However, as defined in this volume, this refers to the order in which the learner needs increased skill, not to a preconceived sequence in a basal text. The persistent life situations requiring the use of intellectual power recur at all periods of life, as do all other persistent life situations. Listening, observing, reading, making ideas clear to others, and the like stretch back into very early childhood. As the learner matures, what changes is the complexity of the situation and the degree of competence needed. With identification of the letter with which his name begins, the five-year-old has begun to use a technique of word analysis that he will refine later in both reading and spelling. The process of division does not start in the intermediate grades but rather when the child first separates anything into two or more parts. Addition has its roots in the first time he says, "Can I have another?" Some idea of the decimal system is gained when Jimmy gets ten pennies in exchange for his dime. Letter-writing begins when two-year-old Sally is helped to make her mark on the letter her mother has written thanking Grandma for the new doll. As situations requiring skills become more demanding, skills become more complex and greater efficiency and more accurate short-cut methods are needed.

Sequential development of skills takes place as the basic techniques called for in some form at every maturity level are refined. This may come somewhat slowly through a series of related situations, each slightly more complicated than the last, or it may come rather quickly when a more difficult task calls for a major reorganization of techniques. Experimentation in the skill areas casts doubt upon the once-accepted idea that an exact number of sequential steps is needed by every child. For example, one ten-year-old could develop considerable skill with fractions under a series of able teachers, each of whom used every classroom situation requiring the use of fractions to build a little more insight. A second ten-year-old, without having had this rich experience, could develop many of the same concepts in a four-week block of intensive work with fractions. In each case, all the experiences leading to accurate concepts have been provided—in the one instance over several years, in the other, in concentrated form.

To develop skills in terms of the demands of new situations, teachers must be thoroughly familiar with the techniques that contribute to competence in each skill area, the ways in which these techniques are interrelated, and the times at which they are most suitably emphasized. A first-grader may use some of the techniques of word analysis to recognize his name but this does not necessarily mean that much emphasis on word analysis and phonetics is appropriate before he has gained enough familiarity with words to be able to identify common sounds when he meets them. A little later, however, it will become very important to stress the techniques of independent word analysis. Skill in dictionary use is not vital in the first stages of spelling. By the intermediate grades, children have enough spelling ability to make it highly desirable to be able to check with the dictionary. The third-graders reading for information have skills appropriate only to the simplest note-taking and outlining. By junior high school, reading abilities are usually refined to the point where it is appropriate to polish such reference skills. The teacher senses when the demands of the situation call for increased skill and whether the learners' present maturity and command of more basic techniques will make additional growth possible. The teacher also decides what experiences will be needed to reach the new level of competence. The sequential development of skills is not denied by this way of working. Responsibility for providing the most appropriate sequence is merely shifted from the specialist who writes the textbook to the teacher who has both special understanding of how the skill develops and insights into the backgrounds and abilities of particular learners.

Growth in skills will continue on into high school, into college, and beyond. The problems normally faced when a child reaches the eighth grade do not call for the competence he will need as an adolescent or an adult. To try to develop adult competence by the end of elementary school is to give practice in isolation which will not necessarily result in understanding the value of the new technique or ways in which it can be used. Perhaps more important, techniques developed in artificial classroom settings when daily life does not call for their use will not be exercised often enough in the daily life of the child to maintain competence. It is almost impossible to keep the many skills required by older learners at high levels of competence by drill alone. As a result, the teacher of the high school class in which techniques first become important may find that little of the previous learning has persisted. If elementary school personnel help children build the skills they will use repeatedly in the situations they actually face, they will go to high school with the ability to use them effectively. This is the sound basis needed by the high school staff as they help learners extend skills and develop the new ones demanded by the increasingly complex situations learners face.

PRACTICE IS IMPORTANT FOR PROFICIENCY IN SKILLS

Proficiency in skills is attained only with practice. This is equally true of the fourteen-year-old striving to improve his tennis serve and of his pal whose accuracy in arithmetical computation is low. However, practice must be planned in relation to individual needs and to the total amount of experience offered in the classroom setting.

Many valuable opportunities for practice are provided through situations in which the skill is actually needed throughout the day and week. For example, opportunities to practice reading skills literally surround the third-grade children who have a bulletin board listing events of the day and long-term plans; who write their daily plans on the blackboard; who receive a letter from an absent classmate; who follow the directions printed in their library corner; who read an announcement for the next assembly program; and who, in addition, are surveying all the materials they can find to learn about the birds feeding at their station.

Some children will need little more than the practice gained through daily activities, while others will require varying amounts of additional drill. How much will depend on the individual learner. Some children grasp a principle when it is first explained and apply it effectively from that point on; others need several days or weeks of help to reach the same degree of proficiency. This does not mean that work on skills must be completely individualized. There will be many times when several class members will have approximately the same need and will work together. There will also be times when the whole class will face a common need for more skill—a new set of reference books all want to use, a map on which projected proportions should be accurate, or a new type of graph to interpret. In all probability, however, the needs of individuals will be met more effectively through flexible grouping and greater small-group activity than is now the case in many classrooms. Such groups would work together for more varied lengths of time—a special-help group in spelling for five weeks; a handwriting session twice a week for a month for five youngsters; a group of poor readers working together, with help, on a difficult reference text needed in a particular unit of work.

The point at which the practice should be given depends upon when the child or group first faces a series of situations in which the more complex ability is needed. In the occasional situations which demand maturity well beyond that of the learners, the skill aspect of the problem would be solved by the teacher. One would not, for example, attempt to teach the details of long division to a first-grader. Help here is more appropriately on the purpose for dividing, with the teacher doing the necessary calculations. At about the fourth grade, where the process is required more often, learners need the practice that results in skill in using long division effectively.

Scheduling of time for practice will depend on the group's activities. In the fifth-grade schedule, discussed in an earlier section, part of the necessary practice was secured during group work on the major class activity, the store. In this case the success of the store depended, in part, on the children's effective grasp of arithmetic principles. Other practice was provided during an afternoon period when children worked on a variety of skills. Sometimes developing a necessary skill may itself become a major activity as happened in a fifth grade in which the teacher helped the children to see that their carelessness in taking notes was impeding much of their work. Other aspects of the unit took second place temporarily and the group took time to discuss what was involved in good note-taking and to practice. Spelling, outlining, summarizing, handwriting, and use of a simple bibliographical form were all involved. After these basic skills had received some attention other activities again became central. But the class continued to be highly critical of the form of each report by identifying weaknesses, and got further practice through daily activities which called for the taking and using of notes.

Some practice will be individual, some will be in small groups, some will involve the whole class. In a first grade of any size, for example, initial help in reading is usually given in small groups. Children who are at somewhat the same level of development work together and meet regularly. At this stage, where so much that must be grasped is complex, regular and frequent help is warranted. Even here, children will at times work together as a class as they read a report of their activities which they dictated as a permanent record or help to phrase a note to parents. At times they will work individually on special library books or practice materials. By the fifth grade it is quite possible that only a few children who find reading very difficult will be working as a regular group. The others may come together in a wide variety of groupings as they encounter special problems in the reading they are doing for other purposes, engage in recreational reading, or use the stories in a basal text for dramatization or for other kinds of practice. This same flexibility is typical of the grouping used to develop any other skill.

Flexibility in grouping allows individuals to proceed at their own rates and to secure special help as needed. Pupils who grasp a process quickly can use their time to better advantage than in drill they do not need. Those who have difficulty should have special help in situations where the teacher does not feel that his step-by-step explanations are delaying the work of the more able.

The materials used for practice will be any which prove helpful in explaining the process and in giving needed experience but will be used in relation to the situation faced and the needs of the learner. Seldom will the sequence in the textbook or workbook be followed from page to page. These materials will become resources, used in the order in which learners need them. Textbooks and supplementary books built to serve as references are needed if the skills are to be developed in this fashion. When pupils have texts in which they can look up the correct form for a business letter or the methods of reducing fractions to decimals, they possess tools which aid immeasurably in their skill development.

LEARNERS NEED TO SHARE IN PLANNING FOR SKILL DEVELOPMENT

The flexibility of a skill development program such as that just described is only possible when children and youth share in the planning. The pupil who knows what he is trying to learn to do, why it is important, and what kind of practice he needs can take a major part in the direction of his own activities. This does not mean less teacher guidance; rather it frees the teacher from routine supervision and allows him to spend full time giving help.

Planning with learners is done partly through group activity in which the teacher helps them identify the skills they lack in the same way as they identify the information required to solve any other type of problem. Plans are made for skill practice just as they are made to follow up any other concern. Periodic checks on progress through discussion and a variety of informal tests will be needed with teacher and learners working together on such evaluations. In addition, learners will be helped to make their own plans and evaluate their own progress. Personal lists of spelling words and compilations of frequent usage errors may be made by each child. Special work sheets for practice in various arithmetic fundamentals may be made available. Individuals may be helped to discover ineffectual aspects of their work habits, methods of discussion, or use of resources, and may add these to their special list of things to be worked on. When learners take an active interest in improving their own skills the effectiveness of the teacher's guidance is increased.

Materials and Equipment for Maximum Growth

The school experiences, described in this and in preceding chapters, call for a wide variety of teaching materials and resources. Because particular topics are not assigned to particular grades, it is no longer possible to designate a filmstrip, a textbook, or a movie as having fourth- or sixth-grade content. What is known about the typical interests and insights of a six-year-old as compared with those of an adolescent serves as a practical guide to the types of information and firsthand experiences likely to be of most value for each age group. Nevertheless, an able second-grader might well engage in activities normally not of much concern to children before they are nine or ten. If he does, the second-grader should have necessary resources available. The same resource may serve varied purposes for learners of different maturities.

Learning to use resource materials effectively is itself a persistent life situation. Just as the experiences of participating in planning and scheduling the day's activities contribute to skills important to the learner in today's world, so do experiences in selecting and using materials.

SCHOOL MATERIALS THAT CONTRIBUTE TO A WIDE VARIETY OF PROBLEMS ARE NEEDED

Few of the experiences proposed in preceding chapters can be effective if reading is the only means of securing information. Within the classroom and school setting a wide variety of resources should be available—pictures, films, filmstrips, recordings, collections, artifacts that can be handled, models, charts, maps, graphs, science equipment, to name some.

Many aspects of school life not usually thought of as teaching aids become so when learners are helped to grow through situations they actually face. For example, children and youth can build fundamental understandings in the area of health as they share in the findings of health examinations and have opportunities to analyze the reasons behind the procedures of the school nurse or doctor. Other insights are acquired as pupils take responsibility for securing medical help for themselves and learn principles of simple first aid. Still other learnings come as they share in setting up an environment which contributes to health in daily living—adjusting seating and lighting to meet individual needs, helping to make the school lunchroom more attractive, using materials and equipment which develop interests and skills in wholesome recreation. Washroom facilities, attractive lunchrooms, play equipment, adjustable classroom furnishings—all help build health understandings. In other areas, too, the services and facilities provided children and youth can make significant contributions to learning when teacher and learners make full use of them for this purpose.

School equipment should be selected and used so as to contribute to skills needed in our technological society. Responsibility for using the radio, projectors, the phonograph, the tape recorder, the mimeograph, typewriters, shop equipment, the motion picture; opportunity to investigate new appliances in the lunchroom; acquaintance with the school heating and ventilating system; opportunity to help repair simple equipment —all offer experiences valuable in modern living. These experiences contribute much to learners' understanding of the world about them, influence the attitudes they build toward the changes going on in society, and contribute to appreciation of the part the machine plays in life today. At the high school and even at the upper elementary level these experiences may include vocational education for those who need it. Shops and laboratories equipped and staffed to provide for increased facility with and understanding of the world of machines should be available to all learners.

The classroom environment itself should be stimulating. A science corner, a sharing table, a bulletin board for current events items, plants, an aquarium, a terrarium, a library table on which new books are displayed, a poet's or writer's scrapbook or special bulletin board, a puppet theater, paints, clay, a play corner for younger children—these and many others enrich the school lives of learners in the elementary grades. Special bulletin boards, social and game rooms, studios or laboratories in which individuals or groups can explore, experiment, and engage in using art, science, music, and other media, are an important part of high school living. From the interests they arouse and the problems they pose come some of the most profitable long- and short-term units of work.

It is particularly important that the classroom environment be rich in areas in which children's experiences have been limited. A five-year-old from an underprivileged home may spend a large share of her first days in kindergarten washing and pressing doll clothes, dusting the play corner, and rearranging the furniture. Children whose musical experiences at home are limited should have opportunities to explore musical instruments at school. A high school group with limited cultural backgrounds may need the experience of entertaining in the well-appointed homemaking facilities. School experiences should not merely help the learner meet the problems he faces in his out-of-school world. They should also expand his horizons and challenge new interests.

A wealth of audio-visual materials and other concrete resources does not in any way reduce the need for books. Because the problems faced by learners do not as a rule fall within typical subject lines or fields, it will be virtually impossible to operate within a single text in any area. Smaller numbers of a greater variety of books are needed as resource materials. The small paperbound books on single topics now appearing in the social and natural science fields, for example, can be very useful. Encyclopedias, dictionaries, almanacs, and other standard reference books are important. School and public libraries can supply biographies, science books, historical novels with authentic descriptions. Daily newspapers, special news reports for children, maps, booklets obtained from civic and industrial organizations, current magazines, are still other kinds of reading material important when situations of everyday life are the basis for school experiences.

Materials used to develop skills in reading, computation, spelling, and language should be equally varied and flexible. It is just as important under the proposed curriculum design, as it is under any other, to provide for a range of abilities. This means smaller sets of books covering several grade levels. Then, too, because the textbook or workbook in number or language will be used as a resource book on a specific problem, it is important to have books where topics are clearly discussed and easy to locate. A textbook or workbook that cannot be used effectively unless its suggested activities are followed in sequence has limited value. Because skill will develop, in part, as teacher and learners set up special practice activities, a variety of work-type materials that can be used flexibly for short practice sessions is very helpful. Books to aid in the development of skills, like reference books, need to serve ongoing experiences, not to govern them.

RESOURCES IN THE OUT-OF-SCHOOL ENVIRONMENT SHOULD BE TAPPED

Any consideration of instructional materials must include those found in the immediate and larger community. Children and youth go on excursions, learn something about eroded land in the community, help in community beautification projects, use the various institutions of industry, attend commercial movies, and use various forms of community transportation. They read the local newspaper, watch television and listen to the radio, and have contacts with community members who come to school for a variety of purposes. The school has a responsibility to guide learners in the use of the community resources which are a part of their experiences.

In addition, the community offers rich resources with which to supplement those of the school in many situations of concern to learners. Teachers talk about budgeting income in terms of realistic family expenditures, banking in terms of the policies of the local bank, government in terms of town affairs. A fifth grade responsible for managing the school store turns to local merchants for guidance in displaying their materials and in keeping their books. Sixth-graders follow the local election in the daily paper, over the radio, through the handbills and printed materials which circulate in the community. A tenth grade seeks information about soil erosion from the new developments in the community, turns to the local legislature to learn about government control of health, and visits the city power plant to follow up some of their questions about electricity. Children in a first grade learn to make simple purchases wisely by going to the local stores and satisfy their curiosity about wild birds by visiting the nearby park.

Some high schools have experimented with more extended contacts with the life of the community through work experiences and through travel. Youth learn about the work of the world, their obligations to employers, the needs of working groups, and the demands of the job by actually working on a job. High school classes have on occasion been able to go to other communities and to live in them for a period of time, becoming acquainted with differing mores and patterns of community action. Week-end trips to the state capitol or other interesting places are quite common.

Community resources also help in understanding situations originating beyond the immediate locality. A group interested in the reports of an invention which has resulted in great saving of time and labor in a textile plant may turn to the industries of their own community to find what similar advances have been made. High school youth following the reports of scientific developments used to improve housing study the projects in their city. A tenth grade concerned about national proposals to provide for the health of working groups investigates what is already being done by their city council. A third grade concerned about a newspaper report of a very serious fire calls upon a representative of the local fire department to see what might have been done to prevent it and to find out what regulations for fire prevention their town has.

Community resources may come into the school as often as learners go into the community. Teachers and pupils call upon parents who have traveled for pictures and articles typical of life in other countries, as well as for firsthand descriptions. They know of the rock collection or the exhibit of butterflies owned by local naturalists. They ask parents and other community members to share their hobbies—a collection of dolls from other lands, the products of a father's workbench, paintings, music, and many others. From the exhibits and pamphlets prepared by local agencies come other resources—a series of pictures or a display showing the steps in the development of a product, a number of bulletins from an experimental farm, government publications. The loan collection from the public library and the exhibit from the natural history or art museum are used so often in this fashion that they need no further mention here.

It is not possible to consider ways of drawing upon community resources without including the adults who are so frequently involved. Many persons who are not members of the professional staff have special competence upon which the school can draw. As community members with whom children and youth associate they can supplement the work of the school. Representatives of various groups—the doctor, nurse, lawyer, engineer, plumber, mechanic, farmer—contribute information about the occupations they represent, and also specialized knowledge about the fields in which they work. Many constructive attitudes toward health can be built in the doctor's office. The plumber who takes time to explain his job to the group of children watching him adds to their growing knowledge of tools and machines. The factory worker can contribute information about technological advances as they affect his occupation. Learners' understanding of the necessity for legal protections can be heightened by their acquaintance with the local judge or the police officer who gives a sound interpretation of the responsibilities of his position. The superintendent of schools can increase student understanding of the function of organized education, the city manager can offer information about community planning. These persons have more detailed information about their special fields than the teacher–specialist whose competence must encompass other areas. Children and youth need this help.

Adults with special talents or interests—musicians, artists, writers, persons with special gifts for interior decoration, woodwork, and adults with unusual hobbies—can also supplement the work of the school. The father who shares his workbench with the boys of the community, or who comes to the school to give special help on a class project, shares a teaching responsibility with the school. The musician who brings his instrument to school and talks with children about it enhances their musical appreciation. A parent interested in photography not only shares an interesting hobby but can add to aesthetic sensitivity, to understanding of the qualities of a good picture, and to knowledge of the scientific processes involved. The special backgrounds of parents and other community members can often make a rich contribution to the school. Parents or grandparents who were born in other countries may be able to provide firsthand information. Community members who have lived in other parts of the country can help learners understand sectional problems. Teachers who are concerned with developing learners' potentialities should be alert to the sources of stimulation and guidance offered by the community.

No discussion of the community as a resource would be complete without reference to the necessity for helping learners discover the educational resources of the community and how they can contribute to special interests and hobbies, and thus to balanced living. Teachers can help learners explore aesthetic resources—a special art class, a puppet-making group, a children's theatre, children's concerts given by the local orchestra. Other possibilities are found in the public library's special services as well as in its books, in the classes in the museum as well as in its exhibits, in the parks, in the demonstrations on the nearby experimental farm. The programs of the various recreational centers, clubs, and youth groups can provide other valuable experiences. The school's responsibility lies in helping learners evaluate these resources—the value of a worthwhile motion picture, a fine news release, an hour of good music—as they bring their concerns about them to the school. Teachers also have a responsibility to help children and youth learn to use these resources in situations in which the school is not involved.

LEARNERS SHOULD SHARE IN THE SELECTION AND USE OF MATERIALS

A persistent problem of living is selecting materials appropriate to the situation at hand. If children and youth are to grow in this ability they should share in selecting materials, in developing plans for using them, and in organizing the physical surroundings in which they live. Potential learnings are many: how to know what sources to use; how to tell rather quickly whether a suggested source is fruitful; how to judge the soundness and reliability of a source; how to arrange materials and equipment with consideration for general attractiveness; how to plan physical surroundings with proper regard for lighting and other factors; how to store materials conveniently; how to conserve materials; and many others. These are problems which are the concern of learners of all ages, expanding as the situations which call for their use increase in complexity.

Still other learnings are possible if children and youth can share in purchasing materials and equipment. Too frequently the board of education, principal, or teacher assumes full responsibility for the selection and purchase of equipment and supplies, and deprives those using the materials of many learnings which come from taking some responsibility in this area. Standardization and centralization of purchasing may reduce the cost of some items, but this method denies valuable experiences to learners and in some cases is a negative factor restricting ideas which call for materials not "listed" or making it necessary at times to use materials not conducive to maximum learning. It is not possible to indicate in May many of the most important instructional materials which will be needed the following September. Basic materials may be ordered through a central office but a portion of the budget should be allocated to the school principal for expenditures by teacher and learners to meet needs as they arise. Supplementary funds can then be used for such purposes as sending for free materials; purchasing additional books, pamphlets, magazines; buying incidental materials needed for parties, construction, experimentation, or costuming.

Flexibility in provisions for obtaining materials and supplies is also necessary. Children and youth can learn much as they share in estimating the quantity of supplies needed, in requisitioning supplies and equipment, in selecting those that best fit their needs, and in anticipating needs so as to be able to secure materials when supply rooms are open. When materials are located in a central place, such as a school materials bureau, the community museum, or library, it is important that arrangements be made for keeping them in a given classroom as long as they are needed, for their prompt return when the need has been met, for a minimum of red tape in requisitioning, and for allowing teachers and class groups or individuals to select materials at their source.

There are also valuable learnings in helping to arrange a classroom. Children and youth can gain much in deciding how to achieve the most convenient working space. Concepts of good design can be developed through taking charge of bulletin boards. Some groups have even refinished battered furniture and made window drapes. Arranging desks so that there is proper light for reading can contribute to good health habits. Making one's surroundings attractive and convenient is a persistent life situation and classroom living has much to contribute.

OPPORTUNITIES SHOULD BE PROVIDED TO EXPERIMENT WITH MATERIALS IN MANY FIELDS

Entirely apart from their contribution to learners as classroom experiences unfold, materials can often add to enriched and balanced living. Children and youth should have available materials which will extend their creative abilities—materials for experimentation with different art media, musical forms, science concepts, foreign languages, dramatic forms. In many elementary school classrooms opportunities for creative work are provided in interest centers set up in various parts of the room. In both elementary and high schools, many valuable experiences can be offered through laboratories in charge of specialists whose schedules are flexible enough to allow time for work with individuals and small groups. Opportunities to develop hobbies and other deep and lasting interests are particularly important in a culture where most persons are facing increased needs to use leisure time wisely.

EQUIPMENT AND MATERIALS SHOULD BE PLANNED FOR FLEXIBLE USE

School equipment as well as materials should be selected and stored with flexible use in mind. This means, among other things, that facilities should be so arranged as to make possible easy communication between groups —elementary and high school, classrooms and laboratories for special work. Facilities should be such that the learner can manage them with a minimum of help—drinking fountains, toilet facilities, windows, playground equipment suited to each developmental stage. Space should be allotted within rooms for small groups and individuals to work on special interests. Ample storage space should be provided for materials and designed to meet the needs of those using them. Consideration also should be given to the necessity for providing for the many different aspects of the learner's growth—possibilities for many types of experiences, equipment which makes it possible to follow many different concerns. Other purposes for which the school is to be used must also be considered—the need for an auditorium for adults, special meeting rooms, equipment for after-school recreation or for vocational education.

Much of the equipment should be mobile. Radios, motion-picture machines, globes, maps, and other audio-visual materials should be available to all groups whenever they are needed. Many of the materials of studios and laboratories should be such that they can be used in the classroom in connection with the particular work under way. One contribution of the teacher who is a specialist might be the maintenance of an up-to-date collection of the most valuable materials in his particular field which could circulate among groups. In addition, teachers who share each other's regular classroom equipment find that in this pooling of resources much more can be available for all. Books, for example, as well as maps and special picture collections, can be lent to other classes. A central materials bureau may facilitate the collection of materials and make them accessible to the school as a whole.

Although mobile equipment, movable furniture, and a building with modern conveniences and colorful walls are desirable, much can be done toward effective curriculum development in buildings which are less functional units. Necessary modifications in the school plant can become the concern of learners and the community working together. Even in poorly planned buildings teachers with initiative and imagination can, with the help of students and parents, eliminate some of the negative aspects. Walls can be made clean and colorful, grounds can be beautified, health facilities can be improved. No effort should be spared to develop community consciousness of the necessity for adequate facilities and materials of instruction. The economy is such that the physical facilities and instructional materials required for the kind of education America wants for its children and youth can be made available.

Beginning the School Year

For the teacher who has not worked in terms of the situations faced by learners, the beginning of the school year may seem the most difficult time. Once an activity is under way it is usually easier to see others following; but how is the start to be made?

MEMBERSHIP IN THE SCHOOL COMMUNITY RAISES PROBLEMS FOR BEGINNING WORK

Working with learners on problems and situations growing out of their responsibilities in the school provides opportunity to begin the work of the year on activities purposeful to them. The school is, after all, their immediate and most important community. It is no imposition upon children or youth to encourage them to undertake activities which make them a part of this community while they learn. Such opportunities can be found in the school paper, the school traffic guard system, a school store or supply room, a lost-and-found department, an attractive bulletin board listing special school events, a school bank, the lunchroom, assembly programs, the library, a materials bureau. A class which has one or more such responsibilities may face from several days to several weeks of intensive group and individual work at the beginning of the school year. Often out of these activities arise other concerns which become the center of extended work. A class which is to publish the school paper may profitably study local papers and the responsibility of the press. The group concerned with suitable celebration of holidays may never before have had the opportunity to investigate historical backgrounds in relation to present-day meanings and implications. The lunchroom helpers may turn to a study of how to select foods of greatest nutritional value and how to decide on a balanced meal, or to a study of the changes needed to make the lunchroom a more attractive place. Teacher and learners, working together in the early fall on responsibilities such as these, can get to know each other, and the teacher can study the needs and concerns of individuals.

EACH CLASS FACES PROBLEMS OF GROUP LIVING

Other situations which arise early in the year come from needs to arrange the classroom for convenient work. Learners sharing in this process will face problems of how to arrange the desks for best lighting, where to put exhibits or collections, what is the most suitable organization of books, what purposes the bulletin board can best serve, what plant life is suited to the particular room conditions, what is needed to make the room attractive. A seventh grade, for example, took the opening days of school to find out what books were in the room and what purposes they served. From this came several days' discussion as to the value of the encyclopedia, the dictionary, and other such standard references, and how they might best be used. In the course of the discussion questions were raised as to how these materials were kept up to date and where one found the latest information. A rather thorough study of the magazines available in the school library and the kinds of information they were most likely to give followed. One result was a simple card file that pupils used all year.

If group members are new to each other and to the teacher, there are also problems of getting acquainted. One ambitious eighth grade published a four-page newspaper to which each class member contributed a six-line autobiography. Members of a sixth grade, artistically inclined, drew pictures of themselves enjoying their favorite summer recreation. The discussion in which these were shared led into a proposal that not enough people knew what fun it was to visit the public library, and plans were laid accordingly. With the teacher's help, a second grade made a rough map of the community on which the children marked their homes and the safest crosswalks to take to school.

There may also be problems of getting to know the school. Learners who are in their first year in junior or senior high schools must become acquainted not only with the physical setup of the school, the organization, the schedule, and the many offerings and resources, but also with the traditions of the student body. Such problems normally lead to short units only, but these are sufficient to develop feelings of group unity and to provide an opportunity for teachers to learn more about the needs and concerns of individuals and the group. Similarly, teachers of kindergartners and first-graders have much to do early in the year to help them become acquainted with the classroom and the school.

INTERESTING EQUIPMENT OR MATERIALS CAN BE A STARTING POINT

At times situations which merit further study center about objects brought into the classroom by learners, teacher, or circumstances. The new books on the library table launch many groups in new activities. A first grade, presented with a frog, spent considerable time learning how to feed and care for it. In one high school new equipment for work in ceramics led many pupils who had artistic inclinations to ask to be in the first group to receive direct instruction. A fourth grade discovered an opaque projector and spent an enjoyable two days sharing pictures of summer vacations. This led to a more extended study of national parks. Such units are not long, but they serve to help get acquainted. Paralleled by the experiences of planning for a school responsibility and making the classroom attractive and livable, and by some beginning activities in reading or language, they would help to make a varied and full day.

COMMUNITY LIFE THROUGH THE SUMMER TOUCHES THE SCHOOL

Learners bring to school all their summer experiences—the report of a trip, a new toy, a shell or rock collection, a new method of building bird houses, the story of a summer job. Elementary school teachers often plan for sharing or conversation periods in order to tap these interests. Homeroom sessions in high school sometimes serve this same purpose. Two types of units might develop from such sharing sessions. One would be the proposal to follow up some situation that strikes the interest of the group. The other would be to make more specific plans for such sharing periods—perhaps to set up a museum corner or to post travel pictures on the bulletin board.

Community developments may touch learners very directly. In one school the children returned in the fall to find new sewers being laid in the street beside the school. This interest led to a number of different activities, depending on the maturity of the classes concerned. In another school, a new annex was under way. Near a third, slums were being razed for a new housing development. Members of a high school heard during the summer that their building was to become a junior high school the following year. To what schools were they to go? What could they do to make this last year memorable?

Teachers working under this type of curriculum design are alert to the concerns learners bring to school. Some of these will involve only individuals or small groups, but some will be centers of interest for an entire class. Learners who live in the same community have many experiences in common which could conceivably become part of their school curriculum. Some of these experiences, uppermost in their thinking when they begin school in the early fall, lead to profitable early units.

ACTIVITIES MAY CARRY OVER FROM THE PRECEDING YEAR

Children and youth who spent the preceding year working under this type of curriculum design may have closed the term by recording phases of their activities which they should explore further and situations which they would like to investigate. They will return to school with questions they did not have time to look into the year before and with others which have arisen over the summer. Even before the group settles down to serious consideration of how best to begin the year, the teacher will have been approached with many different requests. From this point planning takes place much as usual.

A definite source of help to the teacher in studying the needs of his learners are the records of the previous year—if these are designed to provide data needed by teachers in this kind of program. Records can help in understanding the characteristics of the group, in noting individual interests and needs, in knowing the nature of previous experiences and the responses made to those experiences, in recognizing present competencies, and in locating shortages and gaps which former teachers felt were present. Study of the charts in Chapter 6 in relation to the records of learners' previous experiences may suggest other important learnings.

Basically, beginning the school year is a matter of capitalizing on the many types of concerns and interests that will be common to learners who are of about the same maturity, who live in the same community, and who face all the typical problems of getting acquainted and developing ways of living and working together that must be faced when thirty or more individuals share the same facilities. Learners come prepared to participate in beginning the year's work, and bring an accumulation of needs, interests, and concerns resulting from the lives they have lived and the experiences they have had. The teacher's share is to provide insight into the needs of the group—the result of a careful study of their records—and professional skill in understanding children and youth.

Related Readings

ALBERTY, HAROLD B. *Reorganizing the High School Curriculum.* Revised edition. New York: The Macmillan Company, 1953.

ALEXANDER, WILLIAM M., AND PAUL HALVERSON. *Effective Teaching in Secondary Schools.* New York: Rinehart & Company, Inc., 1956.

ANDERSON, VERNON. *Principles and Procedures of Curriculum Development.* New York: The Ronald Press Company, 1956.

ASSOCIATION FOR SUPERVISION AND CURRICULUM DEVELOPMENT. *Creating a Good Environment for Learning.* 1954 Yearbook. Washington, D.C.: The Association, 1954.

ASSOCIATION FOR SUPERVISION AND CURRICULUM DEVELOPMENT. *Guidance in the Curriculum.* 1955 Yearbook. Washington, D.C.: The Association, 1955.

ASSOCIATION FOR SUPERVISION AND CURRICULUM DEVELOPMENT. *The Three R's in the Elementary School.* Washington, D.C.: The Association, 1952.

BAXTER, BERNICE, GERTRUDE M. LEWIS, AND GERTRUDE M. CROSS. *The Role of Elementary Education.* Boston: D. C. Heath & Company, 1952.

BECK, ROBERT H., WALTER W. COOK, AND NOLAN C. KEARNEY. *Curriculum in the Modern Elementary School.* Englewood Cliffs, N.J.: Prentice-Hall, Inc., 1953.

BROGAN, PEGGY, AND LORENE K. FOX. *Helping Children Learn.* Yonkers-on-Hudson, N.Y.: World Book Company, 1955.

BURTON, WILLIAM H. *The Guidance of Learning Activities.* Second edition. New York: Appleton-Century-Crofts, 1952.

BUTLER, FRANK A. *The Improvement of Teaching in Secondary Schools.* Third edition. Chicago: University of Chicago Press, 1954.

CASWELL, HOLLIS L., AND ARTHUR W. FOSHAY. *Education in the Elementary School.* Third edition. New York: American Book Company, 1957.

EDUCATIONAL POLICIES COMMISSION. *Education for All American Youth; A Further Look.* Revised edition. Washington, D.C.: National Education Association, 1952.

FAUNCE, RONALD, AND NELSON BOSSING. *Developing the Core Curriculum.* Englewood Cliffs, N.J.: Prentice-Hall, Inc., 1951.

GANS, R., C. B. STENDLER, AND M. ALMY. *Teaching Young Children.* Yonkers-on-Hudson, N.Y.: World Book Company, 1952.

GRAMBS, JEAN D., AND WILLIAM J. IVERSON. *Modern Methods in Secondary Education.* New York: The Dryden Press, Inc., 1952.

HANNA, LAVONE A., GLADYS L. POTTER, AND NEVA HAGAMAN. *Unit Teaching in the Elementary School.* New York: Rinehart & Company, Inc., 1955.

HERRICK, VIRGIL E., JOHN GOODLAD, FRANK ESTVAN, AND PAUL EBERMAN. *The Elementary School.* Englewood Cliffs, N.J.: Prentice-Hall, Inc., 1956.

HURLEY, BEATRICE D. *Curriculum for Elementary School Children.* New York: The Ronald Press Company, 1957.

LANE, HOWARD, AND MARY BEAUCHAMP. *Human Relations in Teaching.* Englewood Cliffs, N.J.: Prentice-Hall, Inc., 1955.

LEONARD, J. P. *Developing the Secondary School Curriculum.* Revised edition. New York: Rinehart & Company, Inc., 1953.

LINDBERG, LUCILE. *The Democratic Classroom.* New York: Bureau of Publications, Teachers College, Columbia University, 1954.

MIEL, ALICE M., AND ASSOCIATES. *Cooperative Procedures in Learning.* New York: Bureau of Publications, Teachers College, Columbia University, 1952.

MIEL, ALICE, AND PEGGY BROGAN. *More Than Social Studies.* Englewood Cliffs, N.J.: Prentice-Hall, Inc., 1957.

MORRIS, GLYN A. *Practical Guidance Methods for Principals and Teachers.* New York: Harper & Brothers, 1952.

MOUSTAKAS, CLARK E. *The Teacher and the Child: Personal Interaction in the Classroom.* New York: McGraw-Hill Book Company, Inc., 1956.

NOAR, GERTRUDE. *The Junior High School Today and Tomorrow.* Englewood Cliffs, N.J.: Prentice-Hall, Inc., 1957.

OTTO, HENRY J. *Social Education in the Elementary School.* New York: Rinehart & Company, Inc., 1956.

TABA, HILDA, AND DEBORAH ELKINS. *With Focus on Human Relations.* Washington, D.C.: American Council on Education, 1950.

WEBER, JULIA. *My Country School Diary.* New York: Harper & Brothers, 1946.

WILES, KIMBALL. *Teaching for Better Schools.* Englewood Cliffs, N.J.: Prentice-Hall, Inc., 1952.

9

PROVIDING FOR INDIVIDUAL DIFFERENCES

A democratic society cannot afford to waste the potential talent of any individual. One of the two-edged problems facing educators in such a society is how to insure each individual's maximum development while providing for the skills and attitudes basic to the cooperative solution of common problems. Further, the democratic value of equality does not mean identical opportunities for all. If democracy is not to mean mediocrity, equal opportunity in education should not mean a common program for all. Talent is as truly wasted when the budding scientist or engineer drops out of school as it is when a slow learner is sent into the world unequipped for the work of which he is capable. Talent is also wasted if a learner has neither opportunity nor encouragement to pursue a special interest, whether this interest is music, art, wild life, mechanics, science, cooking, ancient history, or any other socially valuable area.

How does the proposed curriculum design accommodate individual differences? Three questions suggest themselves. What is implied for the grouping of learners? What is implied for meeting individual needs within the regular classroom setting? What special adjustments are called for in meeting the needs of the exceptional pupil? The general direction of solutions to these problems has been touched upon at various times in the three preceding chapters. This chapter attempts to synthesize the suggestions.

Functional Grouping of Learners

In spite of research on individual differences, the question of how to group learners is still one of the most controversial faced by educators. A candid appraisal of the arguments often used to support one procedure or to criticize another indicates misunderstanding of the issues involved, both by the public at large and by educators themselves.

While research data regarding individual differences exist, there is little conclusive evidence to elevate one way of grouping learners above any other. It is necessary for teachers, administrators, and the public to have a clear picture of the differences among individuals and of the goals likely to be achieved within a given procedure for grouping.

ANY PROPOSAL FOR GROUPING MUST BE MADE IN THE LIGHT OF KNOWN FACTS REGARDING INDIVIDUAL DIFFERENCES

One fallacy underlying some discussions of grouping of learners is the assumption that there is even development in all aspects of an individual's growth. It is assumed, for example, that grouping pupils on the basis of intelligence scores will place all the able readers, the best mathematicians, and the most mature learners in the same group. While there is a positive correlation between intelligence and these other factors, these relationships hold only for large numbers of youngsters and not necessarily for an individual pupil. An attempt to classify learners on the basis of intellectual ability may not substantially reduce the range of reading or arithmetic skills. Similarly, classification by reading scores could place together in a group both an intellectually able child with a temporary difficulty in learning to read and an efficient reader with somewhat limited intellectual ability.

It is possible to reduce the range of abilities and group learners for specific teaching purposes, but such groupings should be recognized for what they are—a reduction in range of differences in some particular abilities. No matter what criteria are used for grouping the class will still include individuals with a wide variety of interests and aptitudes, abilities and motivations. In this sense, there is no really homogeneous group but merely a group which has been selected on the basis of certain similarities.

Where more than one section of a grade or class is to be formed, naturally some kind of selection process must be used. This may be entirely random choice or it may be based on more or less specific criteria. Whatever combination of criteria is used, the limitations must be kept in mind. If a typical intelligence test is readministered, for example, it would not be unusual for the intelligence quotients of at least half of the class to vary ten points or even more. The longer the time lapse between the first and second tests, the greater the variation is likely to be. Even a competently administered, individual test score may vary as much as five points from one testing to the next. The standard error of measurement on most tests is such that a youngster scoring 118 may be as able as one who scores 123. Furthermore, intelligence, like most human capacities, is so distributed that many more individuals are clustered around the mean, or average, than are found at the extremes. Setting up two so-called homogeneous groups on the basis of intelligence test scores, then, actually separates the few learners at each end of the scale, makes a possible distinction in a few others, and classifies either as A or B students many who might, on a retest, appear to be candidates for the alternate group.

Similarly, a score on a reading test does not indicate by itself whether the child is on a plateau or in a period of accelerated growth. Neither does it always indicate whether the score was earned by painstakingly slow work—correct as far as the time allowed—or rapid but inaccurate work. Further, a score on a reading test does not, alone, show whether a child has limited intellectual ability and will acquire new skills slowly, or whether he is likely to forge ahead rapidly. Such limitations characterize the scores on almost any standardized test that might be used for grouping purposes. Attempts to combine or average scores in order to use two or more criteria do not necessarily solve the problem and sometimes hide important factors which affect success in learning.

Chronological age, which is a familiar basis for grouping, is no more likely to guarantee a class with similar interests, abilities, or even physical development than any other basis for grouping. Eight-year-old Jean, in the third grade, with a recorded IQ of 135—reading sixth-grade books, tall, heavy, eager to play with nine- and ten-year-old neighbors in her block—may be much more at home in school in an older group. Her classmate, Sally, of approximately the same age and IQ, may be small, physically immature, timid, and likely to seek the companionship of six- and seven-year-olds at play. Transferring Sally to a nine-year-old group would place her in a situation where she could make few, if any, social contacts except through her intellectual ability. Under the type of classroom activities through which Sally can be given ample opportunity to use her alert intellectual curiosity, her total development is likely to be much better rounded if she remains with eight-year-olds where she will feel more secure socially.

These are some of the facets of individual differences. They suggest that no matter what the system of classifying learners, teachers must be prepared to provide individual and small-group experiences to meet individual needs. They also make it clear that the problem of setting up class groups is extremely complicated and cannot be solved by referring to the results of some test scores.

ANY METHOD OF GROUPING SHOULD BE APPRAISED IN THE LIGHT OF VALUES HELD

Discussions of the pros and cons of various methods of grouping learners often seem to stress only one of the many values the schools are actually seeking to achieve for children and youth. Those who are most vehement about so-called homogeneous groups usually stress academic progress. These persons talk about not holding back or neglecting the able child and about giving slow learners a fair chance. On the other hand, those who argue for heterogeneous grouping tend to talk about the democratic value of equal opportunity for all. This ideal is sometimes misinterpreted to mean that all learners should have identical experiences. Actually, what is desired is the development of skills and attitudes important in working cooperatively with other persons of all levels of ability. However, there is nothing that makes the chronological age group uniquely valuable as a means of developing these techniques. It could be argued that the development of the skills needed in cooperative action cannot be achieved without many experiences with groups of chronological ages different from one's own.

Effective grouping, in terms of meeting the goals of the proposed curriculum design, should achieve three aims. First, opportunity should be provided for the maximum development of individual capacities—for developing areas of interest and ability and for strengthening weaknesses. Learners should have the stimulation of others whose abilities and interests are similar and the opportunity, if needed, for step-by-step guidance in a group working at the same pace. They should have experiences which are challenging and yet within their range of successful attainment.

Second, opportunity should be provided for development of those skills in social relationships essential in a democratic society—for developing ability in leadership and followership, and in playing other roles such as that of an authority or a questioner in groups of varying abilities, capacities, and needs. To develop these skills, learners need opportunities to work with groups where the contributions of the various members are quite different—where Bill's precise plans can be appreciated although he needs help with his reading; where Jill, who knows all the answers, discovers that others' opinions also have to be respected; where Dale, who learns very slowly, is recognized as just the right person to carry out a simple but responsible part in the class project.

Third, opportunity should be provided for development of wholesome attitudes regarding one's self and others—becoming realistic about one's strengths and weaknesses as well as appreciating those which others bring to a group enterprise. Self-understanding is important for seeing one's obligation to society and for self-fulfillment. The pupil who constantly excels and dominates his group may actually not possess the competence needed to contribute significantly to a more able class. He needs to develop a realistic perception of his own potentialities. Grouping methods should not contribute to erroneous concepts of self and of others, but should help individuals make more realistic appraisals.

EVERY LEARNER SHOULD HAVE A FEELING OF "AT HOMENESS" IN HIS CLASS GROUP

The above points do not argue for an indiscriminate grouping of learners of the same chronological age any more than they do for classification on the basis of test scores. If all-round development is to result, a learner must have a feeling of security in his class group and feel that he can contribute from an intellectual as well as from a social point of view. This suggests grouping learners of approximately the same level of general maturity, regardless of exact chronological age, intelligence, social maturity, or academic achievement. Maturity, in this sense, is best described as a complex combination of factors for which there is as yet no standard formula; it must be determined by the best judgment of experienced persons.

Such grouping would tend to bring together learners of approximately the same chronological age, but age would not be the sole deciding factor. Special strengths or weaknesses in such areas as social adjustment, physical development, intellectual power, would all enter into the decision. Friendships and antagonisms, emotional disturbances, special talents and interests, and in some cases the judgment of teachers as to whose personality or the temper of which group would most likely help a particular child might all play a part in deciding to which class a learner might be assigned.

This means of setting up classes may reduce the range of certain needs and abilities in a given group somewhat, but it does not do so by classifying learners as being in the A, B, or C groups. It would not preclude bringing together a group of learners of very limited intellectual ability in order to provide a total situation less confusing, more routine, and more secure, nor would it set any given intelligence level as the sole criterion as to whether or not a learner should be placed in such a group. Neither would it prevent setting up a class of intellectually able learners in order to make possible certain kinds of specialized activities within their range of competence.

INTERAGE GROUPING FOR LEARNING OFFERS AN IMPORTANT AREA FOR EXPERIMENTATION

Pupils can be grouped for learning on many bases other than age. It is important for learners to have opportunities to work with individuals of differing ages and levels of development. This is one aspect of learning to understand other people. Interage grouping may also offer the special stimulation some pupils need. A gifted ten-year-old who has deep science interests, for example, might be unhappy if he were with twelve- or thirteen-year-olds on a full-time basis, but could be a valued member of a science club or an advanced science class.

At the elementary school level there have been a variety of attempts to modify traditional class organizations by setting up interage groups. Some schools arrange for children to work together in ungraded primary groups until it is apparent that they have attained the maturity to go into the intermediate unit. Attempts have also been made to do away with grade level classifications and to call classes by the teacher's name (Miss Sweet's class) or by the age range represented (seven- to nine-year-old group). Such means of breaking away from traditional grading and promotion approaches allow for better placement of learners according to maturity and for interage experiences.

At the high school level similar flexibility has been tested with students moving into advanced areas after demonstrating achievement, regardless of actual time spent in class. Here grouping on the basis of age tends to disappear and classes can be arranged according to maturity, interest, special aptitude, achievement, or other bases. High school youth have been given opportunities to pursue areas of special talent and interests in greater depth and breadth than is usual through seminars, advanced-level sections, and accelerated groups. Music classes, for example, are made up of youth interested in learning to perform on an instrument or to sing in a choir, regardless of age or grade level. The science–mathematics workshop may have students who are unusually able regardless of their actual years of schooling. The drama group or the homeroom may cut across all age and grade levels.

Laboratories and special-interest centers where any member of the school may work alone or with others under the guidance of a teacher with particular competence have been established. In some secondary schools part of the day, or a half day once a week, is set aside for such activities. In these centers, the group working on a special project may represent high talent and interest but a wide age range.

Some schools that have various kinds of service groups are experimenting with another type of interage activity. Student councils, social functions, projectionists clubs, athletic activities, and other such projects may well be the concern of all ages and levels of development. Opportunities are sometimes provided for older learners to take special responsibility for younger ones. This may mean helping with an after-lunch play period in the elementary school or serving as a "big brother" or "big sister" to a member of an entering high school group.

Related to these adjustments is the plan for assigning a teacher to a class for more than one year. At the elementary school level, this may mean living and working with the same group for two or three years. At the secondary school level it may mean that one teacher will act as adviser or guide for a group over the entire high school period. This may include spending extended time with a group the first year of high school and continuing to have teaching and guidance contacts throughout the remaining years.

Such adjustments have important implications for grouping and grading. By breaking from the traditional patterns, many kinds of flexibility are possible. By allowing more freedom for the learner, without taking him completely away from the group best suited to his general maturity, the possibility for meeting his special needs is increased. Grouping, whether within the class or the school, thus becomes an instrument used to foster learners' growth. It is a means of facilitating maximum individual growth by providing for each learner freedom to work with others who have common interests, face the same problems, or have the same needs. It is also a means for taking into account the individual's need for secure social relationships.

Meeting Individual Needs Within the Classroom Setting

It is not realistic to talk about how to set up groups within a school without also considering what is to happen within each class. Grouping facilitates certain kinds of learning experiences—it does not insure them. There must still be a teacher who understands learners, who is skilled in identifying individual needs, who can interpret effectively the records from preceding years, and who will be with his class a sufficient length of time to get to know each pupil well. Grouping within the total class must be flexible if learners with similar needs are to be brought together, if gifted learners are to be in some groups that challenge them to the full extent of their ability, and if learners with problems are to have sufficient opportunities for special guidance. Special groups must be established as needed within the class, whatever the original basis for grouping. Learners must still have the opportunity to change to other groups as new problems require.

EACH CLASS SHOULD BE WELL KNOWN BY AT LEAST ONE TEACHER

The most desirable organization for achieving the proposed type of curriculum design is one in which a single teacher has major responsibility for guiding the experiences of a particular group of learners. At the elementary school level, specialists in such areas as music, art, and possibly science, would be available to work with the children on special projects but would not have programs of activities in these areas isolated from the other experiences of the group. At the high school level, a homeroom or guidance teacher, working with the core class, would come to know individuals well enough to give sound counseling on questions of how to get the most effective help in areas of special need or interest.

When one teacher knows the learners in a class well and works with them in relatively long blocks of time, the opportunities to meet individual needs are increased. The more time an insightful teacher spends with a group, the more aware of individual needs and talents he is likely to be. The flexibility in scheduling allowed by large time blocks makes possible more efficient provision for a variety of activities and enables the teacher to give learners more help as individuals or in small groups.

SOME ALL-CLASS PROBLEMS ARISING FROM COMMON CONCERNS ARE NEEDED TO DEVELOP FEELINGS OF GROUP UNITY

The general pattern of experiences in a class would normally include one or more all-class concerns around which certain of the day's activities would revolve. Several sources of such concerns have already been indicated. As part of the school community, learners undertake responsibilities which will raise certain common problems. Out of the problems of living together will develop some common concerns. Since they are more or less at the same maturity level other common interests will emerge. As members of the same town or city, reading the same newspapers, watching the same television programs, sharing the same community recreational facilities, they will have concerns in common.

These common problems become the center for planning all-class activities. Some problems and situations will call for brief discussion by the class as a whole while others will lead to an extensive series of activities in which considerable individualizing of responsibilities will take place. Regardless of the extent of the experience, these common concerns or problems provide the group purposes which hold the class together as a unit, and also provide points of reference which give meaning to at least part of the small-group and individual activities which are included in the total day. Other relatively brief but regular activities coming from living and working in the same room also serve to hold the class together as a group—a sharing or conversation period, requests from the student council to be acted upon, lunch money to be collected, housekeeping responsibilities. But even in these activities which develop group unity, there are differences in the kind and amount of individual participation.

TIME FOR SMALL-GROUP AND FOR INDIVIDUAL CONCERNS SHOULD BE DEFINITELY SCHEDULED

While all-class experiences are an important aspect of the work that goes on in any class, individuals and smaller groups will also have concerns. Planning and scheduling should allow for three types of activities—all-class, small-group, and individual. At the elementary school level, the schedule will be more flexible and, at times, more complicated than the typical class organization in which groups established for practice in the fundamental skills may work at different levels but where single units are the center of class work in areas such as social studies, science, and health. Under the latter organization, individualization is secured within the subject units by allowing groups to work on subproblems of their own choosing. The times would be less frequent when one group in science would be working on magnets while a second learned how to develop film and a third made an intensive study of the trees in the neighborhood. Under the proposed design, all-class involvement in all problems would be somewhat less frequent and the times when smaller groups could engage in individual activities would increase.

Time for individuals to work on their own concerns is important. At the elementary school level, a period may be set aside for individual activities and a sharing period be scheduled wherein individuals report on their projects. It would also be possible for an individual to undertake a special task in relation to an all-class or small-group problem—to use his talent to construct a model, to look up information, to interview family friends and report back his findings. At times, an individual might disassociate himself from a group problem to pursue some special concern.

At the secondary school level, similar opportunities for small-group and for individual activities can be arranged. However, the scheduling would be more structured than that necessary when teacher and learners are together for the entire day. Some time for pursuit of individual concerns can be a part of total class planning. Additional time may be provided before or after school, in studio or laboratory periods, during an activities period. On occasion, it will be necessary to work with other teachers so that students can have adequate blocks of time. This method is used when class groups go off on a field trip for a day or part of a day; the same principle can apply for one or two students who need additional time for a particular activity.

INDIVIDUALS WILL PLAY DIFFERENT ROLES IN GROUP ACTIVITIES

Further possibilities for meeting the needs of individuals within a class setting lie in the different roles the learner may play in a group activity. Special groups can be organized on many bases and for many purposes. Frequently in developing skills, the basis is the learner's present level of proficiency. Thus, in reading, a group of limited readers may work together regularly with the teacher giving help while a group of excellent readers may be encouraged to explore library facilities. At times specific skills rather than general reading level may provide the grouping. Joan, who reads at fourth-grade level with painful precision and accuracy, and Jerome, who dashes through the same material with little attention to details, may need to work with groups receiving entirely different kinds of instruction. Even in skill development, interest may be the factor that determines the group—as when children read books on several difficulty levels to prepare for story-hour sharing.

In working on common problems, groups may be based on interest, with each child choosing the aspect of the problem of concern to him. Groups can also be organized with regard to need, with each learner working in the area in which he realizes he knows the least. At times grouping may be for the purpose of locating information and at other times groups may work on specific aspects of a job such as an art committee, a resources committee to search the library for available books, an excursions committee to consider community resources to be tapped.

Sometimes a combination of special talent and interest draws a group together. In high school this might result in an advanced science, mathematics, or foreign language class elected by individuals who choose to make this an area of specialization. At the elementary school level, it could be a special science, art, or hobby group for whose activities time is provided in the schedule.

A pupil may serve the group in a way that provides opportunity to contribute from an area of strength or a talent. Third-grade John, who is a good reader but usually reads too rapidly for a skilled oral performance, is asked to help a group of poor readers locate some of the information that they need. John's major learning in this group activity is to read aloud more effectively. The others listen for the facts they want. Bill, who traveled through the mountains last summer, serves an as expert adviser to the mural group but has to look up some information himself to be sure. Alex has an opportunity to extend his artistic talent as the artist-in-chief. Sandra shares her collection of colonial dolls with a ninth-grade group who are interested in the history of costume design.

On occasion, the major contribution of a group activity for some learners may be the experience of learning to work cooperatively with others. Robert, who writes well and whose command of English is good, may learn a great deal about leadership as editor of the school paper although he may not add appreciably to his present English skills. Joyce, whose special interest is costume design, may join the committee responsible for the costumes for the ninth-grade play. What she learns about costume design may be relatively small in comparison to the techniques of organizing a complicated group venture.

The teacher who is concerned with helping a talented pupil fit into a typical group sometimes talks about "extra" assignments or about "releasing" the pupil from regular assignments. The possibilities for grouping and for varied experiences within a group, just described, suggest other solutions for this problem. There would be no "extra" assignments, but instead there will be ample opportunity to take on responsibilities that call for advanced work in areas of talent or interest. There would be no "release" from assignments that others in the class are completing, but instead pupil–teacher planning will enable each child to make the most of whatever aspects of the total situation best meet his needs. The goal would be to provide the kinds of educational experiences which are appropriate and adequate for each individual.

FLEXIBILITY IN GROUPING IS ESSENTIAL

The importance of flexibility in grouping for facilitating teaching–learning cannot be overemphasized. Participation in one group should not freeze the student there. The child who shows marked improvement should be able to shift to another group concerned with an aspect of a skill which will be a challenge to him. The pupil who needs additional practice should be free to join another group which is receiving special help without feeling any stigma attached to so doing. Even within a group of approximately the same general ability there will be certain aspects of the work which some learners will not need to stress. For example, in a group concerned with long division, only one or two may need added help with multiplication. When several groups are cooperating on a common enterprise it may be advisable for a learner who begins work with one group to change to another when the second seems to offer more to him or when his special contribution is needed. Since teacher and learners are evaluating growth and planning together, in whatever group the individual is placed he should understand why he is engaged in the particular activities undertaken. The pupil can adjust to changes from group to group and to varying roles and purposes when he knows why. In a degree commensurate with his maturity and insight the learner shares in the planning that provides for his special needs.

THE LEARNER'S ABILITY TO WORK INDEPENDENTLY IS AN IMPORTANT ASSET IN MEETING INDIVIDUAL NEEDS

An assumption underlying the preceding discussion of possible ways of providing for individual differences is that learners will profit from taking on as much independent responsibility as their maturity will allow. When learners are carrying out agreed-upon plans, teachers are free to give intensive help to individuals and to small groups. This is another important aspect of meeting individual needs within the regular classroom setting.

Learners are not being neglected when they work independently as long as they have guidance, purpose, and direction. In fact, they can be helped to develop skills important in later life—to lay out clear plans, to foresee difficulties, to collect the materials needed for a specific task, to locate the information needed to solve a problem, to evaluate work in progress and judge what still needs to be done and what help is needed, to help keep a project moving ahead as a leader or follower.

These skills begin to be acquired in kindergarten and first grade and become increasingly important as learners become more mature. One of the most valuable contributions that can be made to a gifted child, for example, is to teach him how to pursue his interests independently without the step-by-step direction of others.

What becomes the teacher's pattern of activity in the day's work? The following are illustrative descriptions of teachers at work.

In a **first grade,** the day began with routine housekeeping activities—a time when brief conversations with individuals were held. Then the class was called together for a sharing period, with the teacher acting as group chairman. Following this the work for the time block was planned—an all-class activity involving the completion of the construction of a class flower store—and detailed plans for each group were checked. As the class went to work, the teacher was free to help where most needed—consulting with the children who were to be clerks, helping with the measuring of the paper to go on the counter. An evaluation session to take stock ended this period. After a break for rhythms, plans were again checked for the last part of the morning. Some children were working with paints, some completing work-type reading activities, some finishing individual aspects of the flower store. With plans clear, the teacher worked with two groups in reading activities, taking time between groups to make sure no one had forgotten his plans or had run out of work. Immediately after lunch the class discussed an excursion to a local flower store with the teacher serving as chairman and helping to record the information gained for an experience chart. Following this, each child drew a picture for a bulletin-board display of the aspect of the trip that interested him most. As this individual work went on the teacher worked with a group of beginning readers and then circulated, helping individuals write captions to their pictures. After a recess break came number activities, some centered around plans for the store. The teacher started two groups with work-type activities, spent about five minutes making sure no unusual problems had arisen, then worked directly with a third group. The last half hour was used to prepare an announcement about the store to take to other classes. At this time the teacher was free to give individualized help with handwriting and spelling.

In a **fourth grade,** the teacher's day started with a planning session. After the schedule for the day was blocked in detail, the children checked on plans for finding out more about the modes of transportation important in today's world. Following this, groups went to work. The teacher spent a few minutes with each group, making sure that plans were clear, and then worked with a selected group of poor readers on their aspect of the problem. A check on how the independent work was progressing was made at the end of the time block, the teacher acting as class chairman as the groups reported. A skills period followed the recess break. After checking a list of possible activities with the class, the teacher worked with one group on reading problems, then called together a special spelling group. During this time other children were carrying out work plans, using practice materials, working with spelling partners, using a class-prepared check list to edit written work. The teacher spent the last fifteen minutes of this block of time checking on individual progress. In the afternoon, plans for creative writing experiences led to individual writing for a class magazine. This provided the teacher an opportunity to confer with individuals on language problems. Following a period for music activities the class returned to pursue several group problems related to science interests. During part of this period the teacher worked with each group in turn, and for part of the time called from the groups individuals in need of special number experiences.

At the **high school level,** in a three-period block devoted to the general education core, the teacher began with a planning session as students scheduled their activities for the morning. Some individuals moved immediately to the school or class library for information about the origins of water-supply problems the community was facing. One or two students stopped to talk with the teacher about individual plans or problems they were encountering in their search for facts. Other students, members of committees already set up, gathered around tables in the room to plan next steps. The teacher moved among these groups, staying with a committee for a time to help them with a problem. Half way through the period, some of the members left to meet with the two representatives from the Bureau of Water Supply who were coming to talk with the students the following day. Before leaving, the students reviewed with the teacher the material they were to use in briefing the city officials. The entire class reassembled near the end of the period to discuss problems encountered and to plan their time with the resource people the following day. The teacher led this discussion.

In a class which had only a single period, the teacher engaged in essentially the same kinds of activities. He worked with the total group, with small groups, with individuals, sometimes for shorter periods of time and sometimes for blocks of time—but these blocks were over a period of several days rather than during a single day. Subgroups met for the entire period for each of three or four days—the equivalent of a single three- or four-period block.

PUPIL–TEACHER PLANNING IS BASIC TO EFFECTIVE INDIVIDUALIZING OF ACTIVITIES

Pupil–teacher planning is essential for effective use of the varied means of meeting individual needs. The values have already been mentioned. Individuals are helped to identify their own particular strengths, weaknesses, and special concerns so that they know why they are engaging in certain activities. Because each individual knows what he is doing, and why, he can move from one activity to the next and can pursue several parallel activities without confusion. When plans are clear, individuals can move forward with constructive activities while the teacher gives help to pupils as needed. Learners who know what they are doing realize when they need help and can also help the teacher to analyze problems and plan where his help is most needed.

If the teacher is to be free to work with individuals, planning is as essential with younger children as it is with those who are more mature. The adjustments needed for younger children and for groups of limited intellectual ability were outlined in Chapter 8. The planning sessions for an immature group would cover shorter time periods. The teacher would use shorter work periods and make more frequent checks on progress, sometimes circulating from group to group and at other times calling the class together for evaluation sessions. The independent work undertaken by the learners would not be as complex. Work-type activities connected with skills would not be complicated and simple directions would be used. At the high school level, students can be expected to take major responsibility, both in planning class activities and in helping to determine desirable individual experiences. Youth at this age are more capable of seeing both short- and long-range planning needs.

Making Adjustments for Exceptional Pupils

Some learners, by virtue of special talents or disabilities, are classified as exceptional. The term is used broadly today and includes pupils whose intelligence quotients are such that they are classified as intellectually gifted, slow learners, educable, or trainable; those who have physical handicaps requiring some adjustments in normal living; and those with special talent in such areas as music or art. A school program that meets individual needs must provide for the special problems of such learners.

Although no complete census has been made, samplings indicate that because of the way in which individual capacities are distributed in normal population groups, the exceptional child or youth is literally the exception. Approximately two children out of one hundred have IQ's of 138 or better on the Stanford–Binet Scale and four out of one hundred would score IQ's of 75 or below on the same scale. Two out of three hundred have hearing losses sufficient to require special teaching, and one out of five hundred are either blind or require special sight-saving equipment. Children with special health problems number two out of every three hundred. Figures on talented children in fields such as music or art are much more difficult to secure, since no reliable tests exist in these fields. Nor is it safe to estimate from the numbers of persons whose mature talents have been recognized because there is no way of telling how many learners with talent might have been discouraged by restricted school programs. The most liberal estimates suggest that about 12 per cent fall into one of the above categories of exceptional children and youth.

In small school districts, therefore, the problem of meeting the needs of the exceptional pupil may be a matter of adjusting programs for as few as one or two or as many as eight or ten learners from each of the categories mentioned above, scattered over many grades. Even in large cities it is unusual to have enough children in any one category at the elementary school level to form a full-sized class unless one goes beyond the area served by a single school. In high schools drawing from many elementary schools, the possibilities are somewhat greater for setting up certain types of special classes, if these seem desirable, without going beyond the boundaries of the school district.

The needs of such learners must be met, however, through some type of school adjustment. It is appropriate to ask whether a curriculum developed in terms of the persistent problems of living has anything to offer in the education of the exceptional individual and whether the general ways of working with learners outlined above offer possibilities for meeting the needs of these pupils.

THE EXCEPTIONAL PUPIL DIFFERS PRIMARILY IN DEGREE

In planning for the exceptional child or youth, it must be remembered that in some ways he is merely at a point near one end of a continuum. He is not a person whose needs, interests, and ways of learning set him completely apart. This is particularly important in thinking about intellectual differences. The child with an IQ of 135 may not be significantly different from the child whose IQ is 130. He may not differ much in his general approach to learning from the child whose IQ is 125. Similarly, there may be no marked difference between Billy whose IQ is given as 70 and John who has a recorded IQ of 80. In fact, what is known—or not known—today about measuring intelligence would cause any teacher to be extremely cautious in classifying a child on the basis of a single test, no matter how carefully it was administered.

While pupils who are completely blind and those who have never heard speech represent extraordinary learning problems, in that a sense normally appealed to is not functioning in terms of interests and needs, and the general principles governing motivation, generalizing, forgetting, and other aspects of the learning process, they are on a continuum.

Youngsters with partial sight or hearing can fit very well into classes with normal children, as can those with cardiac conditions or some other physical handicap.

Pupils with special talent in music or art, with special linguistic ability or mechanical gifts, may be found in any of these groups. The results of research indicate that children classified as intellectually gifted are somewhat more likely to be talented, to be freer of physical handicaps, to be taller and heavier than the average child. Conversely, children classified as slow learners, intellectually, are likely to have more than their share of other disabilities. This evidence does not necessarily hold true for any individual child.

Any realistic discussion about meeting the needs of exceptional children or youth must focus on learners as individuals, each with his unique pattern of strengths and weaknesses, his special experience background, and his particular ways of adjusting to his talent or his handicap, and must consider these individuals as being much the same as other learners in their general needs and in the principles governing how they learn.

THE EXCEPTIONAL PUPIL MEETS PERSISTENT LIFE SITUATIONS

Regardless of the talent or the handicap, an exceptional individual still faces persistent life situations. He must meet health needs, manage his money, prepare himself to earn a living, communicate with others, use various modes of transportation, make wise purchases, vote and take his part in other community enterprises, get along with others. If it is desirable for the typical learner to be helped to develop the knowledge and skills to meet such problems as they recur in increasingly complicated situations, it is equally desirable for the atypical learner to do so.

The difference lies in the exact nature of the situation faced and in the special equipment, or lack thereof, that the learner brings to it. The slow learner, for example, cannot be expected to generalize as readily or to seek as extensive explanations. Since his insights are more limited, he may not face certain intellectual problems as early as does the typical child. He will read, respond to abstract number symbols, and become curious about certain aspects of his environment later. He will need to develop many habits through repeated experiences in arriving at and using the solutions to the problems he faces. For example, through repeatedly washing his hands he acquires a technique that helps prevent the spread of disease. Such experiences must be planned and may include washing before lunch, after a lavatory break, in preparation for handling food for a class party, prior to acting as an assistant in the lunchroom, and so on. Each experience adds a little more to his ability to meet the persistent life situation of keeping healthy. Each experience is concrete and is discussed, although he is not expected to grasp much more than a minimum explanation of the nature of disease germs. This he can understand, but he will grasp the basic idea later than the typical child.

In contrast to the slow learner, an intellectually able pupil may generalize rather quickly from one hand-washing situation to others (although his teacher, too, checks in the new situation to make sure that the generalization is operating). He may grasp concepts regarding the way diseases spread much more readily, and be more interested in following medical discoveries, in asking about wonder drugs, in wanting to know how his polio shot protects him.

It is important to note that the intellectually gifted pupil has just as much need to learn to live effectively in his world as does the slow learner. Often in a school system where it is possible to propose a program for slow learners centered around the actual problems of living, the curriculum considered ideal for the able pupil is strictly of a traditional college-preparatory nature. He studies geometry while the practical mathematics class studies stocks and bonds, insurance, and problems of wise investment. He studies Latin while his less able colleagues learn typewriting and shorthand. He traces the history of ancient man while his friends study community problems. He completes a laboratory course in chemistry while others who are less able discuss the application of science to daily living. Such a program does not necessarily take advantage of the usual characteristics of gifted pupils which give different dimensions to some of their persistent problems—their ability to think, create, initiate, relate, generalize, conceptualize. The mere fact that the able learner is in a traditional college-preparatory program does not mean that he is having the kinds of educational experiences which are adequate or appropriate for him.

The pupil who is blind or deaf will face exactly the same persistent life problems in some areas as does the individual who sees or hears. He must get along with others, select a balanced meal, vote as an adult. In other areas the special handicap requires special adjustments. The blind learner faces problems of transportation different from those of the pupils who can see. He must acquire techniques for securing help or for identifying his location in a familiar neighborhood. A learner with any physical handicap will have different needs in facing the problem of keeping healthy from one with normal health. Physical or intellectual handicaps call for different answers to the problem of earning a living. However, the problem remains the same; the methods of achieving the goals for the particular learner are different.

The learner with special talent in music, art, or mechanics faces the problem of how to secure the specialized education he needs in order to make the most effective use of his talent. This has implications for his hobbies, for his choice of individual activities and elective courses, and probably for his vocational choice. Beyond this, however, most of the situations he must deal with are similar to those faced by any other learner.

A teacher or a curriculum committee concerned with proposing experiences for slow learners, for intellectually gifted individuals, or for children or youth with special talents or handicaps, can develop a list of persistent life situations in a fashion similar to that outlined in Chapters 5 and 6, and then give particular attention to realistic goals for learners with particular needs. A curriculum committee working on a proposal for slow-learner classes developed the following classification for persistent life situations.[1]

1. *Learning to Keep Healthy* involves the essential habits, attitudes, and skills necessary for developing and maintaining the body through nutrition, exercise, bodily care, rest, and those necessary for the prevention and treatment of illnesses.
2. *Learning to Live Safely* involves the essential habits, attitudes, and skills necessary for safety in play, in work, in locomotion, and in emergency.
3. *Learning to Understand One's Self and to Get Along With Others* involves the essential habits, attitudes, and skills necessary to understand and adjust one's strengths and weaknesses, to develop moral and spiritual values basic to our democratic society and the ability to get along with others (such as peers, family, groups, authorities, opposite sex, strangers, etc.) in social relationships.
4. *Learning to Communicate Ideas* (3 R's) involves the essential habits, attitudes and skills that are commonly referred to as speaking, listening, reading, writing, and arithmetic.
5. *Learning Wise Use of Leisure Time* involves the essential habits, attitudes, and skills necessary for locating desirable sources of recreation and participating in wholesome activities.
6. *Learning to Travel and Move About* involves the acquisition of the essential habits, attitudes, and skills necessary for transporting one's self in the neighborhood, within the city, and to distant places, whenever the need arises. (Note: Safety in locomotion is covered in #2, *Learning to Live Safely*.)

[1] Preliminary draft of a curriculum proposal for slow learners, Cincinnati Public Schools, Cincinnati, Ohio. Quoted with permission.

7. *Learning to Earn a Living* (*Vocation*) involves the essential habits, attitudes, and skills necessary to be a good worker, knowing what jobs are available for him, preparing for and getting a job.
8. *Learning Homemaking* involves the essential habits, attitudes, and skills necessary for the feeding, clothing, and housing of oneself and one's family.
9. *Learning to Appreciate, Create, and Enjoy Beauty* involves the essential habits, attitudes, and skills necessary to develop and maintain an attractive environment, to develop and maintain an attractive appearance, and to express oneself through a variety of media (crafts, music, art, dancing).
10. *Learning to Handle and Adjust to One's Social, Technological, and Physical Environment* involves the essential habits, attitudes, and skills necessary in using social amenities and customs, using tools and mechanical equipment, and in understanding and adjusting to the physical environment.
11. *Learning to Manage One's Money* involves the essential habits, attitudes, and skills necessary for budgeting one's income to gain the maximum advantages from expenditures.
12. *Learning to Be a Responsible Citizen* involves the essential habits, attitudes, and skills necessary to understand one's heritage, to understand and participate in government and its processes, and to understand and exercise one's rights, privileges, and responsibilities as a citizen.

The specific objectives suggested by the teachers under the persisting problem of LEARNING HOMEMAKING with regard to the feeding of oneself and one's family are given below. Other objectives regarding clothing, housing, and care of children were worked out in similar fashion. The age ranges given are for the typical class groupings as set up in the city for which this course of study is planned.

PERSISTING PROBLEM 8—LEARNING HOMEMAKING

Six- to Nine-Year-Olds

1. Knows where common foods come from
2. Experiences buying food items in store
3. Helps prepare some simple foods
4. Experiences eating different and new foods
5. Begins to practice simple table manners

Nine- to Twelve-Year-Olds

1. Begins to shop independently for some food in neighborhood store
2. Plans, buys, and prepares simple snacks for classroom parties, picnics, and lunches
3. Engages in simple preparation of food
4. Knows, selects, and eats foods that help keep one healthy

SIX- TO NINE-YEAR-OLDS

6. Uses spoon, fork, and knife
7. Helps clean up after meals

NINE- TO TWELVE-YEAR-OLDS

5. Knows which foods are usually eaten at certain meals
6. Knows importance of eating three regular meals daily
7. Knows and practices basic table manners
8. Knows how to set a table
9. Knows how and when to use spoon, fork, and knife

TWELVE- TO FIFTEEN-YEAR-OLDS

1. Begins to understand how to buy food skillfully and economically
2. Prepares simple meals independently
3. Knows some of the basic skills in meal planning
4. Knows what foods make up a good breakfast, lunch, and dinner
5. Understands the importance of eating balanced meals
6. Understands the importance of practicing good eating habits, such as regular meal hours, pleasant atmosphere, eating together as a family

FIFTEEN- TO EIGHTEEN-YEAR-OLDS

1. Performs skillful and economic buying of food for family
2. Prepares nutritious and economical meals for family and self
3. Plans balanced meals for family and self
4. Knows healthful methods of storing and preserving food
5. Knows adequate sanitary measures in the handling and preparation of food
6. Helps others in the family practice good eating habits

The problem areas suggested for a class with many gifted learners might be developed in a similar way. The gifted learner has persistent problems in human relations, vocational competence, consumer effectiveness, use of leisure time, health and safety, and other such areas just as do all learners. But, because he is gifted, he has potentialities which may make some of these problem areas qualitatively different. For example, because he is intellectually able, other pupils may regard him as "different" and may develop positive or negative attitudes toward him which pose persistent problems of being accepted and understood which other learners might not have to face in the same ways. Because of his potential, his parents may have aspirations for him or may make demands on him which individuals with lesser abilities do not have to face. His skills and knowledge make possible certain kinds of learning experiences which, while desirable for all children, are essential for his further development. The talented musician, for example, must practice his instrument daily. This raises certain problems in his own development, his use of time, and his relations with others. Teachers studying a group of their gifted pupils could discover the persistent areas which are similar for all learners and those which are distinct or qualitatively different for the gifted, developing a guide similar to the one illustrated for the slow-learner group.

THE EXCEPTIONAL PUPIL LEARNS IN THE SAME WAYS AS DO ALL CHILDREN AND YOUTH

The same general learning principles apply whether a learner is classified as gifted, slow, handicapped, or talented, with the only difference being one of degree. This means that pupil–teacher planning will be important, that learners will need to have goals clear, that experiences will develop around problems meaningful to the group, that individual and small-group activities will be important to meet special needs.

The pattern of all-class, small-group, and individual activities for a class of exceptional children would be very similar to the pattern for a more typical group. The differences would be occasioned by the intellectual maturity of the class or by the special adjustments dictated by a particular talent or handicap. For a group of slow learners, for example, the pattern might more nearly resemble that of a primary grade with more definite guidance, simpler activities, more step-by-step planning, shorter periods of independent work. For individuals with special needs for rest or for physiotherapy, the program would be adjusted accordingly. For learners who are deaf, problems of acquiring speech would be given more time than is normally devoted to language experiences. These are adjustments to the needs of learners however; they are not fundamental changes in teaching methods.

THE REGULAR CLASSROOM SETTING OFFERS POSSIBILITIES FOR MEETING THE NEEDS OF EXCEPTIONAL PUPILS

All the suggestions in the preceding section for adjusting to individual differences point to possibilities for meeting the needs of the exceptional pupil within the regular classroom setting. In small school systems this is frequently the only possible solution. In larger systems there is a trend toward not isolating the child or youth whose needs are not greatly different. The level corridors of the modern one-story school may be as suitable for a learner with a cardiac condition or for a pupil on crutches because of poliomyelitis as the special orthopedic school. A child using a hearing aid may fit very well in a regular classroom. Mature learners who are blind or deaf, but have learned to read and write Braille or to lip read, have had very successful high school or college careers.

What are some possibilities for meeting individual needs suggested in the preceding sections? At the elementary school level, for example, an activity of concern to the entire class will present opportunities for individuals to work on various aspects of the problem. The slow learner would be given a relatively routine responsibility, the intellectually gifted child would have a more complicated part of the job, and the child with special talent would find some use for it. In addition, there would be other times when small groups or individuals would have opportunity to pursue special concerns. This allows for the special interest or ability of the gifted child and for special activities of a simpler nature for the slow learner. Balanced growth would be assured by helping learners to identify areas of weakness and by giving special help with such problems. Within the class, the exceptional child usually can find one or two others with similar abilities or needs. This would be particularly true of the gifted pupil, the slow learner, or the one talented in music or art. For certain experiences those learners with similar abilities can work as a group. Finally, the general classroom organization would be such that the teacher would have time to give individual help and to assist with work on special problems.

In a high school class many of the same possibilities exist as are found at the elementary school level. In addition, the opportunities for specialized education through electives and through work with specialists provide even more avenues for individualizing instruction for maximum self-fulfillment.

Much has been written recently—with some real basis—regarding the dangers of neglecting the gifted pupil and devoting too much time to the slower learner when both are in the same room. While this is not a criticism to be passed off lightly, it is important to identify clearly what the special needs of the gifted learner are. It is quite possible for an overzealous teacher to devote full time to a gifted group and still allow many of their potentialities to go unrealized. The gifted learner needs to develop, in keeping with his maturity, habits of efficient independent work. He should be able to plan, to follow through with his plans, to locate information independently, to read widely and critically. He should develop deep interests and have opportunities to pursue them. He should be intellectually curious and unwilling to stop with superficial answers, and he should have one or more areas of special concern in which he is becoming expert. The gifted pupil should develop ability to make a realistic evaluation of his own strengths and weaknesses and should be able to offer suggestions regarding experiences that will contribute to his own growth. He should acquire skills in getting along with people of all levels of ability, both as a leader and as a follower. He needs an environment that is stimulating and the encouragement to develop his potentialities as fully as possible. To achieve these objectives the gifted learner must have relatively longer stretches of uninterrupted time as he matures in order to complete the independent projects of which he is capable—but under teacher guidance. The experience of working with others of differing ability levels, far from holding back the gifted learner, may make an important contribution to his total development.

In the regular classroom, then, the teacher planning to meet the special needs of thirty-five or so individuals can organize his schedule so that it allows for a certain amount of individualized help and individualized activities. He must do this to provide for the normal variations which exist in any group. When the group contains one or more learners whose deviation from the average is sufficient to merit the classification of exceptional, the individualization is especially important.

SOLUTIONS TO PROBLEMS OF MEETING THE NEEDS OF EXCEPTIONAL PUPILS MUST CONSIDER ATTITUDES

Any solutions to the problem of how to meet the needs of the exceptional pupil should be appraised in terms of the attitudes being developed. This includes not only the learners' attitudes but those of parents and teachers as well.

From a mental health point of view, it is important that each individual have a realistic sense of his own strengths and weaknesses, and that any grouping which is used should not establish unrealistic attitudes. Such attitudes may occur, for example, if a gifted child develops the feeling that he is distinctly superior to all other learners in all areas, or if the slow learner feels that his contribution is always second rate. Parents can sometimes build false expectations because of failure to understand the implications of the system of grouping being used by the school.

Even the teacher, whose technical understanding of individual differences should be strong, is sometimes lulled into a false security. Whatever the method of grouping, learners still have to be considered as individuals. It is all too easy, for example, to assume that the capacity of slow learners is limited, and fail to provide the challenging experiences that will allow these pupils to make the most of their abilities, or to label the gifted child with a genuine deficiency in a specific skill as lazy and fail to give him necessary help. Whenever a teacher feels that because he has the "gifted group" or the "slow learners" they can be treated as a homogeneous class, individual needs will fail to be met. There will always be a range of experience backgrounds, of maturity, of talents and interests, of strengths and weaknesses, of skills—reading, oral and written expression, and computation. There needs to be a thoughtful interpretation of this fact to teachers, parents, and learners themselves if this range is to be accepted and understood.

EXPERIMENTATION WITH METHODS OF GROUPING EXCEPTIONAL PUPILS IS NEEDED

Since the days of the Dalton and Winnetka plans and the early yearbooks on grouping, such as the Thirty-fifth Yearbook, Part I, of the National Society for the Study of Education, many more opinions have been written regarding desirable methods of grouping to meet the needs of exceptional children and youth than there have been research studies. While it has been assumed for some time that if a learner is below a certain level in intellectual ability it is difficult for him to follow the activities of a typical group, there is much controversy regarding the best way in which to meet the needs of the gifted individual. Questions of the degree to which children and youth with physical handicaps should be isolated from normal learners are also raised. Such problems will not be solved satisfactorily until research evidence has been secured and the necessary value judgments on which some decisions about grouping rest are checked against the findings.

Obtaining such research evidence is not easy. It is always difficult to disentangle the influence of an able teacher from the effect of the class organization. It also is necessary to decide what evaluation criteria should be used. Certainly, it would be too narrow a base merely to measure progress in academic areas or the development of special talent. Further, the possibilities are much more varied than the alternatives of setting up a special class or leaving a learner with a regular group. There are possibilities for released time to pursue a special interest, for a specialist to supplement the work of the regular teacher in order to meet the special needs of the pupil who has a vision or a hearing loss. There are also possibilities for interest groups that cut across age levels.

The contributions of any special adjustments should be evaluated in terms of the results of the most flexible programs possible in the normal classroom setting. Here, too, research is needed, for it is likely that many schools are not yet making full use of the potentialities of the regular classroom to meet individual needs. Tied up with this problem are general questions of class size and of class organization within a school. What might a careful study of individual growth patterns indicate in deciding on promotions or retardation? What are the possibilities of doing away with age lines, of having primary schools or intermediate schools, of making it possible for a teacher to work with learners for more than one year?

American schools are committed to providing equal educational opportunities for all children and youth. If these opportunities are to be truly equal, they cannot be identical for all learners. "Providing for individual differences" may be a truism, but it certainly is more difficult to realize than many theorists and practitioners believe. The difficulty may be caused in part by the curriculum design under which most schools have been operating.

Related Readings

ANASTASI, ANNE, AND JOHN P. FOLEY. *Differential Psychology: Individual and Group Differences in Behavior.* Revised edition. New York: The Macmillan Company, 1949.

BERTHOLD, CHARLES A. *Administrative Concern for Individual Differences.* New York: Bureau of Publications, Teachers College, Columbia University, 1951.

BUTLER, FRANK A. *The Improvement of Teaching in Secondary Schools.* Third edition. Chicago: University of Chicago Press, 1954.

CRUICKSHANK, WILLIAM. *Psychology of Exceptional Children and Youth.* Englewood Cliffs, N.J.: Prentice-Hall, Inc., 1955.

FEATHERSTONE, WILLIAM B. *Teaching the Slow Learner.* New York: Bureau of Publications, Teachers College, Columbia University, 1951.

GOODENOUGH, FLORENCE. *Exceptional Children.* New York: Appleton-Century-Crofts, 1956.

JEWETT, ARNO J., AND J. D. HULL, editors. *Teaching Rapid and Slow Learners in High Schools.* Washington, D.C.: U.S. Office of Education, 1954.

KELLEY, JANET A. *Guidance and Curriculum.* Englewood Cliffs, N.J.: Prentice-Hall, Inc., 1955.

KIRK, SAMUEL, AND G. ORVILLE JOHNSON. *Educating the Retarded Child.* Boston: Houghton Mifflin Company, 1951.

KOOS, LEONARD V. *Junior High School Trends.* New York: Harper & Brothers, 1955.

NATIONAL SOCIETY FOR THE STUDY OF EDUCATION. *Education of Exceptional Children.* Forty-ninth Yearbook, Part 2. Chicago: University of Chicago Press, 1950.

OTTO, HENRY J. *Curriculum Enrichment for Gifted Elementary School Children in Regular Classes*. Austin: University of Texas, 1955.

PASSOW, A. HARRY, MIRIAM GOLDBERG, ABRAHAM J. TANNENBAUM, AND WILL FRENCH. *Planning for Talented Youth*. New York: Bureau of Publications, Teachers College, Columbia University, 1955.

SCHEIFELE, MARIAN. *The Gifted Child in the Regular Classroom*. New York: Bureau of Publications, Teachers College, Columbia University, 1953.

SHEVIAKOV, GEORGE V., AND FRITZ REDL. *Discipline for Today's Youth and Children*. Revised by SYBIL K. RICHARDSON. Washington, D.C.: National Education Association, Association for Supervision and Curriculum Development, 1956.

WILES, KIMBALL. *Teaching for Better Schools*. Englewood Cliffs, N.J.: Prentice-Hall, Inc., 1952.

10

USING THE RESOURCES OF THE WHOLE SCHOOL AND THE COMMUNITY

The effectiveness of the experiences in any one classroom depends, in no small measure, on the organization of the entire school. At least four major problem areas can be identified. What are the implications for the effective use of specialists—in music, in art, in other subject fields? What are the programing considerations which should enter into questions about the length of the school day and year? How can every aspect of the school—the lunchroom, the library, the nurse's office—be used to contribute to effective growth? What is implied for articulation—from grade to grade, from one school level to another, from school to college?

Making Effective Use of Specialization

In the proposed curriculum design, the homeroom or grade teacher has a central responsibility for guiding the experiences of his class. But no teacher, however able, can provide all the help needed by a group of learners, whether they are beginners, learners in the intermediate grades, or youth in high school or college. In this rapidly changing world, it would be impossible for any one person to be fully and equally proficient in all the facets represented by the varied situations which learners face. Specialists are needed to help learners to explore problems as deeply and insightfully as desired, to understand the place of specialization in modern society, and to learn how to use the services of experts in improving the quality of their daily living. At all school levels learners with special talents and interests need the stimulation that comes from the leadership of an able teacher who is deeply immersed in his field.

How to secure adequate specialization in the school personnel, how to organize the program so that the specialist can make an effective contribution, and how to coordinate efforts effectively, are problems that should be considered.

SPECIALIZATION MAY RESIDE IN A HOMEROOM TEACHER, IN A SPECIALIST SERVING THE ENTIRE SCHOOL, OR IN COMMUNITY RESOURCES

Since all major areas of human experience are involved in the persistent life situations learners face, specialization, even at the elementary school level, must be broadly defined. Certainly, the so-called "special" areas—art, music, physical education, science—make an important contribution to total development, but specialization should not be limited to these alone. Any area may become one of specialization when particular competence is required to make a contribution to the solution of a problem. At times the problems faced by learners call for special help in such areas as government, economic structures, human relations, health, historical backgrounds, and many others.

The kind of specialization required and the way in which it can be provided vary with the size and type of school and the community resources available. In a small school, for example, it may be that staff members other than the regular corps of classroom teachers cannot be made available. In this case specialization is probably best secured by building a faculty with complementary strengths and leaving least adequately represented on the staff the area or areas in which strong community resources exist. In a larger school, specialists in various areas may be regular staff members.

The specialist need not always be a school staff member. All appropriate resources of the community can and should be used in extending and enriching the experiences of learners. The school should seek to make the whole community a resource area, using special skills, interests, and talents wherever they are found. At times children and youth will use these resources by going into the community and, at other times, special community resources will be made a temporary part of the school. Lay persons who understand the purposes of modern education are usually glad to act as consultants in their particular area of expertness if the needs and ways of operating are made clear to them.

THE PERSISTENT LIFE SITUATION FACED BY LEARNERS IS THE KEY TO THE WAY IN WHICH THE SPECIALIST SERVES

In the past, and in some situations still, special teachers take over a class for a set period and teach a particular "lesson." Often the experience bears little relationship to the rest of the learners' work. The specialist, teaching many different groups in a day, cannot possibly determine the real needs and interests of the learners. This practice violates the principles of curriculum development which are proposed here.

The initial responsibility of both classroom teacher and specialist is to work together, each contributing to the maximum growth of learners from his particular background of experience and understanding. The classroom teacher helps acquaint the specialist with the learners' characteristics, their experiential backgrounds, and the particular problems they face. The specialist, on the other hand, explores possibilities and potentialities in areas in which the experiences of the homeroom teacher are limited. The learners' problems determine the type of specialist help needed. There are at least three kinds of situations in which such assistance will be required.

First, there are times when the knowledge and methodology of a special area is required to solve a particular aspect of a problem and the teacher lacks the necessary insight and experience. In a study of how the community was settled, one subgroup needs to locate indigenous folk songs and dances, and turns both to the music specialist and to a physical education expert for help. Other pupils find conflicting dates and seek assistance from the local historian with background in research. Unable to find a satisfactory answer to why a certain crop was particularly successful another group turns to the science specialist for aid, while still another works with the librarian to seek out the folk tales of the period. A high school class concerned with clearer understanding of the issues behind a local bond issue needs expert help in mathematics, economics, and civic government to answer their questions. It is this kind of assistance from specialists that builds genuine respect for the various subject fields, even though they are not the organizing centers for the curriculum.

Second, assistance will be required to secure balanced satisfactions in living by developing outlets for creative expression, hobbies, and special interests. There will be times when small groups, individuals, or the whole class embark on projects all within a special field—learning to dance, writing for a school magazine, sharing poetry, exploring art media, listening to music, developing pictures, collecting or dressing dolls in period costumes, operating an amateur radio station. Such projects would involve the needed specialist for an extended block of time. At the elementary school level, projects may be started under the classroom teacher whose preparation should provide at least minimum competence in special areas. Help from the specialist would then be sought at the point where the classroom teacher's competence is insufficient. Possibilities for scheduling such help are suggested in the next section.

At the high school level, opportunities to explore widely would be scheduled in some areas through the specialized aspects of the educational program. But even here it will be necessary to bring in additional assistance when a particular study goes beyond what the teacher can bring to its solution. The research chemist may come to the chemistry class or the radar technician to the physics class to open up their particular areas to youth. One community set up "apprenticeships" enabling high school youth to work on a part-time basis with various individuals to get the feeling of a particular vocational or professional area. Plans to encourage such exploration for junior high school groups have been tried by scheduling opportunities for youth to discover their specialized interests and aptitudes through contacts with competent resource people. This is done through regularly scheduled time blocks, plus flexible opportunities to stay with certain areas for extended experiences.

A third need for the expert guidance of the specialist is created by the fact that some learners with special talents or interests need opportunities to explore these areas far more deeply than the average student. A pupil with a leaning toward science or mechanics, or one with a strong love of history, is just as much part of this group as is the talented musician, the artist, the pupil with dramatic ability, or the one whose special interest is writing. Individual needs are not being met adequately unless such talents are receiving recognition. Through the encouragement of such talents and interests the school helps to develop the scientists, musicians, historians, writers of tomorrow as well as to meet the needs of those who will find these competencies simply avenues for expression and self-fulfillment.

EFFECTIVE USE OF SPECIALISTS REQUIRES FLEXIBILITY IN SCHEDULING

The varied ways in which the services of specialists may be used emphasize the need for flexibility in scheduling. Ideally, the specialist should have time both to work "on call" with class groups and to be available on a regular basis for individuals or groups pursuing interests of a long-term nature.

If staff members who serve as regular classroom teachers are also specialists in certain areas, careful planning is essential if learners are to secure necessary assistance from such individuals. This aid may come through individual conferences, through resource materials which the specialist makes available directly to learners, or through their own classroom teacher who has consulted the specialist and perhaps secured materials from him. In some cases it will mean developing a program sufficiently flexible to enable the teacher–specialist to leave his own group for a block of time to work with another requiring his help or an arrangement whereby the work of two groups may be combined. The lunch period can be extended to allow for conferences with staff members other than the classroom teacher. Time set aside for special-interest groups is another possibility. In the high school a teacher may serve as coordinator for the core program of one class for a half day and as specialist in his particular field for the other half. Other teachers may serve as specialists for the full day.

If there are specialists on the school staff in addition to classroom teachers, thought must be given to how their services can best meet the varied needs just discussed. Normally, some time would be set aside to go to classes requiring special help, or to assist subgroups volunteering to work on a particular problem. There would also be time for learners from one class or, particularly at the high school level, from several classes to spend extended periods of time on a given area of study. The study might extend for an entire semester or end after a four-, six-, or eight-week period. Some open time would also be desirable for workshop activities with individuals or small groups who are pursuing special concerns.

The daily schedule of the activities of an art specialist at the elementary school level might be as follows:

9:00–12:00	On call during the morning for work on special problems. (These might include showing a third grade how to use finger paints more effectively, advising on perspective in a fourth-grade mural, helping a second grade get clay gifts for mother ready for firing, and advising a sixth grade on the construction of mobiles to be made from nature collections of leaves, nuts, and shells.)
12:00– 1:30	Lunch, and time to confer with teachers needing special materials.

1:30– 2:30 Laboratory period for children making puppets. (This is a four-week commitment, two afternoons a week, involving a fourth grade. The other three afternoons a week are given to children selected from two sixth grades with special interest in ceramics. This, too, is a four-week commitment.)

2:30– 3:30 Open laboratory for individuals. (This period parallels free work periods in many classrooms so that children needing help can come from several groups. Other specialists in the school have the same open laboratory period. Schedules on the various doors, on which children sign up in advance, help prevent overcrowding.)

The daily schedule for the science specialist in a small high school which is part of a twelve-year school might look something like this:

9:00– 9:50 Senior science class meets.

9:50–10:40 Senior science class additional time three days a week. (A 100-minute block—when combined with the nine o'clock period—for laboratory experiences and individual research; time for consulting with students about individual work or planning with student laboratory assistants.)

10:40–11:30 Junior science class meets.

11:30–12:20 Junior science class additional time three days a week. (A 100-minute block for laboratory experiences and individual experimentation; time for student consultation, planning with students who are to present demonstration to a sixth-grade class; time for observing classes and preparing materials and equipment needed by classes or teachers in other departments or grades.)

12:20– 1:10 Lunch.

1:10– 2:00 Sophomore science class meets.

2:00– 2:50 Freshman science class meets.

2:50– 3:40 Meeting with interested elementary school teachers to plan, prepare, and select equipment and materials; time for advanced science workshop or individual research and experimentation, individual counseling and planning, observation in classrooms.

These schedules provide opportunities for the specialist to observe learners in their work and to help them on problems best carried out in their regular homerooms. He also has time to develop a resource laboratory where he is available to work with individuals and groups and to give help to other teachers. The classroom teacher and the specialist plan jointly in the interests of learners; the classroom teacher and the specialist plan jointly with learners.

Programing to Meet Learners' Needs

The flexibility desirable in scheduling activities from day to day, in grouping, and in providing for the help of specialists should be extended to the total school day and school year. Two basic ideas underlying the preceding discussions are also important here. First, the whole learner comes to school; his in-school experiences are affected by, and in turn affect, his out-of-school activities. Second, the school's special responsibilities are met most effectively when its work is viewed in relation to that of other individuals and groups playing a part in the education of children and youth. The school year and the school day should be planned in relation to the needs of learners reflected against the individuals and groups with which they live. The length of the school day and of the school year, as well as the scheduling of activities within the day and the year, must take into account community backgrounds and facilities. Scheduling aspects of the school program in which all are involved (such as lunch and play periods) should also be planned with the overall problems posed by the particular community in mind.

THE LENGTH OF THE SCHOOL DAY SHOULD VARY IN DIFFERENT SCHOOLS

Some of the characteristics of the community in which learners live may influence decisions regarding the appropriate length of the school day. The fact that almost all children in a rural school must travel by bus may determine the length of the day. In another community where mothers work until late afternoon, the school day may well be extended to six o'clock for those who wish it. In still another community where little provision is made in home or neighborhood for after-school recreation, the day may be lengthened to include this type of activity. Such factors as the following should also be taken into account in determining the length of day: the distance learners travel to and from school, the means of transportation, the age of the learners, the needs of older boys and girls for work experiences, the staff available, the nature of educational opportunities afforded by the homes and community agencies, and the particular role of the school in that community. The school that provides for balanced growth is responsive to factors such as these and varies the length of its program to adjust to them. At other times the school may take the leadership or cooperate in securing better community provisions to meet these problems.

THE LENGTH OF THE SCHOOL YEAR SHOULD VARY IN DIFFERENT COMMUNITIES

Like the school day, the school year should vary with the types of educational opportunities offered to children and youth when the schools are not in session. Teachers must ask what happens to learners during vacation periods and during the long summer holiday. Certainly the problems of children and youth continue, and youngsters face many important persistent life situations during those weeks. How are they dealing with them? What guidance are they receiving? What negative approaches to persistent life problems emerge because of inadequate guidance? These are questions that every educator and community member must answer for all learners. Can educationally sound answers be given in widely varied communities where schools each conform to a ten-month school year?

The length of the school year should differ according to the needs of those concerned. For example, children from homes where adequate provision is made for a worthwhile out-of-door summer program may well have a two-month period away from the school. But thought should also be given to children and youth who will play on city streets during these months, to children who must prepare two main meals while their parents are at work, to the child whose parents are overanxious about his scholastic development and keep him to a strict study schedule through the summer months, to the youth whose work experiences are rich in potential learnings which are not being realized because of lack of guidance. A curriculum designed with concern for the all-round development of the learner requires a different length of school year for different schools and even for individuals within the same school. For some schools and for some learners it will mean a nine- or ten-month year, for others it will mean an all-year school—but such decisions would not be uniform for all communities.

Whether the school lengthens its program will also depend upon what other educational agencies there are in the community. In some cases the school can make its best contribution directly and will provide for the extended program within its own staff and facilities. In others the greatest contribution will come through working with community groups—cooperative supervision of a playground, availability of school facilities under the supervision of community groups, close cooperative relations with employers, participation in the planning groups of community councils.

A longer school day or an all-year school should not necessarily mean that the curriculum will provide only the types of activity now included. The program itself must be differentiated as to the nature of experiences, the time distribution for various activities, and the placement of activities. Extending the school year to include the summer months may, for some schools, mean the development of a school camp; for others, the extension of the recreational program or of work experiences under guidance, or the sponsoring of travel experiences; and for still others, the provision of essentially the same type of activities as those included in the regular school year but with a different time distribution in keeping with the needs occasioned by summer weather. Such modifications will call for adjustments in the professional day and year as well as in salaries and schedules.

SCHEDULING OF ASPECTS OF THE DAILY PROGRAM INVOLVING ALL LEARNERS SHOULD VARY TO MEET PARTICULAR NEEDS

Like the length of the school day and year, the organization of a schedule for lunch, play periods, or use of special facilities will be most effective if made with the nature of the community from which learners come in mind. For example, planning for rest, lunch, and recreational periods which will meet the needs of growing children and youth calls for consideration of such factors as distance from home to school, whether parents are at home to prepare meals, what community recreational facilities are available, and the like. In one school a majority of the youngsters may live too far away to go home for lunch. In another, where they go long distances for lunch, the period may need to be lengthened if health factors are taken into account. In some cases children who do not have adequate facilities for rest in their homes may even need time for sleep in school. Recreation facilities in the community may be so inadequate, or out-of-school work responsibilities so heavy, that extensive school time should be allowed for these activities in one situation, while in another community and home provisions may do much to meet this need. These examples could be multiplied for each phase of the program. Flexibility is always necessary if the program is to be balanced, both in range of persistent life situations dealt with—not necessarily in any one day, but over a period of time—and in variety of experiences provided to meet group and individual needs.

Providing Continuity of Growth Through Articulation

Continuity is a basic principle of curriculum development. Progress from grade to grade and from one unit of the school system to the next should be smooth. Under subject-centered curriculum designs, continuity is provided by assigning specific topics within a subject to different grade levels and by repeating topics at intervals so that learners come back to a more detailed study of an area when they are more mature.

In the proposed curriculum design there is no such assignment of topics from grade to grade. How, then, is continuity attained? What will happen if the learner moves to another school system with a different curriculum design? What will happen if he enters a traditional college? The answers to these questions have already been suggested in Chapters 5 and 8 in the discussions of how the focus and activities of a unit of work are determined and of how organized bodies of subject-matter will be used and skills developed. Here the principles suggested earlier are summarized.

THE VARIOUS UNITS OF THE SCHOOL MUST BE CONCEIVED AND OPERATED AS A WHOLE

The preceding sections imply that the same principles governing the selection and guidance of experiences at the elementary school level also apply in the secondary school. Those who would test the proposed design in action would be guided by common principles from the nursery school through the highest educational level.

The teacher at each level must study the situations and problems most likely to face his learners, but all teachers must work together toward the development of consistent balanced growth in meeting persistent life situations. Just as no special problem should be assigned to one grade, so no special group of problems should be assigned with certainty to an educational level. Each teacher must take learners where he finds them, depending on general principles rather than specific recommendations or patterns for his guide. There must be essential agreement as to over-all objectives and values sought so that each teacher has a clear understanding of the world into which the young adult is going and what is likely to be expected of him.

To achieve continuity, each teacher must be thoroughly familiar with the general characteristics of learners at the age level which is his special responsibility, and with the developmental tendencies of those older and younger. It is important, too, that record systems be devised so that the teacher can know the details of learners' previous experiences. Where several teachers are working with the same learner, as is frequently the case, it is important that they have time to share information about him.

The achievement of articulation that makes for maximum growth calls for cooperative planning at many levels. Within the school the whole professional staff must plan together. Between elementary and secondary schools working with the same learners there should be interschool curriculum committees, interschool visitation, and cumulative records that accompany learners as they move from one situation to another.

THE PERSISTENT NATURE OF LIFE SITUATIONS PROVIDES A GUARANTEE OF CONTINUITY

The fact that life situations recur and that learners meet new aspects of the same general problem provides continuity from grade to grade, and from one school level to the next. As suggested in Chapters 5 and 8, continuity is defined and evaluated in terms of increasing insight into persistent life situations. These are the threads about which concepts, information, and skills develop. Continuity in terms of an expanding grasp of the logic of a given subject field will be secondary, but will undoubtedly be achieved at least at a level satisfactory for a later study of the subject as an entity if such is desired. Such devices as time lines and references to chronology in history, discussions in the sciences that indicate interrelated areas of research, and study of number theory in mathematics have been suggested as means through which teachers help learners become acquainted with subject fields even though subjects are not the organizing elements of the curriculum.

PUPIL–TEACHER PLANNING ASSURES ARTICULATION

The problem faced by a given group of learners is viewed as an opportunity to use old learnings and to develop new ones, not as a convenient peg on which to hang a predetermined body of subject matter. The planning that goes on as teacher and learners explore the possibilities of the new problem provides articulation. Teacher and learners identify not only what is already known but also areas requiring more study. If the new problem represents a significant demand for new knowledge or skills, time is taken for as extensive a study as is required to fill the gap. If the new problem calls mainly for a reorientation of facts already well established, the study may be brief. By their joint identification of new needs, pupils and teacher together plan to supply whatever experiences are needed to allow for smooth articulation between the previous learnings and the present situation.

For the individual learner who has already developed considerable competence in an area, repetition of previous experiences is avoided by the assignment of a new aspect of the problem, by an opportunity to serve as an expert in an area of particular competence, or perhaps by an opportunity to explore some different concern altogether. Here, as with the group, joint planning determines the next steps that will make for the smoothest articulation with past learnings.

At the high school level, the planning that provides for smooth articulation may involve more teachers. The learner and his homeroom counselor will plan a tentative program and check it from the point of view of the balance it provides and the direction it indicates. The homeroom counselor may then work with specialists and resource people in planning the final program for the learner. Because there are more choices to be made and because more specialists are involved in working with the high school youth, cooperative planning is especially important to insure continuity and relationship among varied kinds of experiences.

METHODS OF WORKING HELP TO GUARANTEE SUCCESSFUL ADJUSTMENTS TO NEW SITUATIONS

One of the significant implications of the Eight-Year Study [1] was that school systems could depart markedly from the traditional college-preparatory courses and still develop the skills, information, and attitudes essential to success in college. Learners who can apply a scientific approach to the solution of problems, who possess the requisite skills for locating and for critically analyzing needed information, who know how to tap existing resources, who can express themselves clearly and listen intelligently to others, who can evaluate their own strengths and weaknesses, and who are able to make intelligent plans and carry them out, possess some of the skills essential to success in new situations.

Either an individual or a group, so prepared, can move with relative ease to a curriculum developed more specifically on a grade-by-grade basis. In many subject areas, pupils will bring real strength from intensive study of various persistent life situations. In areas where gaps occur, they are well equipped to do the independent study needed to fill in such

[1] Wilford M. Aikin, *The Story of the Eight-Year Study, With Conclusions and Recommendations* (New York: Harper & Brothers, 1942).

gaps. Furthermore, the general skill in getting along with people and in adjusting to the flexible programs described should result in ability to analyze the new situation and to adjust to it without undue frustration.

THE NATURE OF THE LEARNER HAS IMPLICATIONS FOR ARTICULATION

Those who feel that a learner will be handicapped in going into the next grade or educational level if he has not had contact with a prescribed amount of subject matter sometimes assume that what is written into such courses of study represents exactly the learnings the pupil will take with him to his next contact with the same subject area. Nothing could be further from the case. Facts not used continuously are likely to be forgotten, no matter how efficiently taught. When the next contact with a special aspect of a subject field comes several years later, as it might in an area such as American history under a typical spiral design, the loss may be considerable. No matter what the curriculum design, no teacher assumes that all learners will come equipped with the skills and knowledges indicated in the course of study.

Another safeguard against serious handicaps if a learner comes to an advanced study with limited information has been mentioned in previous chapters. This lies in the ability of the more mature learner to grasp concepts rapidly. Time is relative in learning—spending ten hours on a topic in grade five does not mean saving ten hours of an eighth-grader's time. Depending on the topic, it may actually mean very little saving of time. The teacher starts where the learner is and provides as much or as little experience as his maturity demands to meet the new problem successfully.

The choice is not between one curriculum design that achieves continuity by designating subject matter and another that fails to achieve continuity because no such assignments are written down. Regardless of the curriculum design, the problem of achieving continuity is basically one of putting to effective use knowledge of how learners mature and the way learning takes place.

Using the Whole School and the Community As Sources of Learning Experiences

Throughout the preceding discussion a number of ways have been outlined in which the whole school community can be used to contribute to the learner's development. If the curriculum consists of all the experiences of learners under the guidance of the school, it is important that all these experiences point in the same direction. Going through the cafeteria line, walking down the halls, sharing the playground with children of different ages and interests, are all sources of fruitful learning experiences. A summary follows of suggested ways of using the facilities of the entire school community as a source of experiences for children and youth.

BEING OF SERVICE IN A SCHOOL COMMUNITY CAN PROVIDE OPPORTUNITIES FOR IMPORTANT LEARNINGS

Some of the most vital all-class problems come from the obligations that groups take on as part of the school community. Learners do not come to a classroom isolated from the remainder of the school. They live in the school community as truly as their parents live in the town, village, or city. Opportunities for classes to serve the school community include running the lost-and-found department, managing the school store, publishing the school paper, assuming responsibility for the play activities of younger children, running a rainy-day series of lunch-period movies, initiating a school clean-up campaign. With such opportunities to serve, students must have authority for self-direction of some activities. Student councils without actual authority to make decisions lack the vitality of learning which comes with real government. Such budgets of power should be worked out by pupil–faculty–administration groups to insure that qualitative learnings will emerge.

EXPERIENCES OUTSIDE THE CLASSROOM CAN SUGGEST PROBLEMS FOR CLASSROOM STUDY

Not only do special service responsibilities provide the basis for fruitful classroom experiences, but so do problems arising incidentally in parts of the school beyond the classroom doors. The teacher should be alert to these. Criticism of the choice of food in the school lunchroom could lead into a fruitful study of the problems of quantity buying and cooking, or into discussions of what should be the characteristics of a good school lunch. The overbearing attitude of a pupil on safety patrol could raise problems in a third grade of how to get along with people. To improve dull and uninteresting hallways could be a special problem assumed by an art group. Problems of safety in the halls or on the playground could be important class concerns. The teacher working in terms of the concerns of learners watches for all such genuine problems.

THE SCHOOL ITSELF IS A RICH LABORATORY OF RESOURCE MATERIALS

Not only can teachers and learners make full use of the genuine concerns resulting from the experience of living in a school community, they can also utilize the school as a rich laboratory of resources. This may involve taking the first-graders down to see how the school is heated; inviting the engineer to discuss the ventilation system with a fifth grade; asking the school physician to explain a health examination; visiting the nurse's office; asking the principal or business manager to help in a high school study of a proposed tax levy for school buildings; planting and caring for a school garden or some window boxes to make the front of the building more attractive.

Learners also secure valuable experiences as they actually work with school equipment. They may be responsible for the motion-picture projector, for running an opaque projector, for typing the stencil for the school paper, for running the mimeograph machine. At the high school level, particularly, many valuable work experiences can be provided within the school. Such experiences are often especially important in the education of slow-learning children who need repeated experiences in situations where there is sympathetic guidance and where they may return to classrooms and discuss special problems which they have encountered.

LEARNERS BECOME INVOLVED IN COMMUNITY ACTIVITIES WHEN THE WHOLE SCHOOL OPERATES AS PART OF THE COMMUNITY

Because the school has a part to play in community leadership, there are numerous ways in which learners can become realistically involved in community problems through the school. Many types of cooperative relations with businesses are possible. For example, on Hallowe'en the children may volunteer to decorate store windows. This not only prevents vandalism but also provides for an important cooperative experience. Or learners operating a school store may work closely with several merchants in the immediate vicinity.

Illustrations are numerous of children and youth involved in community problems. A fourth grade in a small town started an active campaign against flies and mosquitoes. Through their efforts, and those of other community members who cooperated, considerable progress was made toward covering garbage containers and cleaning up other breeding places. A sixth grade in a large city school, wishing to add beauty to their own homes, worked with the teacher and their parents to build window boxes and to plant flowers that added color to their neighborhood all summer. In many schools children, parents, and interested community members have jointly undertaken to beautify the school buildings and grounds. New equipment has been constructed by interested groups when funds were not available to purchase it. Buildings have been painted, trees planted, school gardens laid out. School and community—parents, children, and others who were concerned—have cooperated in activities to raise funds for the school. A bazaar in which all work together, a spring festival, a Christmas concert, are common activities. Planned wisely they serve to give learners an opportunity to work cooperatively with persons of various age groups.

Necessary services in some communities have been developed through cooperative planning in which teachers and pupils have had a large share. One rural school operates a meat-packing plant for the neighborhood; another runs a bank to serve both school and community; a third manages a local cooperative; and a fourth grows an experimental garden plot in which new types of products are tested. In one city a health clinic was planned jointly by parents and school. In another, an after-school recreation program was set up for the children whose parents work. In a district where children come to school from long distances a lunchroom operated by school and community was established. Children and youth take an active share both in planning and in carrying out such enterprises.

Work experience, as a means of becoming acquainted with certain aspects of community life, has already been mentioned. Its value is enhanced when employers, youth, and school counselors work closely together evaluating the learnings that result, analyzing needed competencies which the school can help to build, and identifying other experiences that can be valuable. Community groups and individual citizens also contribute by pointing out new vocational horizons. The professions are changing as radically as other vocations, and new service occupations are developing. Community members can work with the school to help learners see new possibilities and new needs. Whether or not this leads to actual work experiences for high school youth, it can result in a variety of discussion groups, in firsthand study, and in acquiring information through printed materials, all of which give some understanding of changing occupational patterns.

Preparing young people to leave the school for the world they will help make is an all-community job. Youth and children serving the community with and without adults; the school identified in the councils of the community as a genuine force; the community contributing to education in expert advice, in planning, in materials, in practical experience —these spell modern education to meet modern life. They mean a contribution to the good life of the immediate community and the better life of all men.

The right to share in community affairs by voting comes late in the United States. Our society has no common religious or cultural induction into adulthood. The schools can help to meet this need for preparing competent citizens by planning opportunities for the cooperative sharing of thought and work by youth and adults. The more frequently youth and adults function together in community undertakings, learning those things both must know, the better the understanding of community needs and of the persistent problems they face as citizens.

Related Readings

ASSOCIATION FOR CHILDHOOD EDUCATION. *Grouping: Problems and Satisfactions.* Washington, D.C.: The Association, 1954.

ASSOCIATION FOR SUPERVISION AND CURRICULUM DEVELOPMENT. *Creating a Good Environment for Learning.* 1954 Yearbook. Washington, D.C.: The Association, 1954.

CLAPP, ELSIE R. *The Use of Resources in Education.* New York: Harper & Brothers, 1952.

CRONBACH, LEE J., editor. *Text Materials in Modern Education.* Urbana, Ill.: University of Illinois Press, 1955.

DALE, EDGAR. *Audio-Visual Methods in Teaching.* Revised edition. New York: The Dryden Press, Inc., 1954.

LINDBERG, LUCILE. *The Democratic Classroom.* New York: Bureau of Publications, Teachers College, Columbia University, 1954.

OLSEN, EDWARD G., editor. *The Modern Community School.* New York: Appleton-Century-Crofts, 1953.

ROBERTS, DOROTHY M. *Partners with Youth.* New York: Association Press, 1956.

WITTICH, WALTER ARNO, AND CHARLES F. SCHULLER. *Audio-Visual Materials, Their Nature and Use.* Revised edition. New York: Harper & Brothers, 1957.

11

MAKING EVALUATION AN INTEGRAL PART OF THE CURRICULUM

Evaluation is part of every experience. Everyone engages in evaluation in some form or another—evaluation of self and of others who are friends or associates or individuals to whom society delegates responsibility, and evaluation of institutions and events.

What role does the evaluation process, which is so integral a part of everyday living, play in curriculum development? What should be the nature of the values sought? What kinds of data are needed and how will they be collected? What records are required? How can tne growth of the learner be shared with parents and others? How is the total educational program to be evaluated and by whom?

The Nature of Evaluation in Curriculum Development

Evaluation was a part of every illustration of teachers ana ıearners at work in preceding chapters. What purposes did it serve and who was involved? This section points up principles implicit in earlier discussions. Although the focus here is on the proposed curriculum design, all teachers face similar problems in deciding what purpose evaluation is to serve and whom to involve in the process.

EVALUATION IS AN INTEGRAL PART OF EVERY LEARNING SITUATION

Evaluation is a part of the learning process itself. Appraisals of the learner's growth and development are the bases for deciding next steps. Such appraisals are made by teachers, by pupils, and often by parents and community members as well. As a high school teacher plans with his group, they recognize that their understanding of the major activities of their city government is quite limited. A fourth-grade teacher discovers that many in his class still lack the necessary techniques for effective discussion. A teacher of sixth-graders makes plans with three members of the group for special help to develop essential reading skills. In a first grade a teacher decides to delay organized instruction in reading for the less mature in the group to allow time for more oral language experiences. From such day-by-day appraisals come the teacher's decisions as to how to guide ongoing experiences and when to introduce new ones.

Evaluation is a continuous process for the teacher guiding experiences in terms of the needs and interests of his group seen in the light of persistent life situations. It is no less so for the teacher working under a curriculum organized around subjects. On the basis of today's discussion, a science teacher decides that additional laboratory work tomorrow would be helpful. Noting inadequate concepts of the relation of topography to climate, a teacher of social studies plans for appropriate visual aids. In an eighth-grade English class a group studies the rejection slips on the selections submitted for the school paper and, with teacher guidance, decides what is needed to improve their writing. A sixth-grade health class lists the questions about the circulation of the blood that they want to answer. Regardless of the curriculum design, successful teaching involves evaluation at every step.

THE PURPOSE OF EVALUATION IS TO PROMOTE GROWTH

The primary purpose of evaluation is to promote further growth. It is a process for guiding action, not merely passing judgment. While evaluation certainly involves making judgments, these are for determining the extent and quality of progress toward goals identified and accepted by both teacher and pupils. Jerome and his teacher look at the way he is turning a piece of wood on the lathe and decide that, while progress has been made over the past week, more practice still is in order. The sixth-graders decide that the committee reporting on progress in air travel has done a fine job of locating information but does not have effective skills of organizing and presenting it. The eleventh-grade class pools present information on an international relations problem and decides that Donald and Marie, particularly, have more reading to do. These judgments of the present strengths or weaknesses of groups and of individuals are not ends in themselves, but lead to further action.

Involved in the continuous process of evaluation is periodic collection of test or other data as a means of determining progress. In some instances, these intermittent summary evaluations may lead to the recording of letter grades or marks. However, these are not used to motivate learners but rather to translate judgments the pupils have already been helped to make and understand regarding their present accomplishments and needs into conventional symbols for recording purposes.

THE LEARNER HAS A CENTRAL ROLE IN EVALUATION

To be able to evaluate one's needs and appraise one's competence, to be able to make sound choices and decisions, to be able to propose next steps and take necessary action—these are signs of developing maturity. Such growth occurs as teacher and learners discuss proposals for a new study and together decide what areas most need exploration. It is contributed to by the long-term and daily planning periods through which teacher and learners cooperatively study the development of an activity and revise their plans in the light of progress made and new needs indicated. Growth also comes as the teacher alerts learners to necessary new skills, or to areas in which extended practice is indicated, or to situations where incorrect judgments and generalizations have been made. Growth in self-evaluation comes as the learner and teacher, with or without the parent, sit in conference to inventory progress made and difficulties met, to identify concerns not yet provided for, and to outline plans for next steps.

As learners evaluate they are helped to clarify purposes and to understand the reasons for next steps. In addition, they also learn how to use the processes of evaluation as a guide to decision-making. Like other persistent life situations, the need to evaluate one's activities and to lay new plans is continuous from early childhood through adulthood.

PARENTS AND OTHER LAYMEN HAVE AN IMPORTANT PART TO PLAY IN THE EVALUATION PROCESS

Parents and other laymen share in the evaluation process in two important ways. First, they help teachers gain better understanding of learners by providing significant information about learners' needs and about the way concepts and skills acquired in school are used in the out-of-school setting. Second, joint pooling of experiences can lead to plans for cooperative action in which the school, the home, and other community agencies supplement and support each other in the guidance of young citizens. This may involve joint determination of goals, cooperation to extend learners' awareness of educative possibilities in the community, common action to eliminate situations which undermine desired growth, agreement as to which agency is best equipped to offer a particular kind of experience and guidance, or determination as to how the school and other agencies can modify their practices to provide for consistent growth in dealing with the same persistent life situations.

Determining the Values Sought

The first and basic step in evaluation is clarifying the goals and values to be reached. The key concept in evaluation is value. How the teacher and pupils together clarify goals and establish purposes has been illustrated in the preceding discussion of planning and developing experiences with learners. For learners, goals are usually set by the problem with which they are dealing—the knowledges, skills, concepts, and attitudes required to publish the next edition of the school paper, to discuss the issues involved in sharing natural resources with other states and countries, to judge the statements of a radio commentator. Teachers, however, need broader insights for they must be able to study present situations in terms of future growth.

PERSISTENT LIFE SITUATIONS ARE THE BASES FOR LONG-RANGE GOALS

For the curriculum design under discussion, long-range goals are defined in terms of growth in ability to deal with persistent life situations learners meet in their day-to-day experiences. In this design value is placed on increased command of the skills, concepts, attitudes, information, and ways of behaving required to cope efficiently and competently with today's world.

In spelling out such goals the teacher must first think about the persistent life situations learners face. The framework may be an analysis such as the one in Chapter 6, or a similar one developed by the teachers in a particular school system. In terms of whatever analysis best fits his ways of working, the teacher will then outline the understandings, attitudes, skills, and ways of behaving needed to deal effectively with each of the situations listed. The discussions preceding each area in the analysis of persistent life situations given in Chapter 6 do not give goals in detail, but they point out the importance of the particular area and thereby suggest the general nature of desired goals.

In a changing world, goals stated in terms of growth in ability to deal with persistent life situations will change as research uncovers new data and provides new generalizations or better ways of working. Constant reappraisal of long-range goals is necessary. In the complete set of goals there must be some that relate to the skills of living in a world of change —to the persistent life situations of using a scientific approach to the study of problems and of using appropriate resources.

GOALS HAVE ADDED MEANING WHEN STATED IN TERMS OF BEHAVIOR

Stating goals—skills, understandings, attitudes—in behavioral terms indicates the kind of evidence that will show whether the goals are being realized. Major value is placed upon the learner's ability actually to apply the knowledge, generalizations, and skills he has acquired. For example, goals relating to the persistent life situations of participating as a group member may be stated in such terms as:

Points out weaknesses or limitations of a proposal
Offers counterproposals when in disagreement
Abides by group decisions after pointing out disagreement
. . .

Similarly, the pupil knows what he is trying to accomplish when, as he deals with the persistent life situation of understanding the ideas of others, he is working toward goals in reading skills such as:

Checks on reliability of sources when seeking facts
Uses index to locate desired information
Skims reading matter to find section bearing directly on inquiry
Reads and interprets factual material accurately
. . .

Such statements clearly identify bases for evaluation. Evidence can be gathered by both learners and teacher to show whether individuals are behaving in the manner indicated and under what circumstances. In the light of this evidence further needs in the area can be determined. Both for teacher and for pupils, goals stated in terms of behavior become tangible items toward which pupils can work.

Another example of the kinds of statements resulting when goals are stated in terms of behavior may be helpful. Whatever the age of the pupil, the area of health is one with which all teachers and parents are concerned. Among the behavioral goals in this area the following might be listed:

Selects and partakes of balanced meals
Selects and prepares foods with reference to their nutritional elements
Regulates ventilation and lighting to contribute to healthful living
Selects clothing suited to temperature needs
Adjusts activity to temperature conditions
Secures needed balance of rest and activity
Develops needed skills for relaxation and activity
Uses health routines necessary to well-being
Recognizes symptoms of common communicable diseases
Uses social efforts to protect health—immunization, quarantine, health examinations
Knows and selects sound sources of assistance both to protect health and in caring for illness and injury
Uses first-aid measures in caring for illness and injury
Uses safety measures in everyday activities (using scissors, carrying chairs, putting articles in proper places)
Supports social efforts to foster good health (sanitation, disease control, safety measures)
Adjusts to or takes steps to correct physical defects
Adjusts to personal limitations—physical, intellectual, emotional
Responds with equanimity to success and failure
Makes choices and resolves conflict situations
Establishes secure relations—both social and working relationships
Expresses emotions constructively

Readers who study this illustrative list in relation to the analysis of persistent life situations on pages 155 to 157 will recognize its source and will undoubtedly think of other behavioral goals. Curriculum committees who have prepared analyses of persistent life situations in considerable detail will already have at hand useful bases for developing lists of behavioral goals.

Over-all goals, such as those just given, are achieved gradually and take on new meanings as learners mature. Some teachers and curriculum committees will want more detailed statements for specific age groups. Some will also want to indicate specific skills, attitudes, generalizations, and basic ideas required to deal effectively with persistent life situations. Whatever the decision as to the way in which goals are stated, the teacher should be concerned about assuring that what is taught is effectively translated into behavior which is based on as much understanding as the learner is capable of and as is required for the effective handling of his problem. In terms of the learners with whom he is working, each teacher asks: What are the situations with which my pupils are struggling? How do they meet these situations? How can they be helped to take the next step toward a more complete realization of the behavioral goals basic to dealing with persistent life situations in this area?

GOALS MUST BE SEEN IN RELATION TO THE MATURITY AND CAPACITY OF INDIVIDUALS

Behavioral goals are not fixed standards. As suggested in the preceding discussion, statements of goals prepared by curriculum committees may well include more specific objectives for varied maturity and capacities —for young children, for intermediate-graders, for adolescents, for adults. Even when behavioral goals are differentiated in terms of age levels they should not represent the same standards for all members of a class. Any such arbitrary standard will set for some individuals goals for which they are not ready and which they will consistently fail to attain while, at the same time, it will permit others to fall far short of the achievement of which they are capable. For example, the goals relating to understanding and dealing with science concepts should not be the same for Jim, a tenth-grader, who has been curious about science phenomena and has worked in his basement laboratory since he was a fifth-grader, as they are for his classmate Sarah who has had little or no work in this area prior to entering junior high school. Jim is excited about science, reads widely in the field, shows special competence in working in the area, and wishes and is ready to make this a field of special study. Sarah, on the other hand, is growing in understanding and interest, but the work has value for her mainly as it relates to general education—to the personal and social problems with which all individuals are confronted.

Jim's and Sarah's interests and abilities also suggest that the total group of long-range goals should not be the same for everyone. With strong science interests and high intellectual ability, Jim should achieve goals different from those desirable for Sarah whose vocational interests are those of a homemaker. Goals for either of these adolescents will differ somewhat from those of the equally able youth whose deep interest lies in foreign languages. This is the basic problem of deciding what is appropriate as general education and what represents specialized education.

Similarly, the long-range goals will differ for groups of learners who have special learning difficulties, unusual capacities, or unique community backgrounds. Goals in the area of health for the mentally retarded pupil may go little beyond such specific behaviors for the six- to nine-year-old as washing his face and hands under supervision and taking some responsibility for bathing and showering; for the twelve- to fifteen-year-old group, performing such daily habits of cleanliness independently and habitually; for the fifteen- to eighteen-year-old, being able to help younger children in carrying out such routines. These same behavioral goals are important for all learners, but they are normally achieved earlier with little help from the school. In like manner, the teacher identifying goals for the intellectually gifted pupil keeps in mind his unique ability to deal with abstract concepts, to see relationships, and to integrate his experiences.

Growth in one area must be evaluated in terms of total growth. For example, Susan's general intellectual ability may suggest that she is capable of more advanced thinking in arithmetic. But she may be handling competently all the situations calling for arithmetic confronting her while, at the same time, she is struggling to overcome patterns of English usage learned at home. In planning experiences with Susan, the teacher would weigh her potential growth in mathematics against goals in language usage. Ability, mental and physical health, feelings, work habits, home background, standards and values held, human relations, problem-solving ability—these and many other factors affect the goals desirable for any one individual at a particular time.

Proposals that growth be evaluated in terms of each individual's ability, maturity, and balanced development should not mean that any degree of proficiency which satisfies a learner himself will be acceptable. Nor will this basis of evaluation result in little or no impetus to do a good job or in few experiences with the hard realities of a competitive world. Several assumptions about how the teacher will operate, underlying the illustrations in preceding chapters, suggest that evaluation can be in terms of individual needs and potentialities without undesirable results. When evaluation is an integral part of the teaching–learning process, pupils are continually encouraged to take realistic looks at both their strengths and their weaknesses and to participate in planning next steps. Learners are not protected from failure, and they must face the reality of not being chosen for a job because of inadequate skills. Also, teachers feel responsible for helping learners set higher standards. Perhaps more basic, however, is the psychological assumption that any individual engaged in an activity which he sees as purposeful, worthwhile, and important will not do a haphazard job of it. Teachers working under this curriculum design have as their objective adults who put their best into an activity because they have had long years of satisfying classroom experiences in meeting their full obligations to themselves and to the group. Further, there is an underlying assumption that those individuals most likely to make effective contributions as adults are those who have faced up to realistic appraisals of their own strengths and weaknesses as children and youth. The problems of today's world demand adults who will "hitch their wagons to stars"—but in terms of goals that have some basis in reality.

Gathering Data on Which to Base Evaluation

After specifying desired goals, the next step in the evaluation of pupil growth is to gather data which show the learner's progress in achieving these objectives. Often the effectiveness of the new experiences provided for learners depends on how accurately present achievements are appraised. Since evaluation is a part of every learning experience, techniques for gathering data regarding pupil progress consist, in part, of those which the teacher uses to study day-to-day behavior. However, in addition to a sensitive, continuous alertness to progress and to problems, the teacher must also have techniques for systematizing classroom observations when special evidence is needed, for making effective use of tests, and for giving pupils an appropriate share in the data-gathering process.

DAILY ACTIVITIES SHOULD BE STUDIED TO REVEAL NEEDS AND EVIDENCE OF GROWTH

Many decisions as to next steps will be made on the basis of the teacher's interpretation of the day-to-day behavior of children and youth. The evidence upon which to base evaluations is always available.

Evidence is at hand whenever choices are made. Jim was involved in the evaluation process as he started to throw paper on the playground, hesitated, and then walked several yards to the trash can. So were these children and youth . . .

Sue started to clean up the sink but soon turned from the job, saying, "Someone else can clean up."

"There isn't much time, I won't wash my hands before lunch."

"I could do this more neatly, but maybe Miss Robertson won't care."

"Working to get a community center is the business of the grownups who run our city—not of high school students."

"We can start the new work. We haven't finished our present jobs, but . . ."

The choice made, the stand taken, the action proposed, provide evidence for evaluation of growth toward desired goals. Observing this behavior, the teacher decides what new help is necessary.

Evidence is also available when planning next steps. As groups or individuals evaluate their work, they note the progress made and decide on changes in plans for next steps. This is the meaning of Bob's proposal—"Some of the children weren't very much interested in getting bicycle licenses when we made our talks in the various rooms. We can make posters to remind them." It is the action being taken by these learners . . .

"People in our block are not very careful about covering refuse. Maybe it will help if I . . ."

"Mr. Roberts of the City Planning Commission was very nice but not hopeful that the Commission would be interested in our proposal. Should we continue? . . ."

In planning with learners the teacher appraises the proposal coming from the group, thinks about the insight or lack of insight revealed, decides whether it is appropriate to suggest related problems or whether what has been proposed is, for the moment, as far as the group can be expected to go.

The generalizations upon which learners are acting provide another type of evidence. Because persistent life situations do recur, there will be opportunities to see how generalizations learned in one situation are actually being used . . .

"But why do we need a bond issue? Can't the board just vote the money? . . ."

"I think it's right that there are rules for using the new swimming pool. After all, everybody worked to raise the money and a few people shouldn't be allowed to ruin it. . . ."

"Sure, I voted that some of the Student Council money be used for a campaign to help students become better citizens of Washington High and our community by caring for public property. When we were working for our community center I certainly found out how important it is for everybody to help maintain public property. . . ."

These youngsters are expressing through various immediate problems the depth of their understanding of the basic generalization that public property is supported and maintained by all members of the community and each is responsible for its upkeep. Their teachers would appraise the adequacy of the understanding in terms of the maturity of the individuals and the group. Is the group concerned with the bond issue ready to expand their limited understanding that parents' money is involved? What of the last group—are there individuals who still reveal inadequate understanding of the responsibility of all the members of a community for the maintenance of its property? Not what conclusion is voiced today, but how well it operates several weeks hence in a related problem is the basis for the evaluation.

SYSTEMATIC OBSERVATION IS NEEDED

Sometimes in the give-and-take of daily work the teacher finds himself uncertain of what growth really has occurred. Evidence may be clear for many of the group, but for a few the picture may be clouded. It is also possible to become so involved with certain problems that other aspects of growth do not get the careful look they merit. It is helpful from time to time to make more systematic observations . . .

"They sounded very clear and sure of themselves when we talked about the responsibility of older children for safety on the playground, but I wonder if they really act on it. . . ."

"That was a beautiful job of illustrating and analyzing propaganda techniques, but Darline, Larry, and Anne were quiet. I wonder if they really . . ."

"The more I think about the discussion at noon today about the need for community resources for leisure-time activities, the more I realize how little I really know about my group's sources of aesthetic satisfaction. . . ."

Systematic observation of children and youth as they engage in daily activities in and out of school can provide important evidence. The teacher may select a problem or one aspect of behavior and, for a given period of time, look specifically for evidence in this area. A record of observations of an individual's or group's behavior in typical situations may be made and the accumulated evidence analyzed. Formulating behavioral goals before the observations are made is helpful . . .

"These behaviors should be typical of my group in the lunchroom. Is this what I am really seeing? . . ."

"We have been concentrating on better library techniques. I'm just going to sit back and watch next time to see whether they . . ."

Conferences with pupils, parents, or both are another means of systematically collecting evidence. There may be an informal exchange of ideas, an evaluation of progress and plans for further work, or a meeting to work on a special problem. While the teacher is responsive to the needs of the others in the conference, it is still possible to collect specific evidence . . .

"John has been enjoying many library books here, but he seldom takes them home. I was wondering . . ."

"What do you think your committee needs next, Judy? Have you some plans? . . ."

Work done by individuals—drawings, outlines, notes taken to guide the learner in an oral presentation or a discussion, autobiographies, creative expression of ideas in writing, diaries, or logs—can afford still another source of evidence . . .

"Here is my handwriting folder. Every two weeks I put in something I have written. I am doing better."

"I can use the tables I need for figuring out chemistry problems much more easily—and more accurately, too—as you will see in this paper."

"These are my first drafts and here are the final stories. See how much less proofreading people have to do for me now."

"I think I can stick to the point and develop an idea with pretty good logic. As a check Miss Hempel is going to read the outline of my argument for the community center which I hope will be used in the paper. . . ."

TESTS AND EXAMINATIONS CONTRIBUTE CERTAIN KINDS OF EVIDENCE

Both standardized and teacher-made tests have a place in the evaluation process. There are many kinds of standardized instruments available to inventory or appraise pupil growth. The potential contributions of standardized tests and some of the precautions necessary in using them have been discussed in relation to identifying the concerns of learners in Chapter 7 and to meeting individual needs in Chapter 9. Intelligence or general aptitude tests help to estimate the general level of intelligence and such over-all types of competence as problem-solving ability and verbal competence. Achievement tests contribute to the teacher's insights into the learner's present understandings and skills in a particular area or areas. There are standardized measures (tests, inventories, scales) of specific aptitudes, interests, attitudes, personal-social adjustment, problem-solving, and health and physical development.

Some of the safeguards which must be observed in using tests are particularly important when their contribution to evaluation is considered. First, the teacher should keep in mind that evaluation and measurement are not synonymous. Brian in grade five, with the mental age of a third-grader, may achieve a grade score of 3.8 on a standardized arithmetic test. His classmate Sandy, with the mental age of a sixth-grader, may achieve a standardized test score in arithmetic of 5.0 on the same test. Brian's score may be evaluated as satisfactory progress. For Sandy the score might mean a need for more stimulation in mathematics.

Furthermore, under a curriculum in which teachers and learners set goals jointly, national norms do not have the same meanings in all subject fields. Even in areas such as reading or spelling, where the content of the typical standardized test is not likely to differ much from the experiences of the group, it is important to appraise the evidence regarding present skills and knowledge against the behavioral goals held for the particular group. This does not mean a lowering of standards or a depreciation of skills. While some standardized test scores below the norm will be considered adequate in terms of the present problems facing the group, other scores at or above the norm may be considered inadequate for the situations with which learners are dealing.

It is also important for the teacher to remember that no matter how carefully the test is administered, the score may not represent the learner's true capacity. Examination of Sandy's test paper in arithmetic could reveal careless work habits. It may also be that she has just transferred from a school where tests have been used as threats, and taking them has become fraught with emotion. Many factors may enter into a low score—actual lack of knowledge or skill, limited reading ability, emotional tensions, physical handicaps, gaps in special areas that invalidate an otherwise good performance. The pupil's achievement motivation or his attitudes toward school and school-related activity may also affect his response. This does not mean all scores are questionable and, therefore, without value. Rather, the fact that so many variables can affect the score suggests that caution be exercised in interpreting test results. A well-constructed, standardized test properly used can be very helpful to teacher and pupils in evaluating growth.

Earlier, the ultimate test of growth was defined in terms of behavior. Evidence with regard to the achievement of many behavioral goals is secured through observation of pupils in day-to-day living. However, attempts have been made to develop paper-and-pencil tests that focus on the learner's ability to reflect upon, relate, and organize ideas in responding to situational questions. While such questions do not assure behavioral responses in an actual situation, the reaction given provides on an intellectual level a test of the pupil's control of desired goals. Among the areas in which there has been experimentation in building standardized tests are those of critical thinking, problem-solving, and propaganda analysis.[1]

A teacher-made test can often prove to be the most effective evaluation instrument, since it can be built in terms of tasks appropriate for a particular group. Pupils who have embarked on a study of measurement because of inaccurate proportions in several classroom models take a test on terms and problems similar to those causing the difficulty. Members of a reading group record their oral reading on a tape recorder and then complete a check list of difficulties. A high school social studies class writes on several essay questions to demonstrate their present level of thinking about the unit just completed. Such classroom tests are particularly helpful when they are planned for jointly by teacher and pupils as an aid in appraising progress and as a guide to next steps.

Situational tests are also being developed and used by teachers. Mr. Jackson, concerned with testing student insight into appropriate behavior, built test questions such as the following for use with his tenth-graders . . .

> An automobile is moving along an icy road when the rear wheels suddenly begin to skid toward the ditch at the side of the road. What should the driver do to keep the car on the road? Why?
>
> Soon after obtaining her license, Mary was driving along the highway at medium speed when the car in front suddenly slowed down. Unable to stop quickly enough, Mary bumped the rear of the front car. What instructions would you give Mary which would help her to avoid such accidents?
>
> On returning home from the movies one evening, Jim and his family smelled gas as soon as they entered the front door. What should Jim's father do in order to reduce the potential danger? What precautions should he take?
>
> During a severe cold spell, some of the water pipes in Jack's home froze. How could Jack get the water running again quickly and safely?

Miss O'Brien, working with a sixth-grade group, used the following questions at various times . . .

[1] J. Wayne Wrightstone, Joseph Justman, and Irving Robbins, *Evaluation in Modern Education,* Chapter XX (New York: American Book Company, 1956).

> Mary Jane, Bill, and Sarah have been nominated for the office of president of the student council. What qualifications would you consider in making a decision as to the person for whom you would vote?
>
> Jack can either have a regular newspaper route delivering the local evening paper at a stated salary or can sell papers on a downtown corner on a commission basis. What things should he know about and take into account in making his decision?
>
> The class responsible for the school paper needs to make a decision as to whether to make a nominal charge for the paper or to take care of costs through advertising. What stand would you take if you were a member of the class? Why?

Teachers have also been using situational tests in which the pupils' responses to a problem or incident require insights into social values and relationships . . .

> Edward is new in your school, but it is at once evident that he has a physical handicap which makes it difficult for him to run easily. The usual playground activity at this season of the year is "soft-ball" baseball. Would you choose Edward for your team? Should he be asked to join either team? What is your reason for the decision made?
>
> The class was waiting to begin its work after a recess period. Paul and Vernon were at the coat closet debating who should pick up a cap that had been knocked down, each accusing the other of being responsible for knocking it off the hook. Larry, who sat near the coat closet, picked up the cap and put it on the hook. Do you think Larry did the right thing? Why?
>
> The sixth grade was planning a trip that involved a cost of approximately one dollar for each member of the group. Two children indicated that they probably could not ask their parents for that much money. What do you think should be done? Why?

Tests which provide an opportunity to use ideas in concrete situations, or to show how concepts are implemented, are built on the theory that something can be said to be learned only when the individual can and does use it appropriately. This does not mean that standardized tests of skills or information have no value. Rather, it points to the importance of selecting tests which evaluate the goals toward which individuals and groups are working. It suggests that goals must not be compromised to meet test content, and that other types of tests should be devised when standardized tests do not relate to or fail to cover agreed-upon objectives.

No single measure, or even a battery of measures, can justifiably be trusted implicitly as a basis for evaluating learners' aptitude or achievement. Yet in some school systems teachers and learners face state examinations or tests for admission to college. Teachers in such situations can find reassurance in the fact that learners who have had experiences with intelligence and achievement tests as aids in evaluation will not face any unusual problems in taking college-level tests in the same areas.

If the tests cover specific content—current events, science, history, literature—learners working under any curriculum design or using any textbook that does not happen to stress the facts selected as important by the test makers will be at a disadvantage. Teachers who are realistic face the problem of using such tests with learners, helping them to become aware of the types of questions they may be asked and of any general techniques in test-taking likely to be useful. This is a vital life situation to pupils whose scores may determine a high school certificate or college entrance.

Keeping Functional Records

Something more than numbers or symbols are needed for the records so essential in the evaluation process. Decisions regarding next steps should be supported by specific evidence of growth. If they are to be functional, records must be planned so that it is possible to gather the necessary data within the boundaries of an active school day, and to have these data available in usable form. All teachers have the responsibility of maintaining effective day-to-day and cumulative records, and of helping learners as well as interested adults share in the process. Regardless of the curriculum design, effective evaluation is impossible if ample evidence is not available.

EFFECTIVE RECORDS ARE COMPREHENSIVE

All the significant aspects of growth essential for dealing with persistent life situations should be considered in developing any plan for records which will give a comprehensive picture of the child or youth—growth in individual capacities, in social participation, in dealing with environmental factors and forces. This requires data concerning the individual's health, physical capacities, emotional adjustments, and growth patterns; his mental characteristics, his talents and aptitudes; his values and attitudes; his social relationships; his ability to function effectively in his environment—the whole realm of his interests, aspirations, and goals. Such records should also give the essential facts about the learner in relation to his home and community backgrounds and his in-school and out-of-school experiences.

To show the learner as a developing person, records must be continuous and cumulative, including both positive and negative aspects of the individual's development. Teachers at times hesitate to include statements about negative characteristics on the ground that these may change as the learner develops and are subject to later misinterpretation. Cumulative records should show such change. To fail to include a negative characteristic when it is a factor will mean an inaccurate or incomplete total picture at the particular time, and again when the record is referred to at a later date. It is assumed, of course, that records will be used professionally. They are service tools and must be used to serve the end for which they are designed.

Well-selected evidence, as comprehensive and as objective as possible, should enable those using cumulative records to see the individual in action and to agree or disagree with the interpretations made of the learner's growth and competence.

SIGNIFICANT INCIDENTS OF DAY-TO-DAY BEHAVIOR SHOULD BE RECORDED

Day-to-day anecdotes of significant incidents are an essential part of a record which gives a clear and accurate picture of the learner as a developing person. Knowing what to record and how to record it is a skill that is developed through practice. It is neither possible nor profitable to collect anecdotes for each pupil every day, nor will all incidents in which a pupil is involved be equally valuable in depicting his growth.

In part, decisions as to when an incident should be recorded would hinge on whether the evidence it supplies has been lacking or merely substantiates already ample data. For example, a suggestion that was well timed and helped the group to move ahead in their discussion may be an important incident to enter in Jane's record—it relates to a needed area of growth and the evidence is specific. To report a similar incident for Bill may be quite unnecessary at this time because of comparable anecdotes already recorded. In deciding whether to record an incident, it is also important to consider whether the behavior is characteristic or atypical. For example, the fact that Jim, in anger, closed his book with a slam need not be recorded since his reactions in other trying situations suggest that this particular episode is not characteristic behavior. There are, of course, dangers in the teacher's including or excluding incidents on the basis of his own judgment. The significance of an incident can sometimes be determined only when the event or action is seen in relation to earlier and later behavior. An incorrect impression regarding a pupil may color the teacher's interpretation. For example, too readily classifying Jim's slamming his book shut as atypical and failing to record it may conceal evidence indicating that Jim seems to have endless tolerance of the inadequacies of others but no patience with himself when his extremely good intellectual ability fails to unlock a problem.

Anecdotal records, of course, cannot be collected during a busy school day unless some incidents are selected for recording and some omitted. However, the possibilities suggested by Jim's case indicate that at times, or for specific learners, it may be important to collect evidence systematically and with as few subjective judgments as possible regarding what to include and what to omit. Sometimes this is done by sampling techniques. For example, the teacher decides on one or two fifteen-minute intervals that are typical of the total day and collects anecdotes during these periods.

Whatever anecdotes are recorded should be specific in that they report exact behavior—what was said or done—and give enough of the setting or the circumstance surrounding the behavior to provide those using the records with the facts necessary for a correct interpretation of the incident. A single comment or incident noted on a small pad may be a useful way to collect notations. These notations may be filed in the appropriate pupil's folder or in a card file under each child's name. The recordings relating to a given learner can be reviewed periodically, and those incidents that provide significant evidence of the nature of growth, whether it be forward or a retrogression, can then be made part of the individual's permanent record.

When teachers look at the anecdotes in the literature on record-keeping, they often feel that the practical job of collecting such data is impossible. How can one do so much writing, even for a few incidents a day, and keep class work moving ahead at the same time? Actually, a very brief notation is often sufficient for expansion later in the day before the details are forgotten. The first statement in each of the following illustrations is the abbreviated comment made while teaching or as classes are changing. The second statement shows the more complete recording made at the close of the school day or when a free period made it possible to write more fully.

MARY K. 10/25

Count change—lunch

Mary counted change for Wanda who was having trouble with her lunch money

FRANK 12/10

Keep money—my job

Wanted another child to keep his lunch money. Then added, "No, I'd better keep it. If it is lost, you would be to blame. It's my job."

John C. 11/15

Sun–star—relating ideas

Reference read said nearest star was a light year away. "That can't be right because the sun is the nearest star and it is about ninety-two million miles away. That is much less than a light year."

Sue Ellen 2/7

Voting age—factors take account of

"Of course, you have a right to your point of view on lowering the voting age—but have you taken into account the difference in education provided today—not only by schools but by radio and TV? Young people know a lot more than they did when the original law was passed."

Janet 2/14

Bond issue—color words, innuendo

Suggested that speeches and arguments pro and con for bond issue for the new high school be analyzed with reference to use of color words and innuendo (1) to test the soundness of the arguments and (2) to be prepared to react to questions raised by parents and other members of community.

On some days a number of such anecdotes will be recorded, on others only a few. Seldom will there be daily entries for each pupil. On some days notations will deal with the behavior of a few individuals; on other days single incidents for a number of pupils will be recorded. The teacher who records four or five significant anecdotes each day will have substantial cumulative records for use in evaluating pupil growth and progress.

SAMPLES OF PUPILS' WORK PROVIDE IMPORTANT RECORDS AND CONTRIBUTE DIRECTLY TO TEACHING

Keeping functional records takes time. Of course, anecdotes are not the only kind of specific evidence. Samples of pupils' work can be an important part of the cumulative record and contribute directly to teaching, and collecting such samples need not involve extra work. For example, in a fifth grade children analyzed their own handwriting, clipped their first samples into notebooks, together with plans agreed upon with the teacher, and at intervals added new samples and new evaluations. Eventually summaries of progress toward more legible writing were added to the permanent record, but for much of the year the children's working plans served as part of the cumulative record. In an eighth grade it was decided to file a brief signed review for each library book read. This provided both teacher and pupils with the needed evidence regarding breadth of recreational reading and depth of insight. Eventually each pupil wrote an evaluation of the year's work. To this summary the teacher added his own comments and filed it in the cumulative record. In a tenth grade it was agreed that group-work skills would improve more rapidly if each committee evaluated itself at the end of each session. These records of evaluation—partly check sheets the youngsters had helped to prepare and partly their comments—provided many insights regarding growth and were filed in the cumulative folders.

The possibilities for collections of pupils' work are many. Notebooks can be studied for evidence of increased skill in note-taking and reporting. Tests and individual lists of word difficulties can be kept in a special spelling notebook. Individual or class folders can show growth in creative writing. Dioramas, bulletin-board displays, exhibits, and murals developed around a particular area or problem, can be examined for evidence of growth. Samples of completed projects may be included in the pupil's folder.

Cumulative records should contain other types of samples of learners' work. Any standardized tests should be filed at least for the year. Some classroom tests can also be filed. At times, teacher and learners may plan to do the examples on a workbook page or a teacher-prepared mimeographed sheet, or write an assigned summary in order to have added objective evidence.

Eventually accumulations of work samples must be sorted and summarized. Sometimes the teacher may do this alone, but more often teacher and pupils make these decisions together as they develop new plans or decide what sort of report should go to parents. Such concrete evidence is just as important to a teacher whose problem is to help a learner and his parents realize where insights into a social-studies unit on Ancient Greece are limited, as they are to a teacher concerned with helping a learner plan for new experiences in relation to a persistent life situation. In neither case will a score on a final examination tell the story.

CAREFUL SELECTIONS FROM DAILY RECORDS MAKE UP THE PERMANENT RECORD

The daily notations of pupil behavior, tentatively filed, as well as the accumulations of samples of work, should be reviewed intermittently to select those items which are sufficiently significant to become a part of the pupil's permanent record. Kept up to date, the cumulative record shows changes in behavior and the ways in which the individual is overcoming weaknesses and limitations noted at an earlier time. Such a periodic review of the notations and samples of work will help to bring to the teacher's attention instances where few or no recordings have been made for certain individuals over a period of time and the need for more definite evidence. The selection of items for the permanent cumulative record takes time. But the very process of selection contributes to the teacher's better understanding of individuals and serves as one additional basis for the planning of next steps with individuals and groups.

The items selected to become a part of each pupil's permanent record, carefully dated, can be transferred to the permanent cumulative record form. Standard sheets, 8½ by 11, each headed with one of the major areas of desired growth, can serve as effective forms for making the recordings easily accessible and usable. These may be filed in a single folder for each pupil, or in a series of folders each representing an area of desired pupil growth. The latter may prove more functional since work samples take up considerable space. At the end of the year a final consolidation should be made into a single folder for each pupil to be passed on to his next teacher. Following are illustrations of such record forms, showing recordings in several areas.

Name: Robert Jenkins *Grade:* 2

Physical Health

Absence

10/23 Absent with cold (2 days)
11/15 " " " (entire week)
12/10 " " " (3 days)
12/17 . . . .

Safety

9/10 Reminded Robert three times of safe way to carry chairs.
9/27 Picked up chair with legs extending in front of him—put down—and picked up by back with legs down.
10/18 Robert reminded Cathy of safe way to carry chair.
11/2 . . . .

Name: George Graham *Grade:* 6

Making Ideas Clear and Understanding Ideas of Others

Written Communication

9/9 Autobiography (see attached)—needs help with spelling and use of the comma and semicolon. Vocabulary limited.

9/12 Story for school paper, *Rocket Away,* shows imagination hampered by vocabulary. Fewer spelling errors. Went to dictionary three times to check spelling while writing this story.

10/20 See George's list of "punctuation demons" attached.

11/20 Thanksgiving editorial for school paper (see attached)—points are clear, well organized, no spelling or punctuation errors.

12/5 . . . .

Name: SUE ELLEN BLACKSTONE *Grade:* 10B

PERSON-TO-PERSON RELATIONS

Giving and Taking Commendation and Criticism

2/3 Made no effort to enter discussion after Jim said, "I don't think your suggestion would work. You forget that many of the fellows work on Saturday."

2/7 Seemed quite pleased when Don thanked her for help with a math problem she had grasped quickly.

2/14 Said "Yes" and withdrew from the discussion when Janet asked whether Sue thought the argument she quoted and supported on the bond issue had been checked against the available and known facts.

2/28 Responded with "I don't think that is necessary" to Dorothy's suggestion that the points made in the article for the school paper would be more effective if stated in simpler language. Responded with "I sure tend to use ten-dollar words—I'll look at it again" to the teacher's later comment, "The point we have just been making with Phil of using simple direct wording also applies to you. I think Dorothy was right about the suggestion she gave you."

3/10 . . . .

With each item dated and other illustrative behaviors added as the days and weeks pass, the permanent cumulative record gives a picture of the growing learner as he copes with the range of persistent life situations.

If the teacher is in a self-contained classroom and is responsible for the total growth of the learner, he will record evidence in each area of desired growth. If, on the other hand, the program is departmentalized and the teacher is responsible for work in selected areas, he will contribute primarily to records that relate to those areas of growth. However, growth relating to physical and mental health, person-to-person and group relationships, use of intellectual powers and sound methods of work, and communication, will be the concern of all or many teachers even in a departmentalized program.

Different methods of bringing the recordings of various teachers together in a composite record are used. In some instances, the homeroom teacher or adviser receives the items selected for the permanent record by the various teachers working with the student and is provided time to record the evidence on the appropriate permanent form. The homeroom teacher or adviser thus serves as the coordinating agent in developing pupil records. In other schools, the teacher in a particular instructional area assumes responsibility for developing the permanent record relating to that area of the individual's growth and receives from other teachers pertinent items which they may have noted in their contacts with the pupil. Whatever the system, the records should be readily available to all persons concerned with a particular group of learners, and every teacher will find it helpful to see the learner "whole" and to be able to refer to growth in areas other than those for which he has major responsibility.

While evaluation is an integral part of the learning process, and records are an important tool in evaluation, they should be a service tool and not require time and energy that should be directed toward other aspects of guiding learning. Just as the process of making day-to-day recordings of growth can involve learners and become an integral part of the learning experience rather than an extra task for the teacher, so can the process of selecting items for a permanent record. The fifth-graders described earlier selected the samples of their handwriting for the permanent record. The eighth-graders learned something about their own reading habits as they wrote summary evaluations. Fourth-graders selected the creative writing they felt best represented their work for the month. The selected items became part of a permanent record, but the process of choosing developed sensitivity to effective writing and aroused new interest. One group of tenth-graders, in preparation for planning conferences with their homeroom and core teacher, made a tentative selection of the items they thought should be included in their permanent records and used these in deciding what they should try to achieve through the work they next undertook.

ALL WHO ARE CONCERNED WITH THE LEARNER CONTRIBUTE TO AND USE CUMULATIVE RECORDS

Previous illustrations have shown how teacher and learners can be involved in the record-keeping process and how they can use such records. To be able to look without undue emotion at both positive and negative aspects of growth is an important part of development toward maturity for each pupil. Learning to use the evidence in his record includes interpreting data contributed by different individuals, dealing with situations in which he differs with the recorded statement, and identifying areas in which he can contribute added evidence.

Parents, too, should contribute to and use records. For younger children, parents can share with the school, in the form of anecdotal statements, happenings in out-of-school hours that suggest progress or special needs and interests. These may be written by the parent or by the child with the parent's help. Parents can encourage older children and youth to take time to prepare a memorandum to file in their cumulative records and thus share their out-of-school experiences with those counseling them at school. Parents can do much to contribute to or to negate pupil growth and understanding of the importance of self-evaluation by the way in which they respond to records which are shared with them. Thoughtful and understanding reactions by parents encourage children and youth to respond positively to self-evaluation, to see the efforts of home and school as closely related to their interests, to better understand the interlocking nature of their work and that of their teachers and their parents.

Reporting Pupil Progress

Increasingly, as the purpose of evaluation becomes that of promoting growth rather than passing judgment, earlier forms of report cards are becoming inadequate. New ways of sharing wider and more varied information with pupils and parents are necessary. The problem of developing adequate methods of reporting is one that must be faced regardless of curriculum design. New procedures are being tested in many schools.

DESCRIPTIONS OF BEHAVIORAL GROWTH ARE NEEDED TO REPORT PUPIL PROGRESS ADEQUATELY

Adequate information about a learner's progress can be shared with his parents only when there is some way of providing a more accurate picture of progress than letter or percentage grades can give. If the learner is to deal competently, at his maturity level, with the everyday situations he faces, and the persistent life situations which are involved, his progress must be viewed with reference to change in behavioral responses in dealing with these situations.

Systems of reporting that rely entirely on single grades, percentages, or ratings, without qualifying statements, fail to give essential information to either parents, pupil, or teachers of the grade to which he is transferred or promoted. If a single grade is used, how should it be interpreted? If the grade represents an evaluation of the pupil's growth in terms of his potentiality, it may not indicate his progress in relation to a general standard. If it is his achievement toward a general standard, it cannot show whether this achievement is satisfactory in terms of his potential. Is a very able learner to be rated *A*, for example, when in effect he is coasting only slightly ahead of his classmates? Is a slow learner to be told over and over again by *D*'s and *F*'s that he is a failure because his best is not as good as that of others in his group? On the other hand, parents, other teachers, and pupils themselves will be hopelessly confused if the grades for these two learners are reversed.

School systems have attempted various compromise efforts in grading. Some use two grades, one indicating achievement and the other the learner's progress in terms of his own potentiality. Some have developed general agreement as to the meaning of the grades—learners of limited potentiality working up to capacity will not receive less than *C; A*'s will not be given to pupils unless their achievement measures up to their capacity. However, even though such agreements have the virtue of facilitating consistent interpretations of letter grades by teachers in a given system, they fall far short of conveying adequate information about learners.

Letter grades or percentages fail to solve another fundamental problem. Achievement in any area comes from a complex combination of understandings, concepts, and skills. If a grade of *A* or *Excellent* is reported for Alice's work in reading, does it mean that she reads material of a certain level of difficulty, that she reads accurately, that she reads with a particular speed, that she reads varied types of materials with ease, that she varies her reading techniques according to the nature of the material and her purpose? It is most unlikely that Alice meets each of the suggested criteria with equal excellence. To break an area into its major behavioral components and report a separate grade for each will help some. But there are still other problems, for Alice may read at a particular speed when engaged in recreational reading or working in the social studies but at a much slower rate when working with materials relating to the natural and physical environment. The many facets of learning in any area, and their interrelationships within a field and between fields, suggest that better ways than the usual grade must be found for reporting pupil growth adequately.

Conferences can be used to describe behavioral growth. Conferences with parents, or with a learner and his parents jointly, are probably one of the most effective means of sharing progress. These face-to-face situations offer opportunity for a give-and-take discussion of ideas that contributes to clear communication and for the use of concrete illustrations to clarify meanings further. Teacher, parents, and pupil can learn much in a conference situation. For pupil and parent the conference should contribute further to understanding the goals of the school, the ways in which the learner and his teachers have been working toward these goals, and the obstacles met. In the give-and-take of a conference it is often easier to help parents, or parents and pupil together, think through realistic expectancies. Standardized test records can be interpreted and samples of work examined at such conferences. The conference can also include planning next steps for each participant, all directed toward further growth of the learner. For the teacher there may be new insights regarding the parent and the home situation, parent relations with the learner, ways in which the home does and can contribute to pupil progress, and ways in which home and school can work together.

To realize the potential in a conference and to make it possible in the teacher's heavy schedule, careful planning is required. The teacher must consider how to open the discussion of pupil progress, how to use data from the pupil's cumulative record—whether to refer to the records at once or whether to urge the parent or learner to raise questions first—the pupil's part in the conference, and the importance of a written summary statement which the pupil and parent may take away from the conference. A written notation of major points, to be used as a guide during the conference, may be a part of this planning. The individual conference requires time. Because time demands are heavy, some teachers feel that conferences can be held only when especially requested either by the parent or the teacher. Various methods are being used to provide some time for conferences within school hours. In some schools pupils are dismissed early on certain days or engage in activities which free the homeroom teacher. Other schools make the services of substitute teachers available.

There are other problems in using the conference to report pupil progress. In some situations parents are not at ease with the English language or the teacher with their native tongue. When both parents work, or when parents are hesitant because of dress or home conditions to meet the teacher face to face, problems are created. Often the parents with whom the teacher is most anxious to confer are those who find it most difficult to arrange a time. Adolescents sometimes do not wish their parents to come to the school or the teacher to visit in their home. These are not insurmountable problems. Joint pupil–teacher planning of the conference will overcome some difficulties. To establish a workable system of conferences frequently takes careful all-school planning and the cooperative efforts of the parent–teacher association.

Written statements can be used to report pupil progress. Either as a supplement to, or as a substitute for conferences, schools are using a variety of forms of written communication. One of the most common is the check list of areas of growth in which each aspect of growth is checked as *Good, Satisfactory,* or *Poor,* and space is provided for discussing in greater detail one or more of the items. Some schools have moved toward listing major areas of growth with space for a brief descriptive comment regarding each. Still others are using a letter as a means of communication, the teacher preparing a series of paragraphs dealing with aspects of growth which he wishes to discuss with the parent.

The written descriptive statement can be a valuable means of communicating pupil progress if statements are incisive and really describe behavioral growth. Study of letters to parents often reveals that statements are very general—"It is a joy to have Mary in the fifth grade," "Jim has been making steady progress in his work in geometry," "Sue is a most cooperative member of the group." Such statements, while pleasing to hear, have the same limitations as a letter or percentage grade in that they really do not communicate. In what ways is Sue cooperative, under what conditions? What kind of progress is Jim making—has he memorized a number of theorems and their proofs, can he work originals, does he see how to use basic geometric concepts where they apply in situations of everyday living? Letters also often show that teachers omit aspects of growth or, under the pressures of the total reporting job, use somewhat meaningless stereotypes for all but one or two areas.

One seventh-grade teacher, in an effort to help parents to relate pupil growth to the ongoing class activities, sent them a two-part written communication.[2] The first part, which was duplicated for the parents of all the pupils, described the work in which the class was engaged. The following excerpts are illustrative.

DESCRIPTION OF SEVENTH–GRADE PROGRAM

News Discussions and Reports

This is a period usually coming the first thing each day and requiring from one to two hours. We use the newspapers as a beginning point for this work, but they by no means form the sole basis for our study and discussions. We use several children's magazines and newspapers and we make use of geographies, histories, and encyclopedias nearly every time we come together. The first thirty or forty minutes of the period are given over to study, research, and preparation of reports by the children. The remainder of the period is spent in reporting and discussing the material which the children have gathered. Maps and charts are used constantly in connection with these dis-

[2] Adapted from a report prepared by Dr. Helen Strickland when a member of the laboratory school staff of the State Teachers College, Troy, Alabama.

cussions. The following topics are indicative of the range and depth of our news periods.

1. *U. S. Government*

   DEVELOPMENT OF THE SUPREME COURT

   We have followed rather closely the events which have reshaped the policies of the Supreme Court. Children, having had their first introduction to this body through our discussions, have gained a good understanding of its place and function in our government and its relation to the other branches. Through this study they have been introduced to the Constitution, its history and purpose.

   DEVELOPMENT IN CONGRESS

   The meeting of Congress in September and its work on the Neutrality bill proved an interesting study for us. Here the children saw the importance of the United States as a world power and began to sense some of the intricacies of its international relations. They followed the bill as it went through Congress and became better acquainted with the process of law-making. . . .

The second part was different for each pupil and described how the particular learner related himself to the class work—his strengths and limitations. Any activities in which he individually was engaged were also shared with the parent. The excerpts which follow are taken from the report to Frances' parents.

REPORT OF FRANCES' CONTRIBUTIONS TO THESE ACTIVITIES

NEWS DISCUSSIONS, REPORTS, AND READING

In connection with our study of news, Frances has made a number of excellent reports on current social problems relating to government, foreign policy, and public welfare. She has the ability to sustain interest in a problem over a comparatively long period of time. In connection with each of the above she worked for a period of several weeks, reporting to the class and the teacher as she found information which was important and which she thought would be of interest to them. She is developing effective techniques for handling problems of an intellectual nature. She uses the *Readers' Guide* and follows up references found there quite satisfactorily. She handles articles from such magazines as *Harper's, Reader's Digest,* and *Time* with comparative ease. Her interpretations always involve much thinking and show a consistent tendency to think below the surface of what she reads. She has shown remarkable progress recently in her ability to use words. Her vocabulary is unusually rich and varied for a child of her age. It is well that this tendency to find new words and to use them as often as possible be encouraged at home.

Social Relationships

Frances needs to be more objective about her work and her ideas. She is still too easily upset by a difference of opinion on the part of the teacher or another child. There is, however, much improvement noted in this direction since this time last year. She is conscious of her tendency to be impatient with other members of the class and works toward taking care of this problem.

This form of written communication has the merit of helping parents to understand what is taking place in the school and what the work means for the child. It also has a definite structure which contributes to specific reporting in a number of areas and thereby serves as a safeguard against omissions, general statements, and comments which have little meaning because of lack of concrete evidence.

Other teachers have found a three-column report form a useful way of assuring specific statements regarding growth supported by evidence. Some parents find such an outline form easy to grasp quickly. Opportunity is provided in the *Analysis* column to show present behavioral values and how they relate to desired goals. In the *Evidence* column two items of evidence can be reported, the first of which shows the individual's behavior at the beginning of his work or at the last time of reporting, and the second indicates the present stage of action or behavior. The third column, *Recommendations,* allows for suggestions for next steps. Such a summary sheet can be used to call attention to each major area of growth. If pupils are familiar with this method of summarizing their progress and understand the content of the record, they can be the necessary interpreters of the report. The following illustrate such a record of progress in two areas of growth.

Name: Sue Ellen Blackstone *Grade:* 10B
Date: 3/27/'—

Person-to-Person Relations

Analysis		*Evidence*	*Recommendations*
Disagrees with a point of view without personal antagonism	2/7	"Of course, you have a right to your point of view on lowering the voting age—but have you taken into account the difference in education provided today—not only by schools but by radio and TV? Younger people know a lot more than they did when the original law was passed."	

PERSON-TO-PERSON RELATIONS

Analysis	*Evidence*	*Recommendations*
	3/15 "I can't agree with some of the proposed plans for the dance but don't we need to look at each of them in the light of our major purpose?"	
Accepts criticism in good spirit from those having a status role, not from peers	2/3 Made no effort to enter discussion after Jim said, "I don't think your suggestion would work. You forget that many of the fellows work on Saturday." 2/28 Responded with "I don't think that is necessary" to Dorothy's suggestion that the points made in the article for the school paper would be more effective if stated in simpler language. Responded with "I sure tend to use ten-dollar words—I'll look at it again" to the teacher's later comment, "The point we have just been making with Phil of using simple direct wording also applies to you. I think Dorothy was right about the suggestion she gave you."	Help Sue Ellen from time to time to analyze incidents recorded in her cumulative record to note difference in her response when: 1) *she disagrees* with a point and *offers criticism* 2) *she reacts* to similar *criticism from her peers* Try to devise ways of helping her in on-the-spot situations. (Sue Ellen will need to share in making proposals.)

Name: GEORGE GRAHAM *Grade:* 6
Date: 12/7/'—

MAKING IDEAS CLEAR AND UNDERSTANDING THE IDEAS OF OTHERS

Analysis	*Evidence*	*Recommendations*
Written communication clear in meaning and structurally correct; accurate spelling; limited vocabulary	For growth see attached samples of written material under date of: September 9 (Autobiography) November 20 (Thanksgiving editorial for school paper)	Encourage George to turn attention now to vocabulary—just as he has gained in spelling through use of the dictionary, help him use it for "substance" words when written work shows use of same word several times

MAKING IDEAS CLEAR AND UNDERSTANDING THE IDEAS OF OTHERS

Analysis	*Evidence*	*Recommendations*
Informal conversation clear and interesting; oral presentations for which he has prepared are clear, to the point, and well given (except for overuse of *and*); contributions in group discussion are often involved and difficult to follow	Children seek out George in informal conversation situations 10/2 George selected to represent the class in the Community Chest assembly 11/30 George elected to vacancy in Student Council. Feeling of children rather well expressed by Jack, "I vote for George. He meets all of the qualities we set up for our representative except 'Presents ideas clearly in discussion.' Sometimes he has trouble, but he has good ideas even if he doesn't say it so well. And maybe this will help him."	Involve George in small-group situations as a means of building self-confidence Record on tape a small-group conference and analyze with George to help him see the problem

High school youth and older children in the elementary school can be helped to make such summary evaluations independently and in conference share and compare them with those prepared by the teacher. Together, teacher and learners can then build a joint statement to be shared with parents.

Informal notes can add to understanding of progress. In addition to the periodic summary evaluation, better understanding between home and school and effective encouragement to learners can come through informal evaluative statements. This kind of statement, which usually relates to a particular activity or area of progress, can be written and shared at any time that pupil or teacher feel it would be of interest to the parent. As suggested by the following illustrations, the informal note may refer to a particular achievement, request help which the parent can best give, or present a problem which is baffling and with which little progress is being made. How many and when such notations are sent is an individual matter for each pupil.

Dear Mother and Dad,

Miss Hanley and I want you to know that I am doing much better in spelling. The story I wrote was selected to be sent to the school paper. There wasn't one word misspelled. I am more careful about using the dictionary when I am not sure how to spell a word.

Your son,
Don

Dear Mrs. Walter,

Billy is now reading a wide range of books and is ready to use books from the public library. Both Billy and I would appreciate your help in making it possible for him to secure a library card. Thank you.

Sincerely,
Dorothy Green

Dear Mrs. Morley,

Your son and I have been trying to work out a work–study schedule that will provide a proper balance for Ralph. We have run into certain difficulties which we would like to talk over with you. Ralph will talk with you about these and a possible time for a three-way conference.

Sincerely,
Gertrude Walsh

REPORTS OF PROGRESS SHOULD RELATE INDIVIDUAL DIFFERENCES TO ACCEPTED BEHAVIORAL GOALS

Does the principle of individual differences suggest that evaluation should be in terms of the learner's own potentialities and limitations without reference to generally accepted standards? Should parents know how their children stand in relation to a common set of values or goals toward which all individuals work? What about the pupil who transfers from school to school? What is required by college entrance boards?

Whatever plan is used for relating the learner's level of development to desired competence, an important area of learning for every child and youth—one of life's persistent situations—is to recognize realistically the progress he is making, his limitations and strengths. He needs to be helped to see his competencies in the light of standards generally held as desirable and necessary for the goals he hopes to attain.

Helping parents appreciate a child's growth in relation to his own potentialities without reference to more general standards can result in misunderstanding. Picture the confusion of tne parents who receive periodic progress reports indicating that Sally is doing satisfactory work in reading, and tnen at the end of the term are advised that she should not be promoted because of her limited reading skills. The explanation that the periodic reports were based on the satisfactory gains Sally was making in terms of her abilities and limitations while the final report was in terms of a set of grade standards in reading may be plausible but difficult to accept. John's parents may also be confused if they are repeatedly told that he is doing unsatisfactory work in science, when they have ample evidence that his interests in this field are much wider than those of his friends. This situation can readily occur with an exceptionally able pupil completely disinterested in science activities available in school. The confusion is one brought about by failure to distinguish between evaluation in terms of the learner's own rate and level of development and that indicated by predetermined goals. When parents and pupils can realistically relate individual growth to generally accepted standards and values, more adequate decisions will be made regarding school and college work as well as vocational choices. Such understanding develops more readily, for reasons indicated in earlier sections, under methods of reporting that involve conferences and letters to parents than it does under systems that rely strictly on grades.

For the most part, school and college officials are aware of the weaknesses of grading systems. Teachers in elementary schools are increasingly including in transfer records brief comments that refer to the pupil's level of development in relation to generally accepted standards. It is commonly recognized by colleges that grades from a high school or measures such as rank in class reflect to some extent the caliber of the student body of that school. Many colleges give their own entrance examinations. Typically, these provide measures of college aptitude (or general intelligence), reading ability, and perhaps skills in English usage or in mathematics. Qualitative statements are usually requested from high school principals and counselors as well as transcripts of grades. Some colleges follow a rather generous admission policy with careful guidance of the student in his first year of college work and thoughtful policies regarding selective elimination and redirection of students. In general, school systems that develop various types of descriptive statements that relate the pupil's development to generally accepted standards are able to provide adequate reports of progress when pupils transfer to other schools or make application for admission to college.

REPORTS OF PROGRESS SHOULD NOT BE MADE FOR ALL PUPILS AT THE SAME TIME

Teachers and administrators should realistically recognize that the written descriptive reports under discussion are time-consuming. Ways to assist the teacher as much as possible—clerical help, forms that supply headings and other fixed data, time in a teaching schedule to work on records—should be explored. One solution with merit, both from the standpoint of the teacher's time and the needs of learners, is to abandon fixed report periods in favor of reporting progress or planning conferences at times when they are likely to be most helpful to the individual, his teacher, and parents. Not all pupils will reach the point of needing to evaluate their progress and plan next steps at the same time. At a particular time one learner and his parents will profit by taking an over-all evaluative look while another will find it helpful to reflect on progress in a single area. Thus, to use evaluation as a learning experience to meet the needs of individuals means that reports of progress will not be made for all pupils at the same time.

Other values accrue when reports of pupil progress, in conferences or through written statements, are not all scheduled at the same time. Evaluation is made an individual matter and parents are discouraged from comparing their child's work with that of a neighbor's child. Children and youth are not embarrassed by questions from eager peers about their progress. And, equally important, teachers are not faced with the almost insurmountable task of preparing from twenty to forty or more reports within a week or so. Preparing a large number of reports in a limited time often results in a tendency to use clichés rather than definitive statements, as well as fatigue which impairs teaching efforts.

CHANGING METHODS OF REPORTING PUPIL PROGRESS IS A GRADUAL PROCESS

Despite all the problems mentioned in the preceding sections, parents and teachers are still most familiar with letter grades or percentages as means of reporting progress. Changing to other methods requires careful planning and the participation of all concerned. When committees of parents and teachers work together on the problem of how best to convey information about learners, those most directly concerned with the communication process are involved in making any changes. "What should we be telling you about your children?" is the key question, not "Shall we do away with letter grades?" Often it is advisable to continue to use the established form of reporting while introducing the new. In one school the descriptive letter sent along with the usual letter-grade report card to parents of first-graders was the "new." It resulted in such parent reactions as: "Why, that is just the way Paul acts at home," "Your letter certainly helped us to see the problems our daughter faces," "You really do know Frances and we appreciate what you are doing for her," "I must see that Dan takes care of his own clothes—by following up after him I am undermining what you are trying to do." These were responses parents sent to the teacher after receiving the usual report card plus the descriptive letter. So worthwhile did they find the letter that at a PTA meeting these parents asked if a similar report might not be sent for their older children. Thus one teacher's experiment in reporting led to a change in the total school policy on ways of sharing information regarding pupil progress.

Positive first steps are helpful. In one school a system of conferences was established gradually by first inviting the parents of next year's kindergartners to visit the rooms where their children would be in the coming fall. The pattern of visiting the school and talking with the teacher was established under circumstances where no possible negative evaluations of their own youngsters were in the offing. From this, visits by these same parents in the fall was an easy step. Over the next three years the conference system was gradually extended to all six grades.

A reporting system is only useful if it contributes to understanding of growth. Any changes toward more effective communication can come about only as new skills and insights are acquired. This takes time and study by teacher, pupil, and parent if reporting is to contribute to the educative process.

Evaluating the Educational Program

Evaluation of the individual and of the group of which he is a part also serves to indicate needed change in various aspects of the educational program. Curriculum development and guidance of learners are two parts of the same whole. The responses of learners to curricular experiences condition the nature of the guidance needed and the guidance given modifies the nature of worthwhile subsequent curriculum experiences. Those responsible for the education of children and youth must evaluate the total program continually.

As suggested in earlier sections, parents and other laymen make a fundamental contribution to evaluating the growth of children and youth. So can they contribute in evaluating the effectiveness of the educational program. Several channels through which parents and other laymen can share in the evaluation of the total program have already been indicated. Active cooperation between parents, community members, and teachers in understanding learners better leads inevitably to evaluation of what is now being done. As teachers, parents, and other lay persons in the community jointly study the persistent life situations which learners face, they will move toward discovering areas of living in which no one is giving adequate help. Cooperative planning of how each may best supplement the work of the others always involves evaluation of what is needed and how well it is being provided. Parent study groups, parent–teacher–pupil groups, planning councils of representatives of all educational agencies, should meet regularly to consider how well present attempts to supplement each other's efforts are meeting the needs of learners, and to clarify long-term goals.

Children and youth have an important place in this process. They contribute to the development and evaluation of their curriculum as they share in the planning day by day, and as their needs and concerns become the basis for school experiences. They can also add much if they are given the opportunity to express the ways they think present experiences are helping them and what else they would like to be able to do. What does it say of the attitudes being built at home and in school when learners indicate their wishes about school to be "To pass," "Not to be held back," "To be the smartest boy in class," "To make all *A*'s"? What can be learned from those who ask for "More shop work," "A science lab where we can really carry on experiments," "More time for art," "A kitchen where we can cook hot lunches"?

Like the evaluation of individuals and groups, evaluation of the educational program must be based on the goals and values sought. The test of the curriculum is whether or not children and youth are learning to live in ways that lead to successful handling of the problems facing them now and to successful living as adult members of society. The experiences of living and working together in school should be reflected in home and community life in ways that make for the best society that it is possible to achieve.

Those who would appraise the school curriculum of children and youth must be concerned with every aspect which affects it. Evaluation of the curriculum, then, must include consideration of the experiences with which learners are being helped to deal, school organization and administrative relationships which affect these experiences, school–community relationships as they affect curricular and out-of-school experiences, and the behavior of children and youth as they carry on their daily lives.

ARE THE LIFE SITUATIONS OF LEARNERS CENTRAL IN THE CURRICULUM?

This volume proposes that the curriculum must help each individual to become competent not only while in school but also when he leaves school—in his home and family relations, his work and leisure-time activities, his spiritual and civic-social life. The school is concerned with guiding learners in the complex situations of home, school, and community, viewed in the light of the persistent life situations which are a part of them. Those who would appraise the degree to which the program is meeting this criterion must answer such questions as the following . . .

Are children and youth being helped to deal with experiences which stem from their interests, needs, and concerns of everyday living . . .

Is provision made for needs about which learners are not articulate as well as those about which they are articulate?

Is provision made for needs and interests of individuals as well as of groups? for all levels of ability?

Are needs and interests so guided that individuals extend their capacities and talents?

Are needs, concerns, and interests revealed and better understood because learners share in the selection, development, and evaluation of their experiences?

Are the everyday experiences of children and youth dealt with in the light of the persistent life situations which are a part of them . . .

Are persistent life situations which are a part of everyday living at home, in the neighborhood, at church, at work, at play considered?

Are persistent life situations dealt with in their changing and more complex forms as children and youth mature?

Are children and youth being helped to deal with the range of recurring life situations . . .

Are learners helped to deal with situations that require maximum individual capacities—are they learning how to keep well, mentally and physically; are they growing in power to reason and have they the intellectual tools with which to work; are they learning the satisfactions of aesthetic expression and appreciation; are they developing moral and ethical standards and the will to act upon these standards?

Are learners helped to meet situations which involve social participation—are they building wholesome relationships with other people; are they becoming effective group members; are they learning the techniques of intergroup action?

Are learners helped to respond to situations which involve environmental factors and forces—are they growing in ability to understand and use their natural environment; are they learning how to use technological resources to serve human needs and welfare; are they coming to understand and work effectively with economic, political, and social structures and forces of the local community, the nation, and the world?

Are children and youth helped to deal with persistent life situations in ways that develop basic understandings, generalizations, and skills that are effective guides in dealing with the same persistent life situations as they are met later . . .

Are generalizations and understandings reached based on seeing relationships among facts and events?

Are generalizations appropriately used in meeting new situations?

DOES THE SCHOOL ORGANIZATION AND ADMINISTRATION CONTRIBUTE TO MAXIMUM GROWTH?

Those who believe that all factors in a situation affect the learning that takes place will appraise the organization of the school and its administrative policies and practices as carefully as they do the experiences with which children and youth are being helped to deal. An organizational setup or an administration that hinders teacher–pupil working relationships, or that prevents full cooperation and participation by teachers, pupils, parents, and other community members, will seriously handicap even the master teacher and his pupils in achieving many of their purposes. On the other hand, leadership which gives direction and support to teachers, parents, boys and girls, and interested persons in the community helps to develop schools which serve positively all the children and youth of that community. Evidence of positive leadership and school organizations that facilitate learning are many. They are not subject to statistical count or to any other measure of an exact nature. Rather they are found through watching teachers and learners at work in the classroom, in the halls, in the lunchroom, on the playgrounds, in their organizations—in the responses made to such questions as . . .

Does every aspect of the school contribute to the development and implementation of democratic values . . .

Is there a democratic atmosphere throughout the school—between teachers and learners; administration and teachers; learners, teachers, and custodial staff?

Is each learner aware of the goals of the school and does he participate at his level of ability in the organization of the school and its curriculum to achieve these goals?

Do children and youth assume responsibility for values and attitudes implemented in the halls, in the lunchroom, on the school grounds, and in the classroom?

Are class organization and time schedules adjusted to the demands of the work at hand . . .

Is there flexibility in grouping which meets individual needs and yet assures that one teacher knows the total development of the learner well enough to be able to give sound advice and guidance to him?

Does a flexible use of time blocks allow learners to complete work of concern to them without being hindered by artificial time barriers?

Is there provision for children and youth to become active in those community organizations or activities which touch their lives significantly?

Are adequate and appropriate human and material resources available . . .

Are the materials and equipment used suited to the situations learners face?

Is there opportunity to use specialists in the school and community —the custodian, the lunchroom manager, special teachers, competent laymen—as resources in providing educational experiences of value?

Is there continuity of experience as the learner moves through a grade, from grade to grade, from elementary to high school, from high school to college or into community life . . .

Is there a coordinated and well-organized plan of recording the growth and development of each individual?

Does each learner have a share in determining what he will undertake and in evaluating his success?

Is there follow-through on individuals which allows the school to see wherein it has succeeded or failed in helping them to make adjustments to the succeeding experiences?

Does positive leadership on the part of the administration facilitate continued growth of learner and teacher . . .

Are there adequate time provisions for carrying out the full scope of the teacher's work with parents, in the community, with colleagues in joint planning and study of common problems and interests, as well as opportunity to know well each learner for whom he is responsible?

Is there opportunity for children and youth to assume and carry out responsibilities commensurate with their abilities?

Do all those affected by administrative policies share in their development?

ARE SCHOOL–COMMUNITY RELATIONSHIPS DEVELOPED IN THE BEST INTERESTS OF LEARNERS?

Evaluation must be concerned with the experiences which children and youth are having both in and out of the school; all these experiences make up the learner's total curriculum. The school cannot operate independently of the home, the community, and the many agencies serving children and youth. The fact that the same persistent life situations are a part of aspects of the learner's life at home, in school, and in the community, suggests that the school must work with these other agencies if the full life of the learner is to be considered. The effectiveness of school–community relationships must be appraised by asking such questions as . . .

Do the school and community plan together in the guidance of children and youth . . .

Are channels of communication provided through which school, parents, and community agencies can pool their understanding of learners?

Is the total community aware of the basic goals and functions of the school?

Do community members share in constructive evaluation of the work of the school?

Do youth-serving agencies work together to coordinate and complement their efforts?

Is full use being made of the community as a laboratory for learning to live in society . . .

Do community members share their special talents or information with the school?

Do children and youth make use of community resources pertinent to their needs and interests?

Are children and youth learning to know their community and its functioning through working with community groups on joint enterprises?

Are school and community working together for a better community . . .

Do school and community work together on community problems (quality of motion pictures shown, child safety, juvenile delinquency)?

Are community improvements directly traceable to the interests and activities of children and youth (utilization of community resources for better food, recreation, health, self-expression through the arts, sports, and hobbies)?

Does the school share its resources with the community?

Are the services of the school as an institution or of individual staff members sought in community undertakings?

DO CHILDREN AND YOUTH ACT ON THE BASIS OF DEMOCRATIC VALUES?

The final test of the curriculum lies in the actions of children and youth as they take their places as responsible members in home, school, and community life. The ultimate goal is to help children and youth deal effectively with life problems in terms of democratic values. Questions such as the following must be asked by the teacher, the administrator, parents, and other community members as they watch children and youth in action, as they see them eventually take positions of leadership and responsibility in the community . . .

Are children and youth competent to deal with the situations and problems of their everyday living . . .

Are pupils becoming responsible members of the family group?

Are they becoming responsible community members, participating in various community enterprises such as those carried on by the church, by recreational, social, and economic groups?

Is each individual competent to pursue further education or take a job suited to his ability?

Is each pupil using his leisure time constructively for himself and his group?

Is each learner finding sources of allegiance and spiritual values?

Are children and youth able and willing to act on reasoned judgment?

Do children and youth act on the basis of democratic values . . .

Do learners take action, in keeping with their maturity level, to assure the rights and responsibilities of others of different races, of different religious, vocational, economic, or educational status?

Do they recognize their right and responsibility, and that of others, to contribute their best efforts to solving common problems?

Are actions based on a scientific approach to the study of problems?

Do children and youth have faith that man has the ability and power to improve his life . . .

Do pupils achieve constructive solutions to their own problems?

Do they share actively in solving local problems in ways that are for the common good?

Are they helping to build a better America among the nations of a world dedicated to cooperative action and peace?

Do learners meet their problems and their world with zest and dedication?

IS EVALUATION A CONTINUOUS PROCESS BASED ON CONSIDERATION OF EVIDENCE?

Evaluation of the educational program, like the evaluation of pupil progress, is a continuous process and one which must be based on evidence gathered as teachers and learners work together and as teachers, parents, other laymen, and administrators together consider the educational program and the developing behavioral responses of children and youth. The best in education will be realized when every experience of learners is worthwhile from the standpoint of the individual and of society, when every experience is one which helps to develop boys and girls, men and women, able to meet their problems of daily living with competence and maintain their ideals.

Related Readings

ADAMS, GEORGIA S., AND THEODORE L. TORGERSON. *Measurement and Evaluation for the Secondary-School Teacher*. New York: The Dryden Press, Inc., 1956.

AMERICAN ASSOCIATION OF SCHOOL ADMINISTRATORS. *American School Curriculum.* Thirty-first Yearbook. Washington, D.C.: The Association, 1953.

ASSOCIATION FOR SUPERVISION AND CURRICULUM DEVELOPMENT. *Guidance in the Curriculum.* 1955 Yearbook. Washington, D.C.: The Association, 1955.

GREENE, HARRY, ALBERT JORGENSEN, AND J. RAYMOND GERBERICH. *Measurement and Evaluation in the Elementary School.* New York: Longmans, Green & Company, 1953.

GREENE, HARRY, ALBERT JORGENSEN, AND J. RAYMOND GERBERICH. *Measurement and Evaluation in the Secondary School.* New York: Longmans, Green & Company, 1954.

HARRIS, FRED E. *Three Persistent Educational Problems: Grading, Promoting, and Reporting to Parents.* Lexington, Ky.: Bureau of School Service, College of Education, University of Kentucky, 1953.

REMMERS, H. H., AND N. L. GAGE. *Educational Measurement and Evaluation.* New York: Harper & Brothers, 1955.

SHANE, HAROLD G., AND E. T. MCSWAIN. *Evaluation and the Elementary Curriculum.* New York: Henry Holt and Company, Inc., 1951.

STRANG, RUTH. *How to Report Pupil Progress.* Chicago: Science Research Associates, 1955.

TABA, HILDA, AND OTHERS. *Diagnosing Human Relations Needs.* Washington, D.C.: American Council on Education, 1951.

THOMAS, R. MURRAY. *Judging Student Progress.* New York: Longmans, Green & Company, 1954.

THORNDIKE, ROBERT L., AND ELIZABETH HAGEN. *Measurement and Evaluation in Psychology and Education.* New York: John Wiley & Sons, Inc., 1955.

TORGERSON, THEODORE, AND GEORGIA SACHS ADAMS. *Measurement and Evaluation for the Elementary-School Teacher.* New York: The Dryden Press, Inc., 1954.

TRAXLER, ARTHUR E., AND OTHERS. *Introduction to Testing and the Use of Test Results in Public Schools.* New York: Harper & Brothers, 1953.

WILLEY, ROY DE V. *Guidance in Elementary Education.* New York: Harper & Brothers, 1952.

WRIGHTSTONE, J. WAYNE, JOSEPH JUSTMAN, AND IRVING ROBBINS. *Evaluation in Modern Education.* New York: American Book Company, 1956.

Part IV

TEACHERS AND LEARNERS AT WORK

12

GUIDING A YEAR'S WORK IN A FIFTH GRADE

Preceding chapters contain many examples of teachers and learners at work. For the most part, these are activities scheduled for only part of the day and lasting for a matter of days or weeks. It is relatively easy to see the details of a single unit of work growing from a group concern. This is an experience common to many teachers and learners. But how do activities unfold day after day and month after month? How can a teacher identify enough genuine problems of high educative potential to provide a rich school year? What roles will teacher and pupils play in the planning process? Is it actually possible to meet the needs of groups and of individuals adequately?

Nothing short of a detailed report of a full school year can answer the above questions. Such complete records are not available. However, many teachers have developed portions of their programs in the manner discussed in preceding chapters. With these situations as guides, it is possible to project the experiences of a group of learners for a complete school year.

A fifth grade has been chosen to illustrate the unfolding of a year's work. Because the key to the program lies in the planning process, a good part of this chapter is in dialogue form. An attempt has also been made to show what Miss Thomas, the teacher of this class, was thinking as she appraised the educative possibilities of new situations and problems and helped her class to make decisions. Space does not permit a full description of the activities through which each experience was developed, nor is it possible to present the complete data found in the teacher's records for each child. The reader will need to supply from his own experience such details regarding the children, their backgrounds, and the exact teaching procedures.

Subsequent chapters look at a year's work from two other vantage points. Chapter 13 examines a pattern of activities contributing to general and specialized education. A tenth grade is used as an illustration. Chapter 14 analyzes the contributions of a year's work to growth in ability to deal with persistent life situations. Here the activities of a first grade are the focus.

The Children and Their School

Miss Thomas' fifth grade has thirty-five children ranging in age from nine years four months to eleven years five months. Most of the class are ten or eleven years old. Bill, who is the youngest, is an exceptionally mature boy from a family of five children who have been given a large measure of responsibility at home. Physically he is about average for the group and intellectually he is one of the most able. Alice, who is the oldest, has had recurring illnesses through her school years. She is tall for her age, but awkward in sports and tires easily. Intellectually she is about average for the group.

IQ's from tests given in grades two and four vary somewhat for each child and range from 85 to 150. The class median falls at about 105. David, who is the least able intellectually, has had two individual tests which show approximately the same results. He is ten and one-half, somewhat smaller physically than the average child in the group, and one of the least able in use of fundamental skills. On repeated intelligence tests five other children have shown a range from 88 to 95. Three of these, and two others of considerably greater intellectual capacity—Joe and Myra—have less grasp of the fundamentals of reading, spelling, or arithmetic than is required to carry on their regular activities. Standardized achievement tests administered near the end of the fourth grade confirmed teacher judgment and previous records about this need. The most capable intellectually are Bill, who has already been mentioned, and ten-year-old Joan, who as an only child has been a constant companion of her parents. Her relationships with other children in the group are friendly but casual. She reads extensively, but is erratic in carrying out group responsibilities.

These children live in a midwest community of about one hundred and fifty thousand population. It is in the center of a farming region and serves smaller towns within a radius of approximately fifty miles. In recent years industrialization has spread rapidly, and the expansion into residential districts has left a slum area in the older part of the city. The population is the typical mixture of races, nationalities, and religions which results when early immigration waves are followed by influxes of workers needed in various industries.

The school is located in a part of the city where the older homes of wealthy families and modern apartments for professional people border the flats of those who are underprivileged. Wide ranges of socio-economic backgrounds and of racial heritages are represented in Miss Thomas' class. Children from families of considerable wealth and from those which verge on poverty are both to be found. Doris Jean and Peter are from large families living in two-room tenement apartments. Peter comes to school as clean as a ten-year-old boy can be expected to be, dressed in clothing which is invariably carefully mended. His parents draw upon the services of the public health nurse as needed. Doris Jean, on the other hand, rarely appears in a clean dress. Her hair is seldom combed and her hands and face sometimes have a layer of grime. During the past year four letters were written to her mother before permission was granted to have her teeth attended to at the dental clinic. Mary Anne's family has lived in one of the old brick mansions for three generations; her father is president of a local insurance company. Jerry's father manages one of the departments in a local store; his home is a moderate-priced apartment.

Tomi is a Japanese-American whose parents lived for a time in a relocation center; her parents operate a restaurant. Jean Marie, Jimmy, and Henry are Negro. Jean Marie's mother is a packing clerk in one of the large department stores and her father is employed by the department of public works. Jimmy's mother is a teacher and his father a lawyer. Henry's mother is a public health nurse; his father died shortly after he was born. Theresa and Anthony are of Italian parentage. They are twins, next to the youngest in a family of six. Their father, who worked in one of the local factories, was recently seriously injured and the family is managing on his compensation. Esther is the daughter of a Jewish doctor. Irving is also Jewish; his father manages a branch of one of the city's large dry cleaning establishments. Sarah's father owns a local grocery store.

About three-fourths of the children have been in the school for three or more years. Theresa and Anthony moved recently from another city. John came from Los Angeles where he had been in a large school. Catherine's family moved to the city from their farm recently when her father decided to work for a farm implement company. She had previously been in a one-room rural school. Jerry came from a large eastern city. Several others had transferred from other schools in the city.

The school consists of a kindergarten and the first six grades. From here the children go to a three-year junior high school about a half mile away. Grouping in the two classes at each grade level is heterogeneous and the organization is that of the usual self-contained classroom. No special teachers are available, but the staff has been built with complementary interests. Mrs. Gaynor, one of the fourth-grade teachers, has exceptional talent in art. Miss Thomas, teacher of the fifth grade whose activities are being described, has a strong science background. Mr. Bush, who has a sixth grade, has more than the usual understandings and abilities in the social studies. Mr. Jamison, in addition to serving as assistant principal, takes special responsibilitiy for team sports. Other teachers have similar special interests, talents, or backgrounds.

The school's services to these youngsters are augmented by medical and dental clinics, a lunchroom for those who cannot go home at noon, and a recreational program for those whose parents are not home when the school closes. Play space in this particular neighborhood is rather limited. Five blocks from the school there is a small park. During the summer certain streets are closed to traffic to provide more space. Several churches in the neighborhood offer club activities of various sorts. In addition, the razing of a building next to the school has made it possible to expand the school playground.

The school building is old. Classrooms are of average size without many modern improvements. A well-planned maintenance program has kept equipment in good condition and classroom walls painted in attractive colors. Books and supplies are sufficient for the needs of the various groups but not lavish. Program development in the school is supplemented by an active all-city supervisory program that gives help when needed but allows considerable freedom for the faculty of any one school to work in terms of the needs of its particular learners.

In planning for the year, Miss Thomas has as a guide cumulative records for each child who had been in the school in preceding years. These contain not only the usual information regarding family backgrounds, standardized test scores, and health records but also copies of the letters of evaluation to parents, summaries of the year's work provided by previous teachers, and samples of typical work for each child. A check of these cumulative records before school began helped Miss Thomas note individual strengths and weaknesses. From her study of the reports of the preceding year's activities, she was able to reach tentative conclusions regarding persistent life situations to which previous activities had contributed richly and those with which more experience might prove of value. An analysis made by the school faculty, similar to the Master List on pages 155 to 165 of this volume, provided one basis for judging balanced growth and identifying potential areas of need. In addition, as science specialist, Miss Thomas had from time to time been called on for help by the children now in her class, even from the first grade on. She had had a number of contacts with them as fourth-graders and knew, firsthand, some of their experiences and needs. She and the class had shared in a conference the preceding spring when they had agreed to assume the management of the school store as their all-school responsibility. How this came about is described in more detail in the next section. Miss Thomas had the summer to consider the potential learnings in this activity as they related to what she already knew about the group. All these sources of information contributed to her preplanning as she prepared to meet her class in September.

Beginning the Year's Work

Two main concerns became the centers of group activities in this fifth grade when school started in the fall. One was major responsibility for the management of the school store. After several years of discussion and experimentation, the faculty had become convinced of the educational possibilities in providing opportunity for children to participate in the management of various aspects of the school organization. It was the practice to ask one of the fifth grades to assume responsibility for the school store, while the other fifth-graders were responsible for the materials bureau in the library. Late in the previous spring the two fourth grades and their teachers, the teachers to whom they were to go in the fifth grade, and the principal had conferred on these problems. Among the factors that the teachers weighed heavily and helped the children to consider was that Miss Thomas' group, as fourth-graders, had branched into a number of activities which acquainted them very well with the use and proper care of reference materials, whereas the other class had, among their several areas of study, explored the problem of purchasing foodstuffs wisely and had developed many of the economic concepts and skills needed in the store. In the third and fourth grades the latter group had not focused their attention specifically on types of reference materials.

The school store was open for twenty minutes in the morning and again at noon, and offered for sale a variety of school materials not supplied by the board of education. Once in a while classes used it for special sales of cookies or fruit. Supplies were ordered through the principal's office but the class in charge was responsible for taking inventory, deciding what to order, sending in the order form, checking and displaying merchandise, determining selling prices, keeping accounts, making and recording sales.

The second major concern was the organization of the classroom to secure attractive and convenient working conditions for the year. This was one of the first responsibilities of every class each fall, as teachers felt that learners could work more effectively in an environment which they had helped arrange. A petty cash fund was available for small purchases. Standard books and supplies were delivered to rooms before school opened, but generally were put in temporary storage places until the children arrived. Matters of arranging desks were also decided by teachers and children together. More teacher leadership in room arrangement was given to the younger children, but the general policy was to help children of all ages share in decisions regarding the most effective organization of the materials they used. As learners grew, teachers helped them develop increased sensitivity to the beauty of their surroundings, to effective ways of using the space and materials with which they had to live, and to the health factors involved.

AN ALL-SCHOOL RESPONSIBILITY CALLS FOR EFFECTIVE PLANNING—OPENING THE SCHOOL STORE FOR BUSINESS

Plans for the store and for arranging the classroom got under way immediately. As the children arrived on the first day of school questions and opinions were many. Before all were present, an excited group clustered around Miss Thomas.

"When do we open the store?" said Bill. "Last year they didn't have it open for two weeks and that's too long. The kids need to get stuff sooner than that."

"You have to take stock first," answered Sarah, speaking from the background of what she had heard of her father's experiences. "When you manage a store you have to be sure your supplies are right."

"We can get it started in a week if we all work at it," said somebody else.

"Miss Thomas, wouldn't it be a good idea to leave our room just the way it is until we get the store going?"

"But this is so hard to get around in. If we're going to get the store open we need space here to work in; you can't do it all down there." Peter's experiences with a large family in a small space urged caution.

"Now that we're all here," said Miss Thomas, "suppose we sit down. There are some new people with us this year who don't know anything at all about the school store, and the office wants us to fill in these registration forms."

Theresa and Anthony, John, Catherine, Jerry, and children who had transferred from other schools in the city were introduced. Miss Thomas helped them tell a little of their background and questions from the group elicited much more. Then the registration blanks were filled in and attention turned back to the store.

"I guess we don't even know ourselves just what we're in for," said Bill. "We used the store a lot last year and we used to tell the kids what we didn't like about it, but we never did find out what had to be done."

"They left a final report just as you did," reminded Miss Thomas. "Wouldn't we be wise to make use of their experience? I brought it up from the office today in case we needed it."

The report, filed when a class concluded the year's work in its school job, contained a description of the activities the group found the job entailed, the special responsibilities they felt had to be assumed, and the recommendations they made for the next year. The report on the store was about fifteen typed pages. In mentioning it this early, Miss Thomas short-cut a step that might have taken several days or weeks of investigation into the nature of store management and the kinds of tasks to be undertaken. The choice was deliberate. The immediate problem was to get the store under way as rapidly as possible. This was the first school responsibility undertaken by this class in which efficient rapid planning was needed. Among other problems was the persistent life situation of how to use appropriate resources effectively—in this case the advice of the "expert." Learning about the practical details of management and organization could be developed on the job later; this was the time to take the group one step further in their ability to appraise and make appropriate use of the suggestions of others.

"You read it to us," suggested David, who avoided reading things for himself if he possibly could.

"No, that would take too long," said Joan.

"Does it have parts?" asked Jean Marie. "Could we divide it up and each group read a part?"

"I was going to suggest something like that," said Miss Thomas. "The report has a section on how the store operated, another section on the jobs they had to do to make it work, and a third giving their recommendations for things they thought needed changing."

"That would start us off," said Jimmy. "But we don't have to do it their way, do we?"

"Not at all," replied Miss Thomas. "We're in charge of it this year."

"Well, we'd better get it going first." Bill came back to his original point. "Or we won't have any customers to try new things out on."

The children broke into smaller groups to study the three sections of the report, with the understanding that each group would give a summary of the important items to be considered in getting the store started, and would add their own suggestions. For this work individuals selected the section in which they were most interested. Bill asked for the part on how the class had actually organized for work. Sarah was more interested in finding out how the store operated—she had spent some time around her father's store in the summer. Joan, whose sensitivity to the needs of cooperative group work was none too strong, but whose alert mind often produced the original ideas which the others carried out in practical detail, was encouraged to study the recommendations. Special care was taken to see that the new children found their places in the groups. Miss Thomas took much of the responsibility for this.

When the children separated into groups it was ten o'clock. Since it was customary to schedule recess periods on the crowded playground, their morning had to be broken at 10:30. It was agreed that groups would take the full half-hour to study the previous record and would prepare their reports after the recess period. Miss Thomas stayed long enough with each group to give whatever help was needed in getting under way and then went back to her desk to make a final check on the registration information due in the office by noon.

Miss Thomas' main concern at this point was to use the abilities of her group to best advantage in helping them make plans. Later, when initial success had been achieved and a feeling of security in their ability to manage the store had been established, individuals could be encouraged to take on responsibilities which would demand considerable growth. There was plenty for everyone to learn in these initial sessions.

About 11:15 the class reassembled. As the spokesman selected by each group reported on the particular section studied, Miss Thomas listed important points on the blackboard.

Things to Be Done Immediately	Helpers Needed Immediately	Things to Plan for Later
Check inventory of supplies	People to work on inventory	Selling Christmas cards
Order needed supplies	Committee on needed supplies	Selling more kinds of notebooks
Arrange supplies (displays, drawers for extra stock)	Committee on displays and price tags	Candy
Price stock and make out price tags	Committee to set prices	
Get sales checks from office	Committee to get sales checks	
Plan for publicity—*The Monthly Star*		
	When Store Opens	
	Salesclerks	
	Cashier	
	Manager	
	Supply department	
	Advertising staff	

By noon each item had been discussed in enough detail for the whole group to know roughly what was involved.

The children returned after lunch eager to go to work immediately on their plans. Since the store was the most pressing problem they faced, it seemed best to Miss Thomas to allow them to push ahead with plans as rapidly as they could. The lists on the board were re-examined for serious omissions and it was decided that they provided a good working base.

"What suggestions do you have about how to start?" asked Miss Thomas.

"Why don't we just divide up into the committees we've listed and start in?" said Joe. "Each committee can make its own plans."

"But won't an inventory take a lot of time?" asked Esther. "We can't set prices till we know what we have to sell, and we can't display it or even put it away."

"Last year's class left an inventory. All we need to do is check it," answered Tomi. "But when we get done with it somebody'd better be ready to order new supplies and to put price tags on them and get them out where people can buy them."

"We'd better elect a manager right away," suggested Irving. "And he can tell us all what to do."

"Do any of us know enough about it yet to begin to manage it all?" asked Miss Thomas.

"No." "Gosh, no." "Nobody except you, Miss Thomas." "She hasn't done it before either."

"But we've got to stick together." Irving clung to his point. "You can't just have committees doing anything they want to do."

"Is the inventory our first step in getting our supplies ready to be sold?" asked Miss Thomas. The class agreed that it was.

"Then what would happen if we made our plans to get that done? After we know how many people it will take and how they can work best, then perhaps we could decide what steps those who are left could take."

"That sounds O.K. Then we'll at least be started."

"Last year's class wrote a lot of suggestions as to how to do it," said Joan. "They said it was the thing that held them up so long."

"Why don't you read us what they recommended about taking an inventory?" suggested Miss Thomas.

On the basis of the previous report it was decided to use four teams of two people each to do the inventory. Certain supplies were allotted to each team and the job was organized so that each person in the pair would check the work of his partner.

This full hour of concentrated discussion was beginning to tell on the less mature in the group and when Jerry, who was feeling his way into the new situation, asked if it might be possible to see the store children and teacher agreed enthusiastically. The next twenty minutes were spent taking turns investigating the small room that was used as the store—the counter, storage space, display facilities, and general equipment. As they examined the store, they decided that the space was large enough for the work of those doing the inventory while the other jobs could be done in the classroom.

When they returned to the classroom Miss Thomas again asked about arranging the room.

"Before we leave today, shouldn't we do some thinking about our own living quarters here? You are all going to need your own places to put things and it won't help the store if we start losing things up here."

"If we just choose desks and lockers now, we'll be all right until the store gets going."

"We can find the supplies all right in the cupboard and we can arrange them later."

"But aren't we going to do anything more with the room? It isn't nearly as nice as ours was last year."

"We can plan it better when we know the store's going O.K."

These comments indicated that the room was not the urgent problem at the moment and that no difficulties in choosing desks or lockers were likely to arise. Nor would it apparently be serious to leave the room relatively untouched for a while. Temporary decisions about desks were confirmed and lockers selected before the group disbanded for the day.

SELECTION OF STORE PERSONNEL CALLS FOR RECOGNITION OF INDIVIDUAL ABILITIES

The next morning the children turned immediately to the store. Although those working on the inventory were anxious to start, they remained with the class long enough to help decide how other committees were to be formed. The majority wanted to set up the entire store personnel at once so that they would know what their first offices would be. However, the committee which had studied the report of the personnel from the previous year pointed out that there were certain immediate jobs to be done and that yesterday's plans had called for committees to do these things first. Necessary supplies had to be secured, prices set and price tags made, and equipment secured from the central supply office.

"Can't the store staff do those jobs, Miss Thomas?" asked Doris Jean. "The manager could order the supplies."

"That would be the supply department," said Anthony, who was beginning to feel he could share in suggestions without being called upon directly.

"The clerks would have to help order," added Myra. "They'd be the ones who would know what people are buying."

"No, they just sell things," said Henry.

"All of which means that we still don't know just what we want our regular staff to be able to do, doesn't it?" summed up Miss Thomas. "Shall we take time to try to decide that today or had we better work in committees for a day or so until preliminary plans are under way and then talk again about our staff?"

In the ensuing discussion Miss Thomas pointed out the advantages of informal committees for the work of the next day or so. She saw in the final decisions as to store personnel an opportunity to develop considerable insight into the care needed to provide adequate personnel for a complex job. By encouraging the group to postpone the discussion until they had time to think it over, she made it possible to carry on the practical work of getting ready to open the store without sacrificing an important learning experience to the needs of the moment.

Committees were established. The group working on needed supplies secured the estimate used the previous year for the first two months and began to make a tentative order sheet, pending the final checking of the spring inventory. Another group studied the report of how prices were set the year before. A third committee, knowing in general what was to be sold, began to talk about posters, displays, and advertising. The inventory teams went to the store to start work. Since the major purpose was to make effective plans rapidly and to execute them with dispatch, Miss Thomas continued to capitalize on strengths in the group. David, whose mathematical ability was very limited but whose sense of the dramatic was fairly good, went into the displays and advertising group at her suggestion. So did Joe. Myra and two others who were not very able in mathematics were helping check the inventory. Esther and Tomi who were recognized by the group as two of their best mathematicians were appointed, one to work on the order sheet and the other on prices. Children who were new to the class were helped to find assignments that would probably not make overwhelming demands on their skills, and Miss Thomas made a special point of observing how they were fitting in as she went from group to group. She also had opportunities to appraise their skills as she chatted with them before school, observed how well they followed directions in filling in the registration forms, and listened to their comments in the first group sessions.

Until the recess period the committees worked independently developing plans for what they had to do. Her previous acquaintance with the class as fourth-graders had led Miss Thomas to believe that their work habits were quite mature and her present observations confirmed this. Accordingly, she felt free to leave the majority at work in the classroom while she spent a little time in the store helping the inventory group get started. She then returned to the classroom and after recess worked with each group in turn. By noon tasks were clear and well-formulated plans were under way.

In the afternoon the groups returned to their tasks after a sharing session in which they reported progress. Word had been received from the school library at noon that the annual display of new books was ready. A choice of the last hour in the afternoon or the first the next morning was offered to this particular fifth grade. As the day had been relatively unbroken they decided to take the afternoon visit and spent the last hour talking with the librarian and examining the books. Several in the group selected recreational reading matter, and the store displays and advertising committee arranged to return to see what suggestions they might find in some of the books.

On the morning of the third day committees were ready to report. The floor was first turned over to the inventory committee, followed by the reports from the groups estimating supplies and prices. Throughout the year this class was to learn a good deal about the relation of supply to demand and of price to profit. At this point, however, there was little experience on which to build except the report of the last year's group. Prices, it was decided, had better be continued as of last year. A quick check at the principal's office had indicated that no great changes in the cost prices had occurred. Several children thought it advisable to order all supplies for the year at once, notably Irving, who liked to see things finished quickly. Miss Thomas raised several questions pointing to the wisdom of the group's taking things a step at a time and expanding as they learned their business. As a result the first order was a conservative one, following last year's general recommendations.

While it was important to hear from all committees, several activities broke up a session of sitting, listening, and discussing that would have been too long for even the most mature members of the class. Mr. Jamison asked for a half-hour following the recess break to talk with both fifth-grade classes about the program of organized games. Committee reports were followed by lively discussions that included opportunities to get up to examine materials, such as price tags and books for salesclerks. There was also a short meeting to hear a report from the sixth-grade safety guards.

By noon, committee reports had all been made, discussed, modified, and approved. Meanwhile, the sixth-graders sent a notice that an "Extra" edition of *The Monthly Star* would come out at the end of the week. Writing an announcement of the opening of the store was added to the activities of the afternoon. A check of the list of things to be done immediately showed the following as the next practical steps: making out the requisition sheet for the central supply office, picking up the extra supplies, arranging supplies, making out price tags, and securing the sales checks and other forms needed by the clerks. Bill and the inventory group added that it would help if the supply shelves were relabeled. Miss Thomas suggested that the cashier and sales staff would probably need some practice before they began work. Accordingly it was agreed that early the next morning the class would select the sales force and decide what they should be able to do.

By two o'clock the class had reorganized to carry out its next tasks.

In contrast to the relatively heavy amount of listening and discussing in the morning, this was an afternoon of overt action. Since none was too experienced in writing announcements, the entire class, at Miss Thomas' suggestion, talked over in general what should be said. Alice, Mary Anne, and Jerry were then delegated to phrase the announcement, and at 2:30 the class again broke into small groups.

Esther and two of her committee, with the help of Miss Thomas, made out the requisition sheet. The display and advertising staff, having received suggestions as to a color scheme, went to the store to try it out. The children who lettered best began to remake the labels for the supply shelves. There was some discussion as to whether Mrs. Gaynor, fourth-grade teacher and specialist in art, should be called upon for special help in lettering. In the end it was decided that clarity was the most important factor and that requests for Mrs. Gaynor's time had better be limited to help with posters and other items where artistic quality was more important. Several other children cut the labels the right size. As they finished, two of the boys took them down to the store and tacked them up, under the general supervision of Bill and Mary Anne who knew the shelves from their work on the inventory. Another group made out price tags. These activities afforded Miss Thomas many more opportunities to appraise language, spelling, and writing skills. Later that day all went down to survey the showcases and to discuss the poster needed outside the door. Here, they decided, was a time when Mrs. Gaynor should be asked to give advice.

The schedule for Thursday, planned with reference to the things still to be done, looked as follows:

9:00–10:00	Class meeting—Discussion of the proposed announcement for the paper; check on progress in arranging supplies and labeling; discussion of kind of poster needed. (Miss Thomas reported that Mrs. Gaynor could meet with them in the afternoon if by then they had anything ready for her suggestions.)
10:00–10:30	Drafting individual designs for poster.
10:30–10:45	Recess.
10:45–11:45	Discussion of what clerks and a cashier should be able to do; giving arithmetic skills test (addition, subtraction, making change) to locate for first clerks persons having greatest competency; selection of clerks and cashier in light of qualifications.
11:45– 1:00	Lunch.
1:00– 1:45	Conference with Mrs. Gaynor regarding poster. (While this was going on Miss Thomas met with the fourth grade to advise them on setting up a terrarium.)

1:45– 2:45	Special practice period for clerks and cashier—Children pretended to be customers and the clerks made out sales checks, added bills, made change. (Three children continued to work on the posters and others continued to letter signs for the shelves and make out price tags.)
2:45– 3:15	Check on progress. (At this time plans were made to appoint other store officers on Friday.)
3:15– 3:30	Clean up.

On Friday the discussion of store personnel continued. General abilities needed for each office were listed, and decisions as to who should fill the various posts for this first time were made in terms of ability. The children agreed that the effect on their trade would be best if, for the first few weeks, each did the thing he knew most about. During these weeks others could prepare for specific jobs. Miss Thomas encouraged careful group discussion before decisions were made.

"Irving had better be manager," said Peter. "He likes that best."

"Yes, but he tells us to do too many things at once and we're going to have enough to do without being bossed around." It was David speaking from experience in trying to grasp a series of complex suggestions given too quickly.

"There are several other jobs which need good organizers," pointed out Miss Thomas. "Remember how important we said it was to have persons who would keep very careful records in our books."

"What about Jerry? He's new here but his Dad's a store manager."

"But I don't know how your store runs; it had better be someone this time who has been here."

"How about Bill or Mary Anne?" suggested one of the inventory committee. "They know exactly where everything is."

"Bill helped study the report on how they worked together on things last year and that's what we need," said someone else.

"Bill'd be a good one," chimed a second voice. There were several nods and expressions of agreement.

"What do you think about Bill for this first round?" asked Miss Thomas. "Does he sound like the best prepared?"

Bill became the manager. Irving was appointed head of the committee to keep records; other children were selected for or chose other responsibilities. In all the staff consisted of:

Manager
Assistant manager
Six clerks—three to work in the morning and three in the afternoon
Two cashiers—one to work in the morning and one in the afternoon
Four record keepers

Four members of the supply department
Three members of the advertising staff

It was decided to ask the present staff to continue for at least two weeks. Then a system of rotation was planned so that most children would be able to try every task. The positions of manager, assistant manager, cashier, and record keepers, they decided, would need to change more often if each person were to have a turn. One week's tenure was decided upon. So that all might be made aware of problems and participate in solving them, it was agreed that an hour at the end of each day would be set aside for discussion until the store was running smoothly. Later these planning periods occurred less frequently. It was decided also that a record of the work of each group would be helpful to those who took over next and would make the final report easier to write. Detailed plans for these records were made during the next week as the various groups started to work.

During the latter part of the week, while the details regarding store personnel were being settled, other immediate problems continued to provide variety in the school day. Time was taken to appoint persons to collect lunch money, to water plants, and to take care of other immediate routine housekeeping responsibilities until more elaborate plans could be developed for making the classroom an attractive place in which to live. Bulletins from the principal's office were discussed. On their own first, and then with the rest of the school, the children practiced fire drills. Recess breaks were lengthened to allow for some active games when the time in the classroom seemed weighted with quiet work.

INCREASED SKILLS ARE NEEDED FOR STORE EFFICIENCY

Much that was done during the first two days of the second week pertained in some fashion to the routine running of the store. More signs were needed, sales slips ran out, and a host of other details kept individuals and small groups active. Children who were not members of the staff for the first weeks found much to do in helping with these extra tasks. By the end of the second day a serious problem had been identified.

"They're waiting too long in line and they don't like it," said Bill.

"It takes too long to make change," explained one of the clerks. "We need another cashier."

"Well, I can't go fast if I can't read what you write on the bills," countered Tomi.

"That's right," agreed one of the record keepers. "I tried to check one account of what was sold from the bill and I couldn't make out half of it. Some of them were added wrong, too."

"Are we beginning to see the trouble?" asked Miss Thomas. "Is it our cashier who is slow or are our clerks inaccurate, or are there other problems?"

More discussion produced the evidence that the clerks were not writing legibly enough when they tried to make out the bills rapidly, that their spelling was poor, and that they were slow and inaccurate in their addition. A suggestion that the clerks be fired and replaced by those whose handwriting was more legible was vetoed by Miss Thomas.

"How many situations have we faced already this year where handwriting and spelling were important? Think for a minute."

"The librarian made me do my card over," said Theresa.

"The sixth grade had to come back and ask about our announcement for the paper, and that was good writing."

"My father said he couldn't figure out half of the letters I wrote from camp this summer."

"Then what about it?" Miss Thomas came back to the original suggestion. "Do we solve the problem by firing the clerks?"

"Guess some of us better practice some writing," said Myra.

"Now what about the arithmetic? When else have we had trouble with that?" Miss Thomas went on.

The list of problems on the board finally included adding the inventory, adding sales checks, subtracting to see how much was sold, making change, multiplying when people bought more than one of an item, long division in deciding how to cut posters and labels most economically.

"The clerks had better start practicing," said David with satisfaction as he saw himself out of the skills picture for a little longer.

"We'll all be clerks before we're through," said Henry. "And we don't want this happening all over again next time."

"I'd rather not be a clerk than practice adding"—this from David.

"So would I," said Joe. "You do the clerking. We'll help somewhere else."

"What jobs have we on the list that don't need accurate calculation?" asked Miss Thomas.

Nothing could be checked off except being a member of the advertising staff.

"But right now we're trying to figure out how large our ads should be and having to divide to find out how many words we can put on a line," said the chairman of that committee. "We don't want you unless you can do some of the work after you get the ideas and we haven't time to figure it out for you."

"We'll let you sweep the floor," said Irving, "but you don't get to put things away and help check prices if you can't add them right."

"Besides, everybody has to be able to help with everything or the rest of us won't get turns," added Esther. "I don't want to keep on making change all year just because nobody else wants to learn how."

"That's right," chimed in several others.

The children had made the point with only a little guidance from Miss Thomas. There was no room in this class for people who were not willing to carry their share. Whether or not one was interested in a skill, if it was needed as part of the job it was his responsibility to develop it. Plans were made to schedule a daily period to work on skills—usually the hour from 9:30 to 10:30, but shifted according to other demands on the schedule.

With Miss Thomas' help, and the samples and suggestions in various textbooks and worksheets, each individual analyzed his own difficulties. Several who were slow but wrote very legibly began to work on speed. A spelling list was begun, drawing on the words the clerks needed to use. This was soon expanded to include words from letters, newspaper announcements, and other situations in which correct spelling was essential. All tested themselves on this list and made up individual lists of words they could not spell.

Arithmetic needs were analyzed in the same way. On the basis of the typical demands of the store, Miss Thomas mimeographed a series of graded practice sheets. Tomi, Esther, and Peter, whose arithmetic skills were well above average, did two or three of the most difficult with complete accuracy in record time and went back to their handwriting and to other skills where their strengths were not as great. Joe, David, and one or two more of the least able formed a small group for regular instruction. Others were aided in identifying weaknesses which demanded help for more limited periods of time. Long division was a problem for many. Several were still inaccurate in the use of multiplication tables, and a few still tended to use fingers to help with addition. As these deficiencies were identified special practice was provided. Miss Thomas worked with groups and individuals until the need and the method for improvement were clearly seen, helped provide plenty of practice materials, and then came back to check progress and give extra help. Pages from workbooks provided some of the practice. In the standard arithmetic texts were a number of other exercises. These became reference materials for the group. This was only the beginning of a series of arithmetic experiences for these children. As the year went on and new problems arose demanding other arithmetic skills, provision was made for these new needs in the practice sessions.

The store continued to take from a quarter to half the group time for nearly all the first month. Almost everybody was involved from 8:30 to 9:15 every morning and from 12:40 to 1:15 in the afternoon. This allowed for the twenty-minute periods during which the store was open for business and for some leeway on either side for opening and closing and for checking accounts. As problems arose with regard to the duties of various groups they were worked through in large- and small-group planning periods. This seemed an appropriate time to widen understanding of the responsibilities involved and the skills needed in running a business establishment. However, the emergency was over once the customers were actually able to buy things easily and attention could be turned to other aspects of group living.

TECHNIQUES OF COOPERATION DEVELOP IN MAKING THE CLASSROOM A DESIRABLE PLACE IN WHICH TO WORK

As problems of running the store began to be solved, the classroom became a center of interest. First in order was the permanent arrangement of books and supplies. This was done quickly, as much skill had developed through handling this responsibility for several years previous. However, the cupboard space was different, and it was a somewhat larger room which allowed a little more freedom in arranging desks.

"Let's keep the dictionary and the encyclopedia and the magazines away from our library corner this year," suggested Jimmy, capitalizing on experience from the fourth grade. "Too many people just go back to look over the books and it disturbs those who are trying to look up something special."

In like manner decisions were made for placing other materials where they could be used most effectively. Books and equipment were quickly cleared away and attention turned to beautifying the room and keeping it tidy.

"Miss Thomas, do we have to have committees again this year? Can't everyone just be careful when they use things?" It was Doris Jean speaking, her hair and dress suggesting that the joy of helping make one's living quarters tidy was a rare experience. "It takes so long to straighten things up."

"How do you think it would work?" Miss Thomas turned to the group.

"We tried it last year in our school and it didn't," said John positively.

"Tell us why, John."

"It's all right for around your own desk. But it doesn't matter how careful you try to be, somebody's got to straighten out things like books. Of course it helps the committee if people are careful."

"Then let the people who like to clean up do it and the rest of us will do something else," said Doris Jean.

Again the growing feeling of group responsibility provided the answer before Miss Thomas needed to raise the point.

"Nobody likes to do it. It's just that you can't get your work done and neither can anybody else if you can't find things."

"And everybody should take a turn. We don't need to have as large a committee as we had last year."

"Why doesn't Miss Thomas make out a work sheet and we'll just follow it?"

"Sure, we've got too much to do to bother."

Miss Thomas did as requested. With another class the opportunity to plan how to delegate responsibilities might have involved important learnings. These children understood what was involved and had done a much more complex delegation of duties in the store. There was little of new educative value to be gained in having them work the parallel classroom situation through in detail.

Curtains were decided against. Last year's experience indicated there was too much dirt in the neighborhood to keep them attractive very long. Plants, however, were wanted. Miss Thomas, it has already been pointed out, had special competence in science. Her staff responsibility included the supervision of a small laboratory from which equipment could be borrowed and in which about ten children could work at once, helping to keep the science books and pamphlets in the library up to date, and consultative service as needed by other teachers and children.

"We should grow some plants this year, Miss Thomas, especially with you right here to help us," said Joan.

"Yes, you grow such nice ones upstairs," said Peter, whose crowded tenement home had little room for much beauty.

"Maybe I could get my uncle to send us some cactus," suggested John.

"That would be interesting." Miss Thomas picked up the opportunity both to help a new child become established and to acquaint the group with another part of their country. "Why don't you write him and see?"

"I could get us a slip of the flowering maple we had on our farm," offered Catherine. "It's beautiful."

"We've never had one in the school, Catherine," said Miss Thomas. "Many of the classes would be interested in it."

"Sweet potatoes are always fun to watch."

"I know how to grow an avocado."

"We take in begonias from our garden and they grow all winter. I could bring one."

"Mother would show us how to make flower arrangements." This from Tomi.

"Why don't we see how many kinds we could grow?"

"Put them all along the window ledges."

"Get just one of everything."

"Could we, Miss Thomas?"

Plans were made. John wrote to his uncle during one of the skill periods. Miss Thomas and several children who did not remember exactly how a letter should be headed helped him find a sample in the English textbook and criticized the result before it was mailed. Later, thank-you letters for the box of cacti offered opportunities for each member of the class to write.

PLANTS IN THE CLASSROOM PROVIDE A SOURCE FOR MANY LEARNINGS

In the children's desire for interesting plants, Miss Thomas saw two possibilities for growth. One was in learning how to care for them and in understanding the adjustments needed by way of light, water, soil, special fertilizers, and the like. The other was the possibility of learning something of other parts of the country from the plant life. In her thinking about previous experiences of the class and her analysis of their present understandings as indicated by their conversations, Miss Thomas had come to some tentative conclusions that further opportunities to work with living things would help to round out an area of inexperience. Accordingly, as the plants came in she made books available on how to care for them and encouraged the group to start a list of questions that should be answered if the plants were to thrive. As an avocado, a sweet potato, some grapefruit seeds, and the slip from the flowering maple were added she began to raise questions as to where they had come from. Interest in plants from different parts of the country grew and resulted in a decision to write for something typical of each major region. Working in groups, the children gathered all the information they could about the plants of the South, the Northwest, the Middle West, the Southwest coast, the Northeast, and the Southeast, and as reports were made groups chose one or two plants from each region and sent for them. Miss Thomas guided them in selecting plants which would survive under the classroom or laboratory conditions without an undue amount of care. She helped them find where to send for plants and informed them about quarantine restrictions. A large map of the United States was used to indicate where each new plant had come from. This was not the first acquaintance with other parts of the United States for this class. The previous year current transportation tie-ups and several floods had caused them to make a rather extensive study of the topography of the country, but little had been done with its plant life.

As each group was responsible for writing a business letter to secure its plants, all took time to review the form they needed, and good handwriting and spelling were given further impetus. Reference reading was rather extensive, both to find what plants were wanted and to find how to care for them. The children decided that a brief history of the plant and the care it needed should be written out so that those in other groups and visitors could have the information. This led to careful consideration of how best to write brief descriptions and give clear directions.

From the reading about plants came the need for practice in another skill. Even Bill was bogged down at times by Latin names and technical terms.

"Try the glossary at the back," suggested Miss Thomas after the first attempt to report on material by reading aloud. "It gives the pronunciation of the words. So would your dictionary."

This was the first time this year that reading material had contained a large amount of difficult technical terminology. Good word-analysis skills did not always do the job when the words were not within the children's speaking vocabulary. Yet a minimum number of technical terms were needed to read and to discuss intelligently the information secured. All worked to develop more skill in using common diacritical marks as an aid to pronunciation. In addition, the children began their own glossary of technical terms which they posted on the bulletin board for reference.

Miss Thomas took the pronunciation problem as an opportunity to help several of the weak spellers see the importance of identifying the syllables in their words and worked with them in a special group for several weeks helping them to develop better methods of studying words. She also set up a special reading group for David, Joe, Myra, and three others who were finding the regular reference work far too difficult. These children spent part of their time in this special group working together on simpler materials about plants. They reported on these to the others in their group. The rest of their reading time was spent with a variety of work-type and story materials selected to give additional practice in the techniques in which they were weak. During the period set aside for individual work on skills this group met regularly for help.

INDIVIDUAL AND SMALL-GROUP INTERESTS PROVIDE PARALLEL ACTIVITIES

Meanwhile individual interests and wishes were making themselves felt.

"Miss Thomas, there are all those swell new books in the library. When are we going to have time just to read?"

"I collected interesting rocks all summer at the lake, and I thought you might help me find out what they are."

"Are we going to have time to build any more airplane models this year?"

"I wish we could have some special music in our room again this year." Alice's illness had given her opportunities to explore the satisfactions in music, and several others were also interested. "Last year we made scales by filling glasses with water."

"Did you know that you can also do it with wood?" asked Miss Thomas. "It is much easier to carry around and keep in tune. Would you like to try?"

"I'd like to have time to write a really good continued story for the paper," said Joan. "I did one last year, but it wasn't very good."

"I wish we could just have time to paint anything we wanted to." Theresa's love of color was showing up. "Last year in our school we always had to draw a picture about something we were doing."

"And make some more clay things," added Jimmy. "That was a lot of fun."

During the year these and many other individual and small-group interests were given outlets. Normally about an hour a day was set aside for such activities. As interesting things developed, part of this time was devoted to sharing experiences and to helping other children learn to enjoy the same kinds of activity. Miss Thomas kept in mind her responsibility for bringing in new possibilities and for encouraging and helping the child who was timid or needed extra assistance with techniques. Again, the children's cumulative records aided in indicating gaps in experiences and possible areas of interest.

In order to allow individual children to draw upon special help wherever it resided within the school, the teachers regularly returned to their classrooms at 12:45. For the next half hour they were available by appointment for consultation. To facilitate this procedure each teacher helped his own children clarify their problems so that they went to the expert with their questions clearly in mind. Not all the children in any one class necessarily used this opportunity every day. Many remained in their own rooms. The classroom activities in each room during this noon period were individual or small-group enterprises that needed a minimum of direct leadership. This meant that the teacher could work with children from other classes without interruption. A schedule, blocked off into fifteen-minute intervals, was posted on the bulletin board outside each room for children to sign. This noon period served individuals and small groups almost entirely. When an entire class needed extensive expert help, teachers often exchanged classes.

THE COMING ELECTION ADDS TO UNDERSTANDING OF SOCIAL STRUCTURES

A new all-group interest came into the picture in late September with the ensuing local elections.

"My dad says we'll have no more new things done in the city if Mr. Walters gets to be mayor," said Sarah.

"Oh, no! He'll be much better than the mayor we have now," replied Mary Anne.

"Next year Mr. Duncan says he'll tear down all these buildings and put up new ones," added Jean Marie.

"Who told you that?" asked Miss Thomas. Recognizing in this current community concern an opportunity to help the children grow in their understanding of the bases on which government candidates are chosen, she decided to help them expand their interests. Previous elections had been given cursory attention, but the maturity of the children had not been such that there was much to be gained in extended study. Even now there was danger that unwise guidance would push them into making judgments and expressing opinions for which they had little background. The aspect of the problem which seemed most fruitful was to study how one learns about candidates, what dangers of misrepresentation there are, and why it is important to have an informed electorate. Ten-year-olds could not be expected to judge the soundness of platforms. Accordingly, Miss Thomas began to challenge their opinions.

"Peter, who said that it would mean a smaller police force?"

"My father."

"Where did he hear that?"

"Read it, I guess."

"My father says it won't make any difference at all, he says the city will get run anyway," Esther came into the discussion.

"Oh, yes, it will make a difference—that's why people vote," from Bill.

"They just like to get turns; there are good salaries in those jobs," contributed Anthony.

"Did it matter to us which people held our store jobs?" questioned Miss Thomas.

"Sure, because we wanted a good store."

"What things do you know of that the city government does for all of us?" Several suggestions were made.

"Then is it important to have the right people?" They decided that it might be.

"How did we decide who were best qualified for our store positions?"

"We knew them."

"We've worked with them before."

"Do you think the people in the city know our candidates for mayor and council that well?"

They decided it was impossible. Then how did people find out? You can't just take what anybody tells you, he might be wrong. You can't be sure that what a candidate says is exact, he may be stressing his own position too much. Through the next month the group investigated the means by which a city gets to know its candidates. Radio programs, local meetings, campaign speeches, newspaper and magazine reports, previous histories of candidates, were among the sources studied in an attempt to judge the kind of information secured and the probable accuracy. For the more able children, this was an opportunity to do rather wide independent exploration. Those of more limited ability used more obvious resources and developed somewhat less complete generalizations.

OTHER SCHOOL AND COMMUNITY CONCERNS ARE INCLUDED IN THE CURRICULUM

Meanwhile other short-term, all-group activities continued to develop. Rarely was there a time when a special problem, occupying from a day or two to a couple of weeks, was not on the schedule. Physical examinations were held during the second week at school. These presented an opportunity to build further health understandings. As the examinations were a yearly affair, the children were acquainted with the routine and had a general background of understanding. Several children protested at this interruption of their other activities. Miss Thomas recognized this as evidence that the basic health concept back of a yearly check-up was still not understood and discussed with the group why the examination needed to be repeated each year. She also took time to discuss what the examination consisted of and how it was administered. This served to orient new children and to recall the process to others. Then, as reports came back indicating special needs, she worked with the problems of each child, contacting homes, explaining recommendations, and helping plan what needed to be done.

Other activities arose from events of current interest. A disastrous fire in a supposedly fireproof building led to some investigation of how a building is made fire resistant and to a study of the school fire-prevention system. The report of another new plane which traveled much faster than sound brought both boys and girls to school with many questions. The detailed scientific data were beyond the understanding of most of the children but the general principles could be outlined. A request from the lunchroom committee that children try not to waste food called for one discussion period on why it made any difference and two more on how children could help at home and at school. An influx of all sorts of pictures and clippings led to the establishment of a bulletin board on which current events of interest were posted and from which, at intervals, came concerns that were followed up in some detail.

The problems stemming from typical current interests were given some recognition in the daily sharing and planning periods. Time was or was not found for a more careful study, depending on what other activities were pressing and how deeply the problem concerned the children. In addition, Miss Thomas kept in mind the question of how much the new interest would contribute to balance and continuity of growth. In thinking this through, study of the children's records in the light of the faculty analysis of persistent life situations was of help. She encouraged study of the problems listed above, but let go by, with only brief discussion, such items as the report of an automobile race which contributed nothing but a passing thrill, the story of a new synthetic process which could not be explained without considerably more mature ability to understand chemical processes than most of the class possessed, and an interest in the opening of a new stationery store in the neighborhood which offered experiences duplicating what the children were already learning in their own store.

WORK UNDER WAY SHOWS VARIED ACTIVITIES WHICH GIVE DESIRED BALANCE

Thus the group activities were launched in September. October found the store running smoothly and several related projects well under way. The advertising staff had started a small-group study of effective newspaper advertisements and had one bulletin board filled with samples. All had been interested in more attractive displays and as a group they paid a visit to the grocery store owned by Sarah's father. He had come back to talk with them. A small group interested in posters had volunteered to produce new signs periodically. These children met regularly with Mrs. Gaynor.

Study of the new plants went on apace. Individuals delved further into plant families and with Miss Thomas' help labeled the plants that were related. No special effort was made to involve children of limited ability in this aspect of the project although they examined the labels with interest. Bill and Catherine became very curious about the effects of different kinds of care—Catherine, from her farm experience, saying that soil and water and fertilizer made a real difference, and Bill, with his city background, saying he didn't think it would matter much. Here was an opportunity for experimentation through which everyone could learn something about a scientific approach to problems, and Miss Thomas helped Catherine and Bill set up a simple experiment using a variety of soils. The results later became the center of class interest. Bill was also encouraged to explore the question of why federal laws prohibited importing plants from other countries—a matter that had concerned him since his plan to have plants from the whole continent had to be given up.

Study of the election drew to a close as Election Day approached. There was a suggestion that the children make classroom campaign speeches for their own candidates; but so interested had they become in seeing how adults decided on candidates that they felt they had no time to "play elections" as one of them phrased it. "Our vote doesn't matter and we all know all we want to about voting anyway," said another. "What we want to see is how the real election comes out."

Individual interests continued strong. A wooden xylophone was made with the help of Miss Thomas and one of the first-grade teachers who was a specialist in music. A model airplane group and an "artists" group worked ahead steadily and Joan gathered two or three other "literary enthusiasts" into her short-story projects. David began to see improvement in his reading and forged ahead even at times when his group did not meet.

A typical schedule in October looked like this:

8:45–10:00 Store and work period—This time was taken regularly in the store or the classroom to clear up store responsibilities. Individuals or small groups worked on reading, spelling, arithmetic, or oral or written expression needs, letters were corrected before being mailed, stories checked before sending them to the newspaper, and the like.

10:00–10:30	Organized instruction in a skill area—This was a flexible period. It was not always used, but allowed time for Miss Thomas to work with the entire group on a needed skill without losing the opportunity of giving individual help. Sometimes it was placed earlier in the morning and lasted longer if a new concept was difficult.
10:30–10:45	Recess—Two days a week this period was scheduled for rhythms or other physical education activities and extended from 10:15 to 10:45.
10:45–11:45	Study of plants—This included detailed planning, care of plants, reference reading, writing and making reports, experimentation, and the like.
11:45–12:45	Lunch.
12:45– 1:15	Conferences with other teachers—During this open period children worked on their own interests, either with another teacher or in their own classroom. Children who went home for lunch and those who did not need special help usually did not return to this individual work until 1:00.
1:15– 2:15	Study of election—This hour included discussion, examining papers and other materials, writing reports, and the like. This period, the work session in the morning, and the period after recess were used somewhat interchangeably.
2:15– 3:00	Special problems—This time was given to short-term concerns of the group such as some special local problem; a visitor from the community; special plans for an assembly program.
3:00– 3:25	Planning—The children used this period for any needed check on progress during the day, consideration of time schedule for the next day, items of major importance not planned for, and similar topics.

Late in October there was added the task of helping the other fifth grade decorate the upper hall for a Halloween party. This was part of a school–community celebration which provided fun without vandalism in this crowded city section. Through this project Miss Thomas helped some of the children, whose academic status was limited, to secure group recognition and leadership experience.

The Next Milestone—Getting Ready for Christmas

Space does not permit such a detailed description of the rest of the year. In the briefer outline which follows, the reader will need to picture the same cooperative processes going on and the same method of expanding concerns being used.

Early November had seen the conclusion of the study of the election. By the middle of the month the study of plants was also drawing to a close. A careful account of the history of each plant, where and how it was secured, and the care it needed had been written up; the results of Catherine and Bill's experiment with different soils had convinced them and several others that care actually did make a difference. The class had held open house so that the rest of the school and their parents could share their collection.

CREATIVE EXPRESSION FINDS AN OUTLET THROUGH LANGUAGE

The writing of original stories and poetry now began to receive more attention. The newspaper staff issued a call for stories and poems, and since Joan and the small group working with her were the only ones this year who had had any extended experience in this area Miss Thomas urged the others to try. Given courage by the acceptance of their advertisements and announcements about the store, and by the appearance of two group articles about their plants, the class began to experiment further with writing for publication. Soon a bulletin board contained class efforts, posted before final decisions were made as to what to submit to the editors of the paper. Although Miss Thomas used caution about suggesting any models, the children themselves began to be more sensitive to good plots in the books and stories they read, and to the quality of poetry. As a result a much greater amount of recreational reading began to balance the heavy load of reference work which many of the children had been carrying.

Interest in recreational reading was heightened by the coming of annual Book Week. For their share in the program the group decided to do a series of reviews of the books of two of their favorite authors. This meant finding how many books each author had written and deciding which ones to talk about. Individuals volunteered to read the books and review them for the class. After the choices were made, the question of what, from the audience standpoint, makes a good book review was raised by Miss Thomas. The children went back to the reviews they had already heard and proceeded to criticize and draw up standards. For effectiveness in the auditorium they planned large illustrations of two or three of the best scenes in each book. This afforded an opportunity to encourage some of the children who had not yet attempted very much pictorial art.

Since she saw the need for even broader exploration in recreational reading if there were to be balance in the total program, Miss Thomas continued to make generous allowance for library periods. As children began to talk about Christmas gifts she asked how many liked to get books for Christmas.

"I always get two or three," said Bill, "but they are not always the ones I like."

"Aunt Mary thinks if there's a baseball on the cover I'm sure to like it," said Jerry.

"They never give me boys' books and I think they're swell," added Mary Anne.

"Would a list of your favorite authors and the books you've already read help out?" asked Miss Thomas.

The idea was accepted. For the rest of the month and the first two weeks in December the preparation of these lists was a major project. Children shared books with one another and added to their lists of favorite authors and titles. Miss Thomas took care, as did the librarian, to work with David and the others whose ability was still limited so that their lists would contain simpler books.

MAKING GIFTS PROVIDES ANOTHER OUTLET FOR CREATIVE EXPRESSION

Interest in gifts for others paralleled the preparation of book lists for themselves. By early December almost all individual activities had turned to the making of gifts. Here the only limits were imagination, ability to carry out an idea, and materials with which to work. The back of the classroom was turned into a workshop and a common supply cupboard containing all the work materials that attics and storerooms at home and the school supply department could provide. This was drawn upon as needed by all children. Everything was welcomed, from old newspapers and colored pictures to ribbons, remnants of materials, bits of wood, and a variety of bottles and cans to be turned into flower containers.

At the same time the store provided another intensive activity. It was a school custom for each class to contribute to the Community Chest at Christmas. This year the fifth grade saw the store as one means of helping by undertaking to sell handmade greeting cards if pupils would make them. This necessitated considerable preplanning. How to approach other classes, who should explain the project to them, how many cards to ask for, what standards to suggest cards should meet, when they should be ready, how much they should sell for, how to advertise to parents, which of the store committees to make responsible for various extra jobs, were all problems to be solved.

A CHRISTMAS ASSEMBLY CONTRIBUTES TO UNDERSTANDING THE CUSTOMS OF OTHERS

Parallel with other activities came plans for the Christmas assembly which, in this school, was a program shared by all classes. As the children talked about what might be appropriate, discussion turned to the variety of ways of celebrating Christmas.

"We decorate the tree late Christmas Eve, so the baby won't see it until the morning," said Bill.

"We always sing carols," contributed Joan.

"We go to church on Christmas Eve," said Anthony, "and there's always a manger with the Baby."

"We don't have your Christmas," said Sarah, "but we have the Festival of the Lights, and it's very beautiful."

"Tell us a little about it, Sarah," said Miss Thomas, who saw in the comments and questions the need for most of the children to broaden their understanding of other religious groups.

Sarah, with Esther and Irving helping, explained some of the Channukah ceremonies but had trouble answering many of the questions. It was suggested that her mother, or Esther's or Irving's, might come to school some day and tell the group more, or that they find out more about the observance.

"How much do you know about how children in other countries celebrate Christmas?" queried Miss Thomas. No one knew very much and she elaborated on some of the most interesting customs.

"Why couldn't we tell some of that at assembly?" asked Joan. "I'll bet the others wouldn't know either—we would just pick out the most interesting things."

"Yes, and maybe sing some of their songs," added someone. "I know a lovely French one that we sing at home each year."

"And let Esther or Irving tell about their Festival too."

Not differences alone but basic similarities were the roots of the simple program that evolved. Four countries were selected, together with the Jewish Festival and a typical American Christmas. For the next week children read to discover the songs of each group, when gifts were given and how, what was done on Christmas Day, and any special points of interest. The timing of the assembly did not allow tableaux but it did allow a song, the description of each Christmas celebration, and the display of a large picture representing the most striking characteristics of each.

Famous Christmas pictures, stories, and legends were studied as the program was prepared and many of the familiar carols were sung. This enterprise lent itself to a rich experience with aesthetic resources and Miss Thomas capitalized upon it.

Both of Esther's parents and the mothers of Irving and Sarah came to school to explain more about the Jewish Festival. Later the whole group visited the crèche in a nearby church. The adults involved did not attempt to go deeply into basic religious concepts with children of this age, but helped them feel the larger meaning behind the symbolism—the joyfulness of the season, the expression of love and good will which Christmas presents, the message of liberty of Channukah, and the recognition of something greater in the world than human selfishness.

OTHER ACTIVITIES PARALLEL PLANS FOR CHRISTMAS

Short-term group activities continued to arise from interest in the daily paper, the community nearby, family happenings, and the school itself. Among others were the following:

Some discussion of good movies arising out of conversations about what children had done over the week end and carried far enough to start thinking about ways of selecting movies to be seen.

Parts of three days spent making different kinds of decorations for the school Christmas tree and other decorations for their room and the store. (David was one of those who took the lead in this.)

A brief exploration of the purposes of the Community Chest to which the proceeds from the sale of greeting cards were going.

Time with the physical education teacher learning some of the dances of the countries whose Christmas customs were being studied.

What skills were drawn upon during the period? A backward look highlights the following:

The account-keeping necessary to determine the earnings from the sale of greeting cards.

A variety of calculations needed in making Christmas gifts—estimating costs and amounts of materials needed, measuring.

Continued practice by clerks and auditors of the skills needed in the store.

Writing book reports.

Making announcements, writing advertisements and letters regarding the sale of greeting cards.

Writing stories and poetry for the school paper.

Writing descriptions for the assembly program—these were written by small groups and edited by the class as a whole.

Study of correct punctuation as needed by individuals.

Individual study of common errors in English occurring in speaking and writing.

Continued work on individual spelling lists.

Speaking before the assembly.

Judging recreational reading and doing a variety of such reading.

Continued use of reference materials.

Outlining and note-taking needed to secure the information about the Christmas festivals.

Continued practice of reading skills by the group who still found the reading done by the majority of the class a difficult process.

Budgeting of time in planning daily schedule and carrying out work projects.

Individual and small-group activities continued to be scheduled much as they were in September. Among other things they included:

Continued experimentation with a variety of media providing creative activities.

Considerably more individual writing of poetry and stories. (Joe, to whom spelling and writing had never had much appeal, was given great praise for one poem and began to ask for help with his technique.)

A wide variety of activities needed to make gifts for parents—these included tie racks, ash trays, woven pot holders, clay paper weights, napkin rings, pan holders, flower holders containing slips from some of the plants.

Individual exploration of special interests in books to be placed on the gift book list.

Contacts with other groups within the school came partly on the initiative of this class, partly from others:

Open house to share the collection of plants.

Cooperation in the Book Week program.

Sharing in Thanksgiving and Christmas assemblies.

Contacts with other classes with regard to the sale of greeting cards.

Continued contacts with the staff of the school paper.

Continued contacts with the customers in the store.

Several conferences with the lunchroom committee who were now working on better behavior during mealtimes.

The community continued to be a rich resource. Children went to it to secure information and brought community problems back to the school. During November and December community contacts of importance to these learners included the following:

Visits to local bookstores and to the public library in preparing the book lists—these were mainly individual contacts.

Following the election—children did not go out to the polling booths, but the daily papers and other reports came in to them.

Home contributions of materials with which to make Christmas gifts.

Letters to parents regarding the greeting card sale and contacts with parents at the sale.

Visits from the parents of Esther, Irving, and Sarah, and from Theresa and Anthony's parents to discuss Christmas customs.

Visiting the nearby church to see the Christmas crèche.

The Christmas assembly closed the activities for December and the children, each bearing a plant that needed special care over the holiday, and the Christmas gifts they had made for their families, left for the vacation period.

Continuing Problems Take on Added Meaning in the New Year

Some of the problem areas which were centers of study during the fall took on new meaning as the year progressed. As the children gained experience new developments opened up additional possibilities for exploring continuing problems.

THE STORE MAKES FURTHER CONTRIBUTION TO UNDERSTANDING OF ECONOMIC PROBLEMS

In January the store again became a matter of major concern. A semiyearly inventory and audit of books were the custom. At first the children wanted to omit the whole thing until June; but Miss Thomas, knowing the dangers of leaving financial matters too long unchecked, raised questions about the obligations undertaken when one is responsible for funds.

"If we operated on a profit," she explained, "and someone had made a mistake, who would suffer?"

"Ourselves," admitted one of the children. "We just wouldn't have it to use."

"Who suffers if we've made any mistakes under our present system?" she went on.

"I suppose the school supply department doesn't get paid, but they give us lots of things anyway, so it wouldn't matter much."

"Where do you think their money to buy the supplies comes from?"

Without pushing the question of taxation too far, Miss Thomas helped the children to do enough investigating to see that their parents were indirectly involved and that they, in their small business, were strictly accountable for their share of the funds. Several of the fathers who owned their own businesses were asked and they verified the need for frequent checks on stock and accounts. Accordingly a midyear inventory was made, the accounts were brought up to date and passed on to the school secretary for an official check, and the store's financial status was pronounced sound.

FURTHER STUDY OF PLANT LIFE CONTRIBUTES TO UNDERSTANDING OF NATURAL PHENOMENA

While the inventory was going on, the study of plants came back into the picture. Considerable reading had been done in October about the typical plants of various sections of the country, but at that time the problem was to collect sample plants and to learn how to care for them. The effect of climate on plant life and the causes of weather conditions had not been a center of much exploration by this group in previous years. They had done a little in relation to floods, tornadoes, and other striking weather conditions, and had learned how to read weather maps in order to try to predict clear weather for their outdoor activities; but many of the basic concepts of the effect of climate had been only slightly developed. This was a persistent life situation which they were meeting indirectly in caring for plants, and it seemed an appropriate time to help them become conscious of it. Such a problem also offered an opportunity to review and expand earlier concepts.

Now Miss Thomas began to raise further questions as to why the plants needed such different care, and why they were such different types.

"Why don't we find cactus around here?" she asked. "Why are the orange groves in California, Florida, and Texas?"

The children were intrigued. They lived in a farming belt and had been interested in the descriptions of the foliage in other parts of the country. Now they turned to maps, reference books, and weather reports to see what they could find out. In the work which followed, they traced the causes of climatic conditions, the effects of mountains and prevailing winds on rains. Several children became interested in the effect of weather on the nation's food supply and made a study of the sources of the various plant products. Later in the spring, when most of the group were absorbed in other things, these children continued in their individual activities to watch the paper for reports of the weather in the areas in which they had been most interested. All reviewed and expanded their previous notes on typical plants to include general descriptions of foliage. In addition they proceeded north and south from this country to see what the foliage would be like.

"Canada wouldn't have very much of anything because it's so cold up there," averred Myra.

"It would all be trees," said another child.

"Has anyone ever been there?" asked Miss Thomas. Mary Anne had been to Montreal, but no one had been farther north.

"Why don't you get out your maps and see?"

The group investigated. The reading which followed dispelled many false ideas about the Canadian climate. Likewise, a study of a map indicating the vegetation of Central and South America gave considerable insight into the climate and general vegetation to the south. The entire class did enough reading and group map study to develop general understandings. Small groups read and reported on a number of additional questions in detail.

With the reports on neighbors to north and south, the study terminated. Miss Thomas deliberated about raising questions which would include the whole world and decided against it. Concepts regarding the effect of climate had been amply illustrated by this time. The problem which had meaning for the children was solved when the interest in their own plants and how they came to be different was satisfied. The investigations of Canada and Central and South America were a logical way to test the generalizations arrived at in lands of similar topography. Further study might have helped the children accumulate a few more facts about other lands, but it would not have added much that was new to the concepts toward which they were working.

Parallel study of how to read various kinds of maps came at the same time. The children had done some of this before, but had never needed a map so constantly. They also branched into a great variety of reference books—atlases, geography textbooks, magazines, encyclopedias, and others. Periodic help had been given all fall as individuals used these materials. Now they worked as a group—reviewing techniques of using their major reference books, ways of taking notes, how to find things independently in the library, how to use a table of contents and an index. Charts showing altitude, rainfall, prevailing winds, and the like also came into the picture and were made the center of special study.

MIDYEAR BRINGS THE NEED FOR SELF-INVENTORY

In the middle of January there was added the problem of midyear reports to parents. Children and teacher worked together on it. While informal communications and intervisitation between home and school were frequent, the custom of the school was to send letters to all parents twice a year. Each teacher was free to summarize the child's growth as he wished. For a year before this plan was adopted parents and teachers had met together discussing the problem. As a result, parents felt they were part of the plan and were reasonably secure in interpreting the letters.

In earlier grades these children had shared in decisions about items to be included in their cumulative records and in writing reports. Now an attempt was made to widen their responsibility.

"What do you think your parents ought to be told about you this year?" asked Miss Thomas. "Suppose we start a list."

The list on the board included:

Our store—what we've learned about keeping accounts, making change, writing more plainly.

What else we have been studying as a class and what each of us did—our plants, our Christmas play, our study of climate.

How much better we are in reading (from David who was at last sure he was making progress).

What we have learned about writing stories.

What special things each of us has done.

Work habits.

Miss Thomas suggested that parents might also be interested in how the children were becoming better able to work together. There had been considerable teaching and learning in the area of human relationships as the year went on. Irving, after several minor positions in which he tried not to give "too many orders," had made a highly successful store manager during the rush of the greeting card sale. Most of the class had grown in ability to respect the opinions of others in discussion and to take criticism. Doris Jean still needed to be reminded that the papers lying around her desk held up everybody else, but she was trying. Joan, after failing to carry out part of her responsibility with regard to writing letters for plants in the early fall, was gradually moving back to the place where the class was willing to trust her with an important job. Theresa had begun to overcome a little of the extreme shyness that she manifested in the new group in the fall. Alice, whose illness made it difficult for her to participate fully in physical activities, had displayed real leadership capacities in the making of the wooden xylophone.

It was planned that each child would write briefly his report of what he had done thus far during the year—both as a member of the group and as an individual. Then he would discuss with Miss Thomas what should be said about his skills and his growth in group relationships. This part she would write after agreement was reached. The conferences were learning experiences in themselves, as progress was reviewed and plans for next steps were outlined. These conferences and the planning needed to make the reports of group and individual activities meaningful extended for approximately three weeks. The final copies were typed by the office so that duplicates would be available for the children's individual record folders.

FLOODS IN THE NETHERLANDS EXTEND UNDERSTANDINGS OF OTHER PEOPLES

Early February brought the first extensive exploration of the lives of people of another country. The Christmas study had contributed a little about modern life in other lands, but the focus had been largely upon customs. Previous reading about Canada and Central and South America had drawn upon concepts from human geography but was centered largely on climate and foliage. As the last of the reports on climate were being made, a series of disastrous storms and floods were reported from the Netherlands. Papers were full of pictures and appeals for contributions toward relief.

The children's questions and comments as they brought in clippings for the bulletin board indicated many stereotyped impressions of the Netherlands. "It would all be under water if a dyke broke. They watch them all the time. I read a story of this boy. . . ." "Don't the windmills help pump the water somehow?" "They'd feel funny if they wore the clothes we sent to them; they don't dress like us. . . ." "They do too, my mother says. . . ." "I read where they skate to school. Would all that flood water freeze?" "If they can't plant their tulips, what will they have to sell?"

The problem represented a combination of interest in new aspects of climate and weather and concern about a people whom their parents were asked to help. Miss Thomas saw in it an opportunity to replace some stereotypes with more accurate understandings of another people, and recognized that many of the concepts involved were well within the grasp of ten-year-olds. At about this same time the papers also carried reports of a political revolution in another European country. Although some of the pictures and headlines were more dramatic, the concepts needed to understand the problem were well beyond these children. Consequently, clippings about the revolution were discussed only briefly.

As a start, the children made a list of questions they wanted answered. Miss Thomas helped by challenging false generalizations and by suggesting some questions herself. Then she and the librarian helped the group to find materials that would give a fair picture of modern Holland. Since some of the most urgent questions related to geographical understandings, maps came back into use. So did the globe, in an effort to find out just where the Netherlands was in relation to the United States and Canada. Pictures in the daily papers were useful, particularly in dispelling notions that clothing was different and that cities so far away could not possibly look like those in America. Films were a help, and the elementary supervisor who had been to Europe the preceding summer came to share her slides. She was also able to assist in locating a German exchange teacher who knew Holland well. The afternoon spent asking this young woman questions and seeing at firsthand a suit and shoes looking much like their mothers' but purchased overseas added to the sense of reality with which the children approached pictures and films.

Because this unit offered many opportunities for the children to work independently, Miss Thomas was able to keep an eye on those youngsters whose understandings were likely to be the most limited and to offer additional explanations. During time when the children were reading, she made a special point of checking on difficulties the less able readers were facing. A number of the books supplied by the library were quite simple, and the bulletin-board displays helped to provide much information in picture form.

As the boys and girls read, looked, and talked, new questions arose. They were interested in the numbers of bicycles on the streets and began to draw some comparisons about standards of living. Previous interests in vegetation led to a study of Dutch agriculture. A report of the activities of the Dutch Royal Family offered opportunities to expand concepts of democracy. "Do the people of Holland have a Congress like ours?" "How could they if they have a queen?" "Well, what about England—they have a queen but they have a democratic government, too." The history of the rise of European nations was not explored extensively, but Miss Thomas simplified and related enough of the story to explain to the children why there were so many small European countries speaking so many different languages. Bill, with several of the boys, carried on a special study of the polar air route from Chicago to Amsterdam.

Unusual customs were touched on only incidentally. The emphasis was upon securing facts that would answer questions about the Netherlands today, not on amassing odd and interesting bits of information for their own sake. Individuals who became intrigued with aspects of the culture peculiarly Dutch were helped to follow these leads and to report their findings to the class. Throughout, the stress was on the underlying similarity of human problems rather than on surface differences in customs. "Why might their way be different from ours?" they were asked by Miss Thomas. "How does it fit with what you know about their history, their climate, the size of their country? What is different about our country that might make us do it differently?"

THE SCHOOL CAFETERIA CONTRIBUTES TO PERSISTENT PROBLEMS IN THE AREA OF HEALTH

Health problems came strongly into the picture again in late February and March. The school cafeteria, which was used by many of the youngsters, provided two standard, well-balanced plate lunches. Miss Thomas' class had accepted this in times past, but with growing ability to manage their own lives came protest.

"I don't see why we have to take a vegetable if we don't want it," said one of the group.

"My mother says it's good for you," answered someone else.

"That's what mine says about milk," contributed Alice, "but I still don't like it."

"Could we ask the lunchroom committee to let us choose what we like, Miss Thomas?" asked Doris Jean, whose meals at home left much to be desired.

"Before we do, we had better be sure we know what we're doing," said Miss Thomas. "Why do you think they plan a lunch which has the kind of things you are given?"

"It's supposed to be good for you," seemed to be the most firmly fixed generalization in the group. Miss Thomas pressed the point. "What makes it good? Would it be just as good if you had all dessert and no milk?" They thought not. "How do you know?" They weren't sure. "It makes you sick," "Your teeth decay," "You'll get too fat," were among the comments indicating that a persistent life situation heretofore dealt with incidentally might well be made focal.

Starting with the generalization previously developed—that it made a real difference what you fed plants—the children pushed on to consider what might happen if human beings were fed different things. They were not ready to do much experimentation with the chemistry of foods, but they could comprehend the descriptions of the values of various foods as described in several health and science textbooks and a number of charts and diagrams. Miss Thomas considered the possibility of experimenting with white rats but decided against it. The problem was to find why the school lunch was made up as it was and why the children were urged to take it all. How to balance meals, not what happens when one does not, seemed to be the concept needing further exploration.

The children made a study of what all persons need to sustain health and went on to draw the analogy that human beings, just like plants, require different kinds of balances, and that Alice, whose doctor prescribed milk and a diet calculated to add weight, might well need a different balance in her meals than Jean Marie and Anthony who were quite chubby. They analyzed a series of typical school lunches to see what nutritional elements were included, and then went on to examine their own food for a week, including the school lunch. The emphasis was not on an exact prescription of certain foods, which some families might not be able to obtain, but on a sensitivity to the need for securing a desirable variety of foods through appropriate combinations of what one could get.

Near the end of the study the practical aspect of quantity buying came in, as well as some awareness of the needs of younger children. "They can't stock everything we'd like any more than we can in the store," they decided. "They're operating on a cost basis too." Further, "If little children have not studied about selecting balanced foods perhaps the safest thing is to be sure they are given a good meal, even if we don't always like it," they concluded. "But," added Bill, "if their teachers could show them how, then we all could have more chance to choose."

THE SCHOOL STORE INTRODUCES PROBLEMS OF CREDIT BUYING

Once again the store became a concern of the class as a whole. Irving, now one of the cashiers, conceived the idea that charge accounts paid once a month would make things much simpler for everyone.

"Not this year," he said, "but if we could plan it, next year's class could start it in the fall."

The children were aware that many parents had charge accounts and that many more bought on the installment plan. This was not a problem that could be taken very far with this class as the mathematical concepts and necessary experiences were limited. The children did, however, satisfy themselves as to what kind of accounts would need to be kept, the nature of the bills that would have to be sent, and the calculations needed. They decided that their annual report should include their findings, but the recommendation was that it sounded like too much work if next year's store managers wanted to have time to do anything else.

Someone raised the question as to why stores bothered with charge accounts at all and the children explored some of the more obvious advantages to both customers and firms. They also took time to straighten out the difference between a charge account and installment buying and to do some simple calculations of the increase in the cost of the article when one paid on time. This was their first acquaintance with percentage and led into enough arithmetic to get the concept clear. This new way of expressing numerical relationships was used again in June when they decided to include in the report of the store a comparative statement of the amount of this year's business and that of the previous year.

FURTHER MUSICAL EXPERIENCES CONTRIBUTE TO AESTHETIC EXPRESSION AND APPRECIATION

In March, and on into April, a new aesthetic interest was developed. For the first time this year, one of the school's several portable record players was free for an extended period of time in the fifth grade. While there had been much informal sharing of musical experiences, extensive group work had been limited to the Christmas and one or two other assemblies. Now the class was encouraged to explore recently added records. Few had ever seen a symphony orchestra; but over past years, with the help of several teachers who played various musical instruments, a number of pupils had become interested in the different instruments. They spent several periods with the teacher who knew the most about music to learn more about the records to which they were listening. In April this interest turned to radio and television programs—first those which provided more music and later to an analysis of the serials and other programs which they saw or heard.

OTHER ACTIVITIES PARALLEL OR ARE PARTS OF MAJOR GROUP EXPERIENCES

Small-group and individual activities during these three months were varied. Many of the individual activities continued to arise from special talents, hobbies, or interests—Miss Thomas continuing to urge children to explore varied media. Finger painting, soap carving, and work with clay, for which facilities were not available at the beginning of the year, came into the program now. As April approached, a small nature group was formed to study the returning birds. Children from several other classes joined this group. With better weather came a demand for organized teams and more outdoor play.

Short-term group interests continued to have their sources mainly in the ongoing life of the world about the children. A survey of some of those which were typical would show:

A brief study of why it was necessary to quarantine all the dogs in the neighborhood after a rabies outbreak.

Some exploration of a new city sales tax—caused mainly by concern as to whether a similar tax should be charged in their store.

Following the work of the Red Cross for several days as they met the needs of a flood disaster area in a neighboring state.

Some discussion of what a threatened fuel strike might do to their city—their interest was mainly on what supplies were available in the city and when someone found this reported in the paper the group was satisfied.

A short period spent on how to save paper—brought on by a request from the principal's office that supplies be used carefully.

Finding out about the baby bears born in the zoo.

Individual and group work on fundamental skills continued to grow out of constant demands for these skills. During the three-month period the following were included:

The calculations needed to make the midyear inventory and audit of the accounts—teams again did the inventory but the whole group checked the auditor's work.

Study of charge accounts—the calculations needed to decide how much price increase was represented by installment buying.

Calculating food values in meals and graphing them.

Reference reading to find out about climate.

Study of reference books—the way to use them; the values of different kinds, use of various parts of reference books such as table of contents and indexes. Even the less able readers examined the books and contributed to this study.

Learning how to read maps in connection with the study of weather. (David, who still did not read very well, discovered that interpreting maps was fun and became one of the "experts.")

Learning how to read charts and graphs in connection with the study of the weather. Learning how to read bar graphs in study of foods.

Writing the report letters to parents—deciding how to explain the year's activities so that parents would understand.

Note-taking and continued wide reference reading on the Netherlands.

Reference reading of more technical detailed material regarding diets.

Continued reading of a wide variety of recreational books throughout the period. (Joe, Myra, and several of the less able readers found in the simpler books in the library a source of great pleasure.)

Regular help for individual children who were weak in particular skills, and short-term practice groups as specific problems arose.

What contacts led these children out into the rest of the school? The following were their major efforts:

A series of conferences with the school secretary, who checked their accounts.

Visits to the school dietitian to ask about lunch menus.

Participation in a musical assembly sponsored by the sixth grade.

Helping for several days with the kindergarten children on the playground. (Bill and Jerry proved most efficient with overshoes and wraps.)

Visiting a fourth grade to see their collection of articles from Mexico.

Helping a second grade care for several plants which were not flourishing.

Continued contacts through the store and the school paper. New methods of advertising were tried out, and from time to time individual and group stories were published.

Sponsoring a sale of lost-and-found articles for the first grade which was responsible for this department.

They continued to draw upon the community and go out into it. Had the details of their activities been given, one would have found the following:

Visits to three fathers to get advice on the need to make the January inventory. (Sarah's father, who was nearby, was one of these.)

Contacts with all homes through the report letters—parents in most cases came to the school for additional conferences with Miss Thomas.

The visits of the elementary school supervisor and the exchange teacher in relation to the study of the Netherlands.

Individual investigation of family charge accounts and installment buying —various children reported back what their parents said the advantages and disadvantages were.

A trip to the city conservatory to see different kinds of plants.

A trip to the weather bureau to find out how weather is predicted.

The study of radio programs and movies brought the community to the school.

Spring Brings New Problems

With the change of weather and the arrival of spring, the children faced new problems and concerns. Spring meant new activities and the emergence of different situations. As the pupils carried on their activities in the open—playground, neighborhood, park—new aspects of some persistent life situations appeared.

BICYCLES CALL FOR SAFETY MEASURES

Bicycles appeared on the scene in large numbers as the spring weather approached. A local police officer visited the school with the request that children be reminded of traffic regulations. After a joint meeting of all bicycle riders, at which the traffic officer made various suggestions, individual classes took up the problem as they saw fit. In Miss Thomas' room only about one-third owned bicycles, but a third more rode their friends' bicycles regularly, and only two children were not interested in learning to ride. Consequently, bicycle safety became a short but intense problem of group consideration. The safety guides suggested by the police officer were studied carefully. Children added others from their own experiences. Some time was spent considering the importance of keeping bicycles in good repair. The two youngsters who did not intend to ride bicycles were allowed to go on with other activities during the latter discussion periods. One had several library books he wanted to finish and welcomed the opportunity to read them. The other, Alice, went further with some finger painting—a skill that she had just learned.

A COMMUNITY PROJECT LEADS TO A STUDY OF PIONEER DAYS

The school year, which had been rich in its contacts with parts of the economy and in its challenges to become acquainted with geographic aspects of the Western Hemisphere, had not offered many opportunities to widen understandings of the history of our country. Miss Thomas might have raised enough questions at the time of the Thanksgiving assembly to stimulate some reading, but she knew that understanding of the way in which the country was first settled was fairly clear. The study of the election also had potential historical implications, but only if the children were required to accept a purpose that was not really theirs. Furthermore, many concepts regarding political history are quite complex.

In the spring, the local Historical Society purchased and made plans to renovate one of the oldest homes in the city. In the articles about the early history of the city appearing in the paper when the plans were announced, the children were surprised to learn that the site of an early fort was quite near their school. The newspaper reported a marker in the park only a few blocks away. Nobody remembered seeing it, and a committee volunteered to find it. They came back with a copy of the inscription, but no one was very clear as to what it meant. Why a fort? There were Indians around; this much was definite. Were there other settlements nearby? Did the pioneers stop here or go on? Who were the first settlers? Mary Anne was sure her family had lived in their house for a long time. John said his grandfather's father went all the way to California. Theresa and Anthony said their parents had been born in Europe. Miss Thomas asked if people were able to go across the mountains before there were trains. Here, "Westerns" on television helped and several children gave graphic, if somewhat inaccurate, descriptions of covered-wagon days. Pictures of articles being donated to the Historical Society raised other questions about early ways of living. Through many of the preliminary discussions it was apparent that the children's sense of chronology was vague. Here was a point at which the history of their country touched closely the lives of this particular class. The concepts needed seemed within their grasp and their questions indicated definite gaps in understanding. Miss Thomas encouraged further study by elaborating upon questions already being raised and by suggesting areas they had not thought of.

The study that followed extended for almost two months. As a start, the children decided to get their dates straight. It was hard to talk about the people who built the old fort unless one knew where they had come from and who they were. The class went back to the first colonies and started a time line. All knew about the Pilgrims, but they were surprised to learn how many other early settlements there were, and from how many countries in Europe the people came.

"I always thought the Pilgrims came first," said Bill.

"And people away up in Canada, too!" exclaimed John.

"We were in Montreal last summer," said Mary Anne, "and lots of people still speak French."

"We were in St. Augustine," said Alice. "There were markers to tell us about the history."

Because the main concern was with the movement west, Miss Thomas helped to give the sequence of the early settlements. In story form, she traced enough of the history of the early wars and the Revolution to clarify understanding of why the United States and Canada, both English-speaking nations, were separate countries, and how it was that some people in Canada still spoke French. Then the class focused on the history of the settlement of their own state. Here Miss Thomas called for the help of Mr. Bush, among whose strengths in the social science field was a special interest in the state's history. Together they supplied reading matter and helped the children identify landmarks in the city that could be visited. Persons from the local Historical Society came to serve as consultants. Two of the mothers spent a Saturday driving twelve of the class members to a nearby town to see points of historical interest. Previous skills with maps were capitalized upon, and a relief map was developed so that the routes taken by the settlers could be more clearly understood. The librarian helped by supplying stories of pioneers which gave accurate descriptions of homes and family life.

After questions regarding the settlement of the local community were answered satisfactorily, the class carried the chronology on to the settlement of the West Coast. They traced the trails through the mountains with great interest, using the story materials at hand to fill in the details of the hardships that must have been endured. Here they put to good use concepts developed in the earlier study of vegetation as they considered the country through which the settlers would have traveled.

There were a number of fruitful smaller projects. All the children were interested in the lives of the people who had made such perilous trips. Groups took on special assignments to discover how they traveled, what the first houses must have looked like, what they had to do to get clothing and furniture when stores were not nearby. While no experience in a twentieth-century classroom could be expected to give great insight into the realities of pioneer living, it was possible to show children who were used to purchasing in stores what could be done with one's hands. They made soap and candles, and went to see a loom owned by one of the mothers whose hobbies were weaving and collecting antiques. Mary Anne's mother had some old coverlets and pewter. The school principal showed them his flintlock gun.

There were related experiences in creative expression. Joan took the chairmanship of a group of the better readers who explored stories of famous heroes of American folk tales—Paul Bunyan, Johnny Appleseed,

Pecos Bill. Another group delved into biographies of famous pioneers—Daniel Boone, Davy Crockett. Still another explored the songs, ballads, and dances of the period and then went on to learn modern western music which they taught to the class. For the school paper they wrote a brief history of the settlement of the city. They also presented the Historical Society with a map indicating spots in the city they thought would interest other boys and girls.

This was a unit in which one small project after another was completed and shared. There seemed to be no call for an elaborate culminating activity. The children invited their mothers and fathers to share their work, but the program consisted largely of informal reports by the children who had been most actively involved in that particular part of the project.

END OF THE SCHOOL YEAR APPROACHES AND PLANS ARE MADE FOR VACATION

As the children concluded their study of how their city was settled, they began to give more attention to the question of recreation facilities for the summer. Parents whose children had to stay in the city asked for help in planning how to keep them occupied. In cooperation with the other fifth and the sixth grades the children surveyed the play facilities in the neighborhood. Groups of children explored the facilities in the nearby parks. Recreation leaders from community clubs and the local Y came to the school to talk about possibilities. The result was a leaflet compiled by the sixth grade which all children took home to their parents.

About the time that this project gradually began to take up more of the school day, so did the store. A final inventory had to be made and the closing report written. Selling terminated two weeks before the end of school to get this done. As each group leaving their special department had left a report for the incoming staff, there were cumulative records of the year's suggestions. It was decided that the last incumbents would compile these into one set of recommendations for their department and that each set would then be studied and revised by the class as a whole. With Miss Thomas' help this was done. The final inventory and a list of the prices used and the materials sold were added, and the complete report was filed in the central office for the next year's store operators.

Since it was the custom for both sixth grades to work together on the school paper, no spring meeting was needed to decide on next year's school responsibility. The class did, however, meet with the sixth-graders, who were going on to junior high school and so would not be available in the fall, to hear a little about the responsibilities involved.

PARALLEL ACTIVITIES CONTINUE TO THE CLOSE OF THE SCHOOL YEAR

Short-term activities continued to take up a certain amount of time each week. The last three months of the school year saw the following among those which were most important:

Discussion of the need for recent community steps to control mosquitoes and flies.

Several days' deliberation as to how best to get rid of insects which had appeared on some of the plants.

Starting plants to take home for family window boxes.

Some investigation of magazine reports of new prefabricated houses—how they would be built, what materials would be used.

A few days of follow-up discussion of a travel film shown to the whole school.

Contacts with other parts of the school during this period were as numerous as ever:

Sharing in the April assembly.

Meeting with the sixth grade to learn about the school paper.

Working with the other fifth and the sixth grades on the study of recreation facilities.

The community continued to be a rich source of experiences. Parents, organizations, the representatives of the city's law enforcement agencies, all played their part:

A visit by a representative of the local police force to talk with bicycle riders.

A visit to the zoo to see the baby animals.

A study of city traffic regulations.

Visits by various persons in connection with the study of pioneers.

Consideration of the plans of the Historical Society.

Visits to the nearby recreation facilities available in the summer.

Visits from recreation leaders to tell about summer opportunities.

Sending a leaflet to parents about summer recreation opportunities.

A backward look over these as well as other activities through the year, as revealed in the children's cumulative records, their notebooks, and folders of samples of their work, served as the basis for the final reports to parents. The process was the same as in February. However, Miss Thomas took special pains to provide summaries in the cumulative records both for individuals and for the class as a whole to serve as a guide for the sixth-grade teacher. The children suggested special items to record and selected samples typical of their work to add to individual permanent records.

With the storing away of books so that next year's class could readily find them, the gathering together of paintings, clay models, soap carvings, hobbies, and other individual enterprises which had not yet been taken home, final reading of the store report which the school secretary had typed, and some last discussions of recreation facilities for the summer, the year drew to a close.

A Summary Look

The year's activities of this fifth grade illustrate in action many of the principles discussed in preceding chapters. How valuable a year was it for these boys and girls? What made it so? A summary look may be helpful.

BALANCED DEVELOPMENT WAS PROVIDED

In Miss Thomas' cumulative records for the year would be found indication of balanced growth in terms of persistent life situations. There was variety in the problems receiving major emphasis. The store contributed understanding of economic structures and forces. Social and political structures were prominent in the study of the election, the investigation of the problems of the Netherlands, the study of the settlement of their own country, and the exploration of community recreation facilities. Understanding of natural phenomena grew through the studies of plants and climatic conditions.

Understanding of technological resources, though not a central problem in any of the units, was needed to throw light on others. In the study of plants, problems of modern techniques of irrigation and farming arose. Some insights into the way business machines make office work more efficient grew out of the store. Attempts to understand the lives of settlers brought modern inventions sharply into focus.

Person-to-person relationships were constantly involved as the members of the class learned to work together and cooperated with others in the school and the community. Effective group membership was basic to the successful operation of the store and to every other group activity undertaken during the year. Intergroup relationships were a part of each contact with other class groups and extended into the study of how pioneers helped each other, the election, and the problems of the people of the Netherlands.

Health was a central issue in the study of the meals offered by the school cafeteria, in the health examination, and in the consideration of safety regulations regarding bicycles. It was also a matter of daily consideration in the ventilation of the classroom, provision of adequate light for work, precautions against the spread of colds, and many other problems. Aesthetic expression and appreciation were focal in the Christmas assembly, in the writing of stories for the school paper, in preparing book lists for Christmas, and, in the spring, in the study of records and musical instruments. This problem area was also part of almost all aspects of keeping the classroom and store attractive. Growth in ability to use intellectual powers was needed in relation to every problem and involved much by way of more accurate calculations, making ideas clear to others, and in turn understanding their efforts at communication. There was also need for added skill in planning, in setting up a problem for study, in solving it, and in evaluating the results. Questions of moral choice and responsibility entered into many phases of the year's work and were extended by direct discussion into national and world relationships in the study of the Netherlands, in the spiritual values represented by the Christmas season, and in discussions of responsibilities in the store.

Short-term projects made other contributions to these same areas. So did individual activities. By the end of the year each child had combined intensive exploration in several areas encompassing problems in which he was very much interested with wide but less thorough acquaintance with many others. In those areas in which there had not been active participation there had at least been appreciation of the efforts of others as completed work was shared with the class. In the sixth grade these children would again study everyday situations of concern to them, guided by a teacher able to see the relationships between these daily concerns and persistent life situations, and skilled in building from present understandings and competencies toward further growth.

CONCERNS OF LEARNERS WERE THE STARTING POINT BUT TEACHERS' INSIGHTS ENRICHED THESE CONCERNS

Miss Thomas' contribution to the growth of her group was significant. Activities were not restricted to the insights and expressed wishes of ten-year-olds. As the person responsible for the growth of these thirty-five boys and girls, Miss Thomas made a continuing study of their strengths and weaknesses. She also studied the potentialities of each new problem in the light of her learners' maturities and backgrounds. In planning sessions she gave the leadership that challenged inadequate understandings and helped to identify new problems and to set broader purposes. Acting as a democratic leader she encouraged children to think. Decisions were based on information and thoughtful appraisal. As a resource person she put her mature insights and special preparation at the disposal of the group. This did not mean that she imposed upon them projects for which they could not see the value. Rather, she stood ready to facilitate plans when it seemed likely that a direct contribution from her would be of more value, educationally, than encouragement to solve the problem independently.

In many ways, the staff of the entire school combined to provide an environment that was stimulating, and one that posed genuine problems for boys and girls. The policy that each class take on a real and important responsibility for the welfare of the school community resulted in some major concerns. Then, the interlocking of these responsibilities involved classes in still other problems. The fifth grade wrote for the sixth-grade paper, helped the first grade with a sale of lost-and-found articles, and shared responsibilities for assembly programs. Sometimes, as indicated in the lists of contacts with the rest of the school given at the end of preceding sections, the children served as resource persons for other classes.

The plan the teachers had set up to schedule their time so that each could make his special talents and interests available to other classes also helped to provide an enriched environment. Children with special talents were able to find persons to encourage them. For groups, too, persons were available when needed who could challenge them to look at broader aspects of a problem and who could direct them to appropriate resources or give help with new skills. For teachers this sharing of talents was important. It is scarcely possible, even at the elementary school level, for one person to have the necessary insights to give effective guidance in meeting all persistent life situations. When resource persons are at hand for consultation, each teacher's guidance of his own group is more effective.

The classroom environment also was stimulating. There were ample materials and adequate bulletin-board space. The resources of the library were available when needed. There was room to undertake a project as extensive as the one with plants. Then, too, children used the entire community as a resource. As the lists closing each of the preceding sections indicate, they went into the community for information and they brought community interests to school. Sometimes, as with the request for study of the matter of safety on bicycles, community members brought a problem to the school. This was not a setting where a teacher waited until a child happened to mention a concern. It was a classroom in which children were encouraged to be alert about the world around them. There were opportunities to discuss events of interest and a permissive atmosphere which encouraged raising questions and making suggestions.

INDIVIDUAL AND GROUP NEEDS WERE A PART OF THE YEAR'S WORK

Differentiated responsibilities in all-class activities, short-term projects, and individual activities all helped to meet individual needs.

A backward look at the types of problems that became the focus of attention for the entire class may indicate how a teacher might expect all-class concerns to arise. The store was one such concern. This was a problem faced by the children because it was a vital part of their school community. The election, another group concern, is illustrative of the way in which all the members of a class are likely to be involved in some major community event. The study of plants and the later study of the settlement of the West illustrate that children of about the same age are likely to display common concerns in a new and exciting challenge to intellectual curiosity if it is within their general interest level. The study of bicycle safety late in the spring is illustrative of a problem not necessarily seen as immediately vital by all members of the group, but one in which they can readily accept a purpose if it is made clear to them.

Individual needs were met, even within all-class projects. This is one way in which the enthusiastic interest of a whole class is maintained in a common enterprise. The children started their work in the store with assignments that not only used their talents but appealed to them. Catherine and Bill went ahead with their special experiments with plants. Joan sponsored the group reading American folk tales. While all developed certain common understandings from each group problem, many youngsters pursued individual concerns to competence of considerable depth.

Individuals were also encouraged to follow up special interests. Time was definitely scheduled for this. Many of the short-term projects listed at the end of each of the preceding sections were the major concerns of small groups, explored by them, and then shared with the class. Some of these interests remained constant throughout the year. Alice was urged to put her musical talent to use. Joan wrote her stories. Bulletin boards helped to encourage others to write. There was time to experiment with art, and media were available. Specialists on the staff could give time to talented pupils.

Weaknesses were not neglected. Ineffective clerks worked on improving their arithmetic skills. Regular help in reading was given to Joe, Myra, and several others. Short-term practice groups were set up whenever weaknesses became apparent. Very early, children were helped to see that competence was important. With Miss Thomas they evaluated their own strengths and weaknesses and made plans for the help they needed. The situations in which they were working helped to make needs apparent, and Miss Thomas was alert to difficulties and ready to point them out if the children themselves did not sense them.

PROVISIONS WERE MADE FOR DEVELOPING FUNDAMENTAL SKILLS

The skills referred to at various points in this description of a fifth grade at work indicate the high level of competence demanded if learners are helped to meet efficiently their problems of daily living. As the children completed their reports to parents at the close of the year they could look back on the following as some of the more important areas of skill development:

Translating the year's business in the store into percentages and graphs.

Calculations needed to determine prices, to take a periodic and a final audit and inventory.

Reference reading to find out about plants, weather.

Note-taking and continued wide reference reading on the Netherlands.

Discovering more skillful ways to use reference books.

Learning how to read maps, charts, and graphs in connection with the study of weather, foods, the Netherlands.

Reading historical texts and fiction regarding the Westward Movement.

Reading autobiographies, in whole or in part, of famous pioneers.

Reading American folk tales.

Reading a wide variety of recreational books.

Writing letters—letters to parents reporting progress, thank-you notes to community members who had worked with them, letters ordering supplies.

Writing the final report on store activities.

Writing articles and stories for the school paper.

Taking part in group discussions and presenting reports orally to the class.

Informal reporting to a parent audience as the study of the settlement of the west closed.

The sequence in which each skill was developed was determined by the situations faced, not by textbooks. As much time as was needed was devoted to the steps required to achieve the new level of competence. Individuals were encouraged to share in evaluating their strengths and weaknesses. Work sheets and individual evaluation instruments helped each child to concentrate on his own problem and particular need. This did not preclude group activities in which children with similar needs worked together. For those whose skills were least adequate these regular sessions, designed to build needed skills, were a commitment lasting the full year.

ACQUAINTANCE WITH THE CULTURAL HERITAGE WAS BROAD AND DEEP

This is not a year's work that can be pigeonholed easily into a typical schedule of social studies, science, and health. Yet the problems studied called for considerable depth in exploring these and other bodies of subject matter. Nor is this a year's work that follows an organization traditionally accepted as logical, in the sense that it stays within the boundaries of American history or Old-World backgrounds and covers its given area in chronological sequence. Yet the total learnings over the year are not inconsequential. They have considerable breadth, and a topic once accepted for extensive study is thoroughly and carefully worked through.

Typical of a ten-year-old's ability to grasp concepts of time and space, the greater share of the generalizations related to the world of today and to the community in which the children lived. The store developed many economic concepts. The election helped to expand insights into the process of government. Understanding of the role of law-enforcement agencies was extended through the discussions of rules for riding bicycles. Health concepts and understandings, too, were related to problems that were immediate—the health examinations, the school lunchroom. The creative arts also had their place. Insights developed largely in relation to problems of present living—what makes for an effective exhibit, what decorations are most appropriate for an all-school party, how a classroom can be attractively decorated and still be functional. Science interests centered around plants in their own classroom, weather, and climate.

However, starting with immediate concerns did not mean confining all activities to the present and near-at-hand. This class found meaning in looking at the past in their study of the settling of the West; they extended their geographic understandings to cover a large part of the hemisphere through their study of the relation of climate to vegetation; and they expanded and clarified generalizations about other peoples through their Christmas program, and through the study of the Netherlands.

Whatever problem was the center of a major study, the children were helped to develop it to the point that its setting and its relation to other areas of study were clear. Concern with the nation's early settlement, for example, was chiefly with the children's own community and the Westward Movement. However, Miss Thomas helped them to sketch in the related early history, and to see, through their time line and their maps, where their study fitted in. They did not cover all the details of the earlier settlements, but they were made acquainted with the essential relationships to give perspective to their study.

While the major units of work in the year's activities do not stay within the traditional logic of a subject field, concepts developed in one unit were drawn upon in another about as extensively as one would expect them to be were the series of units from a single subject field. What the children knew about plants contributed to the study of the relation of vegetation to climate. This expanded concept was useful in understanding a country in another part of the world—the Netherlands. When the problems of the early settlers became the focus of attention, skills with maps and concepts regarding weather and vegetation were again very important. This is an example of the way in which a persistent life situation recurs. It is this fact that provides some of the reassurance that there will be continuity of growth even though there is no fixed, preplanned selection of topics.

The selection of areas for major study may have seemed somewhat fortuitous. This is true, in the sense that a curriculum developed in terms of the needs and concerns of learners must be responsive to the way in which a concern actually appears to a given group. However, this is not a matter of waiting and hoping that a problem that is really "worthwhile" will arise. It is a matter of choosing, in the light of potential contributions to growth, from among the many worthwhile problems that do arise. Had the opportunity to explore adaptations of vegetation to different climates not occurred through the study of plants, it might have arisen through reports of summer holidays, interest in why severe storms take certain routes, pictures of parts of the country or of other lands where vegetation is unfamiliar. Had an Historical Society not been active, there might have been a state centennial celebration, a display in a local store of changes in clothing styles over the past two hundred years, a reference to the Civil War in the daily papers, a television pioneer series. This does not mean that every teacher must be on the lookout every year for problems that will lead to specific pieces of subject matter. Miss Thomas' class might well do much less with American backgrounds in the sixth grade and expand their understanding of Old-World backgrounds or perhaps of the peoples of the Far East. However, it might be that these children would continue to expand their interest in American backgrounds in the sixth grade and not face a genuine need for extensive study of European backgrounds until they reached the junior high school. Miss Bing's fifth grade next door might have done much less with American backgrounds this year, and might be encouraged to develop more of these understandings as sixth-graders.

The breadth and depth of the children's exploration into their cultural heritage need to be appraised in terms of the activities of individuals and small groups as well as of the class as a whole. The lists of parallel activities show how wide these contacts were. Putting into practice the principle that persistent life situations will recur and that concepts are built slowly, Miss Thomas helped the children to pursue these parallel interests far enough for accurate solutions to the immediate problem without necessarily going into all related areas. Furthermore, by acknowledging these wide interests she sent on to the sixth grade learners with active intellectual curiosity and a zest for knowledge.

13

CARING FOR YOUTH'S SPECIAL NEEDS— A TENTH-GRADE PROGRAM

While the intellectual, physical, and personal-social characteristics of adolescents are quite unique, the problems youth face are, as illustrated in Chapter 6, variations of recurring life situations. At the secondary school level, learners are able to grapple with these problems with greater depth and breadth of insight and understanding. They are capable of a more mature grasp and use of the resources available for help with problem solution. Their interests may also be broader and deeper. Their needs for specialized activities are greater, as are their capacities to profit from such activities.

The work of a tenth grade is described in this chapter to illustrate activities typical of a year's program—highlighting some of the ways in which persistent life situations recur at this level, and indicating ways in which help is provided individuals and groups in meeting these situations. Similarities to the descriptions of the first and fifth grades, whose experiences are included in this part of the volume, will be apparent. Among these similarities are: activities based on the group's problems, supplemented by the teacher's judgment of how to increase the learners' ability to deal with recurring situations; student efforts as an integral part of the planning; students as active participants in the learning process; teachers concerned with developing a unified, integrated program to which each part makes an important contribution; use of many resources in working on the problems faced; and considerable flexibility in all aspects of the school program. These common elements, taken together, are some of the important features which differentiate, both at elementary and at secondary school levels, the curriculum design outlined in this volume from other proposals.

Curriculum planners who would provide for youth's special needs have some unique problems to solve, however. Because learners at this level have the ability to grapple with persistent life situations with greater depth and breadth of insight, the help of specialists must be available for longer periods of time. Variations in interests, coupled with maturing intellectual ability, complicate the problem of securing effective balance between general education and specialized education—of providing the extended experience required by youth with special talent, interest, or concern. In varying degrees, depending on the concerns and maturity of individuals, there are also problems of providing extended acquaintance with specific subject fields. The basic principles of curriculum development, which underlie the activities of learners, are essentially the same at every age. The specific learning experiences and their organization will vary with emerging maturity.

The Setting for This Tenth-Grade Program

The tenth-graders whose activities are described should be pictured as living in a community with a population of about thirty thousand. They are in one of two secondary schools, each with approximately nine hundred students in grades seven through twelve. These youth represent a cross section of abilities and of socio-economic, racial, ethnic, and religious backgrounds. Their educational plans are quite varied; some on completion of high school will go directly to work while others will go into post-high school educational programs. In both organization and physical plant, the school is designed to be a comprehensive high school, attempting to meet the common as well as the special needs of its student population. The other high school is similar, and the student's home location is the determining factor as to which one he will attend. There is no specialized high school in this community.

THE PROFESSIONAL STAFF HAS MANY COMPETENCIES

The work of each grade group centers in a core program, with time for special courses, short-term projects, and individual activities under the guidance of specialists. The teachers responsible for core programs have rather broad academic and cultural backgrounds, with some specialization in one or two fields. In all but two cases one area of specialization is English, the social sciences, or the natural sciences. The core activities of one of the ninth grades are guided by Miss Duggan whose special interest is foreign languages, and an eleventh grade is advised by Mr. Santole whose major interest is mathematics. All teachers responsible for core activities, except Miss Harvey who works with the seventh grade in which the core comprises the major part of the students' program, offer courses or individual guidance in their fields of special interest during one or more of the periods when they are not with their core group. Since they are responsible for the homeroom activities and general guidance of the students in their core groups, all have at least two periods weekly for work with individuals, for record-keeping, and for the many other activities necessary if guidance is to be effective.

Other teachers in the school are specialists in art, music, mathematics, science, foreign languages, industrial arts, vocational education, home economics, business education, and health and physical education. As indicated above, some specialists also teach core classes. Their classrooms are equipped as laboratories where it is possible for an entire class to work easily or for individuals and several small groups to work at the same time. As a rule, specialists are available to give help as needed in the core programs. They meet with classes in their homerooms, or remain in the laboratories, where individuals or groups come for help on problems being studied in the core. The librarian, the nurse, the psychologist, student personnel workers, and the administrators comprise the rest of the staff. The over-all ratio is approximately one staff member to twenty students. From thirty to thirty-five students are in each core class.

COURSES AND LABORATORIES SERVE A VARIETY OF FUNCTIONS

As the teachers planned, during several years of intensive curriculum study, how to meet the needs of these high school youth, they recognized the importance of different types of courses and special offerings. First, they saw the value of a generous block of time, under the guidance of one teacher who would know the group well, in which students could work on problems that cut across subject fields. A **core program** varying in time allotment with the maturity of the group is planned to serve this purpose. Second, the importance of specialists to help on problems growing out of the core program was recognized. This requirement is met by arranging the schedules of specialists so that part of their day can be devoted to **serv-**

ice units lasting for blocks of time that range from two or three weeks to several months, and part to **service on call** to the core classes. Third, the faculty realized that opportunities must be provided for individuals or groups to explore deeply a problem area or a subject field. **Service courses** meet this need. In addition, some part of each specialist's schedule is allotted to the **guidance of individuals** with special interests, abilities, or needs in his particular field, and to making resource materials available to individuals and groups—both teachers and students.

The core program for each group grows out of problems significant for them. The core program for each group offers opportunities for teacher and students to work together on aspects of persistent life situations important to them. Any area of subject matter is drawn upon. The aim is gradual growth in ability to deal with the recurring problems of living as they confront high school youth. Units at this level are usually longer than those in the elementary school, in keeping with the increased maturity of the group and their ability to explore more deeply to find solutions to their problems. However, short-term projects still have their place, and it is not uncommon to have two or three parallel activities under way, at times with little relationship to each other, at times correlating closely. Both general background understanding and ability to use fundamental skills are built through the work of the core program.

The amount of time devoted to the core decreases gradually from practically full time in the seventh grade to a two-period block in the twelfth. The tenth grade spends three periods of its seven-period day in core activities. The two-and-a-half hour core block, plus fifty minutes of physical education and recreation, constitute the morning program. Special courses and individual projects are undertaken in the three afternoon periods.

The core classes meet in rooms designed and equipped for many kinds of activities. The rooms are large enough to allow freedom of movement and flexibility of furniture arrangement. There are individual and group work tables, file cabinets, storage facilities, bulletin-board and blackboard space, display areas, and book shelves. The variety of instructional materials is arranged so as to be readily accessible to students and teachers. These rooms, like those used for special courses, are viewed as core laboratories and serve as a focal place in which classes operate. Students and teachers are free to move out to the rest of the school and into the community for essential learning activities.

Service courses meet many needs. In considering what service courses should be offered, the faculty had to decide how to plan a program sufficiently flexible to provide for growth in ability to deal with persistent life situations as the students actually faced them and, at the same time, to provide the intensive study that the maturity of these youth required. While there had to be considerable flexibility in terms of special problems, schedules had to be at least partially planned in advance. This was important, not only for the most effective use of the specialists' time but for the most effective guidance of individuals.

In their preplanning, the faculty as a whole and the specialists in particular fields used several guides. They predicted, from their study of the persistent life situations typically faced by adolescents, certain problem areas in which persistent situations could appropriately be grouped and to which specialists in a given subject area seemed most likely to make important contributions. For example, one of the science specialists offers a service course on current scientific developments, designed to help students with special science interests explore the day-to-day situations they face. The home economics department typically offers at least one service course centering around situations which recur in problems of home management. For the past three years, persistent problems in the area of consumer education have been another popular focus. The English service courses include a communication arts study and a drama and play production group. The social studies specialists typically offer a course in trends in American democracy to which students bring special concerns in understanding developments in their own country.

Service courses are not static. As work in the core programs or new community or national concerns suggest the need for special help in other areas, courses are added or present offerings are replaced. While service courses are the responsibility of specialists in the particular field most closely related to the problem area, the actual situations faced often cut across subject fields and call for cooperative teaching or for advice or resource materials from other specialists. To this end time is provided for consultation periods as well as for informal contacts.

In their preplanning, the teachers also determined subject areas and sequences most likely to provide for the needs of youth ready for special study, and planned for service courses in these areas as well. Thus, for example, the English specialists offer several courses which center attention on various aspects of literature. There are also opportunities to work intensively within the areas of physics, chemistry, and biology. Foreign languages are available. So are courses in shorthand and typewriting. Work in mathematics is possible, on both elementary and advanced levels.

In addition, needs for some special skills were predicted. As a result, two clinics were planned by the English department. One provides special help in oral English and speech. The other provides special aid in the mechanics of written expression—spelling, grammar, structure. Similarly, a mathematics laboratory offers remedial help as well as opportunities for individuals to delve into new areas. Reading problems are, for the most part, handled by the core teachers who are in the best position to adjust the day-to-day reading demands made upon their classes and to provide help to individuals that is appropriate to their needs and to the problems they are facing. Each teacher of a service course is also responsible for guidance with the unique reading problems his course poses.

Some of the service courses carry titles which are similar to those found in more familiar programs but, actually, they are quite different in nature. A major difference is in the method rather than in the content. Classes are organized and scheduled to meet specific student needs. Flexible use of personnel and physical and material resources to provide certain kinds of learning experiences mark the program in this school. Even though a service course is offered for several consecutive years, the work of each new class is developed with reference to the needs of the particular group and the special ways in which persistent life situations recur in their daily living. For example, while many of the same concepts were developed ultimately, a beginning course in physics started one year with a study of sound which centered in the tolerance of the human ear for loud and dissonant noises. Another year, the crucial questions raised by the group assembling for beginning physics in the fall were those involved in launching a space satellite.

Service courses meet two, three, or four periods a week, depending on the nature of the problems being studied. Some are one semester in length, some two or more. Some are offered every year, some are given in alternate years, and others are offered to meet a particular demand and are not repeated, depending on the best judgment of the staff as to the needs of individuals and developments in their world.

Special help to individuals comes in several ways. Another type of service from specialists is giving help on a short-term basis to individuals and groups. Service on call to core classes, service units developed around special problems, and clinics or laboratories in which individuals can pursue projects or receive special help are the means for providing short-term aid. The special help is for students who have talents and interests requiring extended or intensive work as well as for those who need remedial assistance. At least one laboratory period in which the work is highly individualized for the latter purpose is offered in each field. Similarly, open or unassigned periods of both core and other teachers serve for conferences for individual guidance, for additional special work with individuals or small groups following up aspects of core activities, and for work with class committees, student council committees, and others concerned with the ongoing social and community life of the class or school. Periods for clinic or laboratory work are staggered during the day so that those most in demand are not scheduled at the same time. The amount of time given to these types of activities varies in terms of the individual students and the nature of the work being developed in the central or core part of the program.

Service units are developed on a short-term basis when needed to clarify or amplify a particular piece of work being considered in the core. For example, as a core class is working on a particular problem and finds that its members lack the specific skills, knowledge, or insights to cope with the situations it faces, specialists may be called in or time may be scheduled during the day for a short service unit to acquire the necessary understandings and skills.

Many service courses and laboratories are available from which to choose. The offerings available to the student and his counselor are varied and many. Some have already been mentioned. In addition to the English service course in drama and play production and the courses in literature, there is a writers' group, a class in journalism, and one dealing broadly with communication arts. The two clinics previously mentioned serve individuals and small groups facing many types of problems. The editors of the school paper, students called upon to make announcements in assembly, the group in charge of the central bulletin board, and others are often found in the English laboratory, as are the students with special ability who desire critical appraisal of their work.

Similarly, in the field of the natural sciences, there is a course relating basic scientific and mathematical concepts, in addition to the previously mentioned offering in current scientific developments and the several courses centering in the areas of physics, chemistry, and biology. There are courses which develop needed understandings and concepts in the sciences through the study of applied mechanics, food chemistry, photography, and the application of scientific principles to the maintenance of physical and mental health. Some of these courses stress underlying theory, basic ideas, and technical competencies, while others place emphasis on the practical application. Special periods provide opportunities for individuals and small groups to investigate projects or areas of interest through experimentation, research, and intensive study in school and commercial laboratories.

Among the most popular courses offered by the social studies group is the study of developmental trends in American democracy, mentioned earlier, which deals with historical backgrounds as these influence and condition current trends. Other courses have as their focus the study of government and governmental agencies, European backgrounds and international relations, current problems in national and international events, geographic backgrounds of economic problems. As a service to the rest of the student body, one social studies group analyzes current news and, with the cooperation and assistance of the special teachers in English, presents a ten-minute summary, with comments, over the public-address system during the noon hour. Another student group examines basic current issues through the study of their historical roots. In the laboratory section there are normally several groups going more deeply into selected current problems and one or two exploring other areas that draw heavily upon historical backgrounds.

The mathematics department offers a course dealing with consumer mathematics relating to persistent problems of buying, selling, saving, and investing, and additional courses focused on basic mathematical concepts and processes and drawing on algebra, geometry, trigonometry, calculus, and logic. The latter courses are more theoretical in nature and stress basic relationships and meanings. Many of the common mathematical needs of today's citizens are met through the core activities, but the laboratory, as previously mentioned, offers both remedial help and individual opportunities to delve into advanced fields. One year a group interested in architecture worked in the mathematics laboratory and were assisted by art and shop specialists. Often current economic problems are discussed by students who need special help. Student council activities requiring statistical procedures of various kinds call for service units provided through this laboratory.

French, Spanish, and Latin are the languages taught regularly. Language courses are concerned with the people and their way of life, their cultural background, the history and structure of the language, and the written and oral communications. All language teachers use literature, art, music, and drama to help the students develop desired skills and understandings.

Activities in home economics vary with the needs of the group. The courses built around concerns of home management and consumer problems, and the persistent life situations recurring in these immediate concerns, have already been mentioned. The service course built around consumer problems has been developed cooperatively with the staff in mathematics and business education. The laboratory or workshop in home economics allows for a wide variety of individual enterprises. Problems of refreshments for a class party, of proper costumes for a play, of choice of a winter coat, and many others find their way to this center.

The specialists in vocational and business education offer work for those who are interested in developing only general competence in the field and also for those with special talents or interests in these areas. The offerings of these departments are not restricted to preparation for specific skilled and semiskilled jobs, but include opportunities for increased insights into the structure and operation of the business, financial, and industrial worlds. There are courses in typewriting open to all students, and courses in shorthand, bookkeeping, and office practice for those who expect to use these skills vocationally. There are also offerings in economics, the consumer and the law, and introduction to business.

Music and art specialists provide several kinds of courses and laboratories. School orchestra, band, and choral groups meet during these periods. Individual practice rooms are also available. The art laboratories are open for individual activities, even when classes are in session. Both the art and music departments combine with the English group to offer a series of courses on "the arts." These courses aim to develop appreciation and understanding and may or may not lead to added production skills. Their special focus varies with the interests and needs of the particular class.

The physical education laboratories are devoted to corrective work or to the development of special skills in such areas as creative dance, rhythms, or gymnastics and recreational pursuits such as tennis, golf, and the like. While competitive sports are not emphasized, there are opportunities to participate in such team games as football, basketball, baseball, and soccer.

SCHEDULES ALLOW FOR FLEXIBILITY

Space does not permit the full picture of the scheduling required to provide the varied services just outlined. Nor is it possible to present the exact schedules maintained year after year. Flexibility in scheduling is at the heart of the program. Nevertheless, time for service courses is specifically set, and periods during which laboratories are open or specialists on call for service to core groups are established.

Mr. Keith, core teacher of the tenth-graders whose program is described in this chapter, also offers service courses in European backgrounds and international relations, both for beginners and for advanced pupils. He is available for service units and for individual help in these same areas. His schedule, typical of teachers working with core courses, is as follows:

8:30–11:00	Core class.
11:00–11:50	Monday, Tuesday, and Thursday—conferences with teachers of other groups in need of resource materials; Wednesday and Friday—guidance conferences and record-keeping for homeroom group.

11:50– 1:00 Lunch.

1:00– 1:50 Monday, Wednesday, and Friday—advanced service course on European backgrounds; Tuesday and Thursday—partial responsibility for individual conferences in the social studies laboratory.

1:50– 2:40 Monday, Wednesday, and Friday—beginning course on European backgrounds; Tuesday and Thursday—social studies laboratory.

2:40– 3:30 Monday, Wednesday, and Friday—available for short-time service units; these units are sometimes scheduled during Tuesday and Thursday laboratory periods.

Miss Adamson, a teacher with full-time responsibility as an English specialist, is one of those who works with the clinic concerned with problems of the mechanics of English usage. She is also the sponsor of the school paper and is in charge of a service course in journalism. Her schedule illustrates that of the specialist with major responsibility for service to individuals and small groups, and is as follows:

8:30– 9:20 Available for conferences with paper staff. All Friday morning devoted to paper staff.

9:20–10:10 Beginning writers' group meets Monday, Wednesday, and Thursday.

10:10–11:00 Journalism class meets four days a week.

11:00–11:50 Available for conferences with core teachers, planning for individual needs, working on laboratory schedule and record-keeping.

11:50– 1:00 Lunch.

1:00– 3:30 Clinic open five days a week; help for individuals and groups scheduled by Miss Adamson in conference with core teachers.

In the field of business education, there is need for regular courses stressing particular skills. Accordingly, Miss McKay's schedule is similar in some respects to the schedule she might have in a high school where the basic curriculum organization is around subject fields:

8:30– 9:20 Monday, Wednesday, and Friday—advanced typewriting; Tuesday and Thursday periods extended to 11:00 for service units with various office-practice groups.

9:20–11:00 Monday, Wednesday, and Friday—available for consultation with core groups, paper staff, other groups with special problems of printing or duplicating.

11:00–11:50 Beginning typewriting class—five days a week.

11:50– 1:00	Lunch.
1:00– 2:40	Supervision of groups securing special on-the-job experience in office practice in the school offices.
2:40– 3:30	Second beginning typewriting class—five days a week.

The major difference between schedules of these teachers and those of a staff working under a more traditional curriculum design is in the flexibility of class meetings in time, regularity, structure, and nature. Some groups meet regularly for large blocks of time; or a single student may meet for one or two periods with a teacher in a clinic or laboratory. Some classes meet for a few days or weeks only, others for a full year.

GUIDANCE IS THE KEY TO PROGRAM QUALITY

The key to the quality of growth which results from this program lies in the guidance given to each individual. Over the six-year secondary school period, it is seldom that two students have exactly the same program. The teacher of the core program is responsible for helping each of his students to evaluate the progress and growth he has made, to decide on the special activities which seem best to fit his needs, and to see the relationship between and among the various activities included in his program. Courses are selected and activities undertaken because of the promise they give of help with concerns and interests of the learner selecting them, rather than because he has now reached the point in the curriculum where these courses have been placed. The student meets each new experience, understanding why he is in the particular course, service unit, or laboratory, and aware of some of the things he expects from it. As the work develops, he is helped to identify other needs and interests which guide his further activities in the course and his selection of subsequent experiences.

Major responsibility for whatever help each individual needs in adjusting to the social and academic demands of the school is in the hands of the core teachers. The school nurse, the principal, and the other teachers stand ready to provide information and to give assistance as required. After considerable experimentation it was found helpful for the teacher of the core program to stay with the same group for two or even three years. This not only provides for better continuity of growth through the core program activities but also for much more effective guidance of individuals as the teacher works with the same students over a longer period of time. The core teachers meet regularly with other staff members to discuss the nature of service courses and laboratories required.

Special teachers, core teachers, other professional personnel, and the school administrators have as their guide an analysis of persistent life situations similar to the Master List provided on pages 155 to 165 in this volume. In planning with individuals, this analysis is used as a guide to balanced development. In addition, both core teachers and groups of specialists have engaged in cooperative research studies to determine more exactly the types of problems faced by the students they teach and the contributions of specific subject areas to these problems. Cumulative records, together with the core teachers' previous experiences with the individual students in their groups, help to point out areas in which experience has been extensive and others in which it has been limited. While there is concern that each individual be helped to develop, to the full extent of his ability, the competencies needed to cope effectively with the persistent life situations faced by all adults, provision is also made to meet the needs of individuals whose capabilities allow them to proceed to higher levels of specialization.

In scheduling activities, teacher and students together consider areas which have been, or are likely to be, a part of the core activities, areas of weakness in which clinical help should be sought, and talents or interests in which special help or advanced study seems desirable. These plans, as learners become more mature, are often blocked out beyond the current year, teacher and student together deciding what is immediate and what should be included at a later stage. From time to time such tentative plans are revised. Vocational considerations and college plans are an integral part of this process. Planning conferences often include other staff members as information in a particular area or special help concerning the demands of a vocation is called for. However, the major responsibility for this type of planning and guidance rests with the core teacher. It is for this reason that two periods of the core teacher's regular weekly schedule are set aside for special guidance.

The Activities of the Core Program

The core program of the tenth grade, whose activities are described briefly in this chapter, is taught by Mr. Keith, a teacher with a strong background in the social sciences and considerable preparation and interest in natural science. The thirty-five students range in age from fourteen to sixteen, and in intellectual ability from two or three who are considerably below average to a number who are very able. The group is typical of other classes in the school. They represent a cross section of the student body, coming from all kinds of socio-economic, religious, ethnic, and racial backgrounds. Except for the students who have moved into the community recently, most of the class members attended one of the four neighborhood elementary schools. The majority have been together through the elementary grades and for three of the six years of secondary school.

The differences and similarities among these youth are many. Besides variations in abilities, the cumulative learnings and diverse experiential backgrounds have resulted in different achievement patterns. Their varied attitudes toward self, school, family, peer and adult relationships, success and failure are rather firmly developed. Their learning patterns and study habits are fairly well established. Interests have deepened and have become more focused as students have been called upon to choose from the many alternatives they face as adolescents in school, at home, and in the community. Rapid physical growth and changes in body structure have intensified varied adjustment problems. Personal-social development tends to bring these students together in groups and the desire for peer recognition and acceptance has become dominant. Marked variations in abilities, motivations, interests, and achievements are not matched by equal differences in personal-social relationships among these students. They tend to dress very much alike and, in a number of ways, conform to the current established norms. A few are definitely planning to go to college. Several of the girls are interested in secretarial work. Many of the others are still uncertain about post-high school plans.

A variety of activities characterized the core program of this tenth grade. Space does not permit a detailed description of the day-by-day interweaving of activities such as that given in Chapter 12 for Miss Thomas' fifth grade. To make clear the types of experiences, the ways of working, and the flexible scheduling, the description that follows is organized around major areas in which the students' activities centered. Actually, the schedule for any day often included more than one problem area. Priorities depended on the stage reached in the particular project. At times the three-period core block was devoted almost entirely to the activities of individuals and small groups as they sought information on a related group of topics or made reports; other times the period was divided among two or three parallel projects. Sometimes information-seeking and preparation of reports were relegated to work at home or to periods scheduled for individual help in the afternoon while a special school or community problem demanded full attention during the core period.

The planning that kept this complex schedule clear to all concerned was similar to that engaged in by pupils of other grade levels. However, Mr. Keith's group was better able than younger classes to project long-term goals, to work independently over more extended periods, and to prepare individual work plans and hold to them.

Mr. Keith became the homeroom-core teacher of this group in the ninth grade and brought this background to the beginning of their work in the tenth grade.

LIVING IN THE SCHOOL COMMUNITY IS A SOURCE OF MANY LEARNINGS

As the class came together in the fall, the students and Mr. Keith attended to general matters of organization so that the work of the year would proceed smoothly. Final evaluation at the close of their ninth year had enabled each individual to make plans for service courses and laboratory work to be taken, but some time was needed to check schedules and make changes in individual programs. Problems were identified during the first morning and individual conferences scheduled to work them out. Schedules had to be developed for the two new students who had joined the group for the first time, having moved to the community during the summer. The new class members were introduced to the group and, in the afternoon, familiarized with the general way of working in the core group. Time was also taken during the first morning to arrange the classroom. Since it was the same room used by this group the previous year, organizing for work was mainly a matter of putting away supplies and arranging materials conveniently.

During the year, short but profitable learning experiences continued to arise from the problems the students in this class faced or were asked to consider as citizens in the school community. All-school activities and special responsibilities for various services to the school were under the general leadership of a student council which functioned through inter-grade committees. Each class was represented on the council and on one or more of the subcommittees. During the early weeks of the fall a number of council or committee items came to the homerooms for consideration—the report of the assembly committee for final approval, a request for suggestions of student needs to be considered in developing a recreational reading center in the library, a proposal that a nominal charge be made for the school paper in order to finance certain other student activities, a list of council committee appointments for approval. In addition, the class had to elect a new council representative, make decisions regarding last year's final reports and recommendations, and make plans for its own social and recreational activities.

Mr. Keith and the other teachers saw in such situations opportunities for the students to acquire practical experience in dealing with many of the persistent problems of working as a cooperative group and of participating in "local" government, and sought to give the council and the class committees definite responsibilities and freedom, under guidance, to carry them out. Regularly during the school year requests calling for action by the homeroom group came from the council representative, council committees, or class officers. In turn, the sensitivity of the students to the needs of their school community often caused them to initiate plans. Teachers and administrators were sometimes directly involved. A request for more opportunity to work with plastics resulted in a new course offered by the art teacher. The tenth grade's concern with the length of the lines at lunch resulted in a request for a study of the problem which finally led to the posting of menus in classrooms so that less time would be taken in choosing food. A follow-up council analysis of student needs in the lunchroom led to a revised menu. The school paper is an active organ through which student opinion makes itself known and was frequently used by members of this tenth grade. Two members of the class served on a library committee that worked regularly with the librarian reviewing and publicizing new books.

Teachers also saw the potential contributions of these activities to the area of person-to-person relationships. From discussions of the kinds of activities which make for a good time socially, what the function of the hosts or hostesses should be on different occasions, what refreshments are desirable, and whether amenities suitable for a picnic are acceptable at a dance, came many valuable learnings. Others came merely from associations in a social setting, testing out ways of making friends, learning how and when to become part of the "crowd," finding out when conformity is important and when to maintain individuality. Teachers working with their groups in these school activities learned much about the needs of individuals, and this later became the basis for special guidance.

During the year the tenth grade regularly spent a part of each Friday morning discussing whatever all-school or class needs had arisen during the week. The length of these discussions naturally varied with the nature of the problems. Final work on some student council proposal sometimes took a good part of the morning or was carried over into the next few days. Since the core class served as the homeroom for these students, the problems concerned with school citizenship and the effective functioning of the school community became the focus for some of their activities. Classroom living also provided many opportunities for learning how to participate effectively as a group member—helping to formulate policy, select leaders, carry out plans. A study of that part of last year's evaluation which dealt with the class's operations was made early in the year for leads in finding ways to improve their working together through increasing their own skills. The class spent whatever time was necessary studying its own processes of living and working together. As a consequence, student government, both in the classroom and in the school, was more than mere mechanical participation in a series of minor decisions. Rather, it was an integral part of the students' learning activities through the generalizing, concept-building, and skill development which accompanied the actual discussion and decision-making.

A YEAR'S STUDY EXTENDS UNDERSTANDING OF PERSISTENT PROBLEMS OF LIVING TO THE INTERNATIONAL SCENE

The first major area of study entered upon by this tenth grade actually came from their activities of the previous year and continued to be a center of attention over the entire year.

September: An interest from the preceding year carries over. As ninth-graders, the group had followed with interest news reports of national and world affairs. A discussion of events which occurred during the summer led to sharing views on the existing crises in several parts of the world. Opinions of causes and suggestions for possible solutions came freely from class members but without much factual basis or depth of understanding. Several students, remembering their experience from the previous year, soon called attention to the inadequacy of what was happening in this discussion and to the need for a more systematic approach.

Mr. Keith saw in these evaluative comments an opportunity to build on understandings developed the preceding year. Both as a way of getting acquainted in the ninth grade and as a means of helping individuals begin to share in evaluating their present growth and planning next steps, he and the class had worked out a set of *Class Goals* at the beginning of the year. Over the year the skills, attitudes, and areas of knowledge which the class had listed and on which they had reached consensus had been used as criteria for selection of study topics, as guides to activities, and as bases for self-evaluation. In the total list were items such as the following:

To learn how to judge news reports in press or on radio or television

To learn how to differentiate between fact and opinion

To learn how to take part effectively in discussions

To learn how to discuss events and ideas, not personalities

To understand the background of important events

While final evaluations in the spring had been carried out in the light of these goals, it seemed appropriate to look back at them now with reference to the attitudes toward accurate information that were being expressed.

Duplicate copies of the goals were available in the file cabinet. The students reviewed the way the goals were evolved and how they were used last year. They spent a little time evaluating their preliminary discussions in the light of these goals and decided that more skills were to be learned in the tenth grade. High though the interest in world crises was, they decided to postpone further discussion for the time being and give attention to the restatement and revision of the objectives which would help direct their studies this year. Mr. Keith had found in the past that time taken to organize the class and to work out guides for planning and for behavior actually averted a great deal of later difficulty. Learning to participate effectively in a working group was a goal with which both the class and the teacher were concerned, and these initial activities contributed toward that end. The revised list continued some of the items from the past year which they felt needed additional attention. New items were added and some old ones deleted. The goals were of several kinds, some dealing with knowledge and understandings, some with increased insights and skills into various processes, and some with growth in personal-social behavior.

After revising the class goals and preparing sufficient copies for each student to have one for his own use and another to share with his parents, the class returned to the discussion they had begun two days earlier. With Mr. Keith as discussion leader, the students started to work out a study plan which would give them a clearer picture of what these world crises actually were, what had contributed to them, what effect they had on the United States, what America's role was, and how these trouble spots might affect the students personally. With the information they already had, the students began to see several things: the crisis areas, although in widely separated parts of the world, seemed to be related to each other; America's foreign policy was being tested in each trouble spot; and whatever developments occurred would affect Americans rather directly in some way.

Mr. Keith saw in the discussion and questions the opportunity to expand concepts of government and the forces that influence it, and to develop certain fundamental insights into the problems faced by nations living and working together. There was also the possibility of extending understandings, developed the previous year, basic to such persistent problems as the distribution of goods and services, the provision of legal protections needed to guarantee the welfare of all, the responsibility engendered by possession of natural resources, and the need for conserving resources, as these problems affect and relate to international relations. In the ninth grade this group had worked intensively with some of these problems in studies focused on situations or issues such as those involved in public versus private development of natural resources, the causes of price rises, the status of public schools, and exploration of the technological system and the effect of automation on labor and industry. However, they had extended their insights to the international scene only as they had reported on current news. Hence, the new interest seemed likely to contribute both to deeper insights and to balanced growth. Accordingly, when the group came together to discuss the problems they wanted to go into more thoroughly, Mr. Keith helped to sharpen some of the issues which they were raising and to point to possibilities. Solutions to problems of international relationships, in the sense of formulating acceptable policies, were obviously impossible. But clear identification of the demands being made by nations, understanding some of the most important factors which influence them, and expanded insight into a significant phase of government were within the ability of the group.

Obviously not all students had an equally intense interest in this area of study, nor were they able to grasp the problems involved in the same way. This was particularly true of the slower learners. But past experience with the core program had taught them that there would be many different aspects of the problem and that these could be approached in varied ways so that each student would help and be helped to find an aspect he could handle and from which he would profit. For example, some would use many advanced sources of information while others would rely on less difficult, more limited materials. All would be concerned with securing help in improving their varied reading skills at whatever level they were working.

The resulting study began by identifying the major trouble spots. Despite much previous work with maps, a number of the group were somewhat hazy as to exact locations. A first step was to use a large map of the world to locate crisis areas more accurately. Meanwhile, all turned to newspapers and magazines for current information about the situations. This search was preceded by a discussion of what materials to study, what to look for, and how to collect needed information. A check was made to see that all students did not turn to the same materials and that all available sources would be covered. A similar plan was made to monitor programs on the local radio and television stations. After several days, students reported on their findings and attempted to list the troubles and issues which seemed to be involved. While many had already taken sides, they recognized that "right" and "wrong" were not clear. They also found that the actions of some friendly nations did not seem to be on the "right" side and that at times America's role was neither clear nor consistent in these various situations.

October: Preliminary explorations eventuate in plans for a specific project. The initial reports and the discussions which followed the preliminary investigations pointed up a number of problems on which to focus. With several points at which to take hold, the class decided the first step would be to get additional information about the peoples, cultures, resources, pressures, and tensions in the various nations under discussion. Because so many countries were involved, the decision limited this aspect of the study to four somewhat contrasting nations. Next, the class members discussed what they needed to learn and how they might go about it.

This phase of the study extended for several weeks and many different kinds of activities were undertaken. One early class discussion centered on the question of what should be studied to understand another culture. Mr. Keith helped the students identify aspects of their own way of life which would be important for someone else to understand. These items became the guides for areas to be studied. Students quickly listed such aspects as geography, government, resources, economy, and technological development. From their discussion, they added other items including family life, standards of living, arts, music, religion, history, and similar cultural aspects more personal than population figures and production statistics. Means for securing these varied kinds of information were also part of the early planning.

Study committees were then organized and each began to plan its own method of procedure. Mr. Keith spent time with each of the four groups, helping them to clarify their plans, suggesting possible activities, and indicating some of the available personnel and material resources. Individual, small-group, and whole-class activities followed. At times, students worked with Mr. Keith intensively for a period. For example, a number of high-ability students who were especially interested worked with Mr. Keith in a study of the historical method, tracing the development of the modern state from its beginnings through analyses of some of the forces which helped to shape it. These students used college-level materials for information not otherwise available. Similarly, several students with below-average reading ability received remedial help from Mr. Keith in order to improve their skills in using materials needed in the study. The same kind of differentiated help was provided when groups were working on written reports.

Committees and individuals consulted with other teachers for guidance in finding information about the arts—graphic, music, building, dramatic, literary, and others. Students investigated the natural resources and technological development of the country of their special concern with the help of Mr. Keith and one of the science teachers. Economic geography was drawn upon frequently, and understanding of other nations grew as the students examined what information they could find about industries and trade needs.

This search for information and synthesis of findings continued until late October. The original four working committees maintained their initial membership although varied groupings emerged with particular needs. Members from several of the groups met to pool their efforts in some areas, and at times they worked together to acquire specific kinds of learnings which all needed. At other times, the whole class met together to see a film or meet with a special consultant or to hear a progress report. Although there was a great deal of independent and small-group activity, the total class participated in certain studies as a group.

November: A phase of the study is brought to a close. In early November the phase of the year's study described above culminated with a series of reports. Each report dealt with the committee's findings about a particular nation and its culture, and took at least two core periods. The method of reporting varied from group to group, although all tried to answer the specific questions raised in their early planning. Presentations made use of such means as a panel discussion, a display of art objects, a demonstration of native music, a talk using slides and charts to present the country's history, and a debate. One group passed out samples of special pastries which came from the country they had studied. Several days of discussion followed the presentations as the class examined the generalizations and relationships which they saw. Basic points were stressed and some of those raised were marked for possible further study. Included among these were questions about the American foreign policy, the role of the United Nations, and the possible effects of nuclear developments on the existing crisis situations.

Before proceeding, the class evaluated its activities and progress. The study of other countries was not, of course, the only activity going on during the three-hour block assigned to the core program. As stated earlier, a session every Friday was devoted to problems relating to the work of the student council or other all-school activities. The difficulties of locating accurate information for the study of international relations led to a variety of individual and group projects. There was a parallel interest in plays and play production, described in the following section, that eventually led to a rather broad consideration of many persistent problems in the area of communication. The mid-November evaluation took all these activities into account. Several kinds of evaluation were made—class, work group, and individual. Using the class goals as a guide, the students examined their growth in the areas listed and decided which needed additional attention.

Mid-November to mid-March: A second phase of the study calls for extended plans. Each of the group presentations had reported on the United States' relationship with the four nations studied. Consideration of America's role had given rise to a number of questions: Who makes American foreign policy? What influences American foreign policy decisions? What part does each of the branches of government have in determining foreign policy? What are the similarities and differences in foreign policy among American political parties? How do elections influence American foreign policy? Can the individual citizen do anything about foreign policy? Are there relationships between domestic and foreign policy?

These questions, which seemed to Mr. Keith to present excellent opportunities to help the students to develop deeper insights into persistent problems in the area of participating in local and national government, became the bases for a second phase of the study. The questions were refined and groups were organized much more rapidly with numerous shifts from the earlier committees. This study drew heavily on both current affairs and history. One committee centered its attention on the historical backgrounds of American participation in international affairs from colonial times. A study of the governmental and political structure of the United States involved a second group. A third committee examined American foreign policy as it related to the four nations studied earlier. Still another group worked on the relationships between domestic and foreign policy. The fifth committee studied the relations between the United States and the United Nations. The reports of the last two committees eventually gave direction to further studies—one on nuclear developments and another on the role of the United Nations in world trouble spots.

The work procedures followed in this study were essentially the same as in the earlier one. Again the emphasis was on how to find information, how to separate facts from propaganda, and how to understand facts as accurately as possible, on appraising problems in the light of these facts, on drawing generalizations and meanings, and on building relationships. Of major importance was the group's growing awareness of the paucity of reliable information. Textbooks disagreed on the interpretation of trends and sometimes even on facts. Often data which the class felt were needed to throw light on an event were completely lacking. Current information was even more contradictory than that which was available in earlier materials.

In carrying this work forward the activities in the core period were again quite varied—at times the entire period was given to planning or to reports and discussion, at others to individual and group study in the classroom or in the library, at still others to a combination of one or more of the types of activities just mentioned. As with the earlier unit, parallel activities called for variation in time allotments. When the study was first launched, almost full time was devoted to it. Later, groups worked on their own for part of the period, while the entire class considered problems of locating and evaluating information for the remainder of the period. Student council requests continued to receive attention. In mid-December, extensive plans to present a class play took up almost full time for several days and committee work related to the major study went ahead in the evenings and in special conferences with other teachers in afternoon periods. There were times, too, when problems not included in the original plans for the study of foreign policy were given priority. At one point, for example, the total group spent several days discussing the influence of nuclear weapons on foreign policy. This discussion emerged from a preliminary report of the group studying the relationships between domestic and foreign policy. The class decided that the whole area of nuclear development warranted further study later and marked this for additional time later. The same thing occurred in the early discussion of the group looking into the relations between the United States and the United Nations.

The resource persons and the way they were used were equally varied. While Mr. Keith was the major resource person for the group, the librarian or other teachers with special abilities came to the classroom as requested, and individuals or small groups went to the appropriate laboratories for help on particular aspects of the study. As specific skills were needed in the development of the study they were made a part of the core program, were stressed in service courses which individual students were taking, or were made a unit of individual study in clinic or laboratory, depending on how universal the need was and where help could best be given. The balance between independent or small-group activity and more formal, direct instruction varied with the particular need. Just as materials were selected which were appropriate, instructional methods varied with the particular problem and the kinds of learnings desired.

This study of American foreign policy (its history, structure, and development) and the examination of the role of the United States in the various trouble spots of the world took about four months of the class's core period. When a group felt it had reached an appropriate point, time was scheduled for reporting to the total class. These reports, however, did not come at the same time since committees did not always complete their work at the same time. Each report was made when the committee was ready and when time could be scheduled through curtailment of other activities.

Mid-March to June: Interests explored partially during the study of foreign policy receive full attention. As committee reports began to bring the class study of American foreign policy to a close, there was time to turn back to problems in the area of nuclear development. Entirely apart from the fact that this was a problem that alert adolescents in the twentieth century could not escape, Mr. Keith saw in this interest an opportunity to help his class explore problems related to the persistent life situation of using technological resources for social good and also a means of providing balanced development. In the ninth grade this class had explored problems related to the use of technological resources in a unit on the effect of automation in local factories. Up to this point in the tenth grade, understandings in the area had been drawn upon and enlarged only incidentally.

The study of nuclear energy and its impact on domestic and foreign policies in America and other countries extended far beyond the class's original plans. As a consequence, they had to revise their plans several times during the progress of the study. Mr. Keith and one of the science teachers served as major consultants. The first phase involved the scientific and technical aspects of nuclear energy. The entire class met for a single period for several days to study the basic principles involved in the release of nuclear power. Many different kinds of materials were available, ranging from highly technical resources to simplified pamphlets, films, and filmstrips. The students were somewhat surprised to find the wealth of materials available from governmental, industrial, and educational sources. Students with particular interest and ability in science and mathematics used more advanced sources and, in some instances, prepared their own charts and diagrams to explain their findings to the other students.

From this focus on the scientific bases, the class moved on to other aspects of nuclear development—military, economic, and social. The effects of the use of nuclear weapons on military establishments interested all students. Here again they found much technical and nontechnical information available. At one point, one of the mathematics teachers was asked to come in and explain the processes needed to compute the release of energy. A news announcement that a plane had been hit by its own rockets stimulated the students to study this phenomenon in greater detail from the technical standpoint and the problems involved.

Economically, the possible peaceful uses of nuclear energy intrigued many students. The effects such uses could have on the relatively underdeveloped countries and on nations with critical power shortages were studied. Two students made a special report on what might happen if atomic energy replaced oil as a fuel, as coal has been in many instances. The transition from the economic to the political-social aspects of nuclear power was relatively easy since the students soon found that it was impossible to separate the various phases as clearly as they would like.

The study of the peaceful and martial uses of atomic energy frequently brought them to considerations of the role of the United Nations in both of these aspects. Eventually, a unit on the United Nations—its structure, purposes, and operations—was carried on through a study of how the problems related to nuclear developments had been and were being handled. The roles played by different UN agencies were many, and, in the evaluation which followed, the students decided that focusing on this one basic problem provided an opportunity to see the whole organization without becoming lost in the myriad of its other activities.

Throughout the year's work in the core, attention was turned again and again to the original questions raised in the discussion of the world's trouble spots. The class followed current affairs closely, particularly those events related to their central concern. For example, they read with interest reports of the meetings of foreign ministers but in studying the material available they stressed the recommendations being made and did not attempt to pass judgments or suggest policies. They came to the close of their year's work in this area with deeper convictions as to the complexities of international relationships, heightened understanding of the common problems faced by all groups, increased insight into the functioning and roles of their own government, and a greater sense of the need to withhold judgments until all facts are available and can be studied. In addition, there were varied learnings as students had pursued individual interests and attempted to develop needed skills. Evaluation was an integral part of the learning process, with frequent return to the class goals to check on group and individual progress and direction.

NEED FOR RELIABLE INFORMATION LEADS TO STUDY OF HOW TO LOCATE AND USE RESOURCE MATERIALS

Related projects centering in the problems faced by these students in locating accurate information were mentioned earlier. This was a year that contributed much to skills important in dealing with persistent life situations such as understanding the ideas of others, using sound bases for interpreting information, and using source materials appropriately. Small units were developed through the year, some involving the entire class, some the committee directly faced with the problem. Frequently, part of the three-period core block was scheduled for these units. Occasionally, solutions to the problem of securing information were so crucial to the larger study that all other work stopped to allow for full attention to them.

In September and October, parallel with the first stages of the foregoing major studies, was a short but profitable study of the sources of information. It began when the members of the group realized the shortcomings of the local newspaper as a means of securing reliable data. As magazine and other current sources confused facts and opinions, gave conflicting facts, or appeared to place emphasis upon only one side of the question, the class reviewed and extended learnings in this area. Experiences in previous years had built sound techniques of reading newspapers for most of the group, but their acquaintance with other sources of international information was slight. At Mr. Keith's suggestion the students wrote to the information agencies of the various governments officially represented in this country, asking for current publications, and for the rest of the year the class was on several mailing lists. To make comparisons they wrote to the Department of State to find what this country made available to its citizens and to other nations, and were soon inundated with official publications of different kinds. They also found that their congressmen could be quite helpful in getting materials for them.

As the year progressed, various magazines and current bulletins issued by national groups or by such organizations as the Foreign Policy Association or the American Association for the United Nations were studied with more critical eyes. Here the librarian made a fundamental contribution to new techniques, as few of the students had built adequate skills in locating current material of the magazine or pamphlet type. The students also acquired additional skills in locating biographical details they felt were necessary for the interpretation of a writer's point of view. In the ninth grade these students had spent time considering the purposes of propaganda and the ways it can be most effective. This area was given further attention as they compared the materials put out by various national groups, noted the effect of different headlines or phrasing upon the total impression given by newspaper articles, and appraised the effectiveness of the representation of their own country in the Department of State bulletins.

Some attention was given to the study of semantics and word usage, to critical thinking, and to reflective reading. Students were helped to increase their skills in skimming, outlining, and annotating materials. Mr. Keith provided help as he met with committees concerned with particular problems. Committee members also helped each other develop habits of accurate thinking as they gained enough background to challenge individuals who spoke without evidence or who jumped to conclusions. Mr. Keith helped students with limited reading ability to locate simpler reading matter, and, at the same time, improve their skills, and scheduled regular work periods for these pupils. For two weeks in the early fall, they worked with him on problems of note-taking. A little later in the year they made plans with him to develop special vocabulary lists. Often he found a few minutes to talk over reading problems with individuals. In addition, four of these youth reported for three afternoons a week to the clinic on the mechanics of written expression sponsored by the English department.

During the extended study of American foreign policy, when textbooks proved inadequate in giving necessary historical backgrounds, previous understandings about the use of instruments of communication were tested and expanded. At this time a number of the group who were studying the historical novel, as part of the year's service course, pointed to the value of the literature of a nation as background for interpreting its history. With the help of the teacher of this course and the librarian this small group built up a reference collection which was used by the whole class, but particularly by the committee concerned with the historical backgrounds of American participation in foreign affairs. The interests of the tenth grade in turn influenced the course on the novel when the group taking it raised problems about the folklore of nations and encouraged the entire group to explore that area. While this study was secondary for the tenth grade it proved very rich for those in the English group.

Mr. Keith, who wanted the year's study to develop not only increased sensitivity to the problems of understanding other people, but also growth in ability to use a wide variety of sources in building that understanding, encouraged the students pursuing special interests in art, music, and physical education to discover what contributions those areas might make. Some of this help was secured during the laboratory periods sponsored by specialists in these areas; in some cases service courses allowed individuals to take on special projects. Two students who had elected one of the elementary courses in "the arts" found that they were already involved in a project that related to the major class problem very closely and shared their studies with the group. Other members of the class joined these students and, as a result, the early November reports on other countries included demonstrations of typical art, music, and dance forms. Because of the demands of other aspects of the study this phase was not investigated in great detail, but enough was done to build further awareness of the variety of forms through which it is possible to gain and give information and to show interrelations between the problems of a people and their art, music, and literature. During the spring, parallel interests in various forms of dramatic expression again took many of the group back to persistent problems of using media other than language to express ideas.

EFFECTIVE MEANS OF COMMUNICATION AND PROBLEMS OF MOLDING PUBLIC OPINION ARE RECURRING INTERESTS DURING THE YEAR

A study of plays and play production was a parallel interest throughout the year although it did not require a consistent allotment of time. It was almost dormant at times as other problems demanded more attention; at others it was worked on intensively. The total study was more nearly a series of closely related units, each having its own culmination, in contrast to the study of world crisis situations which took the full year before many satisfying conclusions were reached.

Several factors contributed to the class interest in dramatic forms. As eighth-graders, the group had experimented with this area in assembly programs and had found the medium a very satisfying means of expression. In the ninth grade several who showed special talent and interest elected the service course in drama and play production. From time to time they had reported their most interesting experiences to the rest of the group. Because the concerns of the majority in the drama group were focused largely on play production, the possibilities of radio, television, and motion picture as modern dramatic forms had been touched upon in the ninth grade only enough to draw general comparisons. This brief contact, however, coupled with many home and community experiences, was sufficient to cause some members of the group to be eager to find a way to go on with this study. The interest was apparent when the class made plans in the spring and again in the fall, although it was not so universal as concern about foreign policies.

Mr. Keith, knowing that the group as a whole had not had many extended experiences with aesthetic forms of expression and recognizing from their comments that they had equally limited backgrounds from which to appraise the dramatic possibilities of such instruments as the motion picture, television, and radio, saw the contribution that such a study could make to balanced development. However, he hesitated to have the entire class swept along too quickly by a purpose that was vital only to a vocal few. In September, as plans were made by the whole class for the preliminary exploration of crisis situations, the small group who were most interested in problems of dramatic expression were given time to outline the questions they especially wanted to consider. These questions were to be presented to the whole class as a possible basis for study, and final decision was withheld until then. Meanwhile, plans moved ahead in the study of foreign policy. Mr. Keith worked on their plans with this drama group, and, in his own planning for guiding them, drew upon faculty analyses of persistent life situations in the area of aesthetic expression and appreciation and upon conferences with members of the English department. In October, documentary films used in connection with the early phases of the study of other cultures provided new impetus. The drama group, even from its rather limited background, pointed out several weaknesses in the films and raised many more questions than they could answer.

Radio and television forums as a means of influencing public opinion and the effectiveness of dramatic forms as against other methods of disseminating information became topics of increasing interest as the study of sources of information in relation to foreign news proceeded. In addition, the class decided on a short play as their contribution to a school assembly, and again those who had somewhat more background raised searching questions as to the effectiveness of the production. The entire class realized that these questions, now expanded to include several on the merits of dramatic forms of expression in molding public opinion, were related to their problems and presented an important area of investigation.

The first large all-class enterprise was the assembly play. Plans began to be formulated in mid-November, and by mid-December the full core time block was required for several days to bring these plans to fruition. All had a hand in helping prepare the script and later in the details of production, lighting, and costuming. Where questions hinged on technical aspects of lighting and sound effects, Mr. Keith was the chief source of help. The teacher in charge of the drama service course met with the group at regular intervals when dramatic form was under consideration.

In January the class turned back to the initial concern with radio, television, and the motion picture as related to dramatic form and to the dissemination of information. By this time, plans for the study of American foreign policy were well under way, and individual energies could be divided between the two studies. Until mid-March these two interests ran parallel with varying allotments of time to each. Three groups were formed. One was concerned with the effectiveness of documentary films. A second studied the methods used by a selected group of radio and television commentators and forums. A third, more interested in the aesthetic and recreational aspects of drama, undertook a study of a variety of popular television programs and attempted to discover what makes a good motion picture. Background reading, together with the pooling of personal opinions and actual contact with selected films and programs, led to the establishment of tentative standards and the identification of effective techniques. These conclusions were then tested by the class in reviewing new films and programs.

Community relationships and contacts with other parts of the school occurred frequently during this study. To secure a list of popular films and programs, and some firsthand opinion about them, the group interested in dramatic productions used a modest questionnaire on a sampling of their own high school population. The results were tabulated, analyzed, and checked against other available data. An interview with the managers of the motion-picture theaters provided much information about Class B pictures, standards of production, buying on a circuit, and ways of testing audience reaction. The entire class spent several sessions at the local radio station watching the production of plays and questioning the technical and acting staffs. The local news commentator and a member of the community who had recently appeared on a radio panel came to the school to provide more information. The group concerned with documentary films spent some time with the instructor responsible for the visual aids center for the city schools, examining the kinds of materials available. Through the year, with Mr. Keith's help, this group previewed and helped to select the films most suitable for their other class projects. In addition, they visited other classes to see different types of films.

Group membership in these enterprises was shifting. Although each student had primary obligations to one group, he was welcomed as a participating observer in others as long as his obligations to his own group were not neglected. When an experience, such as a new and worthwhile community contact, seemed important for all members of the class, preliminary plans were made by the group directly responsible, then shared with and checked by the entire class so that all could take part.

Throughout this study of dramatic forms, major emphasis was placed on effective communication with others, on ways of molding public opinion, and on dramatic effect in relation to these, rather than on the scientific aspects of the problem. The class, on the whole, did not possess sufficient scientific background in this area to go very deeply into the latter phase without extensive additional study. In view of the complex nature of the problems already under way such study did not seem advisable. Mr. Keith satisfied the immediate desire for such information and provided in several ways for future pursuit of science interests. First, with the help of the various technical experts contacted during the study and five members of the class who were taking advanced work in science, he gave simplified explanations of the technical problems most seriously in need of consideration if the group was to understand the adaptations in production techniques demanded by the medium used. Second, in helping individuals decide on service courses for the spring term and the following year, he encouraged several other members to enter classes which would build scientific backgrounds. Third, in his records summarizing the year's work, he indicated the need for further experiences to develop ability to deal with natural phenomena and technological resources, and discussed this recommendation with the class. As a result they went into the eleventh grade aware of their limitations in the depth of scientific understanding required by some of the current problems, and desiring further experiences in this area.

All read widely in connection with the various aspects of this study, not only to secure needed information but because of their growing interest in drama. In selecting suitable materials the class received help from the librarian, from those class members who had or were having contacts with the service course on the drama, and from the teacher who worked with this group. As the work progressed some of the students branched from a study of the problems of dramatic form to writing essays, editorials, and short stories for the school paper, testing in a related field what they had learned about molding public opinion and audience reaction. Help on this phase was provided partly through the core program and partly through the writing clinic.

In the early spring, while a week of opera was presented in the community by the local amateur group, many of the class availed themselves of the opportunity to become acquainted with another art form and spent several periods with the specialists in music and physical education following up questions relating to music and the dance. Here again it seemed that detailed study would make too great a demand on an already full schedule.

In the late spring, with the study of nuclear energy well under way, Mr. Keith encouraged the study of another important aspect of the persistent life situations of using dramatic forms of expression and molding public opinion. The fields of advertising and public relations seemed so closely related to these problems and so important in their effect upon everyday living that he felt it was appropriate to help his group see the relationships. As they turned from the practical problems of using varied means of communication to more general discussion of the effects of different types of appeal, he raised the question of advertisements. This topic had been considered from time to time by the members of this group as problems arose, but it had not, up to this point, been placed in relationship to other means and reasons for appealing to human desires, prejudices, and emotions. For the last six weeks attention centered on review and analysis of the appeals used by the advertiser. Economic concepts entered into the study of advertising at this time only in general terms as the costs were touched upon. In general, group attention continued to center on identifying the type of appeal and the reasons why it was or was not effective. At the end of the study a series of recommendations based on their findings in this study was sent to the poster committee for all-school activities, which had asked for new ways of arousing interest.

UNDERSTANDINGS ARE EXTENDED THROUGH SERVICE TO THE COMMUNITY

This class, as were others, was involved from time to time in community relationships. A brief description of one such activity illustrates their involvement. In January a student council project led to a short but intensive class study. The city council was considering the purchase of a lake adjoining the community for development as a recreational center for swimming, boating, picnicking, and skating. To appraise the needs of the young people of the community, the two high schools offered to make a survey of the present recreational facilities and needs of all school children. The teachers encouraged the student council to enter upon this study because they saw that in addition to the values of sharing actively in a community enterprise, there would be opportunities for learners to grow in their awareness of human needs for relaxation and balanced satisfactions in living. They also saw possibilities for further growth in ability to set up a problem, collect information, and interpret results. Although the councils of the two high schools were jointly responsible for the planning, and prepared a questionnaire to be sent to each family with children under twenty-one years of age, as a first step each core class was asked to discuss and criticize the questionnaire. This request held much interest for these tenth-graders who were planning their own school survey to determine popular films and motion pictures.

The first reaction of the majority of Mr. Keith's tenth grade was that if the student council discovered what active games people wanted to play and what facilities were available, all necessary information would be collected. The fact that lack of time and money to seek recreation was a factor to be considered had not occurred to them, nor had the effect of crowded living quarters and the community's shortage of parks. In addition, those parts of the questionnaire regarding the use of present community resources furnished new understandings of the variety of ways in which a community meets the persistent life situation of providing for the social welfare of its residents. Discussion also increased understanding of the importance of providing for the needs and capacities of different age-groups, of the value of supplying means of satisfaction through the use of aesthetic resources, of the importance of providing a variety of activities to enable individuals to secure balanced satisfaction in living, and of the necessity of considering the needs of the majority in such an enterprise.

As the questionnaire and plans for the survey were discussed, understanding was built of the importance of accurate information, of the background data needed to interpret facts correctly, and of the problems of proper sampling to secure reliable information. Accuracy of wording in the questionnaire was discussed by all classes but final editing was done by the members of the writers' course with the help of the school psychologist who had advanced training in research techniques. Plans for canvassing the neighborhood involved discussion of the best way in which to approach people as well as the need for favorable advance publicity. The latter was the final responsibility of a student council committee but suggestions came from all classes. The tenth-graders, fresh from concern with radio and television as sources of current information, stressed these media.

Other activities went along regularly as this special job was done. It coincided with a period in the study of American foreign policy which required individual and committee work to collect information, and for over a week most of this was done out of class. Plans at this point also included the study of radio, television, and motion pictures. Time was budgeted to allow for work on both problems, and special difficulties of the foreign policy committees were dealt with in early morning planning sessions or in conferences with Mr. Keith. The class devoted one entire morning to extensive discussion, critically appraising the questionnaire and making plans for their share in the canvas. A careful long-view plan for each study helped. Within the larger time block the scheduling problem was mainly one of arranging for necessary committee meetings and designating a point at which those committees were to report back to the group. Normally the last fifteen to thirty minutes of the morning were set aside for considering progress, next steps, and the schedule of activities for the following day.

It was March before the results of the questionnaire were sent back from the student council, which had worked jointly with the council from the other high school. A mathematics class had undertaken the tabulation. For the tenth grade the findings had significance as these gave added information about the needs of their own community. Several children whose backgrounds were most limited with respect to socio-economic problems and four others whose interests were very definite along this line spent a series of laboratory periods following up a number of specific questions. For several other classes the very graphic picture of a small slum section in their community led to detailed studies. A ninth grade decided to learn more about what modern science can do to provide inexpensive housing. A twelfth grade, already concerned about the problems of full employment, sought more information about the income levels of the groups which reported the greatest lack of facilities.

Providing for Needs Through Service Courses and Laboratory Activities

What were these tenth-grade students doing during the other half of the day when not in core class and physical education? How were these activities guided so as to make for effective total growth? Typical opportunities available for the rest of the day have already been mentioned. The students normally elected two or more service courses. Another period was spent in laboratory activities, some lasting for the entire semester or year, others of shorter duration—working in a clinic, in a studio, in a directed reading program, in special library activities. Since service courses met only two, three, or at the most four days a week, schedules also allowed time for library work other than that carried on in connection with the core.

GUIDANCE IS PROVIDED IN THE SELECTION OF SERVICE COURSES

Part of the guidance process has already been shown. Always in the early fall, at midyear, and again toward the close of the academic year, each student met with his homeroom core teacher to appraise progress, review general plans for the year, and discuss desirable next steps in the light of indicated needs. At these points decisions were made as to elective courses and laboratory and workshop activities. Courses were selected with a variety of factors in mind, and care was taken to provide opportunity for each individual to specialize in one or more areas of genuine talent or interest. Several students in Mr. Keith's group were doing advanced work in science. A number were working in the field of English. Six, with college-entrance requirements in mind, were in their third year of foreign language study, while several others were taking the introductory courses which dealt with the cultural backgrounds of another country, including its literature in translation. Three of the girls and one of the boys were on the way toward specialization in home economics—the boy through a vocational interest in hotel management. Business and vocational education drew a number who were preparing for commercial or industrial work after graduation from high school. Advanced classes in mathematics were undertaken by several of the young "scientists," a number of the business education group, and several who found the same personal pleasure in figures and formulas as did some of their fellows in music and art. There were three with special talent in music and two pursuing advanced work in art. The various offerings in the field of the social sciences provided special study for those who found that the core program did not allow sufficient opportunity to explore related areas in detail.

Shortages and weaknesses evidenced in previous experiences, viewed in the light of the present core program, also influenced decisions regarding the selection of service courses. Two of the boys, who found it difficult to deal with the equations needed for their study of chemistry, were advised to take special work in algebra. Several who, in the first semester's work on drama, showed little depth in their appreciation of literature, were encouraged to join a second-semester class centering on wide reading of both prose and poetry. Selection of the course built around international problems and involving considerable world history was not recommended as an elective for many of the tenth grade at the close of the year because of the extended experience provided in this area by the core. However, two students who were especially concerned with securing insight into world problems did elect it for their eleventh-year program.

Because of the flexibility in the offerings in all departments, considerable planning was necessary to coordinate and integrate service courses nd laboratories. Core teachers and specialists met at frequent and regur intervals to evaluate, plan, and make recommendations for individuals nd groups of students. Each staff member tried to approach the planing sessions with ideas about the contribution his area could make to he development of the individual and the nature the offering would have to take in order to make this contribution. Flexibility was in terms of specific purposes.

INDIVIDUALS ARE HELPED TO ENGAGE IN ADVANCED STUDY THROUGH WORK IN LABORATORIES

Beyond the major service courses, in which from twenty to forty students were normally enrolled, provision for greater specialization by individuals or small groups was made through the laboratory and clinic periods. Several members of the tenth grade engaged in such advanced individual work—two students with special musical ability, a third equally gifted in art, and a fourth seeking special help with problems of home management. As the group progressed through the eleventh and twelfth grades individual work of an advanced nature would be in greater evidence. Extensive individual attention was possible in this curriculum setting and there was more flexibility in the problems attacked and ways of working. Teachers worked with groups or individuals as needed, and a regular daily schedule was not necessary.

SHORT-TERM AND REMEDIAL NEEDS ARE ALSO MET THROUGH WORK IN LABORATORIES

Evaluation from day to day, in terms of the demands of the core program and of problems faced in service classes, indicated other needs which were met through clinical or laboratory experiences. Much of the help in fundamental skills needed by the several members of the group was given directly in the core class. However, from time to time many individuals and a number of groups visited the speech or writing clinics—for general remedial help over a semester, for short-term help on difficulties, for advice on a technical problem in relation to some special project. Other clinics and laboratories, as indicated when the organization of the school was described, served similar purposes. Individual work continued until the weakness was overcome or the special problem solved.

In addition, these laboratory periods were used for special help on technical problems arising in the core program. When the group recommending historical novels found they needed help, they went to the library, to their literature class, and to the teacher in charge of the reading and writing clinic. As technical problems in science arose small groups went back to clinic or service course to work out solutions. Specialists in music and art were consulted in the same way when help was needed on the characteristic art and music of other lands. The homeroom teacher assumed responsibility for making general plans when these needs arose and for keeping, with the help of teachers of service courses and the individuals in his group, records which would give a clear picture of the students' experiences and growth through such activities.

A Summary Look

These were the activities for the year. Although the work drew heavily on persistent problems involving social relationships, economic-social-political structures, the use of intellectual powers, and aesthetic satisfactions, there was also some consideration of problems of moral choice and responsibility, health, the natural environment, and the technological world. If it were possible to fill in the preceding outline of the year's work a number of day-to-day problems, now only implied, would appear. One apparent problem is raised by the range of differences among the tenth-graders. These differences exist, of course, regardless of the curriculum design. By using recurring life situations as the basis for selection and organization of learning experiences, specific activities were planned and carried on which provided for these many variations and similarities. Programs were differentiated in the light of individual needs but planned to provide for balanced growth, for capitalizing on special strengths and caring for weaknesses.

MANY SUBJECT FIELDS WERE USED IN GENERAL AND SPECIALIZED EDUCATION

Studies extended understandings into many areas: American government and political structure, nature of other cultures, relationships among nations and peoples, interrelatedness of various aspects of living in a critical world situation. The subject matter of the social sciences, the natural sciences, mathematics, music, art, home economics, physiology, the language arts, and foreign languages were all used. The skills demanded for effective use of intellectual powers continued to be built. Cooperation in a piece of research, finding new sources of reference, writing a play, writing and making reports, discussing, asking questions of members of the community, drawing maps to scale—these are only a fraction of the problems that arose. Individual, small-group, and class concerns all had their place, through activities during the core program and through special periods in the afternoon. Both the core and service courses contributed to the general education of the students while, at the same time, they provided for special needs. The extent and nature of these contributions to balanced growth varied with the core's emphasis on general education and the special periods on individual needs.

LEARNINGS HAD DEPTH AND MEANING FOR THE STUDENTS

Emphasis was not on the acquisition of circumscribed knowledge but rather on understanding the meanings of basic concepts and on building relationships among various experiences in dealing with persistent life problems. Increased knowledge and appreciation of the cultural heritage was a central goal which students attained in different degrees of depth. Optimum use of resources at one's own level was another objective which received considerable attention. Students worked at improving their basic reading skills, for example, by using materials appropriate to their level as the basis from which to grow. When students shared common resources, they used these in ways contributing to their own development while fulfilling common group needs.

INSTRUCTIONAL PROCEDURES VARIED WITH PURPOSES

Instructional methods used in the core, service courses, and laboratories varied with the specific purposes of each, and activities were selected on this basis. Some classes used lectures and discussions extensively because these procedures seemed most appropriate for the kinds of learnings desired. Other classes seldom used these procedures but planned activities stressing individual research and experimentation. Part of the planning processes involved the selection of the means for developing skills, attitudes, understandings, and values. Evaluation usually included a look at the effectiveness of the procedures used.

PLANNING AND GUIDANCE WERE AT THE HEART OF THE PROGRAM

Many kinds of planning took place at several levels: teacher–student, teacher–group, teacher–teacher, teacher–student–specialist, professional staff. Evaluation of individual and group progress was an integral part of the program essential for further planning and guidance.

To tell the whole story the activities of this year would have to be seen in relation to the full sweep of elementary and high school experiences. Teachers of these children in the lower grades built the understandings that were utilized and expanded here. Teachers of the next two high school years continued the process. Those to whom these students went for special activities opened other areas, provided opportunities to explore more deeply, and supplemented the activities of the core. All must be seen together and in the perspective of twelve years of growth to give the total picture.

14

A FIRST GRADE DEALS WITH PERSISTENT LIFE SITUATIONS

Earlier chapters have stressed the fact that persistent life situations are met in many ways—sometimes as problems meriting extended study, sometimes in day-to-day situations calling for exercise of present skills and knowledge, sometimes in experiences where the learner's maturity forestalls all but the simplest explanation. Sometimes a single problem is the focus; more frequently several are involved. The process of curriculum designing is one of living with learners, helping them use present generalizations in new situations, and expanding their insights. In a year's work with children, what opportunities will there be to develop competence in dealing with persistent life situations? Ways in which individuals might face specific situations are suggested in the charts on pages 169 to 321. But what might be the pattern in which such situations would arise for a primary class in the course of a school year?

The activities of a first grade are the focus of this chapter.* The discussion is organized around the major areas proposed in Chapter 6 for grouping persistent life situations—health, intellectual power, aesthetic appreciation and expression, and so on. Teachers of older groups will

* This chapter was contributed to and reviewed by Miss Ruth Green, Department of Education, University of Minnesota, Duluth Branch.

identify parallels in the experiences recurring in the lives of their learners. Those who teach older children of limited intellectual ability may find the description of the relatively more simple and less extensive activities of this first grade helpful in pointing the way to experiences of value to their groups. Here, as with the tenth grade, space does not permit a detailed description of the way in which the experiences were developed or of the teacher–child relationships which the story of the fifth grade in Chapter 12 tried to portray. The reader will need to supply these details from his own experiences with children.

The Children and Their School

Miss Miller's first grade is made up of thirty children. They live in a town of about five thousand population. Fifty miles away is the nearest large city. The community is a center for the truck farmers within a radius of about thirty miles. Branches of larger industries—a frozen food plant, a firm specializing in plastic novelties, a chemical concern—provide other occupations. Neither extreme poverty nor great wealth is present.

The school is one of four elementary schools. It is small, containing a kindergarten and one class in each of the eight grades. The building is new and well equipped. Classrooms are large. The first-grade room has ample space for the tables needed for thirty children, a workbench, a library corner, a clay table, a play corner, a piano, and adequate space for rhythms or for small groups to gather to read, to plan, or to carry out other group activities. Supplies and equipment are readily available but classrooms are not overstocked. A small petty-cash fund makes purchases possible as the work of the year reveals additional needs.

Classes are organized on a self-contained basis. One teacher who specializes in music and another who combines a strong science background with special preparation in home economics serve the elementary schools as consultants. Each school has a librarian and two schools share a nurse. The classroom teachers, like those in the school attended by the fifth grade described earlier, have complementary strengths. Miss Miller has sufficient musical ability to meet most of the needs of her group and, in addition, possesses considerable talent and interest in other areas of aesthetic expression—the dance, creative writing, and a variety of graphic art forms.

The children range in age from five and one-half to seven. Two children who transferred from other towns did not attend kindergarten. Two others are repeating the first grade. One was ill at intervals during most of the previous year and parents, teachers, and principal felt that a second year with the beginners would be a more satisfying experience than trying to fit into the second grade. The other child remaining with Miss Miller for a second year was one of the youngest children in the room a year ago, physically very small and with less than average co-ordination, shy with others, and apparently of less than average intellectual ability. Placement with the less mature children of the incoming first grade seemed likely to provide more security and a better learning situation for this child than would promotion to the second grade.

Within the class there is a typical range of ability and maturity. Throughout the year the usual problems of learning to get along with others, finding how to plan and how to fit into the plans of larger groups, learning to take responsibility for various aspects of one's living, were faced by individuals in differing degrees of seriousness. For several of the least mature, these remained major problems during the entire year.

The Way They Work

The nature of the children's classroom experiences and the ways in which they are developed reflect the same basic principles that guided the work of the older children whose activities have been described in the two preceding chapters. The adjustments are those called for by the immaturity of six-year-olds. "Units of work," or unified experiences, are developed from the daily life situations faced by the children. In general, these units are of shorter duration than those of older children. The activities undertaken in connection with them are somewhat less elaborate and are guided in more detail by the teacher. However, these children, like those in the upper grades, help to lay the plans for the units and work at times as small groups or individuals on aspects of special interest.

It is not uncommon for the class to return from time to time to the same problem or to related aspects of it. Over the entire year, for example, these children had recurring opportunities to explore the possibilities of language as a means of creative expression. Storytelling, listening to stories, and later reading them continued throughout the year. Sometimes creative expression through language was the focus of intensive activity as the group cooperated in preparing an illustrated book about community helpers or contributed to the school paper. At other times stories were secondary to other language experiences. The playhouse constructed in one corner of the classroom was another focus of recurring interest. At first all turned to problems of construction, decoration, and arrangement of furniture. The completed house was the center for dramatic play shared by the entire group for several weeks. Then it became a center of major interest mainly for the immature children, who continued to use it for many play activities. Later it was the chief stage property for group dramatizations—furnishings and decoration being adjusted to needs. For a few days in February it was rebuilt into a post office so that the class mail on St. Valentine's Day might be properly delivered.

Needs for fundamental skills develop, as they do at other ages, out of the ongoing activities of the children. Here, as at other levels, practice in skills becomes part of the program as the need is recognized by teacher and learners. With this class, as with older children, daily life situations provide much effective practice. Captions added to pictures, names signed to bulletin-board lists, notices put up for committees, announcements sent to other classes, stories placed in the paper—all these demanded ability both to read and to write. Situations arose daily requiring ability to explain directions to others, to make a point in a group, to tell about the object brought from home, to ask a question, to communicate for many other purposes. Planning, budgeting time, and using effective methods of work also came into the picture daily as the children decided how best to carry out activities, learned to keep equipment where others could find it, carried plans through to a conclusion, evaluated how effective plans had been.

The general organization of the program reflects the needs of younger children for rest and relaxation, for physical activity, for opportunity to learn to work with other children as individuals or in small groups, for time to complete a project at one's own pace. Normally, group planning was the last activity of the day. This meant that children arrived in the morning knowing what they were going to do and needing only a brief conference with Miss Miller to get started.

The schedule for a typical day might be as follows:

8:40– 9:00 Arrival of children, outdoor clothing put away, informal "socializing" or work responsibilities (collecting lunch money, caring for plants and pets), brief check on plans for first work period.

9:00–10:00 Work period relating to a current interest or problem. (Time given to individual, to small-group, and to total-class work varies with the problem at hand and the attention span of individuals. The total class may be exploring interests in the construction project near by; groups may be working on preparations for a party, with invitations, favors, shopping lists, decorations, or other necessary items being made or assembled. There is provision for individual interests—painting, clay work, reading—as group responsibilities are completed. Miss Miller may recognize that several children are

	ready for some definite instruction on a word-recognition skill, the improving of manuscript skills, or review of some earlier material, and may gather this group together and work with them for as long as is necessary or profitable.)
10:00–11:00	Midmorning lunch, rest, and active play. (Rest may include lying on small rugs on the floor, sitting quietly listening to phonograph or piano music or the singing of the teacher, playing with puzzles, or some other individual quiet activity. Active play may include informal games and rhythmic activities.)
11:00–11:45	Activities relating to fundamental skills. (Varied experiences with reading, number, and language skills—"news," storytelling, dictating and reading stories for the school paper, reading simple stories in books, working on number skills.)
11:45–12:45	Lunch.
12:45– 1:45	Work period. (Similar to one in the morning—at times a continuation of work begun in the morning, more often exploration of a second area of interest.)
1:45– 2:00	Break for story or game.
2:00– 3:00	Individual or group work in creative expression. (Singing, using musical instruments, painting, simple dramatizations, puppet plays, hearing stories on phonograph records.)
3:00– 3:30	Sharing work accomplished, planning for tomorrow.

Throughout the day children are encouraged to be independent in securing and putting away materials, books, and other articles. They are taught to think through problems and plans as a group, in small groups, or individually. Miss Miller is far from a bystander, but neither does she dominate; rather, she enters actively into all plans in a leadership role. She assists children in solving their own problems and offers help and suggestions as needed. She frequently introduces a unit of work, knowing from her previous work with the group that they are ready for it, that it meets a need, and that the interest of the group can be counted on. Her guidance is necessary to insure that all have a chance to participate, that all—even minority—suggestions are received and considered, that interests and thinking are widened and extended. The schedule of work for the day is flexible in terms of the developing needs of the group.

Contacts with other parts of the school and with the community are as numerous for these children as they were for the two classes described in preceding chapters. They wrote for the school paper, managed the Lost-and-Found Department of the school, shared in assembly programs, visited other classes and, in turn, were hosts to other classes, purchased supplies in the school store, shared in keeping the halls attractive by taking charge of the bulletin board outside their classroom. Parents came to help with school activities. Children brought objects from home to share with their friends. A new building under construction a block away, the community clean-up week, the articles in the nearby store—all became sources of experience.

Experiences Through Which Persistent Life Situations Were Faced

What were the everyday concerns of the children in this first grade? What were some of the experiences through which they faced the persistent problems of living? With younger children the problem of giving a picture of the year's program is complicated by the wide variety of activities undertaken for relatively short periods of time, by the number of different concrete experiences provided for individuals and groups within the framework of one activity, and by the amount of concomitant teaching in the course of day-to-day living which makes a fundamental contribution to growth. These are factors which the reader is asked to keep in mind in considering the pages which follow.

HEALTH NEEDS ARE PART OF MANY EXPERIENCES

As the children carried on accepted health practices and were given simple explanations of the "why" behind these practices, understandings and competencies basic to maintaining good health were built. They learned to relax during rest periods. The midmorning lunch helped to develop understandings related both to social behavior and to health. Problems of toileting, of washing hands, of drying them well to prevent chapping, were prominent at the beginning of the year. The box of paper tissues on Miss Miller's desk supported understandings of the purposes served by a handkerchief.

Necessary adjustments in classroom facilities to protect health led to still other understandings. Although the ventilation and heating were centrally controlled, each teacher watched the temperature of his own room. Many children were interested. By January several had learned to read the classroom thermometer and became self-appointed guardians of the room temperature. The children were encouraged to share in decisions as to when lights in the classroom needed to be turned on. When the library corner was arranged they helped to decide where the chairs should be placed so as to have the best light on books. How to sit when writing, when to pull shades to protect eyes from the glare of sunlight, how to hold books when reading—all became situations that had to be met. Finding chairs and tables of the right size for the very tall and the very small people added other learnings.

Changes of weather brought questions of what clothing to wear, the need to remove wet clothing in the classroom, why rubbers are necessary, how to keep hands from chapping when playing in the snow. During inclement weather teacher and children together decided whether play periods should be out of doors. Games appropriate for very warm and very cold days were considered in midwinter and again in the late spring.

Safety precautions led to other understandings. Individuals learned to use scissors, hammers, and other tools properly. How to hold these articles when walking and where they might be most safely stored were a part of learning to live together in the first grade. How to carry chairs safely was another item. The class took time to find what precautions should be observed in using playground slides, jungle gyms, and other equipment. Near the time of the first fire drill the children discussed fire-drill regulations and why it is necessary to have fixed rules at such times. Traffic on the street corners around the school was heavy enough to demand a safety patrol and members of this patrol came to the first grade to discuss their responsibilities and to explain the need for cooperation. The children also talked about precautions they should take on unpatrolled streets. The classroom was equipped with a hot plate on which the children did some cooking from time to time. As they helped with this they learned about the problems of handling hot pans and of placing such articles safely where they cannot be tipped over. Day-to-day events —a glass jar broken, someone running down the stairs, a bumped head caused by too many people at the drinking fountain, skinned knees as two children racing down the hall tripped each other, ice in snowballs— gave many other opportunities for both direct and incidental teaching of safety measures.

Other learnings grew out of experiences associated with the nurse's office. Children who had been ill reported there on returning to school and children who did not feel well or were thought not to be up to par were sent to the nurse to be checked. In their discussion of the reasons for this the children were unable to understand much of the scientific background of disease control, but they did acquire some concept of the need to protect others from disease and of the importance of taking prompt precautions when illness occurred. Why one should not come to school with a bad cold was a recurring question as children found themselves kept at home, away from the activities they enjoyed so much. A number of cases of chicken pox led to understandings of what it means to have a disease spread and the need for isolation. The annual medical examination, first aid for cuts and scratches, inoculations of a number of the group, dental appointments at the school or with family dentists, opened other avenues of exploration.

Several children with special difficulties were the sources of other health experiences meaningful both for the individuals involved and for the group. Three wore glasses and needed to be reminded of them from time to time. Two, on doctors' recommendations, took milk at midmorning lunch. One with an allergy could not handle the pet guinea pig. Another could participate in only a limited amount of physical activity. The children discussed these difficulties, not to gain much knowledge about the reasons for them, but to secure general understanding of the need to adjust to and provide for individual health needs.

In addition to the experiences just described, and many others occurring from day to day, a number of more extended activities made direct contributions to health understandings. Several times during the year the children cooked their lunch at school in a cooperative venture that reached far beyond the health field in the experiences it provided. The preplanning included some discussion of the kinds of food which make up a good meal, why it is important to take a little of everything, what size of helping one should take if not sure he will like a certain food, what is needed by way of washing food and keeping it clean until it is served. The meals themselves added to previous understandings growing out of midmorning lunch experiences—how fast to eat, what to talk about, whether to ask for second helpings, what to do if one does not like the taste of certain foods.

Caring for Josephine, the pet guinea pig, added to health understandings as well as to ability to care for animal life. Her diet needed balance, too, and the children, Miss Miller, and Mr. Banks, the science consultant, studied what would be necessary. A menu was developed and posted above her cage. The individuals responsible for her care followed it carefully. The children also discussed the needs of their various pets at home for food, water, baths, and adequate living quarters. *Our Pet Book* resulted, containing a picture of each pet and the child's account of the care it was given. Josephine's life and care, written as a group effort, occupied the first pages.

Prior to the annual health examination another short study was undertaken to find out what the doctor did, what his instruments were for, what the examination consisted of, how the nurse helped, why parents were asked to be present if they could.

Provisions for growth in ability to meet emotional and social needs, another aspect of health, were so much a part of every activity and involved such sensitivity to the complex needs of individuals that brief descriptions can give very little of the picture. Many of the experiences that helped to build these understandings also contributed directly to more effective person-to-person relationships, to becoming a cooperative group member, and to building bases for moral choice and responsibility. Billy, at the beginning of the year, had no apparent way of achieving status in the group except by shoving or hitting. Gradually he was helped to find ways of using his artistic talent and gift for construction to achieve the same end. Shy little Janie was helped step by step to contribute to the group and to find friends who took her into their activities without overwhelming or dominating her unduly.

Special care was taken to help Marian, who wept when things went wrong, learn how to analyze the difficulty and make more constructive plans as to what to do next. Andy, who threw things when disappointed, was also helped to learn how to take more effective steps in getting what he wanted and to see why individual interests must at times give way to the plans of the group.

Paul, who tended to dominate most group enterprises at the beginning of the year, gradually learned to adapt his plans to the desires of others through repeated experiences in which he was helped to think through the reasons why other children were beginning to refuse to work with him. John, who was extremely doubtful of his ability to succeed in any new area, was given freedom to explore a variety of media in situations in which there were few obvious standards against which he could find his work wanting. Step by step he was encouraged to take on more difficult group responsibilities after he had succeeded in simple ones.

Miss Miller and Joanne's mother worked together to increase her independence. Miss Miller helped her learn how to put on her own clothing and care for her own materials at school. Joanne's mother worked on providing needed affection without answering unnecessary appeals for such help at home. With Miss Miller's help, several parents made provision for wider play experiences with other children after school hours, or for opportunities to take special friends home for meals or for play over the week end. Some mothers whose children were finding the problems of learning to play with the group most difficult formed a special play group for out-of-school hours.

Children for whom certain aspects of the classroom activities were difficult were helped to discover other ways through which they could make contributions to the group. All were given help in overcoming weaknesses as these were identified, and all were encouraged to explore a variety of media to find satisfying means of self-expression. All learned much about how to carry out plans independently, to take responsibility, to make choices which considered others, and to overcome disappointments by planning how best to achieve purposes through other means. These are problems on which many years of consistent help are necessary. Questions of how best to meet social and emotional needs are not solved as simply and as quickly as these illustrations might seem to imply.

INTELLECTUAL POWERS DEVELOP FROM THE DEMANDS OF REAL SITUATIONS

It is not possible to describe in the space available the wealth of experiences calling for growth in ability to make ideas clear, to understand the ideas of others, to deal with quantitative relationships, to use effective methods of work. In this section only a few of the year's activities are described to show some of the fundamental skills that were needed and the kind of learnings which resulted.

In the beginning, as was true throughout the year, the children varied greatly in the techniques and skills which they possessed and the steps for which they were ready. Two or three children were already able to read simple preprimer materials and a like number, at the other end of the scale, gave no evidence of interest in or ability to work with any printed matter. In language skills, several expressed themselves clearly and without difficulty. Janie, partly because she found any contribution to a group difficult, relied mainly on a single "yes" or "no." About a third could count accurately into the twenties, several could tell time, and reactions in daily activities showed some well-developed concepts of quantity and of relationships such as "less than," "more than," "half of," "as much as." Two or three had acquired the names of some of the smaller numbers but showed very little understanding either of the quantities they represented or of what counting really meant.

Work habits were equally varied. Several were already very competent in deciding what they wanted to do, in helping to clarify group purposes, foreseeing needed steps, and keeping them in mind over several days with few additional reminders. Others found it extremely difficult to stay by an agreed-upon plan for as much as fifteen minutes. Some were accustomed to getting their own materials and to moving ahead on a project with a minimum of supervision. Others, in spite of their kindergarten experience, were at Miss Miller's side at almost every turn.

In the early fall, one of Miss Miller's primary concerns was to develop independent work habits and feelings of at-homeness in the room, while she gave herself opportunity to become better acquainted with the needs and capacities of individuals. She knew that habits of independent work would be important when the time came for giving individuals or small groups special help with skills. The program gave each child opportunity to become part of the group and to learn his way around the room. One of the group's activities during the first few weeks was to explore the classroom. Lockers were labeled and decisions made about what to keep in them. The easel, the workbench, the picture-book shelf were examined. The children discovered the blocks with which they later constructed their playhouse and learned how to use them. They decided where to set up a play corner with the dolls and toy furniture. They made tentative decisions as to where it would be best to keep certain supplies and discussed how many children could work at once at the clay table, the easel, and the workbench. Miss Miller gave much guidance for there were many points at which beginners could not foresee complications.

Over the first six weeks, the children gradually renewed acquaintance with the rest of the school. They talked with the principal, the secretary, the custodian, the special teachers, and some of the teachers and children of other grades. They again learned to find their way to the playground, the drinking fountain, the lavatories. They found out about the boiler room, the gymnasium, the auditorium, the science and home economics laboratories. The librarian told them stories and showed them books. The superintendent of schools dropped by to chat and explained a little about his work.

One of the first activities calling for extended planning came when the children talked about what they had done during the summer. Souvenirs brought by various children who had been away from home over the summer provided a source of much conversation and an interesting exhibit corner—shells from the seashore, snapshots taken on a trip, an Indian drum, a bit of petrified wood, some stones from the neighboring lake, a snakeskin found when on a picnic. Then, to get better acquainted, they planned a class bulletin board. Individuals brought in snapshots and Miss Miller helped to write captions. "This is Ricky's dog. His name is Tipsy." "Janie learned to swim." "Bill lives here."

Another early class activity involved constructing and furnishing the playhouse. The children included such satisfying details as wallpaper, curtains, small window boxes containing real geranium plants, a mailbox, and a doorbell which really rang, thanks to a fourth-grader's knowledge of dry-cell batteries. There were other types of group experiences suggested and guided by Miss Miller—singing, listening to stories, experimenting with rhythms, playing games. The children were encouraged to explore the various opportunities in the room for individual activities—the easel, the workbench, crayons and paper, the blackboard, clay, blocks, and toys. In addition, the problem of opening the Lost-and-Found Department, which was their special all-school community service, was soon raised.

This combination of individual and group activities, rich in its opportunities to develop skills in group living and effective independent work habits, was the setting in which Miss Miller began to plan definite work on the development of writing, reading, speaking, and number skills. The opportunities were legion. Reading, writing, speaking, and listening were inextricably interrelated in the children's experiences. Oral expression was an integral part of every activity. Learning how to take part in a discussion, to present ideas to others, to describe an experience, to make an announcement, to use music and other art forms to supplement language, are aspects of oral expression obviously demanded by a program such as this. Miss Miller encouraged informal conversation and frequently planned a period in the early part of the morning to share home activities and interesting objects before the regular work of the day began. Storytelling was an activity enjoyed by many from the beginning. Miss Miller often gathered together small groups for this purpose. Later in the year, the children engaged in many kinds of creative oral expression when they developed a puppet theater. They also enjoyed many experiences in informal dramatization, from dramatic play in their playhouse to dramatizing their favorite stories.

From the first they needed written records—captions to their pictures, names on lockers, committee rosters, plans, reminders of special events, lists of classroom responsibilities. Soon bulletin boards and walls displayed a variety of functional records dictated by the children and written in manuscript by Miss Miller.

The first direct reading instruction came as the children and Miss Miller turned to these records for help. Several children could recognize a number of words from the start. These youngsters, and one or two others who showed rapidly growing ability to identify words, made up the first group Miss Miller gathered together for special reading instruction. Other groups were soon established. By November nearly two-thirds of the class were receiving regular help in reading. The others still did not demonstrate the skills in independent word recognition that indicated readiness for successful reading. However, these youngsters were in a classroom where reading was an integral part of daily living and shared in many activities in which there were opportunities and encouragement to work with words. By February only two very immature children had made no progress in learning to read.

Part of the help in reading came through small groups that met rather regularly. The period from 11:00 o'clock on, indicated in the schedule given earlier, was usually devoted to work in skill development. Reading activities were included in this time. Parts of the early morning and the early afternoon periods also served frequently for this purpose. Miss Miller had in the classroom the beginning books from a number of series of basal readers. She also had many interesting, simple library books and supplementary readers. However, work with these materials was only a small part of the total classroom reading experiences. Whenever the children used records or found it necessary to communicate in writing they also faced needs and opportunities to read.

Whatever the nature of the reading experience, Miss Miller was guided by her understanding of the skills a good reader must acquire and the typical way in which these develop. She knew, for instance, that before any real progress can be made a child must have sufficient maturity and experience to be able to distinguish the general configuration of one word from that of another and she realized that some youngsters would come to her with this capacity while others would need many months to develop it. Miss Miller was aware of the importance of comprehension as a basic reading skill and realized that beginning readers needed to know how to use picture and context clues as an aid in understanding what they read. She recognized that to read independently one had to be able to work out the pronunciation of a word for oneself, but she also knew that the discovery of pronunciation elements is facilitated if youngsters have a stock of familiar words from which to make comparisons. She knew, too, that some children could acquire this stock of words rapidly and with a minimum of repetition, but that others had to meet the same words in many different settings before they could be remembered. She helped Peter, Mark, Billy, Joanne, Gary, and Curtis to use the orderly introduction of new words that the preprimers provided because this systematic approach suited them better, and gave them a kind of security. But John, Clancy, Barbara, and others were able, after a careful beginning, to use word-attack skills very effectively and to work out many new words independently. These children forged ahead into many types of reading materials.

With the wealth of reading experiences connected with daily activities, the children were building and using a reading vocabulary at a faster rate than the use of readers alone could achieve. Miss Miller continued to use a combination of readers, library books, and activity-connected reading material throughout the year. Word-analysis skills were taught as they were needed and could be used, and drills were geared specifically to recognized deficiencies of individuals as and when they could be of most help to them. Much reading was done for specific information and understanding in connection with units of work; recreational reading was continuously encouraged.

Miss Miller kept careful records of each child's progress in the skills. For her record of reading progress, for example, she included material read, pages, errors or difficulties, help or drill needed, and notes. "Notes" might include such remarks as: "Enjoyed humor in the story; craves more excitement—look for this type for him," or "Read smoothly today and understood it. Seems to have very little difficulty at this level."

Writing skills also grew out of and contributed to ongoing classroom activities. The writing that took place in connection with building the playhouse provides an illustration. Letters were at first dictated by the children and written in manuscript by Miss Miller. These oral experiences were definite preludes to their own written expression. The following letter written to the custodian is an example of such dictated letters:

October 1

Dear Mr. Powell,

We are building a playhouse.

The hinges are too hard to put on.

Can you help us?

We need to borrow a drill for

the screw holes, too.

Do you have one?

Your friends,
The First Grade

Later a few of the children were able to copy such a letter from the blackboard where Miss Miller had written it as it was dictated.

Requests, thanks, and questions were the reasons for numerous other letters. Lists of committees were posted on the bulletin board and the children wrote their own names under their choices. Captions under pictures collected for ideas were supplied by Miss Miller and the children.

The first actual practice in writing was done with the children's own names. While kindergarten experiences had developed some skill in this for many of the children, the letters were not too well formed. By the time the playhouse was completed, all the first-graders could write their own names clearly in manuscript and most of them could write more than this. Some had acquired a good deal of skill. The class decided to invite their parents to see the playhouse and the invitation was composed. It was decided that each child would write an invitation to his parents. Some could write, others simply copied from the model.

Dear Mother,
Please visit school.
Visit on Wednesday at two.
You will see our playhouse.
Love,

The children "addressed" the envelopes with the single word "Mother." Everyone signed his own name and also put his name in the return-address corner of the envelope. There was pride in even this small amount of skill.

Later on, letters provided many occasions for additional learnings in this field. The children wrote to a mother thanking her for the plants provided for their playhouse, to other classes inviting them to attend a puppet play, to the librarian about planning a special story for them, to a second-grade child who read to them, to Miss Miller when she was home ill for a few days, to the fourth grade thanking them for the invitation to see their rabbit, to the sixth grade asking for help in making book covers, and to their mothers telling about a change in the school schedule.

As the year progressed, the children's activities involved increasing use of reading, writing, speaking, and listening. Contributions to the school newspaper, at first dictated by the children and written by the teacher, were later put on the blackboard, and copied by "reporters" who delivered them to the sixth-grade newspaper staff. By the end of the year several children could compose simple contributions of their own for the paper, needing only occasional help in the spelling of new words.

Plans for the day were recorded on the board and were read and checked by the group. A bulletin board for the children's use contained such reminders as: "Bring milk money tomorrow," or "Tomorrow and Friday are holidays." The responsibility for writing these notices was turned over to the children as soon as they were able to take it. Lists of purchases, permission slips, plans, and so on, were made for each trip taken by the group. Thank-you letters for favors by parents and other groups in the school were frequent. The reading of a recipe was necessary when cooking was to be done.

A class scrapbook was kept, containing snapshots of the group engaged in various activities with a caption below each picture, stories and accounts of trips and experiences composed by the children, and clippings from the school and city papers of special interest to this group. Letters to the group from classmates and friends were also saved and inserted in the scrapbook. By the end of the year the scrapbook was a valuable log of first-grade activities and could be read by most of the group. The children also helped to dictate reports of special activities they wanted to share with their parents. Some of these were fastened together to form large books and placed on an easel where all could read.

Storytelling, which in the early fall was a valuable oral language experience, also served to encourage reading skills. Small books, typed by Miss Miller and illustrated by the children, were built from the stories children dictated. In the beginning these dictated stories were often read to the group. Later in the year many children were able to read them for themselves. From time to time simplified versions of a story, mimeographed and stapled into small separate covers, were the basis of group reading activities.

Spelling problems arose with increasing frequency as reading and writing skills developed. They were handled in several ways—all calculated to develop the attitude that correct spelling is important. In the beginning the writing job often involved copying correctly a letter or a notice which Miss Miller had written from the children's dictation. When the writing was confined to a special topic, a list of important words was posted. Typically, the bulletin board had one or more such lists—Winter Words, Words for Get-Well Cards, Lost-and-Found Words, Words About Our Tree. In addition, toward the middle of the year when independent reading and writing skills were further developed, Miss Miller set aside one card holder in which she began to keep an alphabetized set of flash cards containing words frequently used.

The children also learned to look for necessary words in the labels on their exhibits and in their classroom records. Miss Miller was always available to write words on request for individuals. As the children developed increased skill in analyzing words for themselves, many tried to apply the same principles in spelling. This led to some interesting games with rhymes and informal discussions of sounds. While definite spelling lessons were not part of the experiences of this first grade, Miss Miller did a great deal to develop a "spelling conscience" on the part of all children and to make them aware of the basic interrelationships between spelling, reading, and the sounds of words. This was the spelling readiness that made for successful experiences in the second grade.

In the same way daily experiences required additional skill in using numbers. Individuals, small groups, or the entire class worked to develop necessary skills. Each day the children listed and then counted the names of absentees for the report sent to the office. Chairs for committees had to be counted to be sure of the right number. Concepts developed, such as: How many more do we need? We have too many—

how many? Three on this side and four on that side—how many do we have? Is it enough? Birthdays and the placing of candles required similar mathematical operations. Curtains for the playhouse called for people who could measure. Children responsible for getting paper for groups working at their tables needed to know how many pieces to bring. And they needed to be able to tell the time. Planning for a party demanded use of measuring for the cooking experiences, shopping with real money for supplies, making and counting invitations, favors, napkins, place cards; counting and arranging chairs for guests.

Sometimes mathematical solutions were used to resolve disputes. When Frances and Sophie were allowed by the group to eat the leftover frosting, an argument soon arose.

"Sophie, that's not fair, you're taking more than half!"

"I am not! I have a bowl and you have a bowl."

"But there's *more* in your bowl. Trade, then."

"There is not!"

Barbara came to the rescue with measuring spoons and the two girls measured two teaspoons each.

When the librarian invited the first grade to arrange the bulletin board for February, much planning went into the job. Peter and Anton, armed with yardsticks, went to the library to measure the space available and to write the figures on a diagram. After they returned to their own room, a roll of wide, glossy shelf paper was carefully measured, cut, and spliced to provide background. On this shiny surface, three children did the largest finger painting they had yet experienced, covering the entire space. When this was dry the committee took the paper to the library, fastened it (with the librarian's help) in the right place, and arranged on it the new book jackets the librarian had given them. The caption, "New Books Received This Month," was done in Al's best manuscript with a large crayon. Many had helped, but Peter and Anton pointed out, "It sure would have been awful if it didn't fit!"

As with reading skills, number concepts and skills were the focus of direct instruction. Miss Miller frequently gathered together groups of about the same level of ability to participate in a variety of number activities. Each had his own box of tongue depressors, buttons, and other objects for number groupings. Satisfactions were derived from using these objects to develop number relationships. Small groups also worked together learning to count the lunch money and discovering the number relationships in other classroom problems. Here, as with reading, Miss Miller was guided by her knowledge of the ways in which children develop number relationships and her insight into the types of understandings needed at this age level.

That the development of intellectual power is a complex process and that experiences tend to require a combination of skills—reading, writing, speaking, listening, computing, planning—are illustrated in the first grade's special all-school service, the Lost-and-Found Department. Many skills were involved in addition to the obvious benefits of serving others. Careful group planning was needed at all points—to decide what information should be secured from the child who had lost an article and from the child finding an article, where to keep materials, how to label articles, how to keep paired articles together, who should take charge and for how long, how to prepare an inventory for the incoming managers. Plans for securing essential information resulted in the mimeographing of simple card forms. These were developed by the children and the stencil was typed by Miss Miller.

LOST

What:

Where:

Date Lost:

Lost by:

FOUND

What:

Where:

Date Found:

Found by:

Claimed by:

These cards were filled in by children who lost or found the articles. However, the first-graders gradually learned to read them and by the end of the year were able to tally the results of the year's work from the cards.

It was decided that four children would have major responsibility for the department for a week. Fridays brought the need for an inventory before the department was turned over to new managers. This meant being able to count and to read the inventory. Early in the year items were tallied under the name of the object beside which was pasted a picture to help nonreaders identify it. The managers did the counting and everybody checked the tally. As they grew more adept with numbers the numerals were substituted. By spring the children wrote their own inventory on large sheets of paper. A typical inventory posted in the corner for the new managers read as follows:

FRIDAY INVENTORY

3 pairs of mittens
4 odd mittens
2 sweaters
2 caps
3 hair bows
1 knife

Need for publicity arose when lost articles were not claimed. This led to the writing of weekly notices for the bulletin board.

We have six pairs of mittens
and three odd ones.
Come to Room 101 and
claim your lost things.
The First Grade

Other notices included one announcing the hours when the department was open, signs to show the helpers where to place objects, notices to the Parent–Teacher Association about objects found. As the year went on these notices became longer as the articles were more completely described. Regularly, during the last half of the year, notices were sent to the school paper.

At Christmas, and again in the spring, the children faced the problem of what to do with unclaimed articles. At Christmas the collection was given to the Junior Red Cross for distribution to the needy. The group decided to have the articles dry-cleaned first, and when the bill came, with Miss Miller's help they calculated how much each child had to bring from home as his contribution. Collecting eight cents apiece and counting it to be certain that the sum was correct added other experiences with numbers. In the spring the class disposed of unclaimed articles through a sale. This involved setting a price for each article (older children who were clerks in the school store came in to help), making signs, sending announcements to other rooms, preparing price tags, making change at the sale, counting proceeds, and many other activities. The money from the sale was used to purchase new books for the school library.

Cooking lunch at school is another illustration of the demands of an ongoing activity for the effective use of many skills. Plans for the first lunch included stew as the main course. Lists of the necessary vegetables for the stew were prepared and the amounts determined. This was early in the year and some of the calculations were done through the grouping of tallies—the children who were most efficient checking the process. Some of the problems to be solved were

> One pound of meat will serve six people.
> How many pounds will we need?
>
> We need one small potato for each of us.
> How many potatoes do we need?
>
> We will need about one-half carrot for each of us.
> How many carrots do we need?
> (This was done by having the children stand
> in pairs and counting the twos.)

Similar processes were used to figure how many loaves of bread, how much butter, how much milk. With their completed list the children set out for the nearby store in order to make their purchases. The school petty-cash fund allowed them to pay the bill and make change. The children then figured the cost per child—Miss Miller doing the calculating—and each brought the necessary amount from home.

Letters written to parents asking permission to stay to lunch, plans for various committees, the recipe for the stew, the list of vegetables needed, the final report of the lunch activity so that they would have a plan if they did it again, were among the significant written language experiences. Oral expression was required at all points. The planning involved in order to purchase the necessary articles, to cook the food, to measure and make place mats, to have all committees complete their work so that everything was ready at the proper time, need not be elaborated upon here.

From every activity undertaken during the year came the need to develop increased competence in the use of intellectual powers. Miss Miller capitalized upon each situation faced and planned other opportunities to help her group become aware of similar needs. She taught through the situations which arose in classroom, school, and community, and provided for supplementary planned help as the situation faced and the maturity of the children showed that they required it. Both group and individual efforts had a place.

RESPONSIBILITY FOR MORAL CHOICES IS AN EVER-PRESENT PROBLEM

In the daily problems of living and working together there were many demands for ability to make moral choices. Sharing materials with others, sharing space to work, taking turns in discussion, being willing to do one's share of the less interesting jobs, deciding what to do with the crackers left over at midmorning lunch, and countless other situations called for decisions involving the modifying of personal desires for the sake of others. These were discussed and worked through by actual experience when the occasion arose. Billy, who did not want to relinquish his place at the easel, was helped to see that if others acted the same way he could not get to the workbench when he wanted to. Alice collected the crayons being used by several other children "in case she needed them" and found that her cherished plan to get the pictures hung in the playhouse could not be carried out because others lacked the colors they needed to finish the wallpaper. Bobby, holding three pieces of cloth because he could not decide which he liked best for his puppet, was helped to make the decision so that others could enjoy using the material he liked so much. Janie relinquished an opportunity to take the cracker left over on the lunch plate because "I had the extra one yesterday and it was so good somebody else should have it today." Ruth was helped to see the difference between taking an apple from the fruit basket at home and taking the apple which one of the children had brought for her midmorning lunch. Dwight was helped to return to its owner the knife which had found its way into his pocket.

Writing to children who were ill, making gifts for parents, planning what would be the best entertainment for other children, deciding when to write a thank-you letter, discussing the thoughtfulness of a note written to them, discovering what services others in the school did for them, planning how to take part in an all-school clean-up campaign, discussing how to run their Lost-and-Found Department to give good service to others in the school, added other understandings of the importance of thoughtfulness in human relationships. Here again actual experience did much of the teaching. The music specialist told them how much she enjoyed their note. The child who was ill told what fun the letters had been. The school paper commended them on the effectiveness of their

Lost-and-Found Department. Miss Miller helped them analyze the experiences and drew upon them when similar situations arose.

From the first, individuals were helped to see the importance of integrity in human relationships. Carelessness in putting materials back where they belonged worked hardships on other people. Not carrying out one's responsibility for cleaning his part of the clay table held up everybody else when a favorite record was to be played. Many materials were jointly owned, but if one wished to use those which really belonged to someone else it was necessary to ask him so that he would know where they were. And one tried to remember to return what was borrowed. The rules of the game cannot be changed in the middle; it may help to win this time, but next time it may work against one. Disputes were "talked out," not settled by fists. Those which did arise were settled so that agreed-upon principles were made clear. What was the plan? Had both parties agreed to it? Why did the objectors think it should be changed? Was there anything to support their case? In the light of all the evidence what is the agreement now? What does that mean in terms of the responsibility of each individual?

Potential difficulties were often turned to positive social learnings. John, Clark, Curtis, and Gary had constructed what appeared to be a barricade across the alcove of the room. This served as a challenge to a group of girls. After some loud vocal disputes in which they were told emphatically to "Stay out!," the girls pushed through the barricade, upsetting part of the construction. Miss Miller called the entire group together.

"Maybe the boys could tell us what the difficulty is."

"We don't want the girls going through there."

"Why?"

"We are the bridgekeepers and they pushed the bridge down."

"They spoiled your game?"

"Yes. We don't want the girls going through there."

"What kind of bridge is it? Explain it to us."

"It's the bridge going over the bay."

"Has anyone been over that bridge? What do you do when you cross?"

"You—the cars—go by the men."

"What are the men there for?"

"To take money."

"Oh. It's a toll bridge. And you boys are those men?"

"Yes, and the girls pushed through."

"Without paying toll?"

"Yes. Say, that's right, we have to have toll."

"How do people decide whose turn it is to pay toll and cross the bridge? Vicki, what did your father do when he drove up on the bridge?"

"He had to get in the line. And the line was stopped 'cause a boat was going through and I got out and watched and . . ."

"I did that, too." "I always get out, too." "So do I." "I do, too . . ." (Many were ready and did contribute.)

"Then your father drove up, paid his toll, and went on across?"

"Yes. You have to stay in line."

"Will these ideas help your game, boys?"

"Yes. The girls can come through if they pay toll, and they *have to line up*!"

The toll bridge operated smoothly for several days. Some children made paper money because this seemed to add flavor to the drama. Although sections of the superstructure had to be rebuilt from time to time, willing construction crews did so good-naturedly, and there was respect for the property of others. For this activity to contribute to positive learning, the group needed Miss Miller's help at a crucial moment. She didn't deceive herself into thinking that this had settled disputes for all time, but she did believe that this and many subsequent experiences of talking over problems could be a vital part of learning to live and work together.

Teasing children who were awkward in certain activities, applying thoughtless epithets to other racial, religious, and socio-economic groups, calling attention to personal differences, became the center of other teaching experiences. "Her dad's just a janitor," "You're a wop" (used merely as a phrase to express exasperation with another child), "He's too slow to play with us," and other such expressions were dealt with as the occasion arose. The general tenor of the help given was that people should not be judged by any one characteristic alone. All the things they can do well must be remembered; they are liked because of what they are, not because of where their families were born or the church to which they go.

Questions of obligations to constituted authority were also numerous. Fire-drill rules and the regulations of the safety patrol could be discussed, but had to be observed. Other classes were trying to work as the first grade went to play. When they had agreed to follow the student council's request for soft voices in the hall it was necessary to abide by this agreement. Miss Miller's warning that too many people at the easel would result in spilling the paint was heeded only after those involved had used precious story time to clean it up. Group decisions as to the use of the playhouse, what activities were best during free reading time, what share each should take in the Lost-and-Found Department, assumed the status of definite regulations lived up to by both teacher and children. A group has a right to decide how its members can best live together, but if the decisions are to be of any help people must follow them—this was the conclusion which the children gradually learned to live by even though they did not express it in such adult terms. They also learned that their small group was part of a larger community and began to recognize that there are times when they could not make their own regulations.

Church schools and churches supplied many experiences of a religious nature. In the school celebrations of Thanksgiving, of Christmas, and of Easter, in grace before the midmorning lunch, in talking about what they did in their religious schools, these children were helped to acquire simple understandings of the meaning of these practices and to relate them to the teachings of families and churches.

RESOURCES FOR AESTHETIC EXPRESSION AND APPRECIATION PROVIDE VARIED SATISFACTIONS

Many sources of aesthetic expression and satisfaction were found in the normal experiences of everyday living. Helping care for the classroom built satisfactions in their daily work. The children learned how to keep their own lockers and tables in order. They took pride in attractively arranged lunch tables. They looked with satisfaction on the clean floors around their tables when they left for the night, on the polish of the clay table when they finished cleaning up, on the attractive colors when the books on the library table were arranged. Caring for plants, sharing in decisions as to what plants would be most suitable for their room, helping arrange the bulletin board, and making many of the pictures that went on it and around the walls of the room, all added to growing consciousness of the satisfactions which can come from pleasant surroundings.

Satisfactions in dress and appearance were built in the same way when bright-colored sweaters were admired, clean hands for lunch commented on, combed hair given recognition. Early in the year the children discussed the necessity for hanging wraps carefully and for wearing aprons or smocks when painting or working in clay. Without making distinctions that economic differences could not overcome, Miss Miller helped the children take pride in items of personal appearance that were within the reach of all.

The playhouse added other experiences in providing attractive surroundings. Wallpaper was needed, the class decided, and accordingly a group started to work with long rolls of wrapping paper. The curtains were attractive when finished but not clean, neither was the dress of their favorite doll. Another small group took over here and the freshly laundered articles were admired by all. Furniture for the house was dingy from a year of use. With Miss Miller's help the children repainted it. Arranging the furniture after it was painted, deciding what pictures were needed for the house, and similar details all made their contribution to growth in aesthetic appreciation.

Many resources for aesthetic expression were available in the room. It was equipped with a small piano, two easels, a linoleum floor pad where children could paint, a clay table, a workbench, and the usual supply of paper, crayons, wool, scraps of cloth, beads, and the like. The children were encouraged to explore these media, given instruction on how to use them, and provided ample time to work with them. At times this was individual work and at others a group enterprise. When the playhouse was being furnished, many of the creative efforts were produced for that purpose. When the class began to make puppets and to build their puppet theater, many of the media were used in this enterprise in which all members of the class shared.

The puppets provided many sources of satisfaction. "Bring anything you think will help us make one," they were told. "What things might look like a head?" "What might we use for arms?" The resulting puppets, constructed as each child used the materials he thought were most interesting, were unquestionably products of creative imagination. Producing their puppet plays drew upon a variety of media. Conversation was supplemented by narration, by group songs, by records which were deemed appropriate, by choral speaking where several voices giving their favorite poems seemed needed for added effect.

Christmas gifts, Easter gifts, birthdays, valentines, led to other experiences. The variety of products that came from the workbench, the clay table, the easel, or were manufactured from wool, bits of cloth, beads, paper, and other resources available in the room were numerous.

Musical experiences came almost daily as the children sang favorite songs, experimented with rhythmic activities, set some of their own poems to music, listened to records. The piano remained in the room throughout the year, but the record player was shared with the second grade. *Peter and the Wolf* was one of the favorite records and a source of continued pleasure. The music specialist loaned the children part of her collection of drums, chimes, bells, and other percussion instruments for about six weeks. This was an exciting new area. They learned to distinguish the sounds, to create their own tunes, to listen for rhythms, to create and follow them. Great satisfaction came as they found how they could use the percussion instruments to supplement the piano, and after

dren how much she had enjoyed these gifts and how she had shared them with the other children in her hospital room, the group decided to expand their ideas and to make gifts for other children in the hospital. They continued to do this from time to time until the end of the year. Libby's own contribution was patterned after a commercial game her brother had bought her. It was a fishing game, using a dowel stick to which a string was tied with a magnet for the hook. The children all joined in creating a large school of magnificent fish, all with paper-clip noses. Thank-you letters from hospital officials, from children in the hospital, and from some of their parents were welcome additions to the class scrapbook.

During the year, as they entertained parents and children from other classes, and discussed plans for their parties, these first-graders grew in another area of person-to-person relations—in ability to choose appropriate activities and to act as hosts and hostesses. The parties were very informal; but discussion ahead of time centered around questions of what the guests would most like to do, and what responsibilities individuals should undertake to make the gathering a pleasant one. After the occasion was over, the group considered what would make the next venture still more enjoyable. Thank-you notes to other classes and to individuals who had helped them, as well as some group time after Christmas spent on writing notes acknowledging gifts, added to these understandings.

Experiences in working together, in consulting the special teachers, and in getting assistance from time to time from the school custodian, helped to develop techniques of establishing effective working relationships with others. "He's busy, too. Shouldn't we write him a note asking when he might be able to help us rather than go down and ask him to come right now?" "Have we all of our questions listed to send to Miss Varney so that she will know exactly what kind of help we want?" "Which one could do that the very best for us?" "It doesn't sound as if John had been very helpful; but is there any better way of telling him than just saying he isn't any good?" "Could last week's Lost-and-Found helpers give us any suggestions for this week?" "When the nurse tells us we should stay home, why should we do as she suggests?" "Do you think your mothers might be able to help us with that?" Questions such as these—sometimes discussed by the group, sometimes simply expressed as comments by their teacher, sometimes implied through experience and not expressed at all—added to competencies in adjusting working relationships to the capacities and needs of others, in deciding what service to give and what to expect from others, in learning what guidance to give and what to expect.

WORKING WITH OTHERS DEMANDS EFFECTIVE GROUP MEMBERSHIP

The activities of these first-grade children demanded effective group membership at all points. From the beginning they were helped to plan together. Decisions were arrived at after all who wished to make a contribution had been heard, Miss Miller helping to evaluate the various suggestions that were made. In the beginning it was difficult for the individual to take his appropriate share in the discussion and to accept and act upon a group agreement that had not been the one he wanted. But experience showed that discussion led to many good ideas, that joint decisions, even when they disagreed with one's plans and wishes, led to many satisfactory results, and that one's own proposals, too, were often accepted. Group plans were written where all could see, and as reading skills improved they were used without Miss Miller's help.

Leadership responsibilities at this age were short-term but none the less real. Careful consideration went into decisions as to who should care for the plants, who should be on the various committees for preparing lunch at school, who should be responsible for the curtain in the puppet show, who should deliver the news to the school paper, which children should be made responsible for caring for Josephine. Previous experience, evidence of ability to do the job, former records of responsibility and willingness to stick to the task, were criteria the children considered in making choices.

There was also need, from time to time, to decide when to join a group. Four people are needed to finish painting the library corner furniture and three others are going to wash and press the curtains for the house. Which group to join? Should a person offer to help on a job he already knows how to do or ask a new group to teach him to do another? Several children are going to play ball on the playground and several others are going to the swings. Shall one go with his friends, even though he would rather be playing ball? When one promises to join the children finishing the pictures for the book about vacations, what are his obligations to stay until the job is finished? When has a person a right to decide he is not interested in the work of a group and to leave it for something else?

Enterprises demanding the cooperative organization of the whole class added much to other experiences arising from daily activities. The Lost-and-Found Department was one such pursuit. Those taking charge of the department relied on the children whose responsibility it was the week before for an accurate inventory. Helpers were appointed to see that children who claimed articles filled out the needed slips. Failure to check on this made trouble for the inventory committee. The cooperative noon lunches which have been mentioned in other connections were opportunities in which everyone carried committee responsibility. The class story, dictated after the first luncheon, read as follows:

> Sally's mother came over to help. She put on the meat in water and salt in a big pot at about 9 o'clock. Then our committees started to work. They first washed their hands.
>
> The vegetable committee scraped the carrots and peeled the potatoes and cut them in small pieces. Miss Miller peeled the onions and cut them up for us.
>
> The sandwich committee spread the bread with butter and made sandwiches. They cut them in halves.
>
> The cooking committee took the vegetables to Mrs. Woods when it was time for them to go in.
>
> About 11 o'clock Miss Miller helped the table committee fix the tables in a long row down the middle of our room. It was like one big, long table. Each of us had decorated our table mats and napkins and place cards to put at our places.
>
> The table committee counted out the right number of plates and forks and put out the place mats. Andy forgot to make his and the committee almost left him out. They put a paper towel at his place.
>
> We washed our hands and listened to Barbara read a story while the serving committee served the plates and poured the milk. Then we all had lunch. There were second helpings too. Bobby said he would like to cook lunch at school every day.
>
> After lunch we had a rest. The dishwashing committee washed the dishes and put them away.

INTERGROUP COOPERATION IS NEEDED IN CLASSROOM AND ALL-SCHOOL ACTIVITIES

Enterprises such as the one just described call not only for effective group membership but also for effective cooperative relationships among groups. As they worked together in this way the children learned about the importance of the work of their particular group to the success of the total enterprise. Other learnings came through the various activities in which they worked with other members of the school. As the managers of the Lost-and-Found Department they had one source of contact. Other cooperative experiences came as the children sent group contributions to the school paper, asked the owners of the school store for a price list so that they could practice getting the right amount of money ready ahead of time, prepared their part of the school assemblies, secured the help of a sixth-grade projectionist in showing a motion picture, and turned to the fourth-grader for wiring a bell for the playhouse. All their stories could not be published in the paper; other classes needed space also. The store managers were busy and took several weeks to send them the price list. Their part of the assembly program must be only ten minutes in length as two other classes were sharing the half hour. Here they had to consider other groups.

Intervisitation between classes was frequent and taught more about other parts of the school community. The fourth grade had the biggest map these children had ever seen. The third grade also had a guinea pig, but he wasn't fed the same way as Josephine. The sixth grade made some beautiful book covers and promised that they would do some more if the first-graders wanted them. The second grade borrowed some books about trees to help in a study they were making. The sixth grade also had puppets, but very different from theirs. The first-graders were invited to a puppet show and in turn put on one of their own.

The problems of coming to understand members of other economic, religious, and racial groups have already been touched upon. In the relatively homogeneous community in which these children lived such questions were not prominent. Although these children repeated a few parental reactions and did some of the usual name-calling, their acquaintance with other groups was not broad enough to make these situations very meaningful to them. Miss Miller helped them to build better bases for action where friends and direct acquaintances were involved but did little more. When books or pictures occasionally made reference to other groups she answered questions as directly as she could. "His clothes look funny to us because he lives in another country. He would think ours are just as funny. He needs them to protect him from the heat. What do we wear on hot days?"

EXPERIENCES DURING THE YEAR LEAD TO ACQUAINTANCE WITH THE NATURAL ENVIRONMENT

Acquaintance with natural phenomena came through incidental experiences and through several extensive studies. Problems of deciding on proper clothing to wear out of doors, of caring for the plants in the classroom, of learning how to mix paint and soften clay, of finding that wet paper tears easily, that an iron bar is a better thing to swing on than a wooden broomstick, that snow and rain will chap hands, were among those regularly met.

Caring for Josephine called for other learnings. Did guinea pigs eat what rabbits ate or were they more like dogs? Children needed milk, didn't Josephine? Was the cage too small? Didn't she need more room to run? How often should her cage be cleaned? Should she be in the sunshine or in the shade? These were the questions raised by the children and, as previously indicated, their consideration resulted in a bulletin on how to care for Josephine which was placed beside her cage where all who helped care for her might read.

"Why do our paints get dry?" was another question the children asked, and with Miss Miller's help they investigated. Deep and shallow containers were set out, each holding the same amount of water. Pans of the same size were placed in the sunshine, in the refrigerator in the home economics laboratory, on the radiator, on the easel with the paints, in the darkest corner of the room. Groups watched to see in which the water would evaporate first. Other groups repeated the experiments to be sure there were no errors. Careful records indicated dates and quantities of water and the results added not only to growing understanding of atmospheric conditions but to ability to make ideas clear, to understand ideas of others, to use quantitative relationships, and to use a scientific approach in the study of problems.

Outside the classroom was a large oak tree which intrigued all the children with its dark red leaves and many acorns in the fall. "Our Tree" became a source of interest and curiosity throughout the year. Its leaves were just beginning to turn when school opened in the fall. The children described the colors and compared them with other trees along the street. They examined the acorns and planted one to see if it would sprout. As winter came on they watched the leaves drop off and sought help in finding why their tree had a few leaves left when the others were completely bare. As the outlines of the branches became clear they compared the tree with the elms near by and with pine trees in the park. In the spring they watched for the first leaves and kept track of how fast they grew. "Why didn't they come out as soon as some of the shrubs around the school grounds?" they wanted to know. In the latter part of April a robin built its nest in the branches and the group added a study of bird life to their tree study. They could not see into the nest from their ground-floor room but the eighth-graders who could see the nest from their room offered to help them keep their records and called them to watch when the baby robins finally hatched.

After Christmas one of the boys brought a new magnet to school. While any understanding of the principles involved was out of the question at this level, it was possible to determine which materials were attracted by a magnet and whether different magnets behaved the same way. Miss Miller borrowed a bar magnet from the science laboratory and the children set about collecting the materials to test, sorting into piles those which the magnet attracted and those on which it had no effect. Time was taken to let all members of the group handle the magnets many times. To help them remember which materials they tested from day to day they made two lists. From the discussions of magnets and the materials they attract, attention moved to the ways in which other materials were alike. They had several kinds of paper in their room and they all tore more easily than cloth. Their nails and saws and the beams that held their house together were all metal and they all seemed to be much harder than wood. When water was mixed with it, clay became soft enough to mold, but was very hard and very easy to break after it dried. Discoveries were made of the properties of other materials and discussed from time to time as the year wore on. And Libby's hospital game and the making of fish with paper clip noses recalled learnings about magnets.

Animals and insects brought into the room extended acquaintance with living things. Once in a while children brought their pets to school, and regularly invitations came from other classes to go to see new additions to their rooms. A turtle, a salamander, a garter snake, a rabbit, a family of white mice, were all examined by an interested first grade. In the spring a jar of tadpoles was brought by one of the fathers, and the children had an opportunity to observe this very different form of life. The life cycle was again studied as they watched the development of a monarch butterfly from a cocoon contributed by another parent.

Mention has already been made of the health understandings that grew from watching the thermometer and helping control the heat of the room. Later in the year a thermometer was placed outside the classroom window and the children took great interest in comparing the two temperatures. For part of the winter they kept a weather map recording in picture form what the weather of the day had been. The symbols used in a television weather report were easily copied for this purpose.

Caring for plants in the fall was largely a matter of looking after those in the room—especially those in the playhouse window boxes—and taking care of the occasional flowers brought in from family gardens. At Christmas individual children planted bulbs to be used as gifts. In the spring they decided to try to grow the salad for their last luncheon. The custodian built a window box for them and in it they planted lettuce and radishes, following carefully the directions on the packages of seeds. As the plants came up the children were confronted with problems of thinning out the rows and of giving enough water. The result was a salad—

two small lettuce leaves and an infinitesimal radish—for every child when the last luncheon of the year was held.

A "collections corner" to which children brought interesting objects from home, found on the way to school, or gathered during vacation, led to acquaintance with other natural phenomena. In addition, the group built Question Booklets for the science specialist in which they placed such problems as "What makes it snow?," "Why does ice melt?," "What makes the thunder?," "What are the stars?" These booklets were from time to time presented to Mr. Banks, who then made an appointment with the class to answer as many questions as he could and to tell them as much about their current collections as they wanted to know. Throughout the entire year these simple explanations and demonstrations of scientific principles added richly to their knowledge of the world about them.

TECHNOLOGICAL RESOURCES IN SCHOOL AND COMMUNITY MAKE THEIR CONTRIBUTIONS

First acquaintance with technological resources came from the immediate classroom environment. Miss Miller took time to see that the children knew how to handle the catches on lockers, the drinking fountain, the saws, hammer, scissors, the electric light switch, and the various other tools and equipment of their everyday world. Some were already quite adept with most of these; others required considerable help.

A new building was being erected in the next block and in the children's interest in this development Miss Miller saw an opportunity to build acquaintance with some of the tools and equipment of the building trade and with vocational structures. Accordingly they went on a trip to see what was being done. Construction was just starting, and by visiting at intervals of about two weeks they were able to watch the entire process. The men at work did not have time to stop to answer questions, but Miss Miller could give help with many and Mr. Banks with others. A record was kept of the progress of the building until it was completed, and samples of the materials used went into the collections corner as part of an exhibit. This study not only served to give some acquaintance with the function of tools and machines but added considerable knowledge of how people must work together, of some of the kinds of jobs that have to be done, and of the health problems involved. Questions in this last area arose as they asked about the thickness of the walls, the solidness of the foundation, the ample basement, and the insulation which they saw used.

Later, when the streets around the school were resurfaced, the children became acquainted with other machines and with very different kinds of construction material. This activity also resulted in a series of records as they could not be away from their classroom all the time and wanted some way of knowing what had gone on since the last time they had watched. Practical experience was added to observation in this situation as several, in spite of repeated warnings and cautious testing with fingers, walked on the asphalt being used and discovered firsthand, as they tried to remove it from their shoes later, why it was effective as a surface for roads.

Other learnings came from shorter contacts with the machines important in their school. Heating the school building was an area of considerable interest. Many questions were raised. What is in the radiators? How does heat get to our room? What makes the noise in the radiators? Plans were made to visit the boiler room and to ask the custodian their questions. The group composed a letter which Elizabeth wrote in manuscript and which she and Helen took to the office. When the reply came from the custodian (who had thoughtfully asked the office secretary to type it on the primary typewriter), several of the children could read it. It said merely:

> Yes. Come on down on
> Tuesday morning. I will see you
> then.
>
> Your friend,
> Jim Powell

Their respect for the custodian grew as they heard him explain and watched him operate the furnace and the ventilation system.

At times they watched some of their class materials being mimeographed and, on two occasions, helped turn the handle to see what it felt like to produce the pages. They admired the facility of the school secretary still more when a typewriter was added to their classroom and they discovered how to write with it. When a plumber was needed to fix some drains in their lavatory they took turns watching him.

At the Christmas vacation several children took train trips to spend holidays with relatives and came back filled with new information and questions. This was a matter of general interest as few of the group had spent much time at the railroad station. Miss Miller made plans to take them to the station during a busy time of the day when they could see various types of trains and engines come in. The station master arranged for them to go through a Pullman car on a siding and had a berth made up for them.

Questions about technological resources, machines, and equipment were written in books, along with questions about natural phenomena. Miss Miller, and from time to time Mr. Banks, was asked to explain what the inside of an airplane looked like, how the water comes out of the tap so fast, why one can squirt water so far by putting a finger partly over the tap, why turning a switch makes the lights go on, how the steam shovel working in a downtown excavation operates, what makes the school bells ring, and many others. The answers given were simple, often in terms of what actually happens rather than in terms of why it happens, but they were sufficient to arouse interest in the world of machines surrounding these youngsters and to encourage more questions as they grew mature enough to delve into scientific explanations.

FIRST-GRADERS BEGIN TO LEARN ABOUT ECONOMIC, SOCIAL, AND POLITICAL STRUCTURES AND FORCES

Economic, social, and political structures touched these children mainly through their families and through the immediate school community of which they were a part. Their own share in the school community and the ways in which they used some of the services offered by other groups have already been described. Although the school did not have a council which functioned regularly in the primary grades, the younger children served on committees of the student government where the activities involved were of concern to them. Through this organization and through the much less formal committees and agreements arrived at in their own classroom they took first steps in learning how a community governs itself.

Knowledge of political structures was extended beyond the immediate school community as the children talked with members of the local fire department about the regulations they were expected to obey. Later a police officer came to supplement some of the suggestions of the safety patrol. In the fall the governor came to lay the cornerstone of a new building and they learned a little about who he was, where he lived, and why he should be asked to come to their town. On Arbor Day the mayor spoke in each school and the children learned a little about his position and about the council which governed their city in much the same manner as the student council made decisions for their school. Some of the activities of the President were reported in the local paper, and they made general comparisons between his duties and those of the mayor and the governor. However, there was no effort to go beyond rather general concepts. Other than answering questions as they arose, Miss Miller felt that the most constructive contribution to growth in understanding the processes of democratic government was to be made through helping the children participate functionally in their own classroom activities.

Their community was relatively small and the school doctor and one or two other doctors, several dentists, a judge, two or three ministers, some of the owners of the local stores, the manager of the nearby service station, and the plumber were familiar figures. Through such contacts many children acquired general ideas about the nature of the work that had to be done in a community and the people who did it. Additional information was gained as they visited the various school staff members and as they took time to learn more about the school doctor and nurse, the construction gang building the nearby house, and the road crew who resurfaced the street. Several conversation periods about people who came to their houses—the milkman, the mailman, the delivery boy, the paper boy, the furnace repair man, the doctor—helped to identify other community members. This problem arose when a discussion of how many people helped them in school led to the question of others in the community who give help. Eventually the children developed a book of stories about community helpers. These were dictated by individuals and groups, and some were planned by the class as a whole. Miss Miller had the collection typed on the primer typewriter and mimeographed. Blank pages allowed each child to illustrate his own copy.

Practical experience in carrying out the work of the world came as they brought their classroom activities to successful conclusions, or failed to do so, and in the resulting evaluation discovered certain vital jobs that no one had foreseen. By the end of the year certain members of the group still had to be reminded of their work responsibilities, but most were quite reliable.

Standards of workmanship and the importance to the group of doing the job well were attitudes built from day to day as individuals and groups evaluated work done, decided on next steps, and tried to identify the reasons why certain jobs did not go as well as expected. Billy thought the central beam of the playhouse would be just as good if it merely rested on the walls and brought several blocks down on the heads of the children inside. Paint not properly mixed caused blotches on the paper. Clay that was too moist was not good to work with. They learned to appraise the effectiveness with which they cleaned up after a job, to keep supplies in order, to put scissors and tools back in agreed-upon spots so that others could find them. The need for reminders in situations such as these was to be expected even toward the end of the year, but long before that time the majority could secure what they needed and start on the job to be done with a minimum of help from Miss Miller.

The children learned more about purchasing as they went to the store to secure the food for their first school lunch. Carrots were two prices and sizes, they found, and potatoes were sometimes large and sometimes small. There was a difference in the cost of bread. How many more slices would they get if they took the larger loaf? Was it worth the difference? Was the difference in cost alone? While in the store they took time to look at some of the other merchandise available and to ask about produce which they did not recognize. The school store added other learnings as individuals shopped there regularly. Problems of cost, securing the right change, deciding what to buy, were continuous. At the beginning of the year they visited the store in small groups and were told what was for sale. Then, as a class, they discussed what their parents should know about the store, whether there were any articles in it they really needed, and what arrangements they should make if they wanted to buy things there.

Vacation trips, letters from a classmate who spent the winter in California, and trips taken by various parents led to some questions about other parts of the country. These were usually the center of very short discussions—an object examined, some pictures shown, a brief description by Miss Miller to supplement that given by the child. However, for a while, they had a bulletin board with postcards sent from other places.

Deciding to give the unclaimed articles in their Lost-and-Found Department to the Red Cross led to some preliminary investigation of some of the services performed by that organization. Why could the Red Cross use clothing? Where would it go? Were there children who needed it? Who were they? When one of the mothers who was in the Red Cross came to collect the articles she told them more about the use that would be made of them. Children matched her information with what they knew about what their various churches were doing to give help at Christmas.

Their contacts with the school paper as an instrument of communication have already been mentioned. They used it to publicize the articles they had in their Lost-and-Found Department. Through the paper they issued invitations to the members of the Parent–Teacher Association to look in on their storeroom. They sent news of their own class and found in the paper news of other classes. From time to time a special school policy would be written up as an editorial, or an important announcement would be made through this medium. Until members of the group were able to read the paper Miss Miller read it to them, selecting those parts that were of most interest or that had the most direct effect on their welfare.

A Summary Look

Many more incidents would have to be described and numerous interrelationships pointed out to make the picture of this one year complete. Both in their day-to-day experiences of living together and in their more extended units of work, these children had opportunities to grow in ability to deal with persistent life situations. Their insights were not as deep as those developed with older children, nor were their conclusions as complete. Yet at this level some fundamental bases were laid for successful living. What general guides for other teachers can be drawn from this summary of the year's experiences of these boys and girls?

BALANCED GROWTH WAS READILY ACHIEVED

The way in which the description of the experiences of this first grade has been organized reveals, perhaps more clearly than do the preceding descriptions of the work of the two other classes, how readily balanced growth in dealing with persistent life situations can be achieved. Actually, these opportunities to promote growth in dealing with persistent life situations do not give the full picture of those that would be available over the year. Readers undoubtedly will have identified many other possibilities as they studied the activities of this class in the light of their experiences with their own groups.

Several points regarding the ways in which balanced growth was achieved are important, however. It should be noted that the opportunities to develop increased ability in dealing with persistent life situations included many small incidents of day-to-day living. Much growth came through repeated experiences in handling a situation only slightly different from those met previously. There was no attempt to build major units in every area, although there were a number of extended unit activities before the year was over.

Many of the problems faced by these children are similar to those listed in the charts on pages 169 to 321 which describe the types of daily life situations through which learners in early childhood are likely to meet persistent life situations. However, no teacher would duplicate the situations used as examples in the charts or try to provide experiences that paralleled all the types of situations listed there. Miss Miller used only those situations actually faced by her group. The charts would be useful as a guide in studying the group, but would not prescribe the types of activities in which they should be engaged.

Experiences within the various areas in which the persistent life situations are grouped in the charts were not scheduled on any regular basis. There was no such thing as a block of time on health, followed by a block of time on person-to-person relationships, followed by one on becoming acquainted with the natural environment. The organizing elements for the day's work were the unit activities in which the children were engaged—the class units under way, the skills in which practice was needed, the individual or small-group projects. The style of reporting the experiences of this class does not reveal the chronology of activities, as did the account of the fifth grade. But, like the experiences of Miss Thomas' children, the various units had a central focus, at times in one area and at times in another. Actually, experiences over several days might well yield some contacts with every area. And, in a single unit, the children usually met persistent life situations from several areas. Balanced development, however, was achieved as activities supplemented and reinforced each other over the weeks and months. It was not the result of any scheduling device.

NEW POSSIBILITIES FOR GROWTH EMERGED AS PROBLEMS RECURRED

The description of the experiences of this first grade also reveals how persistent life situations are likely to recur in the lives of learners. As the same problem arose in a slightly different setting, there were opportunities both to help youngsters test out present concepts and to widen their horizons. A rereading of the experiences described under areas such as health or acquaintance with the natural environment, for example, points up the ways in which new possibilities for growth recur in a typical classroom. Examination of the ways in which these new possibilities were handled shows the combinations of short day-to-day experiences and extended units already discussed.

PERSISTENT LIFE SITUATIONS WERE DEALT WITH IN MANY WAYS

The pattern of the year's activities demonstrates the many ways in which persistent life situations can be dealt with. Some, such as those concerning person-to-person relationships and moral choices, were met best as day-to-day situations arose. This would be true even with older learners, although with increased ability to generalize might come explorations within such areas that would assume the qualities of an extended unit of work.

In most areas, the pattern is the combination of short day-to-day contacts and longer units that has already been discussed. The children practiced health habits every day. They also carried out the rather extended plans for cooking lunch at school. With their alert curiosity they posed innumerable questions about the technological aspects of their world. Most of these were answered briefly, but there was also a well-organized study of the way in which a new building was constructed. Some of their explorations in the social world came through day-to-day experiences of living in a school community, but the children also engaged in careful study of the roles of community helpers.

Where the skills of reading, oral and written expression, and arithmetic were involved, consistent help was planned, and was a part of work throughout the year. Increased command of skills was not left to chance. There were many times when ongoing classroom activities supplied ample practice. But care was also taken to assure that the total experiences would lead to consistent growth.

For teachers planning to develop experiences with learners in relation to persistent life situations, the concept that growth in dealing with these situations can come in many ways is important. Failure to recognize this can result, on the one hand, in over-elaborate units in situations where they are not needed. On the other, there could be failure to delve deeply enough or to provide adequate guidance. Helping children meet persistent life situations does not mean "incidental teaching."

A RICH AND STIMULATING ENVIRONMENT CONTRIBUTED TO LEARNERS' GROWTH

These learners, like those in the two preceding chapters, were in a rich and permissive environment which permitted problems of home and community to be brought to school. Miss Miller's children had responsibilities to the school community—for them the Lost-and-Found Department was a major concern. The children were drawn into many other school relationships as they were helped to understand the school regulations for effective living, and as they were invited to share the activities of other classes.

As with Miss Thomas' fifth grade, the classroom environment was rich. It invited exploration, posed many problems, and challenged intellectual curiosity. Some of the explorations of the natural environment grew out of objects the children themselves added to the classroom display tables. Sharing periods made it possible to bring objects of interest to school or to tell about trips or special events. These in turn revealed present interests and stimulated new ones.

Like the learners in the two classes described earlier, these children made a laboratory of the community. They went to watch the new building go up and followed the steps taken in resurfacing the street. They talked with community helpers who came to their homes. As community officials came to school to share in various activities, they expanded their knowledge of local government. The school community as well as the outside community contributed to growth. Other classes shared experiences important to them. The school doctor and the nurse were willing to serve as resource persons. It was possible to examine school duplicating equipment and to visit the custodian to see the heating system.

While the environment was stimulating, this was not an atypical primary room. A pet, display tables, plants, a hot plate, some simple equipment for a play corner, some materials for creative expression, a piano, and even a primary typewriter are not unusual in a first-grade classroom. The secret of good teaching lies in creative use of what is available, not necessarily in elaborate equipment.

FOUNDATIONS WERE LAID FOR A BROAD ACQUAINTANCE WITH THE CULTURAL HERITAGE

These youngsters took their first steps toward broad and deep acquaintance with their cultural heritage. Actually many of their experiences are not much different from those of first grades under other curriculum designs. The typical six-year-old has not yet achieved the intellectual development that will allow him to venture with comprehension into earlier periods of history and into territories remote from his immediate community. As a result, his activities, regardless of the curriculum design under which he is being taught, tend to center in concerns arising from his immediate home, school, and community environment. In investigating why their paints dried out, in carrying out their plan to cook lunch at school, in studying how the new building was constructed, in becoming better acquainted with community helpers, these youngsters were taking typical first steps toward acquaintance with the scientific and social world in which they live. How broad this acquaintance can be when a teacher is consciously attempting to use every challenge within the immediate environment to achieve growth in ability to deal with persistent life situations can be seen in the preceding pages.

Part V

WORKING COOPERATIVELY FOR CURRICULUM IMPROVEMENT

15

STIMULATING AND GUIDING CURRICULUM CHANGE

Building an educational program around the persistent life situations faced by learners requires that curriculum development be a central function of all who guide the learning experiences of children and youth. Because the curriculum for each group of learners develops as they and their teacher work together on the everyday situations with which they are dealing, and on the persistent life problems which are a part of these everyday concerns, improving the quality of this curriculum requires that attention be given to the various forces and factors which affect learning. The process of curriculum improvement cannot be thought of in terms of the production of typical courses of study or printed guides, the preselection of subject content, or the adoption of uniform textbooks.

Fundamentally, improvement in teaching and learning follows from changes in people—changes in their skills, understandings, values, relationships, and use of resources—no matter what the curriculum design may be. Whether the pattern is in terms of separate subjects, subject fields, broad areas of human living, or persistent life situations, the quality of the learner's curriculum will be determined by his day-to-day experiences in the classroom. Therefore, the effectiveness of any program of curriculum improvement must be measured in terms of actual changes in learning experiences.

Curriculum improvement as just defined can be achieved through diverse channels. A first-grade teacher tries a different method of teaching reading to some children and notes the evidence of its effectiveness; three fifth-grade teachers and their pupils cooperatively develop a community resources file; a faculty group re-examines its instructional goals; a child-study committee considers a case history; a committee of teachers analyzes the range and types of learning experiences at a particular grade level; a teacher does advanced work at a nearby college or university; a parent–teacher committee explores better ways of reporting student progress—all are engaged in activities aimed at improving the quality of teaching and learning. Sometimes these efforts are directed rather specifically at a particular phase of the instructional program; sometimes the focus is on the professional development of the teacher himself. Efforts at curriculum improvement may involve individuals or groups of varying sizes. Organization for curriculum planning may be informal and unstructured, or it may be systematized and directed. No single procedure or technique can characterize the varied means by which changes are made in the learning experiences of children and youth.

While the ways in which the quality of learning is improved are many, there must be, in addition to the informal gains made by every capable teacher, a systematic, organized curriculum program which unites, relates, coordinates, and builds the efforts of varied individuals and groups. This chapter is focused on five problem areas of concern to those responsible for planning the educational program: what are the essential characteristics of the process of curriculum development; how can a school system organize for curriculum improvement; how can useful learning experiences be planned for teachers and other curriculum workers; what constitutes effective leadership; and, how can personnel resources be provided? A final section summarizes implications for building a curriculum in terms of persistent life situations. Chapter 16 explores in more detail the special problem of using research as a means for changing the curriculum.

The Process of Improving the Curriculum

Since the first organized efforts at curriculum development, various approaches have been used to bring about changes in educational programs. A study of trends over the past thirty-five years, for example, reveals distinct shifts in emphasis, both in the ways in which school personnel are organized for curriculum planning and in what are conceived to be the goals of program improvement.

In a typical early pattern of organization, the superintendent or some member of the central office set up a structure which assigned to various individuals or groups definite responsibilities for particular steps. For example, a steering or coordinating committee was given over-all administrative responsibility; another committee determined the philosophy and major goals; still another analyzed these objectives; other committees produced new courses of study, usually for a specific subject or grade level and consonant with the objectives approved by the first committees. When these production groups had finished their work, another committee was assigned responsibility for implementing or getting the new courses of study installed, tried out, and used in the classrooms. In some instances, an evaluation committee examined the effectiveness of these guides and courses of study and indicated the need for new machinery to repeat this process in some other area. The whole procedure, however, proved somewhat mechanical. While it brought changes on paper—new courses of study, textbooks, resource guides—the educational experiences of children and youth were not necessarily altered. This so-called administrative approach has its counterpart today in what is known as the centralized approach to curriculum improvement.

Because periodic revisions of materials and documents fell short of achieving desired educational changes, new procedures and processes emerged which departed from this series of mechanical steps. Perhaps most important is an increased emphasis on curriculum development as a social process involving changes in people and their relationships. This approach stresses the significance of involving in curriculum processes the people who are closest to the educational experiences of children and youth. While production of teacher guides and other materials does not cease within this framework, the basic concept is that educational programs can be improved only as the values, skills, understandings, and relationships of individuals and groups are changed. This stress on the process of curriculum improvement is reflected in schools today in the extent to which programs, techniques, and procedures have aimed at deepening the involvement of individuals in bringing about change in the teaching–learning situation.

There have been equally important shifts in emphases in what are seen as desirable goals for a curriculum improvement program. Early organized curriculum efforts were quite comprehensive in nature. The various committees and individuals, closely directed by the central office on system-wide bases, frequently attempted to look at all aspects of the total curriculum. In these early efforts at comprehensive curriculum programs, specialists of all kinds frequently outnumbered teachers in carrying the major responsibility. With this centralized approach, even state courses of study and syllabi were worked out.

In the 1930's there was a shift from the centralized, uniform front to what has since been called the broken-front approach. Teachers were encouraged to initiate studies and practices in areas that especially concerned them. Descriptions of the changes brought about were then circulated to other individuals. As a result, curriculum change might be occurring in a number of aspects of the program at different rates and in different forms. This decentralized approach tended to sideline the wide-based committee and to make the local building unit the operational and planning force for developing the curriculum. In effect, the individual building faculty, with whatever leadership existed, assumed or was assigned the responsibility for improving the quality of the educational program.

A third approach, now growing in favor in systems where there are several school units, is the centrally coordinated approach which attempts to combine the advantages of both the centralized and decentralized patterns while eliminating some of the problems and difficulties. Basically, in this approach there is a recognition of the importance of the efforts of individual schools and the facility with which the personnel can be encouraged and stimulated to attack instructional problems and develop an appropriate curriculum design. At the same time, there is cognizance of the need to coordinate the efforts of several buildings in common areas of instruction. This organization, then, allots to the individual school unit primary responsibility for curriculum planning in areas which are unique to it, while at the same time it fosters and meshes multiple efforts to resolve system-wide problems.

What appear, then, to be trends in approaches to curriculum development may be characterized as follows:

a. Wide-as-possible participation in planning, testing, and evaluating by all persons—professional and lay—who are affected by policy and action decisions

b. Experimentation with procedures and devices for more effective involvement

c. Assignment to the individual school of a more central role in curriculum activity

d. Use of groups and teams for initiating, planning, executing, and coordinating the improvement efforts *e.* Fusion of supervision, inservice education, and curriculum activity to concentrate personnel and process for the improvement of instruction

f. Extension of kinds and uses of consultative services from many sources—central office, state department, universities and colleges

g. Use of cooperative research in the field situation for improving practices

h. Development of more widespread leadership which has as its goal to bring about changes in the perceptions, values, competencies, and knowledge of individuals who create the conditions for learning [1]

The changing viewpoint of what is involved in curriculum improvement—from a relatively mechanical, job-analysis, administrative procedure to a belief which, in effect, makes curriculum planning a new learning experience for all participants—has implications for essential characteristics of the process of improving the educational program.

CURRICULUM DEVELOPMENT IS AN INTEGRAL PART OF THE EDUCATIONAL PROGRAM

Continuous curriculum planning is seen today as an integral aspect of a good educational program. It is a positive process, a constant striving to improve the quality of instruction. Changes in social forces, for example, necessitate changes in school programs; new insights into the nature of learning or revised goals require modifications in existing practices. Discontent with the extent to which desired objectives are being attained is a measure of professional alertness and dedicated educators will transfer dissatisfaction into exploration and testing of promising procedures and programs. Such dissatisfaction does not imply a weak program, a poor faculty, or a critical public. Continuous curriculum improvement is, instead, a health measure for a sound educational system. Efforts to improve the curriculum are, at their sustained best, the opposite of vacillation, instability, or susceptibility to fads. Continuous curriculum development is important, regardless of the particular design. However, it takes on added dimensions when, as in the persistent life situation concept, the curriculum is always developing and flexible, and never a design fixed by textbook or completely preselected subject matter.

[1] Adapted from A. Harry Passow, "Organization and Procedures for Curriculum Improvement," *Review of Educational Research,* 24:221, January 1954.

CURRICULUM IMPROVEMENT DOES NOT TAKE PLACE IN A VACUUM

Curriculum improvement always takes place in a setting in which many factors affect the kind and direction of change. Of these factors and forces, probably the most important are the relationships which link people—pupils, teachers, administrators, supervisors, parents and other lay citizens, consultants. The school is a social institution whose vitality is dependent on the quality of the relationships among the people who teach, learn, and live within it. The teachers have acquired concepts, values, skills, and knowledge through professional and personal experiences—preservice and inservice education, and just living in a culture—which guide their behavior. Teachers, administrators, and other professional and lay persons have established roles and relationships in the school and community. The school system, the district, and the state have evolved rules and regulations, laws, and guides which affect the organization and instructional program of classes. Community perceptions of the role of the school, power and pressure groups, community mores, and social institutions influence what is taught and how it is taught. Such immediate concerns as America's need for additional trained manpower, a mounting rate of delinquency, or an increasing accident toll, can affect the nature of curriculum changes, the way they take place, the organization and procedures used, and the personnel involved.

Curriculum development, therefore, implies more than simply gathering a group of teachers together and giving them a mandate to create a new or different educational program. Schools exist and operate, children live and learn, teachers create conditions for learning, the community furnishes resources and a setting for instruction, the community is part of a larger social structure—all these provide the framework within which those working to improve the nature and quality of learning experiences must function. Curriculum development, then, does not take place in a vacuum. Many factors, particularly the nature of the individuals involved and their existing relationships, affect the kind and direction of the changes made in the teaching–learning situation.

THE TEACHER IS THE KEYSTONE IN CURRICULUM IMPROVEMENT

Whether he sits alone at his desk studying professional literature as a prelude to planning with his students, or trades insights with other staff members, or participates in committee and study-group work, the key person in program development activities is the classroom teacher. Although a curriculum improvement program involves many other persons, the teacher's influence on the school experiences of children and youth is perhaps the most critical. Production committees may write resource guides and courses of study, but the classroom teacher determines how these are used, if at all, and whether they are effective. The administrator may devise a schedule, assign teachers to certain classes, secure materials of a particular kind, but there he often halts; the actual learning situation is the handiwork of the teacher and his pupils. This key role is recognized in current proposals for inservice education, in plans which seek to permit those changes in personal and professional behavior that will better the teaching–learning situation.

Increased understanding of the nature of curriculum improvement has resulted in greater concern for the processes by which effective change occurs. Some schools made maximum efforts to involve teachers, parents, and others in developing educational programs, only to realize that these groups of busy planners made no fundamental changes in the learning experiences of children. Other schools encountered obstacles and resistance to involving teachers in cooperative planning. Participation alone, obviously, is not enough. Therefore, many recent studies of the processes by which curriculum improvement takes place have been focused on the individual—the dynamics within the person which effect changes in his needs, perceptions, and attitudes—and on the social structure—the institutional setting within which the individual works. The prolific yet inconclusive research that has accumulated has suggested insights into the psychology of change as it is brought about within such a social structure as a school. The parallels with general principles of learning are many. In the determination of the conditions for curriculum improvement, in the selection of inservice experiences, in the organization and structure for planning, in the use of resources, in the necessity for leadership, and in the need for evaluation—involving teachers in curriculum development illustrates, basically, the learning process in operation.

CURRICULUM DEVELOPMENT IS DIRECTIONAL, SELDOM FINAL

There are at least three facets to curriculum improvement: continuous appraisal of the existing program in terms of emerging needs; changes where evaluation indicates they are required; and the operation of an effective ongoing educational program while making changes. These three aspects are closely interrelated. The maintenance of a reasonably adequate educational program while moving toward the improvement of particular aspects of it is essential. While a committee of first-grade teachers studies the needs of their children in order to plan for a more effective program in beginning reading, they also provide the most valuable reading experiences they can. Often the results of the committee deliberations are reflected in classrooms long before they appear in a final committee report. Similarly, seventh-grade teachers, planning cooperatively for the initiation of a core program, may develop guides or other materials, and effect certain administrative and instructional modifications as they continue to work with students.

Conceived in this manner, curriculum improvement is a ceaseless process, flourishing in a dynamic, flexible educational environment, in which security and stability exist without complacency or crystallization. This is a concept very different from that of a quarter of a century ago when the intent was for courses of study to be produced, installed, and evaluated. It suggests continuous study of programs. Such study and planning have direction and, while certain phases may be permanently or intermittently terminated, the curriculum development process continues.

CURRICULUM IMPROVEMENT HAS MANY DIMENSIONS

When the goal of curriculum improvement is defined in terms of actual changes in the classroom experiences of children and youth, the creation of better school programs becomes a problem of many dimensions. Some of these involve personnel—classroom teachers, administrators, consultants, lay persons, pupils, and others. Some concern changes in organization, structure, and administration of the instructional program. Still others affect the resources available in the instructional program.

This characteristic of multiple dimensions is of major importance to persons giving leadership in curriculum development. Whether a suggested change is considered with enthusiasm or rejected frequently hinges upon a dimension not directly related to the merits of the proposal. For example, those giving leadership in a school system moving in the direction of a curriculum developed around the persistent life situations faced by learners must be prepared to provide reassurance for teachers regarding the availability of adequate books and other teaching aids. Both parents and teachers may have to be helped to see in detail how skills will be developed and what contacts will be provided with organized bodies of subject matter. Answers to questions about scheduling may have to be spelled out, particularly at the secondary school level. Curriculum development, regardless of the particular design, must go far beyond written proposals for content. Any change that will facilitate the achievement of desired goals is legitimately part of the curriculum improvement process.

CURRICULUM DEVELOPMENT THRIVES UNDER VARIED CONDITIONS

Changes in the values, attitudes, skills, and motivations of professional staff members, in the elements of the teaching–learning situation, in the availability and utilization of personnel and material resources, in school–community organization, in the other facets of an educational program which affect the curriculum, can be accomplished through many procedures and techniques. Curriculum development is not guaranteed by any single attack on common problems.

For example, workshops have been used to stimulate program improvement. These workshops have taken place before, during, or after the school year; they have been sponsored by school systems, professional organizations, nonschool agencies, colleges or universities; the focus and purpose have varied from skill training to exploration and sharing. From such workshops have come important changes in human relations skills as well as other kinds of learnings. The value of the workshop procedure is well established. However, for certain purposes it may be quite inappropriate or futile. The same could be said for study committees, research teams, or any other technique for bringing about program changes. In short, a process as complicated as curriculum improvement cannot be developed by any single means. Change takes place in many ways, through whatever techniques, procedures, and resources are appropriate to the particular situation.

TIME, FACILITIES, AND RESOURCES FOR CURRICULUM IMPROVEMENT ARE ESSENTIAL

Some kinds of curriculum improvement activities simply require the individual teacher's desire to test new ideas. However, qualitatively good curriculum changes usually are the result of creative, intensive work and study. The teacher faced with continuous demands on his time and energy may be unable to approach his problems imaginatively and with the necessary intensity. If curriculum improvement is to become an integral part of the teacher's responsibility, then the conditions for effective participation and planning must be arranged. Time must be made available for curriculum development activities and resources needed for dealing with problems confronting teachers and others must be provided.

At times, it may be necessary to release from classroom instruction individual teachers or even total faculties so that they can participate in meetings, study groups, workshops, and other activities. Consultants and special resource people may be needed for an inservice workshop or committee activity. Special materials may have to be ordered. Money for materials, consultants, scholarships, conference expenses, substitute teachers, supervisory help, and similar items may be the pump primers for curriculum changes. Favorable working conditions are a must if individuals and faculties are to devote time and effort to continuous curriculum improvement.

LEADERSHIP FOR CURRICULUM IMPROVEMENT IS NECESSARY

The term curriculum coordinator is a relatively new one in education. It is an apt description of one of the key functions in organizing to improve instruction. Someone must synchronize and coordinate activities and energies. Leadership for curriculum improvement, whether it emerges from individuals or from groups, sets the scene within which teachers and others may plan directly or indirectly for curriculum activities. Coordination of all the individuals and groups engaged in these efforts is also necessary to facilitate and insure desirable planning, communication, and execution of decisions, and the evaluation of curriculum improvement activities.

Leadership for curriculum improvement can come from many sources and from different individuals. Some persons will be in administrative positions; others, without such official responsibilities, may provide the functional leadership essential for sparking, encouraging, facilitating, and crystallizing plans and experiences which lead to the improvement of instruction.

With increased insights into the process of curriculum improvement, concepts about the nature of leadership in bringing about changes in the conditions which affect teaching and learning have undergone considerable modification. The central function of leadership has become that of harmonizing all aspects of the learning process related to effecting changes in the behavior of individuals who create the conditions for learning.

Organizing for Curriculum Improvement

If the varied activities that make up a program for curriculum improvement are to assume supportive and integrated form, direction, and purpose, then the parts must be related to a continuing, coordinated program. There must be involvement of key individuals, regularized individual and group participation, official sanction and support, machinery through which resources can be located and shared, and workable communication among individuals and groups, so that coordination, planning, and implementation are facilitated. True, curriculum improvement can spring from incidental and informal activities; but cumulative progress is more certain if an organization systematizes ideas and action.

However, system-wide organization for curriculum development cannot be thought of in terms of the neat hierarchies of committees of a quarter of a century ago. Such patterns are a far cry from the multiple approaches to curriculum improvement found in many school systems today. Because leadership is needed and efforts must be coordinated, the actual organizational pattern must be functional—responsive to particular problems as they arise and flexible in terms of changing needs for personnel and resources.

While flexibility in organizational pattern is desirable in achieving improvement under any curriculum design, it is essential when the curriculum develops around the persistent life situations learners face. In the proposed design, the sole purpose of the organizational pattern is to create the conditions under which planning is encouraged, and skills, attitudes, and understandings are changed in the direction of providing better learning experiences for children and youth. Although it is not possible to sketch a single organizational pattern that will achieve this end, a number of criteria can be suggested that should be met if organization for curriculum improvement is to be effective.

THE ORGANIZATION FOR CURRICULUM IMPROVEMENT SHOULD BE CONSISTENT WITH THE SCHOOL'S GOALS AND EDUCATIONAL PHILOSOPHY

The organizational patterns evolved should reflect the purposes and goals of the school. A school program whose primary purpose is to help learners acquire skills, attitudes, and insights to cope with persistent life situations cannot thrive in a structure dedicated to revising subject courses of study. Since concern will be with continuity from first grade through twelfth, opportunities must be provided for teachers of different grades to work together. When the focus is on the persistent life situations faced by learners it is important also for teachers with different areas of specialization to share their insights. Democratic values cannot be learned in an authoritarian climate. The organizational pattern can suffocate program improvement if it conflicts with the goals and purposes of the school.

The changes effected in individuals are determined to some extent by the leadership under which they function. Teachers in a system moving in the direction of a curriculum developed around persistent life situations of learners should themselves be working under leadership which provides experiences in identifying and solving persistent professional problems. Teachers, like any other learners, learn that which they experience. The organizational pattern can contribute to or negate understanding and use of sound educational philosophy, depending on whether it demonstrates a consistent or a contrary point of view.

THE ORGANIZATION SHOULD FACILITATE A VARIETY OF APPROACHES TO CURRICULUM IMPROVEMENT

Because curriculum improvement has many dimensions, the organization under which maximum growth is achieved must provide for a variety of activities. Under the proposed curriculum design, the means used for arriving at effective experiences for boys and girls will, if anything, be more diverse than under patterns that lend themselves more readily to the production of courses of study. However, even where courses of study are being produced, these typically represent only one aspect of the program for curriculum development. In improving the experiences of learners, curriculum activities of teachers may be:

Task-centered—working on a particular, definite job, such as the selection of books and other teaching materials for a classroom library or the presentation of plans for the revision of cumulative record folders. Here the task is more or less clearly defined, and the individual or committee directs attention to ways and means of completing the assignment.

Idea- or policy-centered—aiming at the clarification of concepts or the exploration of ideas or the development of a philosophy, such as the preparation of a statement of elementary school objectives or proposals for use of out-of-school resources. Closely related to the task-centered focus, attention here is on the exploration and examination of ideas and the formulation of policies as guides to action.

Problem-centered—using the methodology of identifying, refining, and working toward solutions of problems. For example, a faculty assesses possible causes for increased student absenteeism or a teacher tries to improve parent–teacher conferences by analyzing present sessions. Groups engaged in action research or appraisal frequently operate with this kind of focus.

Production-centered—producing particular teaching–learning materials or equipment, such as a kindergarten–grade-three committee which prepares a resource guide for its own use, a committee that develops a list of films available locally, or a teacher who builds a radio trouble-shooting board for his science classes. Some kind of product is the goal.

Skill-centered—pointing at the development of certain essential and desired skills, such as the acquisition of new techniques for teaching elementary science, for observing children's behavior, or for conducting small-group meetings. These activities usually provide opportunities for acquiring new skills through practice in some way.

General education- or appreciation-centered—focusing less on a particular phase of the educational program and more on general cultural and professional development. Broadening travel, art appreciation courses, and forums on critical issues in education illustrate this kind of purpose.[2]

There is, of course, considerable overlapping in these various foci of attention and in practice the distinctions are not always clear. They are typical, however, of the range of activities that should be encouraged in an organized program for curriculum improvement. Further, they obviously demand flexibility of organization—in the personnel involved in a given task, in facilities, in time expenditure, in leadership and consultant help. For example, the task of preparing an analysis of persistent life situations as a guide to balanced development might call for the coordinated efforts of several committees, each with representatives from a wide range of grade levels—a structure deliberately large-scale in order to give a maximum number of individuals an opportunity to become thoroughly acquainted with the persistent life situations concept. In contrast, a survey of the day-to-day problems actually faced by learners might be made by teachers working with a specific age range who are anxious to match ideas on classroom procedures; a resource bulletin in an area in which few teaching aids are available might be prepared by a committee of persons with special competence; and two teachers with complementary strengths might test out possibilities for exchanging classes over a two- or three-month period and report back to the faculty group as a whole.

[2] Adapted from Matthew B. Miles and A. Harry Passow, "Training in the Skills Needed for In-Service Programs," *In-Service Education for Teachers, Supervisors, and Administrators.* Fifty-sixth Yearbook of the National Society for the Study of Education, Part I, p. 353 (Chicago: The University of Chicago Press, 1957).

Schools are generally prolific with committees of many kinds. Some of these committees have defined and clarified purposes so that the membership knows what it is doing and goes systematically and effectively about the task of doing it. Other committees have vague or seemingly useless functions, are overlapping and time-consuming. Sensing this, members of such committees are frequently frustrated, angry, or apathetic. The organizational pattern should not only provide for the establishment of needed committees but, at the same time, should arrange for their termination and dissolution when they have filled their particular function or responsibility. Some groups will work for a very short, specified time while others will continue for an indefinite period. Again, the particular function or responsibility should determine the appropriate structure.

THE ORGANIZATION SHOULD ENABLE INDIVIDUALS AND GROUPS AT EACH PLANNING LEVEL TO CONTRIBUTE EFFECTIVELY TO THE TOTAL PROCESS

Under any curriculum design the individual school unit is the organizing base in curriculum development when improvement is defined in terms of changes in the learning experiences of children and youth. When the design develops in terms of the persistent life situations learners face, the role of the individual school faculty in determining the quality of the curriculum is unique. Theirs are the ultimate decisions regarding what to teach. Their sharing of information regarding children and youth, their insights into matters of school organization, and their skill in involving parents and other community members, determine in large measure the quality of the learning experiences.

The individual school unit must be organized to enable persons and groups—including professional staff, pupils, parents, and others—to participate in the planning process. The particular kind of organization appropriate for the building unit will depend on a number of factors, including roles and functions to be performed. The size of the school can affect the roles and responsibilities that individuals and groups assume. In a school where the faculty may number less than twenty many of the planning and executing functions can be carried on simultaneously by the whole group. However, as the size of the school increases, councils or committees may be established to initiate and stimulate planning, with an executive or steering committee to coordinate activities. Work groups on a grade, departmental, or other functional basis may be established for particular assignments. Within each school unit, groups can undertake rather specific projects aimed at bringing about changes in the over-all design or in specific aspects of the instructional program. In some instances this may involve direct learning by faculty or it may mean changes in materials or administrative structure which influence the kinds of experiences provided.

While the individual building is the prime unit in curriculum growth, each building must be linked to others within the system. How to organize for system-wide planning will depend on the size of the system. It will depend, also, upon the particular problems faced. For example, a school system, now working under a broad fields design, which planned to explore the implications of a curriculum developed around the persistent life situations faced by learners would need an organization which differed sharply from that required by a system already working under the latter design but seeking means of meeting more adequately the needs of youth facing the persistent problem of deciding on a vocation. In the former, a rather complex combination of building and city-wide involvement may seem desirable, with extensive use of consultant help, workshops, and other such procedures at the system-wide level. In the latter, a system-wide committee of the teachers most directly concerned and of interested parents and community representatives may suffice.

For some system-wide problems it may be the central office that takes the major responsibility for initiating and stimulating work on curriculum improvement. The central office, in cooperation with all individuals and groups involved, then sets up the necessary committee and work structure, makes arrangements for essential resources to be used, and otherwise directs or oversees the efforts of the various schools individually or as a group. This type of centralized leadership might well be desirable for the system referred to above as being in the first stages of studying ways of developing classroom activities in the light of the persistent life situations faced by children and youth. Consultant help in exploring the implications of the proposal, committee deliberations focusing on a series of agreed-upon problems, and workshops or other means of providing for extended periods for sharing ideas might all be needed on a system-wide basis.

In still another arrangement, the role of the central office may be primarily one of providing services as requested by the individual schools which are operating, for the moment, almost independently of one another. This might occur as individual faculties organized to study the special needs of their pupil population, worked on scheduling problems peculiar to their situation, or planned how best to use the resources of their community. At other times, the staff in a single building may be concerned with developing its own instructional program while, under the coordination of the central office, various aspects of the program which affect other schools within the system are studied and developed through shared efforts of the schools involved. Such a pattern might be useful at a point where general agreements regarding a curriculum approach through persistent life situations had been reached and teachers in individual buildings were testing the design in action. While the key group, at this stage, would be the staff of each school, many developments could well be shared—detailed studies of how persistent life situations seem to recur in the lives of children and youth from particular cultural backgrounds; collections of materials and resources of value in meeting particular problems; methods worked out in individual schools for using the help of specialists; patterns in which the activities of various age groups seem to be developing; systems of record-keeping and reporting to parents.

These three approaches to system-wide organization (centralized, decentralized, and centrally coordinated) imply different kinds of structure for cooperative planning and working at both the system-wide and individual school levels. Decisions relative to structural organization should be made with regard for the nature of the problem to be studied, and the way in which system-wide and building needs can best be related. For sharing resources in the solution of common problems, for coordinating individual efforts, for making available special material and personnel resources, and for integrating the total program, the organization for curriculum improvement for the school system must take into account the special needs at the building level.

In addition to the building and system efforts for curriculum development, there are other desirable levels at which individual and group participation must be planned. Some of these are state and regional arrangements, some are professional organizations, and others involve cooperative study groups associated with universities and colleges of education or with nonprofessional organizations. Procedures which will facilitate individual and group functioning at each of these levels have some elements in common but others which are different.

THE ORGANIZATION SHOULD PROVIDE FOR MAXIMUM COMMUNICATION

Success in bringing about changes in instructional programs depends to a large extent on the freedom provided teachers and their ability to exchange insights, acquire new understandings, and make decisions through various means of communication. As healthy, nonthreatening, enthusiastic relationships are developed within the total social organization and atmosphere of the school, the perceptions which come from face-to-face communication will be clearer and more accurate. Common perspectives can be developed among individuals with different kinds and levels of responsibility and with diverse experiential backgrounds.

Recognition of the importance of freedom to communicate is evidenced in schools today in many ways. School A has converted a small conference room into an attractive teachers' lunchroom; School B begins faculty meetings with a coffee hour. In one building a daily bulletin is issued; in another, teachers make use of a central bulletin board. The halls of one building have been equipped with display cases so that classroom products can be shared; an open-door policy in another encourages much informal intervisitation. The teachers of one school have initiated a series of study-group sessions on problems of teaching arithmetic, accompanied by classroom experimentation; in another, luncheon sessions are regularly used by the teachers of particular grades to exchange ideas about procedures. The science teachers in one system shared teaching techniques in a series of "Here's How I Do It" meetings, some produced on television. The primary teachers in another system sponsored a child-study program.

In addition to providing for communication in face-to-face groups, the organizational structure should be such that everyone who has a stake in a particular policy or decision can keep informed on developments concerning it. Communication is multidirectional, not merely two-way. As school–community relationships multiply, problems of communication grow more complex. In schools today, attempts to solve these problems have included such variations as weekly reports of class experiences dictated by first-graders and duplicated to be taken home, system-wide weekly bulletins, open-door visitation policies for parents, school-sponsored television programs, coordinating curriculum committees or central advisory committees with building and lay representation.

One of the most difficult communication problems is that of transmitting to others the experiences of an individual or a group engaged in a particular aspect of problem-solving. The difficulty arises not so much from transmitting specific pieces of information or findings but from trying to report the feelings and processes which culminated in particular decisions or findings. Several means have proved useful. One technique employed was role-playing a work session so that observers were able to see a critical portion of a meeting re-enacted. Another involved nonmembers of a group in the analysis of some data which a curriculum committee was working with so that the problems encountered could be better understood by all. Still another procedure was one in which a committee shared with the total faculty the evidence and opinions it had available, provided time for deliberation and the making of a decision by the total group, and then shared the decision it had reached from its own study. Organization should encourage exploration of means by which various individuals and groups engaged in curriculum improvement can interpret to others both the content and thought processes of their work.

THE ORGANIZATION SHOULD FACILITATE EFFECTIVE USE OF PERSONNEL AND MATERIAL RESOURCES

To meet the multiple demands involved in curriculum change, specialized personnel resources are essential and should be available. Functional leadership is vital for cooperative planning. Whether in the individual school, in the school system, or on some other level, wherever organized efforts toward curriculum planning are under way, effective leadership is the first essential. Some of the demands on curriculum leadership and the roles to be played are discussed in more detail in a later section of this chapter. Suffice it at this point to note that the role of the resource person, the specialist, has been redefined in recent years. The consultant is less often the expert who comes in with "answers" and more often the specialist who introduces a group to the means which can help secure its goals. While expertness is certainly essential in bringing about change, the role of consultant has shifted to emphasize the wealth of resources, services, skills, and materials that should be made available to individuals and groups working to improve learning experiences.

One concept that is winning wider acceptance is that personnel and material resources are to be found among individuals having widely varied responsibilities—teachers, students, parents, administrative and supervisory personnel—and that they extend into the community and even beyond. The many kinds of resources available can enlarge the school staff's competencies and assist in curriculum development, if effectively applied to teaching. The organizational pattern should make it possible to locate and integrate outside resources in a way which will stimulate their greatest contribution to learning. The organizational network also should enable committees to discover and use the resources available within their own circles.

THE ORGANIZATION SHOULD PROVIDE FOR THE INVOLVEMENT OF STUDENTS AND LAY PERSONS

The concept of a broader participation base in curriculum development efforts has led to exploration and, in some instances, to intensive involvement of pupils, parents, and other citizens in various improvement activities. Student participation has taken the form primarily of cooperative planning of learning experiences rather than involvement in organized curriculum development programs. However, through the student council and similar organizations, students have dealt with special curriculum problems in some schools. Other faculties enable students, particularly at the secondary school level, to meet with committees dealing with such problems as analyzing needs of youth, studying community needs, and setting school policy. In addition to actually working with teachers and parents on specific aspects of the program, students have helped in collecting pertinent data needed for planning and, in several communities, they have developed and kept current personnel and community resource files.

The basis for lay participation in curriculum improvement extends far beyond a public relations or a sales program. Lay persons have been assigned various important roles in program-planning. The rationale for lay involvement stems from a basic belief that persons affected by decisions should participate in their making, that the combined intelligence of many individuals will result in better problem solution, and that the leadership available outside the professional staff should be utilized for optimum planning. The purposes of lay participation in curriculum planning, then, are increasing understandings, sharing of resources, and utilizing competencies wherever located.

Lay persons can participate in curriculum improvement in many different ways. They can help in establishing policy by serving on advisory councils and committees which are dealing with various policy problems. They can contribute in planning activities by working on coordinating councils, acting as resource consultants in areas where they have special competencies, securing and preparing materials for use by teachers and pupils, and participating directly in the various programs and procedures for curriculum improvement. Lay persons may also help in the teaching–learning process rather directly by working with teachers and students in various service and informational roles.

The avenues through which lay participation is facilitated are many. Master files of interested and competent lay persons have been used widely. Various kinds of citizen councils have mushroomed throughout the country, and teacher–citizen work groups have been initiated. In participating in curriculum improvement programs, lay persons should not be given a peripheral role. Their involvement in areas in which they can make a real contribution and support the building of better quality programs for children and youth should be facilitated.

THE ORGANIZATION SHOULD DEVELOP SKILLS IMPORTANT FOR CURRICULUM IMPROVEMENT ACTIVITIES

Closely related to the problem of making the most effective use of personnel is that of helping those involved in curriculum improvement activities to develop the skills they need to make their maximum contribution. Some curriculum development activities require specific skills which the participants may lack. In carrying on effective group activities, such tasks as agenda-building, goal-setting, decision-making, and effective chairing require skills and know-how which can be taught. Education in these areas may be through direct teaching of specific competencies apart from the ongoing activity, or indirectly as a part of the committee operations. If a group is repeatedly encountering difficulties in agenda-building, for example, it may take time to analyze the causes of the blocks and to practice the chairman and member roles which facilitate this phase of cooperative activity. Wherever particular skills are essential for effectively carrying on some aspect of curriculum improvement, opportunities for acquiring these skills through practice should be arranged. Work sessions may be devoted to training in the skills needed for leading group discussions or for carrying on interviews. Time may be taken from a group's activities for the development of evaluation techniques. If programs for curriculum improvement are to be effective, then provision for developing the necessary skills must be made through the organizational structure.

THE ORGANIZATIONAL STRUCTURE SHOULD BE CONSTANTLY RE-EXAMINED

Just as classroom instruction should be continuously evaluated in order to benefit future planning, organization for instructional improvement should be continuously appraised so that the structure meets the particular criteria set up to guide program development. Curriculum improvement programs gain effectiveness from the use of techniques of productive group planning. The kind of improvement activities used, the levels at which planning occurs, the personnel resources who participate, require that organizational patterns be functional, flexible, and purposeful. The particular functions assigned the various units of the school system, the specific responsibilities for leadership and active participation, the kinds of problems, the learnings involved in the solutions of these problems, and the goals to be reached, require the continuous re-examination of the organization and the study of such fundamental questions as . . .

What should be the basic unit for curriculum development in a particular school system?

To what extent should the organization for curriculum improvement be structured or emergent?

What techniques and procedures are most appropriate for bringing about desired changes in the teaching–learning situation?

What kinds of personnel and material resources should be made available?

What kinds of communication problems should be overcome?

Planning Effective Procedures for Improving the Curriculum

The traditional one- and two-day teacher institutes brought together the teachers and administrators within a school system, district, or county for an injection of inspirational addresses designed to return them to their classrooms full of enthusiasm. From this modest beginning have evolved the myriad procedures used to improve educational programs today.

Basic to all planning for activities leading to curriculum improvement is the concept that many of the generalizations about learners and the way in which learning takes place have their counterparts in the process of curriculum development. Just as young learners face persistent life situations, teachers and other curriculum planners face recurring professional problems which call for new insights, skills, understandings, and values. Effective planning for curriculum improvement will provide means for identifying these recurring professional problems as teachers face them, just as planning with learners starts with the immediate situation of concern.

It is just as important to respect individual differences among curriculum planners as among pupils. Teachers vary considerably in competencies, interests, experiential backgrounds, value systems, and almost all other factors. Even the common element of being a professional person has its variants. Some teachers can work most effectively alone, others make their best contribution in group situations. Individuals relate themselves to groups differently: for some the school is a major referrent, while for others it takes second place to some other agency. These individual differences must be taken into account in organizing for curriculum planning.

The learning process, as discussed on pages 66 to 81, describes professional growth as well as the growth of children and youth. Teachers, too, learn in terms of goals that have meaning for them. Like their pupils, teachers establish goals by identifying and attempting to satisfy the wishes of administrators and supervisors when working under conditions where their real concerns or their proposals for action are subtly rejected or altered. Transfer of learning is more certain with teachers, as it is with pupils, if they work in situations similar to those in which they will actually use the new skill, knowledge, or understanding. Furthermore, teachers, as do all learners, have an active, dynamic approach to learning. They need to be involved in the planning and encouraged actively to seek relationships and draw conclusions.

Over the years, curriculum planning has been viewed increasingly as a group process because it is possible in groups to build an atmosphere which stimulates and supports new behavior. This does not mean that individuals cannot work effectively by themselves or that only cooperative efforts will result in effective curriculum planning; rather, many desired goals are achieved more quickly through group procedures. Groups are comprised of individuals who relate to each other in certain ways because they have, or can discover, common interests, needs, concerns, or goals. While activities and products may be of a group nature, learning is individual. Just as the classroom atmosphere affects children's learnings, group procedures can affect curriculum planning.

Groups are at their best when they build support for change, provide a sense of belongingness which arms the individual for an exploration into new ways of behaving, and furnish opportunities for using the combined insights and resources of the individual members in finding solutions to problems. Teachers normally do not expect that pupils come to the classroom already possessing the skills to operate effectively in a group situation, and so they take the time to develop these necessary competencies. Groups of teachers and others new to curriculum improvement may be just as untried at their task as are youngsters; they, too, may need to improve their own skills in working together if they are to succeed.

Because an effective group can provide a climate for growth, for acquiring new values and behaviors, and for experimenting with different kinds of behavior, cooperative group planning has become an important part of curriculum development. However, just as learning is not synonymous with a classroom, neither is curriculum improvement equivalent to a group. In each instance, the nature of the class or group influences the learnings which emerge and are translated into action in the teaching–learning situation.

While the use of groups and committees has become standard procedure, the functions, responsibilities, purposes, and means by which planning leads to effective change involve more than getting people together. Whatever procedures and techniques are used should be selected because they are particularly promising for effecting the desired growth in persons and changes in institutions, materials, and administrative structure. The following criteria can serve as guides in the selection of fruitful means for improving the curriculum . . .

> The procedures and techniques used should facilitate desired growth, acknowledging the individual differences which exist among the participants, and taking into account the needs for individual and group activities.
>
> The procedures should call for resources that either are or can be made available.
>
> Competent leadership should be at work or available for optimum utilization of desirable techniques.
>
> Skills and competencies needed for participation in a particular program or procedure should be considered and, where necessary, provision should be made for developing these skills.
>
> The procedures followed should be those which can be readily coordinated and directed toward building a comprehensive program.
>
> The procedures followed should advance from planning to implementation.
>
> The procedures or techniques should utilize fully the personnel resources available to the building or school system.
>
> The procedures followed should strengthen effective communication among the various individuals and groups concerned in curriculum planning.
>
> The procedures followed should provide for continuous evaluation.

WORKING COMMITTEES CAN FOSTER TEACHER GROWTH

Committees may serve in the process of curriculum improvement in a number of ways. Such committees may focus on a specific area, cut across several areas and some or all grade levels, cope with problems which are school-wide or which involve the entire system. They may meet regularly or intermittently in order to complete a specific assignment. Often the work such committee members do contributes rather directly to their own classrooms.

Illustrative of the committee organization for a major curriculum project is that of the teachers of slow learners whose preliminary analysis of persistent life problems was cited on pages 450 and 451.

This project had its origin in a specific problem. For the first time, classes of slow learners were to be located in the junior high schools of the city. The teachers most directly involved met to plan for desirable learning experiences for these groups. As this small group worked, it became apparent that the problem could not be solved effectively for one age level alone, and that the scope and continuity of the total program merited review. As a result, a long-term inservice education project was planned.

Teachers of slow learners volunteered to affiliate with the project and joined one of four committees, depending on the age range of the children they taught. These committees had a membership of from seven to twelve persons. Although there were some changes in personnel from year to year, from 60 to 70 per cent of the total faculty teaching slow learners was involved. It was possible, by complying with certain board of education regulations, to receive varying amounts of inservice education credit toward salary increments and about half of the group availed themselves of this opportunity. During the first two years of the project the committees met once a month, from four through eight o'clock with a break for dinner. Later, at the request of the group, meetings were held twice a month and ended at six-thirty.

For the first two years, a steering committee composed of the chairman and recorders of the four age-level groups coordinated the work. The functions of this steering body evolved as the project developed. In the beginning when all committees were exploring a variety of possible approaches to a new curriculum, the steering committee served both as a group that did frontier thinking and as a unit for coordinating suggestions from the age-level committees. Later, as thinking began to crystallize around the possibility of using a persisting problems approach, the steering committee devoted considerable time to examining its implications—feeding in problems that had arisen in the subgroups and giving leadership to these groups. As the general approach became clearer, a special committee was delegated the responsibility of refining and phrasing the list of persisting life problems. This committee operated until its task was completed. Late in the second year the function of the steering committee began to take on more of an editorial nature as attempts were made to get group thinking on paper.

For the third and fourth years an editorial committee assumed the combined responsibility of steering, reviewing, and helping to structure first drafts of materials. This new group was composed of persons with special interest in the production aspect of the job. Rather than consisting of committee chairmen and recorders, it was constituted so as to assure representation from each of the age-level committees.

While the special curriculum project proceeded, other committees carried forward other tasks needed for an effective program. One committee reviewed and recommended textbooks, a second group reviewed supplementary books and other teaching aids, and another committee worked on criteria for admissions and policies for the new junior high school program.

A consultant was available from the local university. The city supervisor of special education furnished leadership and consultant help. These two persons served as regular members of the steering and the editorial committees. As the project reached the point where publication could be foreseen, two teachers were freed from their regular assignments for short periods to assist with the task of coordinating and bringing into common style the reports from the various age-level committees.

Communication among the subgroups was aided by the fact that all committees met in a central place and could be called together readily for planning sessions and progress reports. Mimeographing facilities were available and the materials produced served as indicators of progress and as work sheets for later stages of the project. Preliminary teachers' guides, which focused on single persisting life problems, were made available and were used long before the total proposal was ready to be produced as a teachers' manual.

The work of the various age-level committees had differing emphases as aspects of the project were completed and new problems then became focal. The first year was largely exploratory and numerous possibilities were considered and discarded before the proposal that was finally adopted began to emerge. Then the committees considered the proposal as a whole, testing out its implications by applying it to a specific problem—that of personal appearance as related to general health. All members contributed to and reviewed the proposed list of persisting life problems as phrased by the special committee assigned the responsibility of preparing a draft. As the next phase of the work, the age-level committees contributed to and then carefully reviewed specific lists of outcomes for each persisting life problem. They also compiled lists of activities and suggested teaching aids appropriate for achieving the outcomes desired. The group ran into blocks that are typical of all effective problem-solving where the participants are truly free to work out their own solutions—testing ways of reporting, discarding some plans as ineffective and adopting others, and producing some materials that did not fit the plan that eventually evolved. Although many materials were prepared by the age-level committees, the actual work of bringing these materials into common style, deleting overlapping, and sharpening general suggestions was done either by members of the editorial committee or, at the final production stages, by the supervisor of special education and the teachers freed to work with him. However, all writing plans were reviewed by the group as a whole.

Possibilities for future inservice education projects, once the task of producing a master guide for teachers is completed, are readily apparent. Groups working with learners of a single age range may wish to meet to compare notes. Research could be planned to validate the lists of goals which were produced as the best judgment of experienced teachers. Problems will have to be faced of how best to adapt the proposed program to the realities of a high school organization geared for other youth around subject fields. Materials will have to be located, and in many cases may have to be specially prepared to meet the needs of slow learners. Problems of how to provide concrete work experiences at the senior high school level could be attacked. Plans to acquaint new teachers with the program will have to be worked out. Questions will have to be answered as to how detailed the guides for teachers can be without destroying the flexibility that is the heart of the program. Consideration will have to be given to how much subject matter, and what, should be provided for slow learners in helping them meet their problems of everyday living.

This brief account of working committees illustrates the flexibility in organization and procedures used as a means of evolving a new approach to teaching slow learners. Starting on a volunteer basis, the pattern of operation emerged as specific functions had to be performed. Personnel resources were made available and teachers were freed for particular assignments when their special competence was needed. Communication problems were attacked as the committees worked on their studies. Many of the criteria in the preceding section would probably be met if applied to this project.

WORKSHOPS AND SIMILAR INSERVICE OFFERINGS HAVE MANY VALUES

The workshop as a means of bringing about curriculum development has gained rapidly in popularity since its origin in 1936. Today a wide variety of inservice offerings exemplify all or some of the characteristics that are typical of the workshop procedure—focus on problems of real concern to the participants, the opportunity to concentrate one's own efforts on problem-solving, long blocks of work time, availability of special resource personnel, and provisions for members to become acquainted through other than professional activities.

For purposes of clarification, attempts have been made to develop terminology that will indicate more sharply the specific type of organization. A workshop, according to one such delineation,[3] refers to a full-

[3] See Hollis L. Caswell, *Curriculum Improvement in Public School Systems,* pp. 62–63 (New York: Bureau of Publications, Teachers College, Columbia University, 1950).

time or nearly full-time program for at least four weeks, organized primarily around problems of the members, and usually with participation in some common social activities. In distinction, the term work conference is used to refer to a full-time program for two or three weeks, involving group work on special problems, supported by lectures and discussions which may be scheduled in advance, and usually including some social activities. The term conference is used to describe a single meeting called to deal with a specific topic, or a series of meetings extending up to one week in length, and involving lectures and discussions scheduled in advance, and possibly accompanied by small-group work on special problems.

The clinic is somewhat similar in that it, too, is set up to provide an opportunity for learning and problem-solving under expert help. Clinics adapt the procedure used in medicine of presenting specific problems to specialists for analysis, assessment, and help in solving them. One or more consultants or experts may supply the needed direction and assistance in analyzing difficulties and in suggesting possible steps for the solution of a particular curriculum problem. Thus a group of teachers may work with a remedial reading specialist who guides their activity in diagnosing individual difficulties and in cultivating skills they need in working with youngsters.

Many school systems also sponsor two- or three-day teachers' institutes. These usually provide a combination of opportunities for teachers to work, with consultant help, in small-group sessions for several periods on problems of concern to them, and to attend lectures or panels by resource people.

Study groups represent another variety of group problem-solving. These are usually a series of meetings arranged for intensive examination of a particular area, issue, or problem. Study groups may be carried on by a single school faculty or they may be extended to state-wide and regional groups as well. Relatively small groups of from ten to twenty individuals may participate in regularly scheduled meetings in which opportunities are provided for the continuing examination of curriculum problems. A group may engage in intensive study of children over a period lasting as long as three or four years. Some state departments of education have provided guides to help professional and lay groups to look intensively at the tasks of public education and the success of the school in carrying them out.

Workshops, work conferences, and conferences may be generalized or specialized, providing opportunities for groups or individuals to work on specific problems. They may be conducted in a local school, for a particular school system, on a college or university campus, or sponsored by a regional or national professional organization. Clinics may have equally varied sponsorship. Teachers' institutes and study groups are often a very useful form of organization within a single school. However, professional associations, at the local, state, or national level, may also provide study programs of various kinds to increase insights and understandings of children, communities, and curriculum issues.

Workshops and similar procedures can have particular value for groups of teachers working toward a curriculum which poses as many situations where decisions must be made in the individual classroom as does the design proposed in this volume. Intensive blocks of time to work under consultant help could be very valuable to groups working through an analysis of persistent life situations. It might also be possible to use conferences, workshops, and study groups very effectively to help teachers sharpen their own academic backgrounds in areas where college courses may not have provided adequate help—a human relations workshop, a conference on the communication arts, a workshop on consumer education. Clinics can have value as teachers identify problems in working with children and youth on persistent life situations which are part of daily concerns—helping learners identify needs of which they are not aware, guiding the process of generalizing from experiences. Working on these and other problems might include group observation of a teacher at work in a classroom and follow-up discussion of how this teacher deals with the areas which are of interest to members of the clinic. Committees concerned with the location of materials may be particularly important when the curriculum design develops around persistent life situations. Lacking the security of the textbooks so readily available for subject fields, teachers may well feel uncertain as to how to proceed. Groups involved in locating and in producing materials that can serve as teaching aids provide much essential security for themselves and for others.

PARTICIPATION IN SCHOOL OR COMMUNITY SURVEYS CAN CONTRIBUTE TO TEACHER GROWTH

Changes in behavior depend, in part, on new knowledge. Teachers who are involved in school or community surveys can gain many fresh insights that spark changes in classroom procedures. Surveys may be made by the local staff itself, by outside agencies or institutions, or through a cooperative scheme involving both the local staff and the outside agency. Fact-finding surveys may serve as a prelude to planning procedures for achieving curriculum change. They may also stimulate improvement by appraising weaknesses in existing programs, indicating aspects which can be strengthened, or identifying areas which can be starting points for building better programs.

Surveys for gathering facts and opinions and for appraising their meaning have been primarily for guidance in direction and purpose, rather than as the end step in bringing about change. For example, surveys may analyze phases of the school program or of school–community relations, and the data collected may justify recommendations for next steps. A start could be made toward planning experiences with reference to the persistent life situations of learners by a survey of the problems they actually face in a specific area, by an analysis of the competencies they are using in coping with these problems, or by a study of the ways in which community agencies are providing help. If the needs of learners are to be identified accurately, many such studies will be necessary.

SUPERVISORY CONFERENCES STRESS THE IMPROVEMENT OF INSTRUCTIONAL PROGRAMS

Perhaps no leadership role has been so strikingly redefined in the past three decades as that of the supervisor. From a responsibility which was limited to inspection, rating, and overseeing the use of courses of study, the supervisory role has evolved into one of assisting the professional staff to grow in ability to study and solve instructional problems. In some school systems, even the title has been changed to indicate the new responsibilities of educational consultant and helping teacher. Provision of time for teachers to work and plan with such resource persons is an important means of effecting changes in the teaching–learning process. Supervision through individual and group work has become inextricably interwoven with curriculum development. The supervisor as a consultant in curriculum improvement, using appropriate means to work with individuals and groups on specific programs, provides the personnel and material resources needed for improving learning experiences.

Supervisors work with teachers, administrators, parents, and other community persons in varied ways, depending upon the particular problem faced and the kind of help being provided. In working with a teacher, the supervisor may secure desired instructional materials, arrange for resource people, participate in classroom activity, assist in conducting a case study, observe the teaching–learning situation for a later conference to consider problems with which the teacher desires help, and work in other ways on a face-to-face level with individuals. The supervisor may also play varied roles in organizing groups studying diverse aspects of the program. In developing a curriculum around the persistent life situations of learners, the supervisor may provide support for teachers as they develop necessary skills for identifying the concerns of learners and arranging the conditions for optimum learning.

SCHOOL VISITS FOSTER CHANGE

Many school systems have recognized the value of providing for school visitation as a means of encouraging and stimulating professional growth. On some occasions, this may be a teacher who visits a colleague to get help on a special problem or just to have an opportunity to see how someone else handles similar situations. Group visits have also been worked out. Sometimes these are all-day visits with an opportunity to chat over lunch with the teachers observed and a conference period later. In one school system all principals are invited by the faculty of one school to observe their reading program in action; in another community, first-year teachers and several supervisors go to selected schools to observe classes of special interest; in a third system a committee working on problems of after-school recreation visits a school which has been experimenting with techniques in this area. Such visits should include detailed preplanning, practice in and refining of observational skills, and discussion of observations after the visit. Preplanning is essential if visits are to have a clear and definite purpose and if satisfactory opportunities for observing and analyzing situations are to be provided.

Of particular value in situations where teachers are developing a new curriculum design are visitation plans where a teacher, or a group of teachers, volunteers to test out various committee proposals, understanding that they are not expected to work out perfect solutions but to report frankly on problems and difficulties they encounter. In this atmosphere other staff members are invited to drop in to observe, to offer suggestions, and to help to analyze parts of the program.

Where intervisitation is not feasible, teachers have worked out other ways of sharing techniques they have found effective. In one system, the primary teachers planned a series of four conferences for sharing ideas and procedures—one each on science, social studies, arithmetic, and language arts activities. At each of these meetings, which were set up in the classrooms of the host school, teachers with special interests planned demonstrations and exhibited their own teaching aids and the children's work. The program was so planned that teachers could go to the demonstrations of their choice where the particular exhibit was explained and questions were answered. All exhibits were open during the dinner hour, and an after-dinner assembly, with a consultant as speaker, closed the conference.

Not to be overlooked are the values resulting from the informal intervisitation and mutual stimulation that go on in a school when the general climate is nonthreatening. Teachers chat informally over lunch; a bulletin board developed by one class offers suggestions to another; a fifth-grade teacher asks for help in locating easy materials for his less able readers; a fourth grade invites a second grade to a program relating to an area of study and is invited to return the visit; a high school English group shares its progress in choral speaking in an assembly and stimulates projects in other classes; a science seminar puts on a special exhibit; the teachers who work with a youngster having special difficulty meet to plan next steps. All such informal contacts can lead to better learning experiences for children and youth if the possibilities inherent in intervisitation are recognized and fully utilized.

ORGANIZED COURSES ARE A COMMONLY USED TOOL FOR GROWTH

Institutions of higher education have moved a long way toward tailoring programs to the needs of a particular school system or group. College and university courses may be conducted on the campus of the institution or may be set up conveniently near the faculty whose particular needs and concerns provide the focus for the course. More than a few school boards and administrators, in turn, have given financial assistance, time, and encouragement to enable individuals and entire faculties to participate in college courses and programs geared to professional growth. Industrial concerns have also sponsored courses, seminars, and conferences for teachers, using resource personnel from their own ranks or from nearby cooperating colleges. Joint efforts involving industry, business, labor, and service groups have resulted in making regular courses available for professional staff members on a credit or noncredit basis.

PROFESSIONAL CENTERS MAKE FACILITIES AVAILABLE FOR CURRICULUM WORKERS

Creating and keeping up-to-date curriculum laboratories, professional libraries, and instructional materials centers provide teachers and other curriculum planners with opportunities for knowing about effective teaching–learning materials and understanding how to use them. Teachers who have served on committees reviewing professional books and periodicals report enthusiastically about the contribution of such assignments to their professional growth. Curriculum workers who have made surveys of community resources have derived many ideas for improving their own teaching. Opportunities to study and to appraise teachers' guides and similar curriculum materials from other systems are important for deepening insights into approaches used by others. Not only does the experience of sharing in the development of such professional centers contribute to growth, but the centers themselves serve a valuable function in making available to curriculum committees and to individuals the resources with which to work.

PARTICIPATION IN RESEARCH IS AN EFFECTIVE APPROACH TO CURRICULUM DEVELOPMENT

Research of the operational type releases cooperative assaults on instructional problems. Cooperative research as a means of bringing about curriculum improvement is just beginning to be used widely. Basically, the research process involves a more systematic testing of possible solutions to problems than is used in the casual inquiries which accompany much curriculum change. The problem is specified and refined, and attempts are made to work on causes rather than overt symptoms. Because of the promise of research as a method of evolving a sound basis for improving school practices, this procedure is discussed in greater detail in Chapter 16.

Providing Leadership for Curriculum Improvement

As is evident from the foregoing discussion, curriculum improvement requires the cooperative efforts of many persons. The energies and creative efforts of many individuals must be mobilized in the solution of problems related to the education of children and youth. In a cooperative endeavor, leadership may come from many individuals and sources. Those persons who present the necessary competencies or who can develop them, those who control means to goal attainment or who have legal responsibility and authority—and are perceived as possessing or controlling means—may be accepted as leaders. Probably no single aspect of the curriculum improvement process is as critical as the quality of existent and emergent leadership.

The demands of curriculum leadership and the varied roles of functional leaders imply competencies in several different areas—in face-to-face situations with individuals and groups, in curriculum processes and procedures, in the marshaling of resources, in the creation of a stimulating and supportive environment and atmosphere. Beyond this, there is required of curriculum leaders an understanding of the role of the school, of school–community structure and relationships, of child development and growth, of the learning process, of curriculum theory and organization. Curriculum workers may already possess some of these competencies; others will be developed through participation in improvement activities and professional inservice growth.

Creativity in instructional improvement depends, to a considerable extent, on the development of leadership among many individuals—students, teachers, administrators, supervisors, lay citizens, and persons in state departments, universities, colleges, and professional organizations. Opportunities to exercise leadership roles and to derive recognition for these competencies are important for all of these individuals. Participation in curriculum improvement should provide for the emergence of new leaders and should expand competencies for program development.

While the demands on those who exercise leadership functions vary with the particular project, group processes are almost always involved. Because this is so, some rather specific skills, attitudes, and knowledge can be identified as important if leadership is to be effective. Some of the important contributions to group progress that leaders in curriculum development can make are indicated in the pages that follow.

LEADERSHIP SHOULD IMPROVE GROUP EFFECTIVENESS

One of the primary roles of curriculum leadership is to extend the group's skill in the identification of problems, the discussion of ideas, and the formulation of decisions for action in order to advance toward their accepted goal. The curriculum leader can up-grade the problem-solving processes by raising the quality of discussion, helping the group to establish good operating procedures, facilitating the sharing of leadership, and accelerating the group toward maximum realization of its own potential. Because considerable curriculum improvement rests on growth in small-group situations, one of the curriculum leader's key responsibilities is to heighten group effectiveness in cooperative planning. He may serve as chairman or fill other roles essential for a group to attain its desired goals. A mature group—one which is productive and satisfying—is an important asset in working on curriculum improvement.

LEADERSHIP SHOULD IMPROVE COMMUNICATION AMONG CURRICULUM WORKERS

Effective communication can facilitate curriculum improvement; poor communication can block growth. Within working and planning groups and among various individuals and groups, clear channels of communication are essential. Curriculum leadership should facilitate the clear definition of avenues of communication so that ideas, information, and even grievances may be seen, examined, and acted upon. Recent developments of media make it possible to share information, diffuse facts, and explain curriculum planning to a wider audience within and without the school. Communication is a whole complex which can increase understanding of planning and, from that stage, spread identification with and active participation in curriculum efforts. Seeking ways and means which will enhance understanding and facilitate working together can be an important function of curriculum leaders.

One such function relates to writing assistance and the keeping of necessary records. Significant activities, projects, and researches require the maintenance of adequate records through professional direction and clerical assistance. One barrier to some kinds of research is the time needed for clerical processing and recording of data. Reports must be made and communication maintained. These are resources which curriculum leadership can help provide for individuals and groups.

LEADERSHIP SHOULD FURNISH NEEDED EXPERTNESS AND COORDINATION

The very nature of curriculum improvement suggests a continuing need for certain competencies and insights which groups may or may not be able to furnish from within their own membership. While outside experts and specialists have important and useful roles to play, all group members have competencies which should be capitalized upon as an initial step in group development. These resources within the group will have to be extended at times. The use of consultants should be explored, so that expertness which cannot be readily developed within the group can be secured when required.

Curriculum leaders may supply needed expertness in the selection of procedures for changing the curriculum and organizing for instructional planning. Techniques and procedures which can be employed in working toward the improvement of teaching–learning situations require insights, skills, and understandings if they are to be used appropriately and are to bring about desired changes. If a workshop seems desirable, how will it be organized? Someone or some group will have to make necessary arrangements, secure personnel resources, and generally assume responsibility for being sure that the workshop method can lead to the kinds of curriculum development wanted and have reasonable chances for success.

Synchronizing working relationships among the individuals and groups responsible for various phases and services is another responsibility of curriculum leadership. However, such coordination need not be the concern of a single individual; it may well be accomplished through steering committees or coordinating councils. Whatever administrative means are devised, the diverse efforts and activities of individuals and groups must be coordinated and directed if cumulative growth is to result. As specialists in the process of bringing about change, curriculum leaders should guide thinking about possible means for attaining specific goals and the advantages and disadvantages of various alternatives. They should also teach how to evaluate the effectiveness of the procedures which are used.

LEADERSHIP IS NEEDED FOR RELEASING THE POTENTIALITIES OF INDIVIDUALS AND GROUPS

Because the talents, leadership, and active efforts of many individuals are required for curriculum improvement, ways of discovering, releasing, and utilizing these creative skills, knowledge, and insights must be found. In this respect, the leader must find means to motivate and inspire individuals to acquire and use skills, to reduce psychological tensions and barriers by building trust and confidence, to stimulate creativity, and to provide opportunities for exercising leadership and assuming responsibility. Helping individuals with problems in one area may enable them to grow in another. Opening up avenues for free expression and creativity will extend possibilities for personal and professional growth.

In a process which deals primarily with human beings, the relationships among people are paramount. The curriculum leader who recognizes that his major concern is in mobilizing and releasing the energies, interests, abilities, and initiative of individuals must give attention to the significance of human relations in the school groups. The provision of a good physical and social environment has three facets: healthy working conditions, improvement or maintenance of good morale, and freedom from tensions and pressures which block individuals and groups from effective work in curriculum development.

Securing Necessary Personnel Resources

The varied activities that make up present-day programs of curriculum improvement call for many types of personnel resources. The roles played by the consultant or resource person in curriculum improvement efforts are constantly multiplying. Some groups bow to the consultant as an expert who comes in with ready-made answers or solutions to problems; others view the consultant as a nondirective reflector of the group's ideas; and still others consider him a person with competencies needed to attain certain group goals. Since resource persons increasingly are being cast in varied roles, the group and its leaders must define their particular needs carefully. The consultant can provide many services for groups. He can stimulate interest in curriculum improvement and develop enthusiasm for tackling various educational problems. He can furnish the expertness needed to solve particular curriculum problems when, for example, he understands some aspect of the community structure better than do the staff members or he has the particular specialization needed in certain disciplines or in human relations or in a particular process. A consultant can help organize a group, can focus its consideration on the resources available to it, can indicate alternative ways of attacking a specific problem. Or the consultant can serve as a teacher for individuals and groups who are to participate in inservice activities.

In general, the lack has not been in the existence of persons with special competence to assist in curriculum improvement as resource persons, but rather in their identification and utilization. Caution must be observed in the selection and use of any consultant. The following criteria can be used as guides in the optimum utilization of resource persons . . .

> The purposes for which a particular competency or specialization is desired and the specific role the resource person is to play in the group's development should be clarified from the start. Both the resource person and the group should agree as to what the consultant's role is to be.
>
> It should be ascertained that the individual selected has the competencies needed by the group desiring his assistance.
>
> The nature of the group, the problems it is facing, the kinds of help it wants should be carefully explored with the consultant.
>
> The consultant selected should be an individual who is sympathetic, understanding, and willing to begin with a particular group at the level at which he finds them.

The consultant should have two kinds of competencies—one in the actual problem area in which the group is working, and the other in the combination of attitudes and skills that enable him to use his special ability to help the group.

The group should have, or should acquire, the skills needed for using the resource person effectively.

RESOURCE PERSONS MAY BE LOCATED WITHIN SCHOOL SYSTEMS THEMSELVES

Consultants may be found among teachers and others within the school system itself, and among laymen. Many school systems are proud of their personnel who possess specialized competencies and expertness which can be identified and utilized. A personnel-resources file may help in identifying individuals with special talents and abilities within a professional staff or in the community. In larger school systems, experienced personnel with particular competencies can be shared by the various schools if these talents are known. Supervisory and central office persons who are recognized and identified as having resources useful and necessary for curriculum improvement can provide assistance to individuals and planning groups.

In addition to the personnel resources available within its own ranks, a school system can also use individuals from other school systems as consultants. For example, a third-grade teacher, with a special competence in the teaching of art in relation to other study, may provide the leadership needed for an inservice workshop at a nearby school system or for one involving representatives from several schools. Sharing of personnel is increasing as the availability of such individuals becomes better known and schools recognize the mutual advantages to be derived from this practice.

COLLEGES AND UNIVERSITIES ARE SOURCES OF CONSULTANT HELP

Widely used sources of consultant help have been the colleges and universities. Individuals specializing in a particular discipline or having competence in certain processes are available. Many universities and colleges have special organizations from which specific consultative services can be secured. Some of the workshops, conferences, and other professional meetings sponsored by colleges and universities are especially designed to provide consultant services to public schools and their individual staff members.

The study council movement, in which a number of schools join with an institution of higher education to share resources and ideas and to work cooperatively on common problems, has given impetus to the exchange of personnel between school systems as well as to the use of specialists from colleges and universities. From a single study council, organized in the early 1940's in order to combine the resources of many school systems in research, invention, and the diffusion of ideas and practices, this pattern of cooperative activity has spread and dozens of such arrangements now flourish.

STATE AND NATIONAL PROFESSIONAL AND NONPROFESSIONAL GROUPS OFFER RESOURCE HELP

State departments of education and state and national professional organizations provide still other sources of consultant help. The Office of Education of the U.S. Department of Health, Education, and Welfare, for example, has staff members with particular areas of specialization who are available on a limited basis as consultants. Many state departments of education have moved away from inspectional roles and toward furnishing consultation on specific curriculum problems of state or local nature. Where county organizations exist, the same trend—for central office personnel to view themselves as consultants on particular aspects of curriculum improvement rather than as inspectors and administrators—is evident. Some national professional organizations, such as the Association for Supervision and Curriculum Development, have provided direct consultant help to groups. Directories of people with particular competencies in various aspects of curriculum improvement, willing to serve as consultants to school or county or regional groups, have been made available.

Numerous national and regional organizations have made specialists available for planning with teachers and other professionals. Among these are such groups as the National Conference of Christians and Jews, the Anti-Defamation League, the Joint Council on Economic Education, the United States Chamber of Commerce, and the American Federation of Labor–Congress of Industrial Organizations. Some of these groups are service-oriented and others are identified with a particular segment of the American economy or government.

COMMUNITY MEMBERS CAN SERVE AS CONSULTANTS

Parents and other citizens in the community provide additional sources of consultant help. As noted in earlier parts of this chapter, lay persons can be involved in many aspects of curriculum planning and can serve as special consultants in areas in which they have considerable expertness. A resident in one community, for example, had spent a great deal of time as a key government official in the Middle East, acquiring unusual insights into the political, social, and economic situation in that area. The school invited him to serve as a consultant both to the faculty members and to the students engaged in studying conditions in the Middle East. Another school staffed an inservice workshop on the teaching of science with selected volunteers from a local industrial research laboratory. Community-resources files, which list many kinds of available personnel resources, are useful in making these individuals known to the staff and students who can then request appropriate assistance. In addition, many community organizations, agencies, and institutions have specialized personnel who are willing and able to provide planning assistance. Such groups can be found at the local, state, and national levels.

Developing a Curriculum in Terms of Persistent Life Situations

Basically, most of the techniques, procedures, and means of organization for achieving instructional improvements apply equally to developing any kind of curriculum design, since the principles are essentially the same. The preceding sections contain specific suggestions of ways in which typical procedures can serve the purposes of groups concerned with developing a curriculum with reference to the persistent life situations faced by learners. However, those who have leadership functions face some special problems in helping teachers learn how to work in terms of the specific needs and problems of their groups. This is not a design that can be installed or adopted in the same fashion in which fourth-grade teachers working under a broad fields design might decide to use a unit on Australia rather than one on China or in which the high school English teachers might decide to offer a course in journalism in addition to one in grammar.

While the proposed design does not corner any market on good teaching, its development requires that teachers have certain competencies which may not be quite as critical in other curriculum proposals. They must be equipped with the insights, knowledge, skills, and attitudes that will allow them to determine what to teach instead of working according to decisions made for them, at least in part, by courses of study.

Teachers must be particularly skilled in identifying the immediate concerns of learners and in sensing the persistent life situations which are part of them. This calls for adeptness in judging what a concern means to learners and how much attention it merits; for sensitivity in selecting and organizing learning experiences which will provide balance in daily living for children and youth; and for insights into community relationships and the teaching–learning needs they suggest.

Skills in planning cooperatively will have to be developed to a high level of proficiency—planning with students, with colleagues, with community members. Planning skills must also include well-developed techniques for involving resource persons and specialists, providing for individual differences, and making curriculum structure and school schedules flexible.

New techniques for locating appropriate materials may also have to be acquired. Skill in utilizing community resources will be important. Teachers will also need to know how to produce new materials in situations where available texts do not provide necessary information, and how to marshal a variety of teaching aids other than books. Perhaps even more important, many teachers will require help in building their own professional resources. Their college courses may not have contributed to the knowledge and understandings they need to face problems with learners. Essential security in working with learners is hard to build in situations where teachers themselves do not feel certain of their academic background.

Teachers will have to expand their skills in evaluation. Such skills are particularly important under a curriculum design where the richness of the program depends upon individual judgments. Evaluation skills are also important for teachers' feelings of security. Under the proposed design, more than under any other, conscientious teachers are likely to be asking, "But how will we know that they are making sufficient progress?"

Essentially, then, helping teachers move toward a design developed around learners' persistent problems of living is a matter of developing professional competencies, building feelings of security which will encourage such growth, and expanding the personnel and material resources available for teaching and learning.

Just as the proposed design results in flexible patterns of experiences, which are unique for each group of learners and impossible to spell out ahead of time in terms of specific sequences or organization, so the design for curriculum improvement under which a group of teachers moves toward this way of working with learners will be different for each situation. It is not possible to predict what immediate problem of concern to the group might be the starting point; what combination of committees and other learning experiences might develop as the desirable organization for work; or what type of analysis, teachers' guide, or other professional aid might best meet the needs of a specific group. These are matters as integral to the planning of each group as are the ways in which a teacher and his class finally decide to work on a problem unique to their particular situation.

The general guides for curriculum workers which follow might be adapted in many ways in a particular situation. The crucial point is that teachers, in their curriculum development activities, have the same types of experiences in identifying and solving problems under democratic leadership as they will be expected to provide for children and youth . . .

> Begin where teachers and other curriculum planners are. Good teaching is possible under most curriculum designs and should be capitalized on in moving toward a curriculum built with reference to persistent life situations.
>
> Focus on determining the specific needs of learners in a particular school and on assessing how well these are being met. Deeper understanding of learners and the persistent life situations they face can serve as the stimulus for examining the extent to which the existing program provides pupils with experiences needed to cope with these recurring problems.
>
> Analyze the persistent life situations learners face in the local school–community setting. The charts in this volume are the result of one kind of analysis and may serve as a point at which to begin study. They can be used as a guide by a teacher for improving his technique in a particular area or grade. He can examine the meaning of the charts for his own teaching as an initial step toward more comprehensive efforts involving others at some future time. If the design is to be fully implemented in practice, cooperative planning will be essential. But the interest and concern of just a few individuals may provide the stimulus necessary for initiating and building such a program.
>
> Foster a sense of group purpose within the professional staff. The skills and insights needed for cooperative curriculum planning must be developed. For example, just to plan a general education core program requires considerable inservice experience to enable necessary growth in the skills, insights, materials and—most important—security and belief in the core concept. Opportunities must be provided for examining issues and extending understanding through cooperative study.
>
> Provide favorable working conditions to build morale, extend security, and encourage experimentation among staff members. A teacher's morale and sense of well-being, his feeling of freedom from unnecessary tension and pressure, and his general willingness to experiment with new practices, ideas, and programs, can serve as stimuli for his

own professional growth and for working on a cooperative basis with others. Curriculum leaders should build the confidence of staff members, as individuals and as members of a team, in their own personal and professional creativity and growth potential. A feeling of security must be built into the procedures and techniques used in examining problems honestly and in exploring possible solutions, if change in the institutional setting of the school is to be achieved.

Recognize the importance of bringing about change as rapidly as possible but as slowly as necessary. To develop a total curriculum design, comprehensive and inclusive in nature, takes time and effort. A curriculum based on persistent life situations is not yet sufficiently widespread to allow teachers to visit a nearby school to see how it works. Instead, each school staff will find it necessary to evolve its own understanding of the proposed design and develop a curriculum within its own particular setting. A school staff must realize that a process of designing, rather than a rigid structure or pattern, will be involved in moving toward this kind of a curriculum.

While administrative scheduling and the securing of additional personnel and material resources can facilitate changes in some programs, the implementation of a design based on persistent life situations rests squarely on the ability of the professional staff to marshal resources in selecting and organizing learning experiences in such a way that learners are helped to cope with the specific and recurring problems they face.

The development of a curriculum based on persistent life situations can commence in many ways. From the individual teacher, who examines his own teaching in terms of recurring problems the pupils face to see how well these are met, to a total staff studying its own processes and competencies as a step toward creating the flexibility in teaching–learning necessary for the proposed design—the springboards for curriculum planning are numerous. Possible activities for a teacher, a faculty, or some other curriculum group include the following . . .

Assessing the persistent life situations learners face and building an analysis and charts as a guide to planning

Finding opportunities for increasing skills and techniques in studying learners to determine their needs

Producing or locating necessary resource materials for teaching and learning

Engaging in reality practice or role-playing to acquire and extend necessary teaching–learning skills

Learning how to work with individual differences—using group processes in the classroom, differentiating materials and learning activities, and otherwise recognizing and arranging for individual growth

Seeking opportunities for extending insights into community resources, structure, and relationships

Utilizing opportunities for extending general education and self-understanding

Developing the conditions which encourage experimentation within the classroom and school

Schools are maintained in order to create conditions that will provide the richest and most appropriate learning experiences for all children and youth. Therefore, a basic obligation of all those persons who guide the development of learners at every level is the improvement of instructional programs and procedures. There are many means by which existing programs can be assessed, new learnings acquired, and conditions altered to bring about the development of an improved curriculum. To build a curriculum for modern living requires the continuous, cooperative efforts and inspired leadership of all who would help children and youth acquire the means to cope with recurring problems in a changing world.

Related Readings

American Association of School Administrators. *American School Curriculum.* Thirty-first Yearbook. Washington, D.C.: The Association, 1953.

Anderson, Vernon. *Principles and Procedures of Curriculum Development.* New York: The Ronald Press Company, 1956.

Association for Supervision and Curriculum Development. *Action for Curriculum Development.* 1951 Yearbook. Washington, D.C.: The Association, 1951.

Benne, Kenneth, and Bozidar Muntyan. *Human Relations in Curriculum Change.* New York: The Dryden Press, Inc., 1951.

Caswell, Hollis L., and Associates. *Curriculum Improvement in Public School Systems.* New York: Bureau of Publications, Teachers College, Columbia University, 1950.

Doll, Ronald C., A. Harry Passow, and Stephen M. Corey. *Organizing for Curriculum Improvement.* New York: Bureau of Publications, Teachers College, Columbia University, 1953.

Kelley, Earl C. *The Workshop Way of Learning.* New York: Harper & Brothers, 1951.

MACKENZIE, GORDON N., STEPHEN M. COREY, AND ASSOCIATES. *Instructional Leadership.* New York: Bureau of Publications, Teachers College, Columbia University, 1954.

MIEL, ALICE M. *Changing the Curriculum.* New York: Appleton-Century-Crofts, 1946.

NATIONAL SOCIETY FOR THE STUDY OF EDUCATION. *In-Service Education for Teachers, Supervisors, and Administrators.* Fifty-sixth Yearbook, Part 1. Chicago: University of Chicago Press, 1957.

NATIONAL SOCIETY FOR THE STUDY OF EDUCATION. *Citizen Cooperation for Better Public Schools.* Fifty-third Yearbook, Part 1. Chicago: University of Chicago Press, 1954.

SAYLOR, J. GALEN, AND WILLIAM M. ALEXANDER. *Curriculum Planning for Better Teaching and Learning.* New York: Rinehart & Company, Inc., 1954.

SHANE, H. G., AND W. YAUCH. *Creative School Administration.* New York: Henry Holt and Company, Inc., 1954.

SMITH, B. OTHANEL, WILLIAM O. STANLEY, AND J. HARLAN SHORES. *Fundamentals of Curriculum Development.* Revised edition. Yonkers-on-Hudson, N.Y.: World Book Company, 1957.

STOREN, HELEN F. *Laymen Help Plan the Curriculum.* Washington, D.C.: Association for Supervision and Curriculum Development, 1946.

16

IMPROVING THE CURRICULUM THROUGH RESEARCH

Research and experimentation, appraisal and evaluation are processes closely related to effective teaching and instructional planning. For the classroom teacher and other curriculum planners, these are important processes. Research is basically a way of seeking answers to meaningful questions through systematic gathering of evidence about causes and effects in problems. Experimentation is a specific research procedure that calls for the testing of a specific idea or procedure to determine whether it has the desired results in practice. Because this involves trying out ideas in practice, much fruitful classroom research has been in the form of experimentation.

Appraisal and evaluation refer to determining the degree to which accepted values or goals are being attained. These goals may relate to the curriculum as a whole, to aspects of the educational program, or directly to the growth of students. When a school has established well-defined goals, appraisal of the effectiveness of its curriculum design shows the extent to which these aims are being attained. Curriculum evaluation begins with gathering evidence about varied aspects of the program to determine how well the objectives are being attained. Data may be collected to appraise the work of individual students, to assess the value of the curriculum design in effecting behavior changes, or to judge the quality of the materials and procedures used. The concept of evaluation and the techniques discussed in Chapter 11 are applicable in appraising the effectiveness of educational experiences, and many of the same methods are also part of curriculum research.

As stated in Chapter 15, curriculum changes can climax some plan agreed on cooperatively and based either on practical experience or on the recommendations of specialists. On the other hand, curriculum improvement may be brought about by experimentation within the classroom or school system. Research may be used in both of these situations; in the latter, it consists of actual testing by the people involved in the change, while in the former the plan may be devised on the basis of research reports.

Although the scientific movement in education is little more than a half century old, insights and understandings about the research process and methodologies have grown considerably in that period. Early educational research emphasized measurement, studies of teaching methods in specific subjects in order to determine appropriate content and grade placement, and increased insights into the learning process and child development. Those doing the research tended to be college professors, directors of child-study laboratories, and personnel in bureaus of educational research. Teachers were thought of as consumers of research—as persons who would put new techniques into operation once their worth was demonstrated. If they shared in the research process at all, it was to carry out the procedures outlined by the researchers and to cooperate in the collection of data. In the last two decades curriculum research has changed focus, and has grown in scope, methodology, and stature. New methods for collecting and analyzing data in complex classroom settings have been devised. More important has been the increasing interest in the possibilities of involving teachers and other curriculum planners actively in the research process, leading to growth in professional competence and improvement in teaching situations.

Research in which teachers are directly involved bears several names. Of these, the most common are action research and cooperative curriculum research. The term action research has been derived from a basic belief that an individual teacher can undertake research to improve his own practices or to find out how to do his own job better. In this procedure, research and action are inextricably related. Cooperative curriculum research adds the concept of joint efforts of several individuals or a group. These definitions are, of course, somewhat arbitrary.

All research involves a careful, systematic search for more accurate answers to questions or problems, and the distinctions among the varieties of research—experimentation, surveys, historical investigations, clinical or case studies—are normally made on the basis of the kinds of problems tackled, the purposes for the undertaking, the persons involved, the methodologies employed, and the ultimate applications or generalizations. Distinctions are sometimes made between action research and so-called fundamental research. Aside from whether a piece of research is competent or inept, the distinctions seem to be primarily in the end purposes and in the individuals involved. The phases of the research process and the techniques used to collect data need not be essentially different. Action research generally aims to alter the professional practices of the researchers themselves. Fundamental research usually aims at the establishment of basic generalizations or truths which the researcher hopes practitioners will apply to their activities. Because fundamental research aims at broader generalizations and wider application, the techniques used and the procedures followed may necessitate better control of certain conditions than can be applied by persons studying their own activities.

Comparisons between action and fundamental research sometimes result in belittling one in order to extol the virtues of the other. The importance of research as a means for improving the curriculum has been well established. The acquisition of basic insights into educational processes requires no justification. The need is not to support one kind of research over another but rather to encourage curriculum planners to use the most appropriate methodologies in attacking educational problems. For the classroom teacher concerned with improving the educational program in his own situation, the practical problem is how to acquire necessary competencies in the research process which include the ability to use the findings of other individuals and other disciplines as well as skill in engaging in research.

Because the focus of this volume has been primarily on increasing the competence of the classroom teacher and other curriculum planners in providing worthwhile experiences for learners, the use of cooperative curriculum research as a means of improving educational programs is stressed in this final chapter. Three problem areas are discussed: how can teachers develop competence to participate in the research process; in what areas can classroom research be used as a means of curriculum improvement; and how can the conditions conducive to research and experimentation be provided?

Developing Skill in and Understanding of the Research Process

Research as a process is aimed at discovering new ideas or practices as well as testing old ones, exploring or establishing relationships between causes and effects, or systematically gaining evidence about the nature of a particular problem. For convenience, the phases of this process are frequently described in terms of steps, although in reality they are neither neat nor discrete. Instead, there is usually a flow from one phase to another, sometimes back and forth, without clear demarcations. These phases are quite similar to the sequence of the problem-solving process: the problem is identified and refined; hypotheses are formulated or hunches are advanced about its solution; the hypotheses are tested and evidence is collected, organized, and analyzed; and generalizations are drawn from the data and are retested for further validation of conclusions. In a controlled laboratory situation, the research process may closely parallel these so-called problem-solving steps. In the classroom situation, the process flow is usually quite different.

Classroom research may have many different origins. One teacher may be dissatisfied with some aspect of the teaching–learning situation and may undertake research to find ways of improving it. Another teacher may have a hunch about a particular practice which he wishes to try out. In the first instance, the opening phase of the research process may require specific definition and delimitation of the problem area and the formulation of hypotheses for a solution. In the second situation, the hunches are in the form of possible values to be derived from implementing the practice and the problem is clearly defined. In the actual testing, it may soon become evident that the problem was not clearly analyzed and that further refinement is essential before the hypotheses can be reformulated and tested. When research is viewed as a flexible process, not a fixed formula to be followed step by step, then its application in a classroom situation can be better understood and carried forward. The idea of phases in the process helps to build a framework for understanding the total, ongoing process. It is always important to maintain high quality in the operations in each phase of the work if the resulting research is to be worthwhile.

THE PROCESS CAN BE ILLUSTRATED BY REPORTS OF ACTION RESEARCH STUDIES

Reports of classroom experimentation and action research are now appearing increasingly in professional literature. One of the chief values of these published accounts of studies conducted in the school setting by teachers and other curriculum workers, in addition to the generalizations reported from the findings, is the illustration of the process in operation as provided by those who participated in the activity. From such examples, the various phases of the research process are made evident for others to examine as an initial step to increasing their own insights. Research can have forbidding connotations for teachers, conjuring up a mental image of complicated statistical procedures, endless matching of individuals and controls, interminable evidence-collecting, and constant disruption of classroom routines. While some studies may actually conform to this picture, they do not represent the whole of research.

An individual teacher can use research techniques in attacking a problem which he faces in his classroom. One teacher's feelings of dissatisfaction can lead to the definition and delimitation of a problem, and from this to the derivation of hunches, hypotheses, or predictions, the actual testing and gathering of data about new practices, the interpretation of the evidence, and the forming of generalizations about the validity of the hunches. This process can, in turn, lead to the formulation and testing of new hypotheses, as illustrated in the case of a teacher trying to provide for differences in abilities among children.

> A fifth-grade classroom teacher, although concerned over a period of time about individual differences in reading ability among the members in his group, observed that variations among his students this year seemed to be even greater than usual. Aside from the teaching of reading, he noted other problems in planning for and with the youngsters because of these differences in reading achievement, interests, and motivations. He became sufficiently dissatisfied with the situation to search for some way of providing more adequately for these individual differences in reading as a first step toward improving the other aspects of the teaching–learning situation. He began by trying to discover what these differences were and how they manifested themselves. He assembled all the information available in the cumulative records, including results of standardized tests and measures of past achievement. He then studied some of the literature concerning reading and its effects upon other aspects of learning. From his examination of the literature, he decided that the picture of the students was incomplete and that he needed additional data in order to be able to define the problem more specifically.
>
> As a next step, the teacher gave a diagnostic reading test to pinpoint some of the difficulties his students were encountering. He asked for reports on the kinds of materials the students read and had them keep a log of their reading over a two-week period. He obtained information from the parents as to the reading materials available in the home and the nature of the children's reading out of school. From these data the teacher identified a specific problem within the broad area of concern so that it could

be studied. In addition to securing data about the reading skills and habits of the students, the teacher continued to study the literature about individualizing reading instruction. The evidence he collected about the students and the new insights he developed about individualizing reading instruction provided him with some hunches or hypotheses that he could test in his classroom.

This teacher believed that if he set aside more time for working with students in groups of two or three on reading skills, and discontinued the larger reading groups he had been using, then three benefits could result: the students' reading skills would increase, their interests in literature would expand, and their ability to work with similar materials in other class units would grow. He decided to test his hypothesis by providing direct reading instruction to students in very small groups for a two-month period. He continued to collect evidence about their reading skills and interests, and noted their behavior in using printed materials in a study of the community in which they were engaged. Then he tried his direct reading instruction plan and, at the end of the test period, gathered data about growth in the areas with which he was concerned.

In analyzing the evidence, he found that the work in small groups did help attain certain desired goals but that it made little difference in other areas of concern. Analysis of the data suggested some leads for other possible means of individualizing instruction. He believed, for example, that the additional use of multi-level reading materials seemed a good way to meet the needs of different individuals. The teacher then planned to test his hypothesis about the value of multi-level materials in reading instruction.

Groups of teachers can become involved in cooperative research. Often problems are building-wide or are the concern of a group of teachers working at a particular grade level. Research techniques offer possibilities for group problem-solving, as illustrated by the work of some high school teachers.

Some of the faculty members of a small rural high school, in examining the performance of their top students on a state-wide scholarship test, found that, although the pupils did reasonably well on certain parts of the examination, they were far below youth from other schools in understanding and appreciation of the arts, in handling concepts and abstractions, and in their breadth of reading. These were areas in which the teachers saw important educational goals.

The discussion of the findings resulted in several possible explanations. Two teachers raised the question as to whether this was a general condition or something which only occurred with these particular students. Some faculty members volunteered to gather comparable data for students who had taken this examination over the previous four or five years. Their report was submitted at the next meeting of the group and indicated that the condition had been essentially the same for previous students. Many guesses were made as to why the students in this school should do so much more poorly in these parts of the test than students from other schools, especially since the scores were comparable in sections requiring factual knowledge, and low only in appreciations, attitudes, and generalizing skills. Another meeting followed in which members reported additional findings about the experiences of learners in the areas of art, music, literature, and the assimilation of ideas. Other staff members summarized articles and reports about the achievements of youth in other small rural high schools.

After several sessions, the problem began to be clearer and to take on manageable proportions. The teachers decided that the reason their students did less well in certain parts of the examination probably was that they lacked meaningful experiences in these areas. The group hypothesized that if the students were to participate in a seminar, which offered cultural experiences that now seemed to be missing, their attainments in these areas would rise to a point where their understandings would show up favorably in the annual state-wide scholarship examination in comparison with youth from larger urban schools.

The teachers then set up the machinery for testing their hypothesis. Students whose records would cause one to predict that they would achieve the highest results on the examination were invited to participate in a special three-hour session one afternoon each week. Three teachers with differing interests and specializations volunteered to serve as seminar leaders and shifts were made in their teaching schedules to free them for this assignment. These leaders met for weekly preplanning sessions and reported regularly on their activities and problems to a faculty discussion group. A theme was selected and resources were made available. The students helped plan experiences which consisted of listening to symphonic music; reading more mature literature, poems, and plays; viewing television productions; visiting the nearest art museum which was forty-five miles distant; and listening to special resource persons discuss their areas of expertness. In general they explored cultural areas beyond those normally provided in their regular programs. The teachers compiled anecdotal and behavioral data about growth of individual students during the course of the year.

Eventually, these students took the state-wide examination and their scores, particularly in the areas which had concerned the faculty group earlier, were higher than those received by former students during previous years. The faculty group then examined the validity of this test of their original hypothesis and came up with generalizations for further testing. For example, was the provision of the kind of teaching–learning situation which extended the students' cultural orientation and discussion of ideas and concepts the important thing? Assuming it might be, the faculty group began to explore possible modifications in the curriculum design and adaptations in teaching methods which they might try out the following year to see if the values of the seminar could be extended to other students.

Although there are differences between the two examples, one involving a single teacher and the other a group, both show reliance on the systematized problem-solving method. In the case of the fifth-grade teacher, the generalizations from his research experience probably would be applied to his future fifth grades. At the high school level the seminar might lead to a continuation of this approach in the rural school involved, and a report of the findings might encourage other schools to test similar procedures. The brief descriptions of the two studies indicate the significant phases of the research process as they appeared in practice. While these steps are not always clear and distinct, it is possible to separate them for discussion purposes in order to indicate the competencies needed by persons who will conduct research to improve the quality of educational experiences for children and youth.

SPECIFIC PROBLEMS MUST BE CLEARLY IDENTIFIED AND DEFINED

The selection, definition, and delimitation of the specific problem to be studied is a critical phase of the research process. Many problems loom so large or are so ill-defined that it becomes difficult, if not impossible, to formulate and test related hypotheses. The problem area should be compact, and, at the same time, important to the persons who will study it and eventually take action. Significance, however, is only one of the important criteria for problem selection.

Problems which are too broad, too ambitious, or too unmanageable must be refined and narrowed enough to be handled within the framework of the research setting. For example, a teacher concerned about the provisions made for individual differences in his classroom will find that he must first select the more specific aspects of differentiated learning opportunities before he can proceed with study and experimentation which may reduce his dissatisfactions. However, problems can be made too narrow and too specific. The problem that is conceived too narrowly may be manageable but it may also lack significance or potential for providing a basis for generalization. For instance, a teacher may test a very concrete and specific technique for grouping his students in order to individualize instruction. But the procedure may be so atomized in terms of the total learning conditions that it will lack generality and significance. It may be necessary, in order to deal with a particular problem, to attack it in terms of important parts, but in doing so the researcher must keep constantly in view the relationship of each part with the whole.

Problem definition is one part of the research process that cannot be circumvented. Problem areas must be analyzed and refined before research approaches can emerge. The quality of problem definition determines the progress of other phases of the research process and poor problem definition leads to poor research. Problem identification is itself a process comprising several elements: the statement of concerns, identification of problem areas, analysis of the dimensions of the difficulties, examination of the assumptions underlying problems, delimiting the problem to its specifics, and a definite statement of study plans.

Of the many conditions which foster research and experimentation in the school situation, one of the most important is a climate that will provide sufficient security for individuals to feel free to discuss their real concerns and problems without feeling personally threatened. Unless this freedom to express genuine concerns exists, the problems identified may be superficial, innocuous, and "safe." If problems of vital concern are to be raised and their dimensions explored, the group must feel there is an expectation that honest problems exist and that these can be solved in an atmosphere of mutual aid and cooperative thinking.

In a group situation where individual concerns are expressed, their diversity frequently obstructs a clear beginning. One way over this hurdle is to conduct a problem census and to list individual concerns as they are expressed without stopping to discuss or analyze them, except for clarification of meaning or intent of the person suggesting the problem. After various concerns have been listed, the group can then examine the dimensions of the problems in terms of their common elements to find ways of proceeding. In identifying problems it is important to raise questions and not to state answers, for ready solutions may either suggest that fundamental causes are being overlooked or that no real test of a proposal is anticipated. As a group is able to narrow the concerns which it will pursue by stating, analyzing, and refining the problems expressed, it is then in a position to take next steps.

HYPOTHESES MUST BE FORMULATED AS A PRELUDE TO TESTING POSSIBLE SOLUTIONS

Formulating hypotheses or predicting possible means for problem solution is a second phase of the research process. At this point individuals voice their hunches on how to proceed toward desired goals. The two basic elements of a hunch or hypothesis involve the expression of the desired objectives and the means for attaining them. An hypothesis is frequently stated in terms of "if–then"; that is, if some practice is put into effect or some change made, then particular goals will be attained. For example, the fifth-grade teacher in the earlier illustration decided that if he spent more time teaching reading skills directly to groups of two or three students, then certain kinds of growth would result. The high school teachers predicted that if they established a seminar which provided particular kinds of learning opportunities, then participants would attain specific goals.

However stated, the hypothesis should predict what is likely to be the result of a particular action and should be phrased so as to indicate possible solutions to the problem. Consequently, it should be expressed in such a way that the conditions which are to be tested, the way in which the test is to occur, and the possible generalizations which may emerge are clearly stated. The quality of the problem definition can determine the nature of the hypotheses which are posed as possible solutions.

The sources for hypotheses are many. Some hunches emerge as the problem is explored and defined. Sometimes, past experiences of the researcher suggest possible solutions. Or reports of other research may suggest hypotheses. It is important to explore all possible hunches or hypotheses as intensively as is practical, in terms of their clarity and specificity, to see whether they are testable and whether they provide leads to the means for testing. The practicality of an hypothesis, aside from the promise it has as a potential solution to a problem or a source of action and prediction, must be judged by whether techniques for gathering evidence about its effectiveness when tested, are either available or can be developed.

The conditions under which experimentation is being planned can affect the quality of the proposed hypotheses. Depending on the maturity of the group or the kind of leadership which exists therein, proposals for hypotheses may be prematurely criticized, and as a result creativity may be stifled. In cooperative curriculum research, human relations within the group can influence the nature of the proposals to be tried out and the extent to which resources (such as literature, consultants, and personal experience) are used in the formulation of hypotheses to be tested.

HYPOTHESES MUST BE TESTED AND DATA GATHERED ABOUT THEIR EFFECTIVENESS

Following the formulation of an hypothesis, plans must be made for putting the proposed solution into action and gathering evidence of its value as a possible means of bringing about curriculum improvement. Testing an hypothesis means actually putting the change into practice and observing the results. Some preliminary steps may be required. In order to test a particular practice or procedure, new insights, skills, and knowledge may have to be acquired by the teacher, new materials prepared or located, or certain conditions in a particular situation altered. Taking the proposed action, therefore, may require considerable preplanning and acquisition of necessary competencies prior to or concomitant with instituting a reasonable test of a proposal.

Data-gathering and the handling of evidence are other critical aspects of the research process involving the collection of appropriate evidence about the testing of the particular proposal. Carefully formulated hypotheses provide leads to the action to be taken in their testing and, at the same time, should provide guides for the kinds of data to be gathered, analyzed, and interpreted. Gathering some kinds of data may require considerable skill and technical competence. The selection of the techniques and procedures for assembling test data requires an understanding of the nature of evidence, and of its reliability and validity. It requires a knowledge of and skill in selecting methods and research techniques. The varied kinds of behavior studied and the goal attainment may necessitate the use of different evidence-gathering techniques. These were discussed in detail in Chapter 11 as they relate to evaluation of pupil growth and school programs.

While data-gathering as a research technique will have to be somewhat more systematic than that done in the normal collecting of evidence for appraisal, it is often possible to plan so that much of the data gathered will serve for purposes of student and teacher evaluation as well. For example, a teacher who wants to know how his pupils use their leisure time may work out with them a time schedule which they then keep up to date, using occasional class periods to check on progress and problems. If data-gathering is always an added and cumbersome burden, busy teachers may resist participating in the research process even though they are cognizant of the ultimate value of this means for curriculum improvement.

The value of a study rests on the quality of the evidence secured and its analysis and interpretation. Methods of analysis depend on the kind of data, the means by which they are collected, and the alternatives for handling and categorizing them. Good research designs take into account problems of data-handling in the building of a study so that evidence is collected, analyzed, and interpreted in the most appropriate way to provide an adequate test of the hypotheses. Teachers and other curriculum workers who engage in research will constantly have to expand their competencies in this particular aspect. Even professional researchers must constantly acquire new skills and insights as they confront problems in methodology which require abilities they do not have or have not acquired to sufficient degree. Actually working with data and handling evidence is probably the best way of acquiring necessary competence in this area.

CONCLUSIONS MUST BE DRAWN ABOUT THE RELATIONS BETWEEN THE ACTION TAKEN AND THE DESIRED OBJECTIVES

If the action has been taken as planned, and if the evidence gathered has been assessed for validity and reliability, then the consequences of the experimental action or hypotheses can be judged in terms of larger purposes. Specific conclusions should be drawn about the varied aspects of the problem so that those engaged in the study can determine which questions have been answered and which need further testing. Generalizations—within the limits of the problem studied, the hypotheses tested, and the data gathered—can be drawn which will guide the future behavior of the teacher or other curriculum worker. When generalizations are within the limits of the research design and do not extend beyond what is warranted, then it is possible that the researcher will be in a position to retest a particular method with some confidence in his findings. Care in interpreting data and drawing conclusions from tests of hypotheses must be exercised to avoid making overgeneralizations.

Important outcomes of engaging in research are the evolving of new insights into problems and the building of a body of experience which leads to continuous retesting of findings in related situations. Action research provides opportunities to change behavior and grow professionally because it involves the actual use by the teacher of the practices and procedures as part of the research process. The findings, in a sense, are already a part of the persons who have participated in carrying on the study or experiment. The promise of cooperative curriculum research is in its twofold possibilities—as a means for improving the quality of learning experiences directly, and as a method for extending professional growth for further program development.

Using Research in Developing a Curriculum Based on Persistent Life Situations

While research can make important contributions to the solution of curriculum problems and to the improvement of instructional practices, classroom experimentation, per se, is not a panacea. Not all curriculum improvement lends itself to or requires research. Some changes can be effected by exercising good judgment, which may or may not be based on research findings. Some problems can be resolved simply by making available additional resources or experiences of one kind or another.

However, there are many types of problems to which research techniques can make fundamental contributions. These fall in four major areas, as follows . . .

> Diagnosis of Situations—Research can help to extend the basis on which judgments and predictions are made by increasing insights and understandings about relationships which exist between certain causes and effects.
>
> Testing of Practices and Procedures—Research is an appropriate means for testing, in specific situations, the effectiveness of ideas, practices, procedures, or materials which some individuals and a considerable body of literature extol as promising for the improvement of teaching and learning.
>
> Building of Theory—Research is needed in developing and testing conceptual frameworks and theories to guide the teaching–learning process. While fundamental research alone has not provided needed curriculum theory, and it is quite unlikely that cooperative curriculum research alone will do so, both can contribute toward understandings of learners in classroom settings which can help in building theory.
>
> Building of Research and Teaching Skills—Research can contribute to building many competencies which have their counterparts in effective teaching. Some of the same techniques and procedures used in gathering evidence, for example, are equally applicable in evaluating pupil growth. The skills needed in generalizing from research data are not very different from those used in generalizing in other situations.

Research relating to diagnosing a situation, to testing practices and procedures, to building basic educational concepts and theories, and to extending research and teaching skills can be an inherent part of a curriculum planned to help children and youth deal with the situations of daily life and the persistent life situations which are a part of them. Essentially, the proposed curriculum design exemplifies the problem-solving approach in action—as teachers and learners work together on situations in and out of the classroom and as faculty groups look at basic issues and concepts. Specific questions which are suggestive of the problems curriculum workers must solve are indicated in earlier chapters. Chapters 2 and 3, particularly, point to the role of research in providing insights into the characteristics and values of society and the nature of the learner and the way he learns. Questions in these areas that must be asked by those responsible for the experiences of children and youth are outlined. In Chapter 11 questions that merit a research approach in evaluating the total educational program are named. In the pages which follow, the use of research in dealing with these questions is viewed in terms of some of the persistent professional problems of the teacher who implements the proposed design.

RESEARCH CAN CONTRIBUTE TO ANALYSES OF PERSISTENT LIFE SITUATIONS

Charts of the persistent life situations learners face can be developed through research or tested for their accuracy by classroom experimentation. This represents an important area in which teachers' judgments or generalized statements about learners should be supported by data. Studies can be made of the ways in which persistent life situations appear for particular age groups, for the gifted, and for slow learners. What are the recurring problems with which these learners are trying to cope as they carry on their everyday activities in homes and community? What are the immediate situations of special interest and concern to them—those of which they are aware as well as those about which, while just as real, they are not articulate? Because communities differ, teachers will have to acquire insights into the aspects of problems peculiar to their school population. For example, what aspects of their natural environment are learners in a city slum area trying to control? What understandings about technological resources do rural children bring to the learning situation? Phrasing the scope of the curriculum in terms of learners' persistent life situations does not, in and of itself, guarantee that needs will be met. Teachers must have means of translating general analyses into the realities of living for their particular groups.

Translating general analyses into the situations and experiences which have meaning for specific groups and particular individuals also requires continuous study of the effects of a changing world upon learners' lives. Teachers dedicated to helping learners meet persistent problems of living effectively should be aware of the ways in which these problems are altered with a changing world. Television, for example, is sending children and youth to school with experiences and understandings quite different from those of learners of a decade ago. What does this mean for their school experiences—how can these new understandings be used; are there new levels of sophistication about this changing world with which children and youth must cope; what negative influences will have to be counteracted; what does the existence of television mean for such a problem as developing reading interests; what educational possibilities are there in this medium? Youth today is facing military service. What does this mean for high school education? With what problems will the girls, as well as the boys, be expected to deal? Faculties concerned with the situations their learners are actually facing will identify an unending stream of emerging problems.

The proposed curriculum design calls for a high level of insight into the needs of children and youth and into the effectiveness with which these needs are being met. Techniques are required that will aid teachers in developing more accurate understandings of learners and the environments from which they come. The procedures of research offer possibilities for helping teachers to study individuals and groups, to identify the immediate and recurring situations with which they are and should be dealing, to gain insight into ways of working with learners on these problems, and to evaluate the effectiveness of the guidance provided pupils as they meet the persistent problems of living which are a part of their everyday experiences.

RESEARCH CAN ENHANCE UNDERSTANDING OF HOW TO HELP LEARNERS DEVELOP FUNCTIONAL GENERALIZATIONS

An important premise on which the proposed curriculum design rests is that the generalizations most effective for living in today's world are those that are developed as learners are helped to deal with persistent life situations in the ways they actually meet them. This is a premise which requires constant testing in action. Studies are needed to demonstrate how everyday situations can be capitalized upon most effectively. For example, what constitutes the most effective use of subject matter? How will this differ for learners of varying levels of intellectual ability? How "real" does a situation have to be—can a make-believe store or a mock railroad station actually develop the desired generalizations? How are vicarious experiences best used? What difference does the intellectual maturity and experience background of the learners make in determining whether direct experiences are needed? What is involved in the process of generalizing? How can children and youth with differing intellectual ability best be guided in arriving at sound generalizations? Studies that will reveal how effectively generalizations developed in school are transferred to home and community are also needed. If carry-over is not apparent, what hypotheses does this suggest?

RESEARCH CAN PROVIDE INSIGHT INTO PROBLEMS OF HUMAN RELATIONSHIPS

Some of the most significant reports of cooperative curriculum research studies have been those which explored problems of human relations—in the classroom, in faculty groups, as an aspect of the research process itself. A curriculum design which is based upon the techniques of co-operative problem-solving suggests many such studies. Teachers will require help in examining critically their roles as leaders and resource persons. Techniques for studying the roles played by group members, both at the classroom and the faculty levels, and procedures for helping members of a group to make their most effective contributions are important. Under a curriculum which stresses the translation of democratic values into action, insights are needed as to how learners can be helped best to develop these values. Studies will have to be repeated on many maturity levels and in many settings. Such studies might also focus on problems of improving the effectiveness of groups, enhancing morale, and involving parents and other community members in developing the proposed curriculum design.

RESEARCH CAN BE USED TO SOLVE PROBLEMS OF CLASSROOM AND SCHOOL ORGANIZATION

Preceding chapters have indicated many problems of classroom and school organization for which relatively few valid research answers exist today. Even if the accumulation of research in such areas were significant and definitive, the problems merit re-examination in terms of the goals and values of a particular curriculum design. Studies initiated to discover how to meet the needs of individuals most effectively under the proposed curriculum design would be important. Although earlier chapters have spelled out a number of possible solutions, accurate data regarding what actually happens to individuals are vitally needed. School faculties may also find it necessary to study cooperatively problems of scheduling and of how to make the school community an effective learning environment. With reference to the latter, for example, the proposal that learners could take on service responsibilities to the school merits careful appraisal—how does the time expenditure balance what is learned; what responsibilities are appropriate for learners of various maturity levels; what planning is required before such experiences yield the desired learnings?

RESEARCH CAN LEAD TO THE DEVELOPMENT AND EFFECTIVE USE OF RESOURCES

Cooperative efforts to locate, or at times to develop, and test the effectiveness of materials and resources can be of importance under the proposed design. Surveys of community resources and studies of community influences on learners' present generalizations are of particular value. Groups of teachers may study the possibilities of working with many resource books of a pamphlet nature rather than with sets of textbooks. Problems of how to locate materials appropriate to the needs of learners and still of desired reading levels may loom large. Experimentation is needed in finding how to use firsthand resources rather than relying solely on printed materials. Still another area of study which has special significance in the proposed curriculum design is the role of learners in locating resources and of teachers in developing instructional materials. Problems of when and under what conditions the varied kinds and uses of instructional materials are most effective in teaching and learning deserve a research approach.

RESEARCH CAN EXTEND EVALUATION SKILLS

The proposed curriculum design poses many new evaluation problems. Standardized tests and examinations in traditional subject areas alone will not serve. Cooperative studies will be needed to develop more effective evaluation procedures, both for studying learners' growth and for looking at the total curriculum design. Chapter 11 suggests a variety of possible techniques, but studies will be needed to make these effective in individual classrooms and schools.

Not all problems that teachers and other curriculum workers will face in developing the proposed curriculum will lend themselves to a research approach. Many, however, will be solved more effectively if problems are clarified, hypotheses advanced and data collected, and generalizations drawn. Teachers who are involved in the research process will actually use many of the data-gathering techniques that they already use on a day-by-day basis in the process of studying learners and appraising their growth. However, for sound problem-solving, many new competencies must be developed.

Providing Conditions Conducive to Research and Experimentation

The need for research and experimentation as the basis for improving instruction has been stressed in a growing body of literature. While there is evidence that research is used increasingly, teachers are just beginning to realize their own potential as classroom experimenters and curriculum researchers. Although the research process is readily grasped conceptually, unless conditions are created which facilitate its use, teachers and others concerned with curriculum development will continue to use methods involving casual inquiry and discussion when research and experimentation would be more appropriate and would lead to better solutions of teaching–learning problems.

Cooperative curriculum research is research conducted by a group as a means of bringing about change. Because it involves more than a single person, and therefore extends the resources available for conducting studies, cooperative curriculum research can help to create a climate of group support and feelings of mutual security which are important for stimulating experimentation. However, when research is conducted on a cooperative basis, new dimensions are added to the competencies necessary for conducting research—skill in human relations and skill in group processes. Certain conditions are essential in the local situation if either individual or cooperative curriculum research is to be carried on effectively.

A CLIMATE OF FREEDOM TO EXPERIMENT MUST BE PROVIDED

If classroom research is to be undertaken, teachers must work under conditions which encourage freedom to invent, create, explore, and experiment. The school is a social institution and the dynamics within its structure can either facilitate or impede a willingness to experiment with new ideas and relationships. The roles played by the administrative hierarchy, the relationships between the school and the community, the dynamics of the varied groups and subgroups within the professional staff, are just a few of the factors which influence the climate for experimenting.

Curriculum leaders can develop a respect for and an understanding of research and experimentation. If a climate is established which enables both lay persons and professional staff to view education as a dynamic process in which teachers and other curriculum planners constantly seek more effective teaching–learning procedures, then the possibility of admitting the existence of problems which require study and change is enhanced. This need for an atmosphere of mutual understanding and trust was pointed to earlier as basic to good problem identification. In some schools, teachers do not feel it is wise to admit they have problems or that they do not have all the answers and competencies needed to cope with particular situations. The existence of an instructional problem may be viewed as a criticism of the individual teacher or of the school in general.

If the teacher feels that it is wiser to conform or to agree with an administrator or supervisor than to risk possible conflict or censure, he will participate in discussions accordingly, and free expression will be inhibited. On the other hand, if the persons with administrative responsibilities strive consciously to build feelings of mutual trust and confidence so that teachers do not feel threatened by possible penalties, the need for assistance with instructional problems may be expressed more freely. When all persons concerned with the educational program feel free to discuss their problems and need for help, and when all are able to demonstrate respect for an experimental approach to problems faced, then teachers are more likely to find encouragement to use this same approach. The role of the person with leadership responsibilities for curriculum planning is particularly critical in stimulating experimentation and encouraging research for he sets the tone by his own behavior and by the support and encouragement he gives to others. Such support is usually perceived through his actions rather than through his exhortations.

Opportunities for teachers to help one another can stimulate a research approach. Feelings of freedom to state one's problem may emerge when the individual teacher finds that others also have problems. Frequently, the discussion of difficulties and experiences which takes place in the informal atmosphere of a teachers' room may be more realistic than the problems voiced in faculty or committee meetings. This exchange of ideas may help the teacher to recognize that the real concerns which he cautiously expresses to his colleagues in the informal situation are similar to the problems others face. When the same supportive climate is transferred to the more formal structures, teachers and administrators are likely to find that their real problems are faced by others and that these can be discussed with greater profit than the more "respectable" but less important problems. One technique used by a group in getting its members to express real concerns while building an agenda was to ask "What do you want to work on?" This personalizing of agenda items often brings a very different response from the question, "What should the group work on?"

Security and support come with increased ability to work in groups. Maturity in a group is evidenced by the ability of its members to identify quickly and accurately their real concerns, to bring to bear available resources in the solution of such problems, to provide support and security for individuals, and to diagnose and overcome difficulties in the group's own processes as it works toward problem solution. In such a group, members can freely admit personal and professional inadequacies without feeling threatened, and can expect that some help will be forthcoming. For cooperative curriculum research, the development of mature group behavior is an integral first step toward the creation of the necessary conditions for undertaking experimentation. However, the improvement in methods of group work is one very important aspect of cooperative curriculum research, and not the whole of the process. Research skills must be developed as an essential component of cooperative research, for the end goal is the improvement of instructional practices through curriculum research and not simply the acquisition of new methods of group work.

Administrators can build support for research in the community. By involving interested lay persons in analysis of problems with which they can provide help and by channeling lay dissatisfactions into experimental programs, respect for a research approach to curriculum change can be fostered. Because industry, labor, business, and government rely on research and experimentation for the development of new products and increased sales and service, many lay persons have technical understandings and competencies which can be shared with groups working on curriculum improvement. A favorable climate, achieved through school and community cooperation, can extend a feeling of support and encouragement for research and experimentation. In general, parents are concerned that their children secure the best education possible. If they come to see experimentation and research as important factors in attaining this end, they are more likely to aid and accept this approach to curriculum change. Teacher morale is a product of many personal, school, and community forces. Building morale is an important step in encouraging people to invent and create.

Support for individual experimentation is as essential as encouragement of group research. Because of their very personal nature, research into some problems is best done by individuals. When one teacher wants to experiment, he should receive the same support and help from the administrative and supervisory staff as do groups. Wherever there is a desire to explore and experiment, encouragement should be provided insofar as possible. This individual effort may eventually lead to a group undertaking, but personal concerns should be capitalized upon and encouraged. The conditions which facilitate such individual activity may create a favorable climate resulting in larger and more comprehensive group efforts.

TIME, FUNDS, AND OPPORTUNITIES MUST BE PROVIDED FOR RESEARCH AND EXPERIMENTATION

Research, especially research of good quality, requires time and resources. While some kinds of research can be carried on as an integral part of the teaching–learning situation, planning, collecting and analyzing data, interpreting evidence, communicating findings and sharing these efforts with others, require time and resources greater than are normally available to the teacher whose entire day is devoted to classroom situations.

Time for research activities must be arranged. As with almost all curriculum improvement activities, time for planning must be provided. The means for insuring time for teachers to plan and to work on varied aspects of research are many. These include release of teachers from part of their regular load, or administrative arrangements whereby learners are not in school for part of certain days, or various other approaches which enable teachers to participate in research without other undue demands.

Finding time to carry on the activities involved in curriculum improvement, and particularly in cooperative research, is one of the major barriers to effective experimentation. Even where it is not actually a barrier, lack of time may be regarded by teachers as a legitimate obstacle. Administrative arrangements can be made to provide time for study and research by expenditure of funds for substitutes, extension of the professional year with appropriate compensation, development of new schedules, reassessment of time-consuming activities of the professional staff, and provision of clerical and other assistance as a means of relieving teachers of routine but essential activities.

Funds are necessary for carrying on some cooperative curriculum research. Money is necessary for the development and maintenance of a professional library, for purchase of instruments for gathering data, for obtaining necessary instructional materials, or for securing other assistance for carrying on curriculum research. Research materials require budget allotments beyond normal expenditures for teaching aids. For example, in order to improve communication among teachers and groups within a school and within the school system, funds may be needed for developing communication techniques and methods. Reports which make it possible to share ongoing activities or findings may take additional funds for communication.

The crucial role of consultants in facilitating curriculum improvement has been discussed in the preceding chapter. Funds are needed to secure essential services. The effective resource person can provide stimulation, expertness, and assistance which may be extremely helpful in extending the teachers' own experiences as well as in helping groups maintain perspective. The wise selection and use of consultants can facilitate all phases of research, for their help may be needed in developing research skills, extending understandings of the research process, expediting resources for research activities, and building group maturity. Expenditures for adequate consultant service, from within or without the local group, can be among the best investments a school system can make.

Inservice education for cooperative curriculum research is essential. Effective participation in initiating and carrying out cooperative curriculum research requires competencies which group members may lack or which they may not have developed adequately. The many different skills and understandings necessary for carrying on such research can be acquired through education and experience. Some of the necessary insights, knowledge, and skills can be acquired through appropriate courses at colleges or universities. Special sessions can be arranged to provide opportunities for acquiring new learnings concerning the research process. Or, by participating in the research process and stopping when necessary to develop essential research skills, participants can acquire the special competencies needed for qualitative research.

Research on obstacles to experimentation in a particular situation is needed. Many barriers to the initiation and undertaking of qualitative action research have been explored in the literature. Some of these are caused by poor human relations problems, some by personal problems, some by the institutional problems which arise from school and community structure and interrelationships. The general conditions which facilitate research—development of a favorable climate, assistance, and encouragement to experiment; support in terms of morale, time, and human and material resources; and assistance in developing needed competencies—suggest some of the areas which may increase the quantity and quality of studies to improve school practices. However, the manifestation of specific barriers in particular situations may differ considerably. Curriculum leaders may well undertake research to determine the nature of these obstacles to conducting curriculum research in a local school system. One area which needs considerable study, for example, is the personality structure which leads some individuals to be more suspectible to researching and experimenting than others. The effect of the roles and the nature of the leadership provided in a school by so-called status persons can be studied for changes which will stimulate research. Better quality research results as individuals and groups study the research process itself while analyzing the problem to which the process is being applied.

A research attitude is one of the more difficult prerequisites of quality research to acquire. Procedures and techniques, know-how and competence, can be developed if a willingness exists to engage in research on curriculum problems. How research attitudes are acquired and what makes some individuals more disposed to experimentation than others are questions on which studies are needed. Arranging some of the conditions which are conducive to undertaking research may be an initial step toward involving individuals in the process. Personal experience with cooperative curriculum research seems to be one of the best means for facilitating further teacher undertakings of this kind. An important means of acquiring research experience is for the individual teacher to explore a problem which concerns him in his own situation. He may seek resource help, he may share his problem with others eventually, but he can begin by studying his own problem and attempting to do something about it. Once having had a successful experience, he may develop a positive attitude toward experimenting with curriculum changes. If a teacher has actually achieved improvement in some phase of the educational process by conducting research, the individual, and the group as well, may be more kindly disposed to continue to use research and to value the learnings which emerge.

Sharing of research is essential. Many studies involve aspects of larger curriculum problems. Only by sharing research findings can cumulative experiences be acquired which add to knowledge about the teaching–learning situation. Assuming that good quality research has been carried on, findings and generalizations have significance worthy of dissemination and communication. However, much additional study is needed to determine ways of sharing findings and communicating research within a school. Faculty meetings devoted to research-reporting, house organs which report on research findings, and journal articles are just a few of the means of communicating findings to others.

Building a Research Base for a Curriculum for Modern Living

Curriculum improvement requires many different approaches, the use of a variety of techniques, and the combined efforts of all those who would effectively select and organize experiences in developing a curriculum for modern living. A curriculum design will have a shallow foundation if it is based entirely on opinions and value judgments, even though these are the combined insights of persons dedicated to the welfare of children and youth and to the perpetuation of values that society holds dear. There must be a systematic effort to draw upon research. Interdisciplinary studies are needed, and the significant insights of specialists in fields other than education should be marshaled, analyzed, evaluated, and interpreted.

In the total process of evolving a design, the classroom teacher plays many roles. In the area of research, he must be both a consumer and a producer. He must be able to use, intelligently and appropriately, the knowledges and understandings derived from research. He must also be willing to conduct studies of his own and to approach problems he faces in a research fashion. Just as a curriculum built around the actual problems children and youth face creates conditions for maximum growth and learning, the persistent professional problems which are the concern of teachers and other curriculum planners serve to provide the areas which should be studied and in which research should be carried on.

As stated in Chapter 1, this is an age of fear and anxiety, but it is also a time of hope and expectation. The degree to which tensions will be mitigated and promises realized depends, in part, on the ways in which teachers and others meet the challenge of developing education as a positive social force. As a nation, America has made almost unbelievable progress, and yet the problems of everyday living grow ever more complex. While there is faith in the power of education to help children and youth function effectively in the world of today and that of tomorrow, there is little unanimity in convictions about the nature of the curriculum design which will be most useful in attaining this goal.

The fundamental issues which underlie the choices made by those who guide the learning experiences of children and youth must be re-examined in terms of new findings and changing conditions. Alternatives for resolving basic curriculum problems will have to be critically studied and appraised to determine how well they actually contribute to the achievement of desired ends. Ways will have to be found for using the constantly growing body of research reported by educators and specialists in related fields. But at the same time, those who work most closely with learners must extend their competencies in studying the potency of school-guided experiences for helping individuals cope with the persistent life situations they face.

In this volume, a proposal for a curriculum design has been presented. This is not a blueprint for an educational program, but rather it is an expression of a particular set of beliefs applied to the issues involved in curriculum development. One basic tenet has been emphasized repeatedly—that the individual teacher must constantly test and evaluate his own practices as these affect the total program. Only the teacher, working cooperatively with other planners within the framework of the local setting, can translate the proposed design into reality and breathe life into the concept of a curriculum for modern living.

Related Readings

ASSOCIATION FOR SUPERVISION AND CURRICULUM DEVELOPMENT. *Research for Curriculum Improvement.* 1957 Yearbook. Washington, D.C.: The Association, 1957.

BARR, ARVIL S., ROBERT A. DAVIS, AND PALMER O. JOHNSON. *Educational Research and Appraisal.* New York: J. B. Lippincott Company, 1953.

COREY, STEPHEN M. *Action Research to Improve School Practices.* New York: Bureau of Publications, Teachers College, Columbia University, 1953.

FESTINGER, LEON, AND DANIEL KATZ. *Research Methods in the Behavioral Sciences.* New York: The Dryden Press, Inc., 1953.

FOSHAY, ARTHUR W., KENNETH D. WANN, AND ASSOCIATES. *Children's Social Values.* New York: Bureau of Publications, Teachers College, Columbia University, 1954.

JAHODA, MARIE, MORTON DEUTSCH, AND STUART W. COOK. *Research Methods in Social Relations.* New York: The Dryden Press, Inc., 1951.

LINDQUIST, E. F. *Design and Analysis of Experiments in Psychology and Education.* Boston: Houghton Mifflin Company, 1953.

PASSOW, A. HARRY, MATTHEW B. MILES, STEPHEN M. COREY, AND DALE DRAPER. *Training Curriculum Leaders for Cooperative Research.* New York: Bureau of Publications, Teachers College, Columbia University, 1955.

WALLIS, WILSON A., AND HARRY V. ROBERTS. *Statistics, A New Approach.* Glencoe, Ill.: Free Press, 1956.

INDEX

Action research, 706–712
Activities—*See* Experiences
Adolescence, developmental tasks of, 57
Adults, typical and persistent life situations faced by, 169–321
Aesthetic expression and appreciation
  an area of persistent life situations, 149, 159
  experiences of a fifth grade, 550, 552, 562
  experiences of a first grade, 639–641
  experiences of a tenth grade, 604–608
  typical situations faced by children, youth, adults, 224–235
Aims of education, 7–9, 479–484
Analysis of persistent life situations
  as an aspect of cooperative research, 718–719
  precautions in using, 165–167
  problems to be dealt with in, 152–154
  steps in making, 151–154
  use of, 322–332
Analysis of typical situations of everyday living
  aesthetic expression and appreciation, 224–235
  economic, social, political structures and forces, 294–321
  group membership, 248–259
  health, 172–191
  intellectual power, 192–213
  intergroup relationships, 260–267
  moral choices, 214–223
  natural phenomena, 269–285
  person-to-person relationships, 237–247
  technological resources, 286–293
Appraisal—*See* Evaluation
Approaches to designing the curriculum
  broad areas, 87, 97–103
  common goals and points of difference, 106–110
  needs or problems of learners, 87, 103–105, 114–115
  separate subjects, 87, 88–91
  subject fields, 87, 91–97
Areas of living curriculum—*See* Broad areas curriculum design
Articulation of educational program, 468–471

Balance
  in development, 118, 121–125, 325–328, 348–349
  of experiences in a fifth grade, 546–548, 570–571

of experiences in a first grade, 654–655
persistent life situation charts as a guide to, 325–328
Beginning the school year, 426–429
in a fifth grade, 525–548
Behavior
needs and growth revealed by, 480–482, 484–491
records of, 492–498
systematic observation of, 486–487
Broad areas curriculum design, 87, 97–103

Changing the curriculum, procedures for, 19–21, 362–367, 688–692
Charts of persistent life situations as children, youth, and adults face them, 169–321
Child growth and development
characteristics of, 53–66
related to learners' needs, 61–65
Childhood, developmental tasks of, 56–57
Children, typical and persistent life situations faced by, 169–321
Clinics in curriculum planning, 687
Colleges and universities
in curriculum improvement, 691
as source of consultants, 697–698
Committees for curriculum planning, 683–686
Common goals of different curriculum designs, 106–108
Communication
curriculum improvement and, 676–678
leadership and, 694
tenth-grade study of, 604–608
Community
backgrounds affect learning, 337–338
curriculum development and, 26–50
fifth grade and, 544–546, 554, 564–569
first grade and, 620–621
length of school year and, 466–467
relating school experiences to, 351–352
as source of learning experiences, 351–352, 473–475
tenth grade and, 606, 608–610
using resources of, 460–461, 465–467, 471–475, 554, 564–565, 569, 606
Concepts, development of, 73–77, 110, 130–131, 406–407, 719
Conferences
for curriculum improvement, 687, 689–690
on pupil progress, 500–501
Consultants in curriculum planning, 696–699, 726
Contemporary life and education, 26–50
Content of instruction, selection of, 9–11, 86–105, 109–110, 116–117, 130–136, 329–331, 374
Continuity
of experiences, 12, 117, 125–127, 328, 469
of persistent life situations, 125–127, 469
pupil–teacher planning and, 469–470
through articulation, 468–471
Cooperation
as requisite of curriculum development, 693–694, 722–725
of school and community, 125, 325, 337–338, 351, 428, 465–467, 515–516
Cooperative curriculum research, 706–729
Core program, 356–358, 580–581, 589–610
Criteria
for curriculum development, 121–145, 510–517
for selecting experiences, 109–110, 117–121, 345–351
Cultural heritage
acquaintance with, in a fifth grade, 575–577
acquaintance with, in a first grade, 657
bases for organizing, 330, 360, 403–409
as an educational goal, 88–89, 92
persistent life situations and, 130–136, 330–331, 360, 374
selection from, 130–136, 330–331
Cumulative records—*See* Records of learners
Curriculum
See also Approaches to designing the curriculum; Curriculum design; Curriculum improvement; Curriculum issues; Curriculum problems; Experiences
balance in, 118, 121–125, 325–328, 348–349
basic issues in, 3–25
broad areas approach, 87, 97–103
child development and, 53–66
content of, 9–11, 86–105, 109–110, 116–117, 130–136, 329–331, 374
continuity in, 12, 117, 125–127, 328, 469

criteria for selecting experiences, 109–110, 117–121, 130–136, 344–351
definition of, 9, 85
democratic values and, 26–34, 48–49, 516–517
differentiation of, 15–18, 117–121, 141, 432–457, 610–611
elementary school, 352–355
essentials of, 121–145
evaluation of, 510–517
foundations of, 22–23, 26–49, 51–81
general education in, 17–18, 137–140, 356–358
high school, 355–362
individual differences and, 15–18, 117–121, 141, 432–457, 610–612
learners' needs and problems as an approach, 87, 103–105
learning process and, 66–81, 140–142
moving from traditional designs of, 144–145, 331, 360, 362–367, 470
organization of, 11–13, 86–105, 114–117, 360, 365
persistent life situations and, 114–145
place of subject fields in, 133–134, 360, 362–367, 407–409, 613
as continuous process, 117–121
scope of, 9–11, 86–105, 117, 121–125
selection of experiences for, 109–110, 116–117, 130–136, 335–367
separate subjects approach, 87, 88–91
sequence of, 11–13, 86–105, 117, 125–127
society a guide to, 26–49, 142–143
specialized education in, 17, 137–140, 358–359, 613
subject fields approach, 87, 91–97
values and, 26–34, 48–49, 86, 88–89, 92–93, 95, 101–102, 104, 106–110, 516–517
Curriculum design
See also Broad areas; Needs and problems of learners; Separate subjects; Subject fields
areas of common concern, 106–108
defined, 85
points of difference, 109–110
Curriculum improvement
approaches to, 672–677
clinics for, 687
committees for, 683–686
communication and, 676–678, 694
conditions for, 669–670
consultants in, 696–699, 726
defined, 661–662
dynamic aspect of, 667–668
evaluation in, 476–479, 680–681
facets of, 667–669
groups in, 674–676, 682–683
individuals' contributions to, 20, 666–667, 674–676, 678–679
individual school and, 674–675
leadership for, 145, 670, 692–695
method of, 20–21, 662–670
moving from traditional designs in, 144–145, 331, 360, 362–367, 470
organizing for, 670–681
parents and, 325, 351, 678–679
persistent life situations and, 332, 699–703
personnel for, 20, 666–667, 678–679, 696–699
procedures for, 19–21, 362–367, 681–692
process characteristics of, 662–670
research and, 692, 705–729
resources for, 669–670, 691–692, 696–699
setting for, 666
school goals and, 671–672
school visits and, 690–691
skills for, 680
study groups in, 687
supervisory conferences and, 689–690
surveys and, 688–689
teacher's role in, 666–667
trends in, 664–665
workshops in, 669, 686–688
Curriculum issues, 3–25
Curriculum problems
the learner and, 53–66
the learning process and, 66–81
the nature of society and, 35–49
social values and, 27–34

Daily planning, 379–380, 391–392
Daily program—*See* Program; Scheduling
Democratic values and curriculum development, 26–34, 48–49, 86, 88–89, 92–93, 95, 101–102, 104, 106–110, 516–517
Depth of learning, 124, 127–130, 575–577, 614
Designing the curriculum
approaches to, 85–110
concerns of learners the starting point, 114–115, 121, 326–328, 512, 571–573
a continuous process, 117–121
relating everyday concerns to persistent life situations, 115–117, 128–130,

140–142, 148–151, 322–325, 512
Developmental tasks of learners, 56–59, 62
Differences among individuals—*See* Individual differences
Drill, place and nature of, 78, 415–417

Economic, social, and political structures and forces
an area of persistent life situations, 150, 164–165
experiences of a fifth grade with, 544–545, 552, 554–555, 559, 561–563, 565–569
experiences of a first grade with, 651–653
experiences of a tenth grade with, 593–601, 604–608
typical situations faced by children, youth, adults, 294–321
Education
control of, 4–5
foundation areas of, 22–23, 26–49, 51–81
general, 17–18, 137–140, 356–358, 613
goals of, 7–8
history of, 4–5
issues in, 3–25
philosophical foundations of, 22–23
positive social force, 5–6
psychological foundations of, 22, 51–81
social foundations of, 22, 26–49
specialized, 17, 137–140, 358–359, 613
Educational program, evaluation of, 510–517
Elementary school
curriculum experiences in, 352–355
evaluating growth in, 476–499
exceptional pupils in, 446–457
guiding learning in, 369–429
interage grouping in, 437–438
pupil–teacher planning in, 379–397, 469–470
scheduling in, 353–355, 398–399, 400–402
typical situations faced by children in, 174–321
work in a fifth grade, 521–577
work in a first grade, 616–657
Environmental factors and forces
growth in ability to deal with, 147, 150, 268–271, 286–287, 294–295
learning and, 15, 60, 68, 72, 337–338, 351–352, 418–423, 471–475, 656–657
Equipment—*See* Materials
Evaluation
a continuous process, 476–477, 517
defined, 476–477
of educational program, 510–517
functional records in, 491–499
gathering data for, 18–19, 484–491
of growth of learners, 18–19, 476–499
learners' role in, 19, 478
parents' role in, 19, 479, 499–509
purpose of, 477–478
setting goals for, 479–484
in terms of behavior, 480–482, 507–508
in terms of potentialities, 507–508
tests and examinations in, 487–491
values and, 479–484
Examinations—*See* Evaluation; Tests and examinations
Exceptional pupils
attitudes of, 455–456
differences of, 447–453
grouping of, 456–457
learning methods of, 453
needs of, 446–453
persistent life situations and, 448–453
planning for, 17, 379–397
in regular classroom, 453–455
Experiences of learners
balanced growth and, 118, 121–125, 325–328, 348–349
basis for organizing, 11–13, 86–105, 114–117
continuity of, 12, 117, 125–127, 328, 469
criteria for selecting, 117–121, 344–351
in elementary school, 352–355
in a fifth grade, 525–570
in a first grade, 621–653
firsthand, 14–15, 124
guidance of, 369–430
in high school, 355–362
individual and group, 119, 136–137, 349–350, 438–446
in a second grade, 339
in a tenth grade, 589–613
meaningful, 336–337, 345–347, 614
organized bodies of subject matter and, 133–134, 360, 362–365, 403–409, 471
out-of-class, 12, 74, 124, 361, 426–427, 472–473
out-of-school, 325, 337–338, 351, 473–475
persistent life situations and, 347–348

related to everyday living, 322–325, 426–429
selection of, 109–110, 116–117, 130–136, 335–367
sequence of, 11–13, 86–105, 117
typical situations of everyday living and, 167–321
vicarious, 14, 68–69, 124
Experimentation
action research and, 706–712
conditions conducive to, 722–727
defined, 705

Family life, changes in, 40–43
Firsthand experiences, 14–15, 124
Flexibility of curriculum, 117–121
Flexibility in grouping, 437–438, 443
Flexibility in schedule, 353–355, 399–403, 462–464, 467
Forgetting, learning and, 79–80
Foundations of curriculum development, 22–23, 26–49, 51–81
Fundamental research, 707

General education, 17–18, 137–140, 356–358, 613
Generalizations
development of, 73–77, 377–379, 406–407, 719
of exceptional pupils, 449
learning and, 73–77, 110, 130–131, 406–407, 719
maturity and, 73–77, 377–379, 406–407
research on development of, 719
transfer of learning and, 73–77
Goals
in behavioral terms, 480–482, 507–508
individual differences and, 482–484, 507–508
learning and, 69–73, 141
long-range, 479–480
Group experiences
See also Experiences of learners; Individual and group experiences; Small-group and individual activities and interests
balance between, and individual activity, 136–137
Grouping of learners
class unity and, 436–437, 439–440
exceptional pupils and, 456–457
flexibility in, 437–438, 443
functional, 433–438
interage, 437–438
meeting individual needs and, 433–435
values and, 435–436
Group membership
an area of persistent life situations, 150, 160–161
experiences in a fifth grade, 553, 564, 569
experiences in a first grade, 644–645
experiences in a tenth grade, 591, 609
typical situations faced by children, youth, adults, 248–259
Growth of learners
in ability to deal with persistent life situations, 147, 149–150, 170–173, 192–193, 214–215, 224–225, 236–239, 248–249, 260–261, 268–271, 286–287, 294–295
balanced, 118, 121–125, 325–328, 348–349
behavior as a measure of, 480–482
continuity of, 12, 117, 125–127, 328, 469
in dealing with environmental factors and forces, 147, 150, 268–271, 286–287, 294–295
environment for, 15, 60, 68, 72, 337–338, 419, 471–475, 572
evaluation of, 18–19, 476–499
functional records of, 491–499
goals and, 69–73, 141, 479–484
in individual capacities, 147, 149, 170–173, 192–193, 214–215, 224–225
materials and equipment for, 418–426
out-of-class activities and, 12, 74, 124, 325, 337–338, 351, 361, 473–475
rate of, 59–61
report of pupil progress and, 499–510
school organization and, 468–469, 513–515, 720
in social participation, 147, 149–150, 236–239, 248–249, 260–261
tests and examinations and, 487–491
Guidance
central role of, 361–362, 439
in a tenth grade, 588–589, 610–611, 614
Guiding learning experiences
beginning the school year, 426–429
determining ways of working, 13–15, 350–351, 370–379, 404–409, 614, 618–621, 655–656
developing skills, 409–417
helping learners generalize, 377–379, 406–407

planning for and with learners, 379–397
providing a learning environment, 15, 60, 68, 72, 337–338, 419, 471–475, 656–657
providing for individual differences, 432–457
selecting and using instructional materials, 418–426

Health
an area of persistent life situations, 115, 149, 155–157
experiences of a fifth grade, 545–546, 560–561, 563, 565, 568
experiences of a first grade, 621–625
experiences of a tenth grade, 608–610
typical situations faced by children, youth, and adults, 172–191
High school—*See* Secondary school
Hypotheses
formulation of, 713–714
testing of, 714–716

Identifying learners' concerns, interests, needs, 114–115, 322–325, 326–328, 336–344, 484–491
Individual and group experiences
balance between, 136–137
providing for individuals within group experiences, 119, 136–137, 366–367, 438–446
Individual capacities, growth in, 147, 149, 170–173, 192–193, 214–215, 224–225
Individual differences
curriculum differentiation for, 15–18, 117–121, 141, 349–350, 432–457, 610–612
evaluation to recognize, 507–508
goals and, 482–484, 507–508
grouping for, 433–438
independent work and, 440–441, 443
laboratory work and, 438, 612
provision for exceptional pupils and, 17, 442, 446–457
provision for, in a fifth grade, 531–539, 543–544, 573–574
provision for, in a tenth grade, 580, 581–586, 610–613
pupil–teacher planning and, 445–446
recognition of, in group activities, 119, 136–137, 366–367, 438–446
scheduling for, 467
uniqueness of individuals and, 53–55, 59–61, 433–435

Instructional materials—*See* Materials of instruction
Intellectual power
an area of persistent life situations, 149, 157–158
development of in a fifth grade, 526–527, 534–535, 538, 542, 547, 549–550, 552–553, 556–557, 563–564
development of in a first grade, 625–636
development of in a tenth grade, 601–604, 608–610
typical situations faced by children, youth, and adults, 192–213
Interests and needs of learners
balanced growth and, 118, 325–328, 348–349
curriculum development and, 63, 109–110, 114–115
expressed and unexpressed, 123–124
identifying, 114–115, 326–328, 336–344, 484–491
individual and small group, 119, 136–137, 440–441, 553, 573–574
Intergroup relationships
an area of persistent life situations, 150, 161–162
experiences of a fifth grade in, 551–552, 558–560
experiences of a first grade in, 645–646
experiences of a tenth grade in, 593–601
typical situations faced by children, youth, and adults, 260–267
Issues, curriculum, 3–25

Laboratories
as professional centers, 691–692
for student experiences, 358–359, 580–586, 610–613
Leadership for curriculum improvement, 145, 670, 692–695
Learners
See also Exceptional pupils
characteristics of, 53–66
concerns of, 114–115, 121, 326–328, 512, 571–573
developmental tasks of, 56–59, 62
identifying concerns, interests, needs of, 322–328, 336–344, 484–491
effect of environment on, 15, 60, 68, 72, 337–338, 351–352, 471–475
needs of, 61–65
wholeness of, 65–66, 141

Learning
defined, 53*n*
depth of, 124, 127–130, 575–577, 614
environment and, 15, 60, 68, 72, 337–338, 351–352, 418–423, 471–475, 656–657
evaluation in, 18–19, 476–499
of exceptional pupils, 453
experiences and, 14–15, 67–69, 344–352, 370–379, 471–475
forgetting in, 79–80
generalizations and, 73–77, 110, 130–131, 377–379, 406–407, 719
involvement in, 14–15, 77–79
maturity and, 67–69, 412, 471
motivation and, 70–73, 114
persistent life situations and, 140–142
process of, 66–81
purpose in, 14, 69–73, 141
readiness for, 59–60, 68–69
relation of meaning to, 71, 114–115
school community and, 426–428, 471–475, 513–515, 526–531
specialists and, 358–359, 461–462
transfer of, 73–77
Learning environment—*See* Environment
Learning experiences—*See* Experiences
Life situations—*See* Persistent life situations; Typical situations
Long-term planning 379–392

Master List of persistent life situations, 155–165
Materials of instruction
community as a resource of, 420–423, 460–461, 465–467, 471–475
flexible use of, 425–426
identifying needed, through charts of persistent life and typical situations, 331–332
learners' part in selection and use of, 423–425
nature of, 144, 418–425
research in development and use of, 721
use of in a fifth grade, 526–531, 553–554, 564–565, 569
use of in learning, 418–426
use of in a tenth grade, 591–593, 601–604
Maturation
defined, 53*n*
of learner, 53–66
Maturity
generalizations and, 73–77, 377–379, 406–407, 719
goals and, 482–484
learning and, 67–69, 412, 471
skill in planning and, 397
use of resources and, 405
Mental discipline, 73–74
Moral choices
an area of persistent life situations, 149, 158–159
experiences of a fifth grade and, 534, 551–552
experiences of a first grade and, 636–639
typical situations faced by children, youth, and adults, 214–223
Motivation
extrinsic, 70–71
intrinsic, 70
learning and, 70–73, 114

Natural phenomena
an area of persistent life situations, 116, 150, 162–163
experiences of a fifth grade, 541–542, 547, 555–557, 569
experiences of a first grade, 646–649
experiences of a tenth grade, 607
typical situations faced by children, youth, and adults, 269–285
Needs and problems of learners
as an approach to curriculum design, 87, 103–105, 114–115
identifying, 322–328, 336–344, 484–491
nature of, 61–65

Observation of learners
to evaluate growth, 486–487
to identify needs and concerns, 336–342
Organization of curriculum experiences, 11–13, 86–105, 114–117, 360, 365
Organization of school, 468–469, 513–515, 720
Out-of-school experiences, 12, 74, 124, 325, 337–338, 351, 473–475

Parents
curriculum improvement and, 19, 479, 678–679
experiences in home and, 325, 351–352
reporting to, 499–509
Persistent life situations
analysis of, 147, 149–150, 151–168
balanced development and, 121–125

characteristics of, 121–145
charts of and typical situations in daily life, 169–321
continuity of, 125–127, 469
cultural heritage and, 130–136, 330–331, 360, 374
in curriculum development, 114–145, 699–703
defined, 115
in different vocations, 138–140
as experienced in a first grade, 621–654
as experienced in high school, 589–615
increasing complexity of, 127–128
interrelationships of, 322–323
as learners face them, 169–321
major areas of, 149–150
making an analysis of, 151–154
Master List of, 155–165
recurring nature of, 125–127
relating learner and society through, 115–117, 142–143
research in analysis of, 718–719
scope of, 115–117, 121–125, 146–151, 155–168
sources of, 148–149
subjects and, 132–134, 360, 362–365, 403–409
using an analysis of, 322–332
Personnel for curriculum improvement, 20, 666–667, 678–679, 696–699
Person-to-person relationships
an area of persistent life situations, 116, 150, 160
experiences in a fifth grade in, 539–541, 557
experiences in a first grade in, 641–643
experiences in a tenth grade in, 591–592, 609
typical situations faced by children, youth, and adults, 237–247
Philosophy and curriculum development, 22–23
Planning
advanced, by teacher, 392–394
for beginning school year, 426–429
daily, 379–380, 391–392
essentials of effective, 354–355, 379–397, 469–470
for and with exceptional pupils, 17, 379–397
for and with a fifth grade, 526–531
for and with a first grade, 382–389
for and with a fourth grade, 382–390
for and with a ninth grade, 383–391
for and with a twelfth grade, 383–391
illustrative plans, 382–391
long-term, 379–391
maturity and skill in, 397
organized bodies of subject matter in, 132–134, 360, 362–365, 403–409
procedures for curriculum improvement, 362–367, 681–692
pupil–teacher, 340–341, 354–355, 365–366, 379, 394–397, 469–470
scheduling and, 354–355, 391–392
for skill development, 417
skill in, 396–397
unit, 379–391
Political structures and forces—*See* Economic, social, and political structures and forces
Precautions in using analyses of persistent life situations, 165–167
Problem-solving skills, development of, 365–366, 404–406, 470
Procedures for curriculum improvement, 19–21, 362–367, 681–692
Professional growth of teachers, 144, 681–692
Program
See also Scheduling
carrying over interest from preceding year, 429
flexibility of, 353–355, 399–403, 462–464, 467
learners' needs and, 465–467
teachers', 462–464
Progress reports of pupils, 499–509
Psychological foundations of curriculum, 22, 51–81
Pupils—*See* Exceptional pupils; Learners
Pupil–teacher planning, 340–341, 354–355, 365–366, 379–397, 469–470
Purpose, significance of learner's, 14, 69–73, 141

Readiness and learning, 59–60, 68–69
Records of learners
anecdotal, daily, 492–494
functional, in evaluation, 491–499
functional, in identifying needs and concerns, 342–344, 429
permanent, 495–498
samples of pupils' work, 494–495
summary, 501–506
Repetition, avoidance of undesirable, 375–377
Reporting pupil progress
analyses of behavior, not grades, 499–500
changing methods of, 509

conferences, 500–501
descriptive statements, 501–506
informal notes, 506–507
Research
action, 706–712
attitude for, 727
conditions conducive to, 722–727
contribution of, 108, 717–721
cooperative curriculum, 706–729
in curriculum development based on persistent life situations, 716–721, 727–729
in curriculum improvement, 85–86
data collection in, 714–716
defined, 705
in development of generalizations, 719
evaluation skills and, 721
fundamental, 707
funds for, 725–726
in human relationships, 720
hypotheses in, 713–716
persistent life situations analysis by, 718–719
problem identification in, 712–713
process of, 708–716
reports of, 708–712
resources and, 721, 725–727
skill in, 708–716
teacher's role in, 706, 709–712, 728
Resource persons—*See* Personnel for curriculum improvement
Resources
See also Materials of instruction
community, 460–461, 465–467, 471–475, 554, 564–565, 569, 606
location of, by learners, 404–406
research in development and use of, 721
use of school, 471–475, 526–531, 553, 569, 591–593, 606
Role of the school, 7–9, 125

Scheduling
of day's activities, 397–403
in elementary school, 353–355, 398–399, 400–402
for a fifth grade, 534, 547–548
for a first grade, 619–620
flexibility of, 353–355, 399–403, 462–464, 467
in high school, 359–360, 399, 402–403
large time blocks and, 397–399
learners' needs and, 465–467
length of school day and, 465
pupil–teacher planning and, 391–392, 403
for small groups, 440–441, 553, 573–574
of teachers, 462–464
for a tenth grade, 586–588
use of specialists and, 358–359, 462–464
School
articulation of, 468–469
beginning year in, 426–429, 525–548
community and, 125, 325, 337–338, 351, 428, 465–467, 515–516, 564–568, 606, 608–610
length of day in, 465
length of year in, 466–467
research in, 674–675
resources, use of, 471–475, 526–531, 553, 569, 591–593, 606
role of, 7–9
as source of learning experiences, 426–428, 471–475, 513–515, 526–531, 564, 606
School day, length of, 465
School year, length of, 466–467
Scope of curriculum, 9–11, 86–105, 117, 121–125
Secondary school
curriculum experiences in, 355–362
evaluating growth in, 476–499
exceptional pupils in, 446–457
general education in, 356–358
guidance in, 361–362, 588–589, 610–611, 614
interage grouping in, 437–438
pupil–teacher planning in, 379–397, 469–470
scheduling in, 359–360, 399, 402–403
specialized education in, 17, 137–140, 358–359, 613
typical situations faced by youth in, 174–321
work of a tenth grade, 578–615
Selection of learning experiences
criteria for, 109–110, 117–121, 130–136, 344–351
identifying learners' concerns, 114–115, 326–328, 336–344, 484–491
Separate subjects
curriculum design by, 87, 88–91
place of, 133–134, 360, 362–367, 407–409, 613
use in a tenth grade, 613
Sequence of curriculum experiences, 11–13, 86–105, 117, 125–127
Service courses and laboratories, 358–359, 580, 581–586, 610–613
Situation examinations, 489–490

Situations of everyday living
activities and ways of working on, 371–374
delimitation of, 375–377
generalizing from, 377–379, 406–407
meeting new, 470–471
method of approach to, 406–407
typical, 167–321
Skills
for curriculum improvement, 680
developed in a fifth grade, 552–553, 563–564, 574–575
developed in a first grade, 619, 627–632
in group work, 442, 539–541
levels of competence in, 414
methods of developing, 134–136, 409–417
nature of, 107, 410, 411–412
place in curriculum, 107
in planning, 396–397
practice and drill on, 78, 415–417
problem-solving, 365–366, 404–406, 470
in research, 708–716
Small-group and individual activities and interests, 119, 136–137, 440–441, 553, 573–574
Social foundations of curriculum development, 22, 26–49
Social structures and forces—*See* Economic, social, and political structures and forces
Social participation, growth in, 147, 149–150, 236–239, 248–249, 260–261
Society and curriculum development, 22, 26–49
Sources of persistent life situations, 148–149
Specialization, use of, 358–359, 459–464
Specialists, role of, 358–359, 461–464
Specialized education, 17, 137–140, 358–359, 613
Study groups in curriculum planning, 687
Subject fields curriculum design, 87, 91–97
Subject matter
selection of, 330, 374
used as an organized body of knowledge, 132–134, 360, 362–365, 403–409, 613
Supervisor, role of, 690–691

Teacher-pupil planning—*See* Planning
Teachers
activity patterns of, 444–445, 462–464
courses for, 691, 697
curriculum activities of, 666–667, 672–673
preplanning by, 392–394
professional growth of, 144, 681–692
professional persistent life situations of, 138–140, 144
research role of, 706, 709–712, 728
working committees for curriculum improvement, 683–686
workshops and, 669, 686–688
Techniques for identifying pupil needs, interests, concerns, abilities, 322–325, 326–328, 336–344, 484–491
Technological resources
an area of persistent life situations, 150, 163
experiences of a first grade with, 649–651
experiences of a tenth grade with, 600–601, 607
typical situations faced by children, youth, and adults, 286–293
Tests and examinations, 487–491
Traditional curriculum designs
moving from, 144–145, 331, 360, 362–367, 470
using persistent life situations in, 173, 193, 215, 225, 239, 249, 261, 269, 271, 287, 295, 331, 362–367
Traditional subject areas, values of, 331, 360, 403–409
Transfer of learning, 73–77
Typical situations of everyday living at various maturity levels, 167–321

Units of learning
defined, 379–380
flexible use of, 376–377
planning, 379–391

Values
curriculum design and, 26–34, 86, 88–89, 92–93, 95, 101–102, 104, 106–110
democratic, 26–34
educational, 7–9, 479–484
evaluation and, 479–484
grouping and, 435–436
Variability within instructional groups—*See* Individual differences
Vicarious experiences, 14, 68–69, 124

Workshops, for curriculum improvement, 669, 686–688

Youth, typical and persistent life situations faced by, 169–321

PENNSYLVANIA
LIBRARY